www.wadsworth.com

www.wadsworth.com is the World Wide Web site for
Wadsworth and is your direct source to dozens of online
resources.

At *www.wadsworth.com* you can find out about supplements,
demonstration software, and student resources. You can
also send email to many of our authors and preview new
publications and exciting new technologies.

www.wadsworth.com
Changing the way the world learns®

The Police in America

Classic and Contemporary Readings

STEVEN G. BRANDL
University of Wisconsin–Milwaukee

DAVID E. BARLOW
Fayetteville State University

Australia • Canada • Mexico • Singapore • Spain
United Kingdom • United States

THOMSON
WADSWORTH

Senior Executive Editor, Criminal Justice:
  Sabra Horne
Editorial Assistant: Paul Massicotte
Marketing Manager: Dory Schaeffer
Marketing Assistant: Neena Chandra
Advertising Project Manager: Stacey Purviance
Project Manager, Editorial Production: Ray
  Crawford
Print/Media Buyer: Karen Hunt

Permissions Editor: Kiely Sexton
Production Service: G&S Typesetters
Copy Editor: Chris Sabooni
Cover Designer: Yvo Riezebos Design
Cover Image: © Royalty-Free/CORBIS/
  © Phil Schermeister/CORBIS
Cover Printer: Webcom Limited
Compositor: G&S Typesetters
Printer: Webcom Limited

Printed in Canada
2 3 4 5 6 7 07 06 05 04

For more information
about our products, contact us at:
**Thomson Learning Academic
Resource Center
1-800-423-0563**

For permission to use material from this text,
contact us by: **Phone:** 1-800-730-2214
Fax: 1-800-730-2215
Web: http://www.thomsonrights.com

Library of Congress Control Number:
2003105496
ISBN 0-534-62376-X

**Wadsworth/Thomson Learning
10 Davis Drive
Belmont, CA 94002-3098
USA**

Asia
Thomson Learning
5 Shenton Way #01–01
UIC Building
Singapore 068808

Australia/New Zealand
Thomson Learning
102 Dodds Street
Southbank, Victoria 3006
Australia

Canada
Nelson
1120 Birchmount Road
Toronto, Ontario M1K 5G4
Canada

Europe/Middle East/Africa
Thomson Learning
High Holborn House
50/51 Bedford Row
London WC1R 4LR
United Kingdom

Latin America
Thomson Learning
Seneca, 53
Colonia Polanco
11560 Mexico D.F.
Mexico

Spain/Portugal
Paraninfo
Calle/Magallanes, 25
28015 Madrid, Spain

Contents

II POLICE DISCRETION 113

III STRATEGIES OF POLICING 233

About the Authors

Steven G. Brandl

Steven G. Brandl is an Associate Professor in the Department of Criminal Justice at the University of Wisconsin-Milwaukee. His current research interests include police decision-making and behavior, the hazards of police work, criminal investigation, and program evaluation. Brandl has conducted numerous research projects with several major metropolitan police departments. He is the author of numerous articles in professional journals and is the author of *Criminal Investigation: An Analytical Perspective* (Allyn and Bacon, forthcoming) and co-editor of *Voices From the Field: Readings in Criminal Justice Research* (Pope/Lovell/Brandl, Wadsworth, 2001).

David E. Barlow

David E. Barlow is an Associate Professor in the Department of Social Sciences at Fayetteville State University. His research interests include multicultural issues in policing, white collar crime, and the history, ideology, and political economy of crime control in the United States. He has worked in the criminal justice field as a correctional officer, deputy sheriff and university police officer in South Carolina and Florida. Barlow is the author of numerous articles in professional journals, co-editor of the book, *Classics in Policing* (Anderson 1996) and co-author of the book, *Police in a Multicultural Society: An American Story* (Waveland 2000).

Foreword

SAMUEL WALKER

This book contains an outstanding collection of articles that include many if not most of the truly essential readings on the American police. The opening two essays provide a quick overview of police history. George L. Kelling and Mark H. Moore present what has emerged as the consensus view of that history. Hubert Williams and Patrick V. Murphy, meanwhile, offer an important dissenting interpretation.

With respect to the critical issue of police use of force, Egon Bittner's essay on the capacity to use force is essential reading for anyone seeking to understand the police in America. The articles by Robert Worden and James Fyfe explore other important dimensions of police officer use of force, both physical force and deadly force. Controlling crime is central to the police role in society. No discussion of this issue is complete without consideration of the Kansas City Preventive Patrol Experiment, which is included here. The issues of "Hot Spots" policing and the effectiveness of routine criminal investigations are also extremely important and are also covered in this collection.

The last twenty-five years have been a period of tremendous innovation and experimentation in policing. Without any question, the two most important articles that helped to stimulate this movement are James Q. Wilson and George L. Kelling's "Broken Windows" article and Herman Goldstein's seminal piece on problem-oriented policing. Both are included in this collection.

In short, if someone with no background in American policing read the articles in this book, and only these articles, he or she would emerge *conversant* with a solid foundation for understanding the critical issues in American policing.

Professor Samuel Walker
Department of Criminal Justice
University of Nebraska at Omaha

Preface

The purpose of this book is to provide students with a scholarly foundation for understanding police research, theory, and practice. At the core of police literature there exists a collection of major theoretical and empirical works that represent significant contributions to knowledge in the field of policing. At the same time, there is a collection of contemporary works that build directly upon these classics, testing, challenging, and further developing their theories about policing. Textbooks on policing can only provide an interpretation of these readings. *The Police In America: Classic and Contemporary Readings* provides the reader with access to the actual words and ideas offered by scholars in their contributions to police theory and research.

We believe that it is important for students to read for themselves the influential classic contributions that form the core of police research and theory. In doing so, students can evaluate the works directly and construct their own interpretations regarding significance and meaning, rather than relying on others to assess and interpret the works for them. However, reading all these works in their entirety is much more than can reasonably be expected from a student in a single semester course in policing. This collection reproduces the essence of these classic readings in a condensed and manageable format, which makes it possible for students to be exposed to these works without being overwhelmed by them.

Further, this book goes beyond the classics in policing by introducing more contemporary writings that directly relate to, and build upon, these earlier works. It is our contention that studying "the classics" is only useful insomuch as doing so helps us to understand the present. The contemporary works included here serve to demonstrate how the classic works apply to, explain, or fail to explain, current police issues. Bringing classic and contemporary readings together makes the classic police literature come alive and helps today's students recognize the relevance of this literature to contemporary issues and problems in policing.

It is important that we note some of the problems in assembling such a collection of readings. First, there are articles and book excerpts that constitute major contributions to policing literature that are not included in *The Police in America*. Some readings could not be included simply because of space constraints and costly permission fees. Second, the very concept of classics and the inclusion of works widely recognized as classics inherently results in a conservative bias. Identifying a core group of classics in policing reinforces and perpetuates a traditional mainstream perspective that has been taught over many years in the major institutions of higher learning. This book attempts to counter that tendency by including among the contemporary works perspectives that have traditionally been marginalized in the field of policing. Finally, we had to make value choices about which articles would be most appropriate and accessible for our targeted audience. Although the readings are primarily drawn from the most respected scholarly journals in the criminal justice and policing fields, we avoided articles which we thought would be too complex or abstract for most students to understand or appreciate. As a result, it is important to realize that the readings contained here represent *a* scholarly foundation of policing, not *the* scholarly foundation of policing.

This book divides policing literature into three primary sections. Section I, "Police History and Role," contains writings that describe and explain the nature of the police function in U.S. society from a historical perspective. Section II, "Police Discretion," includes works that have examined the causes and consequences of police discretionary decisions. Section III, "Strategies of Policing," presents writings on the effectiveness of the most influential police operational strategies. Each section begins with an Introduction to the readings. These introductions are meant to assist the reader in understanding the main themes of the included articles. Each section concludes with several Questions for Discussion and Review that may be used to stimulate further discussion and thought about the articles. We believe that this collection of readings provides students with a substantial and necessary foundation on which to base an understanding of the police.

POLICE HISTORY

AND ROLE

INTRODUCTION

Social institutions, such as the police, are human constructions that form and develop in relation to various political, economic, and social forces. Today's police did not simply arrive on the social scene abstracted from their past; the role of the police in the United States has been forged over a long period of time. Therefore, any attempt to describe the police and their function must begin with an analysis of their historical development. This section includes readings that place the police in historical context in order to better understand their role in U.S. society.

The first reading of this section, "The Evolving Strategy of Policing," by Kelling and Moore (1988), is a classic presentation of the historical development of municipal policing in the United States. This article describes the traditional and widely accepted viewpoint that the police have experienced three primary shifts in strategy and design, from the Political Era to the Reform Era and finally to the Community Problem-Solving Era. It builds upon the mainstream perspective that the primary role of the police in U.S. society is to fight crime; therefore, each shift is "explained" as evolutionary adjustments intentionally designed to make the police more legitimate in the eyes of the general public and more effective in their struggle to reduce crime. This reading establishes the foundation upon which the rest of the readings in this section can build.

Williams and Murphy (1990), in their article "The Evolving Strategy of Police: A Minority View," directly challenge Kelling and Moore's presentation of history, primarily because Kelling and Moore do not include race as an essential ingredient for understanding the history of the police in the United States. By looking at the same events from a minority perspective, Williams and Murphy identify some glaring omissions by Kelling and Moore. Specifically, Kelling and Moore fail to take into account how slavery, segregation, discrimination, and racism have affected the development of policing and how they have affected the quality of policing in minority communities. This failure to take into consideration minority perspectives and experiences greatly limits the ability of Kelling and Moore's analysis to truly capture the role of police in today's society, particularly in minority communities. Williams and Murphy present a review of how racial dynamics have contributed to the historical development of policing in the United States and how they continue to contribute to its future.

Chambliss (1994), in "Policing the Ghetto Underclass," presents to the reader a snapshot of police in action that is neglected by Kelling and Moore and directly challenges their interpretation that the role of the police is to fight crime. The article by Chambliss also demonstrates that the problems of racism in policing, as presented in Williams and Murphy, are not just historical legacies, but are alive and well in police operations today. This relatively recent ethnographic study of the operations of the Rapid Deployment Unit in Washington, D.C., provides a picture of how the police are involved in much more than just crime control, particularly in urban ghettos characterized by poverty and racial segregation. The activities of police in this context appear to be more about social control than crime control. Chambliss makes the argument that the role of the police and their strategies are shaped by historical, political, economic, social, and racial factors as well as by crime.

The article "A Political Economy of Community Policing," by Barlow and Barlow (1999), takes this perspective a step further by suggesting that the entire historical development of municipal policing in the United States, from the slave patrols in Charleston, South Carolina, in the 1700s to the implementation of community policing in our major cities in the 1990s, can best be explained through an analysis of the police not as crime fighters, but as defenders of the status quo. Breaking from the "evolutionary" approach, this reading explains the shifts in police strategy and organization, as well as more recent developments in community policing, through a historical analysis of the political, economic, and social conditions in which they emerged. Although the historically specific characteristics of the different eras of policing can be explained by the conditions in which they emerged, their ultimate design was to increase the legitimacy of the police and to enhance the ability of police to maintain social order. This reading seriously questions the ability of police reform to fundamentally change the structural conditions of policing in a class society.

The classic excerpts by Egon Bittner (1967), which anchor this section on the Police History and Role, provide the foundation upon which Barlow and Barlow conclude that the fundamental problem with police legitimacy is structural. Bittner, in Chapters Two and Six of *The Functions of Police in Modern Society,* states that the unique ability and authority of the police to use essentially unrestrictived coercive force in a democratic society is the fundamental unifying element which produces three basic structural determinants: (1) police work is a tainted profession; (2) it is inherently crude; and (3) the ecological distribution and development of police reflect a whole range of public prejudices. The central argument by Bittner is that simply altering policing strategies, improving management techniques, and upgrading the quality of police personnel will not resolve these conflicts in the police function. These two excerpts explain how massive transformations and reforms in policing can take place while the fundamental social, economic, and racial conflicts in police community relations remain unresolved.

The Evolving Strategy of Policing

GEORGE L. KELLING

MARK H. MOORE

Policing, like all professions, learns from experience. It follows, then, that as modern police executives search for more effective strategies of policing, they will be guided by the lessons of police history. The difficulty is that police history is incoherent, its lessons hard to read. After all, that history was produced by thousands of local departments pursuing their own visions and responding to local conditions. Although that varied experience is potentially a rich source of lessons, departments have left few records that reveal the trends shaping modern policing. Interpretation is necessary.

METHODOLOGY

This essay presents an interpretation of police history that may help police executives considering alternative future strategies of policing. Our reading of police history has led us to adopt a particular point of view. We find that a dominant trend guiding today's police executives—a trend that encourages the pursuit of independent, professional autonomy for police departments—is carrying the police away from achieving their maximum potential, especially in effective crime fighting. We are also convinced that this trend in policing is weakening *public* policing relative to *private* security as the primary institution providing security to society. We believe that this has dangerous long-term implications not only for police departments but also for society. We think that this trend is shrinking rather than enlarging police capacity to help create civil communities. Our judgment is that this trend can be reversed only by refocusing police attention from the pursuit of professional autonomy to the establishment of effective problem-solving partnerships with the communities they police.

Delving into police history made it apparent that some assumptions that now operate as axioms in the field of policing (for example that effectiveness in

Source: Kelling, George L. and Mark H. Moore (1988). The Evolving Strategy of Policing. *Perspectives on Policing* number 4:1–15. Washington, DC: National Institute of Justice.

policing depends on distancing police departments from politics; or that the highest priority of police departments is to deal with serious street crime; or that the best way to deal with street crime is through directed patrol, rapid response to calls for service, and skilled retrospective investigations) are not timeless truths, but rather choices made by former police leaders and strategists. To be sure, the choices were often wise and far-seeing as well as appropriate to their times. But the historical perspective shows them to be choices nonetheless, and therefore open to reconsideration in the light of later professional experience and changing environmental circumstances.

We are interpreting the results of our historical study through a framework based on the concept of "corporate strategy."[1] Using this framework, we can describe police organizations in terms of seven interrelated categories:

- The sources from which the police construct the legitimacy and continuing power to act on society.
- The definition of the police function or role in society.
- The organizational design of police departments.
- The relationships the police create with the external environment.
- The nature of police efforts to market or manage the demand for their services.
- The principal activities, programs, and tactics on which police agencies rely to fulfill their mission or achieve operational success.
- The concrete measures the police use to define operational success or failure.

Using this analytic framework, we have found it useful to divide the history of policing into three different eras. These eras are distinguished from one another by the apparent dominance of a particular strategy of policing. The political era, so named because of the close ties between police and politics, dated from the introduction of police into municipalities during the 1840's, continued through the Progressive period, and ended during the early 1900's. The reform era developed in reaction to the political. It took hold during the 1930's, thrived during the 1950's and 1960's, began to erode during the late 1970's. The reform era now seems to be giving way to an era emphasizing community problem solving.

By dividing policing into these three eras dominated by a particular strategy of policing, we do not mean to imply that there were clear boundaries between the eras. Nor do we mean that in those eras everyone policed in the same way. Obviously, the real history is far more complex than that. Nonetheless, we believe that there is a certain professional ethos that defines standards of competence, professionalism, and excellence in policing; that at any given time, one set of concepts is more powerful, more widely shared, and better understood than others; and that this ethos changes over time. Sometimes, this professional ethos has been explicitly articulated, and those who have articulated the concepts have been recognized as the leaders of their profession. O.W. Wilson, for example, was a brilliant expositor of the central elements of the reform strategy of policing. Other times, the ethos is implicit—accepted by all as the tacit assumptions that define the business of policing and the proper form for a police department to take. Our task is to help the profession look to the future by representing its past in these terms and trying to understand what the past portends for the future.

THE POLITICAL ERA

Historians have described the characteristics of early policing in the United States, especially the struggles between various interest groups to govern the police.[2] Elsewhere, the authors of this paper analyzed a portion of American police history in terms of its organizational strategy.[3] The following discussion of elements of the police organizational strategy during the political era expands on that effort.

Legitimacy and Authorization

Early American police were authorized by local municipalities. Unlike their English counterparts, American police departments lacked the powerful, central authority of the crown to establish a legitimate, unifying mandate for their enterprise. Instead, American police derived both their authorization and resources from local political leaders, often ward politicians. They were, of course, guided by the law as to what tasks to undertake and what powers to utilize. But their link to neighborhoods and local politicians was so tight that both Jordan[4] and Fogelson[5] refer to the early police as adjuncts to local political machines. The relationship was often reciprocal: political machines recruited and maintained police in office and on the beat, while police helped ward political leaders maintain their political offices by encouraging citizens to vote for certain candidates, discouraging them from voting for others, and, at times, by assisting in rigging elections.

The Police Function

Partly because of their close connection to politicians, police during the political era provided a wide array of services to citizens. Inevitably police departments were involved in crime prevention and control and order maintenance, but they also provided a wide variety of social services. In the late 19th century, municipal police departments ran soup lines; provided temporary lodging for newly arrived immigrant workers in station houses;[6] and assisted ward leaders in finding work for immigrants, both in police and other forms of work.

Organizational Design

Although ostensibly organized as a centralized, quasimilitary organization with a unified chain of command, police departments of the political era were nevertheless decentralized. Cities were divided into precincts, and precinct-level managers often, in concert with the ward leaders, ran precincts as small-scale departments—hiring, firing, managing, and assigning personnel as they deemed appropriate. In addition, decentralization combined with primitive communications and transportation to give police officers substantial discretion in handling their individual beats. At best, officer contact with central command was maintained through the call box.

External Relationships

During the political era, police departments were intimately connected to the social and political world of the ward. Police officers often were recruited from the same ethnic stock as the dominant political groups in the localities, and continued to live in the neighborhoods they patrolled. Precinct commanders consulted often with local political representatives about police priorities and progress.

Demand Management

Demand for police services came primarily from two sources: ward politicians making demands on the organization and citizens making demands directly on beat officers. Decentralization and political authorization encouraged the first; foot patrol, lack of other means of transportation, and poor communications produced the latter. Basically, the demand for police services was received, interpreted, and responded to at the precinct and street levels.

Principal Programs and Technologies

The primary tactic of police during the political era was foot patrol. Most police officers walked beats and dealt with crime, disorder, and other problems as they arose, or as they were guided by citizens and precinct superiors. The technological tools available to police were limited. However, when call boxes became available, police administrators used them for supervisory and managerial purposes; and, when early automobiles became available, police used them to transport officers from one beat to another.[7] The new technology thereby increased the range, but did not change the mode, of patrol officers.

Detective divisions existed but without their current prestige. Operating from a caseload of "persons" rather than offenses, detectives relied on their caseload to inform on other criminals.[8] The "third degree" was a common means of interviewing criminals to solve crimes. Detectives were often especially valuable to local politicians for gathering information on individuals for political or personal, rather than offense-related, purposes.

Measured Outcomes

The expected outcomes of police work included crime and riot control, maintenance of order, and relief from many of the other problems of an industrializing society (hunger and temporary homelessness, for example). Consistent with their political mandate, police emphasized maintaining citizen and political satisfaction with police services as an important goal of police departments.

In sum, the organizational strategy of the political era of policing included the following elements:

- Authorization—primarily political.
- Function—crime control, order maintenance, broad social services.
- Organizational design—decentralized and geographical.
- Relationship to environment—close and personal.
- Demand—managed through links between politicians and precinct commanders, and face-to-face contacts between citizens and foot patrol officers.
- Tactics and technology—foot patrol and rudimentary investigations.
- Outcome—political and citizen satisfaction with social order.

The political strategy of early American policing had strengths. First, police were integrated into neighborhoods and enjoyed the support of citizens—at least the support of the dominant and political interests of an area. Second, and probably as a result of the first, the strategy provided useful services to communities. There is evidence that it helped contain riots. Many citizens believed that police prevented crimes or solved crimes when they occurred.[9] And the police assisted immigrants in establishing themselves in communities and finding jobs.

The political strategy also had weaknesses. First, intimacy with community, closeness to political leaders, and a decentralized organizational structure, with its inability to provide supervision of officers, gave rise to police corruption. Officers were often required to enforce unpopular laws foisted on immigrant ethnic neighborhoods by crusading reformers (primarily of English and Dutch background) who objected to ethnic values.[10] Because of their intimacy with the community, the officers were vulnerable to being bribed in return for nonenforcement or lax enforcement of laws. Moreover, police closeness to politicians created such forms of political corruption as patronage and police interference in elections.[11] Even those few departments that managed to avoid serious financial or political corruption during the late 19th and early 20th centuries, Boston for example, succumbed to large-scale corruption during and after Prohibition.[12]

Second, close identification of police with neighborhoods and neighborhood norms often resulted in discrimination against strangers and others who violated those norms, especially minority ethnic and racial groups. Often ruling their beats with the "ends of their nightsticks," police regularly targeted outsiders and strangers for rousting and "curbstone justice." [13]

Finally, the lack of organizational control over officers resulting from both decentralization and the political nature of many appointments to police positions caused inefficiencies and disorganization. The image of Keystone Cops—police as clumsy bunglers—was widespread and often descriptive of realities in American policing.

THE REFORM ERA

Control over police by local politicians, conflict between urban reformers and local ward leaders over the enforcement of laws regulating the morality of urban migrants, and abuses (corruption, for example) that resulted from the intimacy between police and political leaders and citizens produced a continuous struggle for control over police during the late 19th and early 20th centuries.[14] Nineteenth-century attempts by civilians to reform police organizations by applying external pressures largely failed; 20th-century attempts at reform, originating from both internal and external forces, shaped contemporary policing as we knew it through the 1970's.[15]

Berkeley's police chief, August Vollmer, first rallied police executives around the idea of reform during the 1920's and early 1930's. Vollmer's vision of policing was the trumpet call: police in the post-flapper generation were to remind American citizens and institutions of the moral vision that had made America great and of their responsibilities to maintain that vision.[16] It was Vollmer's protege, O.W. Wilson, however, who taking guidance from J. Edgar Hoover's shrewd transformation of the corrupt and discredited Bureau of Investigation into the honest and prestigious Federal Bureau of Investigation (FBI), became the principal administrative architect of the police reform organizational strategy.[17]

Hoover wanted the FBI to represent a new force for law and order, and saw that such an organization could capture a permanent constituency that wanted an agency to take a stand against lawlessness, immorality, and crime. By raising eligibility standards and changing patterns of recruitment and training, Hoover gave the FBI agents stature as upstanding moral crusaders. By committing the organization to attacks on crimes such as kidnapping, bank robbery, and espionage—crimes that attracted wide publicity and required technical sophistication, doggedness, and a national jurisdiction to solve—Hoover established the organization's reputation for professional competence and power. By establishing tight central control over his agents, limiting their use of controversial investigation procedures (such as undercover operations), and keeping them out of narcotics enforcement, Hoover was also able to maintain an unparalleled record of integrity. That, too, fitted the image of a dogged, incorruptible crime-fighting organization. Finally, lest anyone fail to notice the important developments within the Bureau, Hoover developed impressive public relations programs that presented the FBI and its agents in the most favorable light. (For those of us who remember the 1940's, for example, one of the most popular radio phrases was, "The FBI in peace and war"—the introductory line in a radio program that portrayed a vigilant FBI protecting us from foreign enemies as well as villains on the "10 Most Wanted" list, another Hoover/FBI invention.)

Struggling as they were with reputations for corruption, brutality, unfairness, and downright incompetence, municipal police reformers found Hoover's path a compelling one. Instructed by O.W. Wilson's texts on police administration, they began to shape an organizational strategy for urban police analogous to the one pursued by the FBI.

Legitimacy and Authorization

Reformers rejected politics as the basis of police legitimacy. In their view, politics and political involvement was the *problem* in American policing. Police reformers therefore allied themselves with Progressives. They moved to end the close ties between local political leaders and police. In some states, control over police was usurped by state government. Civil service eliminated patronage and ward influences in hiring and firing police officers. In some cities (Los Angeles and Cincinnati, for example), even the position of chief of police became a civil service position to be attained through examination. In others (such as Milwaukee), chiefs were given lifetime tenure by a police commission, to be removed from office only for cause. In yet others (Boston, for example), contracts for chiefs were staggered so as not to coincide with the mayor's tenure. Concern for separation of police from politics did not focus only on chiefs, however. In some cities, such as Philadelphia, it became illegal for patrol officers to live in the beats they patrolled. The purpose of all these changes was to isolate police as completely as possible from political influences.

Law, especially criminal law, and police professionalism were established as the principal bases of police legitimacy. When police were asked why they performed as they did, the most common answer was that they enforced the law. When they chose not to enforce the law—for instance, in a riot when police isolated an area rather than arrested looters—police justification for such action was found in their claim to professional knowledge, skills, and values which uniquely qualified them to make such tactical decisions. Even in riot situations, police rejected the idea that political leaders should make tactical decisions; that was a police responsibility.[18]

So persuasive was the argument of reformers to remove political influences from policing, that police departments became one of the most autonomous public organizations in urban government.[19] Under such circumstances, policing a city became a legal and technical matter left to the discretion of professional police executives under the guidance of law. Political influence of any kind on a police department came to be seen as not merely a failure of police leadership but as corruption in policing.

The Police Function

Using the focus on criminal law as a basic source of police legitimacy, police in the reform era moved to narrow their functioning to crime control and criminal apprehension. Police agencies became *law enforcement* agencies. Their goal was to control crime. Their principal means was the use of criminal law to apprehend and deter offenders. Activities that drew the police into solving other kinds of community problems and relied on other kinds of responses were identified as "social work," and became the object of derision. A common line in police circles during the 1950's and 1960's was, "If only we didn't have to do social work, we could really do something about crime." Police retreated from providing emergency medical services as well—ambulance and emergency medical services were transferred to medical, private, or firefighting organizations.[20] The 1967 President's Commission on Law Enforcement and Administration of Justice ratified this orientation: heretofore, police had been conceptualized as an agency of urban government; the President's Commission reconceptualized them as part of the criminal justice system.

Organizational Design

The organization form adopted by police reformers generally reflected the *scientific* or *classical* theory of administration advocated by Frederick W. Taylor during the early 20th century. At least two assumptions attended classical theory. First, workers are inherently uninterested in work and, if left to their own devices, are prone to avoid it. Second, since workers have little or no interest in the substance of their work, the sole common interest between workers and management is found in economic incentives for workers. Thus, both workers and management benefit economically when management arranges work in ways that increase workers' productivity and link productivity to economic rewards.

Two central principles followed from these assumptions: division of labor and unity of control. The former posited that if tasks can be broken into components, workers can become highly skilled in particular components and thus more efficient in carrying out their tasks. The latter posited that the workers' activities are best managed by a *pyramid of control,* with all authority finally resting in one central office.

Using this classical theory, police leaders moved to routinize and standardize police work, especially patrol work. Police work became a form of crimefighting in which police enforced the law and arrested criminals if the opportunity presented itself. Attempts were made to limit discretion in patrol work: a generation of police officers was raised with the idea that they merely enforced the law.

If special problems arose, the typical response was to create special units (e.g., vice, juvenile, drugs, tactical) rather than to assign them to patrol. The creation of these special units, under central rather than precinct command, served to further centralize command and control and weaken precinct commanders.[21]

Moreover, police organizations emphasized control over workers through bureaucratic means of control: supervision, limited span of control, flow of instructions downward and information upward in the organization, establishment of elaborate record-keeping systems requiring additional layers of middle managers, and coordination of activities between various production units (e.g., patrol and detectives), which also required additional middle managers.

External Relationships

Police leaders in the reform era redefined the nature of a proper relationship between police officers and citizens. Heretofore, police had been intimately linked to citizens. During the era of reform policing, the new model demanded an impartial law enforcer who related to citizens in professionally neutral and distant terms. No better characterization of this model can be found than television's Sergeant Friday, whose response, "Just the facts, ma'am," typified the idea: impersonal and oriented toward crime solving rather than responsive to the emotional crisis of a victim.

The professional model also shaped the police view of the role of citizens in crime control. Police redefined the citizen role during an era when there was heady confidence about the ability of professionals to manage physical and social problems. Physicians would care for health problems, dentists for dental problems, teachers for educational problems, social workers for social adjustment problems, and police for crime problems. The proper role of citizens in crime control was to be relatively passive recipients of professional crime control services. Citizens' actions on their own behalf to defend themselves or their communities came to be seen as inappropriate, smacking of vigilantism. Citizens met their responsibilities when a crime occurred by calling police, deferring to police actions, and being good witnesses if called upon to give evidence. The metaphor that expressed this orientation to the community was that of the police as the "thin blue line." It connotes the existence of dangerous external threats to communities, portrays police as standing between that danger and good citizens, and implies both police heroism and loneliness.

Demand Management

Learning from Hoover, police reformers vigorously set out to sell their brand of urban policing.[22] They, too, performed on radio talk shows, consulted with media representatives about how to present police, engaged in public relations campaigns, and in other ways presented this image of police as crime fighters. In a sense, they began with an organizational capacity—anticrime police tactics—and intensively promoted it. This approach was more like selling than marketing. Marketing refers to the process of carefully identifying consumer needs and then developing goods and services that meet those needs. Selling refers to having a stock of products or goods on hand irrespective of need and selling them. The reform strategy had as its starting point a set of police tactics (services) that police promulgated as much for the purpose of establishing internal control of police officers and enhancing the status of urban police as for responding to community needs or market demands.[23] The community "need" for rapid response to calls for service, for instance, was largely the consequence of police selling the service as efficacious in crime control rather than a direct demand from citizens.

Consistent with this attempt to sell particular tactics, police worked to shape and control demand for police services. Foot patrol, when demanded by citizens, was rejected as an outmoded, expensive frill. Social and emergency services were terminated or given to other agencies. Receipt of demand for police services was centralized. No longer were citizens encouraged to go to "their" neighborhood police officers or districts; all calls went to a central communications facility. When 911 systems were installed, police aggressively sold 911 and rapid response to calls for service as effective police service. If citizens continued to use district, or precinct, telephone numbers, some police departments disconnected those telephones or got new telephone numbers.[24]

Principal Programs and Technologies

The principal programs and tactics of the reform strategy were preventive patrol by automobile and rapid response to calls for service. Foot patrol, characterized as outmoded and inefficient, was abandoned as rapidly as police administrators could obtain cars.[25] The initial tactical reasons for putting police in cars had been to increase the size of the areas police officers could patrol and to take the advantage away from criminals who began to use automobiles. Under reform policing, a new theory about how to make the best tactical use of automobiles appeared.

O.W. Wilson developed the theory of preventive patrol by automobile as an anticrime tactic.[26] He theorized that if police drove conspicuously marked cars randomly through city streets and gave special attention to certain "hazards" (bars and schools, for example), a feeling of police omnipresence would be developed. In turn, that sense of omnipresence would both deter criminals and reassure good citizens. Moreover, it was hypothesized that vigilant patrol officers moving rapidly through city streets would happen upon criminals in action and be able to apprehend them.

As telephones and radios became ubiquitous, the availability of cruising police came to be seen as even more valuable: if citizens could be encouraged to call the police via telephone as soon as problems developed, police could respond rapidly to calls and establish control over situations, identify wrongdoers, and make arrests. To this end, 911 systems and computer-aided dispatch were developed throughout the country. Detective units continued, although with some modifications. The "person" approach ended and was replaced by the case approach. In addition, forensic techniques were upgraded and began to replace the old "third degree" or reliance on informants for the solution of crimes. Like other special units, most investigative units were controlled by central headquarters.

Measured Outcomes

The primary desired outcomes of the reform strategy were crime control and criminal apprehension.[27] To measure achievement of these outcomes, August Vollmer, working through the newly vitalized International Association of Chiefs of Police, developed and implemented a uniform system of crime classification and reporting. Later, the system was taken over and administered by the FBI and the *Uniform Crime Reports* became the primary standard by which police organizations measured their effectiveness. Additionally, individual officers' effectiveness in dealing with crime was judged by the number of arrests they made; other measures of police effectiveness included response time (the time it takes for a police car to arrive at the location of a call for service) and "number of passings" (the number of times a police car passes a given point on a city street). Regardless of all other indicators, however, the primary measure of police effectiveness was the crime rate as measured by the *Uniform Crime Reports*.

In sum, the reform organizational strategy contained the following elements:

- Authorization—law and professionalism.
- Function—crime control.
- Organizational design—centralized, classical.
- Relationship to environment—professionally remote.
- Demand—channeled through central dispatching activities.
- Tactics and technology—preventive patrol and rapid response to calls for service.
- Outcome—crime control.

In retrospect, the reform strategy was impressive. It successfully integrated its strategic elements into a coherent paradigm that was internally consistent and logically appealing. Narrowing police functions to crimefighting made sense. If police could concentrate their efforts on prevention of crime and apprehension of criminals, it followed that they could be more effective than if they dissipated their efforts on other problems. The model of police as impartial, professional law enforcers was attractive because it minimized the discretionary excesses which developed during the political era. Preventive patrol and rapid response to calls for service were intuitively appealing tactics, as well as means to control officers and shape and control citizen demands for service. Further, the strategy provided a comprehensive, yet simple, vision of policing around which police leaders could rally.

The metaphor of the thin blue line reinforced their need to create isolated independence and autonomy in terms that were acceptable to the public. The patrol car became the symbol of policing during the 1930's and 1940's; when equipped with a radio, it was at the limits of technology. It represented mobility, power, conspicuous presence, control of officers, and professional distance from citizens.

During the late 1960's and 1970's, however, the reform strategy ran into difficulty. First, regardless of how police effectiveness in dealing with crime was measured, police failed to substantially improve their record. During the 1960's, crime began to rise. Despite large increases in the size of police departments and in expenditures for new forms of equipment (911 systems, computer-aided dispatch, etc.), police failed to meet their own or public expectations about their capacity to control crime or prevent its increase. Moreover, research conducted during the 1970's on preventive patrol and rapid response to calls for service suggested that neither was an effective crime control or apprehension tactic.[28]

Second, fear rose rapidly during this era. The consequences of this fear were dramatic for cities. Citizens abandoned parks, public transportation, neighborhood shopping centers, churches, as well as entire neighborhoods. What puzzled police and researchers was that levels of fear and crime did not always correspond: crime levels were low in some areas, but fear high. Conversely, in other areas levels of crime were high, but fear low. Not until the early 1980's did researchers discover that fear is more closely correlated with disorder than with crime.[29] Ironically, order maintenance was one of those functions that police had been downplaying over the years. They collected no data on it, provided no training to officers in order maintenance activities, and did not reward officers for successfully conducting order maintenance tasks.

Third, despite attempts by police departments to create equitable police allocation systems and to provide impartial policing to all citizens, many minority citizens, especially blacks during the 1960's and 1970's, did not perceive their treatment as equitable or adequate. They protested not only police mistreatment, but lack of treatment—inadequate or insufficient services—as well.

Fourth, the civil rights and antiwar movements challenged police. This challenge took several forms. The legitimacy of police was questioned: students resisted police, minorities rioted against them, and the public, observing police via live television for the first time, questioned their tactics. Moreover, despite police attempts to upgrade personnel through improved recruitment, training, and supervision, minorities and then women insisted that they had to be adequately represented in policing if police were to be legitimate.

Fifth, some of the myths that undergirded the reform strategy—police officers use little or no discretion and the primary activity of police is law enforcement—simply proved to be too far from reality to be sustained. Over and over again research showed that use of discretion characterized policing at all levels and that law enforcement comprised but a small portion of police officers' activities.[30]

Sixth, although the reform ideology could rally police chiefs and executives, it failed to rally line police officers. During the reform era, police executives had moved to professionalize their ranks. Line officers, however, were managed in ways that were antithetical to professionalization. Despite pious testimony from police executives that "patrol is the backbone of policing," police executives behaved in ways that were consistent with classical organizational theory—patrol officers continued to have low status; their work was treated as if it were routinized and standardized; and petty rules governed issues such as hair length and off-duty behavior. Meanwhile, line officers received little guidance in use of discretion and were given few, if any, opportunities to make suggestions about their work. Under such circumstances, the increasing "grumpiness" of officers in many cities is not surprising, nor is the rise of militant unionism.

Seventh, police lost a significant portion of their financial support, which had been increasing or at least constant over the years, as cities found themselves in fiscal difficulties. In city after city, police departments were reduced in size. In some cities, New York for example, financial cutbacks resulted in losses of up to one-third of departmental personnel. Some, noting that crime did not increase more rapidly or arrests decrease during the cutbacks, suggested that New York City had been overpoliced when at maximum strength. For those concerned about levels of disorder and fear in New York City, not to mention other problems, that came as a dismaying conclusion. Yet it emphasizes the erosion of confidence that citizens, politicians, and academicians had in urban police—an erosion that was translated into lack of political and financial support.

Finally, urban police departments began to acquire competition: private security and the community crime control movement. Despite the inherent value of these developments, the fact that businesses, industries, and private citizens began to search for alternative means of protecting their property and persons suggests a decreasing confidence in either the capability or the intent of the police to provide the services that citizens want.

In retrospect, the police reform strategy has characteristics similar to those that Miles and Snow[31] ascribe to a defensive strategy in the private sector. Some of the characteristics of an organization with a defensive strategy are (with specific characteristics of reform policing added in parentheses):

- Its market is stable and narrow (crime victims).
- Its success is dependent on maintaining dominance in a narrow, chosen market (crime control).
- It tends to ignore developments outside its domain (isolation).
- It tends to establish a single core technology (patrol).
- New technology is used to improve its current product or service rather than to expand its product or service line (use of computers to enhance patrol).
- Its management is centralized (command and control).
- Promotions generally are from within (with the exception of chiefs, virtually all promotions are from within).
- There is a tendency toward a functional structure with high degrees of specialization and formalization.

A defensive strategy is successful for an organization when market conditions remain stable and few competitors enter the field. Such strategies are vulnerable, however, in unstable market conditions and when competitors are aggressive.

The reform strategy was a successful strategy for police during the relatively stable period of the 1940's and 1950's. Police were able to sell a relatively narrow service line and maintain dominance in the crime control market. The social changes of the 1960's and 1970's, however, created unstable conditions. Some of the more significant changes included: the civil rights movement; migration of minorities into cities; the changing age of the population (more youths and teenagers); increases in crime and fear; increased oversight of police actions by courts; and the decriminalization and deinstitutionalization movements. Whether or not the private sector defensive strategy properly applies to police, it is clear that the reform strategy was unable to adjust to the changing social circumstances of the 1960's and 1970's.

THE COMMUNITY
PROBLEM-SOLVING ERA

All was not negative for police during the late 1970's and early 1980's, however. Police began to score victories which they barely noticed. Foot patrol remained popular, and in many cities citizen and political demands for it intensified. In

New Jersey, the state funded the Safe and Clean Neighborhoods Program, which funded foot patrol in cities, often over the opposition of local chiefs of police.[32] In Boston, foot patrol was so popular with citizens that when neighborhoods were selected for foot patrol, politicians often made the announcements, especially during election years. Flint, Michigan, became the first city in memory to return to foot patrol on a citywide basis. It proved so popular there that citizens twice voted to increase their taxes to fund foot patrol—most recently by a two-thirds majority. Political and citizen demands for foot patrol continued to expand in cities throughout the United States. Research into foot patrol suggested it was more than just politically popular, it contributed to city life; it reduced fear, increased citizen satisfaction with police, improved police attitudes toward citizens, and increased the morale and job satisfaction of police.[33]

Additionally, research conducted during the 1970's suggested that one factor could help police improve their record in dealing with crime: information. If information about crimes and criminals could be obtained from citizens by police, primarily patrol officers, and could be properly managed by police departments, investigative and other units could significantly increase their effect on crime.[34]

Moreover, research into foot patrol suggested that at least part of the fear reduction potential was linked to the order maintenance activities of foot patrol officers.[35] Subsequent work in Houston and Newark indicated that tactics other than foot patrol that, like foot patrol, emphasized increasing the quantity and improving the quality of police-citizen interactions had outcomes similar to those of foot patrol (fear reduction, etc.).[36] Meanwhile, many other cities were developing programs, though not evaluated, similar to those in the foot patrol, Flint, and fear reduction experiments.[37]

The findings of foot patrol and fear reduction experiments, when coupled with the research on the relationship between fear and disorder, created new opportunities for police to understand the increasing concerns of citizens' groups about disorder (gangs, prostitutes, etc.) and to work with citizens to do something about it. Police discovered that when they asked citizens about their priorities, citizens appreciated the inquiry and also provided useful information—often about problems that beat officers might have been aware of, but about which departments had little or no official data (e.g., disorder). Moreover, given the ambiguities that surround both the definitions of disorder and the authority of police to do something about it, police learned that they had to seek authorization from local citizens to intervene in disorderly situations.[38]

Simultaneously, Goldstein's problem-oriented approach to policing[39] was being tested in several communities: Madison, Wisconsin; Baltimore County, Maryland; and Newport News, Virginia. Problem-oriented policing rejects the fragmented approach in which police deal with each incident, whether citizen- or police-initiated, as an isolated event with neither history nor future. Pierce's findings about calls for service illustrate Goldstein's point: 60 percent of the calls for service in any given year in Boston originated from 10 percent of the households calling the police.[40] Furthermore, Goldstein and his colleagues in Madison, Newport News, and Baltimore County discovered the following: police officers enjoy operating with a holistic approach to their work; they have the capacity to do it successfully; they can work with citizens and other agencies to solve problems; and citizens seem to appreciate working with police—findings similar to those of the foot patrol experiments (Newark and Flint) [41] and the fear reduction experiments (Houston and Newark). [42]

The problem confronting police, policymakers, and academicians is that these trends and findings seem to contradict many of the tenets that dominated police thinking for a generation. Foot patrol creates new intimacy between citizens and police. Problem solving is hardly the routinized and standardized patrol modality that reformers thought was necessary to maintain control of police and limit their discretion. Indeed, use of discretion is the *sine qua non* of problem-solving policing. Relying on citizen endorsement of order maintenance activities to justify police action acknowledges a continued or new reliance on political authorization for police work in general. And, accepting the quality of urban life as an outcome of good police service emphasizes a wider definition of the police function and the desired effects of police work.

These changes in policing are not merely new police tactics, however. Rather, they represent a new organizational approach, properly called a community strategy. The elements of that strategy are:

Legitimacy and Authorization

There is renewed emphasis on community, or political, authorization for many police tasks, along with law and professionalism. Law continues to be the major legitimating basis of the police function. It defines basic police powers, but it does not fully direct police activities in efforts to maintain order, negotiate conflicts, or solve community problems. It becomes one tool among many others. Neighborhood, or community, support and involvement are required to accomplish those tasks. Professional and bureaucratic authority, especially that which tends to isolate police and insulate them from neighborhood influences, is lessened as citizens contribute more to definitions of problems and identification of solutions. Although in some respects similar to the authorization of policing's political era, community authorization exists in a different political context. The civil service movement, the political centralization that grew out of the Progressive era, and the bureaucratization, professionalization, and unionization of police stand as counterbalances to the possible recurrence of the corrupting influences of ward politics that existed prior to the reform movement.

The Police Function

As indicated above, the definition of police function broadens in the community strategy. It includes order maintenance, conflict resolution, problem solving through the organization, and provision of services, as well as other activities. Crime control remains an important function, with an important difference, however. The reform strategy attempts to control crime directly through preventive patrol and rapid response to calls for service. The community strategy emphasizes crime control *and prevention* as an indirect result of, or an equal partner to, the other activities.

Organizational Design

Community policing operates from organizational assumptions different from those of reform policing. The idea that workers have no legitimate, substantive interest in their work is untenable when programs such as those in Flint, Houston, Los Angeles, New York City, Baltimore County, Newport News, and others are examined. Consulting with community groups, problem solving, maintaining order, and other such activities are antithetical to the reform ideal of eliminating officer discretion through routinization and standardization of police activities. Moreover, organizational decentralization is inherent in community policing: the involvement of police officers in diagnosing and responding to neighborhood and community problems necessarily pushes operational and tactical decisionmaking to the lower levels of the organization. The creation of neighborhood police stations (storefronts, for example), reopening of precinct stations, and establishment of beat offices (in schools, churches, etc.) are concrete examples of such decentralization.

Decentralization of tactical decisionmaking to precinct or beat level does not imply abdication of executive obligations and functions, however. Developing, articulating, and monitoring organizational strategy remain the responsibility of management. Within this strategy, operational and tactical decisionmaking is decentralized. This implies what may at first appear to be a paradox: while the number of managerial levels may decrease, the number of managers may increase. Sergeants in a decentralized regime, for example, have managerial responsibilities that exceed those they would have in a centralized organization.

At least two other elements attend this decentralization: increased participative management and increased involvement of top police executives in planning and implementation. Chiefs have discovered that programs are easier to conceive and implement if officers themselves are involved in their development through task forces, temporary matrix-like organizational units, and other organizational innovations that tap the wisdom and experience of sergeants and patrol officers. Additionally, police executives have learned that good ideas do not translate themselves into successful programs without extensive involvement of the chief executive and his close agents in every stage of planning and implementation, a lesson learned in the private sector as well.[43]

One consequence of decentralized decisionmaking, participative planning and management, and executive involvement in planning is that fewer levels of authority are required to administer police organizations. Some police organizations, including the London Metropolitan Police (Scotland Yard), have begun to reduce the number of middle-management layers, while others are contemplating doing so. Moreover, as in the private sector, as computerized information gathering systems reach their potential in police departments, the need for middle managers whose primary function is data collection will be further reduced.

External Relationships

Community policing relies on an intimate relationship between police and citizens. This is accomplished in a variety of ways: relatively long-term assignment of officers to beats, programs that emphasize familiarity between citizens and police (police knocking on doors, consultations, crime control meetings for police and citizens, assignment to officers of "caseloads" of households with ongoing problems, problem solving, etc.), revitalization or development of Police Athletic League programs, educational programs in grade and high schools, and other programs. Moreover, police are encouraged to respond to the feelings and fears of citizens that result from a variety of social problems or from victimization.

Further, the police are restructuring their relationship with neighborhood groups and institutions. Earlier, during the reform era, police had claimed a monopolistic responsibility for crime control in cities, communities, and neighborhoods; now they recognize serious competitors in the "industry" of crime control, especially private security and the community crime control movement. Whereas in the past police had dismissed these sources of competition or, as in the case of community crime control, had attempted to coopt the movement for their own purposes,[44] now police in many cities (Boston, New York, Houston, and Los Angeles, to name a few) are moving to structure working relationships or strategic alliances with neighborhood and community crime control groups. Although there is less evidence of attempts to develop alliances with the private security industry, a recent proposal to the National Institute of Justice envisioned an experimental alliance between the Fort Lauderdale, Florida, Police Department and the Wackenhut Corporation in which the two organizations would share responses to calls for service.

Demand Management

In the community problem-solving strategy, a major portion of demand is decentralized, with citizens encouraged to bring problems directly to beat officers or precinct offices. Use of 911 is discouraged, except for dire emergencies. Whether tactics include aggressive foot patrol as in Flint or problem solving as in Newport News, the emphasis is on police officers' interacting with citizens to determine the types of problems they are confronting and to devise solutions to those problems. In contrast to reform policing with its selling orientation, this approach is more like marketing: customer preferences are sought, and satisfying customer needs and wants, rather than selling a previously packaged product or service, is emphasized. In the case of police, they gather information about citizens' wants, diagnose the nature of the problem, devise possible solutions, and then determine which segments of the community they can best serve and which can be best served by other agencies and institutions that provide services, including crime control.

Additionally, many cities are involved in the development of demarketing programs.[45] The most noteworthy example of demarketing is in the area of rapid response to calls for service. Whether through the development of alternatives to calls for service, educational programs designed to discourage citizens from using the 911 system, or, as in a few cities, simply not responding to many calls for service, police actively attempt to demarket a program that had been actively sold earlier. Often demarketing 911 is thought of as a negative process. It need not be so, however. It is an attempt by police to change social, political, and fiscal circumstances to bring consumers' wants in line with police resources and to accumulate evidence about the value of particular police tactics.

Tactics and Technology

Community policing tactics include foot patrol, problem solving, information gathering, victim counseling and services, community organizing and consultation, education, walk-and-ride and knock-on-door programs, as well as regular patrol, specialized forms of patrol, and rapid response to emergency calls for service. Emphasis is placed on information sharing between patrol and detectives to increase the possibility of crime solution and clearance.

Measured Outcomes

The measures of success in the community strategy are broad: quality of life in neighborhoods, problem solution, reduction of fear, increased order, citizen satisfaction with police services, as well as crime control. In sum, the elements of the community strategy include:

- Authorization—community support (political), law, professionalism.
- Function—crime control, crime prevention, problem solving.
- Organizational design—decentralized, task forces, matrices.
- Relationship to environment—consultative, police defend values of law and professionalism, but listen to community concerns.
- Demand—channelled through analysis of underlying problems.
- Tactics and technology—foot patrol, problem solving, etc.
- Outcomes—quality of life and citizen satisfaction.

CONCLUSION

We have argued that there were two stages of policing in the past, political and reform, and that we are now moving into a third, the community era. To carefully examine the dimensions of policing during each of these eras, we have used the concept of organizational strategy. We believe that this concept can be used not only to describe the different styles of policing in the past and the present, but also to sharpen the understanding of police policymakers of the future.

For example, the concept helps explain policing's perplexing experience with team policing during the 1960's and 1970's. Despite the popularity of team policing with officers involved in it and with citizens, it generally did not remain in police departments for very long. It was usually planned and implemented with enthusiasm and maintained for several years. Then, with little fanfare, it would vanish—with everyone associated with it saying regretfully that for some reason it just did not work as a police tactic. However, a close examination of team policing reveals that it was a strategy that innovators mistakenly approached as a tactic. It had implications for authorization (police turned to neighborhoods for support), organizational design (tactical decisions were made at lower levels of the organization), definition of function (police broadened their service role), relationship to environment (permanent team members responded to the needs of small geographical areas), demand (wants and needs came to team members directly from citizens), tactics (consultation with citizens, etc.), and outcomes (citizen satisfaction, etc.). What becomes clear, though, is that team policing was a competing strategy with different assumptions about every element of police business. It was no wonder that it expired under such circumstances. Team and reform policing were strategically incompatible—one did not fit into the other. A police department could have a small team policing unit or conduct a team policing experiment, but business as usual was reform policing.

Likewise, although foot patrol symbolizes the new strategy for many citizens, it is a mistake to equate the two. Foot patrol is a tactic, a way of delivering police services. In Flint, its inauguration has been accompanied by implementation of most of the elements of a community strategy, which has become business as usual. In most places, foot patrol is not accompanied by the other elements. It is outside the mainstream of "real" policing and often provided only as a sop to citizens and politicians who are demanding the development of different policing styles. This certainly was the case in New Jersey when foot patrol was evaluated by the Police Foundation.[46] Another example is in Milwaukee, where two police budgets are passed: the first is the police budget; the second, a supplementary budget for modest levels of foot patrol. In both cases, foot patrol is outside the mainstream of police activities and conducted primarily as a result of external pressures placed on departments.

It is also a mistake to equate problem solving or increased order maintenance activities with the new strategy. Both are tactics. They can be implemented either as part of a new organizational strategy, as foot patrol was in Flint, or as an "add-on," as foot patrol was in most of the cities in New Jersey. Drawing a distinction between organizational add-ons and a change in strategy is not an academic quibble; it gets to the heart of the current situation in policing. We are arguing that policing is in a period of transition from a reform strategy to what we call a community strategy. The change involves more than making tactical or organizational adjustments and accommodations. Just as policing went through a basic change when it moved from the political to the reform strategy, it is going through a similar change now. If elements of the emerging organizational strategy are identified and the policing institution is guided through the change rather than left blindly thrashing about, we expect that the public will be better served, policymakers and police administrators more effective, and the profession of policing revitalized.

A final point: the classical theory of organization that continues to dominate police administration in most American cities is alien to most of the elements of the new strategy. The new strategy will not accommodate to the classical theory: the latter denies too much of the real nature of police work, promulgates unsustainable myths about the nature and quality of police supervision, and creates too much cynicism in officers attempting to do creative problem solving. Its assumptions about workers are simply wrong.

Organizational theory has developed well beyond the stage it was at during the early 1900's, and policing does have organizational options that are consistent with the newly developing organizational strategy. Arguably, policing, which was moribund during the 1970's, is beginning a resurgence. It is overthrowing a strategy that was remarkable in its time, but which could not adjust to the changes of recent decades. Risks attend the new strategy and its implementation. The risks, however, for the community and the profession of policing, are not as great as attempting to maintain a strategy that faltered on its own terms during the 1960's and 1970's.

ENDNOTES

1. Kenneth R. Andrews, *The Concept of Corporate Strategy,* Homewood, Illinois, Richard D. Irwin, Inc., 1980.

2. Robert M. Fogelson, *Big-City Police.* Cambridge, Harvard University Press, 1977; Samuel Walker. *A Critical History of Police Reform: The Emergence of Professionalism,* Lexington, Massachusetts, Lexington Books, 1977.

3. Mark H. Moore and George L. Kelling, "To Serve and Protect: Learning From Police History," *The Public Interest,* 7, Winter 1983.

4. K.E. Jordan, *Ideology and the Coming of Professionalism: American Urban Police in the 1920's and 1930's.* Dissertation, Rutgers University, 1972.

5. Fogelson, *Big-City Police.*

6. Eric H. Monkkonen, *Police in Urban America,* 1860–1920, Cambridge, Cambridge University Press, 1981.

7. *The Newark Foot Patrol Experiment,* Washington, D.C., Police Foundation, 1981.

8. John Eck, *Solving Crimes: The Investigation of Burglary and Robbery,* Washington, D.C., Police Executive Research Forum, 1984.

9. Thomas A. Reppetto, *The Blue Parade,* New York, The Free Press, 1978.

10. Fogelson, *Big-City Police.*

11. Ibid.

12. George L. Kelling, "Reforming the Reforms: The Boston Police Department," Occasional Paper, Joint Center for Urban Studies of M.I.T. and Harvard, Cambridge, 1983.

13. George L. Kelling, "Juveniles and Police: The End of the Nightstick," in *From Children to Citizens, Vol. II: The Role of the Juvenile Court,* ed. Francis X. Hartmann, New York, Springer-Verlag. 1987.

14. Walker, *A Critical History of Police Reform: The Emergence of Professionalism.*

15. Fogelson, *Big-City Police.*

16. Kelling, "Juveniles and Police: The End of the Nightstick."

17. Orlando W. Wilson, *Police Administration,* New York: McGraw-Hill, 1950.

18. "Police Guidelines," John F. Kennedy School of Government Case Program #C14–75–24, 1975.

19. Herman Goldstein, *Policing a Free Society,* Cambridge, Massachusetts, Ballinger, 1977.

20. Kelling, "Reforming the Reforms: The Boston Police Department."

21. Fogelson, *Big-City Police.*

22. William H. Parker, "The Police Challenge in Our Great Cities," *The Annals* 29 (January 1954): 5–13.

23. For a detailed discussion of the differences between selling and marketing, see John L. Crompton and Charles W. Lamb, *Marketing Government and Social Services,* New York, John Wiley and Sons, 1986.

24. Commissioner Francis "Mickey" Roache of Boston has said that when the 911 system was instituted there, citizens persisted in calling "their" police—the district station. To circumvent this preference, district telephone numbers were changed so that citizens would be inconvenienced if they dialed the old number.

25. *The Newark Foot Patrol Experiment.*

26. O.W. Wilson, *Police Administration.*

27. A.E. Leonard, "Crime Reporting as a Police Management Tool," *The Annals* 29 (January 1954).

28. George L. Kelling et al., *The Kansas City Preventive Patrol Experiment: A Summary Report,* Washington, D.C., Police Foundation, 1974; William Spelman and Dale K. Brown, *Calling the Police,* Washington, D.C., Police Executive Research Forum, 1982.

29. *The Newark Foot Patrol Experiment;* Wesley G. Skogan and Michael G. Maxfield, *Coping With Crime,* Beverly Hills, California, Sage, 1981; Robert Trojanowicz, *An Evaluation of the Neighborhood Foot Patrol Program in Flint, Michigan,* East Lansing, Michigan State University, 1982.

30. Mary Ann Wycoff, *The Role of Municipal Police Research as a Prelude to Changing It,* Washington, D.C., Police Foundation, 1982; Goldstein, *Policing a Free Society.*

31. Raymond E. Miles and Charles C. Snow, *Organizational Strategy, Structure and Process,* New York, McGraw-Hill, 1978.

32. *The Newark Foot Patrol Experiment.*

33. *The Newark Foot Patrol Experiment,* Trojanowicz, *An Evaluation of the Neighborhood Foot Patrol Program in Flint, Michigan.*

34. Tony Pate et al., *Three Approaches to Criminal Apprehension in Kansas City: An Evaluation Report,* Washington, D.C., Police Foundation, 1976: Eck, *Solving Crimes: The Investigation of Burglary and Robbery.*

35. James Q. Wilson and George L. Kelling, "Police and Neighborhood Safety: Broken Windows," *Atlantic Monthly,* March 1982: 29–38.

36. Tony Pate et al., *Reducing Fear of Crime in Houston and Newark: A Summary Report,* Washington, D.C., Police Foundation, 1986.

37. Jerome H. Skolnick and David H. Bayley, *The New Blue Line: Police Innovation in Six American Cities,* New York, The Free Press, 1986; Albert J. Reiss, Jr., *Policing a City's Central District: The Oakland Story,* Washington, D.C., National Institute of Justice, March 1985.

38. Wilson and Kelling, "Police and Neighborhood Safety: Broken Windows."

39. Herman Goldstein, "Improving Policing: A Problem-Oriented Approach," *Crime and Delinquency,* April 1979, 236–258.

40. Glenn Pierce et al., "Evaluation of an Experiment in Proactive Police Intervention in the Field of Domestic Violence Using Repeat Call Analysis," Boston, Massachusetts, The Boston Fenway Project, Inc., May 13, 1987.

41. *The Newark Foot Patrol Experiment;* Trojanowicz, *An Evaluation of the Neighborhood Foot Patrol Program in Flint, Michigan.*

42. Pate et al., *Reducing Fear of Crime in Houston and Newark: A Summary Report.*

43. James R. Gardner, Robert Rachlin, and H.W. Allen Sweeny, eds., *Handbook of Strategic Planning,* New York, John Wiley and Sons, 1986.

44. Kelling, "Juveniles and Police: The End of the Nightstick."

45. Crompton and Lamb, *Marketing Government and Social Services.*

46. *The Newark Foot Patrol Experiment.*

The Evolving Strategy of Police:
A Minority View

HUBERT WILLIAMS
PATRICK V. MURPHY

. . . there is an underside to every age about which history does not often speak, because history is written from records left by the privileged. We learn about politics from the political leaders, about economics from the entrepreneurs, about slavery from the plantation owners, about the thinking of an age from its intellectual elite.

—HOWARD ZINN[1]

INTRODUCTION

Kelling and Moore, in their recent interpretation of the strategic history of American policing, succinctly summarize that history as falling generally into three eras: (1) political, (2) reform, and (3) community.[2] This attempt to create paradigms, as with all such attempts, should be seen metaphorically, providing us with ways to crystallize the complexities of history in simplified terms. Seen in this way, their analysis provides useful insights and a clearer interpretation of the changing role of police in American society—at least with respect to the majority in that society. Despite its utility, we find their analysis disturbingly incomplete. It fails to take account of how slavery, segregation, discrimination, and fascism have affected the development of American police departments—and how these factors have affected the quality of policing in the Nation's minority communities. Furthermore, we find Kelling and Moore to be silent on the important role that minorities have played in the past, and will play in the future, in affecting and improving the quality of policing in America. These omissions seriously diminish the accuracy and objectivity of their analysis and make it less useful than it otherwise could be in understanding the past and predicting the future of American policing.

This paper addresses these omissions by adding a "minority perspective." Ours represents a "minority perspective" in two different senses. First, our

Source: Williams, Hubert and Patrick V. Murphy (1990) The Evolving Strategy of Policing: A Minority View. *Perspectives on Policing* Number 13. Washington D.C.: National Institute of Justice.

understanding of what factors have shaped the evolution of policing was shared by only a minority of those participating in the discussions of the Harvard Executive Session on Community Policing. Whereas Kelling and Moore (and many others) attempted to explain the evolution of policing in terms of strategic choices made by police executives who were developing a professional ideology, we see policing as powerfully conditioned by broad social forces and attitudes—including a long history of racism. They see police departments as largely autonomous; we see them as barometers of the society in which they operate.

Second, our view is particularly attuned to how institutions, norms, and attitudes have dealt with racial minorities and how those dealings affected the role of police during each of the eras described by Kelling and Moore. More optimistically, we believe that improvements have occurred in the last several years and that further improvements are possible, although not assured, in the future. We are particularly aware of the implications for African-American minorities, but we believe that the patterns set in these relations have importantly affected relations with other racially distinctive minorities such as Hispanics, Asians, Native Americans, and other people of color.

In this paper, we contend that the strategies of police in dealing with minorities have been different from those in dealing with others, that the changes in police strategies in minority communities have been more problematic, and that, therefore, the beneficial consequences of those changes for minorities have been less noticeable. Specifically, we argue that:

- The fact that the legal order not only countenanced but sustained slavery, segregation, and discrimination for most of our Nation's history—and the fact that the police were bound to uphold that order—set a pattern for police behavior and attitudes toward minority communities that has persisted until the present day. That pattern includes the idea that minorities have fewer civil rights, that the task of the police is to keep them under control, and that the police have little responsibility for protecting them from crime within their communities.

- The existence of this pattern of police behavior and attitudes toward minority communities meant that, while important changes were occurring in policing during our Nation's history, members of minority groups benefited less than others from these changes—certainly less than it might have seemed from the vantage point of the white community and the police executives who were bringing about those changes.

- The Kelling and Moore discussion of the "political era" of policing, a period generally defined by them as extending from after Reconstruction through the first decade of the twentieth century, neglects the early role of the first varieties and functions of police in this country—as well as the legal and political powerlessness of minority communities in both the North and the South. This omission means that their analysis fails to recognize that members of those minority communities received virtually none of the benefits of policing that were directed to those with more political clout.

- Many of the most notable advances in policing brought about by the advent of the "reform era" proved to be elusive, if not counterproductive, for minorities. Several of the hiring and promotional standards, although implemented as antidotes to the rampant nepotism and political favoritism that had characterized policing during the "political era" proved to be detrimental to blacks—just as the time when, to a limited extent, because of their increasing political power, they were beginning to acquire the credentials that would have allowed them to qualify by the old standards.

- The potential of "professional policing" during the reform era was not fully realized—either for minorities or for whites—until the civil rights revolution of the late 1960's and the coming to power of progressive mayors, both black and white, and the police executives appointed by them who were capable of bringing about changes relevant to blacks and other minorities. It was that movement, led primarily by black Americans, and that political empowerment that finally began to produce the putative benefits of professional policing: a fairer distribution of police services, less use of deadly force, greater respect for individual rights, and equal opportunity for minorities within the Nation's police departments. Without that movement, the promise of professional policing would have remained hollow.

- The minority community also played a key role in initiating the era of community policing. It was the riots of the late 1960's—and the election of many black and white progressive mayors, who appointed likeminded police chiefs—that stimulated broad social investments in police agencies, therefore putting the issue of police-community relations inescapably on the minds of police executives and the mayors who appointed them. The fact that police actions triggered many of the riots and then could not control them revealed to everyone the price of having a police department backed only by the power of the law, but not by the consent, much less active support, of those being policed.

- The era of community policing holds potential benefits and hazards for the quality of American policing. The potential benefits lie in the fundamental tenet of community policing: the empowerment of communities to participate in problem solving and decisions about delivery of services based on the needs of individual neighborhoods. The hazards lie in the possibility of excluding those communities that have been the least powerful and least well organized and thus repeating the historical patterns of race relations in the United States. If, however, the more recent trends toward inclusion of African-Americans and other minorities in policing and in the broader society are continued, then community policing might finally realize a vision of police departments as organizations that protect the lives, property, and rights of all citizens in a fair and effective way.

THE POLITICAL ERA:
POLICING THE POWERLESS

Kelling and Moore argue that during the political era, from the introduction of the "new police" in the 1840's until the early 1900's, American police derived both their authority and resources from local political leaders. We maintain that their account is based largely on an analysis of policing in the cities of the northeastern United States, mostly following the Civil War and Reconstruction, and omitting the importance of racial and social conflicts in the origination of American police departments. As such, their analysis omits several crucial parts of the story of policing in America: the role of "slave patrols" and other police instruments of racial oppression; the role of the police in imposing racially biased laws; and the importance of racial and social turmoil in the creation of the first versions of America's "new police."

Most analyses of early American history reflect an understandable, white, twentieth-century bias toward northern, urban, white conditions. While the literature is replete with studies of the growth of law enforcement in northern urban areas in general[3] and northern cities such as Boston,[4] Chicago,[5] Detroit,[6] and New York City,[7] in particular, little attention has been paid to police development outside the urban North. Kelling and Moore reflect a similar bias. Since the vast majority of blacks in the early years of America lived in the South, and about 80 percent of those lived outside of cities, this perspective creates a significant distortion.

Prominent police historian Samuel Walker has noted the difficulty of establishing dates marking the origins of American modern-style policing, that is, a system of law enforcement involving a permanent agency employing full-time officers who engage in continuous patrol of fixed beats to prevent crime. The traditional analyses, based on urban evidence, have suggested that such policing evolved from older systems of militias, sheriffs, constables, and night watches, and culminated in the "new police" of Boston in 1838, New York City in 1845, Chicago in 1851, New Orleans and Cincinnati in 1852, Philadelphia in 1854, St. Louis in 1855, Newark and Baltimore in 1857, and Detroit in 1865.[8] As Richardson points out, however, these analyses neglect that:

> [many other cities with] elaborate police arrangements were those with large slave populations where white masters lived in dread of possible black uprisings. Charleston, Savannah, and Richmond provided for combined foot and mounted patrols to prevent slaves from congregating and to repress any attacks upon the racial and social status quo. In Charleston, for example, police costs constituted the largest item in the municipal budget.[9]

Indeed, as both Walker[10] and Reichel[11] contend, there is a strong argument to be made that the first American modern-style policing occurred in the "slave patrols," developed by the white slaveowners as a means of dealing with runaways. Believing that their militia was not capable of dealing with the perceived threat, the colonial State governments of the South enacted slave patrol legislation during the 1740's, e.g., in South Carolina:

> Foreasmuch [sic] as many late horrible and barbarous massacres have been actually committed and many more designed, on the white inhabitants of this Province, by negro slaves, who are generally prone to such cruel practices, which makes it highly necessary that constant patrols should be established.[12]

Neighboring Georgians were also concerned with maintaining order among their slaves. The preamble to their 1757 law establishing and regulating slave patrols contends:

> . . . it is absolutely necessary for the Security of his Majesty's Subjects in this Province, that Patrols should be established under proper Regulations in the settled parts thereof, for the better keeping of Negroes and other Slaves in Order and prevention of any Cabals, Insurrections or other Irregularities amongst them.[13]

Such statutes were eventually enacted in all southern States. Although specific provisions differed from State to State,[14] most of these laws responded to complaints that militia duty was being shirked and demands that a more regular system of surveillance be established.

In Georgia, all urban white men aged sixteen to sixty, with the exception of ministers of religion, were to conduct such patrol "on every night throughout the year." In the countryside, such patrols were to "visit every Plantation within their respective Districts once in every Month" and whenever they thought it necessary, "to search and examine all Negro-Houses for offensive weapons and Ammunition." They were also authorized to enter any "disorderly tipling-House, or other Houses suspected of harbouring, trafficking or dealing with Negroes" and could inflict corporal punishment on any slave found to have left his owner's property without permission.[15]

Foner points out that "slave patrols" had full power and authority to enter any plantation and break open Negro houses or other places when slaves were suspected of keeping arms; to punish runaways or slaves found outside their plantations without a pass; to whip any slave who should affront or abuse them in the execution of their duties; and to apprehend and take any slave suspected of stealing or other criminal offense, and bring him to the nearest magistrate.[16] Understandably, the actions of such patrols established an indelible impression on both the whites who implemented this system and the blacks who were the brunt of it.

Reflecting the northern, urban perspective, Kelling and Moore begin their consideration of American policing only after the earliest "new police" were established in the 1840's and 1850's. Even so, their analysis neglects to point out the importance of the role played by social discord in general, and the minority community in particular, in the creation of these departments. Phenomenal increases in immigration, rapid population growth, and major changes in industrialization led to more and more people, many of whom were from an impoverished, rural background, settling in an alien urban environment. Conflicts between black freedmen and members of the white urban working class significantly contributed to social unrest.

In 1830 Alexis de Tocqueville toured the United States to study prison reform. Unfamiliar with American norms, he was surprised to discover that there was more overt hostility and hatred toward blacks in the North, where slavery did not exist, than in the South, where it did. Those who challenged the status quo by demanding the abolition of slavery suffered verbal and physical abuse in northern cities.[17] This tension was reflected in a number of race riots in the mid-1830's in America's major cities. New York City had so many racial disorders in 1834 that it was long remembered as the "year of the riots." Boston suffered three major riots in the years 1834 to 1837, all of which focused on the issues of anti-abolitionism or anti-Catholicism. Philadelphia, the "City of Brotherly Love," experienced severe anti-Negro riots in 1838 and 1842; overall, the city had eleven major riots between 1834 and 1849. Baltimore experienced a total of nine riots, largely race-related, between 1834 and the creation of its new police in 1857. In a desperate attempt to cope with the social disorder brought about by this conflict, America's major cities resorted to the creation of police departments. Clearly, this was a case of the political system responding to incendiary conflict within the society at large by demanding that the police be reorganized to deal with those conflicts.

In their discussion of the political era, Kelling and Moore observe that the police found their legitimacy either in politics or in law. For blacks, both before and several generations after the Civil War, neither of these bases of legitimacy provided much, if any, opportunity to shape policing to their benefit. As the authors point out, local political machines often recruited and maintained police in their positions, from foot officer to police chief. In return, the police encouraged voters to support certain candidates and provided services designed to enhance that support. Departments were organized in a decentralized manner, giving officers a great deal of discretion in carrying out their responsibilities. Police officers were closely linked to the neighborhoods in which they patrolled, often living there and usually of the same ethnic stock as the residents.

For those with political influence, this era provided close proximity to power. Good jobs could be had. Special favors could be obtained. The police could be expected to be extremely sensitive to community concerns—or lose their jobs if they were not.

For those with no access to political power, however, the situation was very different. Before slavery was abolished, the issue of black political power in the South was moot. The Constitution itself provides a sardonic reflection on the state of political power assigned to slaves. The group of white delegates assembled in Philadelphia never even considered slave representation, slave votes, or slave power. The only issue was whether a *slaveowner* would enjoy a three-fifths increment of representation for every slave he owned.

During the debate, William Paterson stated bluntly that slaves were "no free agents, have no personal liberty, no faculty of acquiring property, but on the contrary, are themselves property" and hence like other property "entirely at the will of the master." To make certain there was no mistake, the Constitution explicitly prohibited Congress from abolishing the international slave trade to the United States before 1808.

Early American law enforcement officials in slave States were empowered—and expected—to enforce statutes carrying out the most extreme forms of racism, not restricted solely to enforcing slavery. In 1822, for example, Charleston, South Carolina, experienced a slave insurrection panic, caused by a supposed plot of slaves and free blacks to seize the city. In response, the State legislature passed the Negro Seamen's Act, requiring free black seamen to remain on board their vessels while in Carolina harbors. If they dared to leave their ships, the police were instructed to arrest them and sell them into slavery unless they were redeemed by the ship's master. The other coastal slave States soon enacted similar legislation.

Berlin presents this brief synopsis of Southern justice:

> Southern law presumed all Negroes to be slaves, and whites systematically barred free Negroes from any of the rights and symbols they equated with freedom. Whites legally prohibited Negro freemen from moving freely, participating in politics, testifying against whites, keeping guns, or lifting a hand to strike a white person. . . . In addition they burdened free Negroes with special imposts, barred them from certain trades, and often tried and punished them like slaves. To enforce their proscriptive codes and constantly remind free Negroes of their lowly status, almost every State forced free Negroes to register and carry freedom papers, which had to be renewed periodically and might be inspected by any suspicious white.[18]

Police supervision further strengthened the registration system. City officials periodically ordered police to check the papers of all newly arrived free Negroes or investigate freedmen who failed to register or lacked visible means of support.[19]

Outside the slave States, the rights of blacks were only somewhat less restricted. Although Henry David Thoreau and William Lloyd Garrison exaggerated when they called Massachusetts a slave State, their harsh denunciation is a reminder that a black person could be a slave there or in any of the other "free" States because of the protection afforded by the Federal and State constitutions for masters' rights in fugitive and sojourning slaves. It fell to agents of law enforcement, constables and members of the day and night watches, to carry out these laws. By 1800, some 36,505 northern Negroes still remained in bondage, most of them in New York and New Jersey.[20]

Several northern States enacted gradual emancipation statutes after the Revolution. Because such statutes freed only children born after a specified date, however, many slaves remained unaffected, and the freed children were held in apprenticeship until some time in their adult years. The State of New Jersey was typical. In 1804, the legislature freed the children born to slave mothers after July 4 of that year; the child so freed would be "apprenticed" to its mother's owner, men until age 25, women until 21. Only in 1844 did it remove all barriers to the freeing of slaves. Again, these laws were also enforced by the local constable.

Even after the northern States took action to free slaves — ranging from constitutional provisions in Vermont in 1777 to gradual-abolition acts in New Jersey in 1804 and New York in 1817, the legal and political rights of blacks were quite circumscribed. Every new State admitted to the Union after 1819 restricted voting to whites. Only five States—Massachusetts, Rhode Island, Maine, New Hampshire, and Vermont—provided equal voting rights for black and white males. Illinois, Ohio, Indiana, Iowa, and California prohibited black testimony in court if whites were a party to the proceeding, and Oregon forbade Negroes to hold real estate, make contracts, or maintain lawsuits. Massachusetts banned intermarriage of whites with blacks and enforced segregation in hotels, restaurants, theaters, and transportation. Berlin describes a raid in 1853 in which St. Louis police raided well-known hangouts of freedmen, whipped those who were unregistered, and shipped them out of town. Such raids continued for almost a year.[21]

Litwack describes the situation of northern blacks this way:

> In virtually every phase of existence, Negroes found themselves systematically separated from whites. They were either excluded from railway cars, omnibuses, stagecoaches, and steamboats or assigned to special "Jim Crow" sections: they sat, when permitted, in secluded and remote corners of theaters and lecture halls; they could not enter most hotels, restaurants, and resorts, except as servants; they prayed in "Negro pews" in the white churches, and if partaking of the sacrament of the Lord's Supper, they waited until the whites had been served the bread and wine. Moreover, they were often educated in segregated schools, punished in segregated prisons, nursed in segregated hospitals, and buried in segregated cemeteries.[22]

Indeed, as pointed out by C. Vann Woodward, an eminent historian of the South, "One of the strangest things about Jim Crow [the laws and practices separating the races] was that the system was born in the North and reached an advanced age before moving South in force."[23]

With neither political power nor legal standing, blacks could hardly be expected to share in the spoils of the political era of policing. There were virtually no black police officers until well into the twentieth century. Thus, police attention to, and protection for, areas populated primarily by racial minorities was rare during this era.

THE REFORM ERA: POLICING BY THE LAW FOR THOSE UNPROTECTED BY IT

According to Kelling and Moore's interpretation, the basic police strategy began to change during the early 1990's. By the 1930's, they argue, the reform era of policing was in full sway. Strikingly, their discussion completely overlooks the momentous events of the Civil War and Reconstruction, a time of great change in the legal and political status of minorities.

In the earliest days of the Civil War, President Lincoln and other northern politicians insisted that the issue of slavery had little to do with the conflict. In fact, in July 1861, when Congress assembled in special session, one of its first acts was to pass, almost unanimously, the Crittenden Resolution, affirming that the "established institutions" of the seceding States were not to be a military target. To a large extent, this position was dictated by political forces—to keep the border States in the Union, generate support among the broadest constituency in the North, and weaken the Confederacy by holding out the possibility that they could return to the Union with their property, including their slaves, intact.[24]

Eventually, however, as the Confederacy put slaves to work as military laborers and the presence of Union troops precipitated large-scale desertion of plantation slaves, this policy was overcome by events. On January 1, 1863, Lincoln signed the Emancipation Proclamation. Bowing to political reality, however, he excluded from its purview the 450,000 slaves in Delaware, Kentucky, Maryland, and Missouri; 275,000 in Union-occupied Tennessee; and tens of thousands in occupied portions of Virginia and Louisiana.

By 1864, the Senate approved the 13th amendment, abolishing slavery throughout the Union, but it failed to receive the necessary two-thirds majority in the House. Eventually, in January 1865, this amendment narrowly won House approval and was sent to the States for ratification. Although several Southern legislatures were reluctant to lend their support, this amendment was ratified by the end of the year. To some, this not only ended one of America's most shameful institutions but offered the hope of the beginning of a Nation where North and South, black and white, were ruled by one law impartial over all. As we know with historical hindsight, such an interpretation was far too optimistic.

Even at the time, questions were raised about the practical implications of the amendment. James A. Garfield asked, "What is freedom? Is it the bare privilege of not being chained? . . . If this is all, then freedom is a bitter mockery, a cruel delusion." More to the point, Frederick Douglass maintained, "Slavery is not abolished until the black man has the ballot."[25]

In fact, a political vacuum developed between 1865 and 1867 in which the opponents of the extension of full citizenship to blacks were able to exercise great influence. President Andrew Johnson, with hopes of receiving the support of his fellow Southerners in the election in 1868, left the definition of black rights to the individual States. They accepted the opportunity with a vengeance. In addition to prohibiting black suffrage, the provisional legislatures passed the Black Codes, a series of State laws intended to define the freedmen's new rights and responsibilities.

Mississippi and South Carolina enacted the first and most severe Black Codes toward the end of 1865. Mississippi required all blacks to possess, each January, written evidence of employment for the coming year. Laborers leaving their jobs before the contract expired would forfeit wages already earned and, as under slavery, be subject to arrest by any white citizen. A person offering work to a laborer already under contract risked imprisonment or a fine. Blacks were forbidden to rent land in urban areas. Vagrants—under whose definition fell the idle, disorderly, and those who "misspend what they earn"—could be punished by fines or involuntary plantation labor; other criminal offenses included "insulting" gestures or language, "malicious mischief," and preaching the Gospel without a license. In case anything had been overlooked, the legislature declared all existing penal codes defining crimes by slaves and free blacks "in full force" unless specifically altered by law. South Carolina's Code barred blacks from any occupation other than farmer or servant except by paying an annual tax ranging from $10 to $100.[26]

Virtually all of the former Confederate States enacted such laws. Blacks protested most bitterly, however, against apprenticeship laws, which seized upon the consequences of slavery—the separation of families and the freedmen's poverty—to provide planters with the unpaid labor of black minors. Generally, these laws allowed judges to bind to white employers black orphans and those whose parents were deemed unable to support them. The former slaveowner usually had first preference, the consent of the parents was not required, and the law permitted "moderate corporal chastisement."[27]

This entire complex of Black Codes was enforced:

> . . . by a police apparatus and judicial system in which blacks enjoyed
> virtually no voice whatever. Whites staffed urban police forces as well
> as State militias, intended, as a Mississippi white put it in 1865, to "keep
> good order and discipline amongst the negro population."[28]

Sheriffs, justices of the peace, and other local officials proved extremely reluctant to prosecute whites accused of crimes against blacks. In those rare cases in which they did prosecute, convictions were infrequent and sentences were far more lenient than blacks received for the same crimes. For example, Texas courts indicted some 500 white men for the murder of blacks in 1865 and 1866, but not one was convicted.[29]

Largely in response to the Black Codes, Congress passed, over President Johnson's veto, the Civil Rights Act of 1866. This act defined all persons born in the United States (except Indians) as national citizens and spelled out rights they were to enjoy equally without regard to race—making contracts, bringing lawsuits, and enjoying "full and equal benefit of all laws and proceedings for the security of person and property." No State law or custom could deprive any citizen of these rights. Furthermore, Federal officials were authorized to bring suit against violations and made all persons, including local officials, who deprived a citizen of a civil right liable to fine or imprisonment.

To institutionalize the legal implications of the Civil War beyond the reach of shifting political majorities and presidential vetoes, Congress, after a long struggle, passed the 14th amendment, providing, among other things, that equal protection under the law be afforded to every citizen. Although it implicitly acknowledged the right of States to limit voting because of race, they could do so only at the expense of losing a significant portion of their congressional representation.

The 1866 congressional election essentially became a referendum on the 14th amendment — Republicans in favor, President Johnson and the Democrats opposed. The Republicans won an overwhelming victory, large enough to give them well over the two-thirds majority required to override a veto. In contrast, all Southern legislatures except Tennessee repudiated the amendment by enormous majorities.

Frustrated, and sensing its political strength, the Congress passed, again over Johnson's veto, the Reconstruction Act of 1867. This act divided the eleven Confederate States, except Tennessee, into five military districts and stipulated the process by which new State governments could be created and recognized. This process required the ratification of the 14th amendment, writing of new constitutions providing for manhood suffrage, and approval of these constitutions by a majority of registered voters.

After two years of "Presidential Reconstruction," characterized by a lack of commitment to the extension of full rights to blacks, the era of "Radical Reconstruction" began. Given the right to vote, many blacks participated in — and won — election to the new State legislatures. To allay any concerns that the issue had not been addressed completely, Congress passed the 15th amendment, providing the right to vote to all persons, regardless of "race, color, or previous state of servitude," and prohibited the abridgement of that right by Federal and State governments. The Civil Rights Act of 1875 outlawed the exclusion of blacks from hotels, theaters, railroads, and other public accommodations.

The results of black suffrage on policing were not long in coming. Blacks appeared in several southern police departments soon after Radical Reconstruction began, especially where Republicans were in office and where blacks constituted a large percentage of the population. Black police appeared in Selma, Alabama, in 1867; Houston, Texas, in 1870; and Jackson, Mississippi, in 1871.[30] In New Orleans, a majority of whose population was black, a police board composed of three black members out of five appointed a police force that included 177 blacks by 1870.[31]

Such change was not always easy, however. In July 1868, in Raleigh, North Carolina, under the headline "The Mongrel Regime!! Negro Police!!" the Conservative *Daily Sentinel* announced the appointment of four black police officers and concluded that "this is the beginning of the end."[32] Race riots occurred in Jackson and Meridian, Mississippi, because black police attempted to use their police authority over whites.[33]

In 1872, a Republican mayor in Chicago appointed the first black policeman in the North, where black suffrage was not required by Congress. Three years later, a mayor belonging to the People's Party replaced that officer with another black. In 1880, the Republicans won the mayor's office again, resulting in the appointment of four more black policemen. These officers all worked in plain clothes — in part not to offend the sensibilities of racist whites — and were assigned to black neighborhoods, practices adopted in most departments that hired blacks at that time. By 1894 there were 23 black policemen in

Chicago.[34] Blacks were appointed in other cities in the North soon after those in Chicago; in Washington, D.C., in 1874; in Indianapolis in 1876; in Cleveland in 1881; in Boston in 1885.[35]

Lane provides one of the most thorough and fascinating analyses of the political complexities involved in appointing the first black police officers.[36] The approximately 7,000 blacks in Philadelphia's Seventh Ward had become a consistent Republican constituency, accounting for more than 10 percent of the party's vote. During the 1880 mayoral campaign, however, the black vote became a target of both parties' attention. Although the Seventh Ward voted overwhelmingly for the Republican candidate, the winner was Samuel King, a reform Democrat. Mayor King then appointed Alexander Davis and three other black men to the police department.

The selection criteria applied in appointing these Philadelphia officers reflect a common pattern in the choice of the earliest black officers. As Lane points out:

> In an era before any sort of civil service, when many officers were semi-literate at best, the four blacks chosen, although currently trapped in unskilled jobs, were characteristically overqualified.[37]

Davis, although born a slave, had graduated from Lincoln University, worked as a school teacher, and founded a newspaper. Only one of the other blacks appointed at that time had no experience beyond "laboring work."

Despite their qualifications, the appointment of the first black police officers in Philadelphia produced the same responses as were seen in many other cities. Several officers quit the force in protest. The new men were assigned to beats in or near black neighborhoods and immediately attracted crowds of spectators, saying such things as "Ain't he sweet?" or "Is the thing alive?"

As in Philadelphia, most departments, to appease the racial attitudes of whites, did not allow black officers to arrest whites or to work with white officers. Even as late as 1961, a study reported by the President's Commission on Law Enforcement and Administration of Justice found that 31 percent of the departments surveyed restricted the right of blacks to make felony arrests; the power of black officers to make misdemeanor arrests was even more limited.[38]

Miami established a different designation for the two races: blacks were "patrolmen" and whites were "policemen." In Chicago, blacks were largely confined to the Southside districts; in St. Louis, the "black beats" ranged from the central downtown area to the Northside. Los Angeles established a special "black watch" for the predominantly black Newton Station district.

After the initial dramatic changes brought about by the effects of Radical Reconstruction, the situation for blacks — and policing — began to revert to the *status quo ante*. As early as 1867, black suffrage went down to defeat in referendums in Minnesota, Ohio, and Kansas. Moderates within the Republican party began to back away from "extreme radical measures" such as egalitarianism. The Ku Klux Klan, founded in 1866 in Tennessee as a social club, launched a reign of terror against Republican leaders, black and white. In some parts of the South, armed whites blocked blacks from voting. Violence spread, especially in Georgia and Louisiana where, unable to hold meetings, Republicans abandoned their presidential campaign. By 1868, Republicans, the stalwart supporters of black rights, began to lose some of their strength in the South.[39]

By 1872, the presidential election focused on southern policy, the Democrats emphasizing the evils of Reconstruction and the need to restore local self-government. Although the Republicans won, a significant number of former Radicals supported the Democratic ticket, indicating that their campaign themes were more powerful than the returns would indicate.

While political support for Radical Reconstruction waned, debate about whether the 14th amendment applied only to States raged throughout the Nation—and has continued to do so even in the last decade. Presidents Grant and Hayes retreated from strict enforcement of the so-called "Reconstruction amendments." The Supreme Court began to shift away from the broad interpretation of the 13th amendment to the narrower 14th and 15th. This shift, in turn, encouraged legislators to narrow their concerns as well.

In 1874, a long-awaited compilation of the United States laws, known as the *Revised Statutes,* was produced. This document rearranged the Nation's laws into supposedly relevant, logical categories. Inexplicably, however, this rearrangement failed to list the Civil Rights Act of 1866 either in the published text or in the "historical" documentation. Instead, various parts of the 1866 law were scattered throughout the document, under various chapter headings. Civil rights as an independent subject worthy of the attention of lawyers, judges, law professors, and an entire generation of law students was neither easily researched nor, by implication, important. One by one, case by case, the legal rights of blacks were ruled away.

Against this already ominous backdrop came the Compromise of 1877, by which the Federal Government agreed to end Reconstruction, withdraw military forces from the South, and cease enforcing civil rights laws. In exchange, the election of the Republican candidate for president, Rutherford B. Hayes, was assured. The dike that had laboriously been constructed against racist retaliation was suddenly broken. The stage was set for a massive reversal of the gains made in the previous 20 years.

In 1883, the Supreme Court, in deciding five litigations joined as the *Civil Rights Cases,* declared the Civil Rights Act of 1875 unconstitutional. Reflecting the earlier debates over the Reconstruction amendments, the ruling was based on the premise that those amendments prohibited only States, not individuals, from infringing on the equal protection and due process guaranteed to individuals by the Constitution.

Moreover, in 1896, the Supreme Court, in the landmark decision of *Plessy* v. *Ferguson,* found State laws that required segregation of the races in public accommodations to be constitutional, thereby endorsing the proposition that public facilities could be "separate but equal." This decision virtually completed the quarter-century-long process of standing the law established by the Reconstruction amendments on its head. The effects were quickly seen in police departments. In department after department, blacks lost their jobs, either by dismissal or by being forced to resign. The disappearance of blacks from the

New Orleans police department serves as the most dramatic example of this trend. From a high of 177 black officers in 1870, the number dropped to 27 in 1880. By 1900, only five black officers remained; by 1910 there were none. The city did not appoint another black to the police force until 1950.

It is in this context that the Kelling and Moore discussion of the reform era must be interpreted. They argue that police reformers, led by August Vollmer and O.W. Wilson, changed the basic orientation of American policing in response to the excesses of the political era. The paradigm thus adopted, they contend, rejected politics as the source of authority for the police, replacing it with law and professionalism.

In an effort to curtail the close relationship between local political leaders and police, civil service replaced patronage and influence in the selection, assignment, and retention of police officers. Individual police officers were expected to avoid becoming closely associated with, and therefore contaminated by, the areas in which they patrolled. In some cases, they were prohibited from living in their beats. To further eliminate local political influence, functional control was centralized. By the time this era had reached its peak, during the 1950's and 1960's, police departments had become largely autonomous agencies, led by professionals guided by law, immune from political influence.

As dramatic as this change must have appeared to the white middle-class inhabitants of America's major cities, the transition to the reform era was barely noticeable to blacks and other minorities. Relying on law, rather than politics, as the source of police authority had many desirable aspects for those provided full protection by the law. Once again, however, for those who lacked both political power and equal protection under the law, such a transformation could have little significance.

Even the particular mechanisms implemented to bring about reform proved to be of little avail to blacks and other minorities. Civil service examinations, for example, designed to avoid the influence of patronage and nepotism, provided slight consolation for those who had been denied access to quality education. These examinations, which according to some experts, reveal less about the qualifications of the applicants than about the cultural biases of the examiners, winnowed out a far higher proportion of blacks than whites. In Boston, for example, the examiners failed 75 percent of the blacks as opposed to 35 percent of the whites in 1970. In Atlanta, in the same year, 72 percent of the blacks and only 24 percent of the whites failed. In New York, in 1968, 65 percent of the blacks as opposed to 31 percent of the whites failed. Mexicans and Puerto Ricans fared even worse, perhaps because the tests were given in English.[40]

Background investigations, which blacks and other minorities are more likely to fail than whites, also served as a barrier to inclusion. Fogelson reports evidence indicating that investigators rejected 41 percent of black applicants as opposed to 29 percent of whites in St. Louis in 1966; 68 percent of the blacks, as opposed to 56 percent of the whites, were rejected in Cleveland in 1966; and 58 percent of the blacks, as opposed to 32 percent of the whites, in Philadelphia in 1968.[41] He concludes that these disparities were a function of two things, notwithstanding racial prejudice. First, many departments were unwilling to

accept any applicant who had been arrested or convicted for any criminal offense, no matter how trivial—the President's Crime Commission showed that
blacks were more likely to have a criminal record than whites.[42] Second, most
departments were reluctant to hire anyone who was truant from school,
changed jobs too often, associated with known criminals, or had broken military regulations, all of which are more prevalent among blacks and other minorities than among whites.[43] Regardless of the merits of these criteria, their
effect was the same—the exclusion of minorities.

Centralization of control also provided little help for minorities, inasmuch
as it meant that already strained relations with the police officer on the beat
translated into even more strained relations with a distant government downtown. Reduced contacts with local officers meant that limited opportunities to
bridge the racial barrier became even more limited.

In their efforts to attract qualified recruits, the reformers not only raised sal-
aries, increased benefits, and improved working conditions, they also extended
their recruitment efforts. One method of expanding the pool of applicants was
to abolish residency requirements. This reform, although defended by reformers
on professional grounds, handicapped the blacks, Hispanics, and other minorities by slowing down the ethnic turnover in police departments. Without such a
change, as whites fled from the inner cities, the increasing percentage of minorities remaining could have been expected to have been more readily reflected in
the ranks of the police. Furthermore, despite heavy immigration of minorities to
the Nation's urban centers, the competitive edge that had been experienced earlier by the Irish and other white ethnic minorities no longer held sway.

Despite its limitations, the reform era provided, for members of the majority, a marked improvement in the delivery of professional police services. For
members of minority groups, however, the change from the political era, in
which they lacked political power, to the reform era, in which they lacked the
support of the law, meant, for the most part, more of the same. In only 7 of the
26 cities for which the Kerner Commission collected data was the percentage
of nonwhite police officers equal to as much as one-third of the percentage of
nonwhites in the city.[44]

THE COMMUNITY ERA: POLICING
DISINTEGRATING COMMUNITIES

By the late 1970's and early 1980's, according to Kelling and Moore, we had
entered the era of community policing. Although law remained a source of
authority, the police began once again to recognize that, ultimately, they are dependent on neighborhood, or community, support to achieve their goals. Turning to the citizens they serve for consultation, the police realized that more was
expected of them than simply enforcing the law. Looking at people as clients of
their services, the police found that they were also being judged on their ability

to maintain order, resolve conflict, protect rights, and provide other services. In order to be able to remain responsive to community concerns, organizational decentralization was necessary. To remain even more flexible, officers were given authority and discretion to develop responses appropriate to local needs.

To organized, empowered communities, this strategy of policing offered extraordinary opportunities to participate in structuring the nature of police services delivered. As a result of community demands, for example, programs such as foot patrol were revived, long before they were found to be effective in reducing fear and, in some cases, crime. Despite the popularity of such initiatives, a closer examination of the areas in which such foot beats were created reveals one of the serious problems with this approach. In the State of New Jersey, for example, where foot patrol was funded by the Safe and Clean Neighborhoods Program, most foot beats were instituted in areas with strong community or business organizations—or both—with strong support from and access to political leaders. Those without such resources—and those most in need of police services—often found themselves in a long queue.

Although the 1954 Supreme Court decision in *Brown v. Board of Education of Topeka* began to provide blacks and other minorities with their just share of legal rights and remedies, that provision came only with "all deliberate speed." As this glacially slow process continued, something more virulent occurred in minority communities, especially in the inner cities. Those who could afford to do so moved into less crowded, more comfortable, neighborhoods, leaving behind vacant houses—and those who could not afford an alternative. Businesses closed. Tax bases eroded. Among those who remained, unemployment, especially among minority youths, grew markedly higher than among whites. The incomes of employed minorities was significantly lower than that of whites. The quality of education deteriorated. School dropout rates rose precipitously. Infant mortality rates reached alarming levels. Decent, affordable housing became scarce. More and more children were born to unwed mothers. Drug and alcohol use became endemic. Crime and the fear of crime soared out of control.

The convergence of these factors produced a vicious circle. The police, regardless of the era or the strategic paradigm, must, along with families and other community institutions, concern themselves with crime and the fear of crime. The inner cities, where families, schools, jobs, and other community institutions were disintegrating at a rapid pace, presented the police with the most serious crime problems of all. But the police, because of a gross underrepresentation of minorities among their ranks, a lack of sensitivity and understanding of minority concerns and culture, and, therefore, a lack of community support, were least able to deal effectively in the inner cities—precisely where they were needed most.

Frustrated and angry, many blacks came to see the police as symbolizing the entire "system"—those institutions and resources that had been so unresponsive to their needs. Tensions rose, culminating in the series of riots in America's inner cities during the middle and late 1960's. Many Americans had their first glimpse of ghettos as they burned through the night. Reflecting the nature and extent of the underlying problems, Senator Robert Kennedy observed, after visiting the scene of the Watts riot, "There is no point in telling Negroes to observe the law. . . . It has almost always been used against them." Despite the tragic destructiveness of those riots, they did concentrate the minds of the Nation's leaders wonderfully. In 1967, President Johnson appointed the National Advisory Commission on Civil Disorders (the Kerner Commission) to investigate the causes of the disorder and to recommend solutions. In a trenchant analysis, the commission report concluded that "Our Nation is moving toward two societies, one black, one white—separate and unequal." [45] Essentially, they said, what lay behind the riots was a long historical pattern of racism on the part of whites in America. In one of the most forceful passages of their report, the commissioners observed:

> What white Americans have never fully understood—but what a Negro can never forget—is that white society is deeply implicated in the ghetto. White institutions created it, white institutions maintain it, and white society condones it. [46]

Specifically, the Kerner Commission found that many of the riots had been precipitated by police actions, often cases of insensitivity, sometimes incidents of outright brutality. They saw an atmosphere of hostility and cynicism reinforced by a widespread belief among many blacks in a "double standard" of justice and protection. More generally, they concluded that:

> In many ways the policeman only symbolizes much deeper problems. The policeman in the ghetto is a symbol not only of law, but of the entire system of law enforcement and criminal justice. [47]

The report offered five basic suggestions to address this situation:

- Change operations in the inner city to ensure proper officer conduct and to eliminate abrasive practices.
- Provide adequate police protection to inner city residents to eliminate the high level of fear and crime.
- Create mechanisms through which citizens can obtain effective responses to their grievances.
- Produce policy guidelines to assist police in avoiding behaviors that would create tension with inner city residents.
- Develop community support for law enforcement.

Fearful that new conflagrations would occur otherwise, and responding in many cases to newly elected black and progressive white mayors, many departments followed the commission's recommendations. As a result, a number of improvements have occurred that have reduced the barriers between the police and the inner city. Many more blacks and other minorities are now patrolling our streets. Strict rules against the unnecessary use of weapons, brutality, harassment, verbal abuse, and discourtesy have been promulgated and enforced.

The use of aggressive patrol techniques has been curtailed, restricted to those situations in which it is justified. Steps have been taken to ensure adequate patrol coverage and rapid response to calls for service from inner city areas. Open, impartial, and prompt grievance mechanisms have been established. Policy guidelines have been implemented to direct officers' discretion in potentially tense situations. New approaches—storefront offices, adopting (or even organizing) neighborhood groups, addressing the causes of fear—have been put into effect to improve relations with the community.

Because of these changes, the relationship between the police and citizens has improved considerably in the last several years—to a large extent in white middle-class neighborhoods, to a lesser extent in the inner city. Any transition to an era of community policing will be both a cause and an effect of these improvements. But such a transition is far from complete in the inner city. A recent assessment by the Commission on the Cities found that, despite a brief period of improvement, the conditions that produced the dissolution of ghetto communities are actually getting worse. "Quiet riots," the report concludes, are occurring in America's central cities: unemployment, poverty, social disorganization, segregation, housing and school deterioration, and crime are worse now than ever before.[48] These "quiet riots," although not as alarming or as noticeable to outsiders as those of the 1960's, are even more destructive of human life. Under such conditions, it is unreasonable to expect that the residents of the inner city will have the characteristics—whether social, economic, or political—that are required to sustain the partnership required of the community policing approach.

Furthermore, although the police are better prepared to deal with residents of the inner city than they were 20 years ago, they are far from having totally bridged the chasm that has separated them from minorities—especially blacks—for over 200 years. There are still too few black officers, at all levels. Racism still persists within contemporary police departments. Regardless of rules and guidelines, inappropriate behavior on the streets still occurs. Complaints about differential treatment, patrol coverage, and response time persist. And empirical studies have shown that community-oriented approaches that are effective in most neighborhoods work less well, or not at all, in areas inhabited by low-income blacks and other minority groups.

We welcome the prospect of entering the community era of policing. In a dramatic way, this represents a return to the first principles of policing as established in London in 1829. As Critchley so aptly put it, "From the start, the police was to be . . . in tune with the people, understanding the people, belonging to the people, and drawing its strength from the people."[49] Once community policing becomes a pervasive reality, we will have finally approximated the attainment of that goal. We have begun to bring such fundamental changes about in many of our Nation's police departments. But because of the devastation afflicting our inner cities and the inability of our police to relate to those neighborhoods, the areas that most require a transition to the community era will unfortunately be the last to experience such a change.

SUMMARY

Kelling and Moore have contributed a valuable addition to our repertoire of concepts for understanding the strategic history of American policing. Their interpretation of the shifts in policing from a political to a reform to a community era provides useful insights. It is our contention, however, that the applicability of this interpretation is confined largely to the white majority communities of our Nation. For blacks, and to a lesser extent other minority groups, the utility of this analysis is quite limited.

During the political era, for example, blacks were completely powerless, leaving them unable to exert the influence necessary to affect police strategy. According to the paradigm Kelling and Moore posit to have prevailed in the reform era, police strategy was determined largely on the basis of law, which left blacks almost completely unprotected. Finally, the community era requires an empowered, cohesive community to be able to deal with a sensitive, responsive police agency; neither precondition prevails in many contemporary minority neighborhoods.

Significant progress has been made, however. Large numbers of blacks and other minorities have joined — and in many cases have become leaders of — our major departments. The use of violence by police against minorities has declined dramatically in the last decade. Special efforts have been made to provide training to make our police officers sensitive to the needs and concerns of minority communities. Enlightened, better educated police leadership has opened the profession to new approaches and ideas. The rising popularity of community-oriented policing will undoubtedly further improve the relationship between the police and minorities.

We think it is a particularly hopeful sign in this regard that many of the most articulate proponents of community policing are themselves African-American police executives. Their unswerving emphasis, in their statements of values, on the protection of constitutional rights and the protection of all citizens, gives us reason to be optimistic about the future of policing.

Nevertheless, the history of American police strategies cannot be separated from the history of the Nation as a whole. Unfortunately, our police, and all of our other institutions, must contend with many bitter legacies from that larger history. No paradigm — and no society — can be judged satisfactory until those legacies have been confronted directly.

ENDNOTES

1. Howard Zinn, *The Politics of History.* Boston, Beacon Press, 1970:102.

2. George L. Kelling and Mark H. Moore, "The Evolving Strategy of Policing," *Perspectives on Policing,* No. 4. Washington, D.C., National Institute of Justice and Harvard University, November 1988.

3. Robert M. Fogelson, *Big-City Police.* Cambridge, Harvard University Press, 1977. J.F. Richardson, *Urban Police in the United States.* Port Washington, New York, National University Publications, 1974.

4. Roger Lane, *Policing the City: Boston, 1822–1885.* Cambridge, Harvard

University Press, 1967. E.A. Savage, *A Chronological History of the Boston Watch and Police, from 1631–1865.* Available on Library of American Civilization fiche 13523, 1865.

5. J. Flinn, *History of the Chicago Police from the Settlement of the Community to the Present Time.* Montclair, New Jersey, Patterson Smith, 1975.

6. J. Schneider, *Detroit and the Problem of Order, 1830–1880: A Geography of Crime, Riot, and Policing.* Lincoln, University of Nebraska, 1980.

7. J.F. Richardson, *The New York Police: Colonial Times to 1901.* New York, Oxford University Press, 1970.

8. Samuel Walker, *A Critical History of Police Reform: The Emergence of Professionalism.* Lexington, Massachusetts, Lexington Books, 1977:4–6.

9. Richardson, *Urban Police,* n. 3 above: 19.

10. Walker, *A Critical History,* n. 8 above.

11. P.L. Reichel, "Southern slave patrols as a transitional police type," *American Journal of Policing,* 7, 2: 51–77.

12. T. Cooper, ed., *Statutes at Large of South Carolina,* v. 3, part 2, Columbia, South Carolina, A.S. Johnston, 1838: 568.

13. A. Candler, ed., *The Colonial Records of the State of Georgia,* v. 18, Atlanta, Chas. P. Byrd, State Printer, 1910: 225.

14. Alabama: W. L. Rose, ed., *A Documentary History of Slavery in North America,* New York, Oxford University Press, 1976. Arkansas: O. W. Taylor, *Negro Slavery in Arkansas,* Durham, North Carolina, Duke University, 1958. Georgia: R. E. Flanders, *Plantation Slavery in Georgia,* Cos Cob, Connecticut, John E. Edwards, 1967; B. Wood, *Slavery in Colonial Georgia,* Athens, University of Georgia Press, 1984. Kentucky: J. W. Coleman, Jr., *Slavery Times in Kentucky,* New York, Johnson Reprint Company, 1940; I.E. McDougle, *Slavery in Kentucky 1792–1865,* Westport, Connecticut, Negro Universities Press, 1970. Louisiana: S. Bacon, *The Early Development of American Municipal Police: A Study of the Evolution of Formal Controls in a Changing Society,* unpublished dissertation. Yale University, University Microfilms No. 66-06844, 1939; J. G. Taylor, *Negro Slavery in Louisiana,* New York, Negro Universities Press, 1963; E. R. Williams, Jr., "Slave patrol ordinances of St. Tammany Parish, Louisiana, 1835–1838," *Louisiana History,* v. 13 (1972):399–411. Mississippi: C. S. Sydnor, *Slavery in Mississippi,* New York, Appleton Century Co., 1933. Missouri: H. A. Trexler, "Slavery in Missouri: 1804–1865," in H. Trexler, *Slavery in the States: Selected Essays,* New York, Negro Universities Press, 1969. North Carolina: G. G. Johnson, *Ante-bellum North Carolina: A Social History,* Chapel Hill, University of North Carolina, 1937. Tennessee: C. P. Patterson, *The Negro in Tennessee, 1790–1865,* New York, Negro Universities Press, 1968; C. C. Mooney, *Slavery in Tennessee,* Westport, Connecticut, Negro Universities Press, 1971. Virginia: J. Ballagh, Jr., *A History of Slavery in Virginia,* New York, Johnson Reprint Co., 1968; A. Stewart, "Colonel Alexander's slaves resist the patrol," in W.L. Rose, ed., *A Documentary History of Slavery in North America,* New York, Oxford University Press, 1976.

15. B. Wood, *Slavery in Colonial Georgia,* n. 14 above: 123–4.

16. P.S. Foner, *History of Black Americans: From Africa to the Emergence of the Cotton Kingdom,* Westport, Connecticut, Greenwood, 1975: 206.

17. Richardson, *Urban Police,* n. 3 above: 21.

18. I. Berlin, *Slaves Without Masters: The Free Negro in the Antebellum South,* New York, Pantheon Books, 1974: 316–17.

19. Berlin, above: 319.

20. L.F. Litwack, *North of Slavery: The Negro in the Free States, 1790–1860.* Chicago, University of Chicago Press, 1961: 3.

21. Berlin, n. 18 above: 330.

22. Litwack, *North of Slavery,* n. 20 above, p. 97.

23. C.V. Woodward, *The Strange Career of Jim Crow,* New York, Oxford University Press, 1966:17.

24. E.F. Foner, *Reconstruction: America's Unfinished Revolution,* 1863–1877. New York, Harper and Row, 1988: 4–5.

25. Foner, above: 66–67.

26. Foner: 199–200.

27. Foner: 201.

28. Foner: 203.

29. Foner: 204.

30. M. Delaney, "Colored brigades, 'negro specials' and colored policemen: A history of blacks in American police departments," unpublished manuscript, no date: 12.

31. J.W. Blassingame, *Black New Orleans: 1860–1880*. Chicago, University of Chicago Press, 1973: 244.

32. H.N. Rabinowitz, *Race Relations in the Urban South, 1865–1890,* Urbana, University of Illinois Press, 1980: 41.

33. V.L. Wharton, *The Negro in Mississippi, 1865–1890*. New York, Harper and Row, 1965: 167.

34. Walker, *A Critical History,* n. 8 above: 10.

35. Delaney, "Colored brigades," n. 30 above: 20.

36. R. Lane, *Roots of Violence in Black Philadelphia: 1860–1900*. Cambridge, Harvard University Press, 1986: 60–67.

37. Lane, above: 64–65.

38. President's Commission on Law Enforcement and Administration of Justice,

Task Force Report: The Police. Washington, D.C., U.S. Government Printing Office, 1967: 170.

39. Foner, *Reconstruction,* n. 24 above: 342.

40. Fogelson, *Big-City Police,* n. 3 above: 250.

41. Fogelson, above: 251.

42. President's Commission on Law Enforcement and Administration of Justice, *Task Force Report: Science and Technology,* Washington, D.C., U.S. Government Printing Office, 1967: 216–28.

43. Fogelson, n. 3 above: 251.

44. *Report of the National Advisory Commission on Civil Disorders,* Washington, D.C., U.S. Government Printing Office, 1968: 321.

45. *Report:* 1.

46. *Report:* 2.

47. *Report:* 299.

48. F.R. Harris and R. Wilkins, *Quiet Riots: Race and Poverty in the United States,* New York, Pantheon Books, 1988.

49. T.A. Critchley, *A History of Police in England and Wales, 1900–1966,* London, Constable and Company, Ltd., 1967: 46.

Policing the Ghetto Underclass: The Politics of Law and Law Enforcement

WILLIAM J. CHAMBLISS

For the past several years my students and I have been riding with the Rapid Deployment Unit (RDU) of the Washington, D.C., Metropolitan Police. In response to the urban riots of the 1960s Washington, D.C., like many other cities, established specialized riot control units within the police department.[1] These units were specially trained to respond quickly and with force to the threat of riots or urban disturbances. Even in the United States, riots do not happen that often. For the police, the "war on drugs" provided a functional equivalent to riots: the crisis of inner-city drugs and violence.

In all we spent more than 100 hours riding with members of the RDU and other police officers. These observations and discussions with police officers stimulated the reflections that follow on the state of law enforcement in U.S. cities and the impact it is having on the public's perception of crime and the lives of those most affected.

THE RAPID DEPLOYMENT UNIT

Members of the RDU are described by other police officers as the "Dirty Harrys" and "very serious bad-ass individuals." The RDU is deployed in teams of three patrol cars with two officers in each car. While each car may patrol in different areas, they are never so far from one another that they cannot be summoned on short notice to converge in one place. They patrol what Wilson (1987, 1993) calls the urban ghetto: that is, the area of the city where 40 percent of the black population lives below the poverty level.

The RDU organizes its efforts at crime control around three distinct activities: the "rip," vehicular stops, and serving warrants.

Chambliss, William J. (1994) Policing the Ghetto Underclass: The Politics of Law and Law Enforcement. *Social Problems* 41: 177–194. Copyright © 1994 by The Society for the Study of Social Problems. Reprinted by permission.

This paper was presented as the presidential address at the annual meeting of the Society for the Study of Social Problems, August 1993, Miami. Direct correspondences to: Chambliss, Department of Sociology, George Washington University, 2129 G Street NW, Washington, D.C., 20052.

The "Rip"

The "rip" involves the use of undercover agents to buy drugs and to identify the person who sold the drugs. Obviously it is the goal of undercover agents to maintain their cover. How can an undercover agent identify a drug seller to uniformed officers without revealing his or her identity as an undercover agent to the drug seller? The following field notes illustrate how this is done:

Rips: Case No. 1

"It is about 1730 hours on a hot summer day in 1992. Rapid Deployment Unit (RDU) is patrolling the Seventh District. The 7th district police are doing drug raids called 'rips.' An undercover officer approaches a person suspected of dealing drugs and makes a buy of $10 worth of crack cocaine. The officer then walks away. Another undercover officer is watching. The second officer radios uniformed officers and gives a brief description of the offender. The uniformed officers move in and arrest the suspect. The suspect is then taken to a remote street corner where he is photographed and told to look out into traffic. Various cars drive by. One of the cars is being driven by the officer who made the buy. He looks at the apprehended suspect and positively identifies him."

The purpose of this elaborate process is to maintain the secret identity of the undercover officer. If the suspect were arrested immediately the undercover officer would be compromised in the community.

Most "rips" do not go as smoothly as the one described. Suspects often flee or enter a building before the uniformed police can make an arrest.

Rips: Case No. 2

"It is 10:25 at night when an undercover agent purchases $50 of crack cocaine from a young black male. The agent calls us and tells us that the suspect has just entered a building and gone into an apartment. We go immediately to the apartment; the police enter without warning with their guns drawn. Small children begin to scream and cry. The adults in the apartment are thrown to the floor, the police are shouting, the three women in the apartment are swearing and shouting 'You can't just barge in here like this . . . where is your goddam warrant?' The suspect is caught and brought outside. The identification is made and the suspect is arrested. The suspect is sixteen years old.

While the suspect is being questioned one policeman says:
'I should kick your little black ass right here for dealing that shit. You are a worthless little scumbag, do you realize that?'

Another officer asks:
'What is your mother's name, son? My mistake . . . she is probably a whore and you are just a ghetto bastard. Am I right?'

The suspect is cooperative and soft spoken. He does not appear to be menacing or a threat. He offers no resistance. The suspect's demeanor seems to cause the police officers to become more abusive verbally. The suspect is handled very roughly. Handcuffs are cinched tightly and he is shoved against the patrol car. His head hits the door frame of the car as he is pushed into the back seat of the patrol car. One of the officers comments that it is nice to make 'a clean arrest'."

When asked whether it is legal to enter a home without a warrant, the arresting officer replies:

"This is Southeast [Washington] and the Supreme Court has little regard for little shit like busting in on someone who just committed a crime involving drugs. . . . Who will argue for the juvenile in this case? No one can and no one will."

A "rip" is made involving an older (34-year-old) black male.

Rips: Case No. 3

"It is after midnight and the suspect enters a local strip bar. Three patrol cars race up the street and jump the curb to block the entrance. In the process one officer on foot who is nearly hit by a patrol car jumps and tears up his knee on the wet pavement. Three patrol cars surround the front of the establishment. The arrest team charges in the front door with their weapons drawn. The officers retrieve the suspect and drag him out to the hood of the patrol car. The suspect might have walked of his own volition but is never given the opportunity. The suspect denies any wrongdoing and becomes upset and confused by the arrest. He appears to be slightly intoxicated or high on drugs. He is forced to sit down on the front bumper of one of the patrol cars. He is instructed to sit on his handcuffed hands with his legs crossed. The suspect says: 'What is this shit? This is all a bunch of bullshit man. You guys don't got shit on me man. Kiss my ass.' One of the officers responds by forcefully shoving the suspect against the grill of the car. The officer places his flashlight against the side of the suspect's face and presses it hard into the suspect's cheek:
    'Listen shorty, you say one more word and that's your hospital word. I will lay you out in a heart-beat so shut your damn mouth'."

Rips account for approximately one-third of the RDU's arrests. Another 50 percent of their arrests come from vehicular stops and the remainder from serving warrants, observations made of transactions taking place on the street, and responding to telephone calls and tips received through police headquarters.

Vehicular Stops

The RDU patrols the ghetto continuously looking for cars with young black men in them. They are especially attentive to newer-model cars, Isuzu four-wheel-drive vehicles, BMWs and Honda Accords, based on the belief that these are the favorite cars of drug dealers. During our observations, however, the RDU officers came to the conclusion that drug dealers were leaving their fancy cars at home to avoid vehicular stops. It thus became commonplace for RDU officers to stop any car with young black men in it.

There is a nod to legality in vehicular stops in that the officers look for a violation in order to justify the stop:

> Field Notes: As we pass a new-looking BMW with two black men in it the driver of the patrol car says to his partner: "Joe, check out that car for violations." The partner says quickly: "Broken tail light, hit the horn." The siren is put on and the car pulls over.

Any minor infraction is an excuse: going through a yellow light, not stopping completely at a stop sign, or having something hanging from the rearview mirror (a violation of which almost every car in the southeast section of the city is guilty). In addition I was told confidentially by some of the officers, though neither I nor any of my students ever observed it, that if the officers feel strongly that they should stop a car, they will stop it and break a taillight as they approach the car:

> "This is the jungle . . . we rewrite the constitution every day down here . . . If we pull everyone over they will eventually learn that we aren't playing games any more. We are real serious about getting the crap off the streets."

Once a car is stopped the officers radio for backup. The two other cars in the area immediately come to the scene and triangulate the suspect's car: one car comes in close behind and the two other cars form a V in front of the suspect's car.

Vehicular stops occur on an average of every twenty minutes throughout the shift. From our observations, illegal drugs, guns, weapons, or someone who is wanted by authorities are found in only 10 percent of the cars stopped. The officers themselves believe that they find serious violations in "about a third" of the vehicular stops. The following cases typify vehicular stops.

Vehicular Stop: Case No. 1

"12:15 A.M. A car is spotted with a broken headlight. The patrol car pulls over the vehicle and runs the license plate number through the computer. One officer approaches the vehicle from the rear and another approaches on the opposite side of the car. Both officers have their Glocks (guns) drawn. Momentarily the car is surrounded by two other patrol cars triangulating the stopped car. One officer goes to the window of the car and says: 'Good evening. My name is officer —. I am with the Rapid Deployment Unit. Our job is to remove guns and drugs from the streets. Do you have any guns or drugs on your person or inside the vehicle?' The driver of the car says there are none. The officer requests permission to search the car. The individual refuses the officer's request.

The officer begins pressuring the driver with threats: 'You know what happens if you refuse to obey a police officer's request?' The driver says nothing, shrugs and gets out of the car. The car is searched and nothing is found. A check is made for outstanding warrants of everyone in the car. There are none. The suspects are released with a warning to 'never let me catch you with anything, you understand?'"

Vehicular Stop: Case No. 2

"After midnight. The driver of the patrol car points out a car driven by two young black men. He tells his partner to check for violations. The partner says, 'pull 'em over. Broken taillight.'

The officers call for backup. Two other RDU patrol cars arrive and the suspect's car is surrounded by the three cars. Two officers approach the car on each side. The driver rolls down his window, and the officer asks to see his license, which is given without comment. The officer on the other side of the car asks to see some identification of the passenger and is given his driver's license. The licenses are given to a third officer who removes himself to his car to check for warrants and to check the license plate of the car.

The officer on the driver's side asks: 'Can we search your car?' The driver says 'No.' The officer then says, 'You know what will happen if you refuse a police officer's request?' The driver then says 'OK, you can look.' Both occupants are told to get out of the car and the car is searched. The officers find nothing.

Apparently satisfied that there are no drugs or guns in the car, the officer says: 'OK. You can go; but don't let us catch you with any shit, you understand?' The driver nods yes, everyone returns to their cars."

Vehicular Stop: Case No. 3

"Another vehicular stop takes place at 12:17 that follows the same pattern. Again there are two black men in the car. The officers approach the car with their guns drawn and tell the occupants to get out of the car. One officer points to a small piece of white paper on the back seat. The driver of the car is extremely nervous. He keeps putting his hands into his pockets, then pulling them out. He seems to be trying to push his hand through his pants pockets:

'What's in your pants?' The driver responds, 'Nothin', man, nothin'.' Officer: 'Empty pockets, quick.'

The driver seems confused but complies. An envelope containing perhaps two grams of crack cocaine is handed to the officer who opens the packet, smirks and tells the driver to put his hands on the top of the car. The officer on the other side of the car follows suit. Both men are handcuffed and taken to the patrol car. No one says anything."

The RDU does not patrol the predominantly white sections of Washington, D.C. Observations of policing in this area of the city reveal an entirely different approach by the police. There are no "rips" and no vehicular stops unless there is a clear violation. Officers are not looking for cars with black drivers. If a car is stopped other cars are not called as backups, and the officer handles the infraction on his or her own:

Vehicular Stop: Case No. 4

"9:15 P.M. A rusted 1978 Bonneville Pontiac is spotted and the officer witnesses the vehicle making erratic lane changes. The officer follows at a distance of about 100 yards. The vehicle attempts to go through a yellow light which turns red before the vehicle gets through the intersection. The officer hits his siren and pulls the car over. He calls in the license plate number and advances to the driver's side of the car. He has no other officer with him, only the observer. His gun is not drawn. The officer notifies the driver of the offense and he begins to search the car visually. The suspect is asked, 'Can I search your car?' The suspect says yes but the officer declines the offer. The suspect is written up for running a red light, is told to have a good evening, and is released."

Search Warrants

The RDU's third major activity is carrying out search warrants. Based on information received from informants, undercover agents, or observations a warrant is issued by the court to search an apartment or home for various reasons:

Warrants: Case No. 1

"Five RDU officer enter an apartment about 10:45 P.M. Before entering the officers draw their guns, break down the door and rush in. The suspect is spotted, guns are pointed at him and he is told to 'lie down, NOW.' The suspect is handcuffed and taken outside. An elderly woman begins screaming and crying. She tells the officers to put their guns away. An officer goes to her, his gun still drawn, and tells her to 'shut up or I'll pop you in the jaw.' He physically forces her to lie down on the floor face down. The officers leave the apartment, put the suspect in the car and take him to the precinct for booking."

Observations indicate police carry out warrants differently in the predominantly white section of Washington, D.C.:

Warrants: Case No. 2

A warrant is issued by the court for the arrest of a suspected drug dealer wanted for assault and attempted murder. The third district police are in an excited state over the pending arrest. An anonymous tip has provided them with information as to the suspect's whereabouts and a discussion at the station lays out a plan for making the arrest. Twelve officers are dispatched to the house where the suspect is supposedly living. Seven officers surround the house and five others approach the front door. Most, but not all, of the officers have their guns drawn. In the dark it is not possible to see all of the officers, but of those observable three had guns drawn and two do not. It is a few minutes past 1 A.M. when the officers approach the front door. The doorbell is rung and the team leader shouts, "Police, open up." Everyone appears to be on edge. There is no response to the knock or the command. The officers break open the door. Flashlights are shining in every corner, behind furniture and into people's eyes. A terrified elderly woman stands at the top of the stairs and asks what is going on. One of the officers approaches her with calmness and no gun drawn, speaks to her in a low voice, and gently removes her from the house to be watched by the team outside. The suspect is found in the basement behind a water cooler. He is identified and handcuffed. As he is being led from the house one officer says to him. "You sure have a pretty face, buddy boy. See you at the country club."

THE CONSEQUENCES

The prison population in the United States increased by 167 percent between 1980 and 1992, with the greatest percentage increase in drug law violations (see Table 1). The United States today incarcerates a higher percentage of its population than any country in the world: a dubious distinction formerly held by the USSR and South Africa (see Figure 1). And it is minorities, especially young African Americans and Latinos, who are disproportionately arrested, convicted and sentenced to prison. In 1991, African-American males between the ages of 15 and 34 made up 14 percent of the population and more than 40 percent of the people in prison. White males made up 82 percent of this age group but less than 60 percent of the prison population (Statistical Abstracts 1993). Blacks accounted for more than 40 percent of the inmates in state and federal prisons (Table 2).

In Washington, D.C., and Baltimore, 40 to 50 percent of all black males between the ages of 18 and 35 are either in prison, jail, on probation or parole, or there is a warrant for their arrest (Maurer 1990; Miller 1992). Arrests and convictions for drugs play an increasingly important part as a source of criminal convictions. Nearly 30 percent of all state and over 55 percent of all federal prisoners in 1992 were convicted on drug violations (Maguire, Pastore, and Flannagan 1993). Two-thirds of all drug arrests in 1992 were for possession, and only one-third were for the sale or manufacture of drugs. African Americans account for more than 40 percent of all drug arrests (Maguire, Pastor, and Flannagan 1993) despite the fact that self-report surveys show that, except for crack cocaine, whites are three to five times as likely to use drugs as blacks (Bureau of Justice Statistics 1993a; see Table 3). Thus more whites than blacks use illegal drugs and more than 80 percent of the population is white. But 66 percent of the inmates in state prisons convicted of drug offenses are black, and only 33 percent are white (Maguire, Pastor, and Flannagan 1993).

Table 1 Change in State and Federal Prison Populations: United States, 1980–1992

Year	No. of Inmates	Percent Change
1980	329,821	—
1981	369,930	12.2
1982	413,806	25.5
1983	436,855	32.5
1984	462,002	40.1
1985	502,752	52.4
1986	545,378	65.4
1987	585,292	77.5
1988	631,990	91.6
1989	712,967	116.2
1990	773,124	134.4
1991	824,133	149.9
1992	883,593	167.9

SOURCE: Darrell K. Gilliard, "Prisoners in 1992" Bureau of Justice Statistics, U.S. Department of Justice, Washington, D.C.

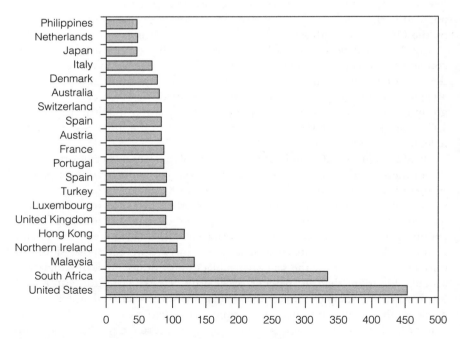

FIGURE 1. Comparative Prison Populations in Selected Countries, 1990 Rate Per 100,000

SOURCES: Nils Christie, *Crime Control as Industry,* London: Routledge, 1993:29 and Australian Institute of Criminology, "Incarceration Rates for the United States, South Africa, and the Soviet Union in Comparison to Europe and Asia," Melbourne: 1991.

Table 2 State and Federal Prisoners by Race, 1991

State Prisoners

White Non-Hispanic	35.4%
Black Non-Hispanic	45.6%
Hispanic	16.7%
Other	2.4%

Federal Prisoners

White	65.5%
Black	31.7%
Other	2.8%

SOURCE: *Sourcebook of Criminal Justice Statistics.* eds. Kathleen Maguire, Ann Pastore, and Timothy J. Flannagan. 1992 Bureau of Justice Statistics, U.S. Department of Justice, Washington, D.C.: USGPO, 1993:622, 634.

Table 3 Self Reported Drug Use By Type of Drug and Race

	RACE AND ETHNICITY		
	% White	% Black	% Hispanic
Heroin	74.5	14.8	10.7
Cocaine	62.0	23.4	14.6
Crack Cocaine	49.9	35.9	14.2
Marijuana	75.1	17.5	7.3

SOURCE: Bureau of Justice Statistics. "Drugs, crime and the criminal justice system," 1992 U.S. Department of Justice, Washington, D.C.: NCJ 133652:28.

Effects on Family and Education

The intensive surveillance of black neighborhoods, and the pattern of surveillance of white neighborhoods has the general consequence of institutionalizing racism by defining the problem of crime generally, and drug use in particular, as a problem of young black men. It further ghettoizes the African-American community and destroys any possibility for normal family and community relations. Young African-American and Latino men are defined as a criminal group, arrested for minor offenses over and over again, and given criminal records which justify long prison sentences. The culture of the black community and the black family is then blamed for high rates of illegitimate children and crime. Crime control policies are a major contributor to the disruption of the family, the prevalence of single parent families, and children raised without a father in the ghetto, and the "inability of people to get the jobs still available" (Anderson 1993; Wilson 1987, 1993).

But the consequences go beyond the destruction of family and community in the ghetto. Scarce resources are transferred from desperately needed social programs to criminal justice. For the first time in history, state and municipal

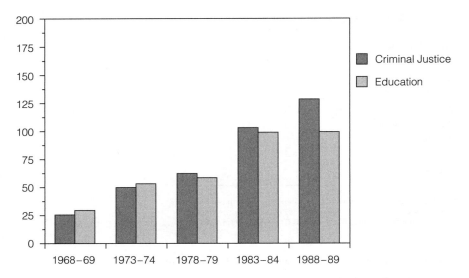

FIGURE 2A. Comparison of Per Capita Municipal Expenditures on Criminal Justice and Education 1968–1989 (in millions)

SOURCE: U.S. Department of Commerce: Bureau of Census, City Government Finances: 1968–69, 1973–74, 1978–79, 1983–84 and 1988–89.

governments are spending more money on criminal justice than education (Figure 2; Chambliss 1991). Nationwide, expenditures on criminal justice increased by 150 percent between 1972 and 1988, while expenditures on education increased by 46 percent. Between 1969 and 1989 per capita spending on criminal justice in U.S. cities (municipal expenditures) rose from $34 to $120 and county expenditures as a percentage of total budget rose from 10 to 15 percent between 1973 and 1989. State expenditures showed even greater increases, rising tenfold from per capita expenditures on police and corrections of $8 in 1969 to $80 in 1989 (Figure 2). State government expenditure for building prisons increased 593 percent in actual dollars. Spending on corrections—prison building, maintenance, and parole—has more than doubled in the last ten years (Chambliss 1991; Maguire and Flannagan 1990; Maguire, Pastore, and Flannagan 1992).

The number of police officers in the United States doubled between 1980 and 1990, and in 1994 the Senate passed a bill, strongly supported by President Clinton, that proposes adding another 100,000 police officers. This is a continuation of a policy begun under the Reagan administration that has seen the federal government increase its allocation of resources for criminal justice without a pause. The War on Drugs, with a budget of $1 billion in 1981, received $13.4 billion in 1993. The government added 700 FBI agents in 1990, an increase of 25 percent, while teachers have been fired in states already suffering from large classes and poor facilities. Welfare for the poor also is severely cut. In real dollars the Aid to Dependent Children program's cash contribution to a mother with two children and no outside employment dropped from $7,836 in 1982 to $4,801 in 1991.

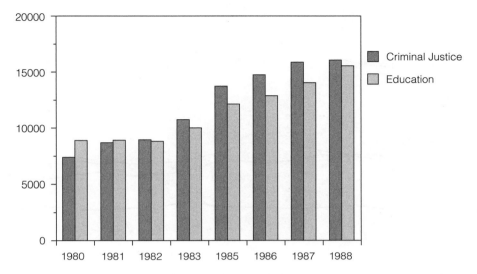

FIGURE 2B. Comparison of Per Capita County Expenditures on Education and Criminal Justice, 1980–1988 (in millions)

SOURCE: U.S. Department of Commerce: Bureau of Census, County Government Finances: 1983–84 and 1988–89.

WHY?

Many reasons have been proposed for the rapid increase in expenditures on criminal justice (or, in the words of Nils Christie, the growth of "the crime industry") in the United States (Christie 1993). One explanation is the alleged increase in crime. There is a general perception that crime, especially violent crime, has increased. The notion of a crime increase is a perception, apparently created by the law enforcement establishment, the media, and politicians. But this is not supported by the facts. The best available data, the findings of victim surveys conducted every year since 1973, show that the crime rate has not changed significantly in the last 20 years (Figure 3).

Victim surveys show also that it is very unlikely that anyone will be the victim of a crime in any given year. More than 90 percent of respondents report that neither they nor any member of their household was the victim of a criminal offense. Indeed, over a lifetime it is unlikely that most people will be the victim of a serious offense. The risk of being a victim of a violent crime in any given year is less than 3 percent (Bureau of Justice Statistics 1992b).

Creating the Perception

The news media and law enforcement agencies use "crimes known to the police," as reported in the FBI's Uniform Crime Reports (UCR), to demonstrate an increase in the crime rate. By the manipulation of data through gimmicks (such as a "crime clock" and percentage increases that appear large because the base is small), the FBI distorts the reality of crime rates and the severity of the

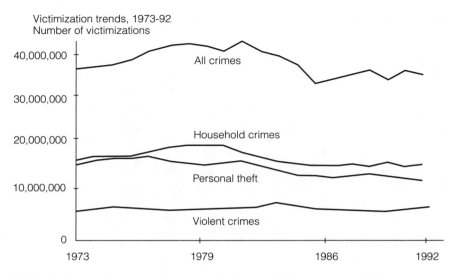

FIGURE 3. Respondents Reporting Being the Victim of Crime by Type of Crime

SOURCE: Bureau of Justice Statistics 1992. "Criminal victimization, 1992." Washington, D.C.

crime problem. The most often cited FBI data are the "crimes known to the police," which consist of crimes reported by the police and crimes reported to the police. Bogess and Bound conclude from their comparison of data from the Uniform Crime Reports and data from the National Crime Victim Survey that most of the increase in crime reported by the FBI between 1975 and 1992 is attributable to an increase in the reporting of crimes to the police, not an increase in the incidence of crime (Bogess and Bound 1993). Furthermore, "the large increase in the incarceration rate [between 1980 and 1992] is attributable primarily to an increase in the likelihood of incarceration given arrest," *not* to an increase in arrests or, inferentially, the crime rate (Bogess and Bound 1993).

For example, the 1992 UCR reported a dramatic increase in the murder rate between 1988 and 1992. The FBI used the report to demonstrate a crime rate increase. What the report failed to mention was that between 1980 and 1987 the murder rate actually declined and the 1992 rate was below that of 1980 (Figure 4). That the murder rate has shown no appreciable increase since the 1980s is particularly noteworthy given the fact that the weapons in use today are more efficient than ever before. Pistols have been replaced with rapid firing automatic weapons that leave a victim little chance of escaping with a wound.

The Seriousness of Crime

If the crime rate has not increased, perhaps the astronomical increase in crime control expenditures and the number of people in prison can be explained by an increase in the seriousness of crime. Data from victim surveys and studies of prison inmates contradict this interpretation as well. For every type of crime reported by victims, the least serious crime is the most common (Table 4).

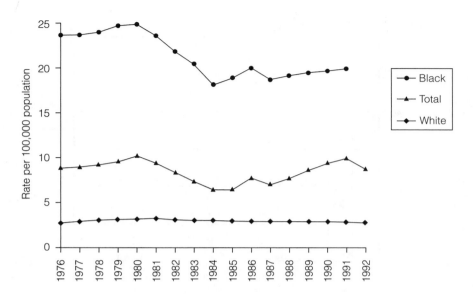

FIGURE 4. U.S. Murder Rate, By Race: 1976–1992

SOURCE: Current Population Reports, F25-1095; Crime in the U.S. and Statistical Abstract of the U.S., various years.
NOTE: Race specific data is for single victim/single offender murders.

Table 4 Estimated Rate of Victimization by Seriousness of Offense, 1992 Rate Per 1,000 Persons Age 12 or Older of Per 1,000 Households

More Serious Offense		Less Serious Offense	
Larceny with Contact	2.4	Larceny without Contact	60.6
Aggravated Assault	8.0	Simple Assault	17.5
Assault Attempted without Weapon	5.8	Assault Attempted without Weapon	12.1
Robbery with Injury	1.6	Robbery without Injury	2.3
Attempted Robbery without Injury	.5	Attempted Robbery without Injury	1.5

Larceny without contact occurs more than 20 times as often as larceny with contact, and simple theft accounts for the vast majority of crimes reported every year. Attempted crimes are reported twice as often as completed crimes (Bastian 1992; Table 4).

About 50 percent of respondents who report being the victim of a crime do not report the crime to the police. When asked why, more than half of the victims say that the crime was "not important enough" or that "nothing could be done about it" (Bureau of Justice Statistics 1992b).

As for people in prison, Austin and Irwin's survey found that more than 50 percent of the prisoners in state and federal prisons are in for offenses that

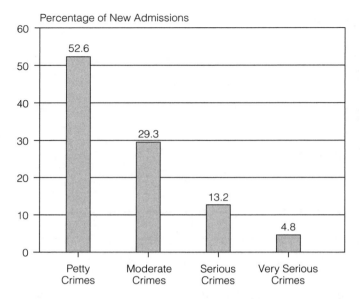

Percentage of New Admissions

FIGURE 5. National Estimate of the Severity of Crimes Committed by Persons Admitted to State and Federal Prisons

SOURCE: James Austin and John Irwin. *Who Goes to Prison?*, San Francisco: National Council on Crime and Delinquency, 1991.

opinion surveys show the general public thinks are "not very serious crimes" (Austin and Irwin 1989; Figure 5). A recent study by the Bureau of Justice Statistics found that more than 20 percent of the inmates in federal prisons were in for drug offenses with no history of violent crime or other felonies (Bureau of Justice Statistics 1994). This indicates that the growth of the crime industry is not due to the seriousness of the crimes.

Crime and Public Opinion

Another explanation for the growth of the crime industry is that lawmakers are merely responding to public opinion. In explaining the creation of President Lyndon Johnson's crime commission and the spate of anti-crime legislation in the 1960s, James Q. Wilson argues that public opinion forced political action. He cites the Gallup Polls in support of this conclusion:

> In May 1965 the Gallup Poll reported that for the first time 'crime' (along with education) was viewed by Americans as the most important problem facing the nation (Wilson 1975:65).

Wilson goes on to say:

> In the months leading up to the Democratic National Convention in 1968 — specifically in February, May and August — Gallup continued to report crime as the most important issue . . . (Wilson 1975:65–66).

Wilson's argument is problematic. The Gallup Polls never showed that crime was perceived by the respondents as the most important problem facing the nation. Every year since 1935 the Gallup Poll has asked a sample of Americans "What do you think is the most important problem facing the country?" Between 1935 and 1993 crime rarely appears as one of the most important problems mentioned, and in the nearly 60 years the poll has been taken, crime is never chosen over other issues as "the most important problem facing the country." In 1989 and 1991 "drugs" and "drug abuse" is frequently mentioned but only once (April 1990) is it the most often chosen. Even when "drugs" is mentioned, crime in the April 1990 poll is seen as "the most important problem" by only 2 percent of the population (Gallup Poll 1989, 1990, 1991).

Wilson's claim that public opinion forced politicians to pass wide-ranging criminal law legislation in the 1960s is simply not supported by the data. In August 1968, a public opinion poll showed for the first time in 20 years that "crime, lawlessness, looting and rioting" was perceived by 29 percent of those asked as one of "the most important problems facing the nation." In the same poll, 52 percent of those surveyed mentioned the Vietnam War as the most important problem facing the United States, and 20 percent mentioned race relations as the most pressing issue facing the nation (Gallup 1972:2107). In fact, between 1935 and 1993 crime was never mentioned as "the most important problem" facing the country in Gallop Polls. (See Table 5.)[2]

One cannot conclude from these polls that crime is not an important issue, but it is safe to say that it is rarely seen as the most important issue. This is particularly significant given a concerted political effort on the part of conservative politicians since the 1960s to create what Cohen calls "a moral panic" over crime (Cohen 1980).

CREATING MORAL PANIC

Crime became a national political issue for the first time in 50 years with the presidential campaign of 1964 when the Republican candidate, Barry Goldwater, sounded the alarm (Cronin et al. 1981:18):

> Our wives, all women, feel unsafe on our streets. And in encouragement of even more abuse of the law, we have the appalling spectacle of this country's Ambassador to the United Nations (Adlai Stevenson) actually telling an audience — this year, at Colby College — that, 'in the great struggle to advance human civil rights, even a jail sentence is no longer a dishonor but a proud achievement.' Perhaps we are destined to see in this law-loving land people running for office not on their stainless records but on their prison record (*New York Times,* September 4, 1964:13).

Goldwater's hue and cry did not strike a resonant chord in the U.S. public. As the *Newsweek* editors observed:

> Remarkably late in the campaign, Barry Goldwater was still a candidate in search of an issue that could score a voting breakthrough . . . [He] did

Table 5 The Most Important Problem Mentioned in Gallup Polls From 1935 to 1990

1935 Unemployment	1965 Vietnam, race relations
1936 Unemployment	1966 Vietnam
1937 Unemployment	1967 Vietnam, high cost of living
1938 Keeping out of war	1968 Vietnam
1939 Keeping out of war	1969 Vietnam
1940 Keeping out of war	1970 Vietnam
1941 Keeping out of war, winning war	1971 Vietnam, high cost of living
	1972 Vietnam
1942 Winning war	1973 High cost of living, Watergate
1943 Winning war	1974 High cost of living, Watergate, energy crisis
1944 Winning war	
1945 Winning war	1975 High cost of living, unemployment
1946 High cost of living	1976 High cost of living, unemployment
1947 High cost of living, labor unrest	1977 High cost of living, unemployment
1948 Keeping peace	1978 High cost of living, energy problem
1949 Labor unrest	1979 High cost of living, energy problem
1950 Labor unrest	1980 High cost of living, unemployment
1951 Korean war	1981 High cost of living, unemployment
1952 Korean war	1982 Unemployment, high cost of living
1953 Keeping peace	1983 Unemployment, high cost of living
1954 Keeping peace	1984 Unemployment, fear of war
1955 Keeping peace	1985 Fear of war, unemployment
1956 Keeping peace	1986 Unemployment, fear of war
1957 Race relations, keeping peace	1987 Fear of war, unemployment
1958 Unemployment, keeping peace	1988 Budget deficit, drug abuse
1959 Keeping peace	1989 Drugs, poverty, homelessness
1960 Keeping peace	1990 Budget deficit, drugs
1961 Keeping peace	1991 Economy, poverty, homelessness, drugs, unemployment
1962 Keeping peace	
1963 Keeping peace, race relations	1992 Economy, unemployment
1964 Vietnam, race relations	

all he could to press the issue of law and order (*Newsweek*, October 19, 1964:27–34).

Gallup Polls taken at the time depict a public more concerned about war, civil rights, poverty and unemployment than crime. Nonetheless, conservative Democrats and Republicans continued to press the issue of crime control after Goldwater's defeat. They focused their attention on Supreme Court decisions such as *Miranda*, *Gideon* and *Escobedo* which gave the accused the right to legal counsel, protection against coerced confessions and the right to remain silent unless a lawyer was present. Congressmen Ford and Senators McClellan, Stennis, Ervin,

Hruska, Thurmond, Bible and Lausche (a formidable conservative block of five Democrats and three Republicans) sponsored the Omnibus Crime Control and Safe Streets Act that legalized wiretapping and "bugging" by federal agents and local police without requiring a court order, authorized trial judges to admit confessions as voluntary after considering "all factors," thus emasculating the Miranda decision, and exempted law enforcement agencies from having to meet the requirements of the 1964 Civil Rights Act therefore allowing federal grants to be given to law enforcement agencies even if they were guilty of racial discrimination (Chambliss and Sbarbaro 1993).

In the 1968 presidential campaign (Nixon vs. Humphrey), Richard Nixon and his running mate, Spiro Agnew (both later to be accused of serious crimes themselves), continued the effort to create a moral panic over "law and order." Nixon attacked the Johnson administration's focus on social conditions as the cause of crime:

> By way of excuse, the present Administration places the blame on poverty. But poverty is just one contributing factor. . . . The truth is that we will reduce crime and violence when we enforce our laws — when we make it less profitable, and a lot more risky to break them (*New York Times,* October 25, 1968:34).

Along with Johnson, Nixon held the Supreme Court responsible for the crime problem. He assailed some of the court's decisions as having "tipped the balance against the peace forces and strengthened the criminal forces" (*New York Times,* September 30, 1968:1).

The Republican and conservative Democrat campaign was apparently somewhat successful for, as noted above, in August 1968 a public opinion poll showed for the first time in 20 years that "crime, lawlessness, looting and rioting" was perceived by 29 percent of those asked as one of "the most important problems facing the nation." It is arguable, however, that the success of the campaign to make crime a major political issue came at a time when riots in the cities and violent demonstrations were taking place throughout the country and "crime" was only mentioned by a significant number of respondents when it was collected together with lawlessness, riots and looting. In any case, the public's concern was short lived, for crime is not mentioned again among the top two or three problems facing the country until 1989 when "drugs" is seen as one of the nation's most important problems.

The years following the Nixon presidency have witnessed a continued assault on civil liberties and an expansion of federal authority in crime control. The Reagan and Bush administrations hammered away at the issue of crime and created the "war on drugs," complete with a "drug czar" and the expenditure of billions of dollars for crime control. Although the public was slow to respond to the barrage, as the Gallup Polls show, in 1989 "drugs" was perceived as one of the two "most important problems facing the country" (Table 5).

The politicization of crime by conservative politicians occurred at a time when the country was deeply divided over the Vietnam War and civil rights. In this historical context crime became a smokescreen behind which other issues could be relegated less important. Crime served as well as legitimation for legislation designed primarily to suppress political dissent and overturn Supreme Court decisions (Chambliss and Sbarbaro 1993).

In addition to these political forces, and partly because of them, the crime control industry emerged as a powerful lobby. Law enforcement agencies control the information available about crime and, as noted above, manipulate the data to serve their purposes. In their effort to create moral panics, and thereby increase their budgets and power, law enforcement agencies are happily joined by the media always hungry for stories that will increase their audience. Indeed, the media has become so dependent on crime news in recent years that in 1993 crime was the most frequently reported subject on television news (Media Monitor 1994). Between 1990 and 1993 the number of crime stories appearing on ABC, CBS and NBC evening newscasts increased from 737 to 1,698.

The crime industry has become so powerful, it is virtually immune from the budgetary cuts experienced by other public services during the recent recession. On those rare occasions when a mayor or governor suggests cutting justice expenditures or even holding steady the number of police officers, propaganda, politicking and arm twisting by police officer associations (often called "benevolent" associations rather than trade unions) and lobbyists with vested interests in supplying equipment and prison facilities quickly reverse the decision. In Prince George's County, a suburb of Washington, D.C., for example, when there was talk of layoffs and pay cuts for police the police officer's association hired a public relations firm and ran television commercials citing increasing crime rates and accusing the county executive of handcuffing police officers with proposed budget cuts. The union spent more than $10,000 in one week on television and newspaper advertisements, and the politicians acquiesced, canceling the proposed budget cuts.

With their newfound success as lobbyists and self-perpetuating bureaucracies, however, law enforcement agencies face some formidable organizational problems, the most important being how to justify their claim to more and more of the taxpayer's dollars. Manipulating data, creating moral panics, and feeding the media crime stories can only go so far. Eventually arrests must be made, successful prosecutions carried out and people sent to prison. For these symbols of effective law enforcement the large population of poor black males is the perfect bureaucratic solution. For here is a population without political clout, with few resources to successfully defend against criminal charges, and a public image as a group in which crime is endemic. Enforcing the law in the black ghetto enables the police, as one officer expressed it, to "rewrite the constitution every day."

A police officer's career and even his annual income is determined by the number of "good collars" he makes. A "good collar" is an arrest for what is defined as a serious violation of the law that culminates in a conviction. Drug arrests qualify. They are among the easiest convictions, the most difficult to defend, and often lead to the longest prison terms as a result of mandatory sentences. But they are organizationally effective only if the person arrested is relatively powerless. Arrests of white male middle class offenders (on college campuses for example) are guaranteed to cause the organization and the arresting officers strain, as people with political influence and money hire attorneys for their defense. Arrests of poor black men, however, create only rewards for the organization and the officer as the cases are quickly processed through the courts, a guilty plea obtained and the suspect sentenced. Organizations reward role occupants whose behavior maximizes rewards and minimizes strains for the organization. In a class society, the powerless, the poor, and those who fit the public stereotype of "the criminal" are the human resources needed by law enforcement agencies to maximize rewards and minimize strains. It is not surprising, but sociologically predictable, then, that doubling the number of police officers in the last 10 years has tripled the number of people in prison and jail, filled these institutions with minor offenders, exacerbated the disproportionate imprisonment of minorities, and institutionalized racist beliefs that make being a young black man synonymous with being criminal.

SUMMARY AND CONCLUSIONS

In the last 20 years the crime control industry has experienced unprecedented growth in the United States. The number of police officers has doubled and, since 1980, the prison population has increased by more than 160 percent. This heady growth has taken place at a time when federal, state, and municipal budgets have been severely strained and other public services cut.

The reasons often given for the diversion of resources from education, welfare and other social services to criminal justice is that a rising crime rate necessitates it and the public demands it. Analysis of crime rates reveals, however, that despite the propaganda of law enforcement agencies and the impression perpetrated by the media, the crime rate in the United States has not changed significantly in the last 20 years. Nor do public opinion polls support the idea that crime has ever been one of the problems perceived as "the most important" facing the country.

The creation of a moral panic over crime was brought about by a coalition of political, law enforcement and media interests that accounts for the growth of the crime industry. First are the political interests of politicians from Goldwater to Clinton in making crime (and drugs) a public issue to gain electoral advantage over their opponents and to serve as a smokescreen or diversion from issues fraught with political danger, such as confronting the budget deficit or health care. Second, a coalition of conservative Democrats and Republicans used crime as a smokescreen to (a) detract from more controversial issues such as Vietnam and civil rights and (b) legitimize the passage of laws that provided law enforcement agencies with more efficient means of suppressing social protest.

Political interests coalesced in the 1970s and 1980s with the growth of a crime industry lobby consisting of organizations representing the interests of police and correctional officers alongside firms profiting from prison construction, the sale of weapons, technology and equipment to law enforcement agencies. The media contributed its part to the creation of a moral panic and young black males particularly, and minorities generally, paid the price in the form of intensive police surveillance, imprisonment and institutionalized racism.

Reversing the process will prove to be more difficult than instituting it. Political leaders will have to show the kind of courage shown by Lyndon Johnson and Hubert Humphrey who defied the conservative platform's call for more police and harsher penalties with pleas for more public spending on schools and jobs. Law enforcement agencies will have to change their reward system to emphasize community policing and rewarding officers who do not have to make arrests in their communities, rather than rewarding those who do. And the media will have to assume some responsibility for educating rather than sensationalizing. Social scientists can play a critical role by conducting studies of law enforcement in the communities most affected and communicating the results to policymakers and the public. It is unlikely, however, that any of these changes will take place so long as we continue to criminalize drugs and provide an incentive for police officers and prosecutors to entrap and arrest people for the possession or sale of small amounts of drugs. The longer it takes, the more lives will be lost and the more the United States will move toward a society permanently divided by race and class into communities that are quasi-police states patrolled by RDU-type police units in search of crime and communities where minor infractions of the law are treated, as they should be, as tolerable indiscretions.

ENDNOTES

1. According to FBI statistics, approximately 10 percent of law enforcement personnel are now employed in specialized police units. In 1992 such specialized units accounted for 25 percent of police departments' budgets (Maguire, Pastore, and Flannagan 1992).

2. Contrary to Wilson's claims, crime was *not* reported in the Gallup Poll of May 1965 as the most important problem: in May 1965 the Gallup Poll did not even ask what respondents thought was the most important problem facing the nation. But in June 1965 the question was asked and the responses were as follows: Vietnam, 23 percent; civil rights, 23 percent; threat of war, 16 percent; prestige abroad, 9 percent; spread of world communism,

9 percent; juvenile delinquency, 2 percent (Gallup Poll 1965).

It is a gross distortion of fact to say, as Wilson does, that "in February, May and August [of 1968] Gallup continued to report crime as the most important issue." Gallup did not ask the question in February. In May 1968 the question was asked and only 15 percent of the respondents named crime including riots, looting and juvenile delinquency as the most important problem, but 42 percent named Vietnam and 25 percent race relations. In August crime, etc. is mentioned by 29 percent as the most important problem, but the Vietnam War is seen as the most important problem by 52 percent (Gallup 1968).

REFERENCES

Anderson, Elijah (1993), "Abolish welfare — then what?" The *Washington Post,* December 31: A23.

Austin, James, and John Irwin (1989), *Who Goes to Prison?* San Francisco: The National Council on Crime and Delinquency.

Bastian, Lisa D. (1992), "Criminal victimization, 1992." Bureau of Justice Statistics, U.S. Department of Justice, Washington, D.C.

Bogess, Scott, and John Bound (1993), "Did criminal activity increase during the 1980's? Comparisons across data sources." Research Report No. 93-280. Population Studies Center, University of Michigan, Ann Arbor, Mich.

Bureau of Justice Statistics (1992a), "Drugs, crime and the criminal justice system," U.S. Department of Justice, Washington, D.C., NCJ 133652:23. (1992b) "Criminal victimization in the United States: 1973–1990." U.S. Department of Justice, Washington, D.C. (1994) "Drug offenders in federal prison." U.S. Department of Justice, Washington, D.C.

Chambliss, William J. (1991), Trading Textbooks for Prison Cells. Alexandria, Va.: National Center on Institutions and Alternatives.

Chambliss, William J., and Edward Sbarbaro (1993), "Moral panics and racial oppression." Socio-Legal Bulletin, Melbourne, Australia.

Christie, Nils (1993), Crime Control as Industry, London: Routledge.

Cohen, Stanley (1980), Folk Devils and Moral Panics: The Creation of the Mods and Rockers. New York: St. Martin's Press.

Cronin, Thomas E., Tania Z. Cronin, and Michael E. Milakovich (1981), United States Crime in the Streets. Bloomington, Ind.: Indiana University Press.

Gallup, George (1993), The Gallop Poll: Public Opinion, 1935–1993, Wilmington, Del.: Scholarly Resources.

Maguire, Kathleen, and Timothy J. Flannagan, eds. (1990), Sourcebook of Criminal Justice Statistics 1990. Washington D.C.: Bureau of Justice Statistics.

Maguire, Kathleen, Ann Pastore, and Timothy J. Flannagan, eds. (1993), Sourcebook of Criminal Justice Statistics, U.S. Department of Justice, Bureau of Justice Statistics. Washington, D.C.: USGPO, 1993.

Maurer, Mark (1992), Young Black Men and the Criminal Justice System: A Growing National Problem. The Sentencing Project, Washington, D.C.

Media Monitor (1994), 1993: The Year in Review: TV's Leading News Topics, Reporters, and Political Jokes, Center for Media and Public Affairs. Washington, D.C.: January/February.

Miller, Jerome M. (1992), Search and Destroy: The Plight of African American Males in the Criminal Justice System. Alexandria, Va.: National Center on Institutions and Alternatives.

Newsweek (1964), "The curious campaign—point by point," October 19.

Statistical Abstracts of the United States (1993), The National Data Book. Washington, D.C.: U.S. Department of Commerce.

Wilson, James Q. (1975), Thinking About Crime. New York: Basic Books.

Wilson, William Julius (1987), The Truly Disadvantaged: The Inner City, the Underclass, and Public Policy. Chicago: University of Chicago Press (1993) The Ghetto Underclass: Social Science Perspectives. New York: Sage Publications.

A Political Economy
of Community Policing

DAVID E. BARLOW
MELISSA HICKMAN BARLOW

INTRODUCTION

Community policing, problem-oriented policing, and quality of life policing
campaigns are the latest in a long line of innovations in policing in the United
States and are currently lauded as our nation's best hope of achieving both
justice and effectiveness in law enforcement. In order to explain contemporary
police practices and policies, it is essential to explore their historical transformations and to analyze how and why they have developed as they have. More
specifically, what is needed are historical analyses which depart from traditional
police textbook accounts. Such analyses must go beyond official explanations
and reject interpretations that present police institutions as simply the product
of social progress. The historically specific institutions and policies of policing
are not the inevitable results of an evolutionary process. Change and innovation do not necessarily mean improvement. Police organizations and strategies
are created by human actors with specific intentions, motivations, and strategies which are not necessarily, or even typically, altruistic or noble. Police institutions and policies are forged within political, economic, and social contexts. Historical analyses of police must account for the ways in which race and
class politics have influenced the specific formations of police in the United
States. The relations and politics of race, gender, and class are part of every aspect of U.S. life, including the institutions and policies of policing.

PRE-INDUSTRIAL POLICE

According to Walker (1980), the first publicly funded municipal police departments were developed in the South and their primary purpose was to preserve
the racist social order and maintain slavery.[1] As part of a larger effort to control

Source: Barlow, David and Melissa Hickman Barlow (1999) A Political Economy of
Community Policing. *Policing: An International Journal of Police Strategies and Management*,
22: 646–674

the growing slave population, public officials in Charleston, South Carolina, established a mounted daytime patrol in the 1740s. By 1837, the Charleston Police Department had 100 officers and the primary function of this organization was slave patrol. The largest item in the Charleston municipal budget was the cost of police (Williams and Murphy, 1990). As Genovese (1976, pp. 617–18) described, "[t]o curb runaways, hold down interplantation theft, and prevent the formation of insurrectionary plots, the slaveholders developed an elaborate system of patrols." These officers regulated the movements of slaves and free blacks, checking documents, enforcing slave codes, guarding against slave revolts, and catching runaway slaves. Walker (1992, p. 6) referred to this "distinctly American form of law enforcement," the slave patrols, as the "first modern police forces in this country."

According to Genovese (1976, p. 22), the slave patrols were made up of mostly poor whites who frequently "whipped and terrorized slaves caught without passes after curfew." Slaveowners and slaves themselves frequently commented on the vicious behavior of the slave patrols, including arbitrary brutality and excessive beatings. Some plantation owners actually attempted to protect their slaves from the patrols while others used the patrols to discipline slaves that resisted their masters. Slaves often developed their own resistance strategies including the use of warning systems, booby-traps, escape systems, and violence. However, the patrols were very successful in accomplishing their main purpose: "they struck terror in the slaves" (Genovese, 1976, p. 618).

The formation of slave patrols is not a trivial event in history and their origin in Charleston is not inconsequential. African slaves and their descendants did not simply acquiesce to their predicament. Resistance took many forms, including work slowdown, breaking of tools, theft, arson, murder, and even armed rebellion. According to Genovese (1976), the most common problem for slaveowners was runaways. When the Dred Scott decision legally denied sanctuary to runaway slaves who escaped to the northern states, thousands of free Blacks[2] went to Canada, Mexico, and Haiti (Loewen, 1995). In fact, one of the primary duties of the Texas Rangers (the first organized state police force, established in 1835) was to retrieve runaways escaping to Mexico (Samora et al., 1979). Slavery was never a practice which was accepted by the enslaved; therefore, a powerful police force was needed to suppress this large population.

For whites, the most frightening form of slave resistance was armed revolt. According to Genovese (1976, p. 615), violent rebellions were frequent enough that "in every decade slaveholders in every part of the South got an occasional jolt from news that normally obedient slaves had killed a master, mistress, or overseer." It is informative to note that Stono, South Carolina, experienced a relatively large rebellion in 1739, shortly before the formation of the Charleston slave patrols. The South Carolina legislation which established the slave patrol indicated that the primary motivation for the creation of this new form of policing was the fear among whites that the militia was unable to adequately control slave rebellions, stating that "[f]oreasmuch as many late horrible and barbarous massacres have been actually committed and many more designed, on the white inhabitants of this Province, by negro slaves, who are generally prone to such cruel practices [it is] highly necessary that constant patrols should be established" (Williams and Murphy, 1990, p. 3). According to Takaki (1993), the fear of slave insurrection was particularly strong in cities, as whites feared that the slaves could more easily congregate and conspire with free Blacks who often worked in the cities. In the cities, Blacks would assemble into groups and become much bolder in their interactions and even confrontations with whites. "Whites feared free blacks in the towns because they suspected them of foul play and conspiracy" (Hawkins and Thomas, 1991, p. 69). The structure of work was dramatically different than on the plantations. "Urban businessmen needed a more skilled and flexible black labour force that would not accept the harsh discipline and social controls so common on plantations" (Hawkins and Thomas, 1991, p. 70). Considering Charleston's critical role in the slave trade, its large slave population, and the highly unstable nature of a slave economy, it is not surprising that Charleston was the site of the first public municipal police force in the United States. Both for the mental peace and physical safety of its white citizenry, Charleston created a police force whose primary mission was to maintain the social order, that is, to preserve the current relations of power which were primarily characterized by racial domination.

From their inception in this country, police have played a pivotal role in maintaining social order and preserving a status quo characterized by inequality, injustice, and racism. When placed in historical context, the maintenance of order does not appear as a neutral function for the equal benefit of all. As long as the social order contains immense inequalities, the maintenance of order is inherently repressive to those on the bottom and enormously beneficial to those at the top. The pattern of policing in defense of the social order continued with the emergence of organized municipal police in the North and Midwest, although the problem population in need of control was not African slaves, but free poor immigrants who filled the seacoast cities during the industrial revolution between the late 1700s and mid-1800s.[3]

INDUSTRIAL POLICE[4]

Although slavery, except as a punishment for crime, was systematically eliminated from the urban areas in the North prior to the nineteenth century, large urban areas had their own problem populations with which to contend, namely free Blacks and recent immigrants who found it increasingly difficult in the mid-1800s to escape urban poverty. These populations were the by-products of an emerging industrial society whose growth began to stagnate in the 1830s. They were economically marginalized populations for whom society had no organized system of provision. Surplus populations are an important asset to industrialists in a capitalist society who have an interest in keeping labor costs down, for they provide an available pool of labor from which industries can draw during periods of labor disputes, strikes, or even contract negotiations (Adamson,

1984). However, surplus populations are also a critical liability to the economic and political system because they are at the bottom of the social stratification system and therefore receive the least benefit from the social order. If the police are to maintain social peace in a society with such sharp and wide class divisions, their efforts must logically be directed toward these surplus populations.

From the 1780s into the 1820s, the United States experienced an industrial revolution, with the large-scale introduction of artisan-produced machines and the steam engine into the manufacturing of goods (Wright, 1979). With accelerated growth and the formation of a world market for industrial goods, the rate of profit for industrialists was very high, which in turn led to high levels of investment and production (Mandel, 1978). A massive number of immigrants, often poor and destitute, were attracted to the United States to build their lives and livelihoods as wage laborers. However, between the late 1820s until the 1840s, economic growth in the United States stagnated, and the three previous decades of unprecedented growth in urban centers led to a host of social problems which the leaders of our young nation were either unable or unwilling to address adequately (Gordon *et al.*, 1982). This period of expanding competitive capitalism produced the slow expansion of the industrial proletariat, i.e., the class of people who sell their labor for a wage (Gordon *et al.*, 1982). Serious concerns about the social order arose among political and economic leaders and the public. One of the most dramatic outcomes of this concern was the development of the first bureaucratically organized, public salaried municipal police in the United States.

This period in U.S. history, from the 1820s to the 1840s, was rife with signs of decline, unrest, and fear (Petchesky, 1981; Lane, 1971; Rothman, 1971; Walker, 1980). Rapid population growth (due to continuing high levels of immigration), increasing class distinctions, high levels of mobility, and increasingly impersonal human and work relationships all contributed to widespread feelings of unrest and disorder (Mohl, 1979). All of these developments contributed to the official and organized action which was mobilized against problem populations (Barlow *et al.*, 1993). In the context of a declining economy, concerns about social disorder came to be expressed as fear of and anger toward the most recent wave of immigrants (Pivar, 1973; Piven and Cloward, 1979; Trattner, 1979).

Another important element in concerns about social order was the apparent escalation of rioting in the 1830s (Walker, 1980). Major rioting occurred in Philadelphia, Baltimore, New York, Cincinnati, St Louis, and Chicago. "To many Americans, the survival of the new nation was at stake" (Walker, 1980, p. 57). Fear and hatred of poor immigrants were exacerbated by the popular notion that these "dangerous classes" lacked the proper level of discipline and thus required control (Silver, 1967). The revolutionary establishment of municipal police closely paralleled the influx of immigrants and concomitant concerns about social disorder. To wealthy industrialists, preserving the social order meant preserving a good business climate by maintaining a stable and disciplined workforce, keeping open the avenues of commerce, and increasing the potential for a high rate of return on investments — profits.

The first municipal bureaucratically organized police departments emerged in this context. The exact dates are subject to debate but a general period is clear. Richardson (1980) locates the creation of the public salaried police department between 1820 and the 1840s. Philadelphia created a modern-style police department between 1833 and 1854 (Walker, 1980). The culmination of the movement toward public municipal police was the development of the first uniformed day and night watch unified into one unit of the New York Police Department in 1845 (Walker, 1980).

The primary role of these newly developed policing agencies was to maintain the social order, including social stratification as it existed at the time of their formation. The greatest perceived threats to that social order were the so-called dangerous classes, i.e., the Irish and German immigrants, free Blacks, and the urban poor in general (Silver, 1967). The dangerous classes comprised the masses of people who derived the least benefit from the current social order. They were perceived by those with power and wealth as dangerous both because of their large number and because of their precarious social and economic position. Of particular concern was that the earlier watch systems were unable to suppress the riots, demonstrations, and strikes that became frighteningly frequent during the 1830s, without the aid of the militia. The industrial police, along with a number of private police agencies such as the Coal Police, the Railroad Police, and company town police agencies hired by industrialists, were used against Irish and German immigrants in the urban seacoast slums to break strikes and suppress hunger riots. Industrial police "also enforced anti-immigrant ordinances on liquor, gambling, and Sunday closing" (Platt *et al.,* 1982, p. 22). Many state legislatures passed laws to regulate drinking habits, particularly targeted against the poor. For example, in 1838, Massachusetts made it illegal to sell alcohol in any amount less than 15 gallons (Richardson, 1974).

Early police agencies also played a critical role in maintaining the stratification of society along racial lines, by regulating and suppressing the activities of free Blacks living in urban areas. According to Hawkins and Thomas (1991), although the North did not have the large slave population with which to contend, northern officials aggressively sought to control the free Black population. Blacks were underpoliced in terms of receiving police protection, but were overpoliced and subject to arrest for such actions as congregating or breaking curfew (Hawkins and Thomas, 1991). The rights of Blacks were only somewhat less restricted in so-called free states than in slave states. Various "free" northern states allowed only white males to vote, banned interracial marriages, and prohibited nonwhites from testifying in court, owning real estate, making contracts, or filing lawsuits (Williams and Murphy, 1990). Police, of course, were responsible for enforcing these racist "Jim Crow" laws, which began in the North and were transported to the South with the abolition of slavery. Therefore, the municipal police departments that emerged in the industrial North played an important role in maintaining the status quo in relations of power by controlling the perceived dangerous classes: the poor, recent Irish and German immigrants, and free Blacks.

This view of pre-industrial policing and industrial policing demonstrates that two distinctly different forms of municipal police operated in the USA during the first half of the nineteenth century.[5] The slave patrols in the South served an important social control function that helped to preserve the Southern political economy — a feudal slave economy. Industrial policing primarily developed in the large cities of the North and Midwest and served a distinctly different social control function, helping to preserve the political economy of competitive capitalism. Both systems of policing were dominant within their own political and economic context and both worked to protect property and facilitate the accumulation of wealth, benefits enjoyed primarily by the upper class. The slave patrols came to an abrupt official end with the end of slavery. However, it was not long before remnants of the slave patrols appeared within the municipal police departments of southern cities.

During Reconstruction, northern occupation of southern cities led to the formation in the South of the type of industrial police agencies that existed in the North. The "problem population" within these southern cities, however, comprised large numbers of recently freed Africans who were immediately transformed into a multitude of severely poor and unemployed. According to Adamson (1983, p. 558), "[c]rime control in the antebellum South was subordinated to race control. With the abolition of slavery, alternative forms of race control had to be found, and race control naturally became a major aim in crime control." A series of state and local laws, often called the Black Codes, were passed throughout the South, legally restricting Blacks to being propertyless rural labor. According to Adamson (1983), the few political and legal rights that were promised by the Radical Republicans were either not forthcoming or were meaningless given the virtually universal economic destitution shared by newly freed slaves. Through both formal and informal racial discrimination, Africans were systematically forced into becoming either sharecroppers or convict laborers. Blacks who refused to become sharecroppers, destined to live their entire life in severe poverty and debt to the landowner, could be arrested simply for having "no visible means for support" and then sentenced to work as free labor at the same plantation (Adamson, 1983, p. 559). Even their freedom of movement was eventually eliminated by the many restrictions placed upon them. The industrial police forces which developed in the post–Civil War South enforced these laws and thus served to preserve the racist social order.

Whites in the North were very apprehensive about the tremendous flood of freed slaves into northern urban areas (Hawkins and Thomas, 1991). Northern police supported many racist legal codes and social norms. According to Hawkins and Thomas (1991, p. 72), as Africans moved into northern cities they were "relegated to the worst jobs and housing along the red light districts teeming with vice and crime." Relentless poverty and racial oppression pushed many of the newly freed Africans into crime and vice, which were then attributed to the innate character of Blacks rather than to the horrible social conditions. Many government officials and police departments used crime by Africans as an excuse to create racist legal codes and to harass, arrest, and jail Blacks at a much higher rate than whites. The industrial police of the North thus systematically preserved their own racist social order.

Immediately following the Civil War, local politics in most large northern municipalities and southern county governments came to be dominated by political machines ruled by powerful bosses (Ostrum *et al.*, 1988). Ostrum *et al.* (1988) argue that the formation of political machines in the South was largely an effort to maintain white supremacy as African slaves were set free and granted citizenship. The political machines adopted a patronage system whereby government officials, political candidates, and even law enforcement officers were carefully chosen by white Democrats. Although in many states, under Reconstruction, the Republican party was able to secure the appointments and elections of a number of white Republicans and African Americans, by 1877 the white Democrats, through political corruption and terrorism, were able to secure nearly complete domination of southern politics (Bennett, 1993; Katz, 1995; Loewen, 1995).

On the other hand, Ostrum *et al.* (1988) attribute the development of the northern political machines to the complexities of providing municipal services and utilities in environments filled with high levels of urbanization, industrialization, and technological innovations. These technological and social changes in the political economy not only made it highly profitable for a corrupt political organization to secure complete control over government contracts and utilities, they made it technically possible for the political machines to dominate the process. In his study of the Chicago Police Department between 1890 and 1925, Haller (1976) provides a vivid illustration of the critical role that the police played in supporting the political machines, as well as the impact that the machines had on the organization and operation of the police. According to Haller (1976), the primary task of the police officer on the beat was to ensure that the dominant political party secured the votes which they needed to stay in power. As opposed to controlling crime, police spent most of their time providing various services to loyal supporters, maintaining a reasonable level of social order necessary for the city and local businesses to operate smoothly, and seeking out every opportunity available to them to make money. The police, as well as prosecutors, judges, and other government officials, were appointed for their political patronage and they maintained their jobs by keeping their benefactors in power. At the same time, they personally participated in highly corrupt money-making ventures to benefit themselves financially (Haller, 1976).

Private police were the primary form of policing in the United States until the late nineteenth century (Harring, 1983). According to Harring (1983), public police agencies of this era were relatively small, fragmented, inefficient, and, most importantly, unreliable. Intimacy between police officers and the public, as well as police officers' loyalty to political machines, made the police unpredictable as agents of social control during periods of social unrest. Private police were employed directly by industrial capitalists. Thus, they had a personal stake in breaking strikes and keeping their employers in business (Spitzer, 1981). In the late nineteenth century, both private and public forms of industrial police lost the ability to guarantee "the kind of stable, predictable, orderly environment that alone permits sophisticated forms of markets to flourish" (Spitzer and Scull, 1977, p. 276). Between 1875 and 1900, a new form of public policing was developed, which we call the modern police force.

MODERN POLICE

The transformation from industrial police to modern police as the dominant pattern of policing in this country took place between the late 1870s and 1920. This transformation was not universal among all police agencies in all regions; nor did it occur in one dramatic moment in history. The changes took place in spurts as different factors impacted upon local governments with different levels of intensity, at different times, encountering varying degrees of resistance. Although industrial and modern police agencies existed contemporaneously, by the 1920s the modern police, primarily characterized by the professional model of policing, emerged as the policing style which nearly every large police department in the United States sought to emulate (Walker, 1980).

A number of factors contributed to the emergence of the modern police department. The overriding impetus was a crisis of legitimacy brought on by various economic, political, and social crises. The legitimacy crisis engulfed not only the police, but also the local political process and municipal governments in general. Municipal agencies, as constructed, were unable to adequately resolve the various crises and it became increasingly difficult to justify their continued existence in their present forms. A number of reformers sought to change the organization of public agencies so that they could respond more effectively to economic, political, and social problems. Legitimacy was of vital concern to police agencies on numerous levels. The police needed the backing of government officials, industrialists, and voters in order to retain or expand their financial and legal support. The police also needed to be seen as a legitimate social control agency in the eyes of the working and poor classes so that they could enforce the law and maintain order effectively and efficiently. As a result, most major police agencies underwent radical changes in their organization at the turn of the century.

The social crisis emerged as the small public and private police agencies which comprised what we have termed industrial police were unable to preserve the social order in the late nineteenth century, particularly during the 1870s. Beginning with a major economic crisis in 1873, social unrest and discontent spread throughout the cities of the United States. Industrialists introduced new, labor-saving technologies, leaving millions of workers unemployed. "Public relief was usually nonexistent, and private charity either insufficient or offered only on the most demeaning terms" (Dubofsky, 1975, p. 20). In New York between 1873 and 1879, demonstrations organized by the unemployed often drew 10 to 15 thousand people who had to be dispersed by mounted police (Piven and Cloward, 1971). In Chicago during the same period, "mass meetings of unemployed, organized by anarchists under the slogan, 'Bread and Blood,' culminated in a march of 20,000 on the city council" (Piven and Cloward, 1971, pp. 43–4). Although these mass demonstrations and accompanying riots were often too much for the local police to handle, the primary threat to the social order in the United States in the late nineteenth century was the class warfare that ensued between industrialists and workers. Some of the most violent industrial conflicts in U.S. history took place between 1865 and 1897 (Dubofsky, 1975). Strikes, lockouts, and worker rebellions are littered throughout this period. Police departments in every major city were on the front lines of the struggle because they were charged with maintaining social order. The years leading up to the twentieth century constituted a critical crossroads for social stability, the labor movement, capitalism, government, and for the police. It is in this context that the form of policing which we refer to as modern police was established.

Much of the violence on the part of workers was directed at the destruction of the factory because the factory was viewed as the cause of unemployment and job insecurity. However, those occupying higher social and economic statuses tended to blame the most recent wave of immigrants for the violence and social unrest of the period, rather than blaming declining economic opportunities. "The American ruling class perceived newer immigrants as particularly prone to violence" (Dubofsky, 1975, p. 8). Business owners often used Black and new immigrant workers as scabs to break union resistance and then proceeded to blame these same groups for causing unemployment among union workers. The anti-immigrant rhetoric played upon the nativist tendencies of workers, who had became angry and afraid in the face of the intense competition for jobs brought about by the economic depression of the 1870s. Many in the labor movement began to claim that poor people, social radicals, Blacks, and recent immigrants were instigating the violence and economic insecurity of the time. Through the criminalization and enforcement of various victimless crimes, lawmakers and government officials launched an assault against the dangerous classes and it was the police officer's job to enforce these racist and class biased laws (Walker, 1980).

Sidney Harring (1983, p. 27) has argued that "beginning with the 'Great Strike' of 1877 and the 'Great Upheaval' of the mid-1880s,[6] the urban police institution was transformed into an efficient, well-organized, and disciplined system that was capable, for the first time, of asserting a powerful regulating effect on urban life—of *policing* urban society." The former signified the decay of industrial policing and the second demonstrated some of the successes of the social experiment of modern policing. According to Harring (1983), police departments organized under the industrial policing style lacked the technology, organization, and sheer numbers to handle effectively such large disputes. In addition, police officers' familiarity with people in their communities, and their extremely informal and personal approach to law enforcement, sometimes led the officers to ignore certain laws as they became sympathetic with the struggle for better pay, living conditions, and job security. Most industrialists continued to use citizens organized into militia to put down strikes. The civilian militia were very prone to violence and often became more riotous than the strikers. The inefficiency of these militia moved industrialists to hire private police (such as Pinkertons) whose brutal forms of repression often inflamed the workers to even greater resistance and violence. In many places, such as Pennsylvania, they were given full police powers, like the "coal police" or the "iron police" for the mines and the "rail police" for the railroads. More often they were deputized for guard duty or for the duration of a strike (Platt *et al.,* 1982). These strategies proved insufficient in putting down the Great Strike of 1877 and eventually the U.S. military had to be called in to maintain domestic order. According to Harring (1983), it was during the 1877 strike that industrialists began to recognize the need for a better disciplined, more efficient, and better organized police force. Partly as a result of this realization, a number of industrialists supported the reorganization of police departments in major cities in the United States, particularly in the North and Midwest. This reorganization is often referred to as the professionalization of police (Walker, 1977; 1980; Kelling and Moore, 1988).

Harring (1983) noted that, in contrast to the failure of local police during the Great Strike of 1877, many reformers interpreted the relative success of local police agencies in maintaining order during the Great Upheaval of the mid-1880s as indicating the value of the changes they were making. Modern policing was still in an embryonic form, but its improved ability to handle the strikes and riots of the 1880s without the use of the military helped to cement the municipal police as the major instrument of social control in urban areas. Because of a variety of organizational, administrative, and technological changes, modern police departments responded to the threat of social disorder with a stronger, more unified, and more effective force of officers than the industrial police system (Harring, 1983). In sum, the revolutionary transformation in the structure, design, and technique of urban police to the modern, professional style was in part due to the failure of police to maintain order during the Great Strike of 1877. The successes attributed to police professionalism, as indicated by increases in technology, discipline, and the size of police departments during the Great Upheaval of the mid-1880s, helped to solidify the transformation and to establish municipal police as the first line of defense for the social order.

The expansion of municipal police was part and parcel of an increase in an array of services provided by municipal governments (Spitzer, 1981). Industrialists had a vested interest in socializing the costs of reproducing the working class, especially during the 1870s and 1880s when the United Sates was experiencing a serious economic crisis, lowering the rate of profit for many investors (Mandel, 1978; Gordon *et al.,* 1982). To socialize the costs of reproducing labor is to spread the expense of education, training, housing, health and welfare, and the maintenance of the social order among a large number of people. In democratic countries, socialization is accomplished by shifting these costs from individual industrialists to governments through taxation. For example, instead of a single mine owner in a company town building schools, training labor, providing housing, sewage, water, and police protection, the workers themselves as well as other businesses are taxed to provide the funds to do these things (Spitzer, 1981).

The other critical factor that helped to convince leaders of government and industry that a strong municipal police department was superior to private police agencies, local militia, and even the military was the issue of legitimacy. For policing in a democratic society to be effective, it must be considered legitimate by the vast majority of the people. That is, the police must be seen as having the right to exercise force because to do so represents the best interests of society in general. If a police agency does not have legitimacy, then it must operate by the use of brute force. In such a case, the society is no longer a democracy but, rather, an authoritarian police state. Private police who worked directly for industrialists, business owners, railroads, wealthy citizens, or mining, lumbering, and steel companies did not have such legitimacy, particularly in the eyes of the workers in these organizations. Therefore, private police had to rely heavily on brute force to obtain discipline and order. Their efficiency and effectiveness declined as more and more people resisted their efforts. As people rebelled against blatant repression by industrialists, the severe brutality of private police often triggered more violence and destruction of property than it prevented. Public police were able to obtain legitimacy, though they were doing essentially the same job as private police had done, because the democratic government represents itself as a neutral entity working on behalf of the people.

Legitimacy was also sought by adopting rationalized formal structures as the basis on which to construct police departments, as well as entire municipal governments. Legitimacy was achieved in this process because widespread faith in theories of modernity during the first half of the twentieth century assumed that the rational formal structure was "the most effective way to co-ordinate and control the complex relational networks involved in modern technical and work activities" (Meyer and Rowan, 1977, p. 342). Police reformers who sought to retain, strengthen, or expand the role of police recognized that, in a rational-legal society such as the United States, adopting this modern model of efficiency operating under the rational rule of law would help police organizations gain legitimacy, stability, and resources (Walker, 1977; Meyer and Rowan, 1977). In the twentieth century, modern U.S. society became filled with rationalized bureaucracies as formal organizations grew more common and more elaborate (Meyer and Rowan, 1977). As police leadership worked to achieve professionalization and modernization, police departments grew more rationalized, impersonal, and institutionalized. Discretion was restricted as the influence of individual police was reduced and the social purposes of the organization were represented as technical rather than social in nature (Walker, 1977; Meyer and Rowan, 1977). Therefore, the historical development of the large bureaucratically organized police department can in part be attributed to a larger movement by government officials to obtain legitimacy for their agencies by adopting the rational-legal formal structure which placed more emphasis on impersonal rules, laws, and discipline, than on individuals.

For many social reformers, the most important impact of this application of a rational-legal model to the operation of political organizations was that it would weaken the power and influence of political bosses and break apart the political machines (Ostrum *et al.,* 1988). The desire of many participants in the Progressive Reform Movement was to dismantle the corrupt political machines which had come to dominate local politics in the big cities (Ostrum *et al.,* 1988). These reform efforts were often strongly supported by industrialists and opposition party members (usually native-born, Protestant, white Europeans), because the political machines were typically built on the support of poor, working class Catholic immigrants. Many industrialists worried about the loyalty of police officers and government officials in the case of massive strikes and felt more comfortable relying on legislators and the rule of law, which they could more readily influence. The police were a primary target of reform, partially because they were seen as the enforcement arm of the political machine. According to Walker (1984), the police were not simply controlled by the political machine, they played an essential role in its survival. The police were "the means by which certain groups and individuals were able to corrupt the political process. These errands included open electioneering, rounding up the loyal voters, and harassing the opponents" (Walker, 1984, p. 85). Therefore, as social reformers sought to challenge the rule of the political bosses, the police became an obvious target for reform. Numerous changes were eventually implemented in most major cities to weaken the direct control of police by the political machine or to remove politics from policing. Central to these reforms was requiring police agencies to operate under formal, rational bureaucratic rules and laws. Many of these changes emerged as the dominant characteristics of the modern police department.

Thus, the professionalization or modernization of police can be seen as a response to the threat of social revolution, declining profits, and a crisis of legitimacy in policing. Professionalization entailed a radical reorganization of police agencies, including the creation of standards for recruiting and training, greater discipline for police officers, increased centralization, bureaucratization, a greater division of labor, new technology, and extraordinary increases in the numbers of officers (Harring, 1983). By 1905, most urban police departments had grown to six to ten times their size in 1865. This increase was not due simply to the increases in the size of cities. Many police agencies grew to twice the number of officers per capita (Harring, 1983).

The innovations which characterize the shift to modern policing include not only the shift to large, centralized, and highly disciplined police agencies, but also the introduction of new technologies and changes in the rights of police officers as employees. According to Harring (1983), the most significant technological developments were designed to make the police department into a more socially sensitive response system. New technologies were applied to make the police capable of responding more quickly and in greater force to potential trouble spots. For example, in 1878 the telephone was applied to police work for the first time in Cincinnati, Ohio. The telephone made it physically possible for police officers and the central command station to communicate directly and in detail about potential disturbances or anticipated strikes. This communication also helped central command to coordinate the police response to these disturbances. Harring (1983) argued that the patrol wagon and signal system was probably the most significant technological innovation in policing of the nineteenth century. This innovation allowed officers to respond more quickly to potential riot situations or the early stages of a strike involving large numbers. The patrol wagon and signal system was set up to allow police to respond much like modern-day firefighters. A number of officers stayed at the central station in barracks. When a signal came in for help, a large number of officers loaded themselves into a horse driven wagon and responded (Harring, 1983).

Harring (1983) further argued that the most significant innovation in the rights of police officers as employees was the introduction of civil service. Some of the major problems of earlier police departments were high turnover rates, poor working conditions, and political corruption. The movement to solve these problems and to reduce the instrumental control of the police by powerful politicians included civil service protections for police. Two such movements occurred almost simultaneously in Milwaukee and Brooklyn in 1884. Another move toward the professionalization of police was the first school of instruction, which was established in Buffalo, New York in 1893 (Harring, 1983; Richardson, 1974).

As modern policing consolidated under the banner of the professional model, the rhetoric of police as professional crime fighters was firmly established as the dominant approach to understanding the nature of police work. According to Walker (1980), "[b]y the late 1920s and 1930s, the crime-fighting model of policing moved to the forefront" of police departments throughout the country, and much of its technology, such as the radio patrol car, airplanes, and psychopathic laboratories, reflected the desire to make the police more efficient crime fighters. Throughout the 1920s and 1930s, the police were a popular focus of reform; however, this reform centered almost exclusively on making police more efficient and effective. The call to reform police departments was typically framed in terms of increased professionalization, with more training, better management, new technology, strict discipline, and complete autonomy from political machines (Walker, 1980). Modern, professional policing dominated law enforcement in major U.S. cities until the mid-1980s, though signs of decay in modern policing appeared during confrontations between police and social activists of the 1960s. During the 1960s police agencies began experimentation toward the contemporary style of policing, which we call postmodern policing.

POSTMODERN POLICE

Beginning in the 1960s, as police clashed with a series of major social movements seeking to change the social order, signs that modern policing was entering a period of decay became visible. Like many other established institutions in the 1960s, police experienced a serious crisis of legitimacy among white college students, African Americans, and even the white middle class. Public faith in professionalization, modernity, bureaucracies, and established institutions began to crumble and the foundation on which police had relied upon for establishing their legitimacy—the law—was no longer sufficient. Police came under serious criticism from nearly every sector of society as being either too repressive or ineffective, or sometimes both. The criticism came from both the left and the right, from practitioners and academics, from activists and politicians, from the inner-city poor and middle class suburbanites, as well as from business leaders. Police themselves began to recognize the limits of modern policing and began to experiment with new forms of policing. Just as postmodern theory[7] critiques faith in modernity as a panacea for social ills, new approaches to policing were often based on a critique of professionalism as a panacea for failures in policing. Police departments began to reject increases in bureaucracy, advances in technology, and enhanced efficiency in management techniques as solutions to the complex problems of policing in a media dominated age. What began to emerge is what we call postmodern policing and we believe that the impetus for and consequence of this radical change are consistent with those of each previous major transition in policing—preservation of the social order.

In the 1960s, police came into direct conflict with numerous, often overlapping social rebellions that challenged the social order. For example, the Civil Rights movement exposed inequality and injustice as it challenged the forms of social control placed upon African Americans. The student movements challenged the "Establishment" and its traditional forms of social restraint. Alongside the political student movements for free speech and in opposition to the Vietnam War, a cultural revolution included anti-materialism, flagrant use of drugs, changes in sexual mores, and contempt for traditional styles and appearances. Mass demonstration and protest often came into direct conflict with the legal system, and the government appeared ill-equipped to control the situation. The decade of the 1960s is often described as a period characterized by a "rising tide of public insecurity and fear of crime in the streets" (Ohlin, 1973, p. 6). Disorder in American streets emerging from the political and social movements of the 1960s came to be conflated with ordinary street crime, via the concept of crime in the streets, and contributed to fears that family, church, school, and particularly the police were losing their grip on society (Chambliss, 1994; Barlow, 1998). As defenders of the social order, and as the most accessible and visible instruments of that social order, police were an integral part of these social conflicts.

The most violent confrontations of the period arose out of African American protests against the oppressions of white society. According to Piven and Cloward (1979), 50,000 people participated in at least one demonstration or another in 1960, and 3,600 demonstrators spent some time in jail. Civil disobedience placed protestors in direct conflict with the police. By the mid-1960s, the direct action campaigns of the Civil Rights movement, typified by the peaceful civil disobedience of Dr. Martin Luther King, Jr., were increasingly met by coercive and violent social control administered by the police. Social disorder reached unprecedented heights between 1964 and 1968, as riots engulfed every major city, and most were sparked by incidents involving the police (Piven and Cloward, 1971; Walker, 1980). The Harlem (1964), San Francisco (1966), and Atlanta (1966) riots and several others were each triggered by the shooting of a black teenager by a white police officer (Walker, 1980). The riots in Philadelphia (1964), Watts (1965), and Newark (1967) escalated from routine traffic incidents. The Detroit (1967) riot developed after a police raid on an after-hours bar in the ghetto (Walker, 1980). Militancy within the Civil Rights movement peaked when 164 civil disorders took place in the first nine months of 1967 in cities across the country (Harris and Wicker, 1988).

The initial reaction to the failure of the police to control the disorder of the 1960s was to increase professionalism and militarization. That is, attempts were made to mobilize the police, nearly at a national level, into a better trained, educated, armed, disciplined, specialized, and technologically advanced fighting unit, capable of suppressing any insurrection. However, at the same time an undercurrent of resistance to this approach was emerging under the name of "community relations."

In the title of their book, *The Iron Fist and the Velvet Glove,* Platt *et al.* (1982) identified the expansion of two distinct forms of policing in the United States. The "iron fist" is reflected in the above described commitment to modern policing, designed to create an elite and very "professional" military organization to wage war on crime and disorder through the effective and efficient use of physical force. On the other hand, the "velvet glove" approach to policing emerged as many observed that "a key lesson from the riots of the 1960s was that purely repressive or overly mechanical and distant forms of official control were usually counter-productive, tending to aggravate the already volatile nature of the urban poor" (Platt *et al.,* 1982, p. 128). Balkan *et al.* (1980, p. 104) argued that:

> [b]ecause of criticism in the late 1960s that the technical and managerial approach to policing would alienate large sectors of the population, the need for the closer police ties to the community were stressed. . . . Community relations programs are another method to persuade people that the police really do exist to serve them.

Community relations programs which were developed beginning in the late 1960s may be viewed as the initial experiments into a radical revolution in policing that is being consolidated today. Walker (1992, p. 21) noted that, through police-community relations programs, police "attempted to improve community relations by speaking at community centers and in schools." In some organizations, these programs grew into ride-along programs, neighborhood storefront offices, fear reduction programs, police academies for citizens, cultural diversity training, police-community athletic programs, and the Drug Abuse Resistance Education (DARE) program. For proponents of modern policing, the major threat of the police-community relations movement was that it initiated efforts to dismantle the wall between the "professional" police crime fighter and average citizens. Advocates of the modern, professional model feared that the police were giving up some of their autonomy and professional status by opening police agencies up to the citizens for support, assistance, and guidance. In general, police-community relations programs were largely marginalized from what was considered "real" police work, as "[t]hey were often little more than public relations efforts, designed to sell the department to the community rather than to change police operations" (Walker, 1992, p. 252). Indeed, public relations and image-management have become the defining elements of postmodern policing.

Another challenge to the structure and organization of modern police was the effort to decentralize policing. One of the first such efforts following the late 1960s was a strategy called team policing. The fundamental thrust of team policing was to decentralize and de-specialize the police so that they could work as a coordinated and relatively self-sufficient neighborhood unit. According to Walker (1992, p. 254), one goal of team policing was "to improve police-community relations by assigning officers to particular neighborhoods for extended periods of time." Largely due to poor planning and limited commitment by the departments, the team policing experiments were not a success. However, the movement to decentralize police decision-making and to localize efforts to confront problems of crime and disorder was later revitalized by Goldstein's (1979) scathing critique of modern policing and his formation of a new policing strategy called "problem-oriented policing." Goldstein (1979; 1990) criticized modern policing's preoccupation with efficient management and its commitment to the rational military bureaucracy. He argued that police departments needed to decentralize their efforts, develop a more fluid management style, and allow more creativity and innovation among the rank and file. Goldstein (1979; 1990) critiqued the professional approach which distanced police from the public being policed. Goldstein argued that, in order to identify and solve problems in the community, it was necessary for the police and the public to become much more connected. This rejection of modern professionalism spearheaded by Goldstein's work, however, did not fully usher in postmodern policing until it was combined with the concept of community policing and its total commitment to image-management.

POSTMODERNITY, COMMUNITY POLICING, AND IMAGE-MANAGEMENT

The phenomenon called "community policing," which emerged in the 1980s and now dominates the rhetoric of nearly every major police department in the United States, fully integrates image-management as an essential component of policing. The logic of community policing is often based on a classic article by Wilson and Kelling (1982) called "Broken Windows: The Police and Neighborhood Safety," in which the authors argue that image-management is not only an important crime prevention tool for the police, but it is essential for communities as well. The basic argument is that if a community presents the image that it is in a state of disrepair and disorder, then it soon will be. As the analogy goes, if a broken window is left unrepaired, then soon all the windows in the building will be broken. Therefore, working together, the police and the community should aggressively address the signals (i.e., untended property and untended behaviors) that send the message that a community is in a state of disorder. Wilson and Kelling (1982) further argued that, even if this effort does not really reduce crime, it improves the quality of life among the citizens by reducing their fear of crime. "Although the police can do little to prevent particular instances of crime, they can reduce the 'disorder' that, as research shows, encourages and facilitates crime" (Bayley, 1994, p. 103). Further, Wilson and Kelling (1982) strongly recommended foot patrols as an important police strategy even though they acknowledged that evaluations of this strategy demonstrate that it does not reduce crime. As Wilson and Kelling (1982, p. 358) noted, what foot patrols do is manufacture an image:

> These findings may be taken as evidence that the skeptics were right—foot patrol has no effect on crime; it merely fools the citizens into thinking that they are safer. But in our view, and in the view of the authors of the Police Foundation (of whom Kelling was one), the citizens of Newark were not fooled at all. They knew what the foot patrol officers were doing, they knew it was different from what motorized officers do, and they knew that having officers walk beats did in fact make their neighborhoods safer.

Based on this logic, community policing blurs image and reality to the point that, not only are they inseparable, distinguishing between the two is unimportant. This approach fits perfectly with the postmodernist concept of "hyperreality," which characterizes media images and reality as so intertwined that our images become real and reality becomes an image (Schwartz and Friedrichs, 1994).

In the language of public relations, police must sell themselves to the public and an essential part of this sales campaign has been to promote community policing as more responsive to the community than the professional (modern) model which preceded it. Police Chief Lee P. Brown (August, 1984), who was one of the first and most successful police chiefs to implement community policing in a major U.S. city, promoted community policing as a clear alternative to the old model of policing that was ineffective in reducing crime and disorder in the 1960s. Bayley (1994, p. 104) argued that "[c]ommunity policing represents the most serious and sustained attempt to reformulate the purpose and practices of policing since the development of the 'professional' model in the early twentieth century." The most significant differences between modern policing and community policing are that the philosophy of community policing encourages the scrutiny of the police by the public, enhances the accountability of the police to the public, provides customized police service, and shares the responsibility for resolving the problem of crime with the public (Brown, 1984). Part of Trojanowicz and Bucqueroux's (1990, p. 5) definition of community policing described it as "a new philosophy of policing, based on the concept that police officers and private citizens working together in creative ways can help solve contemporary community problems related to crimes, fear of crime, social and physical disorder, and neighborhood decay." According to proponents of community policing, involvement of the community in policing is designed to ensure that the police effectively meet the needs of the community. However, meeting the needs of the community is a goal of community policing that appears to be secondary to the goal of utilizing community members to help control crime. Within the community policing model, police now openly admit that they cannot solve crime on their own and they need the community to help them. If community members are more involved in the crime-fighting process, they will be more supportive and co-operative with the police. The idea is to convince the public that the police are in their community to help them and, therefore, to interfere with the police and the performance of their duty is self-defeating and illogical. As Manning (1991, p. 27) pointed out, "[t]he image of community policing is a dramatic one."

Community policing is image-management policing. Even evaluations of community policing concentrate on the public's image of the police. The most common measurements have involved "soft direct indicators" of the public's perceptions about the police and crime (Bayley, 1994, p. 98). In other words, under the rubric of treating the citizen as a customer and being more client-oriented, police often use evaluations that focus on the public's satisfaction with police. These measures of the image of police have become particularly important as most community policing strategies appear to have little effect on the reality of crime. Thus, under the banner of "improving the quality of life," postmodern policing wages war on the image of crime rather than crime itself. Bayley (1994, p. 100) warns that "[p]olice must not be allowed to make performance a 'con game' of appearance management."

Under the surface, the image-management of community policing is a new and potentially powerful social control mechanism. Manning (1991, p. 28) referred to community policing as a "new tool in the drama of control." Klockars (1991, p. 240) stated that community policing "is best understood as the latest in a fairly long tradition of circumlocutions whose purpose is to conceal, mystify, and legitimate police distribution of non-negotiable coercive force." Therefore, the power of community policing is that "[i]t wraps the police in the powerful and unquestionably good images of community, cooperation, and crime prevention. Because it is this type of circumlocution, one cannot take issue with its extremely powerful and unquestionably good aspirations" (Klockars, 1991, p. 257). In other words, community policing evokes powerful positive images that tend to insulate the strategy of social control, and the police operating within that strategy, from critical analysis. Who is against a more responsive police force and stronger communities, greater co-operation between police and the public, and the prevention of crime? An argument by Balkan *et al.* (1980, p. 104) in reference to the earlier police-community relations programs of the 1960s is equally relevant to community policing: "the police were interested not in a real transfer of power from the police to the community, but in more effective management of the community and information gathering. Community-police programs glossed over the continuing repression and arrest of people in poor communities." The logic is that a police department that appears to be "more responsive" to the community can be a more effective agent of social control. In a democratic society, the police are most effective when the iron fist is cloaked in a "velvet glove" (Platt *et al.,* 1982).

That the iron fist of policing is at work in the 1990s, even as the velvet glove of community policing takes center stage, is evidenced by the increase in police paramilitary units and the widespread growth of the criminal justice industrial complex (Kraska and Kappeler, 1997). Kraska and Kappeler (1997) surveyed 548 police departments in the U.S. and report that:

- an overwhelming majority (89 percent) of these departments have para-military units;
- this represents a dramatic increase in the number of such units;
- there is substantial evidence that paramilitary units are becoming normal-ized into mainstream policing; and
- there exists a direct link between police paramilitary units and the U.S. military.

According to Kraska and Kappeler (1997), these findings demonstrate that a notably aggressive turn is being taken by many police agencies in the United States behind the rhetoric of community policing.

Postmodern policing is essentially social control through image control. By convincing the public that they are going to receive a police department that is responsive to their specific needs and is going to be an advocate for the im-provement of the quality of their lives, the police hope to produce a public that will provide them with intelligence information, grant them greater flexibility and authority in dispensing curbside justice, and offer less resistance to their efforts to maintain order. These programs seek to convince people who have every reason to believe that they are being repressed by the social order that those in the front lines of defense of that social order are their friends. But no matter how many town meetings are held, no matter how many baseball cards are handed out, no matter how many "officer friendly" robots appear in inner-city classrooms, the police are mandated to preserve the social order, to maintain the status quo.

CONCLUSION

Throughout the history of policing in the United States, one duty appears to be consistent. The primary role of the police in U.S. society is to maintain the so-cial order. In other words, the police may have numerous functions, including fighting crime and administering DARE programs, but these functions do not define the police, nor can they explain all police activities. Ordinary crime dis-rupts the maintenance of an orderly, productive, and profitable society. The sup-pression of crime helps to maintain order. Under the directive to fight crime, the police are able to investigate potential insurrections, to infiltrate dissident groups, and gather intelligence on individuals that may be conspiring to disrupt the so-cial order, for these activities are usually defined as criminal. The suppression of crime also helps to legitimize the personal intrusions of the police into the per-sonal lives of citizens and it grants police the unique right to exercise legitimate force. Controlling crime is one element of the maintenance of *the* social order.

The preservation of the social order provides an explanation for the emer-gence and formation of the municipal police department. Each transformation that occurred in the formation of the police was triggered and guided by this essential role. The *pre-industrial police* worked to preserve the social order, an order based upon the institution of slavery. The police sought to control African slaves because they were the greatest threat to the social order, with the least to lose and the most to gain if current power relations were transformed. Police activities were molded by this role as they regulated the movement of Africans, punished slaves that challenged the status quo in any way, and protected the "private property" of the slaveowners by not letting the slaves run away. The police played an instrumental role in making the political economy of the pre−Civil War South profitable.

The police agencies formed in the era of *industrial policing* played virtually the same role as the pre-industrial police, except that the political economy was radically different. These police, formed primarily in the industrial North, were responsible for maintaining a different social order. The problem population which posed the greatest threat to this social order comprised recent German and Irish immigrants, as well as a few free Blacks. Similar to the slave community, these groups of people had the least to lose and the most to gain if current power relations were altered. In addition, the suppression of the riots that characterized this period was critical for the preservation of business confidence. For industrial growth, there must be a reasonable predictability that capitalists will receive a return on their investments. When that confidence falls, possibly because social disorder has disrupted the production or consumption of goods, then investments are withheld and economic growth stagnates. By suppressing riots and breaking strikes, the police played a very important role in helping capitalists secure profits from their investments. In so doing, the police preserved the current social and power relations of the time.

When it appeared that the industrial police could no longer effectively preserve the social order, policing underwent another radical transformation. The police changed significantly as they became larger, bureaucratic, more disciplined, better organized, and technologically advanced; however, their core mission remained intact. Through this revolutionary transformation the police became effective at putting down riots and breaking strikes. The *modern police* played a critical role in preventing the labor movement from radically altering the social order and its current power relations. The transformation also helped the police achieve the legitimacy necessary to maintain control adequately. Modern police functioned relatively effectively throughout the first half of the twentieth century; however, in the 1960s they began to lose their legitimacy and their effectiveness. The massive social movements of the 1960s came into direct conflict with the core mission of police. Modern police were not only unable to suppress such strong social movements, they were unable to adequately adapt to the changing social conditions. The traditional activities of modern police actually began to cause more social disorder than they prevented. Thus, a new form of policing was developed to maintain the social order.

Postmodern policing is the latest form of policing to dominate this institution of social control. The primary contemporary threat to the social order has been identified as the young, urban, male, racial minority, particularly the young black male. In many respects, it is he who receives the least benefit from our current social order and, therefore, it is he who has the least to lose and the most to gain from a radical transformation of the social order. In the United States today, brute force and blatantly racist discrimination by the police are no longer socially acceptable. As the police cannot openly rule with a hickory stick and a gun, much more sophisticated techniques are being developed. Postmodernism is characterized by both a rejection of modernity and the blurring of image and reality. Police appear to have moved directly into this new phase within a critique of modern policing and a commitment to image-management. The core mission of maintaining the social order has remained, only now police agencies seek to achieve it with a different set of strategies. Through the image management of community policing, the police hope to obtain enough legitimacy among inner city African Americans to gain their support and assistance in the control of their own people. The use of force by police is couched in the rhetoric of a war on crime that requires war-like mobilizations by police on behalf of the law-abiding public. And it is made more palatable to the communities in which it is most repressive through the rubric of community policing and improving the quality of life. Blatant racism has been institutionalized and made less openly visible. The police now actively sell their new image to the public in order to maintain the legitimacy necessary to function at an efficient level.

In many respects, the above analysis begs the question of why police themselves (most of whom have no direct connection to power and wealth in U.S. society) willingly and enthusiastically engage in the preservation of a racist and class biased social order. In fact, many of the most diligent supporters of community policing among police practitioners are African American police officers and administrators. Thus, the transformation to postmodern policing should not be viewed as simply resulting from a conspiracy among wealthy white male capitalists. Each major transformation in policing has been viewed by most of the general public as a positive and progressive reform. Community policing is no exception. In comparison to Darryl Gates, former chief of the Los Angeles Police Department, community policing advocate Chief Lee Brown is a populist revolutionary. In other words, there is a level at which community policing has the real potential of improving the quality of life in many communities, particularly if it is guided by organizations like the National Organization of Black Law Enforcement Executives (NOBLE) and the Police Executive Research Forum (PERF). However, this examination of the history and political economy of policing demonstrates the folly of believing that the community policing movement is not primarily about social control and maintaining the social order. As stated in *The 1968 Report of the National Advisory Commission on Civil Disorders,* "[p]reserving civil peace is the first responsibility of government. Unless the rule of law prevails, our society will lack not only order but also the environment essential to social and economic progress" (Harris and Wicker, 1988, pp. 17–18). The police are first and foremost the guardians of that civil peace.

ENDNOTES

1. Although the slave patrols were largely publicly funded and were responsible for regulating the behavior of both African slaves and free Blacks, they did not look much like the "modern" police officers. For the purposes of this paper, however, they provide an important point of departure for distinguishing the development of policing in this country.

2. We capitalize "Blacks" to show respect for this segment of the population historically distinguished by skin color.

3. Mandel (1978) identifies the period between 1789 and 1848 as the "Industrial Revolution" because the political economy is characterized by a general transformation from an agricultural base to that of competitive capitalism, with artisan-produced machines, the gradual spreading of the steam engine, and the beginning of the gradual shift in the labor market from farm laborers to industrial wage earners.

4. We use the term "industrial police" to refer to the amalgam of public and private police agencies which derived their character and mission from the industrial political economy.

5. Throughout this paper it should be noted that each of these shifts in the organization of police experience significantly overlap with the other adjustments in policing strategy. In other words, although the model of the modern police may have come to dominate large urban areas, many small southern counties retained the political patronage system well into the 1960s. The diversity of local governments, as expressed by Ostrom *et al.* (1988), suggests that although adjustments in the political economy may have ramifications which reach to the lowest levels of local government, each of these local organizations may respond in differing degrees. In fact, these shifts in policing strategy frequently occur in sports, representing uneven and disjointed developments. The fact that a particular philosophy of policing emerges as a dominant national strategic initiative does not mean all the many and diverse police agencies in this country accept it as their own. Frequently, major innovations in policing have occurred in the largest cities and slowly spread around the country. For the most part, the various forms of policing discussed in this article exist simultaneously with each other depending on region or level in which the police are operating.

6. The "Great Upheaval" of the mid-1880s actually refers to several social upheavals which took place in the 1880s: the 1884 Longshoremen strike in Buffalo, the 1884 street car strikes in Chicago, Columbus, Detroit, and Indianapolis, and Chicago's McCormick strike and Haymarket riot in 1886.

7. See Schwartz and Friedrichs (1994) for a discussion of postmodern theory and its applications to criminology.

REFERENCES

Adamson, C. (1983), "Punishment after slavery: southern state penal systems, 1865–1890," *Social Problems,* Vol. 30 No. 5, pp. 555–69.

Adamson, C. (1984), "Toward a Marxian penology: captive criminal populations as economic threats and resources," *Social Problems,* Vol. 31 No. 4, pp. 435–58.

Balkan, S., Berger, R.J. and Schmidt, J. (1980), *Crime and Deviance in America,* Wadsworth Publishing, Belmont, CA.

Barlow, D.E., Barlow, M.H. and Chiricos, T.G. (1993), "Long economic cycles and the criminal justice system in the US," *Crime, Law and Social Change,* Vol. 19, pp. 143–69.

Barlow, M.H. (1998) "Race and the problem of crime in *Time* and *Newsweek* cover stories, 1946–1995," *Social Justice,* Vol. 25 No. 2.

Bayley, D.H. (1994), *Police for the Future,* Oxford University Press, New York, NY.

Bennett, L., Jr. (1993), *Before the Mayflower: A History of Black America,* (6th ed.), Penguin Books, New York, NY.

Brown, L.P. (1984), "Community policing: a practical guide for police officers." *The Police Chief,* August, pp. 72–82.

Chambliss, W. (1994), "Policing the ghetto underclass: the politics of law and law enforcement," *Social Problems,* Vol. 41 No. 2, pp. 177–94.

Dubofsky, M. (1975), *Industrialism and the American Worker, 1865–1920,* Harlan Davidson, Arlington Heights, IL.

Genovesé, E.D. (1976), *Roll, Jordan, Roll: The World the Slaves Made,* Vintage Books, New York, NY.

Goldstein, H. (1979), "Improving policing: a problem-oriented approach," *Crime and Delinquency,* Vol. 25, pp. 236–58.

Goldstein, H. (1990), *Problem-Oriented Policing,* McGraw-Hill, New York, NY.

Gordon, D.M., Edwards, R. and Reich, M. (1982), *Segmented Work, Divided Workers: The Historical Transformation of Labor in the United States,* Cambridge University Press, Cambridge, MA.

Gurr, T.R. (1980), "Development and decay: their impact on public order in western history," in Inciardi, J.A. and Faupel, C.E. (Eds), *History and Crime: Implications for Criminal Justice Policy,* Sage Publications, Beverly Hills, CA.

Haller, M.H. (1976), "Historical roots of police behavior: Chicago, 1890–1925," *Law and Society Review,* Vol. 10, pp. 303–23.

Harring, S.L. (1983), *Policing a Class Society: The Experience of American Cities, 1865–1915,* Rutgers, New Brunswick, NJ.

Harris, F.R. and Wicker, T. (Eds) (1988), *The Kerner Report: The 1968 Report of the National Advisory Commission on Civil Disorders,* Pantheon, New York, NY.

Hawkins, H. and Thomas, R. (1991), "White policing black populations: a history of race and social control in America," in Hawkins, H. and

Thomas, R. (Eds), *Out of Order: Policing Black People,* Routledge, London, pp. 65–86.

Helmer, J. (1975), *Drugs and Minority Oppression,* The Seabury Press, New York, NY.

Humphries, D. and Greenberg, D.F. (1981), "The dialectics of crime control," in Greenberg, D.F. (Ed.), *Crime and Capitalism: Readings in Marxist Criminology,* Mayfield Publishing, Palo Alto, CA.

Katz, W.L. (1995), *Eyewitness: A Living Documentary of the African American Contribution to American History,* Touchstone, New York, NY.

Kelling, G.L. and Moore, M.H. (1988), "The evolving strategy of policing," *Perspectives on Policing,* Vol. 4, pp. 1–15.

Klockars, C.B. (1991), "The rhetoric of community policing," in Greene, J.R. and Mastrofski, S. (Eds), *Community Policing: Rhetoric or Reality,* Praeger, New York, NY, pp. 239–58.

Kraska, P.B. and Kappeler, V.E. (1997), "Militarizing American police: the rise and normalization of paramilitary police units," *Social Problems,* Vol. 44 No. 1, pp. 1–18.

Lane, R. (1971), *Policing the City: Boston, 1822–1885,* Atheneum, New York, NY.

Loewen, J.W. (1995), *Lies My Teacher Told Me: Everything Your American History Textbook Got Wrong,* The New Press, New York, NY.

Mandel, E. (1978), *Late Capitalism,* Unwin Brothers Press, London.

Manning, P. (1991), "Community policing as a drama of control," in Greene and Mastrofski (Eds), *Community Policing: Rhetoric or Reality,* Praeger, New York, NY.

Meyer, J.W. and Rowan, B. (1977), "Institutionalized organizations: formal structure as myth and ceremony," *American Journal of Sociology,* Vol. 83 No. 2, pp. 340–63.

Mohl, R.A. (1979), "Poverty, pauperism, and social order in the preindustrial American City, 1780–1840," in Hawes, J.M. (Ed.), *Law and Order in*

American History, Kennikat Press, Port Washington, New York.

Ohlin, L.E. (1973), *Prisoners in America,* Prentice-Hall, Englewood Cliffs, NJ.

Ostrom, V., Bish, R. and Ostrom, E. (1988), *Local Government in the US,* ICS Press, San Francisco, CA.

Petchesky, R.P. (1981), "At hard labor: confinement and production in nineteenth-century America," in Greenberg, D.F. (Ed.), *Crime and Capitalism: Readings in Marxist Criminology,* Mayfield Publishing, Palo Alto, CA.

Pivar, D.J. (1973), *Purity Crusade: Sexual Morality, and Social Control, 1868–1900,* Greenwood Press, Westport, CT.

Piven, F.F. and Cloward, R.A. (1971), *Regulating the Poor: The Functions of Public Welfare,* Vintage Books, New York, NY.

Piven, F.F. and Cloward, R.A. (1979), *Poor People's Movements: Why They Succeed, How They Fail,* Vintage Books, New York, NY.

Platt, T., Frappier, J., Gerda, R., Schauffler, R., Trujillo, L., Cooper, L., Currie, E. and Harring, S. (1982), *The Iron Fist and the Velvet Glove: An Analysis of the US Police,* 3rd ed., Synthesis Publications, San Francisco, CA.

Richardson, J.F. (1974), *Urban Police in the United States,* Kennikat Press, Port Washington, NY.

Richardson, J.F. (1980), "Police in America: functions and control," in Inciardi, J. and Faupel, C.E. (Eds), *History and Crime: Implications for Criminal Justice Policy,* Sage Publications, Beverly Hills, CA.

Rothman, D.J. (1971), *The Discovery of the Asylum,* Little, Brown and Company, Boston, MA.

Rusche, G. (1978), "Labor market and penal sanction: thoughts on the sociology of criminal justice," *Crime and Social Justice,* Vol. 10, pp. 2–8, [originally published in 1933].

Rusche, G. and Kirchheimer, O. (1968), *Punishment and Social Structure,* Russell and Russell, New York, NY [originally published in 1939].

Samora, J., Bernal, J. and Peña, A. (1979), *Gunpowder Justice: A Reassessment of the Texas Rangers,* University of Notre Dame Press, Notre Dame, IN.

Schwartz, M.D. and Friedrichs, D.O. (1994), "Postmodern thought and criminological discontent: new metaphors for understanding violence," *Criminology,* Vol. 32 No. 2, pp. 221–46.

Silver, A. (1967), "The demand for order in civil society: a review of some themes in the history of crime, police and riot," in Bordua, D.J. (Ed.), *The Police: Six Sociological Essays,* John Wiley & Sons, New York, NY.

Spitzer, S. (1981), "The political economy of policing," in Greenberg, D.F. (Ed.), *Corrections and Punishment,* Sage Publications, Beverly Hills, CA.

Spitzer, S. and Scull, A.T. (1977), "Social control in historical perspective: from private to public responses to crime," in Greenberg, D.F. (Ed.), *Corrections and Punishment,* Sage Publications, Beverly Hills, CA, pp. 265–86.

Takaki, R. (1993), *A Different Mirror: A History of Multicultural America,* Little, Brown, and Company, Boston, MA.

Trattner, W.I. (1979), *From Poor Law to Welfare State,* 2nd ed., The Free Press, New York, NY.

Trojanowicz, R. and Bucqueroux, B. (1990), *Community Policing: A Contemporary Perspective,* Anderson Publishing Company, Cincinnati, OH.

US Department of Commerce (1975), *Historical Statistics of the United States: Colonial Times to 1970,* Bureau of the Census, Washington, DC.

Walker, S. (1977), *A Critical History of Police Reform: The Emergence of Professionalization,* Lexington Books, Lexington, MA.

Walker, S. (1980), *Popular Justice: A History of American Criminal Justice,* Oxford University Press, New York, NY.

Walker, S. (1984), "Broken windows and fractured history: the use and misuse of history in recent police patrol analysis," *Justice Quarterly,* Vol. 1, pp. 77–90.

Walker, S. (1992), *The Police in America: An Introduction,* 2nd ed., McGraw-Hill, New York, NY.

Williams, H. and Murphy, P.V. (1990), *The Evolving Strategy of Police: A Minority Perspective,* National Institute of Justice, Washington, DC.

Wilson, J.Q. and Kelling, G.L. (1982), "Broken windows: police and neighborhood safety," *The Atlantic Monthly,* March, Vol. 249, pp. 29–38.

Wright, E.O. (1979), *Class, Crisis and the State,* Verso Editions, London.

Further Reading

Coit, M.L. (1975), "The seep westward: 1820–1849," In Time-Life Books (Eds), *The History of the United States,* Vol. 4, Time-Life Books, New York, NY.

The Functions of Police in Modern Society

EGON BITTNER

POPULAR CONCEPTIONS ABOUT THE CHARACTER OF POLICE WORK

The abandonment of the norm-derivative approach to the definition of the role of the police in modern society immediately directs attention to a level of social reality that is unrelated to the ideal formulations. Whereas in terms of these formulations police activity derives its meaning from the objectives of upholding the law, we find that in reality certain meaning features are associated with police work that are largely independent of the objectives. That is, police work is generally viewed as having certain character traits we take for granted, and which control dealings between policemen and citizens, on both sides. Though we are lacking in adequate evidence about these matters, the perceived traits we will presently discuss are universally accepted as present and the

From Bittner, Egon. *The Functions of Police in Modern Society* (1967). Chapter 2, Popular Conceptions About the Character of Police Work, and Chapter 6, The Capacity to Use Force as the Core of the Police Role. National Institutes of Health.

recognition of their presence constitutes a realistic constraint on what is expected of the police and how policemen actually conduct themselves. It is important to emphasize that even while some of these ideas and attitudes are uncritically inherited from the past they are far from being totally devoid of realism. In the police literature these matters are typically treated under either euphemistic or cynical glosses. The reason for this evasion is simple, the Sunday school vocabulary we are forced to employ while talking about any occupational pursuit as dignified, serious, and necessary forces us to be either hypocritical or disillusioned, and prevents us from dealing realistically with the facts and from being candid about opinion.

Among the traits of character that are commonly perceived as associated with police work, and which thus constitute in part the social reality within which the work has to be done, the following three are of cardinal importance.

1. Police work is a tainted occupation. The origins of the stigma are buried in the distant past and while much has been said and done to erase it, these efforts have been notably unsuccessful. (Medieval watchmen, recruited from among the ranks of the destitute and subject to satirical portrayals, were perceived to belong to the world of shadows they were supposed to contain.[1]) During the period of the absolute monarchy the police came to represent the underground aspects of tyranny and political repression, and they were despised and feared even by those who ostensibly benefited from their services. No one can say how much of the old attitude lives on; some of it probably seeps into modern consciousness from the continued reading of nineteenth century romantic literature of the Victor Hugo variety. And it cannot be neglected that the mythology of the democratic polity avidly recounts the heroic combat against the police agents of the old order. But even if the police officer of today did not evoke the images of the past at all, he would still be viewed with mixed feelings, to say the least. For in modern folklore, too, he is a character who is ambivalently feared and admired, and no amount of public relations work can entirely abolish the sense that there is something of the dragon in the dragon-slayer.[2] Because they are posted on the perimeters of order and justice in the hope that their presence will deter the forces of darkness and chaos, because they are meant to spare the rest of the people direct confrontations with the dreadful, perverse, lurid, and dangerous, police officers are perceived to have powers and secrets no one else shares. Their interest in and competence to deal with the untoward surrounds their activities with mystery and distrust. One needs only to consider the thoughts that come to mind at the sight of policemen moving into action: here they go to do something the rest of us have no stomach for! And most people naturally experience a slight tinge of panic when approached by a policeman, a feeling against which the awareness of innocence provides no adequate protection. Indeed, the innocent in particular typically do not know what to expect and thus have added, even when unjustified, reasons for fear. On a more mundane level, the mixture of fear and fascination that the police elicit is often enriched by the addition of contempt. Depending on one's position in society, the contempt may draw on a variety of sources. To some the leading reason for disparaging police work derives from

the suspicion that those who do battle against evil cannot themselves live up fully to the ideals they presumably defend. Others make the most of the circumstance that police work is a low-paying occupation, the requirements for which can be met by men who are poorly educated. And some, finally, generalize from accounts of police abuses that come to their attention to the occupation as a whole.

It is important to note that the police do very little to discourage unfavorable public attitudes. In point of fact, their sense of being out of favor with a large segment of the society has led them to adopt a petulant stance and turned them to courting the kinds of support which, ironically, are nothing but a blatant insult. For the movement that is known by the slogan, "Support your local police," advocates the unleashing of a force of mindless bullies to do society's dirty work. Indeed, if there is still some doubt about the popular perception of police work as a tainted occupation, it will surely be laid to rest by pointing to those who, under the pretense of taking the side of the police, imply that the institution and its personnel are uniformly capable and willing to act out the baser instincts inherent in all of us.

In sum, the taint that attaches to police work refers to the fact that policemen are viewed as the fire it takes to fight fire, that they in the natural course of their duties inflict harm, albeit deserved, and that their very existence attests that the nobler aspirations of mankind do not contain the means necessary to insure survival. But even as those necessities are accepted, those who accept them seem to prefer to have no part in acting upon them, and they enjoy the more than slightly perverse pleasure of looking down on the police who take the responsibility of doing the job.

2. Police work is not merely a tainted occupation. To draw a deliberately remote analogy, the practice of medicine also has its dirty and mysterious aspects. And characteristically, dealings with physicians also elicit a sense of trepidated fascination. But in the case of medicine, the repulsive aspects, relating to disease, pain, and death, are more than compensated by other features, none of which are present in police work. Of the compensatory features, one is of particular relevance to our concerns. No conceivable human interest could be opposed to fighting illness; in fact, it is meaningless to suppose that one could have scruples in opposing disease. But the evils the police are expected to fight are of a radically different nature. Contrary to the physician, the policeman is always opposed to some articulated or articulable human interest. To be sure, the police are, at least in principle, opposed to only reprehensible interests or to interest lacking in proper justification. But even if one were to suppose that they never err in judging legitimacy—a far-fetched supposition, indeed—it would still remain the case that police work can, with very few exceptions, accomplish something *for* somebody only by proceeding *against* someone else. It does not take great subtlety of perception to realize that standing between man and man locked in conflict inevitably involves profound moral ambiguities. Admittedly, few of us are constantly mindful of the saying, "He that is without sin among you, let him cast the first stone . . . ," but only the police are explicitly required

to forget it. The terms of their mandate and the circumstances of their practices do not afford them the leisure to reflect about the deeper aspects of conflicting moral claims. Not only are they required to proceed forcefully against all appearances of transgression but they are also expected to penetrate the appearance of innocence to discover craftiness hiding under its cloak. While most of us risk only the opprobrium of foolishness by being charitable or gullible, the policeman hazards violating his duty by letting generosity or respect for appearances govern his decisions.

Though it is probably true that persons who are characterologically inclined to see moral and legal problems in black and white tend to choose police work as a vocation more often than others, it is important to emphasize that the need to disregard complexity is structurally built into the occupation. Only after a suspect is arrested, or after an untoward course of events is stopped, is there time to reflect on the merits of the decision and, typically, that reflective judgment is assigned to other public officials. Though it is expected that policemen will be judicious and that experience and skill will guide them in the performance of their work, it is foolish to expect that they could always be both swift and subtle. Nor is it reasonable to demand that they prevail, where they are supposed to prevail, while hoping that they will always handle resistance gently. Since the requirement of quick and what is often euphemistically called aggressive action is difficult to reconcile with error-free performance, police work is, by its very nature, doomed to be often unjust and offensive to someone. Under the dual pressure to "be right" and to "do something," policemen are often in a position that is compromised even before they act.[3]

In sum, the fact that policemen are required to deal with matters involving subtle human conflicts and profound legal and moral questions, without being allowed to give the subtleties and profundities anywhere near the consideration they deserve, invests their activities with the character of crudeness. Accordingly, the constant reminder that officers should be wise, considerate, and just, without providing them with opportunities to exercise these virtues is little more than vacuous sermonizing.

3. The ecological distribution of police work at the level of departmentally determined concentrations of deployment, as well as in terms of the orientations of individual police officers, reflects a whole range of public prejudices. That is, the police are more likely to be found in places where certain people live or congregate than in other parts of the city. Though this pattern of manpower allocation is ordinarily justified by references to experientially established needs for police service, it inevitably entails the consequence that some persons will receive the dubious benefit of extensive police scrutiny merely on account of their membership in those social groupings which invidious social comparisons locate at the bottom of the heap.[4] Accordingly, it is not a paranoid distortion to say that police activity is as much directed to who a person is as to what he does.

As is well known, the preferred targets of special police concern are some ethnic and racial minorities, the poor living in urban slums, and young people in general.[5] On the face of it, this kind of focusing appears to be, if not wholly unobjectionable, not without warrant. Insofar as the above-mentioned segments of society contribute disproportionately to the sum total of crime, and are more likely than others to engage in objectionable conduct, they would seem to require a higher degree of surveillance. In fact, this kind of reasoning was basic to the very creation of the police; for it was not assumed initially that the police would enforce laws in the broad sense, but that they would concentrate on the control of individual and collective tendencies towards transgression and disorder issuing from what were referred to as the "dangerous classes."[6] What was once a frankly admitted bias is, however, generally disavowed in our times. That is, in and of itself, the fact that someone is young, poor, and dark-complexioned is not supposed to mean anything whatsoever to a police officer. Statistically considered, he might be said to be more likely to run afoul of the law, but individually, all things being equal, his chances of being left alone *are supposed* to be the same as those of someone who is middle aged, well-to-do, and fair-skinned. In fact, however, exactly the opposite is the case. All things being equal, the young-poor-black and the old-rich-white doing the very same things under the very same circumstances will almost certainly not receive the same kind of treatment from policemen. In fact, it is almost inconceivable that the two characters could ever appear to do something in ways that would mean the same thing to a policeman.[7] Nor is the policeman merely expressing personal or institutional prejudice by according the two characters differential treatment. Public expectations insidiously instruct him to reckon with these "factors." These facts are too well known to require detailed exposition, but their reasons and consequences deserve brief consideration.

In the first place, the police are not alone in making invidious distinctions between the two types.[8] Indeed the differential treatment they accord them reflects only the distribution of esteem, credit, and desserts in society at large. Second, because of their own social origins, many policemen tend to express social prejudices more emphatically than other members of society.[9] Third, policemen are not merely like everybody else, only more so; they also have special reasons for it. Because the preponderant majority of police interventions are based on mere suspicion or on merely tentative indications of risk, policemen would have to be expected to judge matters prejudicially even if they personally were entirely free of prejudice. Under present circumstances, even the most completely impartial policeman who merely takes account of probabilities, as these probabilities are known to him, will feel reasonably justified in being more suspicious of the young-poor-black than of the old-rich-white, and once his suspicions are aroused, in acting swiftly and forcefully against the former while treating the latter with reserve and deference. For as the policeman calculates risk, the greater hazard is located on the side of inaction in one case, and on the side of unwarranted action in the other.

That policemen deal differently with types of people who are thought always to be "up to something" than with people who are thought to have occasional lapses but can otherwise be relied upon to conduct their affairs legally and honorably, does not come as a surprise, especially if one considers the multiple social pressures that instruct the police not to let the unworthy get away with anything and to treat the rest of the community with consideration. But because this is the case, police work tends to have divisive effects in society. While their existence and work do not create cleavages, they do magnify them in effect.

The police view of this matter is clear and simple — too simple, perhaps. Their business is to control crime and keep the peace. If there is some connection between social and economic inequality, on the one hand, and criminality and unruliness, on the other hand, this is not their concern. The problem is not, however, whether the police have any responsibilities with regard to social injustice. The problem is that by distributing surveillance and intervention selectively they contribute to already existing tensions in society. That the police are widely assumed to be a partisan force in society is evident not only in the attitudes of people who are exposed to greater scrutiny; just as the young–poor–black expects unfavorable treatment, so the old–rich–white expects special consideration from the policeman. And when two such persons are in conflict, nothing will provoke the indignation of the "decent" citizen more quickly than giving his word the same credence as the word of some "ne'er-do-well." [10]

The three character traits of police work discussed in the foregoing remarks — namely, that it is a tainted occupation, that it calls for peremptory solutions for complex human problems, and that it has, in virtue of its ecological distribution, a socially divisive effect — are structural determinants. By this is meant mainly that the complex of reasons and facts they encompass are not easily amenable to change. Thus, for example, though the stigma that attaches to police work is often viewed as merely reflecting the frequently low grade and bungling personnel that is currently available to the institution, there are good reasons to expect that it would continue to plague a far better prepared and a far better performing staff. For the stigma attaches not merely to the ways policemen discharge their duties, but also to what they have to deal with. Similarly, while it is probably true that moral naïveté is a character trait of persons who presently choose police work as their vocation, it is unlikely that persons of greater subtlety of perception would find it easy to exercise their sensitivity under present conditions. Finally, even though discriminatory policing is to some extent traceable to personal bigotry, it also follows the directions of public pressure, which, in turn, is not wholly devoid of factual warrant.

The discussion of the structural character traits of police work was introduced by saying that they were independent of the role definitions formulated from the perspective of the norm-derivative approach. The latter interprets the meaning and adequacy of police procedure in terms of a set of simply stipulated ideal objectives. Naturally these objectives are considered desirable; more importantly, however, the values that determine the desirability of the objectives are also used in interpreting and judging the adequacy of procedures employed to realize them. Contrary to this way of making sense of police work, the consideration of the structural character traits was meant to draw attention to the fact that there attaches a sense to police work that is not inferentially derived from ideals but is rooted in what is commonly known about it. What is known about the police is, however, not merely a matter of more or less correct information. Instead, the common lore furnishes a framework for judging and interpreting their work. In crudest form, the common lore consists of a set of presuppositions about the way things are and have to be. Thus, for instance, whatever people assume to be generally true of the police will be the thing that a particular act or event will be taken to exemplify. If it is believed that police work is crude, then within a very considerable range of relative degrees of subtlety, whatever policemen will be seen doing will be seen as crudeness.

In addition to the fact that the normative approach represents an exercise in formal, legal inference, while the structural character traits reflect an approach of informal, commonsense practicality, the two differ in yet another and perhaps more important aspect. The normative approach does not admit the possibility that the police may, in fact, not be oriented to those objectives. Contrary to this, the sense of police activity that comes to the fore from the consideration of the character traits assigned to it by popular opinion and attitude leaves the question open.[11]

Since we cannot rely on abstract formulations that implicitly rule out the possibility that they might be entirely wrong, or far too narrow, and since we cannot depend on a fabric of commonsense characterizations, we must turn to still other sources. Of course, we can no more forget the importance of the popularly perceived character traits than we can forget the formulas of the official mandate. To advance further in our quest for a realistic definition of the police role, we must now turn to the review of certain historical materials that will show how the police moved into the position in which they find themselves today. On the basis of this review, in addition to what was proposed thus far, we will be able to formulate an explicit definition of the role of the institution and its officials.

THE CAPACITY TO USE FORCE
AS THE CORE OF THE POLICE ROLE

We have argued earlier that the quest for peace by peaceful means is one of the culture traits of modern civilization. This aspiration is historically unique. For example, the Roman Empire was also committed to the objectives of reducing or eliminating warfare during one period of its existence, but the method chosen to achieve the *Pax Romana* was, in the language of the poet, *debellare superbos,* i.e., to subdue the haughty by force. Contrary to this, our commitment to abolish the traffic of violence requires us to pursue the ideal by pacific means. In support of this contention we pointed to the development of an elaborate system of international diplomacy whose main objective is to avoid war, and to those changes in internal government that resulted in the virtual elimination of all forms of violence, especially in the administration of justice. That is, the overall tendency is not merely to withdraw the basis of legitimacy for all forms of provocative violence, but even from the exercise of provoked force required to meet illegitimate attacks. Naturally this is not possible to a full extent. At least, it has not been possible thus far. Since it is impossible to deprive responsive force entirely of legitimacy, its vestiges require special forms of authorization. Our society recognizes as legitimate three very different forms of responsive force.

First, we are authorized to use force for the purpose of self-defense. Though the laws governing self-defense are far from clear, it appears that an attacked person can counterattack only after he has exhausted all other means of avoiding harm, including retreat, and that the counterattack may not exceed what is necessary to disable the assailant from carrying out his intent. These restrictions are actually enforceable because harm done in the course of self-defense does furnish grounds for criminal and tort proceedings. It becomes necessary, therefore, to show compliance with these restrictions to rebut the charges of excessive and unjustified force even in self-defense.[12]

The second form of authorization entrusts the power to proceed coercively to some specifically deputized persons against some specifically named persons. Among the agents who have such highly specific powers are mental hospital attendants and prison guards. Characteristically, such persons use force in carrying out court orders; but they may use force only against named persons who are remanded to their custody and only to the extent required to implement a judicial order of confinement. Of course, like everybody else, they may also act within the provisions governing self-defense. By insisting on the high degree of limited specificity of the powers of custodial staffs, we do not mean to deny that these restrictions are often violated with impunity. The likelihood of such transgressions is enhanced by the secluded character of prisons and mental institutions, but their existence does not impair the validity of our definition.

The third way to legitimize the use of responsive force is to institute a police force. Contrary to the cases of self-defense and the limited authorization of custodial functionaries, the police authorization is essentially unrestricted. Because the expression "essentially" is often used to hedge a point, we will make fully explicit what we mean by it. There exist three formal limitations of the freedom of policemen to use force, which we must admit even though they have virtually no practical consequences. First, the police use of deadly force is limited in most jurisdictions. Though the powers of a policeman in this respect exceed those of citizens, they are limited nevertheless. For example, in some jurisdictions policemen are empowered to shoot to kill fleeing felony suspects, but not fleeing misdemeanor suspects. It is scarcely necessary to argue that, given the uncertainties involved in defining a delict under conditions of hot pursuit, this could hardly be expected to be an effective limitation.[13] Second, policemen may use force only in the performance of their duties and not to advance their own personal interest or the private interests of other persons. Though this is rather obvious, we mention it for the sake of completeness. Third, and this point too is brought up to meet possible objections, policemen may not use force maliciously or frivolously. These three restrictions, and nothing else, were meant by the use of the qualifier "essentially." Aside from these restrictions there exist no guidelines, no specifiable range of objectives, no limitations of any kind that instruct the policeman what he may or must do. Nor do there exist any criteria that would allow the judgment whether some forceful intervention was necessary, desirable, or proper. And finally, it is exceedingly rare that police actions involving the use of force are actually reviewed and judged by anyone at all.

In sum, the frequently heard talk about the lawful use of force by the police is practically meaningless and, because no one knows what is meant by it, so is the talk about the use of minimum force. Whatever vestigial significance attaches to the term "lawful" use of force is confined to the obvious and unnecessary rule that police officers may not commit crimes of violence. Otherwise, however, the expectation that they may and will use force is left entirely undefined. In fact, the only instructions any policeman ever receives in this respect consist of sermonizing that he should be humane and circumspect, and that he must not desist from what he has undertaken merely because its accomplishment may call for coercive means. We might add, at this point, that the entire debate about the troublesome problem of police brutality will not move beyond its present impasse, and the desire to eliminate it will remain an impotent conceit, until this point is fully grasped and unequivocally admitted. In fact, our expectation that policemen will use force, coupled by our refusals to state clearly what we mean by it (aside from sanctimonious homilies), smacks of more than a bit of perversity.

Of course, neither the police nor the public is entirely in the dark about the justifiable use of force by the officers. We had occasion to allude to the assumption that policemen may use force in making arrests. But the benefit deriving from this apparent core of relative clarity is outweighed by its potentially misleading implications. For the authorization of the police to use force is in no important sense related to their duty to apprehend criminals. Were this the case then it could be adequately considered as merely a special case of the same authorization that is entrusted to custodial personnel. It might perhaps be considered a bit more complicated, but essentially of the same nature. But the police authority to use force is radically different from that of a prison guard. Whereas the powers of the latter are incidental to his obligation to implement a legal command, the police role is far better understood by saying that their ability to arrest offenders is incidental to their authority to use force.

Many puzzling aspects of police work fall into place when one ceases to look at it as principally concerned with law enforcement and crime control, and only incidentally and often incongruously concerned with an infinite variety of other matters. It makes much more sense to say that the police are nothing else than a mechanism for the distribution of situationally justified force in society. The latter conception is preferable to the former on three grounds. First, it accords better with the actual expectations and demands made of the police (even though it probably conflicts with what most people would say, or expect to hear, in answer to the question about the proper police function); second, it gives a better accounting of the actual allocation of police manpower and other resources; and, third, it lends unity to all kinds of police activity. These three justifications will be discussed in some detail in the following.

The American city dweller's repertoire of methods for handling problems includes one known as "calling the cops." The practice to which the idiom refers is enormously widespread. Though it is more frequent in some segments of society than in others, there are very few people who do not or would not resort to it under suitable circumstances. A few illustrations will furnish the background for an explanation of what "calling the cops" means.[14]

Two patrolmen were directed to report to an address located in a fashionable district of a large city. On the scene they were greeted by the lady of the house who complained that the maid had been stealing and receiving male visitors in her quarters. She wanted the maid's belongings searched and the man removed. The patrolmen refused the first request, promising to forward the complaint to the bureau of detectives, but agreed to see what they could do about the man. After gaining entrance to the maid's room they compelled a male visitor to leave, drove him several blocks away from the house, and released him with the warning never to return.

In a tenement, patrolmen were met by a public health nurse who took them through an abysmally deteriorated apartment inhabited by four young children in the care of an elderly woman. The babysitter resisted the nurse's earlier attempts to remove the children. The patrolmen packed the children in the squad car and took them to Juvenile Hall, over the continuing protests of the elderly woman.

While cruising through the streets a team of detectives recognized a man named in a teletype received from the sheriff of an adjoining county. The suspect maintained that he was in the hospital at the time the offense alleged in the communication took place, and asked the officers to verify his story over their car radio. When he continued to plead innocence he was handcuffed and taken to headquarters. Here the detectives learned that the teletype had been cancelled. Prior to his release the man was told that he could have saved himself grief had he gone along voluntarily.

In a downtown residential hotel, patrolmen found two ambulance attendants trying to persuade a man, who according to all accounts was desperately ill, to go to the hospital. After some talk, they helped the attendants in carrying the protesting patient to the ambulance and sent them off.

In a middle-class neighborhood, patrolmen found a partly disassembled car, tools, a loudly blaring radio, and five beer-drinking youths at the curb in front of a single-family home. The homeowner complained that this had been going on for several days and the men had refused to take their activities elsewhere. The patrolmen ordered the youths to pack up and leave. When one sassed them they threw him into the squad car, drove him to the precinct station, from where he was released after receiving a severe tongue lashing from the desk sergeant.

In the apartment of a quarreling couple, patrolmen were told by the wife, whose nose was bleeding, that the husband stole her purse containing money she earned. The patrolmen told the man they would "take him in," whereupon he returned the purse and they left.

What all these vignettes are meant to illustrate is that whatever the substance of the task at hand, whether it involves protection against an undesired imposition, caring for those who cannot care for themselves, attempting to solve a crime, helping to save a life, abating a nuisance, or settling an explosive dispute, police intervention means above all making use of the capacity and authority to overpower resistance to an attempted solution in the native habitat of the problem. There can be no doubt that this feature of police work is uppermost in the minds of people who solicit police aid or direct the attention of the police to problems, that persons against whom the police proceed have this feature in mind and conduct themselves accordingly, and that every conceivable police intervention projects the message that force may be, and may have to be, used to achieve a desired objective. It does not matter whether the persons who seek police help are private citizens or other government officials, nor does it matter whether the problem at hand involves some aspect of law enforcement or is totally unconnected with it.

It must be emphasized, however, that the conception of the centrality of the capacity to use force in the police role does not entail the conclusion that the ordinary occupational routines consist of the actual exercise of this capacity. It is very likely, though we lack information on this point, that the actual use of physical coercion and restraint is rare for all policemen and that many policemen are virtually never in the position of having to resort to it. What matters is that police procedure is defined by the feature that it may not be opposed in its course, and that force can be used if it is opposed. This is what the existence of the police makes available to society. Accordingly, the question, "What are policemen supposed to do?" is almost completely identical with the question, "What kinds of situations require remedies that are non-negotiably coercible?"[15]

Our second justification for preferring the definition of the police role we proposed to the traditional law enforcement focus of the role requires us to review the actual police practices to see to what extent they can be subsumed under the conception we offered. To begin we can take note that law enforcement and crime control are obviously regarded as calling for remedies that are non-negotiably coercible. According to available estimates, approximately one-third of available manpower resources of the police are at any time committed to dealing with crimes and criminals. Though this may seem to be a relatively small share of the total resources of an agency ostensibly devoted to crime control, it is exceedingly unlikely that any other specific routine police activity, such as traffic regulation, crowd control, supervision of licensed establishments, settling of citizens' disputes, emergency health aids, ceremonial functions, or any other, absorb anywhere near as large a share of the remaining two-thirds. But this is precisely what one would expect on the basis of our definition. Given the likelihood that offenders will seek to oppose apprehension and evade punishment, it is only natural that the initial dealings with them be assigned to an agency that is capable of overcoming these obstacles. That is, the proposed definition of the role of the police as a mechanism for the distribution of non-negotiably coercive remedies entails the priority of crime control by direct inference. Beyond that, however, the definition also encompasses other types of activities, albeit at a lower level of priority.

Because the idea that the police are basically a crimefighting agency has never been challenged in the past, no one has troubled to sort out the remaining priorities. Instead, the police have always been forced to justify activities that did not involve law enforcement in the direct sense by either linking them constructively to law enforcement or by defining them as nuisance demands for service. The dominance of this view, especially in the minds of policemen, has two pernicious consequences. First, it leads to a tendency to view all sorts of problems as if they involved culpable offenses and to an excessive reliance on quasi-legal methods for handling them. The widespread use of arrests without intent to prosecute exemplifies this state of affairs. These cases do not involve errors in judgment about the applicability of a penal norm but deliberate pretense resorted to because more appropriate methods of handling problems have not been developed. Second, the view that crime control is the only serious, important, and necessary part of police work has deleterious effects on the morale of those police officers in the uniformed patrol who spend most of their time with other matters. No one, especially he who takes a positive interest in his work, likes being obliged to do things day in and day out that are disparaged by his colleagues. Moreover, the low evaluation of these duties leads to neglecting the development of skill and knowledge that are required to discharge them properly and efficiently.

It remains to be shown that the capacity to use coercive force lends thematic unity to all police activity in the same sense in which, let us say, the capacity to cure illness lends unity to everything that is ordinarily done in the field of medical practice. While everybody agrees that the police actually engage in an enormous variety of activities, only a part of which involves law enforcement, many argue that this state of affairs does not require explanation but change. Smith, for example, argued that the imposition of duties and demands that are not related to crime control dilutes the effectiveness of the police and that the growing trend in this direction should be curtailed and even reversed.[16] On the face of it this argument is not without merit, especially if one considers that very many of those activities that are unrelated to law enforcement involve dealing with problems that lie in the field of psychiatry, social welfare, human relations, education, and so on. Each of these fields has its own trained specialists who are respectively more competent than the police. It would seem preferable, therefore, to take all those matters that belong properly to other specialists out of the hands of the police and turn them over to those to whom they belong. Not only would this relieve some of the pressures that presently impinge on the police, but it would also result in better services.[17]

Unfortunately, this view overlooks a centrally important factor. While it is true that policemen often aid sick and troubled people because physicians and social workers are unable or unwilling to take their services where they are needed, this is not the only or even the main reason for police involvement. In fact, physicians and social workers themselves quite often "call the cops." For not unlike the case of the administration of justice, on the periphery of the rationally ordered procedures of medical and social work practice lurk exigencies that call for the exercise of coercion. Since neither physicians nor social workers are authorized or equipped to use force to attain desirable objectives, the total disengagement of the police would mean allowing many a problem to move unhampered in the direction of disaster. But the non–law-enforcement activities of the police are by no means confined to matters that are wholly or even mainly within the purview of some other institutionalized remedial specialty. Many, perhaps most, consist of addressing situations in which people simply do not seem to be able to manage their own lives adequately. Nor is it to be taken for granted that these situations invariably call for the use, or the threat of the use, of force. It is enough if there is need for immediate and unquestioned intervention that must not be allowed to be defeated by possible resistance. And where there is a possibility of great harm, the intervention would appear to be justified even if the risk is, in statistical terms, quite remote. Take, for instance the presence of mentally ill persons in the community. Though it is well known that most live quiet and unobtrusive lives, they are perceived as occasionally constituting a serious hazard to themselves and others. Thus, it is not surprising that the police are always prepared to deal with these persons at the slightest indication of a possible emergency. Similarly, though very few family quarrels lead to serious consequences, the fact that most homicides occur among quarreling kin leads to the preparedness to intervene at the incipient stages of problems.

In sum, the role of the police is to address all sorts of human problems when and insofar as their solutions do or may possibly require the use of force at the point of their occurrence. This lends homogeneity to such diverse procedures as catching a criminal, driving the mayor to the airport, evicting a drunken person from a bar, directing traffic, crowd control, taking care of lost children, administering medical first aid, and separating fighting relatives.

There is no exaggeration in saying that there is topical unity in this very incomplete list of lines of police work. Perhaps it is true that the common practice of assigning policemen to chauffeur mayors is based on the desire to give the appearance of thrift in the urban fisc. But note, if one wanted to make as far as possible certain that nothing would ever impede His Honor's freedom of movement, he would certainly put someone into the driver's seat of the auto who has the authority and the capacity to overcome all unforeseeable human obstacles. Similarly, it is perhaps not too far-fetched to assume that desk sergeants feed ice cream to lost children because they like children. But if the treat does not achieve the purpose of keeping the youngster in the station house until his parents arrive to redeem him, the sergeant would have to resort to other means of keeping him there.

We must now attempt to pull together the several parts of the foregoing discussion in order to show how they bring into relief the main problems of adjusting police function to life in modern society, and in order to elaborate constructively certain consequences that result from the assumption of the role definitions we have proposed.

At the beginning we observed that the police appear to be burdened by an opprobrium that did not seem to lessen proportionately to the acknowledged improvements in their practices. To explain this puzzling fact we drew attention to three perceived features of the police that appear to be substantially independent of particular work methods. First, a stigma attaches to police work because of its connection with evil, crime, perversity, and disorder. Though it may not be reasonable, it is common that those who fight the dreadful end up being dreaded themselves. Second, because the police must act quickly and often on mere intuition, their interventions are lacking in those aspects of moral sophistication which only a more extended and more scrupulous consideration can afford. Hence their methods are comparatively crude. Third, because it is commonly assumed that the risks of the kinds of breakdowns that require police action are much more heavily concentrated in the lower classes than in other segments of society, police surveillance is inherently discriminatory. That is, all things being equal, some persons feel the sting of police scrutiny merely because of their station in life. Insofar as this is felt, police work has divisive effects in society.

Next, we argued that one cannot understand how the police "found themselves" in this unenviable position without taking into consideration that one of the cultural trends of roughly the past century-and-a-half was the sustained aspiration to install peace as a stable condition of everyday life. Though no one can fail being impressed by the many ways the attainment of this ideal has been frustrated, it is possible to find some evidence of partially effective efforts. Many aspects of mundane existence in our cities have become more pacific than they have been in past epochs of history. More importantly for our purposes, in the domain of internal statecraft, the distance between those who govern and those who are governed has grown and the gap has been filled with bureaucratically symbolized communication. Where earlier compliance was secured by physical presence and armed might, it now rests mainly on peaceful persuasion and rational compliance. We found the trend toward the pacification in governing most strongly demonstrated in the administration of justice. The banishment of all forms of violence from the criminal process, as administered by the courts, has as a corollary the legalization of judicial proceedings. The latter reflects a movement away from peremptory and oracular judgment to a method in which all decisions are based on exhaustively rational grounds involving the use of explicit legal norms. Most important among those norms are the ones that limit the powers of authority and specify the rights of defendants. The legalization and pacification of the criminal process was achieved by, among other things, expelling from its purview those processes that set it into motion. Since in the initial steps, where suspicions are formed and arrests are made, force and intuition cannot be eliminated entirely, purity can be maintained by not taking notice of them. This situation is, however, paradoxical if we are to take seriously the idea that the police is a law enforcement agency in the strict sense of legality. The recognition of this paradox became unavoidable as early as 1914, in the landmark decision of *Weeks* v. *U.S.* In the following decades the United States Supreme Court issued a series of rulings affecting police procedure which foster the impression that the judiciary exercises control over the police. But this impression is misleading, for the rulings do not set forth binding norms for police work but merely provide that *if* the police propose to set the criminal process into motion, *then* they must proceed in certain legally restricted ways. These restrictions are, therefore, conditional, specifying as it were the terms of delivery and acceptance of a service and nothing more. Outside of this arrangement the judges have no direct concerns with police work and will take notice of its illegality, if it is illegal, only when offended citizens seek civil redress.

Because only a small part of the activity of the police is dedicated to law enforcement and because they deal with the majority of their problems without invoking the law, a broader definition of their role was proposed. After reviewing briefly what the public appears to expect of the police, the range of activities police actually engage in, and the theme that unifies all these activities, it was suggested that *the role of the police is best understood as a mechanism for the distribution of non-negotiably coercive force employed in accordance with the dictates of an intuitive grasp of situational exigencies.*

It is, of course, not surprising that a society committed to the establishment of peace by pacific means and to the abolishment of all forms of violence from the fabric of its social relations, at least as a matter of official morality and policy, would establish a corps of specially deputized officials endowed with the exclusive monopoly of using force contingently where limitations of foresight fail to provide alternatives. That is, given the melancholy appreciation of the fact that the total abolition of force is not attainable, the closest approximation to the ideal is to limit it as a special and exclusive trust. If it is the case, however, that the mandate of the police is organized around their capacity and authority to use force, i.e., if this is what the institution's existence makes available to society, then the evaluation of that institution's performance must focus on it. While it is quite true that policemen will have to be judged on other dimensions of competence, too — for example, the exercise of force against criminal suspects requires some knowledge about crime and criminal law — their methods as society's agents of coercion will have to be considered central to the overall judgment.

The proposed definition of the police role entails a difficult moral problem. How can we arrive at a favorable or even accepting judgment about an activity which is, in its very conception, opposed to the ethos of the polity that authorizes it? Is it not well nigh inevitable that this mandate be concealed in circumlocution? While solving puzzles of moral philosophy is beyond the scope of this analysis, we will have to address this question in a somewhat more mundane formulation: namely, on what terms can a society dedicated to peace institutionalize the exercise of force?

It appears that in our society two answers to this question are acceptable. One defines the targets of legitimate force as enemies and the coercive advance against them as warfare. Those who wage this war are expected to be possessed by the military virtues of valor, obedience, and *esprit de corps*. The enterprise as a whole is justified as a sacrificial and glorious mission in which the warrior's duty is "not to reason why." The other answer involves an altogether different imagery. The targets of force are conceived as practical objectives and their attainment a matter of practical expediency. The process involves prudence, economy, and considered judgment, from case to case. The enterprise as a whole is conceived as a public trust, the exercise of which is vested in individual practitioners who are personally responsible for their decisions and actions.

Reflection suggests that the two patterns are profoundly incompatible. Remarkably, however, our police departments have not been deterred from attempting the reconciliation of the irreconcilable. Thus, our policemen are exposed to the demand of a conflicting nature in that their actions are supposed to reflect military prowess and professional acumen.

ENDNOTES

1. Werner Dankert, *Unehrliche Menschen: Die Verfehmten Berufe,* Bern: Francke Verlag, 1963.

2. G. S. McWatters wrote about the typical policeman, after many years of being one himself, "He is the outgrowth of a diseased and corrupted state of things, and is, consequently, morally diseased himself." quoted in Lane, *op. cit. supra,* Note 2 at p. 69.

3. Erle Stanley Gardner, the prolific detective story writer, reports being troubled by the apparent need for the "dumb" cop in fiction. When he attempted to remedy this and depicted a policeman in favorable colors in one of his books, book dealers and readers rose in protest; see his "The Need for New Concepts in the Administration of Criminal Justice," *Journal of Criminal Law, Criminology and Police Science,* 50 (1959) 20–26; see also, G. J. Falk, "The Public's Prejudice Against the Police," *American Bar Association Journal,* 50 (1965) 754–757.

4. V. W. Piersante, Chief Detective of the Detroit Police Department, has juxtaposed with remarkable perceptiveness the considerations which, on the one hand, lead to dense and suspicious surveillance of certain groups because of their disproportionate contribution to crime totals, while on the other hand, these tactics expose the preponderant majority of law-abiding members of these groups to offensive scrutiny. He stated, "in Detroit in 1964 a total of 83,135 arrests were made . . . of this 58,389 were Negroes. . . . This means that 89 percent of the Negro population were never involved with the police . . ." quoted at p. 215 in Harold

Norris, "Constitutional Law Enforcement Is Effective Law Enforcement," *University of Detroit Law Journal,* 42 (1965) 203–234.

5. Gilbert Geis, *Juvenile Gangs,* A Report Produced for the President's Committee on Juvenile Delinquency and Youth Crime, Washington, D.C.: U.S. Government Printing Office, June 1965; Carl Werthman and Irving Piliavin, "Gang Membership and the Police," in Bordua (ed.), *op. cit. supra,* Note 3 at pp. 56–98.

6. Allan Silver, "The Demand for Order in Civil Society: A Review of Some Themes in the History of Urban Crime, Police, and Riot," in Bordua (ed.), *op. cit. supra,* Note 3 at pp. 1–24.

7. J. Q. Wilson writes, "The patrolman believes with considerable justification that teenagers, Negroes, and lower-income persons commit a disproportionate share of all reported crimes; being in those population categories at all makes one, statistically, more suspect than other persons; but to be in those categories *and* to behave unconventionally is to make oneself a prime suspect. Patrolmen believe that they would be derelict in their duty if they did not treat such persons with suspicion, routinely question them on the street, and detain them for longer questioning if a crime has occurred in the area. To the objection of some middle-class observers that this is arbitrary and discriminatory, the police are likely to answer: 'Have *you* ever been stopped and searched? Of course not. We can tell the difference; we have to tell the difference in order to do our job. What are you complaining about?'" at pp. 40–41 of his *Varieties of*

Police Behavior: The Management of Law and Order in Eight Communities, Cambridge, Mass.: Harvard University Press, 1968.

8. Of primary significance in this respect is that the courts make the same kinds of invidious distinctions even as they follow the law; see J. E. Carlin, Jan Howard, and S. L. Messinger, "Civil Justice and the Poor," *Law and Society,* 1 (1965) 9–89, and Jacobus ten-Broek (ed.), *The Law of the Poor,* San Francisco, California: Chandler Publishing Co., 1966.

9. Reference is made to the evidence that persons of working class origin are more prone than others to harbor attitudes that are favorable to politics of prejudice and authoritarianism; see S. L. Lipset, "Democracy and Working Class Authoritarianism," *American Sociological Review,* 24 (1959) 482–501; "Social Stratification and Right Wing Extremism," *British Journal of Sociology,* 10 (1959) 346–382; "Why Cops Hate Liberals — and Vice Versa," *Atlantic Monthly* (March 1969).

10. Arthur Niederhoffer, a former ranking police official, writes, "The power structure and the ideology of the community, which are supported by the police, at the same time direct and set boundaries to the sphere of police action." at p. 13 of his *Behind the Shield: The Police in Urban Society.* New York: Anchor Books, 1969; Niederhoffer cites an even stronger statement to that effect from Joseph Lohman, a former sheriff of Cook County, Ill., and later Dean of the School of Criminology at the University of California at Berkeley.

11. The normative approach is perhaps best exemplified in Jerome Hall, "Police and Law in a Democratic Society," *Indiana Law Journal,* 2 (1953) 133–177, where it is argued that the structure of police work must be understood as decisively determined by the duty to uphold the law and every police action must be interpreted in relation to this objective. The man on the street, however, approaches police work from a different vantage point. He probably supposes that police work has something to do with law enforcement, but to him this is mainly a figure of speech which does not limit his freedom to decide what the police are really for from case to case.

12. "Justification for the Use of Force in the Criminal Law," *Stanford Law Review,* 13 (1961) 566–609.

13. "At common law, the rule appears to have been that an officer was entitled to make a reasonable mistake as to whether the victim had committed a felony, but a private person was not so entitled. Thus strict liability was created for the private arrester, and be could not justifiably kill, if the victim had not actually committed a felony. Several modern cases have imposed this standard of strict liability even upon the officer by conditioning justification of deadly force on the victim's actually having committed a felony, and a number of states have enacted statutes which appear to adopt this strict liability. However, many jurisdictions, such as California, have homicide statutes which permit the police officer to use deadly force for the arrest of a person 'charged' with felony. It has been suggested that this requirement only indicates the necessity for reasonable belief by the officer that the victim has committed a felony." *Ibid.,* pp. 589–600.

14. The illustrations are taken from field notes I have collected over the course of fourteen months of intensive field observations of police activity in two large cities. One is located in a Rocky Mountain State, the other on the West Coast. All other case vignettes used in the subsequent text of this report also come from this source.

15. By "non-negotiably coercible" we mean that when a deputized police officer decides that force is necessary, then, within the boundaries of this situation, he is not accountable to anyone, nor is he required to brook the arguments or opposition of anyone who might object to it. We set this forth not as a legal but as a practical rule. The legal question whether citizens may oppose policemen is complicated. Apparently resisting police coercion in situations of emergency is not legitimate; see Hans Kelsen, *General Theory of Law and State,* New York: Russel & Russel, 1961, pp. 278–279, and H. A. L. Hart, *The Concept of Law,* Oxford: Clarendon Press, 1961, pp. 20–21. Common law doctrine allows that citizens may oppose

"unlawful arrest," *6 Corpus Juris Secundum,* Arrest #13, p. 613; against this, the Uniform Arrest Act, drafted by a committee of the Interstate Commission on Crime in 1939, provides in Section 5, "If a person has reasonable grounds to believe that he is being arrested by a peace officer, it is his duty to refrain from using force or any weapons in resisting arrest regardless of whether or not there is a legal basis for the arrest." S. B. Warner, "Uniform Arrest Act," *Vanderbilt Law Review,* 28 (1942) 315–347. At present, at least twelve states are governed by case law recognizing the validity of the Common Law doctrine, at least five have adopted the rule contained in the Uniform Arrest Act, and at least six have case law or statutes that give effect to

the Uniform Arrest Act rule. That the trend is away from the Common Law doctrine and in the direction of the Uniform Arrest Act rule is argued in Max Hochanadel and H. W. Stege, "The Right to Resist an Unlawful Arrest: An Outdated Concept?" *Tulsa Law Journal,* 3 (1966) 40–46. I am grateful for the help I received from 35 of the 50 State Attorney General Offices from whom I sought information concerning this matter.

16. Smith, *op. cit. supra,* Note 1.

17. The authors of the *Task Force Report: Police* note that little has been done to make these alternative resources available as substitutes for police intervention; *op. cit. supra,* Note 556 at p. 14.

QUESTIONS FOR
DISCUSSION AND REVIEW

1. Describe the three eras of policing as identified by Kelling and Moore and identify how each differed from the other in relation to their function, organization and relationship to the community.

2. Explain how the Reform Era and the Community Problem-Solving Era of policing, as described by Kelling and Moore, emerged in response to the weaknesses of the eras which preceded their development.

3. Using the information provided in Williams and Murphy, critique the assumptions embedded in the following quote from Kelling and Moore's article: "*Despite attempts by police departments to create equitable police allocation systems and to provide impartial policing to all citizens,* many minority citizens, especially blacks during the 1960s and 1970s, did not *perceive* their treatment as equitable or adequate."

4. According to Williams and Murphy, how have the legal institutions of slavery, segregation, and discrimination shaped the police and their interaction with racial/ethnic minorities?

5. What were the specific characteristics and activities of the Rapid Deployment Units as observed by Chambliss in Washington, D.C.?

6. How do the observations by Chambliss, and the consequences of the "war on crime and drugs" in terms of who is going to prison, suggest that the problems of racism in policing are still relevant today?

7. How do the observations by Chambliss suggest that policing in the ghetto is more about social control than crime control?

8. According to Barlow and Barlow, why did the pre-industrial police emerge in Charleston, South Carolina, and what role did it play in maintaining the slave political economy? What do these historical events teach us about policing today?

9. According to Barlow and Barlow, what critical role have the police played in maintaining the capitalist political economy?

10. According to Barlow and Barlow, how do the specific characteristics of the postmodern police construct a "velvet glove" around the "iron fist" of policing?

11. According to Bittner, what makes police work a tainted profession and inherently crude?

12. According to Bittner, what is the single discriminating quality that characterizes the police or the unique role of the police in U.S. society, and how does that role ensure that the fundamental problem of police legitimacy is structural?

13. If the traits identified by Bittner do in fact define the social reality of police work, and they are structural conditions, what does it suggest about the potential for police reform?

SECTION II

POLICE DISCRETION

INTRODUCTION

Perhaps no other topic in the police literature has received as much attention as discretion. Discretion refers to the autonomy an officer has in choosing an appropriate course of action (Black, 1968; Davis, 1969). Since the police operate with limited resources, and since there is a great deal of uncertainty inherent in many police tasks, the exercise of police discretion is an essential aspect of police work. There is little doubt that the scholarly effort devoted to developing an understanding of police discretion is warranted given the desire for police accountability to the police organization and the public they are supposed to serve. By identifying the factors that influence the decisions of police officers, discretion may be better regulated, and hence the frequency of inequitable and unjust decisions may be minimized.

The research that has been conducted on police discretion can be classified into three explanatory perspectives: research has focused on how officers' traits and characteristics influence their discretionary behaviors (individual level approach), how the structural characteristics of police–citizen encounters affect officers' behaviors (situational approach), and how organizational factors affect officers' behaviors (organizational approach). The six readings included in this section cast light on each of these three perspectives.

The summary report of the Independent Commission on the Los Angeles Police Department (1991) provides a look inside the Los Angeles Police Department in the aftermath of the Rodney King incident. The report attempts to explain why the incident happened and, in so doing, draws upon the individual, situational, and organizational perspectives. The report serves as a contemporary, but non-scientific, example of theory applied to a real-world police problem. Worden (1995), in his article "The 'Causes' of Police Brutality," provides a scholarly example of how these three perspectives can be used to understand police use of force, and police discretion more generally. Worden (1995) identifies and empirically examines the influence of individual, situational, and organizational factors on police behavior.

Each of the remaining readings, all best considered classic contributions to the police literature, focus specifically on different explanatory perspectives of police discretion. Muir (1977), in an excerpt from his book *The Police: Street Corner Politicians,* discusses the role of officers' individual characteristics and traits in police decision making. On the basis of his ethnographic research, Muir explains that a "good" (i.e., "professional") police officer possesses two important qualities: passion and perspective. Passion refers to the belief in coercive power as a means to good ends and to the willingness to invoke power to achieve those ends. Perspective refers to an objective understanding of human dignity. To complete his typology, Muir identifies three non-professional types of police officers: enforcers (those with passion but not perspective), reciprocators (those with perspective but not passion), and avioders (those without passion or perspective). Muir discusses how an understanding of the qualities of officers is important in explaining their discretionary behavior.

Donald Black (1971), in his article "The Social Organization of Arrest," explains how the characteristics of situations affect the decisions of officers. According to Black, the discretionary arrest decisions of officers are most influenced by elements of police-citizen encounters such as the complainant's preferences, the suspect's demeanor, and the evidence available to the police. The empirical generalizations offered by Black are most often supported in the subsequent research that has examined the impact of these factors on police decision making (Worden, 1995).

John Van Maanen (1978), in "The Asshole," calls attention to the role of organizational subcultural influences on officers' perceptions and behaviors. Based on shared understandings of the nature of police work and demands faced by officers, officers categorize, or typify, citizens into several categories: "suspicious persons" (those who are believed to have committed a serious offense), "assholes" (those who challenge and are disrespectful of the police), and "know-nothings" (everyone else). Van Maanen suggests that this classification scheme provides insight into the expectations, thoughts, and feelings of police officers as they organize and make sense of their day-to-day work world. He further explains how these labels guide police actions during street encounters.

The final reading in this section, James Fyfe's (1979) "Administrative Interventions on Police Shooting Discretion," examines the impact of organizational policy (regarding deadly force) in shaping police behavior. His analyses show that upon implementation of policies that limited the use of firearms in the New York City Police Department, the frequency of shooting incidents dramatically declined. Clearly, organizational factors such as administrative rules affect police actions.

In summary, the first two readings of the section provide an overview of how various explanatory perspectives can be used to understand police discretion, and the remaining four readings provide examples of the application of these perspectives.

REFERENCES

Black, Donald (1968) "The Social Organization of Arrest." *Stanford Law Review* 23:1087–1111.

Davis, Kenneth C. (1969) *Discretionary Justice*. Baton Rouge: Louisiana State University Press.

Summary Report
of the Independent Commission

The videotaped beating of Rodney G. King by three uniformed officers of the Los Angeles Police Department, in the presence of a sergeant and with a large group of other officers standing by, galvanized public demand for evaluation and reform of police procedures involving the use of force. In the wake of the incident and the resulting widespread outcry, the Independent Commission on the Los Angeles Police Department was created. The Commission sought to examine all aspects of the law enforcement structure in Los Angeles that might cause or contribute to the problem of excessive force. The Report is unanimous.

The King beating raised fundamental questions about the LAPD, including:

- The apparent failure to control or discipline officers with repeated complaints of excessive force
- Concerns about the LAPD's "culture" and officers' attitudes toward racial and other minorities
- The difficulties the public encounters in attempting to make complaints against LAPD officers
- The role of the LAPD leadership and civilian oversight authorities in addressing or contributing to these problems

These and related questions and concerns form the basis for the Commission's work.

LOS ANGELES AND ITS POLICE FORCE

The LAPD is headed by Police Chief Daryl Gates with an executive staff currently consisting of two assistant chiefs, five deputy chiefs, and 17 commanders. The City Charter provides that the Department is ultimately under the control and oversight of the five-member civilian Board of Police Commissioners. The

This material has been deemed to be in the public domain. From the Independent Commission on the Los Angeles Police Department, 1991.

Office of Operations, headed by Assistant Chief Robert Vernon, accounts for approximately 84% of the Department's personnel, including most patrol officers and detectives. The Office of Operations has 18 separate geographic areas within the City, divided among four bureaus (Central, South, West, and Valley). There are currently about 8,450 sworn police officers, augmented by more than 2,000 civilian LAPD employees.

While the overall rate of violent crime in the United States increased three and one-half times between 1960 and 1989, the rate in Los Angeles during the same period was more than twice the national average. According to 1986 data recently published by the Police Foundation, the Los Angeles police were the busiest among the officers in the nation's largest six cities. As crime rates soar, police officers must contend with more and more potential and actual violence each day. One moment officers must confront a life-threatening situation; the next they must deal with citizen problems requiring understanding and kindness. The difficulties of policing in Los Angeles are compounded by its vast geographic area and the ethnic diversity of its population. The 1990 census data reflect how enormous that diversity is: Latinos constitute 40% of the total population; Whites 37%; African-Americans 13%; and Asian/Pacific Islanders and others 10%. Of the police departments of the six largest United States cities, the LAPD has the fewest officers per resident and the fewest officers per square mile. Yet the LAPD boasts more arrests per officer than other forces. Moreover, by all accounts, the LAPD is generally efficient, sophisticated, and free of corruption.

THE PROBLEM OF EXCESSIVE FORCE

LAPD officers exercising physical force must comply with the Department's Use of Force Policy and Guidelines, as well as California law. Both the LAPD Policy and the Penal Code require that force be reasonable; the Policy also requires that force be necessary. An officer may resort to force only where he or she faces a credible threat, and then may use only the minimum amount necessary to control the suspect.

The Commission has found that there is a significant number of LAPD officers who repetitively misuse force and persistently ignore the written policies and guidelines of the Department regarding force. The evidence obtained by the Commission shows that this group has received inadequate supervisory and management attention.

Former Assistant Chief Jesse Brewer testified that this lack of management attention and accountability is the "essence of the excessive force problem. . . . We know who the bad guys are. Reputations become well known, especially to the sergeants and then of course to lieutenants and the captains in the areas. . . . But I don't see anyone bring these people up . . ." Assistant Chief David Dotson testified that "we have failed miserably" to hold supervisors accountable for excessive force by officers under their command. Interviews with a large number of present and former LAPD officers yield similar conclusions.

Senior and rank-and-file officers generally stated that a significant number of officers tended to use force excessively, that these problem officers were well known in their divisions, that the Department's efforts to control or discipline those officers were inadequate, and that their supervisors were not held accountable for excessive use of force by officers in their command.

The Commission's extensive computerized analysis of the data provided by the Department (personnel complaints, use of force reports, and reports of officer-involved shootings) shows that a significant group of problem officers poses a much higher risk of excessive force than other officers:

- Of approximately 1,800 officers against whom an allegation of excessive force or improper tactics was made from 1986 to 1990, more than 1,400 had only one or two allegations. But 183 officers had four or more allegations, 44 had six or more, 16 had eight or more, and one had 16 such allegations.

- Of nearly 6,000 officers identified as involved in use of force reports from January 1987 to March 1991, more than 4,000 had fewer than five reports each. But 63 officers had 20 or more reports each. The top 5% of the officers (ranked by number of reports) accounted for more than 20% of all reports. . . .

Blending the data disclosed even more troubling patterns. For example, in the years covered, one officer had 13 allegations of excessive force and improper tactics, 5 other complaint allegations, 28 use of force reports, and 1 shooting. Another had 6 excessive force/improper tactics allegations, 19 other complaint allegations, 10 use of force reports, and 3 shootings. A third officer had 7 excessive force/improper tactic allegations, 7 other complaint allegations, 27 use of force reports, and 1 shooting.

A review of personnel files of the 44 officers identified from the LAPD database who had six or more allegations of excessive force or improper tactics for the period 1986 through 1990 disclosed that the picture conveyed was often incomplete and at odds with contemporaneous comments appearing in complaint files. As a general matter, the performance evaluation reports for those problem officers were very positive, documenting every complimentary comment received and expressing optimism about the officer's progress in the Department. The performance evaluations generally did not give an accurate picture of the officer's disciplinary history, failing to record "sustained" complaints or to discuss their significance, and failing to assess the officer's judgment and contacts with the public in light of disturbing patterns of complaints.

The existence of a significant number of officers with an unacceptable and improper attitude regarding the use of force is supported by the Commission's extensive review of computer messages sent to and from patrol cars throughout the City over the units' Mobile Digital Terminals ("MDTs"). The Commission's staff examined 182 days of MDT transmissions selected from the period from November 1989 to March 1991. Although the vast majority of messages reviewed consisted of routine police communications, there were hundreds of improper messages, including scores in which officers talked about beating suspects: "Capture him, beat him and treat him like dirt . . ." Officers also used the communications system to express their eagerness to be involved in shooting incidents. The transmissions also make clear that some officers enjoy the excitement of a pursuit and view it as an opportunity for violence against a fleeing suspect.

The patrol car transmissions can be monitored by a field supervisor and are stored in a database where they could be (but were not) audited. That many officers would feel free to type messages about force under such circumstances suggests a serious problem with respect to excessive force. That supervisors made no effort to monitor or control those messages evidences a significant breakdown in the Department's management responsibility.

The Commission also reviewed the LAPD's investigation and discipline of the officers involved in all 83 civil lawsuits alleging excessive or improper force by LAPD officers for the period 1986 through 1990 that resulted in a settlement or judgment of more than $15,000. A majority of cases involved clear and often egregious officer misconduct resulting in serious injury or death to the victim. The LAPD's investigation of these 83 cases was deficient in many respects, and discipline against the officers involved was frequently light and often nonexistent.

While the precise size and identity of the problem group of officers cannot be specified without significant further investigation, its existence must be recognized and addressed. The LAPD has a number of tools to promote and enforce its policy that only reasonable and necessary force be used by officers. There are rewards and incentives such as promotions and pay upgrades. The discipline system exists to impose sanctions for misconduct. Officers can be reassigned. Supervisors can monitor and counsel officers under their command. Officers can be trained at the Police Academy and, more importantly, in the field, in the proper use of force.

The Commission believes that the Department has not made sufficient efforts to use those tools effectively to address the significant number of officers who appear to be using force excessively and improperly. The leadership of the LAPD must send a much clearer and more effective message that excessive force will not be tolerated and that officers and their supervisors will be evaluated to an important extent by how well they abide by and advance the Department's policy regarding use of force.

RACISM AND BIAS

The problem of excessive force is aggravated by racism and bias within the LAPD. That nexus is sharply illustrated by the results of a survey recently taken by the LAPD of the attitudes of its sworn officers. The survey of 960 officers found that approximately one-quarter (24.5%) of 650 officers responding agreed that "racial bias (prejudice) on the part of officers toward minority citizens currently exists and contributes to a negative interaction between police and community." More than one-quarter (27.6%) agreed that "an officer's prejudice towards the suspect's race may lead to the use of excessive force."

The Commission's review of MDT transmissions revealed an appreciable number of disturbing and recurrent racial remarks. Some of the remarks describe minorities through animal analogies ("sounds like monkey slapping time"). Often made in the context of discussing pursuits or beating suspects, the offensive remarks cover the spectrum of racial and ethnic minorities in the City ("I would love to drive down Slauson with a flame thrower . . . we would have a barbecue"; "I almost got me a Mexican last night but he dropped the dam [sic] gun to [sic] quick, lots of wit"). The officers typing the MDT messages apparently had little concern that they would be disciplined for making such remarks. Supervisors failed to monitor the messages or to impose discipline for improper remarks and were themselves frequently the source of offensive comments when in the field.

These attitudes of prejudice and intolerance are translated into unacceptable behavior in the field. Testimony from a variety of witnesses depicts the LAPD as an organization with practices and procedures that are conducive to discriminatory treatment and officer misconduct directed to members of minority groups. Witnesses repeatedly told of LAPD officers verbally harassing minorities, detaining African-American and Latino men who fit certain generalized descriptions of suspects, employing unnecessarily invasive or humiliating tactics in minority neighborhoods, and using excessive force. While the Commission does not purport to adjudicate the validity of any one of these numerous complaints, the intensity and frequency of them reveal a serious problem.

Bias within the LAPD is not confined to officers' treatment of the public, but is also reflected in conduct directed to fellow officers who are members of racial or ethnic minority groups. The MDT messages and other evidence suggest that minority officers are still too frequently subjected to racist slurs and comments and to discriminatory treatment within the Department. While the relative number of officers who openly make racially derogatory comments or treat minority officers in a demeaning manner is small, their attitudes and behavior have a large impact because of the failure of supervisors to enforce vigorously and consistently the Department's policies against racism. That failure conveys to minority and non-minority officers alike the message that such conduct is in practice condoned by the Department.

The LAPD has made substantial progress in hiring minorities and women since the 1981 consent decree settling discrimination lawsuits against the Department. That effort should continue, including efforts to recruit Asians and other minorities who are not covered by the consent decree. The Department's statistics show, however, that the vast majority of minority officers are concentrated in the entry level police officer ranks in the Department. More than 80% of African-American, Latino, and Asian officers hold the rank of Police Officer I-III. Many minority officers cite white dominance of managerial positions within the LAPD as one reason for the Department's continued tolerance of racially motivated language and behavior.

Bias within the LAPD is not limited to racist and ethnic prejudices but includes strongly felt bias based on gender and sexual orientation. Current LAPD policy prohibits all discrimination, including that based on sexual orientation. A tension remains, however, between the LAPD's official policy and actual practice. The Commission believes that the LAPD must act to implement fully its formal policy of nondiscrimination in the recruitment and promotion of gay and lesbian officers.

A 1987 LAPD study concluded that female officers were subjected to a double standard and subtle harassment and were not accepted as part of the working culture. As revealed in interviews of many of the officers charged with training new recruits, the problem has not abated in the last four years. Although female LAPD officers are in fact performing effectively, they are having a difficult time being accepted on a full and equal basis.

The Commission heard substantial evidence that female officers utilize a style of policing that minimizes the use of excessive force. Data examined by the Commission indicate that LAPD female officers are involved in use of excessive force at rates substantially below those of male officers. Those statistics, as confirmed by both academic studies and anecdotal evidence, also indicate that women officers perform at least as well as their male counterparts when measured by traditional standards.

The Commission believes that the Chief of Police must seek tangible ways, for example, through the use of the discipline system, to establish the principle that racism and bias based on ethnicity, gender, or sexual orientation will not be tolerated within the Department. Racism and bias cannot be eliminated without active leadership from the top. Minority and female officers must be given full and equal opportunity to assume leadership positions in the LAPD. They must be assigned on a fully nondiscriminatory basis to the more desirable, "coveted" positions and promoted on the same nondiscriminatory basis to supervisory and managerial positions.

COMMUNITY POLICING

The LAPD has an organizational culture that emphasizes crime control over crime prevention and that isolates the police from the communities and the people they serve. With the full support of many, the LAPD insists on aggressive detection of major crimes and a rapid, seven-minute response time to calls for service. Patrol officers are evaluated by statistical measures (for example, the number of calls handled and arrests made) and are rewarded for being "hard-nosed." This style of policing produces results, but it does so at the risk of creating a siege mentality that alienates the officer from the community.

Witness after witness testified to unnecessarily aggressive confrontations between LAPD officers and citizens, particularly members of minority communities. From the statements of these citizens, as well as many present and former senior LAPD officers, it is apparent that too many LAPD patrol officers view citizens with resentment and hostility; too many treat the public with rudeness and disrespect. LAPD officers themselves seem to recognize the extent of the problem: nearly two-thirds (62.9%) of the 650 officers who responded to the recent LAPD survey expressed the opinion that "increased interaction with the community would improve the Department's relations with citizens."

A model of community policing has gained increased acceptance in other parts of the country during the past 10 years. The community policing model places service to the public and prevention of crime as the primary role of police in society and emphasizes problem solving, with active citizen involvement in defining those matters that are important to the community, rather than arrest statistics. Officers at the patrol level are required to spend less time in their cars communicating with other officers and more time on the street communicating with citizens. Proponents of this style of policing insist that addressing the causes of crime makes police officers more effective crime-fighters, and at the same time enhances the quality of life in the neighborhood.

The LAPD made early efforts to incorporate community policing principles and has continued to experiment with those concepts. For example, the LAPD's nationally recognized DARE program has been viewed by officers and the public alike as a major achievement. The LAPD remains committed, however, to its traditional style of law enforcement with an emphasis on crime control and arrests. LAPD officers are encouraged to command and to confront, not to communicate. Community policing concepts, if successfully implemented, offer the prospect of effective crime prevention and substantially improved community relations. Although community-based policing is not a panacea for the problem of crime in society, the LAPD should carefully implement this model on a City-wide basis. This will require a fundamental change in values. The Department must recognize the merits of community involvement in matters that affect local neighborhoods, develop programs to gain an adequate understanding of what is important to particular communities, and learn to manage departmental affairs in ways that are consistent with the community views expressed. Above all, the Department must understand that it is accountable to all segments of the community.

RECRUITMENT

Although 40% of the candidates for admission to the Police Academy are disqualified as a result of psychological testing and background investigation, the Commission's review indicated that the initial psychological evaluation is an ineffective predictor of an applicant's tendencies toward violent behavior and that the background investigation pays too little attention to a candidate's history of violence. Experts agree that the best predictor of future behavior is previous behavior. Thus, the background investigation offers the best hope of screening out violence-prone applicants. Unfortunately, the background investigators are overworked and inadequately trained.

Improved screening of applicants is not enough. Police work modifies behavior. Many emotional and psychological problems may develop during an officer's tenure on the force. Officers may enter the force well-suited psychologically for the job, but may suffer from burnout, alcohol-related problems, cynicism, or disenchantment, all of which can result in poor control over their behavior. A person's susceptibility to the behavior-modifying experiences of police work may not be revealed during even the most skilled and sophisticated psychological evaluation process. Accordingly, officers should be retested periodically to determine both psychological and physical problems. In addition, supervisors must understand their role to include training and counseling officers to cope with the problems policing can often entail, so that they may be dealt with before an officer loses control or requires disciplinary action.

TRAINING

LAPD officer training has three phases. Each recruit spends approximately six months at the Police Academy. The new officer then spends one year on probation working with more experienced patrol officers who serve as field training officers ("FTOs"). Thereafter, all officers receive continuing training, which includes mandatory field training and daily training at roll call. The Commission believes that in each phase of the training additional emphasis is needed on the use of verbal skills rather than physical force to control potentially volatile situations and on the development of human relationship skills.

The quality of instruction at the Police Academy is generally impressive. However, at present the curriculum provides only eight hours in cultural awareness training. No more than 1-1/2 hours is devoted to any ethnic group. Substantially more training on this important topic is essential. In addition, the Academy's current Spanish language program needs to be reviewed and current deficiencies corrected. Officers with an interest in developing broader language skills should be encouraged to do so.

Upon graduation the new officer works as a "probationary officer" assigned to various field training officers. The FTOs guide new officers' first contacts with citizens and have primary responsibility for introducing the probationers to the culture and traditions of the Department. The Commission's interviews of FTOs in four representative divisions revealed that many FTOs openly perpetuate the siege mentality that alienates patrol officers from the community and pass on to their trainees confrontational attitudes of hostility and disrespect for the public. This problem is in part the result of flaws in the way FTOs are selected and trained. The hiring of a very large number of new officers in 1989, which required the use of less experienced FTOs, greatly exacerbated the problem.

Any officer promoted to Police Officer III by passing a written examination covering Department policies and procedures is eligible to serve as an FTO. At present there are no formal eligibility or disqualification criteria for the FTO position based on an applicant's disciplinary records. Fourteen of the FTOs in the four divisions the Commission studied had been promoted to FTO despite having been disciplined for use of excessive force or use of improper tactics. There also appears to be little emphasis on selecting FTOs who have an interest in training junior officers, and an FTO's training ability is given little weight in his or her evaluation.

The most influential training received by a probationer comes from the example set by his or her FTO. Virtually all of the FTOs interviewed stated that their primary objective in training probationers is to instill good "officer safety skills." While the Commission recognizes the importance of such skills in police work, the probationers' world is quickly divided into "we/they" categories, which is exacerbated by the failure to integrate any cultural awareness or sensitivity training into field training.

The Commission believes that, to become FTOs, officers should be required to pass written and oral tests designed to measure communications skills, teaching aptitude, and knowledge of Departmental policies regarding appropriate use of force, cultural sensitivity, community relations, and nondiscrimination. Officers with an aptitude for and interest in training junior officers should be encouraged by effective incentives to apply for FTO positions. In addition, the training program for FTOs should be modified to place greater emphasis on communication skills and the appropriate use of force. Successful completion of FTO School should be required before an FTO begins teaching probationers.

PROMOTION, ASSIGNMENT, AND OTHER PERSONNEL ISSUES

In the civil service process for promotion of officers in the LAPD, the information considered includes performance evaluations, educational and training background, and all sustained complaints. The number and nature of any not sustained complaints, however, are not considered. The Commission recommends that a summary of not sustained complaints be considered in promotion decisions, as well as in pay-grade advancements and assignments to desirable positions that are discretionary within the LAPD and outside the civil service system.

This is not to say that a past complaint history, even including a sustained complaint for excessive force, should automatically bar an officer from promotion. But there should be a careful consideration of the officer's complaint history including a summary of not sustained complaints, and particularly multiple complaints with similar fact patterns.

Complaint histories should also be considered in assignment of problem officers who may be using force improperly. For example, a problem officer can be paired with an officer with excellent communications skills that may lessen the need for use of force, as opposed to a partner involved in prior incidents of force with that problem officer. Another example is assignments to the jail facilities where potential for abuse by officers with a propensity to use excessive force is high. As several incidents examined by the Commission made clear, transfer of an officer to another geographical area is not likely to address a problem of excessive force without other remedial measures such as increased supervising, training, and counseling.

Since 1980 the Department has permitted police officers working in patrol to select the geographic area or division for their patrol assignment subsequent to their initial assignment after completion of probation. As a result, sergeants and patrol officers tend to remain in one division for extended periods. The Commission believes that assignment procedures should be modified to require rotation through various divisions to ensure that officers work in a wide range of police functions and varied patrol locations during their careers. Such a rotation program will increase officers' experience and also will enable the Department to deploy police patrols with greater diversity throughout the City.

Under the current promotion system officers generally must leave patrol to advance within the Department. Notwithstanding the importance of the patrol function, therefore, the better officers are encouraged to abandon patrol. To give patrol increased emphasis and to retain good, experienced officers, the LAPD should increase rewards and incentives for patrol officers.

PERSONNEL COMPLAINTS AND
OFFICER DISCIPLINE

No area of police operations received more adverse comment during the Commission's public hearings than the Department's handling of complaints against LAPD officers, particularly allegations involving the use of excessive force. Statistics make the public's frustration understandable. Of the 2,152 citizen allegations of excessive force from 1986 through 1990, only 42 were sustained.

All personnel complaints are reviewed by a captain in the LAPD's Internal Affairs Division ("IAD") to determine whether the complaint will be investigated by IAD or the charged officer's division. Generally IAD investigates only a few cases because of limited resources. Wherever investigated, the matter is initially adjudicated by the charged officer's division commanding officer, with a review by the area and bureau commanders.

The Commission has found that the complaint system is skewed against complainants. People who wish to file complaints face significant hurdles. Some intake officers actively discourage filing by being uncooperative or requiring long waits before completing a complaint form. In many heavily Latino divisions, there is often no Spanish-speaking officer available to take complaints.

Division investigations are frequently inadequate. Based on a review of more than 700 complaint investigation files, the Commission found many deficiencies. For example, in a number of complaint files the Commission reviewed, there was no indication that the investigators had attempted to identify or locate independent witnesses or, if identified, to interview them. IAD investigations, on the whole, were of a higher quality than the division investigations. Although the LAPD has a special "officer involved shooting team," the Commission also found serious flaws in the investigation of shootings. Commissioners' compensation should be increased substantially. They should serve a maximum of five years with staggered terms. The Police Commission's independent staff should be increased by adding civilian employees, including management auditors, computer systems data analysts, and investigators with law enforcement experience. It is vital that the Police Commission's staff be placed under the control of an independent civilian Chief of Staff, a general manager level employee.

The Chief of Police must be more responsive to the Police Commission and the City's elected leadership, but also must be protected against improper political influences. To achieve this balance, the Chief should serve a five-year term, renewable at the discretion of the Police Commission for one additional five-year term. The selection, tenure, discipline, and removal of the Chief should be exempted from existing civil service provisions. The Chief should be appointed by the Mayor, with advice from the Police Commission and the consent of the City Council after an open competition. The Police Commission should have the authority to terminate the Chief prior to the expiration of the first or second five-year term, but the final decision to terminate should require the concurrence of the Mayor and be subject to a reversal by vote of two-thirds of the City Council.

IMPLEMENTATION

Full implementation of this Report will require action by the Mayor, the City Council, the Police Commission, the Police Department, and ultimately the voters. To monitor the progress of reform, the City Council should require reports on implementation at six-month intervals from the Mayor, the Council's own Human Resources and Labor Relations Committee, the Police Commission, and the Police Department. The Commission should reconvene in six months to assess the implementation of its recommendations and to report to the public.

Chief Gates has served the LAPD and the City 42 years, the past 13 years as Chief of Police. He has achieved a noteworthy record of public service in a stressful and demanding profession. For the reasons set forth in support of the recommendation that the Chief of Police be limited to two five-year terms, the Commission believes that commencement of a transition in that office is now appropriate. The Commission also believes that the interests of harmony and healing would be served if the Police Commission is now reconstituted with members not identified with the recent controversy involving the Chief.

More than any other factor, the attitude and actions of the leaders of the Police Department and other City agencies will determine whether the recommendations of this Report are adopted. To make genuine progress on issues relating to excessive force, racism, and bias, leadership must avoid sending mixed signals. We urge those leaders to give priority to stopping the use of excessive force and curbing racism and bias and thereby to bring the LAPD to a new level of excellence and esteem throughout Los Angeles.

The "Causes" of Police Brutality: Theory and Evidence on Police Use of Force

ROBERT E. WORDEN

S ocial scientific theories and evidence concerning police behavior, and particularly research on the factors that contribute to—or "cause"—police brutality, can provide insights into the promise (and pitfalls) of governmental, administrative, managerial, and policy reforms. Indeed, every serious prescription for controlling police brutality rests at least implicitly on some theory of police behavior.[1] Fortunately, over the past 25 years social scientists have given considerable attention to some forms of police behavior, and scholars have made some headway in developing theories that account, at least in part, for these behaviors. The use of officers' authority to make arrests has been analyzed in a number of studies, as has the use of *deadly* force, and a substantial (but still inadequate) body of empirical evidence has accumulated. Unfortunately, very little social scientific evidence has accumulated on the use and abuse of nonlethal force, and little effort seems to have been made to consider whether the theories applied to other forms of behavior apply equally well (or at all) to the use of nonlethal force.[2]

This chapter seeks to connect theories of police behavior with new evidence on the use of force by police. First, I briefly review the theories of police behavior, along with the evidence that bears on those theories, drawing principally from empirical analyses of arrest and of deadly force. I then review the handful of studies that have examined the use of nonlethal force, and evaluate

From *And Justice for All: Understanding and Controlling Police Abuse of Force,* William A. Geller
and Hans Toch (eds.), pp. 31–60. Washington, D.C.: Police Executive Research Forum.
Reprinted by permission.

the data—collected through in-person observation of police officers—on which most of these analyses are based. I then turn to the new empirical evidence on the use of force, which is also based on an analysis of observational data. I conclude by discussing whether and how further research might contribute to the development of theory and to the deliberation about reform.

I. THEORIES OF POLICE BEHAVIOR

Existing research on police behavior reflects the diverse training and backgrounds of those who study the police—sociologists, political scientists, psychologists, and others. Even so, much of this research can be subsumed within three explanatory rubrics: sociological, psychological, and organizational.

A. Sociological Theory

One prominent sociological approach to understanding the behavior of police officers is based on the premise that police behavior is influenced by the social dynamics of police-citizen encounters. For example, Donald Black's sociological theory of law holds that the "quantity of law" is influenced by the social attributes of concerned parties—victims and suspects, or plaintiffs and defendants, as well as the agents of social control themselves (see especially Black 1976).[3] According to this theory, police officers are least likely to take legal or other coercive action against lower status persons—especially the poor, and racial and ethnic minorities—whose accusers are also of low status, but more likely to take such action against lower-status persons whose accusers are of higher status (Black 1980: ch. 1). Somewhat more generally, this line of inquiry has directed analytical attention to the structural characteristics of the situations in which officers and citizens interact: the social class, race, and gender of complainants, and their dispositional preferences—i.e., whether they want offenders arrested, or prefer that offenders not be arrested; the social class, race, age, gender, sobriety, and demeanor of suspects; the seriousness of the offense (if any); the nature of the relationships between complainants and suspects; the visibility of the encounters (whether they transpire in public or private locations, and whether bystanders are present); the number of officers at the scene; and the character of the neighborhoods in which encounters take place. From this theoretical perspective, these "situational" factors (Sherman 1980a) are the cues on which officers form judgments about how incidents should be "handled" (Berk and Loseke 1980–81). Perhaps the most comprehensive and succinct statement of this explanatory approach is Bittner's, which posited that "the role of the police is best understood as a mechanism for the distribution of non-negotiably coercive force *employed in accordance with the dictates of an intuitive grasp of situational exigencies*" (Bittner 1970: 46).

Most empirical research that is grounded in this theory has examined the use of arrest powers (e.g., Black 1971; Lundman 1974; Smith and Visher 1981;

also see Sherman 1980a:77–85). This research has consistently shown that arrest is influenced by the demeanor of suspects—arrest is more likely if the suspect is antagonistic or disrespectful to police (but cf. Klinger 1992, 1994; also see Lundman 1994, and Worden and Shepard 1994)—and by the preferences of complainants (if any)—arrest is more likely if complainants wish to press charges, and less likely if complainants express a preference for informal dispositions. This research has also produced somewhat inconsistent results. For example, some analyses indicate that nonwhite suspects are more likely than white suspects are to be arrested (Lundman 1974; Smith and Visher 1981), while others show that the relationship between race and arrest is either null (Berk and Loseke 1980–81; Worden and Pollitz 1984; Smith and Klein 1984; Worden 1989) or spurious—that black suspects are more likely to be arrested because they are more likely to be disrespectful, and that race has no independent effect (Black 1971; Sykes and Clark 1975; but cf. Black 1980: ch. 5; Smith, Visher, and Davidson 1984).[4] Overall, research of this genre has demonstrated that officers' arrest decisions are influenced by situational factors; but it also shows that at least half of the variation in arrests remains unexplained by this theoretical perspective.

Research on the use of deadly force has dwelt on one hypothesis that is quite compatible with this theory, namely that minorities are more likely to be shot (or shot at) by police. The empirical evidence confirms that minorities are, in fact, overrepresented among the human targets at which police shoot, relative to their numbers in city populations, but it also indicates that minorities are overrepresented among those whose actions precipitate the use of deadly force by police (e.g., Milton, et al. 1977; Fyfe 1980a, 1981b; Blumberg 1981; Geller and Karales 1981b; Alpert 1989; see generally, Geller and Scott 1992). Insofar as this alternative explanation for the racial disparities is captured in the available data (e.g., on felony arrests), this hypothesis—that minorities are more likely to be the objects of police deadly force merely because of their race— has, then, received support in only a few analyses (Meyer 1980, Geller and Karales 1981a:123–25, Fyfe 1982).

B. Psychological Theory

A second approach to understanding the behavior of police officers is psychological. This approach highlights variation among officers in their behavioral predispositions, variation that is obscured by the sociological approach. This perspective directs attention to the outlooks and personality characteristics that presumably produce different responses to similar situations by different officers. This perspective also underlies many propositions (or suppositions) about behavioral differences related to officers' race, gender, and educational background, inasmuch as black officers, female officers, and college-educated officers are supposed to have outlooks that differ from their white, male, less-educated colleagues, and these differences in attitude are presumed to manifest themselves in officers' behavioral patterns. Hypotheses that specify a linkage between attitudes and behavior have intuitive appeal, but social psychological research has shown that people's behavior is often inconsistent with their attitudes; one review of this research concluded that "in most cases investigated, attitudes and behaviors are related to an extent that ranges from small to moderate in degree" (Schuman and Johnson 1976:168).

This theory (or some version thereof) is reflected in portions of the report by the Christopher Commission (Independent Commission on the Los Angeles Police Department 1991), which identified a small group of "problem officers" who were disproportionately involved in incidents in which force was either used or allegedly misused. In its discussion of problem officers, the commission reported its findings, from a survey of Los Angeles Police Department (LAPD) officers, that "a significant percentage . . . agreed with the statement that 'an officer is justified in administering physical punishment to a suspect who has committed a heinous crime' (4.9 percent) or 'to a suspect with a bad or uncooperative attitude' (4.6 percent)" (p. 34). The commission could not link officers' survey responses with departmental data on uses of force or on personnel complaints, and it acknowledged that "the precise size and identity of this problem group cannot be specified (at least without significant further investigation)" (p. 38). However, the commission rejected the alternative explanation that officers' assignments (to active, high-crime areas or to specialized units) produced these skewed distributions of use of force involvement. While the commission focused on what management could and should do after-the-fact, once these problem officers were identified, it implicitly presumed that the outlooks or personalities of these officers are at the root of their seemingly distinctive behavioral patterns.[5]

One more specific hypothesis might be that officers who are predisposed to use force have "authoritarian" personalities (Balch 1972, and more generally, Adorno, et al. 1950). Research on the personality characteristics of police has been concerned primarily with whether officers are psychologically homogeneous and, moreover, different as a group from the general public. These efforts to establish a modal (and pathological) "police personality" have proven no better than inconclusive (Balch 1972, cf. Lefkowitz 1975). Moreover, such analysis is misguided if one seeks to account for behavioral variation among officers. As Toch (in this volume) suggests, these findings do not refute the proposition that those officers who score high on indices of authoritarianism are also those who use force with unusual frequency. Unless research examines officers' authoritarianism or other personality traits as characteristics that vary among officers, then these concepts will be of no value in explaining officers' use of force.

The richest discussions of psychological hypotheses about police behavior can be found in studies that have constructed four-fold typologies of police officers (White 1972, Muir 1977, Broderick 1977, Brown 1981), each typology based on two (or in one case, three) attitudinal dimensions. For example, William Muir (1977) classifies officers according to their outlooks on human nature and their moral attitudes toward coercive authority. Although these four studies together define 16 categories of officers, a careful comparison of the types of officers described in these studies shows that five composite types can be isolated (Worden forthcoming). These types do appear to differ in their propensities to use force.

One type of officer, for which I have borrowed White's (1972) label of the "tough cop," is perhaps the most likely to use force improperly. Tough cops are cynical, in the sense that they presume that people are motivated by narrow self-interest. They conceive the role of police in terms of crime control, focusing especially on "serious" crime, and they see themselves as a negative force in people's lives. They believe that the citizenry is hostile toward police, and they identify with the police culture. They believe that experience and common sense are the best guides in dealing with the realities of the street, and that "curbstone justice" is sometimes appropriate and effective.

By contrast, "problem-solvers" (also White's term) have what Muir (1977) calls a "tragic" perspective: they recognize that people's actions are influenced by complex sets of physical, economic, and social circumstances, and not simple self-interest. They conceive the role of police as one of "offering assistance in solving whatever kind of problem . . . [their clientele] face" (White 1972:72), and thus they see themselves as a positive force. They are skeptical of traditional police methods, as they are unable to reconcile the use of coercive measures with their moral codes. This type of officer is probably the least likely to use force improperly (or at all).

The descriptions of these and the other types of officers (Worden forthcoming) suggest that, if there are officers with pronounced propensities to use force, they share several outlooks that distinguish them from other officers.[6] Officers who are the most likely to use force could be expected to (a) conceive the police role in narrow terms, limited to crime-fighting and law enforcement, (b) believe that this role is more effectively carried out when officers may use force at their discretion, and (c) regard the citizenry as unappreciative at best and hostile and abusive at worst.[7]

Much of the evidence that supports psychological hypotheses about police behavior is impressionistic, based on limited and/or unsystematic observation of officers. The few efforts to systematically test these hypotheses have produced little or no support. Brown's (1981: ch. 9) analysis, based on officers' responses to hypothetical scenarios, indicates that—as hypothesized—there is more variation across than within categories of officers in the ways that they handle common incidents (such as family disputes and drunk driving), but it also shows that officers' behavior is affected by the organizational context in which they work; behavior is not a simple extension of attitudes, as organizational and other social forces can attenuate the impact of attitudes on behavior. Snipes and Mastrofski (1990) undertook a small-scale examination of hypotheses derived from Muir's framework, by conducting in-depth interviews with and observations of nine officers in one department; they found little consistency between officers' attitudes and behaviors, and little consistency in each officer's behavior from one incident to the next. My own analyses (Worden 1989) indicate that officers' attitudes are only weakly related to their discretionary choices—in the initiation and disposition of traffic stops, in the initiation of field interrogations, and in the disposition of disputes. The results of these studies certainly do not constitute evidence sufficient to reject psychological hypotheses, however, and none of these studies examined the use of force. But these findings suggest that the connections between officers' attitudes and behavior are probably more complex (and perhaps more tenuous) than many have supposed.

A larger body of evidence has accumulated on the relationship of officers' behavior to their background and characteristics—race, gender, length of police service, and especially education. Officers' educational background has been the subject of a number of studies, and although this research has shown that education bears no more than a weak relationship to officers' attitudes (e.g., Weiner 1974, Miller and Fry 1976, Hudzik 1978, Worden 1990) and no relationship to the use of deadly force (Sherman and Blumberg 1981), it also indicates that college-educated officers generate fewer citizen complaints (Cohen and Chaiken 1972, Cascio 1977). The reason for this difference is not clear (but see Worden 1990:589).

Similarly, the most systematic comparison of male and female officers shows small or no differences in attitudes other than job satisfaction (Worden 1993). Other research reveals some behavioral differences—in the frequency with which men and women initiate encounters and make arrests—but on most behavioral dimensions the differences are nil (Bloch and Anderson 1974, Sherman 1975, cf. Grennan 1987). One study of the effects of officers' race on behavior (Friedrich 1977:307–319) found that black officers patrol more aggressively, initiate more contacts with citizens, are more likely to make arrests, and more frequently adopt a neutral "manner" toward citizens of either race. Other research has found that black officers are more likely than white officers are to use deadly force, either on–duty (Geller and Karales 1981a, 1981b) or on- *and* off-duty (Fyfe 1981a); but these differences in the use of deadly force can be attributed to black officers' duty assignments and to where they choose to live (also see Blumberg 1982). Finally, analyses of officers' length of service indicate that less experienced officers are more active, in that they patrol more aggressively and initiate more contacts with citizens, and that they are more likely to make arrests, to write crime reports (Friedrich 1977:280–290, Worden 1989), and to use deadly force (Blumberg 1982, cf. Alpert 1989).

C. Organizational Theory

Some approaches to understanding the behavior of police officers emphasize features of the organizations in which officers work. A theory that highlights organizational properties as influences on police behavior would seem to hold the greatest potential as a guide for police reform, since organizational factors are more readily manipulated than are the demeanors of suspects or the outlooks of officers. Unfortunately, organizational analyses of police are seldom undertaken, probably because of the expense and difficulty of collecting comparable data on multiple police agencies, and thus organizational theories of police behavior are not well supported by empirical evidence.

One theory emphasizes the influence on police officers' behavior of the formal organizational structure, especially the system of incentives and disincentives and the content and application of rules and regulations. The principal statement of this approach is Wilson's (1968); his exploratory research formed the basis for the delineation of three organizational styles of policing—the legalistic, watchman, and service styles—and for hypotheses that these styles can be attributed to the orientations of chiefs, which influence officers' behavior through the medium of organizational structure. While Wilson acknowledges that the capacity of police administrators to shape officers' behavior is constrained by the nature of police tasks, he seems to see the glass of managerial influence as half (or partly) full rather than half (or partly) empty. Wilson's study has more to say about the use of the law than about the use of physical force; however, it suggests that improper force is more likely to be used by officers in watchman style departments, usually in response to perceived disrespect for police authority. Some research has tested hypotheses derived from Wilson's framework (Gardiner 1969, Wilson and Boland 1978, Smith 1984) with results that are generally supportive, but only Friedrich (1980), whose study I discuss below, tested hypotheses about the use of force.

Some research on the use of deadly force has shown rather convincingly that administrative controls can have salutary effects on the frequency with which officers use their firearms. Policies that set clear boundaries around the use of deadly force and that provide for effective enforcement (by, say, establishing review procedures) have reduced the number of shootings (Fyfe 1979b, 1982; Meyer 1980; Sherman 1983), especially the more discretionary or "elective" shootings (Fyfe 1988a:184–87). Whether such controls are, by themselves, equally effective in controlling the use of nonlethal force is an open question in the sense that no study has produced an empirical answer. But there is good reason to be skeptical; the use of deadly force is a more visible act—or, more precisely, an act with more visible outcomes—which probably makes this form of behavior more susceptible to administrative controls.

Another theory emphasizes the limitations of formal structure in directing and controlling the behavior of patrol officers and the importance of the informal organization or peer group, i.e., the police culture. According to this perspective, the formal, more obtrusive controls on police—rewards and punishments, rules, regulations, and SOPs—extend to the more observable and, for the most part, more mundane aspects of police work, such as the use of equipment, report writing, and officers' appearance (Manning 1977, Brown 1981, more generally see Prottas 1978). At the same time, the application of unobtrusive controls on police, in the form of socialization and training, is governed by the work group. Analyses of the socialization process are quite scarce, but the available evidence indicates that new officers learn the police craft on the job (not in the academy) from more senior officers, especially their field training officers or FTOs (Van Maanen 1974, Fielding 1988). Rookies are quickly led to believe that their academy experience was merely a rite of passage, that the training they received there is irrelevant to the realities of policing, and that they will learn what they need to know on the street. Thus, according to this line of argument, the police culture is not only the primary reference group for officers but also the principal mechanism of organizational control (to the extent that control is exerted at all) over the substantive exercise of police discretion.

One must be careful not to confuse what has been called the police culture with the cultures of police organizations. "The" police culture is an occupational culture, consisting of outlooks and norms that are commonly found among patrol officers in police agencies. This culture emphasizes the danger and unpredictability of the work environment, the consequent dependence of officers on each other for assistance and protection, officers' autonomy in handling situations, and the need to assert and maintain one's authority (Westley 1970, Skolnick 1975, Brown 1981, Manning 1989). The police culture does not prescribe the substance of officers' working styles so much as it serves to protect officers from administrative scrutiny and sanction and to insulate them from administrative pressures for change (Reuss-Ianni 1983); thus it allows officers the latitude to develop and practice their own styles.[8] These cultural elements can, presumably, be found among patrol officers in all or most police agencies.

One may find variation in the *organizational* cultures of police departments, even while one finds consistency in the elements of the *occupational* culture. Wilson maintains that the administration of police departments produces differing styles both directly, by shaping the calculus on which officers' choices are based, and indirectly, by cultivating a "shared outlook or ethos that provides for [officers] a common definition of the situations they are likely to encounter and that to the outsider gives to the organization its distinctive character or 'feel'" (1968:139). Officers in both legalistic and watchman departments might subscribe to a norm of loyalty, but according to Wilson's analysis, they would differ in their beliefs about the nature of the police role and about the proper use of police authority. Brown (1981) disputes this argument, finding officers with very different individual styles within each of the three departments he studied. These arguments can perhaps be reconciled, inasmuch as any organization that is differentiated by task and authority might well develop multiple subcultures (Reuss-Ianni 1983; Worden and Mastrofski 1989; Jermier, et al. 1991), and even where multiple subcultures exist among patrol officers, one may predominate. Unfortunately, the distinction between the occupational culture of police and the organizational cultures of police departments is seldom made; most previous research has attended to the former but ignored the latter.

The report of the Christopher Commission makes reference to both of these theories. The commission identified LAPD's "assertive style of law enforcement" as a reason for "aggressive confrontations with the public" (Independent Commission on the LAPD 1991:97), and traced this style of policing to a "'professional' organizational culture" that has been cultivated by LAPD administration through training and the incentive structure. Officers in the LAPD are rewarded for hard-nosed enforcement that is likely to (occasionally) produce arrests and (often) bring police into conflict with citizens. The commission further found that the administration of the LAPD fails to discourage the improper use of force, in that (a) the complaint intake process discourages citizens from filing complaints, (b) many complaints that are filed are not substantiated as a result of inadequate resources and procedures for investigating complaints, and (c) the sanctions imposed on officers against whom complaints have been substantiated have been too light, both as a deterrent and as a message that such behavior is inappropriate. Like Wilson (1968), then, the commission concluded that the LAPD's incentive structure influences officers' behavior directly, and that there is a link between the (formal) administrative structure and the (informal) organizational culture. The implications for administrative practice are fairly straightforward: reduce the incentives for hard-nosed enforcement and increase the sanctions for the improper use of force.[9]

But the commission also acknowledged the limitations on the formal structure in controlling police conduct, reporting that "perhaps the greatest single barrier to the effective investigation and adjudication of complaints is the officers' unwritten 'code of silence,' [which] consists of one simple rule: an officer does not provide adverse information against a fellow officer" (p. 168). From this conclusion one cannot easily draw practical implications, and the commission's recommendations do not address this "barrier." Since this culture originates to a significant degree in the nature of the work itself, and is not unique to LAPD or even to policing (see Gouldner 1954), it is not likely to be altered by traditional organizational reforms (Van Maanen 1974, Toch 1979).

This analysis of the LAPD is instructive, to be sure, but it suffers all the limitations of a case study. Indeed, the LAPD depicted in the Christopher Commission report (circa 1991) may represent an extreme and unrepresentative case, where formal and informal organizational forces tend to reinforce one another in producing an aggressive style of policing and an elevated probability of the use of force. Most American police departments are smaller, less bureaucratic, and appear to be less insulated from the communities they serve;[10] as a result, the formal expectations in such departments might be less clearly crime-control oriented, and the potentially restraining influence of administrative controls might be greater. Any characterization of the problem of police brutality must take this variation among departments into account. So, too, must *research* on police brutality, because if large departments can be structured to simulate the relevant conditions that prevail in smaller departments, there is much to be learned by studying small and medium-sized police departments.

Internally, one might expect that in smaller police departments, which typically have fewer levels of hierarchy, administrators could more closely monitor and supervise street-level performance by taking advantage of the less distorted information that flows through the shorter formal channels of communication, and of the greater information that flows through the wider informal channels of communication (Whitaker 1983). In principle, managers in smaller agencies could more directly and hence effectively communicate their priorities and expectations to street-level personnel. In addition, since they need not rely so heavily on statistical summaries of individual performance, managers can base their evaluations of officers' performance on a richer and probably more accurate base of information; consequently, patterns of (problematic) behavior are likely to be more readily detectable, and the incentive system need not emphasize quantifiable, enforcement-related activities at the expense of the more qualitative aspects of police performance. Brown's (1981) analysis, even while it led him to conclude that the police culture is more important than formal organizational structure in shaping the exercise of police discretion, also confirms the expectation that administrative controls are more palpable in smaller departments, where Brown found that officers are more reluctant to take the risk of administrative sanction that they would run by practicing an aggressive style of patrol. Furthermore, insofar as work groups are more stable in smaller departments, immediate supervisors could be expected to more frequently and effectively play an instrumental role in the development of subordinate officers' judgment and moral outlooks (see Muir 1977).

Externally, one might expect that smaller agencies would be subject to closer oversight both by the public and by its representatives. Insofar as smaller municipalities are more homogeneous and their residents are in greater agreement about the delivery of police services, public officials have less latitude in setting policy and priorities (Wilson 1968). Citizens in smaller municipalities also might take a more active part in local affairs (Dahl 1967), so that municipal officials might better apprehend citizens' preferences regarding municipal services. Moreover, if in smaller municipalities public officials—including councillors, mayors, and city managers—play more active roles in policymaking and oversight (Mastrofski 1988), then one might expect that the direction of administrative influence in their police departments would be more toward restraint and less toward aggressive enforcement, inasmuch as aggressive policing could be expected to generate political friction from which the department is not insulated.

II. THEORY AND RESEARCH
ON THE USE OF FORCE

As Reiss (1968a) points out, "what citizens mean by police brutality covers the full range of police practices," including the use of abusive language and seemingly unjustified field interrogations; but "the nub of the police-brutality issue seems to lie in police use of physical force." Of course, some of the problems with which police deal may require the use of force, and under many of these circumstances the line between proper and improper force is a rather fuzzy one; where force is necessary, judgments must be made about the *amount* of force that is reasonable. Whenever judgments must be made, some misjudgments are probably inevitable; such cases of *excessive* force involve the use of more force than is reasonably necessary. Other cases of improper force, however, involve the use of force where *none* is necessary; these are instances of *unnecessary* force. Reiss (1968a) focused mostly on such cases of gratuitous violence by police; he explains:

> "A physical assault on a citizen was judged to be 'improper' or 'unnecessary' only if force was used in one or more of the following ways:
>
> - If a policeman physically assaulted a citizen and then failed to make an arrest; proper use involves an arrest.

- If the citizen being arrested did not, by word or deed, resist the policeman; force should be used only if it is necessary to make the arrest.

- If the policeman, even though there was resistance to the arrest, could easily have restrained the citizen in other ways.

- If a large number of policemen were present and could have assisted in subduing the citizen in the station, in lockup, and in the interrogation rooms.

- If an offender was handcuffed and made no attempt to flee or offer violent resistance.

- If the citizen resisted arrest, but the use of force continued even after the citizen was subdued."

It may be important, for both theoretical and policy purposes, to distinguish between the use of *excessive* force and the use of *unnecessary* force. Although this distinction rests on overt and thus observable behavior, it is admittedly an elusive one, inasmuch as officers not only respond to situations but also help to create them; sometimes, officers' choices early in police-citizen encounters can contribute to the emergence of circumstances that require the use of force (Binder and Scharf 1980, Bayley 1986; also see Klockars, in this volume). Insofar as these two forms of behavior can be distinguished, we may find that they are sufficiently different phenomena that each of them is influenced by a different set of situational, individual, and organizational factors. We may also find that interventions intended to reduce excessive force, such as (re)training officers, have little effect on the incidence of unnecessary force, and, conversely, that other interventions, such as disincentives, have a greater effect on unnecessary force than on excessive force (but cf. Fyfe, in this volume).

Most empirical research on the use of nonlethal force by police is based on data collected through the observation of officers on patrol. Generally, observation of police enables one to collect data on forms of behavior that cannot be reliably measured based on other sources. These are the forms of behavior that are least visible, such as field stops or the resolution of disputes, and that often result in no official record. Observation also enables one to collect data on the setting in which police action takes place; even when such information is contained in officers' reports, it is frequently incomplete or of dubious validity. Analyses of observational data make unique contributions to our understanding of police use of force, since observation by independent observers enables one to enumerate, describe, and analyze instances in which force is used, whether or not they result in citizen complaints or departmental disciplinary actions. Like survey data on victimizations, which uncover the "dark figure" of unreported crime, observational data on police behavior reveal unreported instances of police use of force (see Adams, in this volume).

Observational data are not without shortcomings, as they may be biased as a result of "reactivity"—that is, officers might refrain from the use of force in some instances due only to the presence of observers. But efforts to assess the bias introduced by reactivity suggest that the validity of observational data, in general, is quite high (Mastrofski and Parks 1990); moreover, evidence shows that the relationships between some forms of police behavior and other variables (such as characteristics of the situation) are unaffected by reactivity (Worden 1989: fn 8). As Reiss (1971b:24) observes, ". . . it is sociologically naive to assume that for many events the presence or participation of the observer is more controlling than other factors in the situation." More specifically, based on the results of one observational study (to be discussed below), Reiss maintains that ". . . the use of force by the police is situationally determined by other participants in the situation and by the officer's involvement in it, to such a degree that one must conclude the observer's presence had no effect" (Reiss, 1971b:24, also see Reiss 1968a, 1968b). At a minimum, the bias in observational data is almost certainly no greater, and probably less, than that in archival data.

The first large-scale observational study of police was undertaken by Black and Reiss (1967) for the President's Commission on Law Enforcement and Administration of Justice. This research was conducted during the summer of 1966 in Boston, Chicago, and Washington, D.C. Observers accompanied patrol officers on sampled shifts in selected high-crime precincts. "In the data collection, emphasis was placed upon gaining detailed descriptions of police and citizen *behavior*. . . . The social and demographic characteristics of the participants as well as a detailed description of the settings and qualities of the encounters were also obtained" (Black and Reiss 1967:15; emphasis in original).

Reiss (1968a, 1971a) applied a sociological approach to police brutality in analyzing these data. He describes the incidents in which officers used undue force in the following terms:

> "Seventy-eight percent of all instances where force was used unduly took place in police-controlled settings, such as the patrol car, the precinct station, or public places (primarily streets). Almost all victims of force were characterized as suspects or offenders. They were young, lower-class males from any racial or ethnic group. Furthermore, most encounters were devoid of witnesses who would support the offender. In general, persons officers regarded as being in a deviant offender role or who defied what the officer defines as his authority were the most likely victims of undue force. Thirty-nine percent openly defied authority by challenging the legitimacy of the police to exercise that authority, 9 percent physically resisted arrest, and 32 percent were persons in deviant offender roles, such as drunks, homosexuals, or addicts" (Reiss 1971a:147–149).

Reiss also points out, however, that "many instances where the citizen behaved antagonistically toward the police officer and many encounters with deviants did not involve uncivil conduct or misuse of force by the police" (1971a:149), and, more generally, that police-citizen encounters do not follow a rule of reciprocity in incivility—"whenever incivility occurs in an encounter, the chances are only 1 in 6 that the other party will reciprocate with incivility" (1971a:144).

In a 1980 article, Robert Friedrich reviewed the problems with then-existing research on police use of force and outlined three approaches to explaining police use of force—"individual," "situational," and "organizational"—that correspond to the theories discussed above. From each approach, he pointed out, one can derive a number of specific hypotheses about the use of force; using the Black-Reiss data, Friedrich tested some of those hypotheses to produce what was at that time the most thorough and sophisticated analysis of the phenomenon.

Friedrich found, first, that physical force was used only infrequently by police, and that the use of excessive force was still less frequent. Force was used in 5.1 percent of the 1,565 encounters that involved suspected offenders (and in only one of the remaining 3,826 incidents that involved no suspects). "Excessive" force was used in 1.8 percent of the encounters with suspects, or in no more than 29 incidents.[11]

Friedrich further found that situational, individual, and organizational hypotheses were with few exceptions unsupported by the data. Bivariate and multivariate analyses showed that characteristics of the police-citizen encounters bore the strongest relationship to the use of force, which was more likely if the suspect was antagonistic, agitated, intoxicated, or lower-class, if the offense was a felony, and if other citizens or officers were present. Be that as it may, situational characteristics together had no more than modest explanatory power. The characteristics of officers—their length of service, attitudes toward the job, race, and (among white officers) attitudes toward blacks—accounted for little of the (limited) variation in the use of force. Differences across departments were of marginal significance and, moreover, did not conform to Friedrich's expectations. The incidence of the use of force overall, and of improper force particularly, was (as Friedrich hypothesized) somewhat lower in the "professional" department (Chicago) than in the "traditional" department (Boston); but the incidence of force, and especially of improper force, was (contrary to Friedrich's hypotheses) lowest in the "transitional" department (Washington).[12]

Other analyses of the use of nonlethal force tend to corroborate Friedrich's findings. Analyses of other observational data have shown that force is used infrequently. Sykes and Brent (1980, 1983) analyzed sequences of interactions between officers and citizens, and they concluded that officers "regulate" or control their interactions with citizens primarily by asking questions or making accusations, and secondarily by issuing commands; they found that "coercive regulation [including threats as well as the actual use of force] is rare" (1980:195). Bayley and Garofalo (1989), who conducted a smaller-scale observational study under the auspices of the New York State Commission on Criminal Justice and the Use of Force, found that even in encounters that qualified as "potentially violent mobilizations," police used force in only 8 percent, and that the force "consisted almost exclusively of grabbing and restraining" (p. 7) (see also Adams, this volume).

Croft (1985) analyzed reports of the use of force filed by officers in the Rochester, N.Y., Police Department from 1973 through 1979, along with a comparison sample of arrests in which no force was used. Like Friedrich's, Croft's analysis indicates that the use of force was infrequent—2,397 reported uses of force, and 123,491 arrests over the period—and that it was typically prompted by citizens' actions—threatening or attacking officers and/or other citizens, or attempting to flee. Croft's analysis also suggests that many of the citizens against whom force was used were antagonistic and/or uncooperative, either verbally abusing officers or disobeying officers' commands.[13] Neither gender nor race bore the expected relationship to the use of force. Furthermore, Croft found that some officers were much more likely to use force than others were, even after controlling for officers' "hazard status," or the risk of "being exposed to police-citizen incidents having a potential for use of force" (p. 160); 119 of 430 officers selected for analysis were classified as "high force" officers, who used force in 6.1 percent or more of the arrests they made. However, "high force" officers could not, for the most part, be distinguished from "low force" officers in terms of their background characteristics; officers' use of force was related only to their age and length of service, and was unrelated to their gender, race, education, prior military service, or civil service test ranking. Neither did the two groups differ in their arrest productivity or in their numbers of citizen complaints, internally-initiated complaints, or disciplinary charges. Thus, this analysis of official police records yields results that mirror those based on observational research.

III. ANALYSIS OF THE POLICE SERVICES STUDY DATA

Data collected for the Police Services Study (PSS) afford another opportunity to analyze police use of force based on in-person observations. The PSS was funded by the National Science Foundation and conducted by Elinor Ostrom, Roger B. Parks, and Gordon P. Whitaker. The study was designed to examine the impact of institutional arrangements on the delivery of police services. The second phase of the PSS provided for the collection of various kinds of data about 24 police departments in three metropolitan areas (Rochester, N.Y.; St. Louis, Mo.; and Tampa-St. Petersburg, Fla.); attention focused particularly on 60 neighborhoods served by those departments. During the summer of 1977, trained observers accompanied patrol officers on 900 patrol shifts, 15 in each of the 60 neighborhoods. Observers recorded information about 5,688 police-citizen encounters in field notes and later coded that information on a standardized form; in many cases, narrative accounts of the encounters were also prepared. In addition, the observed officers (and samples of other officers) were surveyed. These data form the principal basis for the analyses reported below.

Compared with the Black-Reiss data and other observational data, the PSS data are broader and deeper. The Black-Reiss study focused on high-crime precincts in three major cities. The departments included in the PSS range in size from one with only 13 officers to one with over 2,000, serving municipalities whose populations range from 6,000 to almost 500,000. Within jurisdictions, neighborhoods were selected with explicit reference to racial composition and wealth to ensure that different types of neighborhoods were represented. The departments and neighborhoods provide a rough cross-section of organizational arrangements and residential service conditions for urban policing in the United States. Thus, the PSS data provide a much firmer basis for generalizing about police practices in American metropolitan areas (and not only in urban, high-crime areas).

A. The Use of Force

While they were observed for the PSS, officers used no more than reasonable force to restrain or move a citizen in 37 encounters.[14] In 23 encounters, officers used force that the observer judged to be unnecessary or excessive;[15] in three of those, officers hit or swung at citizens with a weapon.[16] This analysis will focus on these two categories of behavior, i.e., the use of reasonable force, and the use of improper (i.e., unnecessary or excessive) force. It should be obvious already that the use of force was uncommon, and the use of improper force was rare as a proportion of police-citizen encounters. According to the coded data, reasonable force was used in less than one percent of the encounters, and improper force was used in less than one-half of one percent; in encounters with suspects, who one would presume to be the most likely targets of police force, reasonable force was used in 2.3 percent, and improper force in 1.3 percent. Even so, incidents in which improper force was used represent a substantial proportion of the incidents in which any force (reasonable or improper) was used (Adams, in this volume).

This trichotomization of officers' behavior—no force, reasonable force, improper force—for present analytic purposes should be recognized for what it is: a simplification. Officers' use of force can be conceived (if not precisely measured) along a continuum, say, from minimal force to extreme (even deadly) force; these differences of degree are largely lost in this trichotomy. Moreover, this conceptualization of officers' behavior also obscures differences in the use of improper force, but the PSS data do not permit one to reliably differentiate the use of excessive force from the use of unnecessary force.[17]

Table 1 displays the characteristics of encounters in which reasonable force was used, encounters in which improper force was used, and for reference, all encounters, and all encounters that involved suspected offenders (other than traffic violators). To illustrate, 3.7 percent of all 5,688 encounters involved a violent crime, and 16.8 percent involved a nonviolent crime; 5.8 percent of the 1,528 encounters with (nontraffic) suspects involved a violent crime, and 9.8 percent involved a nonviolent crime. These data indicate that most encounters in which force is used do not take place in seclusion: most transpired in public locations, and in three-quarters a number of bystanders were looking on.[18] All but a small fraction of the encounters in which force was used also involved one or more officers other than the observed officer, and a substantial fraction also attracted a supervisor to the scene. Force was used disproportionately in those encounters that involved violent crimes, and in those that involved automobile pursuits; but most encounters in which force was used—reasonably or improperly—involved neither of these events. It might be added that none of the encounters in which force was used originated as a suspicion stop or

Table 1 Characteristics of Encounters

	All Encounters	Encounters with Suspects*	Reasonable Force Used	Improper Force Used
Type of Problem				
Violent crime	3.7	5.8	21.6	21.7
Nonviolent crime	16.8	9.8	16.2	13.0
Suspicious circumstances	10.0	23.8	13.5	13.0
Interpersonal conflict	8.6	20.8	24.3	13.0
Dependent person	4.8	4.9	5.4	17.4
Morals offense	1.4	3.7	2.7	0.0
Public nuisance	9.1	20.8	10.8	13.0
Traffic	22.6	—	5.4	0.0
Medical problem	1.8	0.1	0.0	0.0
Assistance	8.8	3.9	0.0	0.0
Information	6.3	0.7	0.0	0.0
Internal operations	4.4	3.8	0.0	8.7
Other/miscellaneous	1.7	2.0	0.0	0.0
Car chase	0.9	0.5	2.7	13.0
Location				
Street, sidewalk, parking lot	57.2	55.4	59.5	34.8
Public/commercial bldg.	8.4	7.3	10.8	17.4
Private residence	29.4	30.4	24.3	39.1
Other	5.0	6.9	5.4	8.7
Bystanders				
None	52.3	48.2	24.3	17.4
1–3	29.9	26.1	2.7	8.7
4–10	13.9	18.7	37.8	30.4
More than 10	3.8	7.0	35.1	43.5
Other Officers				
None	62.3	44.5	10.8	4.3
One	23.7	32.0	29.7	17.4
2–5	13.0	21.4	46.1	34.8
More than 5	1.0	2.1	13.5	43.5
Supervisor(s) present	9.9	15.8	35.1	60.9
N	5,688	1,528	37	23

* Excluding those suspected only of traffic violations

police-initiated field interrogation; indeed, few of these encounters were initiated by officers. If the use of force is a byproduct of police aggressiveness, then it would seem not to be a *direct* outgrowth of an "aggressive" style of patrol that involves frequently stopping suspicious persons or vehicles (Wilson and Boland 1978; Whitaker, Phillips, and Worden 1984); it might nevertheless be a consequence of an overly assertive or confrontational posture vis-a-vis citizens in any of a number of different contexts.

Table 2 Characteristics of Citizens

	All Citizens	Suspects Only*	Reasonable Force Used	Improper Force Used
Role				
Suspect	33.0	100	94.9	73.1
Victim	28.3	—	0.0	3.8
Sick/injured person	1.4	—	2.6	7.7
Subject of concern	1.3	—	0.0	7.7
Person requesting service	13.8	—	2.6	0.0
Witness/person with information	18.4	—	0.0	3.8
Other	3.8	—	0.0	3.8
Race				
White	65.3	53.6	35.9	50.0
Black	32.0	43.4	64.1	50.0
Other	2.1	1.9	0.0	0.0
Mixed	0.6	1.2	0.0	0.0
Gender				
Male	59.8	75.6	84.6	72.0
Female	33.9	18.6	15.4	28.0
Mixed	6.3	5.8	0.0	0.0
Age				
Under 18	16.1	30.9	17.9	19.2
19–35	41.9	45.4	53.8	53.8
Over 35	38.7	20.2	28.2	26.9
Mixed	3.3	3.5	0.0	0.0
Sobriety				
Sober	89.7	77.8	42.1	48.0
Drinking/using	6.1	12.8	15.8	8.0
Drunk/stoned	4.2	9.4	42.1	44.0
Mental Disorder	1.3	2.1	12.8	16.7
Weapon				
None in possession	98.8	96.4	84.6	76.9
Possessed gun	0.4	1.1	5.1	3.8
Possessed knife	0.8	2.5	10.3	19.2
Tried to use	0.1	0.2	2.6	7.7
Demeanor				
Detached	1.5	4.3	10.3	3.8
Hostile, antagonistic	1.8	5.0	23.1	46.2
Other	96.6	90.7	66.7	50.0
Fought with officer	0.3	0.9	17.9	57.7
N	8,666	1,819	39	26

* Excluding those suspected only of traffic violations

Table 2 displays the characteristics of the citizens against whom force was used, citizens against whom improper force was used, and for reference, all citizens who were involved in observed encounters and all citizens who were initially regarded as suspected offenders. Most citizens against whom the police used force were suspects. That the police used force against some citizens whom observers coded as sick or injured, or as the subjects of concern,[19] might seem curious; but further analysis, of both the coded data and the narrative data, shows that about half of those were citizens who appeared to have mental disorders. About half of the citizens against whom force was used showed evidence of drinking or drug use, and most of those were drunk. Nearly half of the citizens against whom improper force was used displayed a hostile or antagonistic demeanor,[20] more than half of them fought with the officer, and one-fifth of them had a weapon. Most of the citizens were adult men, and two-thirds of the adults were young adults; half were black.[21]

Table 3 displays the characteristics of officers who used force, officers who used improper force, and for reference, all surveyed officers with a rank below sergeant.[22] In general (and taking into account the small numbers of officers on which some of the percentages are based), the officers who used force (reasonably or improperly) resemble the larger sample of officers in their race, gender, length of service, and educational background; most were white, all were men, their average length of service was about six years, and most had no college degree. Somewhat greater differences can be found along attitudinal dimensions. Most of the officers who used force agreed that police "should help to quiet family disputes when they get out of hand," but most also indicated that police should *not* "handle cases involving public nuisances, such as barking dogs or burning rubbish"; a majority agreed with the statement that "police should not have to handle calls that involve social or personal problems where no crime is involved." Two-thirds of the officers who used improper force, and half of those who used force, agreed that "if police officers in tough neighborhoods had fewer restrictions on their use of force, many of the serious crime problems in those neighborhoods would be greatly reduced"; similar proportions agreed that "when a police officer is accused of using too much force, only other officers are qualified to judge such a case." Almost half of the officers who used improper force, and one-third of those who used force, disagreed with the statement that "most people in this community respect police officers'; three-quarters of the former and over half of the latter agreed that "the likelihood of a police officer being abused by citizens in this community is very high."

B. The Effects of Situational Characteristics

The data presented thus far are useful primarily for describing the incidents in which force was used: Table 1 displays for encounters in which force was used, the percentages with specified characteristics. Table 2 displays for citizens against whom force was used, the percentages with specified characteristics. Tables 4 and 5 lend themselves more to the identification of encounter-level correlates of the use of force.

Table 3 Characteristics of Officers

	All Officers	Reasonable Force Used	Improper Force Used
Race			
White	88.4	83.8	88.9
Black	10.4	13.5	5.6
Other	1.1	2.7	5.6
Gender			
Male	93.6	100	100
Female	6.4	0.0	0.0
Mean Age	30.5	30.5	29.5
Mean Length of Service	6.1	6.2	5.7
Education			
No college degree	68.3	56.8	72.2
Associate's degree	15.8	18.9	16.7
Bachelor's degree	15.9	24.3	11.1
Should quiet family disputes			
No	7.2	5.7	11.1
Yes	92.8	94.3	88.9
Should handle public nuisances			
No	61.6	77.1	83.5
Yes	38.4	22.9	16.7
Should not handle personal problems			
Strongly agree	8.0	13.5	11.1
Agree	24.1	29.7	44.4
Disagree	57.0	51.4	44.4
Strongly disagree	10.9	5.4	0.0
Fewer restrictions on use of force			
Strongly agree	12.4	16.2	27.8
Agree	30.2	35.1	38.9
Disagree	45.7	40.5	33.3
Strongly disagree	11.6	8.1	0.0
Only officers can judge use of force			
Strongly agree	16.8	16.2	11.1
Agree	30.1	37.8	55.6
Disagree	47.9	43.2	33.3
Strongly disagree	5.2	2.7	0.0
Most citizens respect police			
Strongly agree	6.3	2.7	0.0
Agree	69.9	62.2	55.6
Disagree	19.6	29.7	38.9
Strongly disagree	4.2	5.4	5.6
Citizens likely to abuse police			
Strongly agree	11.6	29.7	22.2
Agree	34.7	29.7	55.6
Disagree	47.5	32.4	22.2
Strongly disagree	6.2	8.1	0.0
N	1,069	37	18

Table 4 Use of Force by Characteristics of Encounters

	ALL ENCOUNTERS		ENCOUNTERS WITH SUSPECTS*	
	Reasonable Force Used	Improper Force Used	Reasonable Force Used	Improper Force Used
Type of Problem				
Violent crime	3.8	2.4	9.1	5.7
Nonviolent crime	0.6	0.3	4.0	1.3
Suspicious circumstances	0.5	0.9	1.4	0.6
Interpersonal conflict	1.8	0.6	2.8	0.9
Dependent person	0.7	1.5	1.3	1.3
Morals offense	1.2	0.0	1.8	0.0
Public nuisance	0.8	0.0	1.3	0.0
Traffic	0.2	0.2	—	—
Medical problem	0.0	0.0	0.0	0.0
Assistance	0.0	0.0	0.0	0.0
Information	0.0	0.0	0.0	0.0
Internal operations	0.0	0.8	0.0	1.7
Other/miscellaneous	0.0	0.0	0.0	0.0
Car chase	2.0	5.9	12.5	12.5
No car chase	0.6	0.4	2.2	0.9
Location				
Street, sidewalk, parking lot	0.7	0.2	2.4	0.5
Public/commercial bldg.	0.8	0.8	3.6	2.7
Private residence	0.5	0.5	1.7	1.3
Other	1.3	1.3	2.9	1.4
Bystanders				
None	0.3	0.1	0.8	0.4
1–3	0.1	0.1	0.3	0.3
4–10	1.8	0.9	4.9	1.1
More than 10	6.0	4.6	12.3	6.6
Other Officers				
None	0.1	0.0	0.4	0.1
One	0.8	0.3	2.0	0.4
2–5	2.3	1.1	5.2	0.9
More than 5	8.6	17.2	12.5	25.0
Supervisor(s) present	2.3	2.5	4.6	4.1

* Excluding those suspected only of traffic violations

Table 4 breaks down the use of force by the characteristics of encounters; it displays for encounters with specified characteristics, the percentages in which force was used. The more illuminating set of figures is probably that for encounters with suspects, which are those in which the use of force is most likely in the first place. This analysis indicates that the use of reasonable force

Table 5 Use of Force by Characteristics of Citizens

	ALL CITIZENS (N = 8666)		SUSPECTS ONLY* (N = 1819)	
	Reasonable Force Used	Improper Force Used	Reasonable Force Used	Improper Force Used
Role				
Suspect	1.3	0.7	1.9	0.9
Victim	0.0	0.0	—	—
Sick/injured person	0.8	1.7	—	—
Subject of concern	0.0	1.8	—	—
Person requesting service	0.1	0.0	—	—
Witness/person with information	0.0	0.1	—	—
Other	0.0	0.0	—	—
Race				
White	0.2	0.2	1.2	0.7
Black	0.9	0.5	2.9	1.1
Other	0.0	0.0	0.0	0.0
Mixed	0.0	0.0	0.0	0.0
Gender				
Male	0.6	0.3	2.2	1.0
Female	0.2	0.2	1.5	0.6
Mixed	0.0	0.0	0.0	0.0
Age				
Under 18	0.5	0.4	1.3	0.2
19–35	0.6	0.4	2.3	1.1
Over 35	0.3	0.2	2.5	1.6
Mixed	0.0	0.0	0.0	0.0
Sobriety				
Sober	0.2	0.2	1.1	0.4
Drinking/using	1.2	0.4	2.7	0.4
Drunk/stoned	4.4	3.0	7.8	4.8
Mental Disorder				
No evidence of disorder	0.4	0.2	1.8	0.7
Evidence of disorder	4.5	3.6	10.8	2.7
Weapon				
None in possession	0.4	0.2	1.7	0.7
Possessed gun	5.6	2.8	10.0	5.0
Possessed knife	5.7	7.1	8.9	6.7
Tried to use	20.0	40.0	25.0	25.0
Demeanor				
Detached	3.0	0.8	5.1	1.3
Hostile, antagonistic	5.7	7.6	9.9	11.0
Other	0.3	0.2	1.3	0.3
Fought with officer	28.0	60.0	41.2	47.1

* Excluding those suspected only of traffic violations

and the use of improper force (a) are more likely in encounters that involve violent crimes than in those that involve other kinds of problems, (b) are more likely in encounters that involve automobile pursuits than in those that do not, (c) are more likely in encounters with at least four bystanders, and still more likely in encounters that involve 10 or more bystanders, and (d) are more likely in encounters in which more than one officer is involved, and much more likely in encounters in which at least five officers are involved.

Table 5 breaks down the use of force by the characteristics of citizens; it displays for citizens with specified characteristics the percentages against whom force was used. Once again, the more illuminating set of figures is probably that for suspects. This bivariate analysis indicates that the use of reasonable force and the use of improper force (a) are somewhat more likely if the citizen is black, male, and over 18; (b) are more likely if the citizen exhibits signs of drunkenness or mental disorder; (c) are more likely if the citizen has a weapon, and still more likely if the citizen attempts to use a weapon; and (d) are more likely if the citizen is hostile or antagonistic, and especially if the citizen fights with the officer(s).

Tables 4 and 5 show only bivariate associations; they do not enable one to isolate the independent effects of individual variables, nor do they form the basis for an assessment of the explanatory power of these sets of variables. For example, the citizen's race and demeanor are both related to the use of force. Some previous research has found that the citizen's race and demeanor are both related to arrest, but that when one statistically controls for the effect of demeanor, race has no effect. A multivariate analysis, using suspects as the units of analysis, permits one to impose statistical controls and thus to estimate the independent effects of these variables, summarized in the form of regression coefficients, and it also provides an estimate of the extent to which these variables together account for the use of force.

The results of a multinomial logit analysis are shown in Table 6.[23] This analysis produces two sets of coefficients; one set reflects the estimated effects of the variables on the use of reasonable force, and the other reflects the estimated effects of the variables on the use of improper force. The statistical significance of each coefficient indicates the confidence that one can have in rejecting the null hypothesis that the variable has no effect. Otherwise, however, the coefficients have no intuitive interpretation. Thus the table also presents for each variable (X) the estimated probability that force will be used, i.e., Pr(Y), given that X has the value shown in brackets, and given that all of the other variables have their modal values. The last column shows the estimated change in the probability given that X changes from its modal value to the value in brackets.

Several variables have (statistically) significant effects both on the use of reasonable force and on the use of improper force. Either reasonable or improper force is more likely in incidents that involve violent crimes, and against suspects who are male, black, drunk, or antagonistic, or who physically resist the police. Physical resistance has by far the greatest effect on the use of force. But even when the effects of physical resistance are statistically controlled, suspects' demeanor has significant effects on the use of force. And even when the effects of physical resistance and of demeanor are statistically controlled, suspects' race

Table 6 The Effects of Situational Factors on the Use of Force

Variable (mode)	REASONABLE FORCE			IMPROPER FORCE		
	Coefficient	Pr (Y l x = [ ])	Change	Coefficient	Pr (Y l x = [ ])	Change
Violent crime (0)	1.555*	.01777[1]	.01394	2.436*	.00076[1]	.00009
Nonviolent crime (0)	1.108**	.01150[1]	.00767	−1.582	.00001[1]	.00005
Car chase (0)	1.271	.01341[1]	.00958	4.640*	.00692[1]	.00685
Street, sidewalk, parking lot (1)	0.335	.00274[0]	−.00109	0.928	.00003[0]	−.00004
Public/commercial bldg. (0)	0.397	.00568[1]	.00185	2.144	.00006[1]	.00051
Police station/car (0)	−14.191	.00000[1]	−.00383	−11.096	.00000[1]	−.00007
Number of bystanders (0)	0.034*	.00396[1]	.00013	0.004	.00007[1]	.00000
		.00453[5]	.00070		.00007[5]	.00000
		.00636[15]	.00253		.00007[15]	.00000
Number of other officers (0)	0.141	.00440[1]	.00057	0.293**	.00009[1]	.00002
		.00771[5]	.00388		.00029[5]	.00022
		.01547[10]	.01164		.00126[10]	.00119
Supervisor(s) present (0)	−0.785	.00175[1]	−.00208	0.821	.00015[1]	.00009
Citizen black (0)	1.265*	.01342[1]	.00959	2.133*	.00057[1]	.00050
Citizen male (1)	1.549*	.00082[0]	−.00301	3.440*	.00000[0]	−.00007
Citizen 19–35 (1)	0.711	.00188[0]	−.00195	1.034	.00002[0]	−.00004
Citizen over 35 (0)	0.692	.00761[1]	.00378	1.381	.00027[1]	.00020
Citizen drunk/stoned (0)	1.453*	.01615[1]	.01232	1.992*	.00049[1]	.00042
Citizen mentally disordered (0)	1.479**	.01658[1]	.01275	− 0.226	.00005[1]	−.00001
Citizen possessed weapon (0)	0.990	.01023[1]	.00640	1.600	.00033[1]	.00027
Citizen used weapon (0)	−4.295*	.00052[1]	−.00378	−5.238	.00000[1]	−.00007
Citizen hostile, antagonistic (0)	1.280*	.01361[1]	.00978	2.795*	.00110[1]	.00103
Citizen fought with officer (0)	5.501*	.45310[1]	.44927	7.595*	.06531[1]	.06524

* p < .05, two-tailed test

** p < .10, two-tailed test

has significant effects on the use of force. That officers are more likely to use even reasonable force against blacks might suggest that officers are, on average, more likely to adopt a penal or coercive approach to black suspects than they are to white suspects.[24] For example,

> "Shortly after midnight we received a call of disturbance and [the observed officer] proceeded to the scene without delay. We were the first to arrive and noticed two older women and a man standing on the south side of the street and a large group of younger women standing on a porch on the north side of the street. There was no disturbance upon arrival. [The observed officer] pulled up by the smaller group of people and asked them if they had called the police. They said that they had not. The [officer] apparently assumed (correctly) that the man in the group was the source of trouble, for he told the man that someone had called the police about a disturbance and that it would be necessary for them to go inside. The man (black, 30) said that there was no problem and stood his ground. At this point another [officer] and a friend of the man walked up to our car. [The observed officer] said that whether there was a problem or not they would have to get off the street. One of the women (the mans [sic] mother) told him to go inside but the man began muttering about how no one was going to tell him what to do. It was then that I realized that he was very drunk. [The observed officer] said that if the man didn't get off the street and the police got another call to come out he would be arrested. The man didn't like this at all and began raving about how there was no problem and about how the police were just trying to hassle him. The friend pleaded with the man to come inside but the man would not move and continued his muttering. [The observed officer] got out of the car and placed himself very near the man. He began saying something about not going anywhere and [the officer] told the man that he was under arrest. [The second officer] helped handcuff the man who was being very uncooperative. His friend told him that he was ignorant and asked the [officer] if he could go to the station with them. [The officer] said yes. They placed the man in the back seat of our car and we drove to the station, all the while being accussed [sic] of harassment and racism. The man threatened to kill us and [the officer] said he would have his chance when we got to the station. When we arrived [the officer] took him out of the car but the man started pulling away. [The second officer] grabbed him by the hair and [the observed officer] said that he had originally planned to let the man go when they got to the station but since the man was being such an ass he was going to book him."

In this case, the officer's actions early in the encounter—ordering the man to get off the street, and then confronting and challenging him—were, arguably, precipitous and ill-advised, making it all the more likely that force would later need to be used.

Several additional variables have statistically significant effects on the use of reasonable force, but *not* on the use of improper force.[25] The likelihood that reasonable force will be used rises with the number of bystanders. The use of reasonable force is also more likely if the encounter involves a nonviolent crime, and if there is some evidence that the citizen has a mental disorder. Curiously, the use of reasonable force is *less* likely if the citizen uses a weapon.

The effect of bystanders, and perhaps even of mental disorder, may reflect some officers' judgment that such encounters are best handled with dispatch. For example,

> "We were on routine patrol when flagged down by an [officer] waving a flashlight. He was out of breath from chasing a 'mental', a black woman about 22 years old. We noticed an ambulence [sic] in the parking lot of an apartment complex, and [the observed officer] decided to check it out. The first officer explained that the young woman had been drinking heavily and had put her head through a plate glass window, sustaining minor (but bloody) injuries. Her mother had called both the police and the ambulence because the woman had a history of drinking and mental disorder and might abuse her two children. When the police arrived, the woman ran away, covering about two blocks before the police and her mother caught her. When we arrived, the woman was having a heated discussion with her mother about whether or not she should go to the hospital. A third [officer] arrived. Two National Ambulence attendants were also trying to persuade the woman to go along. She became more and more distraught, and began yelling and cursing the attendants and officers. Lights began appearing in apartment windows, and several people began filtering out toward the confrontation. The woman kept screaming, 'Momma, you done me wrong.' Suddenly, [the observed officer] and the first [officer] grabbed the woman by the arms and began dragging her, kicking and screaming, to the ambulence. She was rather large, and put up a good struggle. The third [officer] and an attendant each had to grab a leg. They threw her on a stretcher. [The observed officer] sat on her legs while the other two officers held her arms and the attendants tied her hands and feet to the stretcher. She cursed and spit at the officers. [The observed officer] bounced on her legs and grinned. (She was wearing a bathrobe and underwear, and the bathrobe lost its effectiveness in the struggle. [The observed officer] mocked the woman, saying that her spit was 100 proof. The mildest epithet used was 'Get your white ass offa me, mother-fucker.' An attendant put a pillow over her face to keep her from spitting.) ★ ★ ★ In reflecting on the case as we patrolled, the [observed officer] mentioned that he had stopped even though there were two officers on the scene because both were young and sometimes indecisive. He said that the officers let the situation drag on too long, that people were beginning to come out of their apartments, and that he had to act. . . ."

This officer apparently believed that the encounter was better resolved before a large crowd formed and the dynamics of the encounter were thereby altered (as Muir [1977: ch. 7] illustrates in his discussion of "the crowd scene").

Two variables have statistically significant effects on the use of improper force, but not on the use of reasonable force. Improper force is more likely if the encounter involves a car chase, even controlling for physical resistance by the suspect. One reason may be that pursuits are emotionally and physiologically intense experiences that are *sometimes*—i.e., in some cases and/or for some officers—"catalytic" (see Toch, in this volume); one would do well to remember that most pursuits do not conclude with the use of excessive or unnecessary force. Another reason may be that suspects' flight is another form of disrespect for police authority, as is a hostile or antagonistic demeanor, which (sometimes) prompts officers to (unduly) assert their authority. Either explanation could account for the following:

> "At about 18:05, we were sitting in the car in a parking lot on the corner of B and LK talking to a patrol supervisor, when a Lilliput [a pseudonym for another municipality] police car went by chasing a motorcycle. Both the patrol car and the supervisor took off after the bike, which had turned onto LK Avenue. We chased him down LK to S, where he turned right and onto LT and back into Lilliput. By the time a Lilliput car and our car stopped him, two other Lilliput cars and another Metro [also a pseudonym] car had arrived. Two Lilliput officers and a Lilliput detective jumped out of their cars, tackled the suspect, roughed him up a bit, and handcuffed him. ★ ★ ★ The suspect was frisked and loaded into the back of a Lilliput patrol car."

The likelihood of improper force also rises with the number of officers at the scene. This finding, too, is open to (at least) two interpretations (Friedrich 1977:93). One is that an officer is more likely to use improper force when other officers are there to provide physical and social psychological reinforcements. Another is that incidents in which improper force is used are also those to which other officers come (or are summoned); according to this interpretation, the presence of other officers is an effect rather than a cause. Unfortunately, the analysis does not permit one to eliminate either interpretation.

In some respects these results parallel Friedrich's, who found that "police use of force depends primarily on two factors: how the offender behaves and whether or not other citizens and police are present" (1980:95). In particular, Friedrich's results show that the use of force is affected by the citizen's demeanor and sobriety. This analysis of the PSS data corroborates these findings: drunkenness, a hostile demeanor, and especially physical resistance all make the use of force more likely. But Friedrich's analysis indicated that the use of force is unaffected by other characteristics of citizens, such as race and gender. The results of this analysis indicate that the use of force *is* affected by race as well as by gender.[26]

The explanatory power of situational factors can be assessed in terms of the success of the model in "predicting" the use-of-force outcomes of these encounters; the proportion of cases that are correctly classified can be compared with the proportion that one could correctly classify based on knowledge only of the frequencies of the outcomes. Given that the use of force is so uncommon, however, predictions based only on the frequencies would be quite accurate. Indeed, one could correctly classify over 97 percent of the cases if one predicted that force was *never* used; if one randomly classified cases to reproduce the frequencies, one could correctly classify 94.6 percent. So overall, the model would seem to have little room for improvement in predictive success—no more than a 5.7 percent improvement over random classification. In fact, the model's predictions correctly classify 97.7 percent of the cases, a 3.3 percent improvement over chance. A fairer assessment of the model, perhaps, is its success in classifying cases in which force was used; random classification would result, on average, in 2 percent correct (one of 49 cases), while the model yields 24.5 percent correct. Furthermore, this analysis also suggests that, together, these situational factors better predict the use of improper force than they do the use of reasonable force. Five of 35 cases (14 percent) are correctly classified as those in which reasonable force was used, while seven of 14 cases (50 percent) are correctly classified as those in which improper force was used.

C. The Effects of Officers' Characteristics

Table 7 breaks down the use of force by the characteristics of officers; it displays for officers with specified characteristics, the percentages who used force. (Table 3 displays for officers who used force, the percentages with specified characteristics.) This bivariate analysis indicates that black officers and officers with college degrees are somewhat more likely to use force, but also that black officers and officers with bachelor's degrees are somewhat less likely to use improper force. The analysis also indicates that the two forms of force bear modest relationships to officers' attitudes. Officers who conceive their role in narrow terms, by excluding public nuisances and personal problems, are somewhat more likely to use force. Officers who believe that force is effective, and officers who believe that the use of force should be regulated by police themselves, are somewhat more likely to use force. Finally, officers whose views of citizens are negative—who believe that citizens do not respect and are likely to abuse police—are somewhat more likely to use force. However, judging from the percentage differences alone, these relationships are as weak as they are consistent with expectations.

Multivariate analyses, using officers as the units of analysis, form a better basis for assessing the impacts of officers' characteristics on their use of force. For such an analysis, one may measure officers' use of force as counts—the numbers of occasions on which each officer was observed to use reasonable force and improper force, respectively—or as dichotomies—whether or not each officer was observed using reasonable force and improper force, respectively. As it turns out, the results are very much the same regardless of the measure and the statistical technique used.[27] Since OLS coefficients are more intuitively interpretable than logit or Poisson regression coefficients, Table 8 displays the results of two OLS regression analyses, one of the use of reasonable force and the other of the use of improper force.

Table 7 Use of Force by Characteristics of Officers

	Reasonable Force Used	Improper Force Used	N
Race			
White	3.3	1.7	948
Black	4.5	0.9	112
Other	8.3	8.3	12
Gender			
Male	3.7	1.8	1003
Female	0.0	0.0	69
Length of Service			
Less than 1 year	0.0	0.0	20
1 to 3 years	3.7	2.1	326
4 to 8 years	3.8	1.7	476
More than 8 years	2.8	1.2	250
Education			
No college degree	2.9	1.8	733
Associate's degree	4.1	1.8	169
Bachelor's degree	5.3	1.2	171
Should quiet family disputes			
No	2.6	2.6	76
Yes	3.4	1.6	974
Should handle public nuisances			
No	4.2	2.4	638
Yes	2.0	0.8	397
Should not handle personal problems			
Strongly agree	5.9	2.4	85
Agree	4.3	3.1	257
Disagree	3.1	1.3	608
Strongly disagree	1.7	0.0	116
Fewer restrictions on use of force			
Strongly agree	4.5	3.8	133
Agree	4.0	2.2	323
Disagree	3.1	1.2	489
Strongly disagree	2.4	0.0	124
Only officers judge use of force			
Strongly agree	3.3	1.1	180
Agree	4.3	3.1	322
Disagree	3.1	1.2	512
Strongly disagree	1.8	0.0	56
Most citizens respect police			
Strongly agree	1.5	0.0	67
Agree	3.1	1.3	747

(continued)

Table 7 (*continued*)

	Reasonable Force Used	Improper Force Used	N
Disagree	5.3	3.3	209
Strongly disagree	4.4	2.2	45
Citizens likely to abuse police			
Strongly agree	8.9	3.2	124
Agree	3.0	2.7	371
Disagree	2.4	0.8	508
Strongly disagree	4.5	0.0	66

Table 8 The Effects of Officers' Characteristics on their Use of Force OLS Estimates

	Reasonable Force	Improper Force
Constant	.199	.138
Race (black = 1)	.003	−.015
Gender (female = 1)	−.079	−.044
Associate's degree	.058	.003
Bachelor's degree	.078**	−.011
Length of service	.003	−.001
Role orientation	.007	−.010
Attitude toward force	.000	.010***
Attitude toward citizens	−.045*	−.017*
Time observed (in 100s of mins)	.061**	.001
R^2	.037	.031
N = 463		

* p < .05, two-tailed test

** p < .10, two-tailed test

*** p < .10, one-tailed test

Only three variables (other than the amount of time for which officers were observed) have significant effects on one or both forms of force. First, officers' attitudes toward citizens—i.e., citizens' respect for police and the perceived likelihood that officers would be abused by citizens—have significant effects both on officers' use of reasonable force and on their use of improper force;[28] officers with more negative attitudes toward citizens are more likely to use force, reasonably or unreasonably. Second, officers' attitudes toward the use of force have a marginally significant effect on their use of improper force (at the .10 level with a one-tailed test); officers with more positive attitudes toward the use of force tend to use force improperly with greater frequency.[29] Third, the effect of officers' education on their use of reasonable force is statistically significant (at the .07 level in the OLS regression and at the .05 level in the

Poisson regression); in particular, officers with bachelor's degrees are more likely to use reasonable force.

Overall, then, officers' characteristics contribute very little to an explanation of the use of reasonable or improper force in these data. In OLS analyses, these variables explain hardly any of the variation—less than 3 to 4 percent—in officers' uses of force. (In logit analyses, this set of variables has practically no predictive power; all of the officers were classified as having not used force.) Furthermore, one might suspect that even these modest relationships are partially or entirely spurious, inasmuch as officers who are assigned to the more active, violent, socially disorganized police districts, in which the use of force is more frequently necessary, might as a result have more negative attitudes toward citizens; those officers might also be those with less seniority, and thus younger, less experienced, and more highly educated. When officers' characteristics are included with situational factors in an analysis using suspects as the units of analysis, only one of these three variables—officers' attitudes toward citizens—has a statistically significant effect, and only on the use of reasonable force. Psychological hypotheses about officers' use of force find some, but not much, support in these analyses of the PSS data.

D. The Effects of Organizational Characteristics

As one might expect, given the infrequency with which force was used in the observed encounters, the incidence of force varies very little across the 24 departments. In 11 departments there were no observed uses of force; in each of five other departments there was only one observed case of reasonable force; and in each of another five departments observers recorded two or three uses of force. In each of the remaining three departments, observers recorded 10, 16, and 19 incidents in which force was used, respectively. These raw numbers are potentially misleading, however, as these three departments were not only the largest departments but also those in which the largest numbers of shifts were observed. Taking into account the varying amount of observation across departments as well as the frequency with which officers in the respective departments encounter suspected offenders, one finds, for example, that the incidence of improper force in three smaller departments equals or exceeds that in the largest departments. But even when the use of force is standardized across departments for the duration of observation, these estimates of the use of force as an *organizational* property rest on a narrow foundation of data collection; in the smaller departments, observation extended over only 15 to 30 shifts, or 120 to about 250 hours.

Rather than use the departments as the units of analysis, one can include the theoretically relevant characteristics of the departments with situational factors in the same model, using suspects as the units of analysis. This approach has the advantage of controlling for the frequency with which officers in different departments confront the kinds of situations in which force is more likely. Three characteristics of the departments, which are featured in organizational theory, can be measured with PSS data.

First, the bureaucratization of the departments can be measured in terms of their size (the number of full-time employees), their levels of hierarchy or vertical differentiation (the number of separate ranks), their degree of specialization (the number of separate units, such as traffic, juvenile, etc.), and the extent to which the departments are civilianized. These characteristics can be analyzed as individual variables, or they can be combined to form a single index of bureaucratization.[30] In either case, bureaucratization is conceived as a continuum, rather than as a dichotomy (or as a synonym for organization).

Second, the priority that the chiefs of the departments place on law enforcement and crime-fighting can be gleaned from in-depth interviews with the chiefs and with other high-ranking police administrators. Respondents' answers to one or more of three questions in these interviews provide some clues to their priorities:

> "(1) Would you characterize the department's emphasis as being one of primarily providing service to residents, as primarily trying to suppress crime, or as something in between?
> (2) Are there any specific departmental policies regarding patrol style or emphasis?
> (3) What kinds of reports do you [does the chief] get on day-to-day operations of your patrol officers? (Probes: What things get brought to the chief's attention immediately? What kinds of indicators does the chief think are important regarding patrol?)"

On the basis of these interview data, three departments appear to have a decidedly "legalistic" or "professional" orientation (Wilson 1968), in the sense that their chiefs place primary emphasis on fighting crime. One chief, for example, told the PSS interviewer that

> "the department's first priority was the suppression and prevention of crime, and its second priority was responding to calls for service. The respondent felt that the department receives many trivial or 'bullshit' calls for service. . . . The department does what it can to respond to all calls, but such calls as these take low priority."

Furthermore, administrators in that department monitored patrol officers' performance through time sheets, filled out by each officer,

> "indicating how much time he spent on a variety of activities and various production measures: hours on patrol, hours traffic control, hours accident investigation, hours special duty, hours court, hours office duty, hours writing reports, hours approved overtime, sick leave, number of field interrogation reports filed, number of miscellaneous investigations conducted, number of complaints investigated, number of accidents investigated, number of non-traffic arrests, number of traffic arrests, number of accident arrests, number of warrant arrests, number of juvenile arrests, number of warnings issued."

This chief's express priority on crime-fighting was reinforced by the department's information system.

Predictably, perhaps, not all chiefs' answers revealed an unambiguous and well-ordered set of priorities. Of course, some chiefs may have been reluctant to tell interviewers that, in effect, "service" was secondary to suppressing crime; they may have shared the orientation, but not the candor, of other chiefs whose departments have been coded as legalistic. But it is equally or more likely that ambiguous answers reflected truly ambiguous priorities. For better or worse, police administrators typically are not compelled to establish clear priorities among the multiple and sometimes competing goals and functions of the police; the LAPD under Chief Daryl Gates may have been exceptional in the clarity of its priorities. Be that as it may, priorities can be communicated, even unwittingly, in the form of activity report categories, the criteria for evaluation, the reasons for sanctions, orders, memoranda, and the like. The PSS interviews with police administrators do not suffice to measure priorities established in these ways, but the measure based on these data certainly represents an improvement over those available for previous research (e.g., Friedrich 1980).[31]

Third, survey data on patrol officers in each department can be aggregated to measure some features of the informal cultures of the departments. Besides the observed officers, all or a sample of the other officers in each department were included in the survey.[32] Their responses to seven questionnaire items, described above for the analysis of officers, reveal wide variation in the collective attitudes of the departments. For example, the proportions of respondents who agreed that police should not have to handle social or personal problems ranged from 6.3 percent in one department to 62.5 percent in another. The proportion of respondents who agreed that fewer restrictions on the use of force would reduce the serious crime problems in tough neighborhoods ranged from 14.3 percent in one department to 69.2 percent in another.

When these variables—bureaucratization, the priority placed on crime-fighting, and the collective attitudes of patrol officers—are added to situational factors in analyses of the use of force, the estimated effect of one organizational characteristic achieves statistical significance: the likelihood that reasonable force will be used increases with the bureaucratization of the department (see Table 9).[33] The effect of bureaucratization on the use of improper force does not achieve a customary level of statistical significance (although it too has a positive sign), and the estimated effects of the other organizational variables are negligible. The inclusion of organizational factors modestly improves the explanatory power of the model: 28.6 percent of the cases in which force was used are classified correctly, compared with 24.5 percent correctly classified based only on the situational factors.

It would seem, then, that compared with officers in more bureaucratized departments, officers in less bureaucratized departments either are less likely to use force when it would be justified, seeking instead to handle problems in other ways, or are less likely to take actions early in an encounter that make it more probable that force will be necessary later in an encounter. These results may thus offer some support for the proposition that in smaller, less bureaucratic departments, administrators can more effectively monitor the performance of

Table 9 The Effects of Organizational Factors on the Use of Force

Variable (mode)	REASONABLE FORCE			IMPROPER FORCE		
	Coefficient	Pr (Y | x = [ ])	Change	Coefficient	Pr (Y | x = [ ])	Change
Violent crime (0)	1.503*	.01541[1]	.01194	2.579*	.00033[1]	.00030
Nonviolent crime (0)	1.127**	.01063[1]	.00716	−1.816	>.00001[1]	−.00003
Car chase (0)	1.662	.01791[1]	.01444	5.567*	.00643[1]	.00640
Street, sidewalk, parking lot (1)	0.339	.00248[0]	−.00099	1.586	.00001[0]	−.00002
Public/commercial bldg. (0)	0.391	.00365[1]	.00018	2.863**	.00009[1]	.00006
Police station/car (0)	−15.956	.00000[1]	−.00347	−12.562	.00000[1]	−.00003
Number of bystanders (0)	0.030*	.00358[1]	.00011	0.010	.00003[1]	.00000
		.0040[5]	.00056		.00003[5]	.00000
		.00543[15]	.00196		.00003[15]	.00000
Number of other officers (0)	0.065	.00370[1]	.00023	0.231	.00003[1]	.00000
		.00480[5]	.00133		.00008[5]	.00005
		.00663[10]	.00316		.00025[10]	.00022
Supervisor(s) present (0)	−0.454	.00221[1]	−.00126	1.485	.00011[1]	.00008
Citizen black (0)	1.043*	.00978[1]	.00631	2.370*	.00027[1]	.00024
Citizen male (1)	1.577*	.00072[0]	−.00275	4.275*	.00000[0]	−.00003
Citizen 19–35 (1)	0.733	.00167[0]	−.00180	0.543	.00001[0]	−.00002
Citizen over 35 (0)	0.555	.00291[1]	−.00056	0.732	.00003[1]	.00000
Citizen drunk/stoned (0)	1.514*	.01558[1]	.01211	2.134*	.00021[1]	.00018

(continued)

Variable (mode)

Variable (mode)						
Citizen mentally disordered (0)	1.243***	.01193[1]	.00846	-0.268	.00002[1]	-.00001
Citizen possessed weapon (0)	1.272**	.01227[1]	.00880	1.859**	.00016[1]	.00013
Citizen used weapon (0)	-19.302	.00000[1]	-.00347	-20.517	.00000[1]	-.00003
Citizen hostile, antagonistic (0)	1.257*	.01208[1]	.00861	3.303*	.00068[1]	.00065
Citizen fought with officer (0)	20.521	.95369[1]	.95022	22.425	.04631[1]	.04628
Legalistic department (0)	-16.435	.00000[1]	-.00347	-14.635	.00000[1]	-.00003
Bureaucratization (a)	0.166*	.00208[b]	-.00139	0.220***	.00001[b]	-.00002
		.00503[c]	.00156		.00004[c]	.00001

* $p < .05$, two-tailed test
** $p < .10$, two-tailed test
*** $p < .10$, one-tailed test
a = 1.13 (see footnote 33)
b = -1.97 (see footnote 33)
c = 3.38 (see footnote 33)

officers, and perhaps that supervision can more frequently extend to the development of subordinates' judgment. These are long inferential leaps, to be sure, but they are consistent with the quantitative results.

These conclusions find some additional support in the interviews with administrators. The chief of one department pointed out that his "is a small enough department to allow [him] to read each crime report every day or two." When asked about the reports that are used to get a feel for day-to-day operations, another chief, whose department was relatively small (with 27 full-time patrol officers),

> "pointed out that he does have the daily activity sheets that comes [sic] in to rely on. But his further comments indicate that he relies at least as heavily on other means of keeping tabs on day-to-day operations. Just listening to the radio, he said, is a good way to tell how things are going. And he pointed out that he can tell by the tone of voice of the officers, the way they are answering calls, whether there is anything wrong, and he said that listening to the men talking around the department is also a good way to keep track of daily operations. He emphasized that not anyone can do this; one has to know the individual officer's personality to be able to tell if the person is quieter than usual."

Needless to say, the chiefs of larger departments are scarcely in a position to take advantage of these sources of information. Larger, more bureaucratic agencies tend to rely on quantitative measures of performance, both of individuals and of the agency as a whole, and the less quantifiable aspects of police performance may thus receive too little attention. Indeed, the chief of one larger department (with 381 full-time patrol officers) "mentioned that a big problem in law enforcement was an overwhelming concern for statistical measures of performance, such as arrest rates, clearance rates, crime rates. [The chief] indicated that many of the statistics are misleading, but that nearly all professional departments use them, people come to expect their use, and it is difficult to come up with other more meaningful comparative measures of police performance."

Quantitative indicators of performance are useful primarily for measuring officers' productivity in enforcement; they reveal little about officers' performance of other police tasks, or even about some aspects of their enforcement activities, such as the judiciousness with which they use force. Police administrators are not blind to this problem. But as the Christopher Commission's analysis suggests, a higher incidence of the use of force may be one consequence of relying too heavily on such performance measures. A decentralized administrative structure, which would permit mid-level managers to monitor officers' performance through a more complete range of information channels, might enable the subunits of a large department to capture some of the managerial advantages of smaller departments (see Brown 1981: ch. 10; Whitaker 1983). An explicit and vigorous commitment to addressing the problems of the community, as the community defines them, might also be a step in the right direction, insofar as it underscores both the multiplicity of the functions that police perform, and the legitimacy of citizen preferences in shaping police policy.

IV. CONCLUSIONS

Analyses of both the Black–Reiss data and the PSS data, as well as of other data, show that physical force is infrequently used by the police, and that improper force is still less frequently used. Is police brutality, then, "rare"? The incidence of the use of improper force is rare in the sense that aircraft fatalities are rare: it is infrequent relative to the large volume of interactions between police and citizens, just as deaths in aircraft accidents are infrequent relative to the large number of passenger-miles flown. That these events are rare does not, of course, mean that no effort need be devoted to making them still more rare. Both types of events are almost certainly inevitable to some degree, so long as neither officers nor pilots are recruited from the ranks of philosopher-kings. But as we extend our understanding of how best to structure and regulate human behavior, we may expect that the frequency of either event can be further reduced.

Analyses of the Black–Reiss data and the PSS data also show that to some extent, the use and abuse of force by police are influenced by characteristics of the situations in which officers and citizens interact. Of course, it would be very surprising indeed to find that the use of force is distributed randomly across police–citizen encounters; that officers are more likely to use force, say, against suspects who offer physical resistance is hardly startling. That officers are more likely to use force—and especially improper force—against suspects who are inebriated or antagonistic (other things being equal) is—if not unexpected—cause for concern. That officers are more likely to use improper force against black suspects (other things being equal) is cause for grave concern. Unfortunately, although these results form the basis for causal inferences, they are open to different interpretations. For example, one might interpret the effect of race simply as the behavioral manifestation of hostile police attitudes toward African-Americans. A somewhat different interpretation was offered by one chief of police (in a private communication with the author), who thought that some of his officers were especially fearful of black suspects; the unstated implication, I take it, is that those officers might either use force preemptively (and unnecessarily) or act (unwittingly) in such a way that provokes resistance to which they must respond with force. These different interpretations, moreover, would seem to have different implications for the form and likely efficacy of managerial interventions. In general, a sociological approach to *explaining* police use of force may not suffice for *understanding* the use of force.[34] Further research on the dynamics of police–citizen encounters in which force is used, with a view toward how those dynamics may be affected by—and the ways in which officers interpret—specific situational factors, could improve our understanding of these results (Worden 1989; Mastrofski and Parks 1990).

Neither this analysis nor previous analyses demonstrate that officers' characteristics or attitudes have a substantively (rather than merely statistically) significant effect on the use of force. Such results are consistent with the negative results of recruit screening (Grant and Grant, in this volume). Even so, this analysis does offer some—albeit weak—support for psychological hypotheses, and perhaps the most prudent conclusion at this juncture is that, if officers' propensities to use force are affected by their backgrounds and beliefs, then those effects are probably contingent on other factors—such as the character-istics of the situations in which officers interact with citizens and the charac-teristics of the organizations in which officers work—and the effects may be interactive rather than additive—that is, officers' propensities to use force may be affected by a constellation of outlooks rather than by each outlook inde-pendent of others. For example, the officers who are most likely to use and abuse force might be those who define the police role exclusively in terms of crime-fighting *and* who are inclined to bend or break rules that regulate their authority in order to bring about outcomes that they consider desirable *and* whose (formal and informal) training has provided them with few alternatives to the use of force; such officers might be more likely to use force *if* they work in (more) bureaucratic agencies that emphasize hard-nosed enforcement, *and* that measure and reward performance accordingly. Put more succinctly, officers' attitudes and personality characteristics may bear a systematic but complex relationship to their use of force.

Research on these questions should be designed to capture these complex-ities. Previous observational studies have not been so designed. For both the Black-Reiss and PSS studies, the units of sample selection (within precincts and neighborhoods, respectively) were shifts. Active or busy shifts were oversam-pled in order to maximize the number of police-citizen encounters that ob-servers could record. For the Black-Reiss study, 589 officers were observed for one or more shifts; the average period of observation per officer was two-and-one-half shifts (Friedrich 1977). For the PSS, 522 officers were observed; more than half of the officers were observed for only one shift, only 60 officers were observed for as much as 24 hours (or about three shifts), and only 24 for as much as 32 hours.[35] But if the use of force is infrequent, and if the distribution of the incidence of force across officers is skewed, then officers should serve as the units for sample selection. Officers who use force most frequently could be oversampled; the sampling frame could be stratified according to the numbers of (sustained or unsustained) citizen complaints, arrests for resisting arrest, use of force reports, or other departmental indicators (including the reports of other officers—see Bayley and Garofalo 1989). The balance of the sample would be composed of other officers with similar assignments, and officers would be weighted for analysis. If observation were extended to include de-briefing officers about individual encounters, to obtain data on the decision rules by which they choose courses of action (Mastrofski and Parks 1990, Worden and Brandl 1990), and if these observations were complemented by a well-conceived survey instrument, then one might conduct a relatively power-ful test of psychological hypotheses.

Finally, this analysis provides modest support for an organizational explana-tion of police brutality. It suggests that elements of formal organizational struc-ture affect the incidence with which force is used. It does not, however, sug-gest that this effect is a simple product of restrictive policies, in terms of which discussions of administrative controls are too frequently cast. The theory on which this analysis is based, and the structural variables that were conceptualized and measured, point toward more fundamental—and less easily altered—features of the organization. Future research should continue to explore the ways in which organizational forces affect the incidence with which officers use force, but it should cast a broad theoretical net, one that reaches beyond policy and procedure with respect to the use of force (and complaints about the use of force). Evidence on these propositions will accumulate slowly, because comparable data on the use of force in multiple departments will be difficult to find or very expensive to collect (see Adams, in this volume). But evidence will not accumulate at all unless research is guided by theory.

ENDNOTES

1. However, the converse—that every theory has implications for reform—is not true.

2. See, for example, Sherman (1980b), whose discussion of violence by police focuses almost exclusively on the use of deadly force.

3. Black holds that the quantity of law can be conceived as a continuous variable, but quantitative research on police has with few exceptions conceived and measured it as a dichotomy.

4. I return to the issue of race below, when I review studies of the use of non-lethal force.

5. See Toch (in this volume) for a more thorough assessment both of the commission's analysis of problem officers and of violence-prone officers more generally.

6. The other types are "professionals," "clean-beat crime-fighters," and "avoiders" (see Worden, forthcoming):

"Professionals . . . are . . . willing to use coercive means to achieve desirable ends, but they use it with a keen sense of when, and in what proportion, it is necessary. . . . [T]hey believe that . . . the application of the law should be tempered by a sensitive appreciation of its consequences, justifying the enforcement of the law in terms of helping people. . . . [T]hese officers are neither overly aggressive on the street nor resentful of legal restrictions on their authority."

"Clean-beat crime-fighters . . . stress the law enforcement function of the police.

. . . [T]hey justify uniform (non-selective) enforcement in terms of its deterrent effect." They are very energetic and aggressive on the street, although they lack the street sense of the tough cop.

"Avoiders . . . [are] unable to cope with the characteristic exigencies of police work. . . . [T]hey prefer to do as little police work as possible, only that amount of work necessary to meet the minimum expectations of supervisors; otherwise, they adopt what has elsewhere been called a 'lay-low-and-don't-make-waves' approach to policing."

7. Aslo see Lester (in this volume).

8. Brown (1981) makes the argument that one of the core themes of the police culture is individualism, and Fielding (1988) maintains that some officers ostensibly go along with the dominant value system but "once confident of their place, and ability to use the necessary justifying rhetoric in relation to their own complex of values, officers begin to move in and through the culture to secure their own ends" (p. 185). However, many other (less convincing) accounts of the police culture tend to highlight the forces that have homogenizing effects, both on officers' outlooks and on their behavioral patterns; little attention is given to the differing interpretations of and conformity with the norms of the culture. For example, Hunt (1985) describes the effects of peers on individual officers' conceptions of proper force and their justifications for the use of force, and while she also observes that some

"violence-prone" officers repeatedly "exceed working notions of normal force" and are "not effectively held in check by routine means of peer control" (p. 336), her analysis does not allow for officers who use less than "normal" force.

9. Such a shift in expectations and incentives could perhaps be effected with the adoption of community policing, which the commission recommended. That such a model of policing—and of police administration—would reduce the incidence of improper force is itself a largely untested (albeit plausible) hypothesis. For a theoretically-rich and illuminating study that offers some support for this proposition, as well as a sobering account of the likely obstacles to implementing this model, see Guyot (1991); also see Goldstein (1987).

10. About half of all local police agencies employ fewer than 10 full-time sworn officers (Reeves 1993:9).

11. Reiss's (1968a) analysis of the same data reports that force was used improperly in 37 cases. Friedrich's analysis rests on the characterizations of the coders, who "examined pertinent passages of the observation reports to determine if physical force had been used and if it was justified in terms of self-defense or the need to make an arrest," while Reiss "had an expert panel decide whether or not force on the order of an aggravated assault was used" (1980: fn. 12; also see Reiss, 1968a).

12. These expectations were based largely on Wilson's (1968) analysis of police styles and the organizational contexts with which they are associated. In the light of more recent research, especially Brown's (1981), it should be clear that these expectations are faulty. For many years, the Los Angeles Police Department was regarded as the epitome of police professionalism; elements of that professionalism, we now realize, may make the use of force *more* likely.

13. Her analysis also shows that when citizens in these incidents verbally abused or disobeyed officers, officers typically responded by issuing a command, whereupon citizens attacked the officers.

14. According to a PSS memorandum (coding update number 3, dated 29 May 1977), this category encompasses "instances where the officer is attempting to make a citizen come with him, or is attempting to separate citizens who are fighting, or similar acts. The sense here is that the officer is restraining or moving the citizen without the intent to beat the citizen."

15. The aforementioned PSS coding memo specifies that this code should be used "for instances where the officer is 'kicking ass'."

16. A gun was *drawn* by one or more officers in each of 53 encounters, and in one of those the gun was fired (albeit at a rattlesnake); another type of weapon was drawn in 33 encounters.

17. The coded data provide little information about the temporal sequences of events. For example, the data indicate whether the citizen fought with the officer and whether the officer(s) used improper force, but they do not indicate whether the force preceded the citizen's resistance or continued after the resistance ceased— a case of unnecessary force—or the force was more than that required to subdue the citizen—a case of excessive force.

18. The location shown in Table 1 is the location at which the encounter began (or at which the observed officer entered). The coded data provide for up to three changes in the location of the encounter, e.g., from inside a house to the front porch, to the squad car, and to the police station. However, these data do not enable one to determine the point (and thus the location) at which the officer(s) used force. The location changed at least once in 26 of the 37 encounters in which reasonable force was used, in 15 to the squad car and in 11 to the police station or jail; both logic and the narrative data suggest that these changes accompanied arrests. The location changed at least once in 13 of the 23 encounters in which improper force was used, in four to the squad car and in seven to the police station or jail. In at least two of these the impropriety consisted of "throwing" suspects into police cars, and in one other it involved excessive force in searching an arrestee at a

jail. Otherwise, it appears that improper force was not observed in these locations.

19. "Subjects of concern" might include, for example, juveniles or drunks—people who could not be expected to care for themselves.

20. Each citizen's demeanor was coded at three points in time: at the beginning of the encounter, during the encounter, and at the end of the encounter. This analysis conservatively uses the citizen's demeanor at the beginning of the encounter, lest we confuse antagonistic behavior that prompts the use of force with antagonistic behavior prompted by the use of force.

21. A small number of the "citizens" coded by observers were actually groups of citizens; if the group was not homogeneous with respect to race, gender, or age, it was coded as "mixed."

22. In some encounters, the officer who was designated as the "primary" or observed officer, and for whom survey data could be connected to coded observations, was not among those who used force. Thus, the figures in Table 3 for officers who used force are based on only the primary officers who were observed to use force, and exclude other officers who used force in the observers' presence.

23. Since I have conceived the use of force as a nominal variable with three categories, I have estimated the parameters of a multinomial logit model, which is the "standard method" (Aldrich and Nelson 1984:37–40) for analyzing a polytomous, unordered dependent variable. As an alternative, one could operationalize the use of force—reasonable and/or improper force—as a dichotomy and apply other multivariate techniques, including the widely used Ordinary Least Squares (OLS) regression; this is the analytic approach that Friedrich (1980) used. In the PSS data, when regression equations for reasonable force and improper force, respectively, are estimated using OLS, some but not all of the findings are congruent with the multinomial logit results. Binomial logit results are largely—but not entirely—consistent with the multinomial logit results. Since OLS regression is not appropriate for dichotomous dependent variables (Hanushek and Jackson 1977: ch. 7; Aldrich and Nelson 1984: ch. 1; and, more generally, King 1989), there is good reason to prefer the logit results. Also see Brehm and Gates (1992) for a discussion of alternative techniques and applications to the Black-Reiss data.

24. Black (1980: ch. 5) comes to a similar conclusion based on his analysis of dispute resolution by police using the Black-Reiss data.

25. This is not the same as saying that for each of these variables the two coefficients are significantly different from one another; to the contrary, in each case the confidence intervals for the two coefficients overlap.

26. The OLS results indicate that race has a statistically significant effect on the use of reasonable force but not on the use of improper force. Perhaps the discrepancy between the results of the logit analysis and those of Friedrich's analysis are methodological artifacts.

27. The two measures of officers' use of force differ very little from one another, inasmuch as no officer was observed to use excessive force more than once, and only seven officers were observed to use reasonable force more than once (five used it twice and two used it on three occasions). Moreover, the estimation of model coefficients hinges neither on the measure nor on the statistical technique that is used. When the use of force is measured as an event count, both OLS regression and Poisson regression (see Inn and Wheeler 1977; and more generally, King 1989) yield comparable results; when the use of force is measured as a dichotomy, binomial logit yields results that are congruent with the OLS and Poisson regressions.

28. This variable is an index formed by summing officers' responses to the two questionnaire items. Neither of the items by itself achieves statistical significance in separate OLS analyses, although both are significant (one at .07 and the other at .03) in the Poisson regression.

29. This, too, is an index formed by summing officers' responses to the questionnaire items about the use of force in

"tough neighborhoods" and about who (if anyone) besides police are qualified to judge allegations of improper force. In a separate analysis, the former item achieves this same marginal level of statistical significance, and the effect of the latter is insignificant.

30. This index is the sum of the standardized variables. Smith's (1984) analysis of the PSS data is based on an index of bureaucratization that was formed in a similar fashion (but using a somewhat different set of variables).

31. It is also nearer the mark of police "professionalism" than are indicators of officers' educational achievement (cf. Smith 1984).

32. Because the survey was intended to collect information relevant to the 60 study neighborhoods, selection procedures generally identified would-be respondents who had responsibilities in those areas—for patrol, supervision, or administration. In the six largest departments, samples of officers and supervisors assigned to those areas were selected, in addition to command staff; in the smaller departments, all officers, supervisors, and command staff were selected. In two departments, samples of all officers were selected, regardless of their assignments to study neighborhoods or to other areas. Overall, of the 1,435 officers selected, two refused to be interviewed, eight could not be contacted, and eight others were not interviewed for unidentified reasons. Aggregated responses in each department are based only on respondents with a rank below sergeant, i.e., those whose primary responsibility is patrol, and who are most likely to use force or have occasion to use force.

33. The results presented in Table 9 are based on a model that omits measures of the collective attitudes of patrol officers, none of whose effects achieve statistical significance; results are available from the author.

The values of bureaucratization on which predicted probabilities are calculated are not modal values, but rather scale values that correspond to hypothetical departments that are more or less bureaucratized: 1.13 is the scale score for a department with 6 ranks, 10 separate divisions, and 200 employees, 25 percent of whom are civilians; -1.97 is the score for a (less bureaucratic) department with 4 ranks, 6 divisions, and 70 employees, 20 percent of whom are civilians; 3.38 is the score for a (more bureaucratic) department with 7 ranks, 12 divisions, and 800 employees, 25 percent of whom are civilians.

34. Black (1976:7) points out that his theory of the behavior of law "predicts and explains . . . without regard to the individual as such. . . . It neither assumes nor implies that he is, for instance, rational, goal directed, pleasure seeking, or pain avoiding. . . . It has nothing to do with how an individual experiences reality."

35. In fairness to the PSS, it should be noted that it was not designed for the purpose of analyzing police brutality.

REFERENCES

Adams, Kenneth (in this volume) "Measuring the Prevalence of Police Abuse of Force."

Adorno, T.W., Else Frenkel-Brunswik, Daniel J. Levinson, and R. Nevitt Sanford (1950) *The Authoritarian Personality* (New York: Harper and Row).

Aldrich, John H., and Forrest D. Nelson (1984) *Linear Probability, Logit, and Probit Models,* volume 45 of Quantitative Applications in the Social Sciences (Beverly Hills: Sage).

Alpert, Geoffrey P. (1989) "Police Use of Deadly Force: The Miami Experience," in Roger G. Dunham and Geoffrey P. Alpert (eds.), *Critical Issues in Policing: Contemporary Readings* (Prospect Heights, IL: Waveland).

Balch, Robert W. (1972) "The Police Personality: Fact or Fiction?" *Journal of Criminal Law, Criminology, and Police Science* 63:106–119.

Bayley, David H. (1986) "The Tactical Choices of Police Patrol Officers," *Journal of Criminal Justice* 14:329–348.

————, and James Garofalo (1989) "The Management of Violence by Police Patrol Officers," *Criminology* 27:1–27.

Berk, Sarah Fenstermaker, and Donileen R. Loseke (1980–81) "'Handling' Family Violence: Situational Determinants of Police Arrest in Domestic Disturbances," *Law & Society Review* 15:317–346.

Binder, Arnold, and Peter Scharf (1980) "The Violent Police-Citizen Encounter," *Annals of the American Academy of Political and Social Science* 452:111–121.

Bittner, Egon (1970) *The Functions of the Police in Modern Society.* Washington, DC: U.S. Government Printing Office.

Black, Donald (1971) "The Social Organization of Arrest," *Stanford Law Review* 23:1087–1111.

———— (1976) *The Behavior of Law* (New York: Academic Press).

———— (1980) *The Manners and Customs of the Police* (New York: Academic Press).

————, and Albert J. Reiss, Jr. (1967) "Patterns of Behavior and Citizen Transactions," in President's Commission on Law Enforcement and Administration of Justice, *Studies in Crime and Law Enforcement in Major Metropolitan Areas,* Field Studies III, Vol. II, Sec. I (Washington, DC: U.S. Government Printing Office).

Bloch, Peter B., and Deborah Anderson (1974) *Policewomen on Patrol: Final Report* (Washington, DC: Police Foundation).

Blumberg, Mark (1981) "Race and Police Shootings: An Analysis in Two Cities," in James J. Fyfe (ed.), *Contem-*

porary Issues in Law Enforcement (Beverly Hills: Sage).

———— (1982) "The Use of Firearms by Police: The Impact of Individuals, Communities, and Race," unpublished Ph.D. dissertation, State University of New York at Albany.

Brehm, John, and Scott Gates (1992) "Policing Police Brutality: Evaluation of Principal-Agent Models of Noncooperative Behavior," paper presented at the Annual Meeting of the Midwest Political Science Association, April, Chicago.

Broderick, John J. (1977) *Police in a Time of Change* (Morristown, NJ: General Learning Press).

Brown, Michael K. (1981) *Working the Street: Police Discretion and the Dilemmas of Reform* (New York: Russell Sage Foundation).

Cascio, Wayne F. (1977) "Formal Education and Police Officer Performance," *Journal of Police Science and Administration* 5:89–96.

Cohen, Bernard, and Jan M. Chaiken (1972) *Police Background Characteristics and Performance* (New York: Rand).

Croft, Elizabeth Benz (1985) "Police Use of Force: An Empirical Analysis," unpublished Ph.D. dissertation, State University of New York at Albany.

Dahl, Robert A. (1967) "The City in the Future of Democracy," *American Political Science Review* 61:953–970.

Fielding, Nigel G. (1988) *Joining Forces: Police Training, Socialization and Occupational Competence* (London: Routledge).

Friedrich, Robert J. (1977) "The Impact of Organizational, Individual, and Situational Factors on Police Behavior," unpublished Ph.D. dissertation, University of Michigan.

———— (1980) "Police Use of Force: Individuals, Situations, and Organizations," *Annals of the American Academy of Political and Social Science* 452:82–97.

Fyfe, James J. (1979) "Administrative Interventions on Police Shooting Discretion," *Journal of Criminal Justice* 7:309–323.

———— (1980) "Geographic Correlates of Police Shooting: A Microanalysis," *Journal of Research in Crime and Delinquency* 17:101–113.

———— (1981a) "Who Shoots? A Look at Officer Race and Police Shooting," *Journal of Police Science and Administration* 9:367–382.

———— (1981b) "Race and Extreme Police-Citizen Violence," in R.L. McNeely and Carl E. Pope (eds.), *Race, Crime, and Criminal Justice* (Beverly Hills: Sage).

———— (1982) "Blind Justice: Police Shootings in Memphis," *Journal of Criminal Law and Criminology* 73:707–722.

———— (1988) "Police Use of Deadly Force: Research and Reform," *Justice Quarterly* 5:165–205.

———— (in this volume) "Training to Reduce Police-Citizen Violence."

Gardiner, John A. (1969) *Traffic and the Police* (Cambridge, MA: Harvard University Press).

Geller, William A., and Kevin J. Karales (1981) "Shootings of and by Chicago Police: Uncommon Crises. Part I: Shootings by Chicago Police," *Journal of Criminal Law and Criminology* 72:1813–1866.

Goldstein, Herman (1987) "Toward Community-Oriented Policing: Potential, Basic Requirements, and Threshold Questions," *Crime and Delinquency* 33:6–30.

Gouldner, Alvin W. (1954) *Patterns of Industrial Bureaucracy* (Glencoe, IL: Free Press).

Grant, J. Douglas, and Joan Grant (in this volume) "Officer Selection and the Prevention of Abuse of Force."

Grennan, Sean A. (1987) "Findings on the Role of Officer Gender in Violent Encounters with Citizens," *Journal of Police Science and Administration* 15:78–85.

Guyot, Dorothy (1991) *Policing as though People Matter* (Philadelphia: Temple University Press).

Hanushek, Eric A., and John E. Jackson (1977) *Statistical Methods for Social Scientists* (New York: Academic Press).

Hudzik, John K. (1978) "College Education for Police: Problems in Measuring Component and Extraneous Variables," *Journal of Criminal Justice* 6:69–81.

Hunt, Jennifer (1985) "Police Accounts of Normal Force," *Urban Life* 13:315–341.

Independent Commission on the Los Angeles Police Department (1991) *Report of the Independent Commission on the Los Angeles Police Department* (Los Angeles: Author).

Inn, Andres, and Alan C. Wheeler (1977) "Individual Differences, Situational Constraints, and Police Shooting Incidents," *Journal of Applied Social Psychology* 7:19–26.

Jermier, John M., John W. Slocum, Jr., Louis W. Fry, and Jeannie Gaines (1991) "Organizational Subcultures in a Soft Bureaucracy: Resistance Behind the Myth and Facade of an Official Culture," *Organization Science* 2:170–194.

King, Gary (1989) *Unifying Political Methodology: The Likelihood Theory of Statistical Inference* (Cambridge: Cambridge University Press).

Klinger, David A. (1992) "Deference or Deviance? A Note on Why 'Hostile' Suspects Are Arrested," paper presented at the Annual Meeting of the American Society of Criminology, November 4–7, New Orleans.

Klockars, Carl (in this volume) "Supervising for Excellence in Police Use of Force: Beyond Prohibitory Performance Standards."

Lefkowitz, Joel (1975) "Psychological Attributes of Policemen: A Review of Research and Opinion," *Journal of Social Issues* 31:3–26.

Lester, David (in this volume) "Officer Opinion About Police Abuse of Force."

Locke, Hubert G. (in this volume) "The Color of Law and the Issue of Color: Race and the Abuse of Police Power."

Lundman, Richard J. (1974) "Routine Police Arrest Practices: A Commonweal Perspective," *Social Problems* 22:127–141.

Manning, Peter K. (1977) *Police Work: The Social Organization of Policing* (Cambridge, MA: MIT Press).

——— (1989) "The Police Occupational Culture in Anglo-American Societies," in William G. Bailey (ed.), *Encyclopedia of Police Science* (Dallas: Garland).

Mastrofski, Stephen (1988) "Varieties of Police Governance in Metropolitan America," *Politics and Policy* 8:12–31.

———, and Roger B. Parks (1990) "Improving Observational Studies of Police," *Criminology* 28:475–496.

Meyer, Marshall W. (1980) "Police Shootings of Minorities: The Case of Los Angeles," *Annals of the American Academy of Political and Social Science* 452:98–110.

Miller, Jon, and Lincoln Fry (1976) "Reexamining Assumptions About Education and Professionalism in Law Enforcement," *Journal of Police Science and Administration* 4:187–198.

Milton, Catherine H., Jeanne W. Halleck, James Lardner, and Gary L. Abrecht (1977) *Police Use of Deadly Force* (Washington: Police Foundation).

Muir, William Ker, Jr. (1977) *Police: Streetcorner Politicians* (Chicago: University of Chicago Press).

Prottas, Jeffrey Manditch (1978) "The Power of the Street-Level Bureaucrat in Public Service Bureaucracies," *Urban Affairs Quarterly* 13:285–312.

Reeves, Brian A. (1993) "Census of State and Local Law Enforcement Agencies, 1992," Bureau of Justice Statistics Bulletin (Washington: Bureau of Justice Statistics).

Reiss, Albert J., Jr. (1968a) "Police Brutality—Answers to Key Questions," *Trans-action* 5:10–19.

——— (1968b) "Stuff and Nonsense about Social Surveys and Observation," in Howard S. Becker, *et al.* (eds.), *Institutions and the Person* (Chicago: Aldine).

——— (1971a) *The Police and the Public* (New Haven: Yale University Press).

——— (1971b) "Systematic Observation of Natural Social Phenomena," in Herbert L. Costner (ed.), *Sociological Methodology 1971* (San Francisco: Jossey-Bass).

Reuss-Ianni, Elizabeth (1983) *Two Cultures of Policing* (New Brunswick, NJ: Transaction).

Schuman, Howard, and Michael P. Johnson (1976) "Attitudes and Behavior," *Annual Review of Sociology* 2:161–207.

Sherman, Lawrence W. (1975) "An Evaluation of Policewomen on Patrol in a Suburban Police Department," *Journal of Police Science and Administration* 3: 434–438.

——— (1980a) "Causes of Police Behavior: The Current State of Quantitative Research," *Journal of Research in Crime and Delinquency* 17:69–100.

——— (1980b) "Perspectives on Police and Violence," *Annals of the American Academy of Political and Social Science* 452:1–12.

——— (1983) "Reducing Police Gun Use: Critical Events, Administrative Policy, and Organizational Change," in Maurice Punch (ed.), *Control in the Police Organization* (Cambridge, MA: MIT Press).

———, and Mark Blumberg (1981) "Higher Education and Police Use of Deadly Force," *Journal of Criminal Justice* 9:317–331.

Skolnick, Jerome H. (1975) *Justice Without Trial: Law Enforcement in Democratic Society* (2nd ed.; New York: John Wiley).

Smith, Douglas A. (1984) "The Organizational Context of Legal Control," *Criminology* 22:19–38.

————, and Jody R. Klein (1984) "Police Control of Interpersonal Disputes," *Social Problems* 31:468–481.

Smith, Douglas A., and Christy A. Visher (1981) "Street-Level Justice: Situational Determinants of Police Arrest Decisions," *Social Problems* 29:167–177.

————, and Laura A. Davidson (1984) "Equity and Discretionary Justice: The Influence of Race on Police Arrest Decisions," *Journal of Criminal Law and Criminology* 75:234–249.

Snipes, Jeffrey B., and Stephen D. Mastrofski (1990) "An Empirical Test of Muir's Typology of Police Officers," *American Journal of Criminal Justice* 14:268–296.

Sykes, Richard E., and Edward E. Brent (1980) "The Regulation of Interaction by Police: A Systems View of Taking Charge," *Criminology* 18:182–197.

———— (1983) *Policing: A Social Behaviorist Perspective* (New Brunswick, NJ: Rutgers University Press).

Sykes, Richard E., and John P. Clark (1975) "A Theory of Deference Exchange in Police-Civilian Encounters," *American Journal of Sociology* 81:584–600.

Toch, Hans (1979) *Peacekeeping: Police, Prisons, and Violence* (Lexington, MA: Lexington Books).

———— (in this volume) "The 'Violence-Prone' Officer."

Van Maanen, John (1974) "Working the Street: A Developmental View of Police Behavior," in Herbert Jacob (ed.), *The Potential for Reform of Criminal Justice* (Beverly Hills: Sage).

Weiner, Norman L. (1974) "The Effect of Education on Police Attitudes," *Journal of Criminal Justice* 2:317–328.

Westley, William A. (1970) *Violence and the Police: A Sociological Study of Law,*

Custom, and Morality (Cambridge, MA: MIT Press).

Whitaker, Gordon P. (1983) "Police Department Size and the Quality and Cost of Police Services," in Stuart Nagel, Erika Fairchild, and Anthony Champagne (eds.), *The Political Science of Criminal Justice* (Springfield, IL: Charles C. Thomas).

————, Charles David Phillips, and Alissa P. Worden (1984) "Aggressive Patrol: A Search for Side-effects," *Law & Policy* 6:339–360.

White, Susan O. (1972) "A Perspective on Police Professionalization," *Law & Society Review* 7:61–85.

Wilson, James Q. (1968) *Varieties of Police Behavior: The Management of Law and Order in Eight Communities* (Cambridge, MA: Harvard University Press).

————, and Barbara Boland (1978) "The Effect of the Police on Crime," *Law & Society Review* 12:367–390.

Worden, Alissa Pollitz (1993) "The Attitudes of Women and Men in Policing: Testing Conventional and Contemporary Wisdom," *Criminology* 31:203–241.

Worden, Robert E. (1989) "Situational and Attitudinal Explanations of Police Behavior: A Theoretical Reappraisal and Empirical Assessment," *Law & Society Review* 23:667–711.

———— (1990) "A Badge and a Baccalaureate: Policies, Hypotheses, and Further Evidence," *Justice Quarterly* 7:565–592.

———— (forthcoming) "Police Officers' Belief Systems: A Framework for Analysis," *American Journal of Police.*

————, and Steven G. Brandl (1990) "Protocol Analysis of Police Decision Making: Toward a Theory of Police Behavior," *American Journal of Criminal Justice* 14:297–318.

Worden, Robert E., and Stephen D. Mastrofski (1989) "Varieties of Police
Subcultures: A Preliminary Analysis,"
paper presented at the Annual Meeting of the Law & Society Association,
June 8–11, Madison, WI.

Worden, Robert E., and Alissa A. Pollitz
(1984) "Police Arrests in Domestic
Disturbances: A Further Look,"
Law & Society Review 18:105–119.

The Professional Political Model
of the Good Policeman

WILLIAM KER MUIR, JR.

He who lets himself in for politics, that is, for power and force as means,
contracts with diabolical powers and for his action it is not true that good can
follow only from good and evil only from evil, but that often the opposite is
true. Anyone who fails to see this, is, indeed, a political infant.

MAX WEBER
"POLITICS AS A VOCATION"
1918

At this point I reveal myself in my true colours, as a stick-in-the-mud. I
hold a number of beliefs that have been repudiated by the liveliest intellects of
our time. I believe that order is better than chaos, creation better than destruction.
I prefer gentleness to violence, forgiveness to vendetta. On the whole I think that
knowledge is preferable to ignorance, and I am sure that human sympathy is more
valuable than ideology. I believe that in spite of the recent triumphs of science, men
haven't changed much in the last two thousand years; and in consequence we
must still try to learn from history. History is ourselves. I also hold one or two
beliefs that are more difficult to put shortly. For example, I believe in courtesy,
the ritual by which we avoid hurting other people's feelings by satisfying
our own egos. And I think we should remember that we are part of a great
whole, which for convenience we call nature. All living things are our

From *Police: Street Corner Politicians*, pp. 47–58. Chicago, University of Chicago Press,
1977. Reprinted with permission.

brothers and sisters. Above all, I believe in the God-given genius of certain individuals, and I value a society that makes their existence possible.

KENNETH CLARK

CIVILISATION

1969

I

Coercion, the power of the sword, is not the only means of power. There are the power of the purse and the power of the word as well. We should keep these two other fundamental techniques of controlling others, reciprocity and exhortation, in mind to get a perspective on the moral implications of coercion.

Reciprocity is a distinct kind of power relationship. Instead of resorting to threats, one individual overcomes the resistance of another by making an attractive exchange. He gives up something he values less and gets in return something he thinks has a greater worth to him. His exchange partner, meanwhile, because his scale of values is different, receives something that he desires more than what he has to surrender. Thus, both are reciprocally enriched.

There is something extremely civilized about the notion of reciprocity. Persons with different possessions and diverse value systems exchange voluntarily in fair and mutually satisfactory trades. Because there is no antagonism on either side, the motives to welsh on a deal or to resist the terms of reciprocity are inhibited by the prospects of continuing the profitable relationship. Diversity, trustworthiness, constructiveness, empathy, self-improvement—all these virtues have their rewards in reciprocal relationships.

The other technique of power is exhortation. Individuals act, not because they are coerced or tempted, but because they think their action is right, because they are persuaded by the "truth" of the matter that they have a duty to fulfill. They will sacrifice gladly, even kill or be killed, for a cause they believe in, even though, without that dedication, they would have resisted the tortures of the barbarian and the blandishments of the devil. Exhortation is a noble form of human control. There is something inspiring about persons working harmoniously, coordinated by their inner convictions, identifying with the well-being of the larger group, bound by words of honor, certain of purpose. When one thinks of the exhortative relationship between a leader and his followers, numerous virtues leap to mind—solidarity, community, selflessness, conscience, inspiration.

Of the three techniques of power—trade and "truth" and threat—only the last, the means we call coercion, seems on first acquaintance mean and barbaric. To be sure, reciprocity and exhortation are not unmitigated goods. In fact, if the powers of the purse or word were to be examined in detail, they would present as many paradoxical and troublesome aspects as does the power of the sword. Each promotes, in the extreme, highly questionable qualities— for example, selfishness (reciprocity) and conformity (exhortation).

But coercion seems of a different order. The human qualities which appear to be required for the practice of coercion seem incompatible with any civilized notion of the good. The moral realm of the person who must recurrently deal with the paradoxes of dispossession, detachment, face, and irrationality is turned topsy-turvy. Coercion creates a situation in which what is effective is at odds on every point with what Lord Acton called "the inflexible integrity of the moral code."[1] The gap between being a good man and a good practitioner of coercion appears unbridgeable. Even if the person in authority would prefer to act in conventionally fair and gentle ways, he can be sure that self-minimization, detachment, remorselessness, and ignorance will be practiced against him, necessitating his self-defense and more, if his desires to put his authority to good purpose are to avail. The tendency of coercive power to corrupt its wielder seems nearly unavoidable.

II

But are there ways to prevent persons in authority from becoming wicked? In his essay, "Politics as a Vocation," the German social theorist Max Weber (1864–1920) probed that question.[2] He framed the problem of coercive power and personality as follows: "He who lets himself in for politics, that is, for power and force as means, contracts with diabolical powers and for his action it is *not* true that good can follow only from good and evil only from evil, but that often the opposite is true. Anyone who fails to see this is, indeed, a political infant."[3] Or, as Weber said elsewhere in the essay, "Whosoever contracts with violent means for whatever ends—and every politician does," exposes himself to the "ethical paradoxes of coercion" and "endangers the 'salvation of the soul.'" Those paradoxes, summed up by Weber as the "irreconcilable conflict" between the "demon of politics" and the "god of love," produce consequences "for his inner self, to which he must helplessly submit, unless he perceives them." If political persons do not anticipate them, if those who undertake coercive power "do not fully realize what they take upon themselves," then the consequence is bitterness, banal self-acceptance, or flight.[4]

Weber constructed a model of "a *mature* man," one who would not "crumble" under the ethically paradoxical pressures which afflict the "professional politician." For purposes of reference, I shall call this construct the professional political model, using "political" in Weber's limited sense to refer to matters involving coercive threats and violence, and "professional" to indicate that the encounters with coercion occur so recurrently as to become routine. Weber's model of a professional politician had two characteristics which in combination reduced the chances of corruption. Weber called them the virtues of "passion and perspective."

1. *Passion: a capacity to "integrate" coercion into morals*. Weber insisted that the "genuine man," the professional political model, harmonized his standards of innocence and his willingness to "stand up arms-in-hand" for the general welfare.

He did not suffer disabling pangs of guilt about the harmful consequences which flowed from recourse to threats and violence. He reconciled the irreconcilable. He felt good about coercive power; he made the consequences of his recourse to threats consistent with those moral codes which regulated and gave value to the conduct of his total life; he knew that his involvement in violence was "principled." Having accomplished "the integration of violence into ethics," the professional political model achieved the "passion" necessary to endure the antagonisms aroused by politics, by coercive power. (The ethical basis for coercion lay in the "causes" served by it and not attainable without it.)

2. *Perspective: intellectual "objectivity."* But an ethic of "principled violence as a means" was not enough, since moral equanimity about coercive means could be achieved not by reconciling but by rejecting the ethical concerns of civilization. Then there would be no guilt because there would be no conscience. For Weber such fundamental moral rejection led to a "really radical Machiavellianism," in which the world was distorted to appear hateful, thereby justifying the violence being used against it. In a word, cynicism was possible.

The model professional politician, however, fought the temptation to distort by cultivating "objectivity." By this Weber meant "the knowledge of tragedy with which all action, but especially political action, is truly interwoven." The professional political model possessed a sense of the meaning of human conduct—a comprehension of the suffering of each inhabitant of the earth, a sensitivity to man's yearning for dignity, and, ultimately, "some kind of faith" that no individual is worthless. In short, the professional political model nurtured a persistent contact with reality. He developed a cognitive efficiency, a "perspective," a capacity for seeing rich implications of meager cues. He developed an inner understanding of the motives of men, a sense of life's rhythms of cause and effect, and a self-suspicion that drove him to find out for himself when what he had been told by frighteners and flatterers did not square with his inner "knowledge of tragedy."

The secret of avoiding corruption by coercive power—i.e., wickedness, banality, or cowardice—was to combine passion with perspective. Once again, to resort to Weber's language, the "good" politician was defined by an ability to forge together "warm passion and a cool sense of proportion . . . in one and the same soul."

III

What is the point of discussing Weber's professional political model in a book on policemen? It turns out to be of the utmost utility in solving the crucial methodological problem inherent in this study. I ask the reader's patience to indulge me in a short excursion into technical matters which may strike him or her as a bit pedantic. I think the point is important enough to take the time.

Recall that what I am trying to do is to explain the development of *good* policemen. The reader and I both know that to derive any value from such an inquiry, we must come up with a sensible definition of what we mean by "good." The problem is a sticky one. Any solution to it is both pivotal and also most deserving of critical scrutiny.

I urge that a reasonable definition of "good" will have to satisfy three criteria: (1) *Independence*—is the definition grounded in terms of a relatively broad range of social concerns and as free of police organizational bias as practical? (2) *Realism*—would a reasonable policeman agree that any assessment made of him in terms of the definition was taking into consideration many of the substantial constraints affecting him? and (3) *Timeliness*—assuming the definition was relatively independent and realistic, could a researcher gather evidence on how a policeman currently measured up to the definition?

In view of these three standards, let me explain why I flirted with, but ultimately rejected, five apparent solutions to the problem of defining the good policeman.

1. *Good is what a policeman's supervisors say it is.* Performance ratings by supervisors were made annually in the Laconia Police Department. Each supervisor reviewed them with both the rated officers and his own superior. The evaluations tended to be knowledgeable and were taken seriously by all parties. The merit of an inside, informed appraisal, however, was undermined by its lack of independence. In making ratings, policemen were writing their own report cards, not only in the sense that an officer's promising development reflected well on the supervisor's abilities but also, and more important, because the evaluations were based on the Laconia Police Department's criteria and not demonstrably on the larger society's.

Under ideal circumstances the administrator's definition of good police work might have been appropriate for the larger society. But it was not necessarily so. In any organization a tendency exists to displace the needs of its clientele for its own good, and the Laconia Police Department was unlikely to be an exception to this general rule. To know whether the organization's goals were congruent with the social welfare, it ultimately was necessary to anchor the evaluative standard outside the organization. For these two reasons, self-inflation and self-deception, I rejected supervisors' ratings as a measure of good police work.

2. *Good is measured by a policeman's performance in recruit school.* Recruit-school grades of the individual patrolmen were tempting because they were so precise in appearance and the recruit school was, to me, so sophisticated. The grades, however, lacked timeliness (as well as independence). Unless one presupposed that good trainees eventually made good police officers, classroom performance was either obsolete or irrelevant. In fact, one of the inquiries made in this research was whether good trainees turned into good police officers.

3. *Good is standing at one extreme or another on a scale created by the police organization for other reasons.* Certain secondary indicators had the merit of automatic and timely collection. Injuries on the job, days of absence from work,

censures and awards, and public complaints about police misconduct were recorded systematically in the department. The difficulty in using these statistics as gauges of merit was their empirical remoteness to the quality of police work. For example, both good and bad policemen could be injured. Injuries were often explicable in terms of beat assignment (and selection for a tough beat, at least arguably, was related to the quality of a police officer). Absences resulted as much from a good officer's having an unbearable supervisor as an unbearable officer's having a good supervisor. And so on. No matter what the secondary indicator, every policeman I met thought it too remote or too equivocal in the individual case to be a decisive measure of police work.

4. *Good is the number of arrests a policeman makes.* The Laconia Police Department required each policeman to summarize his accomplishments on weekly activity sheets. However, it limited the recordable activities to issuing tickets and making arrests. This indicator of activity obviously lacked comprehensiveness. Ticketing and arresting were not the quintessence of police work in most men's minds. The activity sheets omitted to record the family beefs handled well, the crime prevented, the information gathered, the stolen goods recovered, the friends made, the potential delinquents set straight, the commercial relationships ameliorated, the racial cleavages bridged, the hope infused, the help given. Such activities, which frequently animated the policeman, never were tabulated administratively. The activity sheets were, in a word, unrealistic.

5. *Good is a psychiatrist's finding of "not being abnormal."* Psychiatric examinations were made of Laconia policemen initially when they were recruited and followed up a year or two later. The reports of the psychiatrist resulting from this series of examinations overcame some of the liabilities of the first four definitions of a "good" policeman. They were more independent than the ratings of supervisors, more timely than recruit-school grades, more decisive than secondary indicators, and more comprehensive in assessing the whole policeman than the department's activity sheets.

A psychiatric evaluation was based upon a medical "model" of a "bad" man. A Laconia police officer was deemed "bad" if he approached the sick state of schizophrenia, "good" if he was not so sick. The "model" was sensitive to the individual's attitudes, not to his behavior. It searched out his understandings and emotions, and if they resembled those of the "sick" psychiatric model, then he was considered problematic and hence a problem cop. If he saw things with an "unrealism," if he evaluated matters too autonomously, without an adequate appreciation of the complex interrelationships of others around him, then his resemblance to the psychiatric model of the schizophrenic was marked, and he was characterized as abnormal, hence "bad."

Problems with the psychiatric model, however, occurred in two directions. Defining a bad policeman in terms of whether or not he was a sick man was at once too broad and too narrow. Too broad, because it presupposed that "bad" men would be "bad" policemen, that unhealthy attitudes would produce socially destructive behavior. Conceivably, however, "unrealistic" ideas and autonomous value systems might produce beneficial behavior. Martin Luther and Mahatma Gandhi might well have looked sick to the psychiatrists of their day. This is the problem of the attitude/behavior relationship, and we shall come back to it in the next section.

Even more important, the definition of a "bad" policeman was too narrow. By confining itself to detecting "bad" men, it might not identify a great many "bad" policemen. Arguably, the police job could be so demanding that more than a nonsick condition would be required of an individual if he were to do good police work over the long haul. An individual adequate to manage his own affairs might prove inadequate to govern the lives of others. A good man, as determined by civilized standards, able to cope well within the reciprocal and moral conventions of civilization, might be out of his depth in the uncushioned and frightening circumstances of the coercive world. Thus, application of the psychiatric model failed the test of realism.

IV

That is where the professional political model came in. By accepting Weber's assertions, I could identify a "good" policeman in terms of how his "passion and perspective" resembled the qualities of the professional politician. If he felt morally reconciled to using coercion and at the same time he reflected empathetically upon the condition of mankind, he measured up to being a professional, a good policeman.

To be sure, the professional political model was no less based on attitudes than the psychiatric model, which we have just rejected, had been. It did not solve the problem of the attitude/behavior relationship any better. Singling out "passion and perspective" as important assumed, but never proved, that the personal attitudes of a policeman and the actual results of his public actions were somehow positively related. I think there are both logical connections and a factual correlation between the two, but the reader should remain skeptical. Comparing the professional political model with the psychiatric model, however, I must repeat one point. They are both attitude models. The question is, which is the better attitude model for assessing policemen?

The professional political model had some virtues. It was independent of organizational bias, capable of using timely information, and, above all, realistic. Every policeman I asked insisted that the critical and recurrent part of his job occurred when he was the object of the threats of others and when he, in turn, had to influence people to do those things they were little inclined to do of their own accord—to desist from an antisocial act, to give humiliating information, to go to jail. At those times, he could give little in the way of positive inducements to compensate the citizens for their pains. He had only his authority, the threat to harm, to defend or assert himself. He had to extort cooperation because often he could not obtain it by any other means. In that a Laconia policeman often had to rely on his power to harm to prevent himself from being harmed by others, Weber's model of the professional politician seemed to fit the problem of measuring the man to the police job.

Moreover, a further advantage of the two-dimensional professional political model was that it could, theoretically at least, generate three types of nonprofessional policemen: (1) enforcers—police who had passion, but lacked perspective; (2) reciprocators—police who had perspective, but lacked passion; and (3) avoiders—police who lacked both passion and perspective.

V

I carefully analyzed the contents of the first interview of each police officer, young man and old-timer alike. I characterized his attitudes about the motives of mankind and the acceptability of coercion. I looked for clues particularly, but not exclusively, in his answers to these five questions.

1. Now let me get a feeling for what it is like being a police officer in Laconia today. Can you tell me about a particular incident which turned out to be one of the more difficult spots you've been in as a policeman in the field in Laconia?

2. Did anyone ever tell you how to deal with bullies—a pal or a minister or teacher or father or someone?

3. Let me shift gears a minute. I was reading a story of a first-year New York policeman named Gene Radano, and he told of an incident when he pulled over a car, an expensive-looking car, for running a stoplight. Radano said to the young guy who was driving, "I'm sorry, sir, but you just went through that red light. Can I have your license, please?"

The driver was pretty rude, but the policeman kept on being polite and said, "I'm sorry, but from where I was standing you had ample time to stop." The driver wouldn't turn over his license and told Officer Radano to go ahead and arrest him; his father who was a bigwig would have his job. A crowd gathered—about eight or nine people, and when the driver even refused to give his name, Radano decided to take him to the station to be booked. Well, it turned out the guy who was arrested had claustrophobia, a fear of closed places, but nobody knew about it, including him, and when he refused to cooperate even at the station, the lieutenant decided to lock him up and cool him off. When the kid saw the bars of the lockup, however, he began fighting hysterically. In the fight a couple of officers got hurt, but, of course, the young fellow got hurt worst of all, and he ended up in the hospital. Radano's reaction was to blame himself. "If only I'd spoken with more authority in the beginning. Maybe if I'd been stern, it might not have happened. Maybe my courtesy was interpreted by the man as a sign of weakness. Maybe that was what started the snowball rolling downhill." One thing that interested me was the way Officer Radano felt about himself. What do you think of the way he blamed himself for what happened?

4. I have heard policemen talk about each other, and invariably they seem to talk about how one group of men will do things differently from other groups of police officers. What are the different types of police officers which you see, and what are they like, and how do they differ?

5. Let me ask you a personal question: Have you ever had a tough problem in your police work where a decision of yours was right from one angle but wrong from another: say, from a personal or religious viewpoint it may have been right to do something, but from a police angle it was wrong, or the other way around: right from a police angle but not from a personal one.

Among the twenty-eight young policemen, ten (36%) appeared to be professionals. They resembled Jay Justice, whom we met in chapter 2, with his general notion about the dignity and tragedy of human nature and his ability to integrate the use of "proportionate" force into his principles of morality. Five (18%) could be characterized as enforcers. In their first interviews, at least, they resembled John Russo, whom we saw earlier as thoroughly confident in the efficacy of force but somewhat cynical about human society. Six (21%) could be typed as reciprocators, officers like Bob Ingersoll, who had moral conflicts over the necessity of coercion ("hated it," Ingersoll said) and were sympathetic with the citizenry. Finally, seven (25%) fell into the category of avoider. Bill Tubman, with his suspicion, cognitive bluntness toward the subtleties of human detail, and puzzlement about the ethics of force, illustrated this group of policemen.

A tabulation of the twenty-eight young officers would look like Table 1.

In the course of this book, you will become acquainted with most of these individual policemen. Before you do get to know them better, let me utter two essential reservations about the classifications.

First, some men did not readily fall into categories. Some officers were uncertain about their perspectives. Rockingham, for example, a giant, motorcycle-riding ex-military policeman with a musician's sensibilities, was still trying to make sense of a hazy world filled with human suffering, and he wavered almost day to day. Because he had not resolved this conflict in comprehension, his perspective was treated as if it were cynical. Some officers who usually felt good about exercising coercive power (and hence were labeled as having an integrated passion) still evinced considerable discomfort about coercion in some situations. And vice versa: some officers usually troubled by force could take coercive action without the slightest qualm when the conditions were right.

Second, these men were young and, by and large, developing. Some had just begun the domesticating experience of having their own families. Some were taking college courses and confronting systems of ideas in their sociology and history courses that allowed them to recompose their perspectives. Each was increasing in police skills, and each was encountering new aspects of the city and of humanity. Some were likely to encounter difficulties which were going to overwhelm and destroy their development as professionals. Others, like John Russo, thanks to maturation, reassignment, and accident, appeared to change their outlooks and moralities so perceptibly in the several years I observed them as to begin the transformation into professionals.

**Table 1 Classification According to
Professional Political Model**

	MORALITY OF COERCION	
	Integrated	**Conflicted**
Tragic perspective	*Professional*	*Reciprocator*
	Justice	Ingersoll
	Andros	Haig
	Bentham	Hooker
	Chacon	Hughes
	Douglas	Lancaster
	Patch	Wrangel
	Peel	
	Rolfe	
	Tennison	
	Wilkes	
Cynical perspective	*Enforcer*	*Avoider*
	Russo	Tubman
	Bacon	Booth
	Carpasso	Garfield
	Kane	Longstreet
	Kip	Nary
		Rockingham
		Thayer

This last point is the essential one to recall. Development and change were not easy, yet paradoxically were very likely. Development occurred daily; some was constructive, some destructive. One object of this book will be to identify a few of the crucial factors affecting this development.

VI

We have just begun the inquiry by measuring twenty-eight young policemen against the professional political model. Assuming for sake of argument that this typology is "correct" in some way, I want to emphasize that it is still nothing more than a starting point. We need to discover three things.

First, we have to know whether the typology is *useful*. Do policemen whose attitudes place them in these different categories behave differently? Specifically, did the professional policeman, the "good" cop, perform differently (and in some sense, respond more desirably) from the nonprofessional officer? This question, as we shall soon see, produces some very complex answers, and some readers may believe (as I do) that, sometimes, in some situations, the professional may behave *less* desirably than the nonprofessional policeman.

Second, there is the question of *explanation*. What is the dynamic process by which the recurrent use of coercive means produces the perspectives and passion to which the professional political model is sensitive? How does the resort to force build and destroy the attributes measured by Weber's scheme?

And third is the question of *engineering*. How can the corrupting effects of confronting recurrent coercive situations be modulated by human artifice so that desirable development will more probably occur and bad effect will be less likely? Those three questions—usefulness, explanation, and manipulation—constitute the final three parts of this book.

ENDNOTES

1. Lord John Emerich Edward Dalberg-Acton was born the year before Queen Victoria took the throne and died a year after her death. He believed passionately both in the inherent weakness and wickedness of mankind and in the uses of history to hold mankind accountable. For Acton, history recorded the deeds and misdeeds of individuals; it taught future generations about the evil consequences of doing evil; and it punished in perpetuity those men who had escaped punishment too long during their lives. Among the targets he attacked most devoutly were men of politics and men of the cloth; state and church alike, in his eyes, had done immeasurable disservice to mankind.

When Acton's friend Mandell Creighton concluded, in his *History of the Papacy during the Reformation,* that the late-medieval papacy had "been tolerant and benevolent," Acton disputed the point in a review submitted to the *English Historical Review,* of which Creighton was the editor. Creighton's kindly nature made him willing to publish the review despite its "ill-natured" quality, and in the correspondence between the two men concerning some revisions prior to its publication in 1887, Acton remarked, "Power tends to corrupt and absolute power corrupts absolutely." The tenor of Acton's argument is revealed in these excerpts: "I cannot accept your canon that we are to judge Pope and King unlike other men, with a favourable presumption that they did no wrong. . . . Historical responsibility has to make up for the want of legal responsibility . . . ; if what one hears is true, then Elizabeth asked the gaoler to murder Mary, and William III ordered his Scots minister to extirpate a clan. Here are the greater names coupled with the greater crimes. . . . I would hang them, higher than Haman; for reasons of quite obvious justice; still more, still higher, for the sake of historical science. . . . The inflexible integrity of the moral code is, to me, the secret of the authority, the dignity, the utility of history. If we may debase the currency for the sake of genius, or success, or rank, or reputation, we may debase it for the sake of a man's influence, of his religion, of his party, or the good cause which prospers by his credit and suffers by his disgrace. Then history ceases to be a science, an arbitration of controversy, a guide to the wanderer, the upholder of the moral standard which the powers of earth and religion itself tend constantly to depress. . . . Then history . . . serves where it ought to reign, and it serves the worst cause better than the purest."

2. Max Weber, "Politics as a Vocation," in *From Max Weber: Essays in Sociology,* ed. and trans. H. Gerth and C. Wright Mills (New York: Oxford University Press, 1946), pp. 77–128.

3. Ibid., p. 123.

4. Weber summed up these three harmful developments this way: "Will you be bitter or banausic? Will you simply and dully accept world and occupation? Or will the third and by no means the least frequent possibility be your lot: mystic flight from reality . . . ?" (ibid., p. 128.)

The Social Organization of Arrest*

DONALD J. BLACK

This article offers a set of descriptive materials on the social conditions under which policemen make arrests in routine encounters. At this level, it is a modest increment in the expanding literature on the law's empirical face. Scholarship on law-in-action has concentrated upon criminal law in general and the world of the police in particular.[1] Just what, beyond the hoarding of facts, these empirical studies will yield, however, is still unclear. Perhaps a degree of planned change in the criminal justice system will follow, be it in legal doctrine or in legal administration. In any event, evaluation certainly appears to be the purpose, and reform the expected outcome, of much empirical research. This article pursues a different sort of yield from its empirical study: a sociological theory of law.[2] The analysis is self-consciously inattentive to policy reform or evaluation of the police; it is intentionally bloodless in tone. It examines arrest in order to infer patterns relevant to an understanding of all instances of legal control.

Source: Donald J. Black (1971). "The Social Organization of Arrest," *Stanford Law Review,* 23:1087–1092; 1044–1111. © 1971 by the Board of Trustees of the Leland Stanford Junior University. Reprinted with permission.

★The article's findings derive from a larger research project under the direction of Professor Albert J. Reiss, Jr., Department of Sociology and Institute of Social Science, Yale University. The project *was coordinated* at the Center for Research on Social Organization, Department of Sociology, University of Michigan. It was supported by Grant Award 006; Office of Law Enforcement Assistance, U.S. Department of Justice, under the Law Enforcement Assistance Act of 1965, and by grants from the National Science Foundation and the Russell Sage Foundation.

The empirical analysis queries how a number of circumstances affect the probability of arrest. The factors considered are: the suspect's race, the legal seriousness of the alleged crime, the evidence available in the field setting, the complainant's preference for police action, the social relationship between the complainant and suspect, the suspect's degree of deference toward the police, and the manner in which the police come to handle an incident, whether in response to a citizen's request or through their own initiative. The inquiry seeks to discover general principles according to which policemen routinely use or withhold their power to arrest, and thus to reveal a part of the social organization of arrest.[3]

The article begins with a skeletal discussion of the field method. Next follows a brief ethnography of routine police work designed to place arrest within its mundane context. The findings on arrest are then presented, first for encounters involving both a citizen complainant and a suspect, and second for police encounters with lone suspects. The article finally speculates about the implications of the empirical findings at the level of a general theory of legal control, the focus shifting from a sociology of the police to a sociology of law.

I. FIELD METHOD

The data were collected during the summer of 1966 by systematic observation of police-citizen transactions in Boston, Chicago, and Washington, D.C.[4] Thirty six observers—persons with law, social science, and police administration backgrounds—recorded observations of encounters between uniformed patrolmen and citizens. The observers' training and supervision was, for all practical purposes, identical in the three cities. Observers accompanied patrolmen on all work shifts on all days of the week for seven weeks in each city. Proportionately more of our manhours were devoted to times when police activity is comparatively high, namely evening shifts, and particularly weekend evenings. Hence, to a degree the sample overrepresents the kinds of social disruptions that arise more on evenings and weekends than at other times. The police precincts chosen as observation sites in each city were selected to maximize scrutiny of lower socio-economic, high crime rate, racially homogeneous residential areas. Two precincts were used in both Boston and Chicago, and four precincts were used in Washington, D.C. The Washington, D.C. precincts, however, were more racially integrated than were those in Boston and Chicago.

Observers recorded the data in "incident booklets," forms structurally similar to interview schedules. One booklet was used for each incident. A field situation involving police action was classified as an "incident" if it was brought to the officer's attention by the police radio system, or by a citizen on the street or in the police station, or if the officer himself noticed a situation and decided that it required police attention. Also included as incidents were a handful of situations in which the police noticed themselves but which they chose to ignore.

The observers did not fill out incident booklets in the presence of policemen. In fact, the line officers were told that the research was not concerned with police behavior but only with citizen behavior toward the police and the kinds of problems citizens make for the police.

The observers recorded a total of 5,713 incidents, but the base for present analysis is only a little more than 5 percent of the total. This attrition results primarily from the general absence of opportunities for arrest in patrol work, where most of the incidents involve non-criminal situations or criminal situations for which there is no suspect. Traffic encounters also were excluded, even though technically any traffic violation presents an opportunity for arrest. Other cases were eliminated because they involved factors that could invisibly distort or otherwise confuse the analysis. The encounters excluded were those initiated by citizens who walked into a police station to ask for help (6 percent of the total) or who flagged down the police on the street (5 percent). These kinds of encounters involve peculiar situational features warranting separate treatment, though even that would be difficult, given their statistically negligible number. For similar reasons encounters involving participants of mixed race and mixed social-class status[5] were eliminated. Finally, the sample of encounters excludes suspects under 18 years of age—legal juveniles in most states—and suspects of white-collar status.[6] Thus, it investigates arrest patterns in police encounters with predominantly blue-collar adult suspects.

II. ROUTINE POLICE WORK

In some respects, selecting arrest as a subject of study implicitly misrepresents routine police work. Too commonly, the routine is equated with the exercise of the arrest power, not only by members of the general public but by lawyers and even many policemen as well. In fact, the daily round of the patrol officer infrequently involves arrest[7] or even encounters with a criminal suspect. The most cursory observation of the policeman on the job overturns the imagery of a man who makes his living parceling citizens into jail.

Modern police departments are geared to respond to citizen calls for service; the great majority of incidents the police handle arise when a citizen telephones the police and the dispatcher sends a patrol car to deal with the situation. The officer becomes implicated in a wide range of human troubles, most not of his own choosing, and many of which have little or nothing to do with criminal law enforcement. He transports people to the hospital, writes reports of auto accidents, and arbitrates and mediates between disputants—neighbors, husbands and wives, landlords and tenants, and businessmen and customers. He takes missing-person reports, directs traffic, controls crowds at fires, writes dogbite reports, and identifies abandoned autos. He removes safety hazards from the streets, and occasionally scoops up a dead animal. Policemen disdain this kind of work, but they do it every day. Such incidents rarely result in arrest; they nevertheless comprise nearly half of the incidents uniformed patrolmen encounter in situations initiated by phone calls from citizens.[8] Policemen also spend much of their time with "juvenile trouble," a police category typically pertaining to distinctively youthful disturbances of adult peace—noisy groups of teenagers on a street corner, ball-playing in the street, trespassing or playing in deserted buildings or construction sites, and rock-throwing. These situations, too, rarely result in arrest. Some officers view handling juvenile trouble as work they do in the service of neighborhood grouches. The same may be said of ticketing parking violations in answer to citizen complaints. All these chores necessitate much unexciting paperwork.

Somewhat less than half of the encounters arising from a citizen phone call have to do with crime—a felony or a misdemeanor other than juvenile trouble. Yet even criminal incidents are so constituted situationally as to preclude arrest in the majority of cases, because no suspect is present when the police arrive at the scene. In 77 percent of the felony situations and in 51 percent of the misdemeanor situations the only major citizen participant is a complainant.[9] In a handful of other cases the only citizen present is an informant or bystander. When no suspect is available in the field setting, the typical official outcome is a crime report, the basic document from which official crime statistics are constructed and the operational prerequisite of further investigation by the detective division.

The minority of citizen-initiated crime encounters where a suspect is present when the police arrive is the appropriate base for a study of arrest. In the great majority of these suspect encounters a citizen complainant also takes part in the situational interaction, so any study of routine arrest must consider the complainant's role as well as those of the police officer and the suspect.[10]

Through their own discretionary authority, policemen occasionally initiate encounters that may be called *proactive* police work, as opposed to the *reactive,* citizen-initiated work that consumes the greater part of the average patrol officer's day.[11] On an evening shift (traditionally 4 p.m. to midnight) a typical work-load for a patrol car is 6 radio-dispatched encounters and one proactive encounter. The ratio of proactive encounters varies enormously by shift, day of week, patrol beat or territory, and number of cars on duty. An extremely busy weekend night could involve 20 dispatches to a single car. Under these rushed conditions the officers might not initiate any encounters on their own. At another time in another area a patrol car might receive no dispatches, but the officers might initiate as many as 8 or 10 encounters on the street. During the observation study only 13 percent of incidents came to police attention without the assistance of citizens.[12] Still, most officers as well as citizens probably think of proactive policing as the form that epitomizes the police function.

The police-initiated encounter is a bold confrontation between state and citizen. Hardly ever does a citizen complainant take part in a proactive field encounter and then only if a policeman were to discover an incident of personal victimization or if a complainant were to step subsequent to the officer's initial encounter with a suspect. Moreover, the array of incidents policemen handle—their operational jurisdiction—is quite different when they have the discretion to select situations for attention compared to what it is when that discretion is lodged in citizens. In reactive police work they are servants of the public, with one consequence being that the social troubles they oversee often have little if anything to do with criminal law. Arrest is usually a situational impossibility. In proactive policing the officer is more a public guardian and the operational jurisdiction is a police choice; the only limits are in law and in departmental policy. In proactive work, arrest is totally a matter of the officer's own making. Yet the reality of proactive police work has an ironic quality about it. The organization of crime in time and space deprives policemen on free patrol of legally serious arrests. Most felonies occur in off-street settings and must be detected by citizens. Even those that occur in a visible public place usually escape the policemen's ken. When the police have an opportunity to initiate an encounter, the occasion is more likely than not a traffic violation. Traffic violations comprise the majority of proactive encounters, and most of the remainder concern minor "disturbances of the peace." [13] In short, where the police role is most starkly aggressive in form, the substance is drably trivial, and legally trivial incidents provide practically all of the grist for arrest in proactive police operations.

Perhaps a study of arrest flatters the legal significance of the everyday police encounter. Still, even though arrest situations are uncommon in routine policing, invocation of the criminal process accounts for more formal-legal cases, more court trials and sanctions, more public controversies and conflicts than any other mechanism in the legal system. As a major occasion of legal control, then, arrest cries out for empirical study. [14]

V. GENERALIZATIONS

This section restates the major findings of this study in the form of empirical generalizations which should provide a manageable profile of police behavior in routine situations where arrest is a possibility. When appropriate, inferences are drawn from these materials to more abstract proponents at the level of a general theory of legal control. Arrest patterns may reveal broad principles according to which legal policy is defined, legal resources mobilized, and dispositions made. [15]

A. Mobilization

Most arrest situations arise through citizen rather than police initiative. In this sense, the criminal law is invoked in a manner not unlike that of private-law systems that are mobilized through a reactive process, depending upon the enterprise of citizen claimants in pursuit of their own interests. In criminal law as in other areas of public law, although the state has formal, proactive authority to bring legal actions, the average criminal matter is the product of a citizen complaint.

One implication of this pattern is that most criminal cases pass through a moral filter in the citizen population before the state assumes its enforcement role. A major portion of the responsibility for criminal-law enforcement is kept out of police hands. Much like courts in the realm of private law, the police operate as moral servants of the citizenry. A further implication of this pattern of reactive policing is that the deterrence function of the criminal process, to an important degree, depends upon citizen willingness to mobilize the criminal law, just as the deterring function of private law depends so much on citizen plaintiffs.[16] Sanctions cannot deter illegal behavior if the law lies dormant because of an inefficient mobilization process.[17] In this sense all legal systems rely to a great extent upon private citizens.

B. Complainants

Arrest practices sharply reflect the preferences of citizen complainants, particularly when the desire for leniency and also, though less frequently, when the complainant demands arrest. The police are an instrument of the complainant, then, in two ways: Generally they handle what the complainant wants them to handle and they handle the matter in the way the complainant prescribes.

Often students of the police comment that a community has the kind of police it wants, as if the community outlines the police function by some sort of *de facto* legislative process.[18] That view is vague, if not mistaken. Instead, the police serve an atomized mass of complainants far more than they serve an organized community. The greater part of the police workload is case-by-case, isolated contacts between individual policemen and individual complainants. In this sense the police serve a phantom master who dwells throughout the population, who is everywhere but nowhere at once. Because of this fact, the police are at once an easy yet elusive target for criticism. Their field work evades planned change, but as shifts occur in the desires of the atomized citizenry who call and direct the police, changes ripple into policemen's routine behavior.

The pattern of police compliance with complainants gives police work a radically democratic character. The result is not, however, uniform standards of justice, since the moral standards of complainants doubtlessly vary to some extent across the population. Indeed, by complying with complainants the police in effect perpetuate the moral diversity they encounter in the citizen mass.[19] In this respect again, a public-law system bears similarity to systems of private law.[20] Both types seem organized, visibly and invisibly, so as to give priority to the demands of their dispersed citizens. Whoever may prescribe the law and however the law is applied, many sovereigns call the law to action.[21] Public-law systems are peculiar in that their formal organization allows them to initiate and pursue cases without complainants as sponsors. Still, the reality of public-law systems such as the police belies their formal appearance. The citizenry continually undermines uniformity in public- as well as private-law enforcement. Perhaps democratic organization invariably jeopardizes uniformity in the application of legal controls.[22]

C. Leniency

The police are lenient in their routine arrest practices; they use their arrest power less often than the law would allow. Legal leniency, however, is hardly peculiar to the police. Especially in the private-law sector[23] and also in other areas of public law,[24] the official process for redress of grievances is invoked less often than illegality is detected. Citizens and public officials display reluctance to wield legal power in immediate response to illegality, and a sociology of law must treat as problematic the fact that legal cases arise at all.

D. Evidence

Evidence is an important factor in arrest. The stronger the evidence in the field situation, the more likely is an arrest. When the police themselves witness a criminal offense they are more likely to arrest the suspect than when they only hear about the offense from a third party. Rarely do the police confront persons as suspects without some evidence; even more rarely are arrests unsupported by evidence. The importance of situational evidence hardly constitutes a major advance in knowledge. Evidence has a role in every legal process. It is the definition of evidence, not whether evidence is required, that differs across legal system. It should be emphasized that even when the evidence against a suspect is very strong, the police frequently take action short of arrest. Evidence alone, then, is a necessary but not a sufficient basis for predicting invocation of the law.

E. Seriousness

The probability of arrest is higher in legally serious crime situations than in those of a relatively minor nature. This finding certainly is not unexpected, but it has theoretical significance. The police levy arrest as a sanction to correspond with the defined seriousness of the criminal event in much the same fashion as legislators and judges allocate punishments. The formal legal conception of arrest contrasts sharply with this practice by holding that arrest follows upon detection of any criminal act without distinguishing among levels of legal seriousness. Assuming the offender population is aware that arrest represents legislation and adjudication by police officers, arrest practices should contribute to deterrence of serious crime, for the perpetrator whose act is detected risks a greater likelihood of arrest as well as more severe punishment. The higher the risk of arrest, once the suspect confronts the police, may help to offset the low probability of detection for some of the more serious crimes.[25]

F. Intimacy

The greater the relational distance between a complainant and a suspect, the greater is the likelihood of arrest. When a complainant demands the arrest of a suspect the police are most apt to comply if the adversaries are strangers. Arrest is less likely if they are friends, neighbors, or acquaintances, and it is least likely if they are family members. Policeman also write official crime reports according to the same differential.[26] Relational distance likewise appears to be a major factor in the probability of litigation in contract disputes[27] and other private-law contexts.[28] One may generalize that in all legal affairs relational distance between the adversaries affects the probability of formal litigation. If the generalization is true, it teaches that legal control may have comparatively little to do with the maintenance of order between and among inmates.

Yet the findings on relational distance in police arrest practices may merely reflect the fact that legal control operates only when sublegal control is unavailable.[29] The greater the relational distance, the less is the likelihood that sublegal mechanisms of control will operate. This proposition even seems a useful principle for understanding the increasing salience of legal control in social evolution.[30] Over time the drift of history delivers proportionately more and more strangers who need the law to hold them together and apart. Law seems to bespeak an absence of community, and law grows ever more prominent as the dissolution of community proceeds.[31]

G. Disrespect

The probability of arrest increases when a suspect is disrespectful toward the police. The same pattern appears in youth officer behavior,[32] patrol officer encounters with juveniles,[33] and in the use of illegal violence by the police.[34] Even disrespectful complainants receive a penalty of sorts from the police, as their complaints are less likely to receive official recognition.[35] In form, disrespect in a police encounter is much the same as "contempt" in a courtroom hearing. It is a rebellion against the processing system. Unlike the judge, however, the policeman has no special legal weapons in his arsenal for dealing with citizens who refuse to defer to his authority at a verbal or otherwise symbolic level. Perhaps as the legal system further differentiates, a crime of "contempt of police" will emerge. From a radically behavioral standpoint, indeed, this crime has already emerged; the question is when it will be formalized in the written law.

All legal control systems, not only the police and the judiciary, defend their own authority with energy and dispatch. To question or assault the legitimacy of a legal control process is to invite legal invocation, a sanction, or a more serious sanction, whatever is at issue in a given confrontation. Law seems to lash out at every revolt against its own integrity. Accordingly, it might be useful to consider disrespect toward a policeman to be a minor form of civil disorder, or revolution the highest form of disrespect.

H. Discrimination

No evidence exists to show that the police discriminate on the basis of race. The police arrest blacks at a comparatively high rate, but the difference between the races appears to result primarily from the greater rate at which blacks show disrespect for the police. The behavioral difference thus lies within the citizen participants, not the police.[36] This finding conflicts with some ideological conceptions of police work, but it is supported by the findings of several studies based upon direct observation of the police.[37] These findings should be taken as a caveat that in general improper or illegal behavior toward blacks does not in itself constitute evidence of discrimination against blacks. A finding of discrimination or of nondiscrimination requires a comparative analysis of behavior toward each race with other variables such as level of respect held constant. No study of citizen opinions or perceptions[38] or of official statistics[39] can hold these variables constant.

In closing this Section it is important to note that the findings on racial discrimination by the police should not remotely suggest that law is oblivious to social rank. On the contrary, broader patterns in the form and substance of legal control seem at any one time to reflect and to perpetuate existing systems of social stratification. That the degradation of arrest is reserved primarily for the kinds of illegality committed by lower status citizens exemplifies this broader tendency of the law in action.

VI. CONCLUDING REMARKS

A major commitment of this article is to dislodge the discussion from its grounding in empirical findings and to raise the degree of abstraction to the level of general theory. Statements at this level ignore the boundaries and distinctions that ordinarily contain and constrain generalization about law as a social phenomenon. The various subsystems of law—criminal law, torts, contracts, constitutional law, family law, property law, criminal procedure, administrative law—are assumed to contain common elements. As if this aim were too faint-hearted, a general theory of legal control also seeks to discover patterns present in several functional dimensions of law: prescription, mobilization, and disposition; or respectively, the articulation of legal policy, the engagement of legal cases by legal organizations, and the situational resolution of legal disputes. This sort of sociology of law shares with jurisprudence the inclusiveness of its subject matter. Each discipline acts upon a longing for a universal understanding of law. For each, the past shares the relevance of the present, and other legal systems illustrate our own. Unlike jurisprudence, however, sociology of law abjures problems of a normative character; unlike sociology of law, jurisprudence bypasses the ordeal of concrete description.

A closing note should state what the article has not done. Arrest might be examined from a number of other perspectives that have their own vocabulary suited to their own special kind of discourse. For example, arrest may usefully be conceived as one stage in an elaborate processing network, an assembly line of inputs and outputs. This technocratic metaphor has been popular in recent studies of the criminal justice system. Another perspective might see every arrest as a political event. When and how the arrest power is used says much about the nature of a political system and the quality of life within it. Then, too, arrest is part of a job. It is a role performance of a bureaucratic functionary.

Police work may be contemplated as it arises from its rich occupational subculture with standards and values that policemen share and enforce among their peers. And every arrest is enveloped by the police bureaucracy. Not surprisingly, therefore, the arrest practices of individual officers are under some degree of surveillance from their superiors as well as their peers. Finally, a study of arrest can inform and benefit from the sociology of face-to-face interaction. The police encounter is a small group with its own morphology, its own dynamics. What happens in an encounter may have less to do with crime and law than with the demands of situational order, with social etiquette or the pressures of group size or spatial configuration. An arrest may be the only means available to a policeman bent on restoring order to field situation, yet other times it is the surest way to undermine order by making a situation disintegrate.

Some encouragement may be taken from the development of social science to the point where a subject such as arrest can occasion so many diverse perspectives. Diversity of this degree, nevertheless, casts a film of arbitrariness over whatever theoretical framework is chosen. Although the many perspectives available to a study of arrest surely mirror the empirical nature of arrest itself, its theoretical identity is precarious and unstable. Here it is sanction and justice; there, input, coercion, expectation, job, criterion, or gesture. Any single theoretical view of arrest is inevitably incomplete.

ENDNOTES

1. *See generally* E. Schur, Law and Society (1968); Skolnick, *The Sociology of Law in America: Overview and Trends,* in Law and Society 4 (1965) (supplement to 13 Social Problems (1965)); Bordua & Reiss, *Law Enforcement,* in The Uses of Sociology 275 (1967); Manning, *Observing the Police,* in Observing Deviance (J. Douglas ed., forthcoming). The empirical literature is so abundant and is expanding so rapidly that these published bibliographic discussions are invariably inadequate.

2. It should be noted that the article's approach to legal life differs quite radically from the approach of Philip Selznick, one of the most influential American sociologists of law. Selznick's sociology of law attempts to follow the path of natural law; my approach follows the general direction of legal positivism. In Lon Fuller's language, Selznick is willing to tolerate a confusion of the *is* and *ought,* while I am not. L. Fuller, The Law in Quest of Itself 5 (1940). *See* P. Selznick, Law, Soci-

ety, and Industrial Justice (1969); Selznick, *The Sociology of Law,* 9 International Encyclopedia of the Social Sciences 50 (D.L. Sills ed., 1968); Selznick, *Sociology and Natural Law,* 6 Natural L.F. 84 (1961).

3. As used in this article, the broad concept "social organization" refers to the supraindividual principles and mechanisms according to which social events come into being, are maintained and arranged, change, and go out of existence. Put another way, social organization refers to the descriptive grammar of social events.

4. At this writing, the data are over four years old. However, there has been little reform in routine patrol work since 1966. This is in part because of the police work in question—everyday police contact with citizens—is not as amenable to planned change as other forms of police work, such as crowd or riot control, traffic regulation, or vice enforcement. Moreover, the data have value even if they no longer describe contemporary conduct,

since they remain useful for developing a theory of law as a behavior system. A general theory of law has no time limits. Indeed, how fine it would be if we possessed more empirical data from legal life past.

5. This means that encounters involving a complainant and suspect of different races were excluded. Similarly, the sample would not include the arrest of a black man with a white wife. However, it does not mean the exclusion of encounters where the policeman and suspect were not of the same race.

6. Because field observers occasionally had difficulty in judging the age or social class of a citizen, they were told to use a "don't know" category whenever they felt the danger of misclassification. Two broad categories of social class, blue-collar and white-collar, were employed. Since the precincts sampled were predominantly lower class, the observers labeled the vast majority of the citizen participants as blue-collar. In fact, not enough white-collar cases were available for separate analysis. The small number of adults of ambiguous social class were combined with the blue-collar cases into a sample of "predominantly blue-collar" suspects. The observers probably were reasonably accurate in classifying suspects because the police frequently interviewed suspects about their age and occupation.

7. In this article, "arrest" refers only to transportation of a suspect to a police station. It does not include the application of restraint in field settings, and it does not require formal booking of a suspect with a crime. See W. LaFave, Arrest: The Decision to Take a Suspect into Custody 4 (1965).

8. D. Black, Police Encounters and Social Organization: An Observation Study, 51–57, Dec. 15, 1968 (unpublished dissertation in Department of Sociology, University of Michigan). See also Cumming, Cumming & Edell, Policeman as Philosopher, Guide and Friend, 12 Social Problems 276 (1965).

9. D. Black, supra note 8 at 94.

10. In fact, of all the felony cases the police handle in response to a citizen request

by telephone, including cases where only a complainant, informant, or bystander is present in the situation, a mere 3% involve a police transaction with a lone suspect. D. Black, supra note 8, at 94.

11. The concepts "reactive" and "proactive" derive from the origins of individual action, the former referring to actions originating in the environment, the latter to those originating within the actor. See Murray, Toward a Classification of Interactions, in Toward a General Theory of Action 434 (1967).

12. This proportion is based upon the total sample of 5,713 incidents.

13. Much proactive patrol work involves a drunken or disorderly person. Typically, however, arrest occurs in these cases only when the citizen is uncooperative; ordinarily the policeman begins his encounter by giving an order such as "Move on," "Take off," or "Take it easy." Arrest is an outcome of interaction rather than a simple and direct response of an officer to what he observes as an official witness.

14. Earlier observational studies have neglected patterns of arrest in the everyday work of uniformed patrolmen. Emphasis has instead been placed upon detective work, vice enforcement, policing of juveniles, and other comparatively marginal aspects of police control. See J. Skolnick, Justice Without Trial (1966) (patterns of arrest in vice enforcement); Bittner, The Police on Skid-Row: A Study of Peace-Keeping, 32 Am. Soc. Rev. 699 (1967); Black & Reiss, Police Control of Juveniles, 35 Am. Soc. Rev. 63 (1970); Piliavin & Briar, Police Encounters with Juveniles, 70 Am. J. Soc. 206 (1964). Several observational studies emphasizing other dimensions of police work also are directly relevant. See L. Tiffany, D. McIntyre, & D. Rotenberg, Detection of Crime (1967); Reiss & Black, Interrogation and the Criminal Process, 374 Annals of the Am. Academy of Pol. & Soc. Sci. 47 (1967); Project, Interrogations in New Haven: The Impact of Miranda, 76 Yale L.J. 1519 (1967). There also have been a number of studies based upon official arrest statistics. See N. Goldman, The Differential Selection of Juvenile Offenders

FOR COURT APPEARANCE (1963); J. WILSON VARIETIES OF POLICE BEHAVIOR (1968); Green, *Race, Social Status, and Criminal Arrest,* 35 AM. SOC. REV. 476 (1970); Terry, *The Screening of Juvenile Offenders,* 58 J. CRIM. L.C. & P.S. 173 (1967). For a more speculative discussion *see* Goldstein, *Police Discretion Not to Invoke the Criminal Process: Low-Visibility Decisions in the Administration of Justice,* 69 YALE L.J. 543 (1960). *See generally* W. LAFAVE, *supra* note 7.

15. These three functional foci of legal control—prescription, mobilization, and disposition—correspond roughly to the legislative, executive, and judicial dimensions of government, though they are useful in the analysis of subsystems of legal control as well as total systems. For instance, the police can be regarded as the major mobilization subsystem of the criminal justice system. Yet the police subsystem itself can be approached as a total system involving prescription, mobilization, and disposition subsystems. *Cf.* H. LASSWELL, THE DECISION PROCESS 2 (1956).

16. Contemporary literature on deterrence is devoted primarily to the role of sanctions in criminal law. *See,* e.g., Andenaes, *The General Preventive Effects of Punishment,* 114 U. PA. L. REV. 949 (1966). *But see* R. VON JHERING, THE STRUGGLE FOR LAW (1879).

17. Roscoe Pound concludes that the contingent nature of legal mobilization is one of the major obstacles to the effectiveness of law as a social engineering device. *See* Pound, *The Limits of Effective Legal Action,* 27 INT'L J. ETHICS 150 (1917). *See also* H. JONES, THE EFFICACY OF LAW 21–26 (1969); Bohannan, *The Differing Realms of the Law,* in THE ETHNOGRAPHY OF LAW 33 (1965) (supplement to 67 AM. ANTHROPOLOGIST 33 (1965)).

18. *See,* e.g., P. SLATER, THE PURSUIT OF LONELINESS: AMERICAN CULTURE AT THE BREAKING POINT 49 (1970).

19. This generalization does not apply to proactive police operations such as vice control or street harassment, which seldom involve a citizen complainant. By definition, street harassment is the selective and abrasive attention directed at people who are, at best, marginally liable to arrest—for example, a police command to "move on" to a group of unconventional youths. Proactive policing may involve an attack on particular moral subcultures. *Compare* J. CLEBERT, THE GYPSIES 87–119 (1963) *with* Brown, *The Condemnation and Persecution of Hippies,* TRANS-ACTION, Sept. 1969 at 33, *and* W. HAGAN, INDIAN POLICE AND JUDGES (1966).

20. *See* Pashukanis, *The General Theory of Law and Marxism* in SOVIET LEGAL PHILOSOPHY III (H. Babb transl. 1951).

21. This is true historically as well; legal systems usually have made the citizen complainant the *sine qua non* of legal mobilization, except under circumstances posing a direct threat to political order. A well-known example was the Roman legal process, where even extreme forms of personal violence required the initiative of a complainant before government sanctions were imposed. *See generally* A. LINTOTT, VIOLENCE IN REPUBLICAN ROME (1968). A theory of legal control should treat as problematic the capacity and willingness of government to initiate cases and sanction violators in the absence of an aggrieved citizen demanding justice. *See generally* S. RANULF, MORAL INDIGNATION AND MIDDLE CLASS PSYCHOLOGY: A SOCIOLOGICAL STUDY (1938).

22. The norm of universalism reflected in systems of public law in advanced societies is a norm of impersonalism: The police are expected to enforce the law impersonally. But by giving complainants a strong role in the determination of outcomes, the police personalize the criminal law. This pattern allows fellow family members and friends to mobilize the police to handle their disputes with little danger that the police will impose standards foreign to their relationships. At the level of disputes between strangers, however, the same pattern of police compliance with complaints can, given moral diversity, result in a form of discriminatory enforcement. A law enforcement process that takes no account of the degree of intimacy between complainant and suspect may also upset the peculiar balance of close social relationships. *See* Kawashima, *Dispute Resolution in Contemporary Japan,* in LAW IN JAPAN: THE

LEGAL ORDER IN A CHANGING SOCIETY 41 (A. von Mehren ed. 1964).

23. *See, e.g.,* Macaulay, *Non-Contractual Relations in Business: A Preliminary Study,* 28 AM. SOC. REV. 55 (1963).

24. *See, e.g.,* M. Mileski, Policing Slum Landlords: An Observation Study of Administrative Control, June 14, 1971 (unpublished dissertation in Department of Sociology, Yale University).

25. *See* Black, *Production of Crime Rates,* 35 AM. SOC. REV. 733, 735 (1970) (remarks on detection differentials in police work).

26. Black, *supra* note 29, at 740. Jerome Hall hypothesizes that relational distance influences the probability of criminal prosecution. J. HALL, THEFT, LAW AND SOCIETY 318 (2d ed. 1952).

27. Macaulay, *supra* note 27, at 56.

28. For example, in Japan disputes that arise across rather than within communities are more likely to result in litigation. *See* Kawashima, *supra* note 26, at 45. In American chinatowns disputes that arise between Chinese and non-Chinese are far more likely to result in litigation than disputes between Chinese. *See* Grace, *Justice, Chinese Style,* CASE & COM., Jan.-Feb., 1970, at 50. The same is true of disputes between gypsies and non-gypsies as compared to disputes between gypsies. *See* J. CLEBERT, *supra* note 23, at 90. Likewise, in the United States in the first half of the 19th century, crimes committed between Indians generally were left to the tribes. *See* F. PRUCHA, AMERICAN INDIAN POLICY IN THE FORMATIVE YEARS: THE INDIAN TRADE AND INTERCOURSE ACTS 188–212 (1962). In medieval England the same sort of pattern obtained in the legal condition of the Jews. Ordinary English rules applied to legal dealings between Jews and the King and between Jews and Christians, but disputes between Jew and Jew were heard in Jewish tribunals and decided under Jewish law. *See* F. POLLOCK & F. MAITLAND, THE HISTORY OF ENGLISH LAW 468–475 (2d ed. 1898).

29. *See* L. PEATTIE, THE VIEW FROM THE BARRIO 54–62 (1968) (for a stark illustration of this pattern). *See generally* R. POUND, SOCIAL CONTROL THROUGH LAW 18–25 (1942); S. VAN DER SPRENKEL, LEGAL INSTITUTIONS IN MANCHU CHINA: A SOCIOLOGICAL ANALYSIS (1962); Cohen, *Chinese Mediation on the Eve of Modernization,* 54 CALIF. L. REV. 1201 (1966); Nader, *An Analysis of Zapotec Law Cases,* 3 ETHNOLOGY 404 (1964); Nader & Metzger, *Conflict Resolution in Two Mexican Communities,* 65 AM. ANTHROPOLOGIST 584 (1963); Schwartz, *Social Factors in the Development of Legal Control: A Case Study of Two Israeli Settlements,* 63 YALE L.J. 471 (1954); notes 26, 30–31 *supra.*

30. It is at this level that Pound posits his thesis concerning the priority of sublegal control. R. POUND, *supra* note 33, at 33. *See also* Fuller, *Two Principles of Human Association,* II NOMOS 3 (1969); Selznick, *Legal Institutions and Social Controls,* 17 VAND. L. REV. 79 (1963).

31. *See* F. TONNIES, COMMUNITY AND SOCIETY 202 (C. Loomis transl. 1957).

32. Piliavin & Briar, *supra* note 14, at 210.

33. Black & Reiss, *Police Control of Juveniles, supra* note 14, at 74–75.

34. P. CHEVIGNY, POLICE POWER: POLICE ABUSES IN NEW YORK CITY 51–83 (1969); Reiss, *Police Brutality—Answers to Key Questions,* TRANS-ACTION, July-Aug., 1968, at 18; Westley, *Violence and the Police,* 59 AM. J. SOC. 34 (1954).

35. Black, *supra* note 29, at 742–44.

36. Of course, "discrimination" can be defined to include any *de facto* unequal treatment, regardless of its causes. *See* L. MAYHEW, LAW AND EQUAL OPPORTUNITY 59–60 (1968). The evidence in the article simply indicates that blacks are treated differently not because they are blacks, but because they manifest other behavioral patterns, such as disrespect for the police, more frequently than whites. The question of why blacks disproportionately show disrespect for the police cannot be addressed with the observational data. We could speculate, for example, that in anticipation of harsh treatment blacks often behave disrespectfully toward

the police, thereby setting in motion a pattern that confirms their expectations.

Despite the article's finding of nondiscrimination the police officers observed did reveal considerable prejudice in their attitude toward blacks. *See generally* Black & Reiss, *Patterns of Behavior in Police and Citizen Transactions,* in 2 President's Comission on Law Enforcement and Administration of Justice, Studies in Crime and Law Enforcement in Major Metropolitan Areas 132–139. *See also* Deutscher, *Words and Deeds: Social Science and Social Policy,* 13 Social Problems 235 (1966).

37. *See generally* W. LaFave, *supra* note 7; J. Skolnick, *supra* note 14, at 83–88;

L. Tiffany, D. McIntyre, & D. Rotenberg, *supra* note 14; Piliavin & Briar, *supra* note 14 (despite innuendos to the contrary); Project, *supra* note 14, at 1645; n.9. These studies do not report evidence of discrimination or fail altogether to mention race as an analytically important variable.

38. *E.g.,* Werthman & Piliavin, *Gang Members and the Police,* in The Police: Six Sociological Essays 56 (D. Bordua ed. 1967).

39. *See* N. Goldman, *supra* note 14, at 45; J. Wilson, *supra* note 14, at 113; Green, *supra* note 14, at 481.

The Asshole

JOHN VAN MAANEN

"I guess what our job really boils down to is not letting the assholes take over the city. Now I'm not talking about your regular crooks . . . they're bound to wind up in the joint anyway. What I'm talking about are those shitheads out to prove they can push everybody around. Those are the assholes we gotta deal with and take care of on patrol. . . . They're the ones that make it tough on the decent people out there. You take the majority of what we do and its [sic] nothing more than asshole control."

A VETERAN PATROLMAN[1]

I. POLICE TYPIFICATIONS

The asshole—creep, bigmouth, bastard, animal, mope, rough, jerkoff, clown, scumbag, wiseguy, phony, idiot, shithead, bum, fool, or any of a number of

From *Policing: A View From the Street,* P.K. Manning and J. Van Maanen (eds.). Santa Monica: Goodyear, 1978. Reprinted with permission of the author.

anatomical, oral, or incestuous terms—is a part of every policeman's world.[2] Yet the grounds upon which such a figure stands have never been examined systematically. The purpose of this essay is to display the interactional origins and consequences of the label asshole as it is used by policemen, in particular, patrolmen, going about their everyday tasks. I will argue that assholes represent a distinct but familiar type of person to the police and represent, therefore, a part of their commonsense wisdom as to the kinds of people that populate their working environment. From this standpoint, assholes are analytic types with whom the police regularly deal. More importantly, however, I will also argue that the label arises from a set of situated conditions largely unrelated to the institutional mandate of the police (i.e., to protect life and property, arrest law violators, preserve the peace, etc.) but arises in response to some occupational and personal concerns shared by virtually all policemen.

According to most knowledgeable observers, nothing characterizes policing in America more than the widespread belief on the part of the police themselves that they are primarily law enforcers—perpetually engaged in a struggle with those who would disobey, disrupt, do harm, agitate, or otherwise upset the just order of the regime. And, that as policemen, they and they alone are the most capable of sensing right from wrong; determining who is and who is not respectable; and, most critically, deciding what is to be done about it (if anything). Such heroic self-perceptions reflecting moral superiority have been noted by numerous social scientists concerned with the study of the police. Indeed, several detailed, insightful, and thoroughly accurate mappings of the police perspective exist.[3] For instance, learned discussions denote the various "outgroups" perceived by the police (e.g., Harris, 1973; Bayley and Mendelsohn, 1969); or the "symbolic assailants" which threaten the personal security of the police (e.g., Skolnick, 1966; Neiderhoffer, 1967; Rubenstein, 1973); or the "suspicious characters" recognized by the police via incongruous (nonordinary) appearances (e.g., Sacks, 1972; Black, 1968). These reports provide the background against which the pervasive police tropism to order the world into the "for us" and "against us" camps can most clearly be seen.

Yet these studies have glossed over certain unique but together commonsensical properties of the police situation with the attendant consequence of reifying the police position that the world is in fact divided into two camps. Other than noting the great disdain and disgust held by many police officers toward certain predefined segments of the population they presumably are to serve, these studies fail to fully describe and explain the range and meaning attached to the various labels used by the police themselves to affix individual responsibility for particular actions occurring within their normal workaday world. Furthermore, previous studies do not provide much analytic aid when determining how the various typifications carried by the police are recognized as relevant and hence utilized as guides for action by a police officer in a particular situation. In short, if police typifications are seen to have origins as well as consequences, the popular distinction between "suspicious" or "threatening" and the almost mythologized "normal" or "respectable" is much too simple. It ignores not only the immediate context in which street interactions take place, but it also disregards the critical signs read by the police within the interaction itself which signify to them both the moral integrity of the person with whom they are dealing and the appropriate recipe they should follow as the interaction proceeds.[4] Therefore, any distinction of the "types" of people with whom the police deal must include an explicit consideration of the ways in which the various "types" are both immediately and conditionally identified by the police. Only in this fashion is it possible to accurately depict the labels the police construct to define, explain, and take action when going about their routine and nonroutine tasks.

To begin this analysis, consider the following typology which suggests that the police tend to view their occupational world as comprised exhaustively of three types of citizens (Van Maanen, 1974). These ideal types are: (1) "suspicious persons"—those whom the police have reason to believe may have committed a serious offense; (2) "assholes"—those who do not accept the police definition of the situation; and (3) "know nothings"—those who are not either of the first two categories but are not police and therefore, according to the police, cannot know what the police are about.

This everyday typification scheme provides a clue to the expectations, thoughts, feelings, and behaviors of the police. For example, "suspicious persons" are recognized on the basis of their appearance in public surroundings. Such an appearance is seen as a furtive, nonroutine, *de trop,* or, to use Sacks's (1972) nicely turned phrase, "dramatically torturous." Crucially, such persons, when they provide the police reason to stop and interrogate them, are treated normally in a brisk, though thoroughly professional, manner. It is not their moral worth or identity which is at issue, but rather it is a possible illegal action in their immediate or not-so-immediate past which is in question. From the patrolman's point of view, he is most interested in insuring that formal procedural issues are observed. Hence the personal production of a professional police performance is called for and is presented—at least initially.[5] On the other end of the continuum reside the "know nothings," the "average" citizens, who most generally come under police scrutiny only via their request for service. The "know nothing" may be the injured or wronged party or the seeker of banal information and as such is treated with a certain amount of deference and due respect by the patrolman.

"Assholes," by way of contrast, are stigmatized by the police and treated harshly on the basis of their failure to meet police expectations arising from the *interaction situation itself.* Of course, street interaction may quickly transform suspicious persons into know nothings and know nothings into assholes, or any combination thereof. But it is the asshole category which is most imbued with moral meaning for the patrolman—establishing for him a stained or flawed identity to attribute to the citizen upon which he can justify his sometimes malevolent acts. Consequently, the asshole may well be the recipient of what the police call "street justice"—a physical attack designed to rectify what police take as personal insult. Assholes are most vulnerable to street justice, since they, as their title implies, are not granted status as worthy human beings. Their actions are viewed by the police as stupid or senseless and their feelings as incomprehensible (if they can even be said to have feelings). Indeed, as I will show, the police consistently deny an asshole a rationale or ideology to support their actions, insisting that the behavior of an asshole is understandable only as a sudden or lifelong character aberration. On the other hand, suspicious persons are less likely candidates for street justice because, in the majority of cases, their guilt may still be in question, or, if their guilt has been in fact established, their actions are likely to seem at least comprehensible and purposeful to the police (i.e., a man steals because he needs money; a man shoots his wife because she "two-timed" him; etc.). Also, there are incentives for the suspicious person to cooperate (at least nominally) when subject to police attention. The suspicious person may well be the most cooperative of all the people with whom the police deal on a face-to-face basis. This is, in part, because he is most desirous of presenting a normal appearance (unafraid, unruffled, and with nothing to hide), and, in part, because if he is in fact caught he does not want to add further difficulty to his already difficult position. Finally, know nothings are the least likely candidates for street justice since they represent the so-called client system and are therefore those persons whom the police are most interested in impressing through a polished, efficient, and courteous performance.

At this point, I should note that the above ideal types are anything but precise and absolute. One purpose of this paper is to make at least one of these categories more explicit. But since I am dealing primarily with interior, subjective meanings negotiated in public with those whom the police interact, such typifications will always be subject to severe situational, temporal, and individually idiosyncratic restriction. Hence, an asshole in one context may be a know nothing in another, and vice versa. In other words, I am not arguing in this essay that a general moral order is shared by all policemen as their personalized but homomorphic view of the world. Indeed, the moral order subscribed to by police is complex, multiple, and continually shifts back and forth between that which is individual and that which is collective. What I will argue, however, is that particular situational conditions (i.e., provocations) predispose most policemen toward certain perceptions of people which lead to the application of what can be shown to be rule-governed police actions. My objective, then, is simply to begin teasing out the underlying structure of police thought and to denote the features of what might be called the secondary reality of police work.

The remainder of this essay is divided into four sections. The next section, "Patrol Work," describes very briefly certain understandings shared by street-level patrolmen as to what is involved in their work. In a sense, these understandings are akin to behavioral rules that can be seen to mobilize police action; hence they represent the grounds upon which the figure of the asshole is recognized. The following section, "Street Justice," deals with the characteristic processes involved in discovering, distinguishing, and treating the asshole. Some conclusions revolving around the relationship between the police and the asshole are suggested in the next section. And, finally, a few of the broad implications that flow from this analysis are outlined in the last section.

II. PATROL WORK

Policing city streets entails what Hughes (1958) refers to as a "bundle of tasks." Some of these tasks are mundane; many of them are routine; and a few of them are dangerous. Indeed, patrol work defies a general job description since it includes an almost infinite set of activities—dogcatching, first-aid, assisting elderly citizens, breaking up family fights, finding lost children, pursuing a fleeing felon, directing traffic, and so forth. Yet, as in other lines of endeavor, patrolmen develop certain insider notions about their work that may or may not reflect what outsiders believe their work to be. Such notions are of course attached firmly to the various experientially based meanings the police learn to regularly ascribe to persons, places, and things—the validity of which is established, sustained, and continually reaffirmed through everyday activity. Because these meanings are, to some degree, shared by patrolmen going about similar tasks, their collective representation can be detailed and linked to certain typical practices engaged in on the street by the police. Thus, to understand the police perspective on, and treatment of, the asshole, it is necessary also to understand the manner in which the policeman conceives of his work. Below is a very short summary of certain interrelated assumptions and beliefs that patrolmen tend to develop regarding the nature of their job.

Real Police Work

Many observers have noted the pervasive police tendency to narrowly constrict their perceived task to be primarily—and to the exclusion of other alternatives—law enforcement. As Skolnick and Woodworth (1967:129) suggest evocatively, "when a policeman can engage in real police work—act out the symbolic rites of search, chase and capture—his self-image is affirmed and morale enhanced." Yet, ironically, opportunities to enact this sequence are few and far between. In fact, estimates of the time police spend actually in real police work while on patrol vary from 0 percent (as in the case of the quiet country policeman for whom a street encounter with a bona fide "criminal" would be a spectacular exception to his daily tour of duty) to about 10 or 15 percent (as in the case of the busy urban patrolman who works a seamy cityside district in which the presence of pimps, dealers, cons, and burglars, among others, are the everyday rule). Nonetheless, most of the policeman's time is spent performing rather dry, monotonous, and relatively mundane activities of a service nature—the proverbial clerk in a patrol car routinely cruising his district and awaiting dispatched calls (see Cain, 1971; Reiss, 1971; Webster, 1970; and Cummings, Cummings and Edell, 1965, for further discussion on how the police, spend their time).

Within these boundaries, notions of real police work develop to provide at least a modicum of satisfaction to the police. To a patrolman, *real police work* involves the use of certain skills and special abilities he believes he possesses by virtue of his unique experience and training. Furthermore, such a perspective results in minimizing the importance of other activities he is often asked regularly to perform. In fact, an ethos of "stay-low-and-avoid-trouble-unless-real-police-work-is-called-for" permeates police organizations (Van Maanen, 1973, 1974, 1975). Only tasks involving criminal apprehension are attributed symbolic importance. For the most part, other tasks, if they cannot be avoided, are performed (barring interruption) with ceremonial dispatch and disinterest.

Territoriality

A central feature of policing at the street level is the striking autonomy maintained (and guarded jealously) by patrolmen working the beat. All patrol work is conducted by solo officers or partnerships (within a squad to whom they are linked) responsible for a given plot of territory. Over time, they come to know, in the most familiar and penetrating manner, virtually every passageway—whether alley, street, or seldom-used path—located in their sector. From such knowledge of this social stage comes the corresponding evaluations of what particular conditions are to be considered good or bad, safe or unsafe, troubled or calm, usual or unusual, and so on. Of course, these evaluations are also linked to temporal properties associated with the public use of a patrolman's area of responsibility. As Rubenstein (1973) suggests, the territorial perspective carried by patrolmen establishes the basic normative standard for the proper use of place. And those perceived by patrolmen to be beyond the pale regarding their activities in space and time are very likely to warrant police attention.

Maintaining the Edge

Charged with enforcing ambiguous generalized statutes and operating from an autonomous, largely isolated position within the city, it is not surprising that police have internalized a standard of conduct which dictates that they must control and regulate all situations in which they find themselves. At one level, police feel they have the right to initiate, terminate, or otherwise direct all encounters with members of the public. Yet such perceptions penetrate more broadly into the social scheme of things, for police feel furthermore that the public order is a product of their ability to exercise control. The absence of trouble on their beat becomes, therefore, a personalized objective providing intimate feedback as to one's worth as a patrolman. Activity which may threaten the perceived order becomes intolerable, for it signifies to the patrolman that his advantage over the conduct of others (his "edge") is in question. It is a source of embarrassment in front of a public audience, and sometimes it is considered a disgrace to the police uniform if it is viewed by one's peers or departmental superiors. Clearly, such activity cannot be allowed to persist, for it may indicate both to a patrolman's colleagues and to his superiors that the officer no longer cares for his job and has, consequently, lost the all-important respect of those he polices (endangering, it is thought, other policemen who might work the same district). Hence, to "maintain one's edge" is a key concept vis-à-vis the "how to" of police work. And, as all policemen know, to let down the facade (for they do recognize the contrived nature of the front) is to invite disrespect, chaos, and crime.

The Moral Mandate

In light of the above three features of the police frame, it should be clear that police are both representatives of the moral order and a part of it. They are thus committed ("because it is right") to maintain their collective face as protectorates of the right and respectable against the wrong and the not-so-respectable. Situations in which this face is challenged—regardless of origin—are likely to be responded to in unequivocal terms. For example, Cain (1971) writes that when the authority of an officer is questioned by a member of the nonpolice public, the officer has three broad responses available to him. He may (1) physically attack the offender; (2) swallow his pride and ignore the offender; or (3) manufacture a false excuse for the arrest of the offender. What this suggests is a highly personalized view on the part of the police as to their moral position and responsibility, one in which an attempt on the part of the citizen to disregard the wishes of a policeman may be viewed by the police as a profaning of the social and legal system itself. Such an act can also be seen to provoke moral and private indignation on the part of the officer as an individual, thus providing him with another *de rigueur* excuse to locate an appropriate remedy. Since the police personally believe that they are capable of making correct decisions regarding the culpability of an involved party, justice is likely, in the case of an offense to the moral sensibilities of a police officer, to be enacted quickly, parsimoniously, and self-righteously— whether it be the relatively trivial swift kick in the pants or the penultimate tragedy involved in the taking of a life. Thus, the moral mandate felt by the police to be their just right at the societal level is translated and transformed into occupational and personal terms and provides both the justification and legitimation for specific acts of street justice.

This truncated picture of the occupational frame involved in the doing of police work provides the rubric upon which we now can examine the making of an asshole. As one would expect, assholes are not afforded the protection of the more structured relationships police maintain with other of their categories of persons—the suspicious and the know nothings. Rather, they fall outside this fragile shelter, for their actions are seen as "senseless," so "aimless" and "irrational" that recognizable and acceptable human motives are difficult for the police to discover (i.e., from the patrolmen's perspective, there are not legitimate reasons to distrust, disagree with, make trouble for, or certainly hate the police). In this sense, it is precisely the "pointlessness" of an individual's behavior that makes him an asshole and subjects him to the police version of street justice.

III. STREET JUSTICE

Policeman to motorist stopped for speeding:
  "May I see your driver's license, please?"
Motorist:
  "Why the hell are you picking on me and not somewhere else looking for some real criminals?"
Policeman:
  "Cause you're an asshole, that's why . . . but I didn't know that until you opened your mouth."

The above sea story represents the peculiar reality with which patrolmen believe they must contend. The world is in part (and, to policemen, a large part) populated by individuals to whom an explanation for police behavior cannot be made, for, as the police say, "assholes don't listen to reason." The purpose of this section is to explore the commonplace and commonsense manner in which the tag asshole arises, sticks, and guides police action during a street encounter. This stigmatization process is divided into three stages which, while analytically distinct, are highly interactive and apt to occur in the real world of policing almost simultaneously. For convenience only, then, these phases are labeled *affront, clarification,* and *remedy.*

Throughout this discussion it should be remembered that the asshole is not necessarily a suspected law violator—although the two often overlap, thus providing double trouble, so to speak, for the labeled. Importantly, the police view of the asshole as deviant is a product of the immediate transaction between the two and not a product of an act preceding the transaction. This is not to say, however, that certain classes in society—for example, the young, the black, the militant, the homosexual—are not "fixed" by the police as a sort of permanent asshole grouping. Indeed, they are. Yet such bounded *a priori* categories can do policemen little good—except perhaps when dealing with the racial or bohemian obvious—for such stereotypes are frequently misleading and dysfunctional (e.g., the "hippie" who is a detective's prized informant; the black dressed in a purple jumpsuit who happens to be a mayor's top aide; the sign-carrying protester who is an undercover FBI agent). And, even in cases in which *a priori character* judgments are a part of the decision to stop an individual, the asshole label, if it is to play a determining role in the encounter, must arise anew. That is to say, if the asshole distinction is to have a *concrete* as opposed to *abstract* meaning, it must in some manner be tied fundamentally and irresolutely to observable social action occurring in the presence of the labeling officer.

Certainly, a policeman's past experience with an individual or with a recognizable group will influence his street behavior. For example, a rookie soon discovers (as a direct consequence of his initiation into a department) that blacks, students, Mexicans, reporters, lawyers, welfare workers, researchers, prostitutes, and gang members are not to be trusted, are unpredictable, and are usually "out-to-get-the-police." He may even sort these "outsiders" into various categories indicative of the risk he believes they present to him or the implied contrast they have with his own life-style and beliefs. Yet, without question, these categories will never be exhaustive—although the absolute size of what patrolmen call their "shit lists" may grow over the years. Consequently, to understand the police interpretation and meaning of the term "asshole" we must look directly into the field situations in which it originates.

Affront: Challenge

When a police officer approaches a civilian to issue a traffic citation or to inquire as to the whys and wherefores of one's presence or simply to pass the time of day, he directly brings the power of the state to bear on the situation and hence makes vulnerable to disgrace, embarrassment, and insult that power. Since the officer at the street level symbolizes the presence of the Leviathan in the everyday lives of the citizenry, such interactions take on dramatic properties far different from ordinary citizen-to-citizen transactions (Manning, 1974a; Silver, 1967). In a very real sense, the patrolman-to-citizen exchanges are moral contests in which the authority of the state is either confirmed, denied, or left in doubt. To the patrolman, such contests are not to be taken lightly, for the authority of the state is also his personal authority, and is, of necessity, a matter of some concern to him. To deny or raise doubt about his legitimacy is to shake the very ground upon which his self-image and corresponding views are built.

An affront, as it is used here, is a challenge to the policeman's authority, control, and definition of the immediate situation. As seen by the police, an affront is simply a response on the part of the other which indicates to them that their position and authority in the interaction are not being taken seriously. It may occur with or without intent. Whether it is the vocal student who claims to "know his rights," the stumbling drunk who says he has had "only two beers," or the lady of the evening who believes she is being questioned only because she is wearing "sexy clothes," the police will respond in particular ways to those who challenge or question their motive or right to intervene in situations that they believe demand police intervention. Clearly, overt and covert challenges to police authority will not go unnoticed. In fact, they can be seen to push the encounter to a new level wherein any further slight to an officer, however subtle, provides sufficient evidence to a patrolman that he may indeed be dealing with a certifiable asshole and that the situation is in need of rapid clarification. From this standpoint, an affront can be seen, therefore, as disrupting the smooth flow of the police performance. The argumentative motorist, the pugnacious drunk, the sometimes ludicrous behavior of combatants in a "family beef" all interfere, and hence make more difficult, the police task. Of course, some officers relish such encounters. In this sense, ironically, the asshole gives status to the police rather than takes it away. However, since the label is itself a moral charge (and it need not be made salient or verbally expressed), it is open theoretically for rebuttal and evidence may or may not be forthcoming which will substantiate or contradict the charge. Such evidence is gathered in the next analytic stage.

Clarification: Confrontation

Based upon a perceived affront, the patrolman must then attempt to determine precisely the kind of person with whom he is engaged. It is no longer an idle matter to him in which his private conceptions of people can be kept private as he goes about his business. But the patrolman is now in a position wherein he may discover that his taken-for-granted authority on the street is not exactly taken for granted by another. Two commonsensical issues are critical at this point in an encounter. *First,* the officer must determine whether or not the individual under question could have, under the present circumstances, acted in an alternative fashion. To wit, did the perceived affront occur by coercion or accident through no fault of the person? Did the person even know he was dealing with a police officer? Was he acting with a gun at his head? And so on. *Second,* and equally important, given that the person could have acted differently, the officer must determine whether or not the individual was aware of the consequences that might follow his action. In other words, was the action frivolous, naive, unserious, and not meant to offend? Did the person know that his actions were likely to be interpreted offensively by the police? The answers to these two questions provide patrolmen with material (or lack of it) to construct and sustain an asshole definition. Let us examine in some depth these questions, for they raise the very issue of personal responsibility which is at the nexus of the asshole definition.[6]

McHugh (1969) argues persuasively that the social construction of deviant categories is a matter of elimination which proceeds logically through a series of negotiated offers and responses designed to fix responsibility for a perceived deviant act (i.e., a deviant act requires a charge before it can be said to have happened). Police follow a similar paradigm when filling, emptying, or otherwise attending to their person categories. Again, the first item to be determined in this process is the issue of whether or not the person had alternative means available to him of which he could reasonably be expected to be aware. For example, the speeding motorist who, when pulled to the side of the road, could be excused for his abusive language if it were discovered by the officer that the motorist's wife was at the same time in the back seat giving birth to a child. Similarly, juveniles "hanging out" on a public street corner at certain times of the day may be sometimes overlooked if the police feel that "those kids don't have anyplace to go." On the other hand, if it can be determined that there is no unavoidable reason behind the affronting action, the individual risks being labeled an asshole. The drunken and remorseless driver, the wife who harangues the police officer for mistreating her husband after she herself requested police service to break up a family fight, or the often-warned teenager who makes a nuisance of himself by flagrantly parading in public after curfew are all persons whom the police believe could have and should have acted differently. Their acts were not inevitable, and it could be expected that they had available to them conventional alternatives.

Given that there are no compelling deterministic accounts readily available to the patrolman to excuse a particular affront, the officer must still make a judgment about the offender's motive. In other words, as the second issue listed above suggests, the policeman must decide whether or not the person knows what he is doing. Could the person be expected to know of the consequences which follow an affront to an officer of the law? Indeed, does the person even realize that what he is doing is likely to provoke police action? Could this particular person be expected to know better? All are questions related to the establishment of a motive for action. For example, the stylized and ceremonial upright third finger when attached to the hand of a thirty-year-old man is taken by the police very differently from the same gesture attached to the hand of a four-year-old child. Loud and raucous behavior in some parts of a city may be ignored if the police feel "the people there don't know any better." Or the claim that one is Jesus Christ resurrected and is out to do battle with the wages of sin may indicate to the police that they are either in the presence of a "dope-crazed radical hippie freak" or a "soft-brained harmless mental case," depending, perhaps, on the offender's age. If the person is young, for instance, responsibility is likely to be individualized—"it is his fault"; however, if the person is old, responsibility is likely to be institutionalized—"he can't help it, he's a nut."

Summarily, the police have available to them two principles of clarification. One concerns the means available to a person guilty of an affront, and the other concerns the purposes behind the affront itself. If the affront is viewed as unavoidable or unintended, the person is unlikely to be subjected to shabby or harsh treatment at the hands of the police. The asshole, however, is one who is viewed as culpable and blameworthy for his affronting action, and, as the next section details, he will be dealt with by the police in ways they feel appropriate.

Remedy: Solution

The above portrait of the clarification principles utilized by police in labeling assholes suggests that certain typical police responses can be displayed by a simple fourfold typology. Figure 1 depicts the relationship between the police officer's assessment of responsibility for the affront and denotes, within each cell, the typical police response given the various possible assessments.

Cell A represents the subject case of this essay since it involves a flagrant (inexcusable) disregard for the sentiments of the police. To the police, those falling into this category are unmistakably assholes and are therefore prominent candidates to be the recipients of street justice—the aim of which is to punish or castigate the individual for a moral transgression. Persons placed in this category are also the most likely to be placed under questionable arrest. This is not so because of the original intent of the encounter (which often, by itself, is trivial) but rather because of the serious extralegal means utilized by the police to enforce their particular view of the situation upon the recalcitrant asshole—"hamming-up" or "thumping" (beating).[7] And, as Reiss (1971) suggests, the use of force is not a philosophical question to the police but rather one of who, where, when, and how much.

The use of such means requires of course that the officer manufacture post facto a legally defensible account of his action in order to, in the vernacular of the day, "cover his ass."[8] Such accounts in legalese most often take the form of

	YES	**NO**
COULD THE PERSON ACT DIFFERENTLY UNDER THE CIRCUMSTANCES?	YES A Castigate	B Teach
	NO C Ignore	D Isolate

FIGURE 1. Does the Person Know What He Is Doing?

"disorderly conduct," "assaulting a police officer," "the use of loud and abusive language in the presence of women and children," "disturbing the peace," or the almost legendary—due to its frequent use—"resisting arrest." The asshole from this position is subject to a police enactment of double jeopardy—justice without trial in the streets and justice, perhaps with trial, in the courts. And regardless of the outcome in the latter case, there is usually only one loser. I should emphasize, however, that I am not saying the behavior of the asshole may not be brutish, nasty, and itself thoroughly vicious. I am simply suggesting that behavior violating extralegal moral codes used by police to order their interactions—whether it be inconsiderate, barbarous, or otherwise—will be responded to in what police believe to be appropriate ways.

Cell B of Figure 1 also represents serious affront to police integrity, and it too may be an affront which calls for an extra-legal response. An illustration provided by the remarks of a patrolman is useful in this context:

> Those goddamn kids got to learn sooner or later that we won't take a lot of shit around Cardoza (a local college campus). Next time I see one of those punks waving a Viet Cong flag I'm gonna negotiate the little bastard back into an alley and kick his rosy red ass so hard he ain't gonna carry nothing for awhile. Those kids gotta be made to see that they can't get away with this type of thing.

Whether or not such a prediction was actually carried out does not matter, for the quotation itself indicates that "teaching" occupies a particularly prominent position in the police repertoire of possible responses. Thus, the uncooperative and surly motorist finds his sobriety rudely questioned, or the smug and haughty college student discovers himself stretched over the hood of a patrol car and the target of a mortifying and brusque body search. The object of such degradation ceremonies is simply to reassert police control and demonstrate to the citizen that his behavior is considered inappropriate. Teaching techniques are numerous, with threat, ridicule, and harassment among the more widely practiced. Other examples are readily available, such as the morally-toned lectures meted out to those who would attempt to bribe, lie, or otherwise worm their way out of what a policeman sees to be a legitimate traffic citation, the traditional—but vanishing—"kick in the ass" administered to a youngster caught stealing an apple or cutting school. The intent in all these cases is clear. The person must be taught a lesson. And whether the teaching occurs in public or in the back of an alley, the person must be shown the error of his ways.

He has acted perhaps out of ignorance, but nevertheless the police feel they must demonstrate that they will not casually overlook the action. However, I should note that the person in this category will remain an asshole in the eyes of the police until he has apparently learned his lesson to the satisfaction of the officers on the scene. Here a display of remorse is no doubt crucial to the police.[9]

Cell C represents the case in which the police are likely to excuse the affront due to the extenuating circumstances surrounding the affront. When it is clear to the police that there are indeed mitigating conditions, their response is to ignore the error—to pretend, as it were, that such an affront never happened. For example, it is understandable to the police that the victim of a mugging may be somewhat abusive toward them when they interrogate him just after the crime (although there is a fine line to be drawn here). Similarly, if a teenage male vigorously defends the chaste and virtuous intentions of he and his girl friend while questioned by the police in a concealed and cozy corner of a public park, it is understood by the police that the boy has few other acceptable alternative lines available. The police response is typically to adopt a somewhat bemused tolerance policy toward actions which under different circumstances may have produced the orb and scepter.

Finally, cell D in Figure 1 concerns the case of an affront which police take to lie beyond the responsibility of the actor. While such action cannot normally be allowed to continue, the moral indignation felt by police is tempered by the understanding that the person is not aware nor could be easily made aware of the rule-breaking nature of his actions. The police response is to isolate the offender, not to punish him. Thus, the "mental case" is shipped to the county hospital for observation and treatment; the "foul-mouthed child" is returned to those responsible for his behavior; the out-of-state tourist prowling an area close to his hotel but frequented by prostitutes is informed of his "oversight" and told in unmistakable terms to vacate the territory. It is important to note that police feel justified in using only enough force or coercive power to seal off the offender from public (and, by implication; their own) view. To use more force would be considered unreasonable.

It has been my purpose here to suggest that much of what the general public might see as capricous, random, or unnecessary behavior on the part of the police is, in fact, governed by certain rather pervasive interpretive rules which lie close enough to the surface such that they can be made visible. Certain police actions, following the model presented above, can be seen, then, to be at least logical if not legal. Furthermore, much of the power of these rules stems from their tacit or taken-for-granted basis. Indeed, were the rules to be questioned, the game could not continue. However, while these rules are applied in a like fashion by all police in a given interactional episode, the specific situated behavior of a citizen that is taken as a sign which leads to isolating, ignoring, teaching, or castigating a given individual is no doubt quite different across patrolmen. Here, the police game continues as it does because, in part, the asshole label swallows up and hides whatever individual differences exist across patrolmen. Thus, language neatly solves the problem of misunderstanding that would arise among the police were the rules to be articulated and standards sought as to how they should be applied.

IV. SOME CONCLUSIONS

It is possible, of course, to see the preceding ritualized sequence as an isolated and rarely indulged propensity of the police. However, in this section, I will argue that indeed such a sequence and the corresponding identification and treatment of the asshole is intimately related to the police production and represents an aspect of policing that is near the core of the patrolman's definition of his task. In essence, the existence of an asshole demonstrates and confirms the police view of the importance and worth of themselves both as individuals and as members of a necessary occupation. However, several other, somewhat more practical and everyday features of police work insure the ominous presence of the asshole in the police world.

First, the labeling of individuals as assholes can be seen as a technique (although invisible to most) useful to patrolmen in providing distance between themselves and their segmented audiences—to be liked by the people in the street is, in the defensive rhetoric of patrolmen, a sign of a bad cop. By profaning and degrading the actions of another, social distance can be established and maintained—a guarantee, so to speak, that the other will not come uncomfortably close. Thus, the asshole simplifies and orders the policeman's world and continually verifies his classification scheme regarding those who are "like him" and those who are "unlike him." Relatedly the labeling serves also as an immediate call to action, denoting a consensually approved (by the police culture) means for remedying "out-of-kilter" situations.

Second, the label not only describes and prescribes but it also explains and makes meaningful the statements and actions of others. In fact, an entire set of action expectations (i.e., "they are out to make the police look bad") can be ascribed as motives to the asshole. In this sense, the police function in street interaction is not unlike that of a psychiatrist diagnosing a patient. Both explain perceived deviancy in terms of a characterological genesis. Hence, the label implies that a different, inappropriate, and strange motivational scheme is used by the "type of person" known as an asshole. In this manner, an act is made understandable by stripping away whatever meaning might be attributed to it by the actor. Thus, to make sense of the act is to assume that it does not make sense—that it is stupid, irrational, wrong, deranged, or dangerous. Any other assumption would be too threatening.

Third, the labeling process must be viewed as serving an occupational purpose. I suggested previously that the urban policeman is primarily a keeper of the peace yet he defines his job in terms of law enforcement. Furthermore, as others have noted, many patrolmen try to convert peacekeeping situations to those of law enforcement (e.g., Bittner, 1967, 1970; Wilson, 1969; Piliavin and Briar, 1964). Since real police work is seldom available, marginally legitimate arrests of assholes provide a patrolman excitement and the opportunity to engage one's valued skills. Perhaps the police cliché, "a good beat is full of deadbeats," reflects structural support for the asshole-labeling phenomena.

Fourth, the discovery and subsequent action taken when the police encounter the asshole provides an expressive outlet—almost ceremonial in its predictability—for much of the frustration policing engenders. To the patrolman, one particular asshole symbolizes all those that remain "out there" untouched, untaught, and unpunished. Such emotional outbursts provide, therefore, a reaffirmation of the moral repugnance of the asshole. Whether the officer responds by placing the handcuffs on the person's wrists such that they cut off circulation (and not incidentally cause intense, almost excruciating pain) or pushes a destitute soul through a shop window, these actions release some of the pent-up energies stored up over a period in which small but cumulative indignities are suffered by the police at the hands of the community elites, the courts, the politicians, the uncaught crooks, the press, and numerous others. The asshole stands, then, as a ready ersatz for those whom the police will never—short of a miracle—be in a position to directly encounter and confront.

Finally, the asshole can be seen as a sort of reified other, representing all those persons who would question, limit, or otherwise attempt to control the police. From this standpoint, knowing that there are assholes at large serves perhaps to rally and solidify police organizations around at least one common function. Thus, the police are, to a limited degree, unified by their disdain of those who would question their activities. Perhaps one could say that the police represent what Simmel (1950) referred to as an "invisible church" in which the faithful are fused together through their common relation to an outside phenomenon.

Consequently, assholes are not simply obscure and fanciful figments of the bedeviled imagination of the police. On the contrary, they define to a surprising degree what the police are about. And while the internal satisfactions and rewards involved in "slamming around" an asshole may seem esoteric if not loathsome to the outsider, to the patrolman who makes his living on the city streets it is not.

V. POSTSCRIPT

The foregoing description and explanation of an overlooked aspect of urban policing highlights the fact that the police officer is anything but a Weberian bureaucrat whose discretion and authority are checked rigidly. The collective myth surrounding the rulebound "policeman-as-public-servant" has no doubt never been very accurate. By virtue of their independence from superiors, their carefully guarded autonomy in the field, their deeply felt notions about real police work and those who would interfere with it, and their increasing isolation from the public they serve (as a result of mobile patrol, rotating shifts, greater specialization of the police, and the growing segmentation of the society at large with its own specialized and emerging subcultures), police-community "problems" will not disappear. And, since the police view their critics as threatening and as persons who generally should be taught or castigated, one could argue that the explosive potential of citizen-police encounters will grow.

Additionally, if the police become more sensitive to public chastisement, it could be expected that something of a self-fulfilling prophecy may well become a more important factor in the street than it is presently. That is to say, if the police increasingly view their public audience as foes—whose views are incomprehensible if not degenerate or subversive—it is likely that they will also magnify clues which will sustain the stereotype of citizen-as-enemy escalating therefore the percentage of street interactions which result in improper arrest and verbal or physical attack. Thus, the fantasy may well become the reality as stereotypes are transformed into actualities. In fact, the future may make prophetic Brendan Behan's half-jesting remark that he had never seen a situation so bad that a policeman couldn't make it worse.

To conclude, this essay has implied that there is a virtual—if unintended—license in this society granted to police. In particular, when it comes to the asshole, police actions are not governed at all, given the present policies of allowing the watchers to watch themselves. It would seem that something is amiss, and, if the practical morality in urban areas is not exactly inverted, it is at least tilted. If the asshole is indeed a critical aspect of policing, then there is serious risk involved in the movement to "professionalize" the police. As other observers have remarked, successful occupational professionalization inevitably leads to increased autonomy and ultimately increased power for members of the occupation (Becker, 1962; Hughes, 1965). Professionalism may well widen the police mandate in society and therefore amplify the potential of the police to act as moral entrepreneurs. From this perspective, what is required at present is not professional police but accountable police.

ENDNOTES

1. All police quotes are taken from field notes I compiled of conversations and observations taking place during a year of participant observation in what I have referred to anonymously in my writings as the Union City Police Department (a large, metropolitan force employing over 1,500 uniformed officers). The quotes are as accurate as my ear, memory, and notes allow (see Epilogue—eds.). I should note, also, that in this essay I use the terms "police," "police officer," "patrolman," and "policemen" somewhat interchangeably. However, unless I indicate otherwise, my comments are directed solely toward the street-level officer—the cop on the beat—and not toward his superiors, administrators, or colleagues in the more prestigeful detective bureaus.

2. I chose the term "asshole" for the title of this essay simply because it is a favorite of working policemen (at least in Union City). The interested reader might check my assumption by a casual glance at what several others have to say about this linguistic matter. Most useful in this regard are the firsthand accounts police have themselves provided and can be found, for example, in Terkel (1968, 1974); Drodge, (1973); Mass (1972); Olsen (1974); Whittemore (1973); Walker (1969). I should note as well that such labeling proceeds not only because of its functional use to the police but also because it helps officers

to capture perceptual distinctions (i.e., labels are "good to think"). Thus assholes are conceptually part of the ordered world of police—the statuses, the rules, the norms, and the contrasts that constitute their social system.

3. See, for example: Rubenstein's (1973) report on the Philadelphia police; Westley's (1970) study of a midwestern police department in the late 1940s; Wilson's (1968) global accounting of the police perspective; Reiss's (1971) research into police-community interactions; LaFave's (1965) treatment of the police decision to arrest; Cain's (1973) and Banton's (1964) observations on the British police; and Berkeley's (1969) cross-cultural view of policing in democratic societies. What comes out of these excellent works is tantamount to a reaffirmation of Trotsky's famous dictum, "There is but one international and that is the police."

4. For example, Skolnick's (1966) idea that policemen are "afraid" of certain categories of persons distorts the nature of the occupational perspective. More to the point, policemen are disgusted by certain people, envious of others, and ambivalent toward most. At times they may even vaguely admire certain criminals—those that the British police call "good villains" (Cain, 1971). Fear must of course be given its due, but the occasion of fear hangs more upon unforeseen situational contingencies (the proverbial dark alley, desolate city park, or underlife tavern) than upon certain individuals.

5. Certainly this may not always be the case. For example, some "suspected persons," due to the nature of their alleged crime (e.g., child molestation, drug dealing, indecent exposure, political sabotage, assault [or worse] upon a police officer, etc.) are likely to provide a strong sense of moral indignation on the part of the arresting (or stopping) officers. In such cases, once identity has been established to the satisfaction of the police (and it should be noted that errors are not unknown—particularly in these volatile cases), the person suspected is transformed immediately into an asshole and is subject to a predictably harsh treatment. Thus, in effect the label arises from an offense which occurred outside the immediate presence of the officers. However, since the spoiled identity must be reestablished anew in the immediate surroundings, the properties of the "affront" correspond analytically to the more familiar case outlines in the text. And while the distinction has theoretical value regarding the norms of the police culture (i.e., that it is not the denounced per se that is important, but rather it is the denouncer that matters—"says who?"), its practical implications are questionable because patrolmen rarely encounter such situations.

6. In most regards, the asshole is a classic case of the deviant—although not transituationally so. See Matza (1969), Becker (1963), and Cohen (1965) for a systematic elaboration of the ideas which underpin this analysis.

7. By the term "extralegal" I am merely implying that the formal police mandate excludes such moral considerations from actions inducing decisions made by officers on the street. The notion of professional policing makes this explicit when it is suggested that patrolmen must act impersonally without regard to individual prejudice.

8. The "cover-your-ass" phenomena associated with urban policing is described in more depth in Van Maanen (1974). See also Manning (1974b) for a theoretical view of the more general construct, the police lie; and Chevigny (1968) for a presentation of numerous disturbing case studies.

9. Arrests are, of course, sometimes used to teach someone a lesson. However, police believe that in many cases the asshole will arrange his release before the patrolman will have completed the paperwork necessitated by the arrest. And since the affront was moral, the legal justification to "make the case" in court may be lacking. Thus, the classroom more often than not is in the street. Given the opportunity to teach the asshole either by "turning him in" or "doing him in," most police would choose the latter.

REFERENCES

Banton, Michael, (1964) *The Policeman in the Community.* New York: Basic Books.

Bayley, P. H. and H. Mendelsohn, (1969) *Minorities and the Police: Confrontation in America.* New York: Free Press.

Becker, Howard S., (1962) "The Nature of a Profession," in *Education for the Professions,* 61st Yearbook of the Society for the Study of Education, Part 2. Chicago: University of Chicago Press. (1963) *Outsiders.* New York: Free Press.

Berkeley, George E., (1969) *The Democratic Policeman,* Boston: Beacon Press.

Bittner, Egon, (1970) *The Functions of the Police in Modern Society.* Washington, D.C.: United States Government Printing Office. (1967) "The Police on Skid Row," 32, *American Sociological Review,* 699–715.

Black, Donald, (1968) "Police Encounters and Social Organization: An Observational Study." Unpublished Ph.D. Dissertation, University of Michigan.

Cain, Maureen, (1973) *Society and the Policeman's Role.* London: Kegan Paul. (1971) "On the Beat: Interactions and Relations in Rural and Urban Police Forces," in S. Cohen (ed.) *Images of Deviance.* Middlesex, England: Penguin Books.

Chevigny, Paul, (1968) *Police Power: Police Abuses in New York.* New York: Pantheon.

Cohen, Albert K., (1965) "The Sociology of the Deviant Act," 30, *American Sociological Review,* 5–14.

Cumming, E., I. Cumming and L. Edell, (1965) "The Policeman as Philosopher, Guide and Friend," 12, *Social Problems,* 276–286.

Drodge, Edward F., (1973) *The Patrolman: A Cop's Story.* New York: New American Library.

Harris, Richard N., (1973) *The Police Academy: An Inside View.* New York: John Wiley and Sons.

Hughes, Everett C., (1965) "Professions," in K. S. Lynn (ed.) *Professions in America.* Boston: Beacon Press. (1958) *Men and Their Work.* Glencoe, Ill. Free Press.

LaFave, W. R., (1965) *Arrest: The Decision to Take a Suspect into Custody.* Boston: Little, Brown and Company.

Maas, Peter, (1973) *Serpico.* New York: The Viking Press.

Manning, Peter K., (1971) "The Police: Mandate, Strategies and Appearances," in J. Douglas (ed.) *Crime and Justice in America.* Indianapolis: Bobbs-Merrill. (1974a) "Dramatic Aspects of Policing: Selected Propositions." *Sociology and Social Research,* 59 (October). (1974b) "Police Lying." *Urban Life* 3 (October).

Matza, David, (1969) *Becoming Deviant.* Englewood Cliffs, N.J.: Prentice-Hall.

McHugh, Peter, (1969) "A Common-Sense Preception of Deviancy," in J. Douglas (ed.) *Deviance and Respectability.* New York: Basic Books.

Neiderhoffer, Arthur, (1969) *Behind the Shield.* Garden City, N.Y.: Doubleday, 1967.

Olsen, Jack, (1974) *Sweet Street.* New York: Simon and Schuster.

Piliavin, I. and S. Briar, (1964) "Police Encounters with Juveniles." 70, *American Journal of Sociology,* 206–214.

Reiss, Albert J., (1971) *The Police and the Public.* New Haven, Conn.: Yale University Press.

Rubenstein, Jonathan, (1973) *City Police.* New York: Farrar, Straus and Giroux.

Sacks, Harvey, (1972) "Notes on Police Assessment of Moral Character," in D. Sudnow (ed.) *Studies in Social Interaction.* New York: The Free Press.

Silver, Allen, (1967) "The Demand for Order in Civil Society," in D. Bordua (ed.) *The Police: Six Sociological Essays.* New York: John Wiley and Sons.

Simmel, Georg, (1950) *The Sociology of Georg Simmel.* Translated, edited, and with an introduction by Kurt H. Wolff. New York: The Free Press.

Skolnick, Jerome, (1966) *Justice Without Trial.* New York: John Wiley and Sons.

Skolnick, Jerome and J. R. Woodworth, (1967) "Bureaucracy, Information and Social Control," in D. Bordua (ed.) *The Police: Six Sociological Essays.* New York: John Wiley and Sons.

Terkel, Studs, (1968) *Division Street: America.* New York: Random House. (1974) *Working,* New York: Pautheon.

Van Maanen, John, (1972) "Pledging the Police: A Study of Selected Aspects of Recruit Socialization in a Large Police Department." Unpublished Ph.D. Dissertation, University of California, Irvine. (1973) "Observations on the Making of Policemen," 32, *Human Organizations,* 407–418. (1974) "Working the Streets: A Developmental View of Police Behavior," in H. Jacobs (ed.) *Reality and Reform: The Criminal Justice System,* Beverly Hills,

California: Sage Publications. (1975) Police Socialization. *Administrative Science Quarterly,* 20, 207–228.

Walker, T. Mike, (1969) *Voices from the Bottom of the World: A Policeman's Journal.* New York: Grove Press.

Webster, J. A., (1970) "Police Task and Time Study," 61 *Journal of Criminal Law,* Criminology and Police Science, 94–100.

Westley, William, (1970) *Violence and the Police.* Cambridge, Mass.: MIT Press (originally a Ph.D. Dissertation, University of Chicago, 1951).

Whittemore, L. H., (1973) *The Super Cops.* New York: Stein and Day.

Wilson, James, Q., (1967) "Police Morale, Reform and Citizen Respect: The Chicago Case," in D. Bordua (ed.) *The Police: Six Sociological Essays.* New York: John Wiley and Sons. (1968) *Varieties of Police Behavior.* Cambridge, Mass.: Harvard University Press.

Administrative Interventions on Police Shooting Discretion: an Empirical Examination

J A M E S   J .   F Y F E

ABSTRACT

In August, 1972, the New York City Police Department promulgated administrative shooting guidelines and shooting incident review procedures far more restrictive than former statutory "defense of life" and "fleeing felon" justifications for police shooting. Using a database that includes all reported New York City police firearms discharges and serious assaults on police between 1971 and 1975, this article examines the effects of the new guidelines and procedures on shooting frequencies, patterns, and consequences.

Great decreases in "fleeing felon" shootings, "warning shots," and shooting-opponent injuries and deaths were found to be associated with the new rules. This change also appeared to have a favorable effect on line-of-duty officer deaths and serious injuries. The implications of these findings are discussed.

Perhaps the major paradox of the American system of justice is the discretionary latitude it allows many of its police officers in the use of their firearms as a means of "deadly force." While the system—and the society—argue and agonize over the death penalty, police shootings generally draw little attention. It is likely, in fact, that the 1977 execution of Gary Gilmore generated more publicity and debate than did the more than 2500 police shooting deaths that occurred during the ten-year period between that event and the last previous court-ordered exercise of deadly force (Milton et al., 1977:33).

It is true that police use of deadly force differs dramatically from court-ordered death sentences. Police often use their firearms as the last resort against real and imminent peril; they often have no choice but to shoot. Judges who elect to impose the death penalty, in contrast, usually select it from among a range of alternatives after lengthy deliberation in the safety of their chambers. Despite these differences, it is ironic that the system has devised rigid devices to control and review court-ordered death sentences, but has generally maintained a hands-off policy where police decisions to shoot are concerned. Indeed, the

From *Journal of Criminal Justice* 7: 309–323, 1979. Copyright © 1979 Elsevier Science. Reprinted with permission.

system zealously controls the court's power to take lives on evidence of guilt beyond a reasonable doubt, but frequently gives its police a blank check in deciding whether or not to shoot at those they have probable cause to arrest.

POLICE SHOOTINGS

Legal Controls and Review Procedures

While Milton et al. (1977:41–43) detect both a "recent eagerness of the judiciary to impose restraints upon police conduct" and an increase in the number of civil actions alleging excessive police force, police shooting discretion in many jurisdictions is limited only by the broad common law fleeing-felon and defense-of-life rules (National Advisory Commission, 1973:18). In addition, police shooting is often subjected to review procedures of questionable effectiveness (Harding and Fahey, 1973).

The fleeing-felon rule is very briefly, but accurately, described by Wilson as police "authority to use deadly force to prevent escape from any felony charge" (1972). Milton et al., (1977:39) note that this principle was defensible when "virtually all felonies were punishable by death," but question its wisdom in an era in which the death penalty is all but extinct.

An only slightly lengthier definition of the defense-of-life rule is offered by Rhine (1968:834):

[It is the police officer's] general right to use deadly force for defense of self and others against threats of death and serious bodily action. In addition, law enforcement authorities never have a duty to retreat before using deadly force, and may always use this for defense of others solely upon reasonable belief that they are being threatened with death or serious bodily harm.

The most striking features of these guidelines are brevity and breadth. Further, while many states have supplemented them by legislating more narrow and clearly delineated statutory limits on police shooting discretion, the record suggests that police officers are rarely penalized for violating them.[1] The adjudication of violations of either codified common law principles or more restrictive legislative guidelines requires that they be subjected to the criminal process. Here, one finds that, even among those cases that do come before the courts,[2] often the only civilian eyewitness to a police shooting is its subject— if surviving. The only version of a police shooting that comes to court attention, therefore, is likely to be that of the police officer involved. Further, even where alternative versions are offered, the prosecutor must decide to take action if a case is to go to trial. Several reasons have been proposed to explain the reluctance of district attorneys to take these cases to trial. Rhine (1968:856) suggests that it is very difficult to prove criminal intent in police killings. Harding and Fahey (1973:298, 299) point out that elected prosecutors may find that both constituent concern with law and order and the need to maintain a cooperative relationship with police militate against such prosecutions.

Administrative Controls and Review Procedures

The broad nature of legal restrictions on police shooting discretion and the difficulties of enforcing them have led many to argue that police agencies should formulate narrower administrative guidelines and internal procedures for the review of shootings (President's Commission, 1967:189, 190; American Bar Association 1973:125–31). Milton et al. (1977:45–57) report a "clear trend" toward the adoption of such policies. They note also, however, that where administrative standards are operative, they vary widely and are frequently contradictory or (perhaps intentionally) vague. As a result, "their impact on the conduct of police officers is questionable." Further, the adoption of administrative guidelines and review procedures is often resisted by police who perceive such rules as arbitrary restrictions on their ability to defend themselves (Berkley, 1969; McKiernan, 1973). This argument is based on the premise that such regulations would promote police reluctance to shoot when necessary for self-defense out of fear that their split-second, life-or-death decisions will be subject to leisurely second-guessing (Rubinstein, 1973:333).

NEW YORK CITY: A TEST CASE

One agency that has adopted clearly delineated administrative shooting guidelines and review procedures is the New York City Police Department. In August, 1972, that department promulgated Temporary Operating Procedure 237 (T.O.P. 237), a directive that narrowed officer shooting discretion considerably more than did New York's statutory provisions. In addition, T.O.P. 237 established a high-level Firearms Discharge Review Board (FDRB) to investigate and adjudicate all officer firearms discharges.

T.O.P. 237 refined New York's penal law restrictions on police shooting (which are based on the American Law Institute's 1962 Model Penal Code and permit officer use of deadly force to "defend life" or to arrest for several specified "violent felonies") by providing that:

a. In all cases, only the minimum amount of force will be used which is consistent with the accomplishment of a mission. Every other reasonable means will be utilized for arresting, preventing or terminating a felony or for the defense of oneself or another before a police officer resorts to the use of his firearm.

b. A firearm shall not be discharged under circumstances where lives of innocent persons may be endangered.

c. The firing of a warning shot is prohibited.

d. The discharging of a firearm to summon assistance is prohibited, except where the police officer's safety is endangered.

e. Discharging a firearm at or from a moving vehicle is prohibited unless the occupants of the other vehicle are using deadly physical force against the officer or another, by means other than the vehicle. (NYPD, 1972:1)

Except for some minor changes in 1973 (NYPD, 1973:2), these provisions have been in effect since 1972. So too, has the FDRB, which is chaired by the Chief of Operations (the department's highest ranking officer), and which also includes as members two deputy police commissioners and the supervisor of the Police Academy's Firearms Unit. FDRB is empowered to conduct hearings at which it may question civilian witnesses, the officer involved, the officer's commander, or any other officers. Its findings are submitted in the form of recommendations to the commander of the officer involved. These, a review of case dispositions reveals, fall into one or more of the following categories:

1. The discharge was in accordance with law and department policy.
2. The discharge was justifiable, but the officer should be given additional training in the use of firearms or in the law and department policy.
3. The shooting was justifiable under law, but violated department policy and warrants department disciplinary action.
4. The shooting was in apparent violation of law and should be referred to the appropriate prosecutor if criminal charges had not already been filed.
5. The officer involved should be transferred (or offered the opportunity to transfer) to a less sensitive assignment.
6. The officer involved should be the subject of psychological testing or alcoholism counselling.[3]

T.O.P. 237 became the core of this study, which attempts to examine the impact of that directive on the frequency, nature, and consequences of police shooting in New York City.

DATA SOURCES

The primary data for this study consist of 4,904 Firearms Discharge/Assault Reports, (FDAR) or all of those filed by officers who had reported discharging their firearms (N = 3,827) or being the subjects of serious assaults (assaults with deadly weapons that may have resulted in officer death or serious injury) between January 1, 1971 and December 31, 1975. These FDAR reports, supplemented by various personnel records, were converted to computer data and analyzed using the Statistical Package for the Social Sciences (Nie et al., 1975).

We would have preferred to have included in this data set reports on shootings and assaults on officers that occurred during the two or three years immediately preceding 1971. While this endeavor might have strengthened our analysis by providing a clearer description of shooting frequencies and patterns before the promulgation of T.O.P. 237, we were precluded from undertaking it by the unsystematic and incomplete shooting and assault data available.

Of necessity, therefore, we contented ourselves with the inclusion of data on shootings and assaults on officers reported during the nineteen months preceding T.O.P. 237.

A potential weakness of this database (or of any other that consists of incident reports) involves the degree to which events have not been reported or have been inaccurately reported. Because officers who fired justifiably would not be disciplined for shooting but would be charged for failing to report, we concluded that missing data would most often include shootings of questionable justifiability. Even in violative cases, however, officers would be unlikely to omit reports of shootings in which they had (or thought they might have) hit someone or something. They would also be unlikely to omit reports of shootings perceived as likely to be brought to official attention by third parties, including their colleagues. Because of New York City's population density and because its police rarely work alone, it is unlikely that more than a very few police could fail to file incident reports in confidence that their shootings would not otherwise come to light. We concluded that the problem of missing data was of minimal import.

The problem of inaccurate reports was viewed as more substantive. Following the T.O.P. 237 ban on warning shots, for example, we had found a great and unexpected increase in reported accidental "shots in the air" fired by police who "tripped on curbs" while pursuing fleeing suspects (Fyfe, 1978:316−28). FDRB generally recommends disciplinary action against officers who fire warning shots, but usually refers accidental shooters to nonpunitive tactical retraining classes. It is probable, therefore, that this specific pattern change reflects altered reporting behavior rather than changes in actual field behavior. To minimize the effects of this and any other distortions, we attempted to limit our analyses to variables reasonably immune to reporting bias.[4]

ANALYSIS

Shootings and Intra-Community Violence

In related research (Fyfe, 1978:32−106), we had found strong correlations among the geographic distributions of shooting incidents, arrests for felonies against the person, and reported murders and non-negligent manslaughters (Pearson's $r = +0.62$ and $+0.78$, respectively). Therefore, we commenced the present investigation by examining the relationships between these variables over the five years studied. If we found that these associations also existed over time, it would be reasonable to conclude that changes in shooting frequencies were at least in part attributable to these nonorganizational variables.

Table 1, which contrasts annual shooting incidents (which may include one or more officer shooters who fired at the same time and place) with reported criminal homicides and arrests for felonies against the person, presents strong evidence to the contrary. After peaking in 1972, homicides remain fairly constant over the period studied (the relatively large 1973−1974 decrease is only a 7.5 percent decline), while arrests register a regular annual increase and firearms

Table 1 Violent Crimes and Police Shootings by Year, 1971–1975

| | | | | RATIOS | |
Year	Reported Homicides[a]	Felony Arrests[a,b]	Police Shootings	Homicides/ Shootings	Arrests/ Shootings
1971	18.2%	17.1%	21.5%	2.33	47.62
	(1466)	(30002)	(630)		
1972	21.0%	18.9%	27.5%	2.11	41.18
	(1691)	(33070)	(803)		
1973	20.9%	20.1%	19.6%	2.93	61.26
	(1680)	(35163)	(574)		
1974	19.3%	21.7%	16.1%	3.30	80.62
	(1554)	(37971)	(471)		
1975	20.5%	22.2%	15.3%	3.67	86.88
	(1645)	(38922)	(448)		
Totals	100.0%	100.0%	100.0%	2.75	59.85
	(8036)	(175128)	(2926)		

[a]Calculated from: New York City Police Department (December, 1971–1975). *Monthly arrest report.*
[b]Includes murder, non-negligent manslaughter, forcible rape, robbery, felonious assault.
NOTE: Subcell percentages may not total 100.0 due to rounding.

discharge incidents decline annually after a large increase between 1971 and 1972. More specifically, columns four and five reveal considerable variation in annual ratios of homicides/shootings and arrests/shootings before and after the promulgation of T.O.P. 237. In 1971, there were 2.33 reported criminal homicides for every police shooting in New York City; this ratio declines slightly (to 2.11) in 1972, then increases considerably over 1973 and 1974 to a high of 3.67 in 1975. Perhaps most significant for the purposes of police administrators, the table indicates that the annual ratio of arrests/shootings has been nearly doubled over the five years studied (from 47.62 in 1971 to 86.88 in 1975).

T.O.P. 237

The decline in reported shooting incidents in the face of a continuing increase in arrests since 1972 suggests the intervention of another variable. A logical first subject of investigation in looking for such an event is T.O.P. 237, which became effective in late 1972, after which the relationship seems to have changed. Our examination of the association of T.O.P. 237 with decreased shooting frequencies commenced by dividing the five years under study into two-month periods and displaying the number of reported officer shooters and shooting incidents for each, as shown in Figure 1. The two-month observation periods were chosen to refine the trend as far as possible without losing information: they reduce the total of observations from sixty to thirty and allow for the data to be cut September 1, close in time to T.O.P. 237 (August 18, 1972) and its slightly altered successor, I.O. 118 (August 27, 1973).

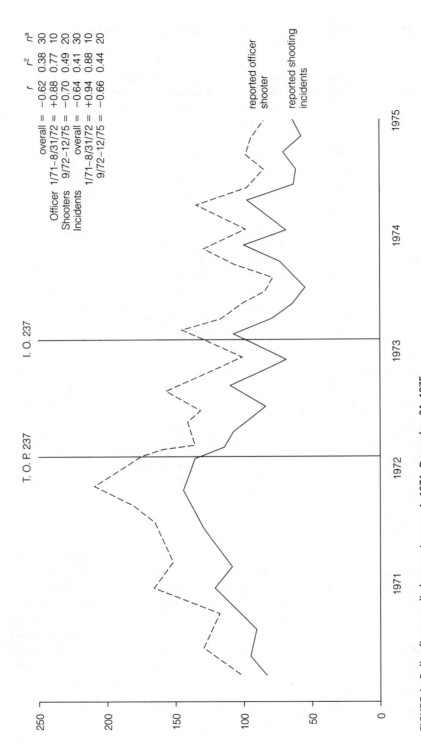

FIGURE 1. Police firearms discharges, January 1, 1971–December 31, 1975

[a]n = number of bimonthly periods.

The chart, and the overall r's of -0.62 and -0.64 for officer shooters and shooting incidents, indicate that both phenomena have fluctuated somewhat, but have been declining steadily since the period during which T.O.P. 237 became effective; "officer shooters" show a peak of 210 during May and June, 1972, decline to 175 during July and August, 1972, and never again reach either level. Similarly, "shooting incidents" peak at 149 during the May–June, 1972, period, decline to 141 during July–August, 1972, and remain below those levels for the duration of the period studied.

One cannot argue, of course, that incident declines are entirely attributable to T.O.P. 237. Indeed, the "shooter" and "incident" r^2 values of 0.38 and 0.41 serve notice that fewer than half these variations are explained by the passage of time. Many other variables over which the department has little or no control (e.g., economic and social conditions, the numbers of officers available for street duty) are certain to have affected these frequencies. On the other hand, splitting the chart at September 1, 1972 produces Pearson's r values of $+0.88$ (officer shooters) and $+0.94$ (shooting incidents) for the earlier period and respective r's of -0.70 and -0.66 for the latter. It is evident, therefore, that T.O.P. 237 was accompanied by rather dramatic changes in the frequencies with which New York City police officers reported discharging their firearms.

I.O. 118

The second department firearms policy statement was I.O. 118, which was issued on August 27, 1973. The major purposes of this directive were to clarify T.O.P. 237's ambiguities and to establish decentralized "area level" review boards,[5] but the document appears at the beginning of a six-month decline in shooting incident frequencies and an eight-month decline in officer shooter frequencies. Some percentage of these decreases may be attributable to a cold weather slump. But the declines continued in the absence of other possible explanations (e.g., the department was, at that time, adding to its ranks; reported homicides and arrests for violent crime did not show similar declines), and are at least as severe and as long as those that followed the issuance of T.O.P. 237.

Because so few observations are included in this second period, it was decided not to attempt to test their possible significance statistically. It would be interesting, however, to continue following the frequencies of shooting incidents and reported shooters consequent to other clarifications, procedural alterations, and minor discretionary changes. If further declines occurred, one might postulate that substantial influence is exerted on shooting frequencies by continuing emphasis on limits to individual officer discretion or the institution of decentralized reporting and review procedures.

Weekly Means

The two-month periods studied thus far are, of course, rather inexact and may be criticized if used as a basis for comparison because they include varying numbers of days. July/August periods, for example, encompass sixty-two days, while January/February includes only fifty-nine (in all years except 1972, which was a leap year). In addition, bimonthly figures do not allow the data to be split precisely at the effective date of T.O.P. 237 (August 18, 1972).

To provide more comparable figures, the five years under study were therefore split at midnight, August 18, 1972, and means of reported officer reason for shooting were computed weekly for each period (period 1 weeks = 85.1; period 2 = 175.7). The results are presented in Table 2. Its column totals reveal that a weekly mean of 18.4 officers reported discharging their firearms prior to T.O.P. 237 and that this figure dropped to 12.9 officers after the directive was put into force (this represents a decrease of 29.9 percent). Further, the table shows important changes in the reasons given by officers in reported discharging of firearms ($p = 0.001$; $v = 0.28$). Indeed, while the weekly mean reported "defense of life" shootings has decreased (from 11.9 to 9.0), the pre-T.O.P. 237 percentage for these shootings (65.8 percent) has increased since the order (to 70.6 percent). Concomitantly, both the weekly mean and percentage of "prevent/terminate crime" shootings (usually fleeing-felon situations) have decreased substantially (from 3.9 and 21.4 percent to 0.6 and 4.6 percent, respectively). Conversely, Table 2 demonstrates that both the weekly means and percentage of suicide attempts have remained relatively constant. As one would expect, T.O.P. 237 has little effect in deterring suicides.

Warning Shots

While Table 2 demonstrates reduced shooting frequencies and varying reported reasons for shooting, it leaves unanswered many questions about other consequences of T.O.P. 237. Its frequencies, for example, are confounded because they include warning shots, which were not treated separately but were coded on the basis of the officer shooter's reported intent. If, for example, a police officer fired a shot into the air in an attempt to stop a fleeing burglary suspect, the shooting would be classified as "prevent/terminate crime" and would be included in Table 2. What Table 2 does *not* provide, therefore, is a measure of T.O.P. 237's effect in reducing shots fired *at* fleeing burglars or other opponents. Instead, it indicates that before T.O.P. 237, 3.9 officers per week reported discharging their firearms to prevent or terminate crimes, regardless of whether or not they fired *at* or over the heads of suspects, and that this mean has subsequently declined to 0.6. Since, in addition to mandating the use of "every other reasonable means . . . for arresting, preventing or terminating a felony . . . before a police officer resorts to the use of a firearm," T.O.P. 237 flatly prohibits warning shots, one might expect that much of the decrease discussed above is attributable to lower warning shot frequencies rather than to reduced numbers of shootings at human targets.

To control for this possibility and to better measure relative frequencies of officers who shot at targets (except, obviously, accidental shooters), Table 3, which excludes all officers who reported firing only warning shots, was calculated. This table presents some important differences from the data in Table 2. Its total (3,413 shooters) indicates that 414 of the shooters reported in the

Table 2 Officer-Reported Reason for Shooting

	Pre-T.O.P. 237	Weekly Mean	Post-T.O.P. 237	Weekly Mean	Totals	Weekly Mean
Defense of Life	65.8% (1016)	11.9	70.6% (1582)	9.0	67.9% (2598)	10.0
Prevent or Terminate Crime	21.4% (330)	3.9	4.6% (103)	0.6	11.3% (433)	1.7
Destroy Animal	4.4% (68)	0.8	11.4% (255)	1.5	8.4% (323)	1.2
Suicide Attempt	0.7% (11)	0.1	0.8% (18)	0.1	0.8% (29)	0.1
Accidental	3.6% (56)	0.7	9.0% (201)	1.2	6.7% (257)	1.0
Other	4.1% (63)	0.7	3.7% (83)	0.5	3.8% (146)	0.6
Totals	40.8% (1562)	18.4	59.2% (2265)	12.9	100.0% (1827)[a]	14.7

NOTE: Chi-squared = 318.82; $p = 0.001$; $v = 0.28$. Subcell percentages may not total 100.0 due to rounding.

[a]All column totals include 18 pre-T.O.P. 237 and 23 post-T.O.P 237 cases in which reason for shooting was not reported.

Table 3 Officer-Reported Reason for Shooting, Excluding Warning Shots

Reason	Pre-T.O.P. 237	Weekly Mean	Post-T.O.P. 237	Weekly Mean	Totals	Weekly Mean
Defense of Life	72.7% (902)	10.6	70.7% (1536)	8.7	71.5% (2438)	9.0
Prevent or Terminate Crime	13.9% (172)	2.0	4.3% (93)	0.5	7.8% (265)	1.0
Destroy Animal	5.5% (68)	0.8	11.7% (254)	1.4	9.4% (322)	1.2
Suicide Attempt	0.9% (11)	0.1	0.8% (18)	0.1	0.8% (29)	0.1
Accidental	4.5% (56)	0.7	9.2% (201)	1.2	7.5% (257)	1.0
Other	2.5% (31)	0.4	3.3% (71)	0.4	3.0% (102)	0.4
Totals	36.3% (1240)	14.6	63.7% (2173)	12.3	100.0% (3413)	13.1[a]

NOTE: Chi-squared = 102.62; $p = 0.001$; $v = 0.17$.

[a]Total weekly mean includes 36 cases in which a reason for shooting was not reported.

previous table had fired only warning shots. Further, most of the reported warning shots (304 of the 414) took place during the period preceding T.O.P. 237. Consequently, the weekly mean number of officers who reported firing "in defense of life" during the early period has declined to 10.6 and the weekly mean "prevent/terminate crime" shooters is almost halved from 3.9 to 2.0.

While this table's exclusion of "warning shots" still leaves significant pre- and post-T.O.P. 237 differences in the mean weekly frequencies of reported reasons for shootings, the differences shrink considerably; indeed, the relative percentage of reported "defense of life" shootings decreases.[6] In terms of weekly shots fired at people, however, this table also demonstrates significant decreases following T.O.P. 237.

T.O.P. 237 and Firearms Discharge/
Assault Generated Injury

In measuring the impact of T.O.P. 237 on officer injury, we chose to include in our analysis only injuries and deaths sustained in the line of duty. In this manner, we eliminated from consideration injuries on which one might reasonably expect that T.O.P. 237 would have no impact (e.g., officer suicides, injuries accidentally suffered while handling or cleaning weapons. This does not, however, limit the analysis to injuries sustained by on-duty officers. Off-duty officers hurt while "taking police action" (e.g., while attempting arrests, stopping and questioning suspicious persons) are defined by the department to have been injured in the line of duty. Thus, for example, an off-duty officer who is shot while attempting to apprehend the perpetrators of a robbery that the officer witnesses is deemed to have been injured only because of his or her status and actions as a police officer. The injury was sustained in response to "duty's call." If, conversely, whether the officer is off or on duty when injured in circumstances that do not involve the performance of the police function or that involve negligence on the officer's part, the injury is defined as non–line of duty. As a case in point, an officer stabbed in a street robbery by individuals who do not know that he or she is a police officer is regarded as having been injured as would any citizen in similar circumstances. The injury, therefore, is classified as non–line of duty. Similarly, an on-duty officer who is injured by, for example, the accidental discharge of a carelessly handled weapon while not engaged in a specific police action, is also recorded as having suffered a non–line-of-duty injury.

Table 4, which presents comparative frequencies of FDAR-generated, officer-line-of-duty injury and death before and after T.O.P. 237, demonstrates that the injury vs. death percentages remained fairly constant across the two periods. Once again, however, one finds that weekly means for injured and killed officers vary considerably. Before T.O.P. 237, 4.4 officers a week suffered non-fatal FDAR-generated, line-of-duty injuries; after T.O.P. 237, the figure declines to 2.5. Similarly, the frequency with which officers are killed in the line of duty drops from 0.2 (one every five weeks) to 0.1 (one every ten weeks).

Table 5, which presents frequencies of known shooting incidents opponent degree of injury for the pre- and post-T.O.P. 237 periods, shows reductions in these frequencies as well. Again, one finds that the relative chances of opponent injury have remained fairly constant across the five years studied. Of opponents whose degree of injury was known to the police, approximately seventy percent suffered no injury, slightly more than twenty percent were wounded and just over nine percent were killed during both periods.

Table 4 Reported Line-of-Duty Injuries Sustained by Officers in Firearms Discharge/Assault Incidents[a]

Officer Injury	Pre-T.O.P. 237	Weekly Mean	Post-T.O.P 237	Weekly Mean	Totals	Weekly Mean
Injured	95.9% (376)	4.4	96.9% (438)	2.5	96.4% (814)	3.1
Killed	4.1% (16)	0.2	3.1% (14)	0.1	3.6% (30)	0.1
Totals	46.4% (392)	4.6	53.6% (452)	2.6	100.0% (844)	3.2

NOTE: Chi-squared = 0.14; p = 0.70; Q = 0.14.

[a]Excludes incidents not involving confrontations with human opponents (e.g., destroying injured animal).

Table 5 Known Injuries Sustained by Opponents in Police Shooting Incidents

Opponent Injury	Pre-T.O.P. 237	Weekly Mean	Post-T.O.P. 237	Weekly Mean	Totals	Weekly Mean
None	69.0% (1043)	12.3	70.9% (1435)	8.2	70.1% (2478)	9.5
Injured	21.8% (329)	3.9	20.0% (405)	2.3	20.8% (734)	2.8
Killed	9.2% (139)	1.6	9.1% (184)	1.0	9.1% (323)	1.2
Totals	42.7% (1511)	17.8	57.3% (2024)	11.5	100.0% (3535)	13.5

NOTE: Chi-squared = 0.03; p = 0.99; v = 0.01.

But in examining the weekly means, we again find considerable reductions in all our categories following T.O.P. 237. Most specifically, Table 5 shows us that New York City police wounded a weekly average of 3.9 opponents and that they killed 1.6 prior to T.O.P. 237; during the period between that intervention and December 31, 1975, these means fell to 2.3 and 1.0, respectively.

While both Tables 4 and 5 present rather striking differences between the pre- and post-T.O.P. 237 periods, several considerations prevent our concluding that these differences are entirely attributable to that directive and they limit the degree to which equivalent reductions might be predicted for other agencies. Simply stated, the reduced frequencies that are presented in both tables are based on two observations made over a five-year period, during which other variables might have been expected to influence police and citizen injuries. Those other variables (e.g., injuries resulting from the unprovoked police assasination attempts by the radical "Black Liberation Army," which were most frequent during the pre-T.O.P. 237 period; police personnel deployment), however, are beyond the scope of the present inquiry.[7] We elected, therefore, to more clearly identify the effect of T.O.P. 237 on police

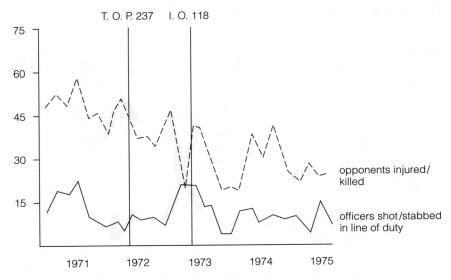

FIGURE 2. Police opponent injuries and deaths and police officers shot or stabbed in the line of duty, (*N* = 30)

and citizen injury by increasing the number of observations in our examination of those phenomena during the five years studied.

Figure 2 contrasts the bimonthly frequency of civilian FDAR-generated deaths and injuries (classified as one entity on the premise that degree of injury is subject to chance variations) with the frequency with which officers were shot or stabbed in the line of duty (including only what are generally the most serious injuries). This figure demonstrates a general decrease in both these phenomena between 1971 and 1975. In addition, the figure reveals that the relationship between citizen injuries and officer shot or stabbed frequencies is subject to considerable variation. In some periods, citizen injuries far outweigh officer shot or stabbed frequencies, while in others, the gap is closed considerably: during May and June, 1973, officer injuries even exceeded citizen injuries. Again, except for these periods, and despite the gross incident and injury reductions cited earlier, the relative risk of FDAR-generated officer or citizen injury or death looks relatively stable.

CONCLUSIONS

Our examination has demonstrated that a considerable reduction in the frequency of police shooting accompanied New York City's direct intervention on the firearms discretion of its police officers. Further, our data indicate that this reduction was greatest among the most controversial shooting incidents: shootings to prevent or terminate crimes, which frequently involve police shots at fleeing felons. To the extent that this New York experience may be generalized to other agencies, therefore, an obvious consequence of the implementation of clear shooting guidelines and their stringent enforcement is a reduction of injuries and deaths sustained by suspects who would face far less severe penalties even if convicted after trial.

Of equal significance to the police administrator is the fact that these shooting decreases were not accompanied by increased officer injury or death. Conversely, since both these phenomena appear to be associated with the frequency of shooting incidents and related citizen injury, both declined pursuant to T.O.P. 237.

In the most simple terms, therefore, the New York City experience indicates that considerable reductions in police shooting and both officer and citizen injury and death are associated with the establishment of clearly delineated guidelines and procedures for the review of officer shooting discretion.

ENDNOTES

This paper is a revision of a paper presented at the Annual Meeting of the American Society of Criminology, Atlanta, Georgia, November, 1977.

1. Kobler (1975:164) reports that only three of the 1,500 police shooters he studied were criminally punished for their actions.

2. It is probable that officers who do violate statutory provisions (e.g., by shooting at fleeing misdemeanants) but who both miss and fail to apprehend their targets do not often come to court attention.

3. Firearms Discharge Review Board cases disposed of with recommendations that include more than one of these categories most typically involve shootings deemed to have violated departmental guidelines and to have indicated that transfers from sensitive (and often desirable) assignments are appropriate. Narcotics officers and other plainclothes personnel who shoot in violation of departmental policy, for example, are often recommended for transfers to administrative assignments or to patrol duty in outlying areas where the chances of encountering circumstances provocative of weapons use are slight. In such cases, we considered the board's recommendation for disciplinary action to be its major and most severe finding and coded dispositions under that single heading. Similarly, because we regarded criminal charges to be the major and most severe finding in all cases in which they

resulted, we included such cases in that single category, although they also invariably involved some departmental disciplinary action. Cases involving criminal charges are held in abeyance by FDRB pending court disposition: officers convicted of criminal use of firearms are then summarily dismissed from the department; all officers acquitted of such criminal charges during the period we studied were subsequently subjected to departmental trials for their actions.

By the time data collection for this report ceased (August, 1976), the Firearms Discharge Review Board had adjudicated 2,155 shootings. Their major recommendations in these cases were as follows:

Within law and and department guidelines	70.8%	(1525)
Retraining in law or tactics	18.3%	(395)
Disciplinary action	7.7%	(167)
Criminal charges	1.2%	(26)
Transfer	0.6%	(13)
Psychological or alcoholic counselling	1.3%	(29)
Total	100.0%	(2155)

4. This attempt was not always successful. In the absence of information to the contrary (e.g., FDRB or judicial findings), we accepted "officer reported reason for shooting" at face value. This exception,

however, affects only our examination of changes in the nature of shootings. It has little or no significance as far as total shooting frequencies are concerned.

5. I.O. 118's only new discretionary parameter was the statement that "(t)he discharge of a firearm at dogs or other animals should be an action employed ONLY when no other means to bring the animal under control exists."

6. A good part of this percentage decrease, however, is due to the great in-crease in frequency in reported "destroy animal" shootings. Had these remained constant at their pre-T.O.P. 237 level (0.8 per week), the post-T.O.P. 237 "defense of life shots at people" percentage would have been 74.6 percent.

7. We conducted detailed examinations of the effects of several other variables on shooting frequency, type, and consequences in Fyfe (1978) and found that they did not significantly alter the findings reported in this study.

REFERENCES

American Bar Association Project on Standards for Criminal Justice (1973). *Standards Relating to the Urban Police Function*. New York: American Bar Association.

Berkley, G.E. (1969). *The Democratic Policeman*. Boston: Beacon Press.

Fyfe, J.J. (1978). "Shots fired: An examination of New York City police firearms discharges." Ph.D. dissertation, State University of New York at Albany.

Harding, R.W., and Fahey, R.P. (1973). "Killings by Chicago Police, 1969–70: An Empirical Study." 4 *Southern California law review*, 6:284–315.

Kobler, R.M. (1975). Police Homicide in a Democracy. *Journal of Social Issues*, 31:163–181.

McKiernan, R.M. (1973). Police Shotguns: Devastating to the Animals. *The New York Times*, February 7:35.

Milton, C.H.; Halleck, J.W.; Lardiner, J.; and Abrecht, G.L. (1977). *Police Use of Deadly Force*. Washington, DC: Police Foundation.

National Advisory Commission on Criminal Justice Standards and Goals (1973). *Police*. Washington, DC: U.S. Government Printing Office.

New York City Police Department (1973). *Interim order 118.*

———, (1972). Temporary Operating Procedure *237.*

———, Crime Analysis Unit (1971–1975). *Monthly arrest report*. December.

Nie, N.H.; Hull, C.H.; Jenkins, J.G.; Steinbrenner, K.; and Bent, D.H. (1975). *Statistical Package for the Social Sciences*. New York: McGraw-Hill.

President's Commission on Law Enforcement and Administration of Justice (1967). *Task Force Report: The Police*. Washington, DC: U.S. Government Printing Office.

Rhine, B. (1968). Kill or Be Killed: Use of Deadly Force in the Riot Situation. 56 *California Law Review*: 829.

Rubinstein, J. (1973). *City Police*. New York: Farrar, Straus and Giroux.

Wilson, J.V. (1972). "Deadly force." *Police Chief*, December; 44–46.

QUESTIONS FOR
DISCUSSION AND REVIEW

1. Based on the Independent Commission Report, explain how what happened to Rodney King (and related incidents) could be considered a result of officer characteristics, situational factors, or organizational factors.

2. Investigators of the Independent Commission on the Los Angeles Police Department stated that without the videotape of the beating of Rodney King there would have probably been no investigation into the matter. Why? What evidence did they present to support their claim?

3. Based on your understanding of the Worden (1995) article, discuss the potential contributions of sociological, psychological, and organizational theories in explaining police behavior. The findings of the study are most supportive, and least supportive, of which perspectives?

4. According to Worden (1995) what are the various types of misuse of force? Are these distinctions important? Why or why not?

5. According to Muir (1977), what is the power of the purse, the power of the word, and the power of the sword?

6. According to Muir (1977), what are the four types of police officers in his typology? What is the role of passion and perspective in defining these types of officers?

7. According to Black (1971), what factors impact police officers' decisions to make an arrest?

8. Are there any similarities between the findings of Worden (1995) and Black (1971)? Explain.

9. Identify and discuss the three groups of citizens identified by the police according to Van Maanen (1978).

10. According to Van Maanen (1978) how does one become identified as a "suspicious person" or as an "asshole"? Based on your own understanding of the police, are there other categories in which the police place citizens? What difference does it make that police officers "typify" citizens?

11. Based on your understanding of the reading by Fyfe (1979), discuss how and to what extent police policy affects police actions.

12. According to Fyfe (1979), why does administrative policy/rules affect the behavior of police officers?

13. Are there any similarities between the findings of Fyfe (1979) and Worden (1995)? Explain.

STRATEGIES
OF POLICING

INTRODUCTION

Organizations develop and implement strategies in order to reach their goals. A primary official goal of the police organization is the control of crime. Not surprisingly, the most significant strategies of the police have crime control as the outcome upon which success is measured. This section of *The Police in America: Classic and Contemporary Readings* contains several studies that examine the major operational strategies of the police (e.g., preventive patrol, criminal investigation, community policing). In considering the strategies of policing discussed here, Peter Manning's (1978) notion of the police organization's "impossible mandate" is enlightening. According to Manning (1978), the public has come to equate the police organization with crime control, and the police have staked out crime control as their territory. The problem is that the police have extremely limited capabilities in controlling crime; hence the "impossible mandate." As a result of this predicament, the police have resorted to the display of symbols and the manipulation of appearances in order to make it look like they are doing something about the problem of crime. Many of the strategies discussed in this section of the book can be considered in relation to this critical perspective.

The first strategy examined is police patrol. In 1972 George Kelling and his colleagues conducted an experimental study to test the almost sacred assumption that routine preventive patrol reduces crime. In comparing the extent of crime across areas with different levels of police patrol, the researchers found few significant differences. These findings led the researchers to the conclusion that preventive patrol may not affect crime as previously thought. Although certainly not without criticism (see Larson, 1973; and Sherman and Rogan, 1995 included here), the study represents a critical piece of knowledge on police strategies and has been the catalyst (at least in part) for innovations in the patrol function, or, as Manning may argue, for more manipulation of appearances. In particular, Sherman and Rogan's (1995) article "Effects of Gun Seizures on Gun Violence" contradicts Kelling et al. by offering evidence to lead one to believe that police patrol activities can have an impact on crime. Sherman and Rogan (1995) have refined our knowledge about the impact of the police on crime. The contemporary reading complements the classic reading.

The second set of readings deal with criminal investigations, particularly the role of detectives in the process. The seminal research by Chaiken et al. (1977), "The Criminal Investigation Process: A Summary Report," came to the conclusion that detectives play a minor role in solving crimes; if crimes are solved they are either solved by patrol officers or because patrol officers collected the necessary information at the crime scene that later led to the crimes being solved. Again, this is another study that was very controversial when its findings were first released. Brandl and Frank (1994), in their article "The Relationship Between Evidence, Detective Effort, and the Disposition of Burglary and Robbery Investigations," noted and addressed the methodological weaknesses of the Chaiken et al. research. Based on their analyses, Brandl and Frank came to the conclusion that, contrary to the views of Chaiken et al., detectives do make a significant contribution in solving many, but certainly not all, crimes.

The third set of readings addresses the strategies of team policing and community policing. Team policing represented one of the first attempts on the part of the police to improve their relationship with the public. Team policing did not last long because it proved extremely difficult to implement. These difficulties are documented and discussed by Sherman, Milton, and Kelly (1973), in an excerpt from their book *Team Policing: Seven Case Studies.* The article written by Maguire (1997), "Structural Change in Large Municipal Police Organizations During the Community Policing Era," provides an analysis of community policing in police departments today and shows that, just as with team policing, community policing is quite difficult to implement. He shows that most police departments claim to have community policing but have actually changed very little as a result. These two readings demonstrate that one needs to have a critical understanding of what is actually being done in police departments.

Herman Goldstein's (1979) article "Improving Policing: A Problem-Oriented Approach" set the stage for the development of community-oriented policing. Goldstein describes the "means over ends" syndrome in which the police essentially become preoccupied with internal management and correspondingly ignore the objectives or outcomes that police activities are supposed to achieve. Goldstein identifies a new way of approaching the police function—one that focuses directly on the ends of policing, one oriented around the identification of problems and the development of solutions to these problems. Although there is little specific reference to "community policing" in this article, this approach lies at the core of the community policing strategy.

The nearly instant classic piece by Wilson and Kelling (1982), "The Police and Neighborhood Safety: Broken Windows," offers a popularized and simplified version of problem-oriented policing. The authors, like Goldstein, emphasize the importance of expanding the police officer's role beyond law enforcement to other areas, namely order maintenance. In addition, they recommend that the police become more focused on crime prevention, although in order to do so, the primary community problem that needs to be addressed is disorder. The authors argue that disorder (e.g., broken windows) and anonymity among residents and between police and residents encourages illegal behaviors. Residents who live in areas of disorder will feel that the area is unsafe. In turn, these feelings reinforce the anonymity among residents and residents tend to avoid one another. According to the authors, such areas are the most vulnerable to serious crime. In such an environment, criminals may believe that the chances of apprehension are relatively slim. It follows then that police efforts directed at reaffirming informal controls, thus providing for the maintenance of order, would lead not only to the reduction of disorder but also to a reduction in actual crime and fear of it. Community policing is portrayed as such an effort.

The final reading, Kraska and Cubellis's 1997 piece "Militarizing Mayberry and Beyond: Making Sense of American Paramilitary Policing," identifies the most recent trend in American policing, the strategy of using military-like units for "normal" police work. Kraska and Cubellis demonstrate that rather than becoming more responsive to the community and more friendly and personable in their interactions with the community, the trend in policing in the United States appears to be toward more aggressive, militaristic, and formal policing, leading to greater violence, discrimination, and tension between the police and the community (also see Kraska and Kappeler, 1997). They demonstrate that there is an increase in the number of paramilitary police units operating in the United States, an escalation of their activity, and a normalization of their operations into mainstream policing. What is particularly interesting is that these developments are often taking place under the guise of community and problem-oriented policing initiatives. If this trend continues, as it likely will, given the new war on terrorism, it may represent the beginning of the future of American policing.

REFERENCES

Kraska, Peter B. and Victor E. Kappeler. (1997). "Militarizing American Police: The Rise and Normalization of Paramilitary Units." *Social Problems* 44:1–18.

Larson, Richard C. (1975). "What Happened to Patrol Operations in Kansas City? A review of the Kansas City Preventive Patrol Experiment." *Journal of Criminal Justice* 3:267–297.

Manning, Peter K. (1978). "The Police: Mandate, Strategies, and Appearances." In P.K. Manning and John Van Maanen (eds.), *Policing: A View From the Street,* pp. 7–31. Santa Monica, CA: Goodyear.

The Kansas City Preventive Patrol
Experiment: A Summary Report

GEORGE L. KELLING
TONY PATE
DUANE DIECKMAN
CHARLES E. BROWN

I. INTRODUCTION
AND MAJOR FINDINGS

Ever since the creation of a patrolling force in 13th century Hang-chow, preventive patrol by uniformed personnel has been a primary function of policing. In 20th century America, about $2 billion is spent each year for the maintenance and operation of uniformed and often superbly equipped patrol forces. Police themselves, the general public, and elected officials have always believed that the presence or potential presence of police officers on patrol severely inhibits criminal activity.

One of the principal police spokesmen for this view was the late O.W. Wilson, former Chief of the Chicago Police Department and a prominent academic theorist on police issues. As Wilson once put it, "Patrol is an indispensable service that plays a leading role in the accomplishment of the police purpose. It is the only form of police service that directly attempts to eliminate opportunity for misconduct. . . ." Wilson believed that by creating the impression of police omnipresence, patrol convinced most potential offenders that opportunities for successful misconduct did not exist.

To the present day, Wilson's has been the prevailing view. While modern technology, through the creation of new methods of transportation, surveillance and communications, had added vastly to the tools of patrol, and while there have been refinements in patrol strategies based upon advanced probability formulas and other computerized methods, the general principle has

Source: George L. Kelling, Tony Pate, Duane Dieckman, Charles E. Brown (1974). *The Kansas City Preventive Patrol Experiment: A Summary Report.* Washington, D.C.: Police Foundation. (Note: Complete report except for tables and reference to them— see document.) Reprinted by permission of The Police Foundation.

remained the same. Today's police recruits, like virtually all those before them, learn from both teacher and textbook that patrol is the "backbone" of police work.

No less than the police themselves, the general public has been convinced that routine preventive patrol is an essential element of effective policing. As the International City Management Association has pointed out, "for the greatest number of persons, deterrence through ever-present police patrol, coupled with the prospect of speedy police action once a report is received, appears important to crime control." Thus, in the face of spiraling crime rates, the most common answer urged by public officials and citizens alike has been to increase patrol forces and get more police officers "on the street." The assumption is that increased displays of police presence are vitally necessary in the face of increased criminal activity. Recently, citizens in troubled neighborhoods have themselves resorted to civilian versions of patrol.

Challenges to preconceptions about the value of preventive police patrol were exceedingly rare until recent years. When researcher Bruce Smith, writing about patrol in 1930, noted that its effectiveness "lacks scientific demonstration," few paid serious attention.

Beginning in 1962, however, challenges to commonly held ideas about patrol began to proliferate. As reported crime began to increase dramatically, as awareness of unreported crime became more common, and as spending for police activities grew substantially, criminologists and others began questioning the relationship between patrol and crime. From this questioning a body of literature has emerged.

Much of this literature is necessarily exploratory. Earlier researchers were faced with the problem of obtaining sufficient and correct data, and then devising methodologies to interpret the data. The problems were considerable, and remain so.

Another problem facing earlier investigators was the natural reluctance of most police departments to create the necessary experimental conditions through which definitive answers concerning the worth of patrol could be obtained. Assigned the jobs of protecting society from crime, of apprehending criminals, and of carrying out numerous other services such as traffic control, emergency help in accidents and disasters, and supervision of public gatherings, police departments have been apprehensive about interrupting their customary duties to experiment with strategies or to assist in the task evaluation.

It was in this context that the Kansas City, Missouri, Police Department, under a grant from the Police Foundation, undertook in 1972 the most comprehensive experiment ever conducted to analyze the effectiveness of routine preventive patrol.

From the outset the department and the Police Foundation evaluation team agreed that the project design would be as rigorously experimental as possible, and that while Kansas City Police Department data would be used, as wide a data base as possible, including data from external measurements, would be generated. It was further agreed that the experiment would be monitored by both department and foundation representatives to insure maintenance of experimental conditions. Under the agreement between the department and the foundation, the department committed itself to an eight-month experiment provided that reported crime did not reach "unacceptable" limits within the experimental area. If no major problems developed, the experiment would continue an additional four months.

The experiment is described in detail later in this summary. Briefly, it involved variations in the level of routine preventive patrol within 15 Kansas City police beats. These beats were randomly divided into three groups. In five "reactive" beats, routine preventive patrol was eliminated and officers were instructed to respond only to calls for service. In five "control" beats, routine preventive patrol was maintained at its usual level of one car per beat. In the remaining five "proactive" beats, routine preventive patrol was intensified by two to three times its usual level through the assignment of additional patrol cars and through the frequent presence of cars from the "reactive" beats.

For the purposes of measurement, a number of hypotheses were developed, of which the following were ultimately addressed:

1. crime, as reflected by victimization surveys and reported crime data, would not vary by type of patrol;

2. citizen perception of police service would not vary by type of patrol;

3. citizen fear and behavior as a result of fear would not vary by type of patrol;

4. police response time and citizen satisfaction with response time would vary by experimental area; and

5. traffic accidents would increase in the reactive beats.

The experiment found that the three experimental patrol conditions appeared not to affect crime, service delivery, and citizen feelings of security in ways the public and the police often assume they do. For example,

- as revealed in the victimization surveys, the experimental conditions had no significant effect on residence and non-residence burglaries, auto thefts, larcenies involving auto accessories, robberies, or vandalism—crimes traditionally considered to be deterrable through preventive patrol;

- in terms of reporting crime to the police, few differences and no consistent patterns of differences occurred across experimental conditions;

- in terms of departmental reported crime, only one set of differences across experimental conditions was found and this one was judged likely to have been a random occurrence;

- few significant differences and no consistent pattern of differences occurred across experimental conditions in terms of citizen attitudes toward police services;

- citizen fear of crime, overall, was not affected by experimental conditions;

- there were few differences and no consistent pattern of differences across experimental conditions in the number and types of anti-crime protective measures used by citizens;

- in general, the attitudes of businessmen toward crime and police services were not affected by experimental conditions;

- experimental conditions did not appear to affect significantly citizen satisfaction with the police as a result of their encounters with police officers;

- experimental conditions had no significant effect on either police response time or citizen satisfaction with police response time;

- although few measures were used to assess the impact of experimental conditions on traffic accidents and injuries, no significant differences were apparent;

- about 60 percent of a police officer's time is typically non-committed (available for calls); of this time, police officers spent approximately as much time on non-police-related activities as they did on police-related mobile patrol; and

- in general, police officers are given neither a uniform definition of preventive patrol nor any objective methods for gauging its effectiveness; while officers tend to be ambivalent in their estimates of preventive patrol's effectiveness in deterring crime, many attach great importance to preventive patrol as a police function.

Some of these findings pose a direct challenge to traditionally held beliefs. Some point only to an acute need for further research. But many point to what those in the police field have long suspected—an extensive disparity between what we want the police to do, what we often believe they do, and what they can and should do.

The immediate issue under analysis in the preventive patrol experiment was routine preventive patrol and its impact on crime and the community. But a much larger policy issue was implied; whether urban police departments can establish and maintain experimental conditions, and whether such departments can, for such experimentation, infringe upon that segment of time usually committed to routine preventive patrol. Both questions were answered in the affirmative, and in this respect the preventive patrol experiment represents a crucial first step, but just one in a series of such steps toward defining and clarifying the police function in modern society.

What the experiment did not address was a multitude of other patrol issues. It did not, for example, study such areas as two-officer patrol cars, team policing, generalist-specialist models, or other experiments currently under way in other departments. The findings of this experiment do not establish that the police are not important to the solution of crime or that police presence in some situations may not be helpful in reducing crime. Nor do they automatically justify reduction in the level of policing. They do not suggest that because the majority of a police officer's time is typically spent on non-crime-related matters, the amount of time spent on crime is of any lesser importance.

Nor do the findings imply that the provision of public services and maintenance of order should overshadow police work on crime. While one of the three patrol conditions used in this experiment reduced police visibility in certain areas, the condition did not withdraw police availability from those areas. The findings in this regard should therefore not be interpreted to suggest that total police withdrawal from an area is an answer to crime. The reduction in routine police patrol was but one of three patrol conditions examined, and the implications must be treated with care.

It could be argued that because of its large geographical area and relatively low population density, Kansas City is not representative of the more populous urban areas of the United States. However, many of the critical problems and situations facing Kansas City are common to other large cities. For example, in terms of aggravated assault, Kansas City ranks close to Detroit and San Francisco. The rate of murder and manslaughter per 100,000 persons in Kansas City is similar to that of Los Angeles, Denver, and Cincinnati. And in terms of burglary, Kansas City is comparable to Boston and Birmingham. Furthermore, the experimental area itself was diverse socio-economically, and had a population density much higher than Kansas City's average, making the experimental area far more representative and comparative than Kansas City as a whole might be. In these respects, the conclusions and implications of this study can be widely applied.

II. DESCRIPTION OF THE PREVENTIVE PATROL EXPERIMENT

The impetus for an experiment in preventive patrol came from within the Kansas City Police Department in 1971. While this may be surprising to some, the fact is that by that year the Kansas City department had already experienced more than a decade of innovation and improvement in its operations and working climate and had gained a reputation as one of the nation's more progressive police departments.

Under Chief Clarence M. Kelley, the department had achieved a high degree of technological sophistication, was receptive to experimentation and change, and was peppered with young, progressive, and professional officers. Short- and long-range planning had become institutionalized, and constructive debates over methods, procedures and approaches to police work were commonplace. By 1972, this department of approximately 1,300 police officers in a city of just over half a million—part of a metropolitan complex of 1.3 million—was open to new ideas and recommendations, and enjoyed the confidence of the people it served.

As part of its continuing internal discussions of policing, the department in October of 1971 established a task force of patrol officers and supervisors in each of its three patrol divisions (South, Central, and Northeast), as well as in its special operations division (helicopter, traffic, tactical, etc.). The decision to establish these task forces was based on the beliefs that the ability to make competent planning decisions existed at all levels within the department and that if institutional change was to gain acceptance, those affected by it should have a voice in planning and implementation.

The job of each task force was to isolate the critical problems facing its division and propose methods to attack those problems. All four task forces did so. The South Patrol Division Task Force identified five problem areas where greater police attention was deemed vital: burglaries, juvenile offenders, citizen fear, public education about the police role, and police-community relations.

Like the other task forces, the South task force was confronted next with developing workable remedial strategies. And here the task force met with what at first seemed an insurmountable barrier. It was evident that concentration by the South Patrol Division on the five problem areas would cut deeply into the time spent by its officers on preventive patrol. At this point a significant thing happened. Some of the members of the South task force questioned whether routine preventive patrol was effective, what police officers did while on preventive patrol duty, and what effect police visibility had on the community's feelings of security.

Out of these discussions came the proposal to conduct an experiment which would test the true impact of routine preventive patrol. The Police Foundation agreed to fund the experiment's evaluation.

As would be expected, considerable controversy surrounded the experiment, with the central question being whether long-range benefits outweighed short-term risks. The principal short-term risk was seen as the possibility that crime would increase drastically in the reactive beats; some officers felt the experiment would be tampering with citizens' lives and property.

The police officers expressing such reservations were no different from their counterparts in other departments. They tended to view patrol as one of the most important functions of policing, and in terms of time allocated, they felt that preventive patrol ranked on a par with investigating crimes and rendering assistance in emergencies. While some admitted that preventive patrol was probably less effective in preventing crime and more productive in enhancing citizen feelings of security, others insisted that the activities involved in preventive patrol (car, pedestrian, and building checks) were instrumental in the capture of criminals and, through the police visibility associated with such activities, in the deterrence of crime. While there were ambiguities in these attitudes toward patrol and its effectiveness, all agreed it was a primary police function.

Within the South Patrol Division's 24-beat area, nine beats were eliminated from consideration as unrepresentative of the city's socio-economic composition. The remaining 15-beat, 32-square mile experimental area encompassed a commercial-residential mixture, with a 1970 resident population of 148,395 persons and a density of 4,542 persons per square mile (significantly greater than that for Kansas City as a whole, which in 1970 with only 1,604 persons per square mile, was 45th in the nation). Racially, the beats within this area ranged from 78 percent black to 99 percent white. Median family income of residents ranged from a low of $7,320 for one beat to a high of $15,964 for another. On the average, residents of the experimental area tended to have been in their homes from 6.6 to 10.9 years.

Police officers assigned to the experimental area were those who had been patrolling it prior to the experiment, and tended to be white, relatively young, and somewhat new to the police department. In a sample of 101 officers in the experimental area taken across all three shifts, 9.9 percent of the officers were black, the average age of the officers was 27 years, and average time on the force was 3.2 years.

The 15 beats in the experimental area were computer matched on the basis of crime data, number of calls for service, ethnic composition, median income and transiency of population into five groups of three each. Within each group, one beat was designated reactive, one control, and one proactive. In the five reactive beats, there was no preventive patrol as such. Police vehicles assigned to these beats entered them only in response to calls for service. Their non–committed time (when not answering calls) was spent patrolling the boundaries of the reactive beats or patrolling in adjacent proactive beats. While police availability was closely maintained, police visibility was, in effect, withdrawn (except when police vehicles were seen while answering calls for service).

In the five control beats, the usual level of patrol was maintained at one car per beat. In the five proactive beats, the department increased police patrol visibility by two to three times its usual level both by the assignment of marked police vehicles to these beats and the presence of units from adjacent reactive beats.

Other than the restrictions placed upon officers in reactive beats (respond only to calls for service and patrol only the perimeter of the beat or in an adjacent proactive beat), no special instructions were given to police officers in the experimental area. Officers in control and proactive beats were to conduct preventive patrol, as they normally would.

It should be noted, however, that the geographical distribution of beats (see Figure 1) avoided clustering reactive beats together or at an unacceptable distance from proactive beats. Such clustering could have resulted in lowered response time in the reactive beats.

It should also be noted that patrol modification in the reactive and proactive beats involved only routine preventive patrol. Specialized units, such as tactical, helicopter, and K–9, operated as usual in these beats but at a level consistent with the activity level established the preceding year. This level was chosen to prevent infringement of these specialized units upon experimental results.

Finally, it should be noted that to minimize any possible risk through the elimination of routine preventive patrol in the reactive beats, crime rate data were monitored on a weekly basis. It was agreed that if a noticeable increase in crime occurred within a reactive beat, the experiment would be suspended. This situation, however, never materialized.

While the Kansas City experiment began on July 19, 1972, both department and Police Foundation monitors recognized by mid-August that experimental conditions were not being maintained, and that several problems had arisen. Chief Kelley then saw to it that these problems were rectified during a suspension of the experiment.

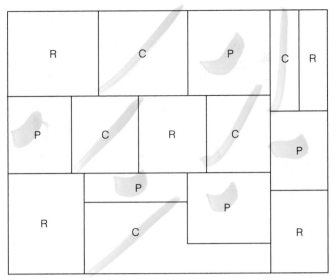

P = Proactive
C = Control
R = Reactive

FIGURE 1. Schematic Representation of the 15-Beat Experimental Area

One problem was manpower, which in the South Patrol Division had fallen to a dangerously low level for experimental purposes. To correct this problem additional police officers were assigned to the division and an adequate manpower level restored. A second problem involved violations of the project guidelines. Additional training sessions were held, and administrative emphasis brought to bear to ensure adherence to the guidelines. A third problem was boredom among officers assigned to reactive beats. To counter this, guidelines were modified to allow an increased level of activity by reactive-assigned officers in proactive beats. These revisions emphasized that an officer could take whatever action was deemed necessary, regardless of location, should a criminal incident be observed. The revised guidelines also stressed adherence to the spirit of the project rather than to unalterable rules.

On October 1, 1972, the experiment resumed. It continued successfully for 12 months, ending on September 30, 1973. Findings were produced in terms of the effect of experimental conditions on five categories of crime traditionally considered to be deterrable through preventive patrol (burglary, auto theft, larceny—theft of auto accessories, robbery, and vandalism) and on five other crime categories (including rape, assault, and other larcenies). Additional findings concerned the effect of experimental conditions on citizen feelings of security and satisfaction with police service, on the amount and types of anti-crime protective measures taken by citizens and businessmen, on police response time and citizen satisfaction with response time, and on injury/fatality and non-injury traffic accidents. The experiment also produced data concerning police activities during tours of duty, and police officer attitudes toward preventive patrol.

III. DATA SOURCES

In measuring the effects of routine patrol, it was decided to collect as wide a variety of data from as many diverse sources as possible. By so doing, it was felt that overwhelming evidence could be presented to prove or disprove the experimental hypothesis.

To measure the effects of the experimental conditions on crime, a victimization survey, departmental reported crime, departmental arrest data, and a survey of businesses were used. While reported crime has traditionally been considered the most important indicator of police effectiveness, the accuracy of both reported crime and arrest data as indicators of crime and police effectiveness has come under scrutiny in recent years. Both types of data are subject to wide degrees of conscious and unconscious manipulation, and to distortion and misrepresentation. Because of these, a criminal victimization survey was used as an additional source of data.

Victimization surveys were first used by the President's Commission on Law Enforcement and Administration of Justice. These surveys revealed that as much as 50 percent of crime was unreported by victims, either from neglect, embarrassment, or a feeling that the crimes were not worth reporting. Although victimization surveys also have their limitations, they can be an important way of measuring crime. Thus a victimization survey was used by the experiment to measure this key outcome variable.

To measure the impact of experimental conditions on community attitudes and fear, attitudinal surveys of both households and businesses (in conjunction with the victimization surveys) and a survey of those citizens experiencing direct encounters with the police were administered. Estimates of citizen satisfaction with police services were also recorded by participant observers.

Overall, in collecting data for the experiment, the [sources listed on the opposite page] were used.

Because many of these sources were used to monitor the degree to which experimental conditions were maintained or to identify unanticipated consequences of the experiment, only findings derived from the following data are presented in this report.

Community Survey

The community survey, which measured community victimization, attitudes and fear, was taken on a before and after basis. A sample of 1,200 households in the experimental area (approximately 80 per beat) was randomly selected and interviewed in September of 1972. In September of 1973, 1,200 households were again surveyed, approximately 600 chosen from the same population as the 1972 survey (for a repeated sample) and 600 chosen randomly from, the experimental area (for a non-repeated sample). Since 11 cases had to be excluded because of missing data, the 1973 sample totaled 1,189.

Commercial Survey

The commercial survey involved interviews conducted both in 1972 and 1973 with a random sample of 110 businesses in the experimental area to measure victimization rates and businessmen's perceptions of and satisfaction with police services.

Encounter Survey
(Both Citizen and Participant Observers)

Because household surveys tend to interview relatively few citizens who have experienced actual contact with the police, citizens in the three experimental areas who experienced direct encounters with police officers were interviewed. Although three survey instruments were developed (one to elicit the response of citizens, a second for the police officers, and a third for the observers riding with the officers) only the observer and citizen responses were analyzed. Identical questions were used as often as possible. The survey was conducted over a four-month period (July through October, 1973). Interviewed were 331 citizens who were involved in either an officer-initiated incident (car check, pedestrian check or a traffic violation) or citizen-initiated incident (one in which the citizen called for police service: burglary, robbery, larceny, assault, etc.).

SURVEYS AND QUESTIONNAIRES

1	Community Survey
	   victimization
	   attitudes
	   rates of reporting
		5	Encounter Survey — Observers
			   attitudes
			   perceptions

2	Commercial Survey
	   victimization
	   attitudes
	   rates of reporting
		6	Noncommitted Time Survey

		7	Response Time Survey observers

3	Encounter Survey — Citizens
	   attitudes
	   perceptions
		8	Response Time Survey
			   citizens

		9	HRD Survey

4	Encounter Survey — Officers
	   attitudes
	   perceptions
		10	Officer Questionnaire

INTERVIEWS AND RECORDED OBSERVATIONS

1	"Player" Observations	3	Participant Observer Interviews
2	Officer interviews	4	Participant Observer Transaction Recordings

---

DEPARTMENTAL DATA

1	Reported Crime	4	Computer Dispatch Data
2	Traffic Data	5	Officer Activity Analysis Data
3	Arrest Data	6	Personnel Records

Participant Observer Transaction Recordings

While the community encounter survey focused on the location of the police–citizen contact, the observer transaction recordings focused on police–citizen interactions in terms of the assignment of the officer involved (reactive, control, or proactive beats). These data were obtained by observers while riding with officers assigned to the experimental area, and involved observer estimates of citizen satisfaction as a result of direct contact with the police. Observations covered all three watches in all 15 beats. As a result, 997 incidents of police–citizen transactions were systematically recorded.

Reported Crime

Monthly totals for reported crime by beat over the October 1968 through September 1972 (pre-experimental) period and over the October 1972 through September 1973 (experimental) period were retrieved from departmental records. Time-series analyses were then performed on these data to produce the findings.

Traffic Data

Two categories of traffic accidents were monitored: non-injury and injury/fatality. Monitoring was maintained over two time periods, October 1970 through September 1972 for the pre-experimental period, and October 1972 through September 1973 for the experimental period.

Arrest Data

Arrest data by month and beat for the experimental year and the three preceding years were obtained from departmental records.

Response Time Survey

Police response time in the experimental area was recorded between May and September 1973 through the use of a response time survey completed by the participant observers and those citizens who had called the police for service. In measuring the time taken by the police in responding to calls, emphasis was placed on field response time (i.e., the amount of time occurring between the time a police unit on the street received a call from the dispatcher and the time when the unit contacted the citizen involved). In measuring citizen satisfaction with response time, the entire range of time required for the police to answer a call was considered (i.e., including time spent talking with the police department operator, police dispatcher, plus field response time).

Methodology and Maintenance
of Experimental Conditions

Because multiple dimensions of the possible effects of the experiment were examined, differing methods of analysis were applied to the data generated. Detailed discussions of these and other factors concerning the experiment's methodology, including a discussion of the sampling error, can be found in the technical report and its appendices. A discussion of the methods used to determine the extent to which desired levels of patrol coverage were achieved, the degree to which experimental conditions were maintained, and whether the criminal world realized that routine patrol strategies had been modified and to what extent patterns of behavior changed as a result can be found in Chapter III of the technical report. In summary, the data sources used to analyze these factors point to the overall maintenance of experimental conditions.

Spillover Effect

One major concern in an experiment of this type is the so-called spillover or displacement theory, i.e., that as crime decreases in one area due to increased police presence, it will increase in other, usually contiguous, areas. This would mean that the effect of the experiment within the experimental area would be offset by counter-effects in other areas. To test this, various correlations between contiguous beats were calculated and analyzed. Except for auto theft, there were no noticeable alterations in the correlations of crime levels. These results, combined with an examination of the actual monthly figures, tend to indicate that, in general, there was no spillover effect. Results of the calculations can be found in the appendices to the technical report.

IV. EXPERIMENTAL FINDINGS

The essential finding of the preventive patrol experiment is that decreasing or increasing routine preventive patrol within the range tested in this experiment had no effect on crime, citizen fear of crime, community attitudes toward the police on the delivery of police service, police response time, or traffic accidents. Given the large amount of data collected and the extremely diverse sources used, the evidence is overwhelming. Of the 648 comparisons made to produce the 13 major findings that follow, statistical significance occurred only 40 times between pairs, or in approximately 6 percent of the total. Of these 40, the change was greater 15 times in reactive beats, 19 times in control beats, and 6 times in proactive beats.

Findings of the experiment are presented in terms of the impact that the range of variation in preventive patrol used in this experiment had upon the following:

- community vicitimization
- departmental reported crime
- rates of reporting crime to police
- arrest trends
- citizen's fear of crime
- protective measures used by citizens

- protective measures used by businesses
- community attitudes toward the police and the delivery of police services
- businessmen's attitudes toward the police and the delivery of police services
- citizen attitudes toward the police as a result of encounters with the police
- estimation of citizen–police transactions
- police response time
- traffic incidents

The tables used in this document to illustrate the findings are summary tables which compress elaborate amounts of data. Presentation of the data in this form presents numerous problems in that much information is lost in summary. For example, actual numbers, direction of the findings, and discussion of those methodologies used for analyses are not included. Because of this, the findings are considered in their most generalized form; the sole issues are statistical significance and whether or not routine preventive patrol, within the range of variation tested, had an impact on the experimental area. The details of that impact are not presented. Consequently, as mentioned earlier, the findings outlined here cannot be used for specific planning purposes.

On the other hand, presentation in this manner allows for an overview, and focuses on only the most significant findings. Given the importance of the issue and the difficulties inherent in proving the effects of such experiments, emphasis is placed on the large amounts of data collected from diverse sources, and the overwhelming tendency of the data to point in a single direction.

EFFECTS ON CRIME, REPORTING AND ARRESTS

Finding 1: Victimization

The Victimization Survey found no statistically significant differences in crime in any of the 69 comparisons made between reactive, control, and proactive beats.

This finding would be expected for such categories as rape, homicide, and common or aggravated assault. For one thing, these are typically impulsive crimes, usually taking place between persons known to each other. Furthermore, they most often take place inside a building, out of sight of an officer on routine preventive patrol. The spontaneity and lack of high visibility of these crimes, therefore, make it unlikely that they would be much affected by variations in the level of preventive patrol.

Given traditional beliefs about patrol, however, it is surprising that statistically significant differences did not occur in such crimes as commercial burglaries, auto theft, and robberies.

Nonetheless, as measured by the victimization survey, these crimes were not significantly affected by changes in the level of routine preventive patrol.

Finding 2: Departmental Reported Crime

*Departmental Reported Crimes showed only one statistical difference among
51 comparisons drawn between reactive, control and proactive beats.*

Statistical significance occurred only in the category of "Other Sex Crimes."
This category, separate from "Rape," includes such offenses as molestation and
exhibitionism. Since this category is not traditionally considered to be responsive to routine preventive patrol, however, it appears likely that this instance of
significance was a statistically random occurrence.

Finding 3: Rates of Reporting Crime

*Crimes citizens and businessmen said they reported to the police showed statistically
significant difference between reactive, control and proactive beats in only five of
48 comparisons, and these differences showed no consistent pattern.*

Of the five instances of statistical significance, three involved vandalism and
two residence burglary. But where statistical significance was found, no consistent pattern emerged. On two occasions the change was greater in the control
beats, on two occasions greater in the proactive beats, and once it was greater
in the reactive beats. Given the low number of statistically significant findings
combined with a lack of consistent direction, the conclusion is that rates of reporting crimes by businessmen and citizens were unaffected by the experimental changes in levels of patrol.

Finding 4: Arrest Patterns

*Police arrests showed no statistically significant differences in the
27 comparisons made between reactive, control, and proactive beats.*

While arrest totals for 16 categories of crime were determined, it will be noted
that in seven categories—common assault, larceny-purse snatch, homicide,
non-residence burglary, auto theft, larceny-auto accessory, and larceny-bicycle
—either the number of arrests was too small to allow for statistical analysis, or
the pre-experimental pattern of arrests was so distorted that statistical significance could not be determined. On the basis of the comparisons that could be
made, however, the conclusion is that arrest rates were not significantly affected
by changes in the level of patrol.

EFFECTS ON COMMUNITY ATTITUDES

Citizen Fear of Crime

The experiment measured community attitudes toward many aspects of crime
and police performance to determine whether varying degrees of routine preventive patrol—reactive, control, proactive—had any significant effect upon
these attitudes. Previous investigators, including Roger Parks and Michael
Maltz, have shown that citizens can recognize, or at least sense, changes in levels of service or innovations in policing.

Thus, through the Community and Commercial Surveys which provided the victimization information used in the previous section of this summary, citizen attitudes toward crime and police were also measured before and after the experiment.

The first attitude measured was citizen fear of crime, determined by (1) a series of questions in the Community Survey designed to probe levels of fear; (2) a series of questions in the Community Survey regarding protective and security measures taken by citizens; and (3) questions in the Commercial Survey about protective and security measures used by businessmen at their places of business.

Finding 5: Citizen Fear of Crime

Citizen fear of crime was not significantly affected by changes in the level of routine preventive patrol.

In the Community Survey, citizen estimates of neighborhood safety and perceptions of violent crimes were obtained. Citizens were then asked what they thought the probability was that they might be involved in various types of crime, including robbery, assault, rape, burglary, and auto theft.

Of the 60 comparisons made between experimental areas, statistical significance was found in only five cases. Three involved the probability of being raped, one the probability of being robbed, and one the probability of being assaulted. The change in the level of fear was greater in reactive beats four times and greater in proactive beats once.

Yet when statistical significance is found, the patterns are inconsistent. For example, all cases in which the change in reactive beats are significantly higher than in other beats are found in the repeated sample. These findings are not confirmed by the non-repeated sample, however. The one area in which control registered the higher change occurs in the non-repeated sample, but this is not confirmed by the repeated sample.

The findings thus lead to the conclusion that citizen fear is not affected by differences in the level of routine preventive patrol.

Finding 6: Protective Measures (Citizens)

Protective and security measures taken by citizens against the possibility of being involved in crime were not significantly affected by variations in the level of routine preventive patrol.

The questions asked of citizens in the Community Survey on this subject dealt with the installation of such devices as bars, alarms, locks and lighting, the keeping of various types of weapons or dogs for protection, and the taking of certain actions, such as staying inside, as preventive measures.

Here, 84 comparisons were made between experimental areas, with statistical significance occurring 11 times. The significance occurred most often (6 times) in those beats where preventive patrol had not changed, that is, in control beats. The change in the reactive beats showed significance three times, and in the proactive beats twice. There is no apparent explanation for the fact that the use of protective measures supposedly increased in the control beats relative to the other two conditions. For the most part, the findings are inconsistent and occur either in the non-repeated sample or the repeated sample but never uniformly in both.

Thus, as measured by the use of protective and security measures, experimental preventive patrol conditions did not significantly affect citizen fear of crime.

Finding 7: Protective Measures (Businesses)

Protective and security measures taken by businesses in the experimental area to protect offices of other places of business did not show significant differences due to changes in the level of routine preventive patrol.

In the Commercial Survey, businessmen were asked such questions as whether they had installed alarm systems or reinforcing devices such as bars over windows, whether they had hired guards, or whether they kept watchdogs or firearms in their places of business.

All told, 21 comparisons were made and statistical significance was found once, where the change in the control beats was the greater as compared with the reactive beats.

Because this was a telephone survey, however, some problems with the findings were evident. Briefly, some businessmen were reluctant to talk about protective measures over the phone to persons unknown to them. This is discussed more fully in the technical report.

The conclusion remains, however, that preventive variations seem to have little effect on fear of crime as indicated by protective measures taken by commercial establishments.

Citizen Attitudes Toward Police

In addition to investigating citizen fear of crime and criminals, the preventive patrol experiment delved into citizen attitudes toward the police. Residents in the experimental area were asked, for instance, about the need for more police officers, about variations in patrol, police officer reputations, and effectiveness, police treatment of citizens, and about their satisfaction with police service.

The attitudes of businessmen toward police were studied in the course of the preventive patrol experiment for a variety of reasons. One was simply that businessmen's attitudes have seldom been studied in the past, although these people are often affected by crime in ways more crucial to their survival than are citizens in general. It is not only the businessman's personal comfort and safety that may be involved, but also the ability to remain in business that may be affected by crime. At the same time, businessmen are often influential in their communities. For these reasons, assessing their attitudes is often crucial to the development of new policing programs. Therefore, businessmen were asked similar questions about police effectiveness, treatment of citizens, and so forth.

While the study of such attitudes is valuable in obtaining the impressions of a significant cross-section of the community, most of the citizens and businessmen interviewed were unlikely to have experienced recent actual contact with the police. Thus, another part of the preventive patrol experiment focused on determining citizens' responses to actual encounters with police officers. To determine such responses, citizens themselves, the police with whom they came in contact, and trained observers were all asked to complete reports on the encounter. Citizens were interviewed as soon as possible after the incident. Separate questionnaires were used, depending on whether the encounter was initiated by an officer or by a citizen.

Finally, a fourth measure was used to determine citizen attitudes. Here, in what has been given the title "Police-Citizen Transactions," the trained observers focused on the outcome of police-citizen interactions in terms of the patrol assignment of the officer involved, that is, reactive, control or proactive.

The next findings deal with citizen attitudes toward police, businessmen's attitudes toward police, police-citizen encounters initiated either by citizens (calls for service) or police (traffic arrests, suspect apprehension, etc.), and finally police-citizen transactions.

Finding 8: Citizen Attitudes Toward Police

Citizen attitudes toward police were not significantly affected
by alterations in the level of preventive patrol.

A large number of questions in the Community Survey were designed to measure citizen attitudes toward the police. As a result, more comparisons were made here than in other cases and more instances of statistical significance were found. Altogether, 111 comparisons were made and statistical significance occurred 16 times. Items with significant differences included the need for more police officers in the city, the reputation of police officers, citizens' respect for police, police effectiveness, harassment, and change in the neighborhood police officers.

Of the 16 instances of significance, the change in reactive beats was greater 5 times, in control beats 10 times, and in proactive beats once, demonstrating no consistent pattern of statistical significance. The indication is that there was little correlation between level of patrol and citizen attitudes.

Finding 9: Businessmen's Attitudes Toward Police

Businessmen's attitudes toward police were not significantly affected
by changes in the level of routine preventive patrol.

Like citizens in the Community Survey, businessmen in the Commercial Survey were asked about their attitudes toward police. Some of the questions in the Commercial Survey were similar to those in the Community Survey and some specially selected with regard to businessmen's interests.

In all, 48 comparisons were made to measure differences in businessmen's attitudes, but no statistically significant differences were found or even approached. The clear indication here is that variations in the level of preventive patrol have no effect on businessmen's attitudes.

Finding 10: Police-Citizen Encounters

Citizen attitudes toward police officers encountered through the initiative of either the citizen or the officer were not significantly affected by changes in patrol level.

Citizen attitudes were measured by both questions asked of citizens themselves and observations of trained observers. Citizens and observers alike were asked about such items as response time, characteristics of the encounter, the attitude and demeanor of officers in the encounter, and citizen satisfaction. Observers in officer-initiated encounters also recorded things not likely to be noted by citizens, including the number of officers and police vehicles present.

Including both citizen-initiated and officer-initiated encounters, a total of 63 comparisons were made and no statistically significant differences were found.

Finding 11: Police-Citizen Transactions

The behavior of police officers toward citizens was not significantly affected by the officers' assignment to a reactive, control or proactive beat.

The finding is distinct from the previous finding in that the focus here is upon the police-citizen interaction in terms of the beat assignment of the officer rather than on the location of the contact. (Many police contacts with citizens take place outside of the officer's beat.) Data were recorded by participant observers riding with the officers.

In all, 18 comparisons were made between experimental areas, and no statistically significant differences were found.

OTHER EFFECTS

Experimental Findings in Regard to
Police Response Time

The time it takes for police officers to respond to a citizen call for assistance is usually considered an important measure of patrol effectiveness. The general principle is that the lower the response time, the more efficiently the police are doing their job.

But there are difficulties in determining how to measure response time given the numerous possible segments involved. For instance, is the response time cycle complete when the first officer arrives at the scene? Or when the last of several officers dispatched reaches the scene? Or when the first officer contacts the person making the call? For the purposes of the preventive patrol experiment, response time was defined as the time between receipt of a call from a dispatcher to the point when that unit contacted the citizen involved. In measuring citizen satisfaction with response time, the entire range of time required was considered, beginning with the citizen's contact with the police switchboard operator.

Response time was studied to see if experimental conditions would have any effect on the amount of time taken by police in answering citizen calls for service. Before the experiment began, the hypothesis was that experimental conditions would affect response time, particularly in proactive beats. It was believed that since more officers were assigned to proactive beats, response time would be significantly reduced in those beats.

Finding 12: Response Time

The amount of time taken by police in answering calls for service was not significantly affected by variations in the level of routine preventive patrol.

To obtain the finding, data were gathered on such matters as distance from the police car to the scene of incident, mean time from receipt of call to start of call, mean time from receipt of call to arrival at scene, and observer's estimate of patrol car speed. Citizen estimates of time and satisfaction were also measured.

In the area of response time, a total of 42 comparisons were made between patrol conditions. Statistical significance occurred only once: in the number of officers present at the scene of incidents in the reactive beats. The reason for this is unclear, but it can be theorized that police officers were exhibiting their concern for the safety of fellow officers and citizens in reactive beats.

While variations in the level of patrol did not significantly affect police response time, the Kansas City findings suggest that more research is necessary. It appears that response time is not only the result of rate of speed and distance, but also reflects the attitude of the officers involved and possibly other variables not investigated in this study.

Experimental Findings in Regard to Traffic Accidents

Does the police visibility through routine preventive patrol have an effect upon traffic accidents? A common hypothesis is that it does, that reduction in patrol, for instance, will be followed by an increase in traffic accidents. Therefore the preventive patrol experiment involved some study of the presumed relationship.

The finding in this area is presented with considerable caution, however, since traffic patterns played no role in the selection of the experimental beats. It is possible (and in fact likely, given the area involved) that traffic patterns in the experimental area are not representative, and thus would not allow for reliable findings. In addition, the findings involved only accidents reported to the department by citizens and do not take into account accidents which occurred but were not reported.

Finding 13: Traffic Accidents

Variations in the level of routine preventive patrol had no significant effect upon traffic accidents.

A total of six comparisons were made in this area, with statistical significance not occurring in any.

SUMMARY AND CONCLUSION:
EXPERIMENTAL FINDINGS

Of the 648 comparisons used to produce the major findings of the preventive patrol experiment, statistical significance between pairs occurred 40 times representing approximately 6 percent of the total. Of these 40 findings, the change in the reactive beats was greater 15 times, in the control beats 19 times, and in the proactive beats 6 times. Given the large amount of data collected and the extremely diverse sources used, the overwhelming evidence is that decreasing or increasing routine preventive patrol within the range tested in this experiment had no effect on crime, citizen fear of crime, community attitudes toward the police on the delivery of police service, police response time, or traffic accidents.

Effects of Gun Seizures on Gun
Violence: "Hot Spots" Patrol
in Kansas City

LAWRENCE W. SHERMAN
DENNIS P. ROGAN

We tested the hypothesis that greater enforcement of existing laws against carrying concealed weapons could reduce firearms violence with a quasi-experimental, target beat/comparison beat design. Over a six-month period in a ten-by-eight-block area with a homicide rate 20 times higher than the national average, intensive patrol near gun crime hot spots produced a 65 percent increase in firearms seized by police. Gun crimes declined in the target area by 49 percent, with no significant displacement to any patrol beat surrounding the target area. Neither gun crimes nor guns seized changed significantly in the comparison beat several miles away.

This report was supported in part by grant 91-DD-CX-KO56 from the National Institute of Justice to the University of Maryland. Findings and conclusions of the research reported here are those of the authors and do not necessarily reflect the official position or policies of the U.S. Department of Justice. The authors present this report in collaboration with the Kansas City (Mo.) Police Department, with special thanks to Police Chief Steven Bishop, Major Dennis Shreve, Deputy Chief James Nunn, Captain John Hamilton, Sergeants Tim Edwards and David Burns, and Ms. Judy Robinette.

Source: Sherman, Lawrence W. and Dennis P. Rogan (1995) Effects of Gun Seizures on Gun Violence: "Hot Spots" Patrol in Kansas City. *Justice Quarterly* 12: 674–693. Reprinted with permission of the Academy of Criminal Justice Sciences.

Can police take more guns off the streets? Would it make any difference for gun crime if they did? The answers to these questions are critically important, almost regardless of the future of gun control laws in the United States. Even if all handgun possession or carrying were banned tomorrow, the gun stock to be controlled would be an estimated three handguns for every 10 persons in the United States (Kleck 1991: Table 2.1). If gun carrying is an essential proximate cause of gun crimes outside the home, then compliance with laws against gun carrying is a key issue for reducing gun crime.

GUN CARRYING AND GUN CRIME

While the literature on guns and violence has focused primarily on gun *density* (Cook 1991; Reiss and Roth 1993: Chapter 6) gun *carrying* is a logical extension and specification of the dynamics of gun density. The two variables may be highly correlated over time, allowing strong relationships to emerge between gun density and homicide (e.g., McDowall 1991). But carrying frequency per gun may be the behavioral mechanism by which gun density is translated into gun crime. Thus it is conceivable that some cities with high handgun density may have lower gun crime rates because the carrying frequency per handgun is lower than in a city with few guns but high carrying frequency per gun. Reports of multiple murders over time committed with the same gun in Washington, DC, where all handguns are banned (Lewis 1995), suggest that carrying frequency per handgun may vary enormously, depending on the social networks and community conditions in which the gun is circulated.

The importance of gun carrying is also suggested by the results of the evaluations of the 1974 Bartley-Fox law in Massachusetts, which created mandatory one-year prison sentences upon conviction for illegal gun carrying. Although the implementation of this law was eventually watered down, the substantial publicity effort and early vigorous enforcement reduced gun homicides as well as gun use in robberies and assaults (Pierce and Bowers 1979; Reiss and Roth 1993:275).

The importance of gun carrying is consistent with the strong geographic concentration of gun crimes. Even in high-crime neighborhoods, most addresses never suffer any gun crimes, while a few addresses experience them repeatedly. Over a two-year period in Indianapolis, for example, gun crimes were reported at only 3 percent of all addresses, with 6,409 gun calls at only 5,024 addresses; after seven gun calls at an address, the probability of further gun calls rose to 100 percent. Concentrations are even clearer at the block level: one block registered 68 calls for service about guns; another, 55; a third, 53; and a fourth, 33 (Sherman 1995). At these gun crime hot spots, the percentage of persons on the streets carrying guns may be far higher than elsewhere in the city.

Gun-carrying hot spots also may attract repeat gun criminals, a clearly documented problem. One study of juvenile arrests in Washington, DC, showed that 373 (17 percent) of 2,176 persons arrested at least once on gun charges were arrested again for the same reason over a six-year period. Fifty had at least three gun charges as juveniles; 10 of these were later charged with murder and five were shot to death themselves (Lewis 1995).

Policing Gun Carrying

These findings are consistent with Wilson's (1994) hypothesis that police can reduce gun violence by more enforcement of laws against gun carrying in high-risk places, by high-risk people, at high-risk times. Kleck offers a similar suggestion:

> [P]olice departments might experiment with increasing street searches and arrests for unlawful carrying, and/or improving the targeting of searches. Even in the absence of increased use of prison sentences for violators, increased carrying arrests might deter the casual, routine carrying of firearms, and thereby indirectly reduce opportunistic robberies. (1991:441).

Most big-city police agencies, however, have done relatively little to test that hypothesis. Rather than focusing on gun seizures as a strategy for preventing gun crime, police have tended to obtain guns reactively in the course of other enforcement duties (Moore 1980). Cities vary widely in both the effort they expend on gun seizures and in the results (Brill 1977). A survey of 1993 gun seizures in 30 large police agencies (Sherman and Bridgeforth 1994) found the highest rate of guns seized per 100 police employees (331 in Phoenix) was seven times as great as the lowest (47 in New York City). The highest rate per 100,000 population (1075 in Chicago) was five times the lowest rate (202 in Long Beach). The greatest variation was in the rate of guns seized per 100 homicides: the rate for the highest-ranking city, Albuquerque (8,333), was 13 times as great as for the lowest ranking city, Los Angeles (639).

Perhaps the most surprising result of the survey was that almost half of the cities surveyed (of all 59 over 250,000 population) responded that they did not know the number of guns seized. Few police chiefs use that number as a productivity statistic, and few annual police reports mention it. Few officers apparently go out of their way to try to find guns on the street. In an 11-month period in 1993–1994, half of the 895 Indianapolis police officers seized no guns at all, while 10 percent of the officers seized over 50 percent of the total 2,318 guns seized (Sherman 1995).

The lack of importance given to seizures of illegal guns may reflect pessimism about the difficulty of replacing guns. Many police agree that an offender from whom a gun is taken can replace that gun within hours. Gun offenders' ability to replace seized weapons, however, should not be taken for granted. As youthful gun violence has exploded—with Washington, DC, juvenile arrests three times more likely than adult arrests to include gun charges (Lewis 1995)—young people's ability to replace guns is increasingly important to total gun crime. Incarcerated felons have boldly told survey researchers that they believed they could obtain a replacement gun "within a few hours," but the reality may be closer to this case reported from Washington, DC:

> One youth told [the interviewer] he had spent more than two weeks hiding in his house after his gun was confiscated when he was frisked entering a local disco. He said he didn't leave the house again until he had obtained another gun (Lewis 1995: A1).

Taking guns away from high-risk persons may not incapacitate them permanently from carrying guns, but it may do so in the short term. It may incapacitate them long enough to allow the cooling of their anger at someone they had planned to shoot. It also may reduce the supply of rent-a-guns (Lewis 1995) widely circulated for criminal purposes. Alternatively, taking guns may specifically deter the confiscatees and may generally deter others from carrying guns in high-gun-enforcement areas, so that they may avoid the inconvenience, expense, and perceived danger (due to lack of self-defense capacity) of temporarily losing access to a gun.

Even if Wilson's (1994) hypothesis is correct, one still might expect some displacement of gun crime to other places besides the targeted gun hot spots. Yet if routine activities theory is correct (Felson 1994), the likelihood that gun crimes will occur outside the hot spots should be substantially lower than within those spots. Fewer interactions with likely victims or antagonists should lead to fewer uses of the weapon, even if the carrying rate remains the same outside the hot spots. Thus the hypothesis that greater enforcement of gun carrying in gun crime hot spots can reduce gun crime overall is at least theoretically plausible. Not for the first time in modern police history, the Kansas City (Mo.) Police Department was the first to put the hypothesis to a controlled quasi-experimental test.

THE KANSAS CITY GUN EXPERIMENT

The experiment developed in 1991 from the first federal grant awarded under the U.S. Bureau of Justice Assistance (BJA) "Weed and Seed" program. The Kansas City (Missouri) Police Department (KCPD) was given wide latitude in planning its Weed and Seed strategy. Shortly after the BJA made the award to the KCPD, the National Institute of Justice (NIJ) awarded the University of Maryland a grant to evaluate the Kansas City effort. This timing allowed the police and researchers to collaborate in planning a focused program with a strong research design.

Because the area already selected by federal officials for the Weed and Seed grant had the second highest number of drive-by shootings of any patrol beat citywide in 1991, the police and academic team designing the experiment chose reduction of gun crime as the principal objective of the program. The program budget for police overtime and extra patrol cars then was dedicated to removing guns from the street as cost-effectively as possible.

Because the program was restricted to one target patrol beat (#144 in the Central Patrol District), the planning team selected a before-after comparison area design. One can argue that the comparison area design is preferable to a citywide trend comparison because citywide trends are more stable than area-level trends; they average out any sharp differences across areas and therefore create a bias toward showing an effect of treating a single area. Area-level trends, in contrast, are more likely to reflect local changes in gun crime patterns, and are less likely than citywide trends to remain stable simply because of their size. The comparison area chosen was Patrol Beat 242, in the Metro Patrol District. It was selected primarily because it was almost identical to Beat 144 in the drive-by shootings[1] in 1991: 25 drive-bys were reported in Beat 242, compared with 24 in Beat 144. Although no special efforts were made to limit police activities in Beat 242, no funds were available for extra patrol time in that area.

The KCPD attempted three different strategies for increasing gun seizures in Beat 144: door-to-door solicitation of anonymous tips, training police to interpret gun-carrying cues in body language, and field interrogations in gun crime hot spots (Shaw 1994; Sherman, Shaw and Rogan 1995). Both the federal funds for extra police patrol and the measurable effects were associated entirely with the third strategy, as described in this evaluation.

Hypothesis

According to the theory, if the added patrols increased gun seizures, gun crime would be reduced in turn. We suggested two possible mechanisms: deterrence and incapacitation. The deterrence theory held that if it became known that police were likely to take away a gun, illegal gun carriers would become less likely to carry guns in the area. The incapacitation theory held that if guns were confiscated from enough potential gun criminals in the area, they would be unable to commit gun crimes (incapacitated)—at least for the time required to obtain a new gun. A third theory—that increased patrol visibility in the area would generally deter all crime—was also suggested.

Neither of the two primary theoretical mechanisms could be examined directly within the limits of the study, although the third could be tested by measuring non-gun crimes as well as gun crimes. The evaluation focused on the basic hypothesis that *gun seizures and gun crime would be inversely related*. From the outset, the team recognized that support for the hypothesis would not prove that more gun seizures cause reduction of gun crime. The design could not eliminate all competing explanations that could be suggested for the results. Yet if an inverse correlation between gun seizures and gun crime was found, it could suggest the value of further research and development. It could also support a policy of extending the patrols, regardless of the exact mechanism that made them effective.

Design and Experimental Period

For 29 weeks in 1992-1993 (July 7 to January 27), the Kansas City Police Department focused extra patrol attention on gun crime "hot spots" (Sherman, Gartin, and Buerger 1989) in the target beat. The hot spot locations were identified by University of Maryland computer analysis of all gun crimes in the area.[2] The extra patrol was provided in rotation by officers from Central Patrol Division in a pair of two-officer cars, working on overtime funded by the U.S. Bureau of Justice Assistance Weed and Seed program. The officers on overtime worked from 7 p.m. to 1 a.m. seven days a week. They were asked to focus on gun detection through proactive patrol, and were not required to answer calls for service.

Although the evaluation concentrated primarily on this first phase of the Weed and Seed grant, additional findings report what happened when the funding of Phase 1 patrols ended (first half of 1993) and when the funding of Phase 2 allowed resumption of the patrols (second half of 1993).[3]

Target and Control Areas

Beat 144, the target beat, is an eight-by-10-block area with a 1991 homicide rate of 177 per 100,000 persons, or about 20 times the national average that year (Shaw 1994:120). In addition to eight murders in 1991, this beat registered 14 rapes, 72 armed robberies, 222 aggravated assaults (142 with firearms), and a total of 349 violent felonies—close to one a day. Table 1 shows that the population of the beat is almost entirely nonwhite, with very low property values for the predominantly single-family detached homes. The rate of homeownership is very high, over two-thirds of all households.

Table 1 also shows that the comparison beat, 242, is similar to the target beat in many ways, although hardly a perfect match—a virtual impossibility in this kind of design. The major difference is that Beat 242 has almost twice as much population and three times as much land area, including a park. Housing prices are somewhat higher in the comparison beat. Both beats have substantial volumes of violent crime, which provide a more reliable basis for assessing trends over time than in beats with less crime.

Treatment Content and Dosage

Four officers at a time (volunteering from the entire patrol district) worked six hours of overtime each night (7 p.m. to 1 a.m.) for 176 nights, and only two officers worked on 24 other nights, for a total of 200 nights, 4,512 officer-hours, and 2,256 patrol car-hours of hot spot patrol. Officers reported spending 3.27 car-hours of the 12 car-hours per night actually patrolling the target area (27 percent), for a total of 1,218 officer-hours of potential gun detection and visible patrol presence in the area. The officers thus spent 70 percent of their time in processing arrests and performing other patrol related duties, as well as in patrol work outside the target area.

Despite their limited time in the area, the officers did a great deal. They were not assigned calls for service except in extraordinary circumstances, but they initiated a high volume of contact with the street population. Both inside and outside Beat 144, the directed patrols issued 1,090 traffic citations, conducted 948 car checks and 532 pedestrian checks, and made 170 state or federal arrests and 446 city arrests, for an average of one police intervention for every 40 minutes per patrol car. There is some evidence that activity levels declined somewhat

Table 1 Characteristics of Target and Comparison Beats

Characteristic	Target Beat (144)	Comparison Beat (242)
Population	4,528	8,142
% Female	53	56
% under 25	38	41
Median Age	32	31
% Nonwhite	92	85
% Age 25+ High School Grad.	53	73
Residential Square Blocks	80	150
Population Density per Mile	7,075	4,308
% Single-Family Housing	84	93
% Land Parcels Vacant	34	14
% Houses Owner-Occupied	63	71
Median Years Owned	12	10
Median Parcel Value	$14,181	$23,953
1991 Firearms-Related Crimes	183	252
(per 1,000)	40	31
1991 Shots Fired Incidents	86	120
(per 1,000)	19	15
1991 Drive-By Shootings	24	25
(per 1,000)	5	3
1991 Homicides	8	11
(per 1,000)	1.77	1.35
7/7/91 to 7/5/93 Gun Crimes	468	712
% Gun Crimes Aggravated Assault	63	57

during the period from October to January, as is usually true of street activity in colder weather (Shaw 1994:243). The average number of car checks made per day, for example, began at its high of 6.5 in July, and declined to its low of 3.2 in November. Time in the target area, miles driven, and traffic citations issued, however, did not change substantially over the first six months.

The actual techniques used by the officers to find the guns varied widely; they included searches incident to arrest on other charges and *Terry v. Ohio* (1968) safety frisks associated with car stops for traffic violations (also see *Pennsylvania v. Mimms* 1977; *Michigan v. Long* 1983). Of the 29 guns seized by officers on hot spot patrols, 10 (34%) were detected during a safety frisk, six (21%) were found in plain view, and 13 (45%) were discovered during a search incident to arrest. Every arrest for carrying concealed weapons had to be approved as to adequate probable cause by signature of a supervisory detective.

The exact nature of the work leading to gun seizures can be illustrated, although not comprehensively, by the following examples:

Safety frisk during traffic stop: When the officer asks the driver for his license, the driver leans over to the glove compartment and reveals a bulge under the jacket on the left arm. The officer grabs the bulge, feels a hard bulk in the shape of a gun, and reaches into the jacket to pull the gun out.

Plain view: As the officer approaches the car he has stopped for speeding, he shines a flashlight onto the floor in front of the back seat and sees a shotgun. Ordering the driver and passenger out of the car, he finds that the shotgun is loaded.

Search incident to arrest on other charges: A driver is stopped for running a red light. The officer asks for the driver's license. A computer check reveals that the driver is wanted for a failure to appear on domestic assault charges. The officer arrests the driver, searches him, and finds a gun hidden inside his shirt.

Many important questions can be asked about these methods and about the "sixth sense" that officers use initially to identify cars and pedestrians to stop. The literature on this question (e.g., Skolnick 1966) tends to stress situational cues out of order, such as a man wearing a heavy coat on a warm day. Yet the wide variety of situational cues that could be "out of order" is virtually impossible to specify. In recent years, for example, General Motors vehicles have been thought more likely to be stolen than others. Thus a GM car with windshield wipers running when there is no rain (suggesting the driver is unfamiliar with the car) can be stopped by an officer on "suspicion." The questions raised most often by critics about these procedures concern the rate of false positives and the potential discrimination entailed in responding to certain patterns of cues. Although such questions are beyond the scope of this study, they merit continuing attention. Yet it is interesting that none of the U.S. Supreme Court decisions even attempt to articulate the substantive bases for police officers' suspicions; they place on the officers the burden of articulating a reasonable basis and implicitly accept as reasonable the facts in the cases cited.

Measures

We measured both police activity and crime. Because the extra patrol hours were federally funded, separate bookkeeping was required to document the time. In addition, the on-site University of Maryland evaluator accompanied the officers on 300 hours of hot spot patrol and coded every shift activity narrative for patrol time and enforcement inside and outside the area (Shaw 1994). We analyzed property room data on guns seized, as well as computerized crime reports, data on calls for service, and arrest records. We made no attempt to conduct victimization surveys, although other papers (Shaw 1994, 1995) report a before-and-after survey of the target and comparison beats conducted in order to measure residents' perceptions of the program.

We counted gun crimes according to computerized offense records showing that a gun had been used in the crime. Actual discharges of the weapon could be determined only by reading the narrative section of the incident reports for every offense in the target and the comparison beat (Shaw 1994).

Analyses

Building on the precedent of previous studies of gun crime policy impact (Loftin et al. 1991), we examined the data using four different models. The primary analyses assumed that the gun crime counts were independently sampled from the beats examined before and after the intervention. This model treated the before–during difference in the mean weekly rates of gun crimes as an estimate of the magnitude of the effect of the hot spot patrols, and assessed the statistical significance of the differences with standard two–tailed t-tests. A second model assumed that the weekly gun crime data points were not independent but were correlated serially, and thus required a Box-Jenkins ARIMA (autoregressive integrated moving average) test of the effect of an abrupt intervention in a time series, computed with BMDP software (BMDP 1990).[4] A third model examined rare events, such as homicide and drive-by shootings, aggregated in six-month totals on the assumption that those counts were independent, using one-way analysis of variance tests. A fourth model also assumed independence of observations, and compared the target with the control beat in a before–during chi-square test.

Displacement tests for gun crime in each contiguous area were conducted with the difference of means, ARIMA, and ANOVA models.

Time Periods

The t-tests compared weekly gun crimes for all 29 weeks of the Phase 1 patrol program (July 7, 1992 through January 25, 1993, when the initial funding for the special patrols expired) with the 29 weeks preceding Phase 1, using difference of means tests. The ARIMA models extended the weekly counts to a full 52 weeks before and after the beginning of Phase 1 patrols in the target area, in order to obtain more reliable estimates of effect size. The ANOVA models added another year before Phase 1 (all of 1991), as well as 1993, the year after the Phase 1 patrols. During that year, hot spot patrols stopped for six months and then were resumed for six months in the second half of 1993, when Phase 2 funding was awarded. These changes offered six periods of six months each; in two of these periods the program was in effect, and in four it was not. We used the chi-square tests to compare 1991–1992 differences in gun crimes for all four quarters, as well as in both half-years, in both target and comparison beats (Shaw 1994).

RESULTS

Gun Seizures

The federally funded hot spot patrol officers found 29 guns in addition to the 47 guns seized in the target beat by other police units during Phase 1 (second half of 1992), increasing total guns found in the beat by 65 percent over the previous six months and almost tripling the number of guns found in car checks in a 260 percent increase over regular policing activities during the experimental period. Overall there was an increase from 46 guns seized in Beat 144 in the first six months of 1992 to 76 seized in the last six months. The ratio of

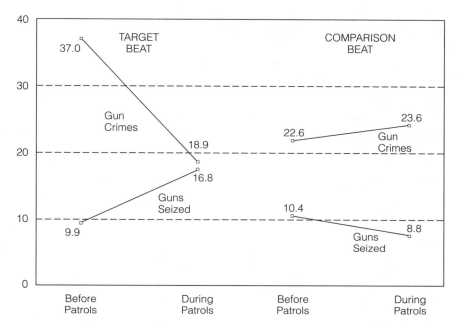

FIGURE 1. Firearm Offenses/Guns Seized per 1,000 Persons, First and Second Half of 1992

guns seized to directed patrol time in the experimental period was one gun per 156 hours, but the ratio to time actually spent in the area (and not processing arrests) was one gun per 84 hours and one gun per 28 traffic stops. Figure 1 compares the six-month rates of guns seized per 1,000 resident population in the first and the second half of 1992 in the target and the comparison beat to the respective changes in 29-week rates of gun crimes.

Most of the guns were removed permanently from the streets. Not all of the weapons seized were carried illegally; about one-fifth (14) of the total 76 guns taken from target area during Phase 1 (and four of the 29 guns seized by the extra hot spot patrols) were confiscated by police for "safekeeping," a practice followed in many police agencies when officers have reason to believe that gun violence may occur otherwise. Although guns taken for this reason are usually returned to their rightful owners upon application at the property room, the process can take several days to several weeks. Illegally carried guns, on the other hand, are destroyed by the Kansas City (Mo.) police and are not returned to circulation.

Trends in Gun Crime

There were 169 gun crimes in the target beat in the 29 weeks preceding the hot spot patrols, but only 86 gun crimes in the 29 weeks during the Phase 1 patrols—a 49 percent decline, with 83 fewer gun crimes (Table 2). This change

Table 2 Gun Crimes 29 Weeks Before and 29 Weeks During Phase 1 Hot Spots Patrol, by Beat

Beat	Before 12/17/91–7/6/92	During 7/7/92–1/25/93	% Change	
Target (144)	169	86		−49%*
Weekly mean	5.83	2.97	$t =$	−3.296
Standard deviation	3.89	2.59	$P =$	.002
Comparison (242)	184	192		+4%
Weekly mean	6.34	6.62	$t =$	.279
Standard deviation	4.03	3.59	$P =$	.781
Adjoining Target				
141	76	57		−25%
Weekly mean	2.62	1.97	$t =$	−.972
Standard deviation	3.09	1.85	$P =$	.335
142	106	84		−21%
Weekly mean	3.66	2.90	$t =$	−1.160
Standard deviation	2.56	2.43	$P =$	.251
143	39	44		+13%
Weekly mean	1.34	1.52	$t =$	.415
Standard deviation	1.97	1.25	$P =$	.679
213	143	158		+10%
Weekly mean	4.93	5.45	$t =$	.475
Standard deviation	4.46	3.86	$P =$	.637
214	104	138		+33%
Weekly mean	3.59	4.76	$t =$	1.487
Standard deviation	2.17	3.64	$P =$	1.43
331	143	175		+22%
Weekly mean	4.93	6.03	$t =$	1.252
Standard deviation	3.08	3.59	$P =$	.216
332	153	160		+5%
Weekly mean	5.28	5.52	$t =$	.166
Standard deviation	4.19	6.58	$P =$	.869
All Contiguous Beats	764	816		+7%
Weekly mean	26.34	28.14	$t =$	.62
Standard deviation	10.11	11.78	$P =$	.537
All Kansas City	4,359	4,287		−2%
Weekly mean	150.31	147.83	$t =$	−.386
Standard deviation	23.82	25.08	$P =$	.701

* t value $P < .05$.

was statistically significant in both a test of differences of means (t–test) for that period and in ARIMA (autoregressive integrated moving averages) model covering the longer 52-week before and after period (Table 3).[5]

Comparison Beat 242 showed a slight reduction in guns seized, from 85 in the first half of 1992 to 72 in the second half. It also showed a slight increase

Table 3 ARIMA Parameter Estimates, Gun Crimes 52 Weeks Before and 52 Weeks After Phase 1 Hot Spots Patrol Began, by Beat

Patrol Beat	Box-Jenkins Estimate	Standard Error	T-Ratio
144	5.788	.433	13.36
Impact	−2.558	.613	−4.17*
242	7.154	.567	12.62
Impact	−.751	.080	−.94
141	2.692	.339	7.95
Impact	−.981	.479	−2.05*
142	3.250	.311	10.46
Impact	−.539	.440	−1.22
143	2.135	.250	8.55
Impact	−.692	.353	−1.96*
213	4.442	.547	8.12
Impact	.500	.773	.65
214	4.308	.418	10.31
Impact	−.192	.591	−.33
331	5.096	.451	11.29
Impact	.346	.639	.54
332	5.847	.730	8.01
Impact	−1.021	1.032	−.99
All Contiguous	27.777	1.375	20.19
Impact	− 2.577	1.945	−1.32

* $P < .05.$

in gun crimes, from 184 in the 29 weeks before the program to 192 in the 29 weeks during the program (Table 2). Neither change was statistically significant, in either 29-week t-tests or the 52-week ARIMA model. Shaw's (1994) analysis of incidents in which shots were fired shows very similar results, confirming the computerized KCPD designation of gun crimes with Shaw's qualitative review of incident report narratives.

Displacement

Although gun crime dropped in Beat 144, none of the seven contiguous beats registered any significant increases in gun crime, as shown in Table 2 for the 29-week before-and-after tests and in Table 3 for the 52-week ARIMA models. Rather than displacing gun crime, some evidence even suggests that the program's benefits were diffused to two of the adjoining beats. The 52-week before-and-after special tests (ARIMA models) showed significant reductions in gun crimes in Beats 141 and 143.

The only suggestion of displacement is that the sum of changes in gun crime across all seven contiguous beats shows a nonsignificant increase of 52 gun

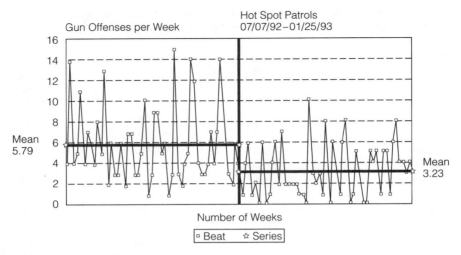

FIGURE 2. Plot of Gun Offenses per Week, 52 Weeks Before and After Hot Spot Patrols, Beat 144 (Experimental Beat)

SOURCE: Kansas City Police Offense Reports

crimes, 7 percent over the "before" period. Although gun crime may have been partially displaced, the displacement was dispersed so well across the contiguous beats that it was not noticeable in any one beat. Even if this were the case, Barr and Pease (1990) have argued that such dispersion is actually a social benefit because high risks of crime are not concentrated on a small number of potential victims. Dispersion helps to make everyone aware of the costs of crime, and may even increase support for public policies that might help prevent crime.

The most likely interpretation, however, is that the small increase in gun crime in the total contiguous areas was due to chance. The two-tailed t-test reported in Table 2 shows a 54 percent likelihood that the 29-week increase was the result of chance. The 52-week before-and-after ARIMA model reported in Table 3 shows a decrease in gun crime in the aggregated contiguous beats, further falsifying the displacement hypothesis, while the target area shows the overall decrease illustrated in Figure 2.

Crime-Specific Effects

Drive-by Shootings Analysis of variance of six-month totals for drive-by shootings showed that these shootings declined during both six-month periods of hot spot patrols (second half of 1992 and of 1993) in comparison to the periods without patrols ($F = 4.8214$, $p = .079$). Beat 242 showed no such difference ($F = .1383$, $p = .725$). The same analyses showed no significant differences in the beats surrounding Beat 144 ($p < .10$). Figure 3 displays the target

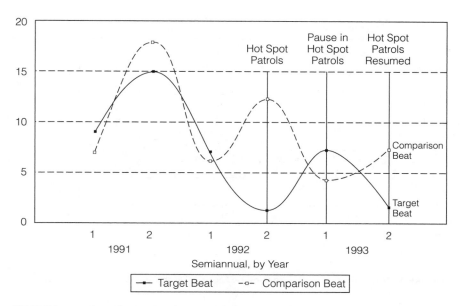

FIGURE 3. Number of Drive-by Shootings (6-Month Aggregates)

and comparison area trends in drive-by shootings, as compiled by the KCPD Perpetrator Information Center.[6]

Homicides Homicides also were significantly lower in Beat 144 during the two six-month program periods than in other half-years from 1991 through 1993 (Mantel-Haenszel chi-square = 4.65, P = .03). We found no significant differences in homicide across those periods in comparison Beat 242 (Mantel-Haenszel chi-square = .36, P = .54) or in any of the contiguous beats (P < .05, although P < .10 in three of the seven).

Other Crimes Neither total calls for police service, calls about violence, property, or disorder crimes, total offense reports, nor property or violent offenses showed any effect of the increased patrol (data are not displayed). We found no significant changes in t-tests of these measures in either the target or the comparison area. The target area hot spot patrols focused primarily on guns, and their effects were limited to gun crimes. Thus, although we cannot say whether the effects were due to crime-specific deterrence or to incapacitation through loss of guns, we can refute the hypothesis of general deterrence due to more visible patrol presence.

Community Attitudes Community surveys before and after the intensive patrols showed that respondents in target Beat 144 became less fearful of crime and more satisfied with their neighborhood than respondents in comparison Beat 242 (Shaw 1994, 1995). Target beat respondents were only marginally

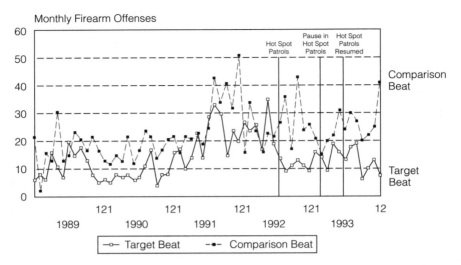

FIGURE 4. Total Offenses with Firearms, by Month, Target and Comparison Beats

more likely to say that the shooting problem had improved and were no more likely to report improvement in overall crime problems, but they were significantly more likely than comparison beat respondents to say that neighborhood drug problems had improved.

Effects of Program Cessation and Resumption

Crimes involving firearms gradually increased again for five months in the first half of 1993 (see Figure 4), in keeping with the usual pattern of police crackdowns (Sherman 1990). After the program resumed in July 1993, however, gun crimes declined in the target area while they rose in the comparison area.

DISCUSSION

Why should seizing 29 more guns in 29 weeks make any difference in gun crime in an 8-by-10-block area? If we assume that there are tens of thousands of handguns in Kansas City,[7] the seizure of 29 handguns might be viewed as a drop in the bucket, an implausible reason for any significant reduction in gun crime. At least three plausible theories, however, explain how the patrols may have caused a reduction in gun crime: high-risk guns, high-risk offenders, and deterrence.

Wilson (1994) argues that most guns are not at immediate risk of being used in crime. Guns seized by police in areas of high gun crime at times of high crime may be at far greater risk of imminent use in crimes than the average handgun. Cook (cited in Reiss and Roth 1993:282) estimates that for each new cohort of 100 guns, 33 uses of those guns in crime are reported. Those uses could be concentrated heavily in the small fraction of that cohort which is carried in gun crime hot spots. In those areas, each gun could be used in hundreds of crimes especially in light of anecdotal evidence about gun loaning and renting.

Even so, criminals may easily replace guns seized by police. Connecting the 29 guns seized to the 83 gun crimes prevented may thus require a further assumption that gun crime is more opportunistic than planned, and is relatively infrequent in any criminal's career. The high proportion of gun crime consisting of aggravated assaults in both the target and the comparison areas, as noted above, is consistent with this argument.

Some gun carriers may be far more frequent gun users than others. If even 10 percent of the 170 state and federal arrests made by the directed patrols captured high-frequency gun users, and if the arrestees spent the next six months in jail on serious charges from outstanding warrants, then the incapacitation of those 17 offenders by the program may have prevented 83 gun crimes for a not implausible average of five gun offenses each, or less than one per month. This effect would not be tied directly to gun seizures, but it may well be an important component of targeting hot spot patrols in an area of high gun crime.

Deterrence of gun carrying may be an even more plausible explanation of reduced gun crime. The 29 extra gun seizures, the 1,434 traffic and pedestrian stops, or the total of 3,186 arrests, traffic citations, and other police encounters could have specifically deterred potential gun criminals who encountered police. Visibility of police encounters in the hot spots also may have deterred gun carrying as a general effect among those who were not checked by police. This argument appears at least plausible enough to suggest that directed patrols can reduce gun crime, regardless of the exact theoretical mechanism. It is not clear, however, whether this explanation is more plausible than attributing the reduction in gun crime to a handful of high-risk offenders who were kept off the streets or at least away from gun crimes by the temporary loss of their guns.

Much is still to be learned about the entire process of gun detection and seizure by police. Until recently, neither police administrators nor researchers showed a strong interest in understanding or encouraging the factors leading to gun seizures. We know little about differences across police agencies or police officers as to their respective rates of gun detection. We do not even know how many more guns could be detected if patrol officers generally received more direction and training in locating guns in the course of their routine activities. We do know from Kansas City that a focus on gun detection, with freedom from answering calls for service, can make regular beat officers working overtime very productive.

Reducing Gun Crime

Now that we know how to increase gun seizures in target areas, the key question is whether that policy will reduce gun crime without total displacement. The Kansas City evidence suggests that it can reduce gun crime without *local* displacement. Only repeated tests of the hypothesis, however, will show whether the policy can produce that result predictably. Even before replications are completed, many cities must decide how to respond to increasing gun crime. Although some might counsel taking no action until more research is completed, it is not certain that inaction is safer. Just as much harm may be done and just as many lives may be lost by waiting for more research as by acting prematurely.

This situation is analogous to the problem of domestic violence arrests in 1984, when an unreplicated experiment suggested that arrest was an effective deterrent (Sherman and Berk 1984). Replications completed eight years later showed that the effects of arrest varied across cities and between employed and unemployed suspects, deterring violence in some instances but increasing it in others (Sherman 1992). Even before these later findings were reported, some scholars have argued that unreplicated experiments with major policy implications should not even be published (Binder and Meeker 1988; Lempert 1989). We offer the present unreplicated quasi-experiment for publication in the belief that police agencies, not scholars, are most able to judge the policy implications of these findings.

Cautions

Nonetheless, we offer our findings with appropriate cautions. Intensified gun patrols in some neighborhoods conceivably could harm police-community relations (but see Shaw 1995), even though no complaints and no legal challenges to the experiment were ever filed in Kansas City. Such efforts at least may waste time and money, especially if they do not reach any minimum threshold of detection probability. Gun hot spot patrols could pose great risks to officers' safety, although no officers were injured in the limited period of the experiment. Most worrisome is the possibility that field interrogations could provoke more crime by making young men subjected to traffic stops more defiant toward conventional society (Sherman 1993) and thus commit more crimes.

All of these hazards are possible but unknown. The trade-off is the well-known risk of gun violence, which is extremely high and is still rising in many inner cities. Firearms crimes in Indianapolis, for example, increased by 220 percent from 1988 to 1993 (also see Rand 1994). The need for action makes the central questions for further research all the more urgent:

1. Can other cities obtain similar results with similar methods in similar target areas?
2. Can cities without federal funding obtain similar results with far fewer patrol hours in the target area?
3. Can city-wide programs obtain the same results Kansas City obtained in one small area, or would displacement erode the apparent benefit?

Answering these questions through further research will require the support of many public officials, but the evidence suggests that support is well-justified.

ENDNOTES

1. As defined by the KCPD Perpetrator Information Center, which classifies drive-by shootings from an ongoing review of incident reports and produces monthly statistics by beat. These statistics are employed in all analyses of those events discussed here.

2. "Gun crime" is defined as any offense report in which the use of a gun by the offender is mentioned. The data presented in this report include the following offense types reported as gun crimes on one or more occasions in either the target or the comparison area during the year before and after the initiation of the hot spot patrols:

OFFENSE TYPE	NUMBER	
	Beat 144	Beat 242
Criminal Homicide	10	30
Rape	6	5
Armed Robbery and Attempts	124	222
Aggravated Assault	293	409
Aggravated Assault on Police	3	1
Burglary	0	1
Simple Assault, Gun Pointed	1	0
Destruction of Property	18	38
Kidnapping	0	1
Casualty Injury, Firearm	2	4
Suicide and Attempts	1	1
Totals	468	712

3. Data on guns seized by beat, however, are available only for the first phase.

4. We identified the model as a "white noise" ARIMA (0,0,0) model by examining the plots of the autocorrelation and partial autocorrelation functions. Because the series spans two years, we examined it carefully for seasonality components. None were found.

We estimated the white noise model using the conditional least squares method.

The equation estimated was $At = 0 + Yt$, substituting the mean of the series $At = 4.510 + Yt$ or the dependent variable. A white noise model contains no ARIMA parameters other than the mean of the series. Examination of the plot of residual autocorrelation added support to the white noise interpretation. The Box-Ljung test (LBQ) for 25 lags is .31 and the critical value is 43.38; this test failed to reject the null hypothesis that the cumulative autocorrelation function is 0 in the population and that the model is acceptable.

We then added an intervention component to the model to account for the introduction of the hot spot patrol in July 1992 as the dividing point of the series. This intervention component is a dummy variable coded 0 before the patrols and 1 thereafter. Examination of the combined model reveals a white noise model with the cumulative amount of autocorrelation in the residuals equal to 0.

5. We had two reasons for extending the ARIMA model to cover 52 weeks before and 52 weeks after the Phase 1 start-up date of July 7, 1992. One is that ARIMA models generally require more data points than the 29 actual program weeks to produce more reliable estimates and to eliminate factors such as seasonality. This is true even though there is no specific minimum requirement. The other reason is that according to police crackdown theory (Sherman 1990), we predicted that the effects of the hot spot patrols would linger as a form of residual deterrence even after they ceased.

6. KCPD data on drive-by shootings in beats contiguous to the target beat are not displayed, but are available from the authors on request.

7. Kleck (1991:18) estimates that there are at least 65 million handguns in the United States, with a population of more than 250 million people. A rough application of this ratio to the Kansas City population of some 400,000 people suggests the presence of at least 100,000 handguns in that city.

REFERENCES

Barr, R. and K. Pease (1990) "Crime Placement, Displacement and Deflection." In M. Tonry and N. Morris, (eds), *Crime and Justice: A Review of Research, Vol. 12.* pp. 277–318. Chicago: University of Chicago Press.

Binder, A. and J. Meeker (1988) "Experiments as Reforms." *Journal of Criminal Justice* 16:347–58.

BMDP (1990) *BMDP2T—Box-Jenkins Time-Series Analysis.* Los Angeles: BMDP Statistical Software, Inc.

Brill, S. (1977) *Firearm Abuse: A Research and Policy Report.* Washington, DC: Police Foundation.

Cook, P. (1991). "The Technology of Personal Violence." In M. Tonry (ed.), *Crime and Justice: A Review of Research, Vol. 14,* pp. 1–72. Chicago: University of Chicago Press.

Felson, M. (1994) *Crime and Everyday Life.* Thousand Oaks, CA: Pine Forge Press.

Kleck, G. (1991) *Point Blank: Guns and Violence in America.* New York: Aldine.

Lempert, T. (1989) "Humility Is a Virtue: On the Publicization of Policy-Relevant Research." *Law and Society Review* 16:513–68.

Lewis, N. (1995) "Court Cases Reveal Arms Buildup among D.C. Youths." *Washington Post,* January 1, p. A1.

Loftin, C., D. McDowall, B. Wiersema, and T. J. Cottey (1991) "Effects of Restrictive Licensing of Handguns on Homicide and Suicide in the District of Columbia." *New England Journal of Medicine* 32:1615–20.

McDowall, D. (1991) "Firearm Availability and Homicide Rates in Detroit, 1951–1986." *Social Forces* 69:1085–1101.

Moore, M. (1980) "The Police and Weapons Offenses." *Annals of the American Academy of Political and Social Sciences* 452:22–32.

Pierce, G. and W. Bowers (1979) "The Impact of the Bartley-Fox Gun Law on Crime in Massachusetts." Unpublished manuscript, Northeastern University, Center for Applied Social Research.

Rand, M. (1994) *Guns and Crime.* Washington, DC: Bureau of Justice Statistics.

Reiss, A.J., Jr. and J.A. Roth, eds. (1993) *Understanding and Preventing Violence.* Washington, DC: National Academy of Sciences.

Shaw, J.W. (1994) "Community Policing Against Crime: Violence and Firearms." Doctoral dissertation, University of Maryland, College Park, Department of Criminology and Criminal Justice.

——— (1995) "Community Policing against Guns: Public Opinion of the Kansas City Gun Experiment" *Justice Quarterly,* this issue.

Sherman, L.W. (1990) "Police Crackdowns: Initial and Residual Deterrence." In M. Tonry and N. Morris (eds.) *Crime and Justice: A Review of Research,* Vol. 12. pp. 1–48. Chicago: University of Chicago Press.

——— (1992) *Policing Domestic Violence: Experiments and Dilemmas.* New York: Free Press.

——— (1993) "Defiance, Deterrence, and Irrelevance." *Journal of Research in Crime and Delinquency* 30:445–73

——— (1995) "Carrying Concealed Weapons: Community Policing against Guns." NIJ research in progress, presented to the U.S. Attorney General, April.

Sherman, L.W. and R.A. Berk (1984). "The Specific Deterrent Effects of Arrest for Domestic Assault." *American Sociological Review* 49:261–72.

Sherman, L.W., P.R. Gartin, and M.E. Buerger (1989) "Hot Spots of Predatory Crime: Routine Activities and the Criminology of Place." *Criminology* 27:27–55.

Sherman, L.W. and C. Bridgeforth (1994)
  Getting Guns off the Streets, 1993:
  A survey of Big-City Police Agencies.
  Washington, DC: Crime Control
  Institute.

Sherman, L.W., J.W. Shaw, and D.P. Rogan (1995) *The Kansas City Gun Ex-*

periment. Washington, DC: National
  Institute of Justice.

Wilson, J.Q. (1994) "Just Take Away
  Their Guns: Forget Gun Control."
  New York Times Magazine, March 20,
  pp. 46–47.

CASES CITED

Michigan v. Long 436 U.S. 1032 (1983)

Pennsylvania v. Mimms 434 U.S. 106
  (1977)

Terry v. Ohio 392 U.S. 1 (1968)

The Criminal Investigation Process: A Summary Report

JAN M. CHAIKEN
PETER W. GREENWOOD
JOAN PETERSILIA

Criminal investigation is one of the more important functions of municipal and county police departments. Yet many police administrators know
little about the nature or effectiveness of their own department's investigative operations and even less about the situation in other departments.

At the request of the National Institute of Law Enforcement and Criminal
Justice, the Rand Corporation undertook a nationwide study to fill some of
these gaps in knowledge.[1] The objectives of the two-year study were—

- to describe, on a national scale, current investigative organization and
  practice;

- to assess the contribution of police investigation to the achievement of
  criminal justice goals;

Source: Jan M. Chaiken, Peter W. Greenwood, and Joan Petersilia (1977). "The Criminal
Investigation Process: A Summary Report." *Policy Analysis,* 3:187–217. Reprinted courtesy of Policy Analysis, University of California Press, Berkeley, California.

- to ascertain the effectiveness of new technology and systems that are being adopted to enhance investigative performance;
- to determine how investigative effectiveness is related to difference in organizational form, staffing, procedures, and so forth.

While the objectives were broad, many questions of potential interest had to be excluded from consideration in order to have a study of manageable size. In particular, the study focused on Part I crimes,[2] thereby excluding analysis of how misdemeanors and vice, narcotics, and gambling offenses are investigated. Also, little attention was paid to personnel practices such as selection, promotion, and motivation of investigators.

DESIGN OF THE STUDY

Several principles guided our study design. First, the research had to be conducted with the participation and oversight of experienced police officials from around the country. Second, information had to be collected from many police departments: single-city studies had already been conducted, and their lack of persuasiveness stemmed from the possibility that the host department was unique in some way. Third, in as many departments as possible, information had to be obtained through direct on-site interviews and observations.

We secured the participation of the law enforcement community by appointing a suitable advisory board,[3] retaining a prosecutor and retired federal and local investigators as consultants,[4] and assembling a panel of currently working investigators. The advisory board reviewed and vigorously criticized our research approach, data collection instruments, findings, and interpretations of the findings. The consultants assisted in designing data instruments and participated with Rand staff in on-site interviews in many locations. The panel of working investigators commented on the validity of our observations in other cities, by comparing them with their own daily experiences, and highlighted important issues that could not be captured by numerical data.

We collected data from a large number of departments by developing a comprehensive survey questionnaire and distributing it to all municipal or county law enforcement departments that had 150 or more full-time employees or that served a jurisdiction whose 1970 population exceeded 100,000. This survey produced extensive information from 153 jurisdictions (of the 300 solicited) on such topics as departmental characteristics, investigators' deployment, investigators' training and status, use of evidence technicians, nature of specialization, evaluation criteria, police-prosecutor interaction, case assignment, use of computer files, and crime, clearance, and arrest rates.[5] For example, the number of officers assigned to investigative units was found to average 17.3 percent of the police force. Thus, the investigative function in the United States costs about $1 billion per year—about the same as the cost of the entire court system.[6]

On-site interviews were conducted in more than 25 of the 153 police agencies. Many of these were selected because they were known to have implemented novel investigative practices that were reportedly successful; others were selected on the basis of their survey responses indicating interesting programs or data resources and a desire to participate. Project staff and consultants visited each of these departments, observing and participating in the operations of the investigative units and discussing their procedures with personnel at various departmental levels. In some cities, Rand staff monitored individual investigators and their supervisors continuously over a period of several days to obtain realistic profiles of their activities.

Some departments gave us previously prepared written evaluations of their investigative programs. In addition, several departments cooperated closely with the Rand staff and provided access to data that were subsequently used in one of the component studies.

One useful data source, located and made available during the course of the survey, was the Kansas City (Missouri) Detective Case Assignment File, which had been maintained since 1971. This unique computer file contained daily information submitted by individual detectives, permitting us to determine, for each investigator and each investigative unit, the time spent on various activities, the number of cases handled, and the number of arrests and clearances produced. The file greatly facilitated our analyses of how detectives spend their time and to what purposes and effects.

Additional sources of information included a computer-readable file of 1972 Uniform Crime Reporting data provided by the FBI and a limited telephone survey of robbery and burglary victims.

FINDINGS

Arrest and Clearance Rates

Several earlier studies, each conducted in a single city or in a small number of neighboring cities, had shown that *department-wide clearance*[7] *and arrest statistics are not suitable measures of the effectiveness of investigative operations*. Our own study, using data from cities across the country, confirmed this observation in several different ways. The implication is that measures of effectiveness related to solving crimes must be defined carefully and can only be interpreted in conjunction with other information related to prosecution of arrestees, public satisfaction with the police, deterrence effects, and so forth. In a study in New York City, published in 1970, Greenwood found that the average number of clearances claimed for each burglary arrest varied from 1 to 20 across the city's precincts, depending primarily on how frequently clearances were credited on the basis of *modus operandi* only.[8] Similarly, Greenberg's 1972 study in six California departments found wide variation in clearance rates because of differences among departments in the strictness with which FBI "exceptional clearance" guidelines were applied.[9] Our own study[10] using 1972 data from all departments with 150 or more employees, showed that the average number of clearances claimed for each arrest for a Part I crime ranged from a low of 0.38 to a high of 4.04, a factor of over 10. The ratio from high to low was even larger for each individual crime type, such as robbery or auto theft. Some departments claim a clearance for an auto theft whenever the vehicle is recovered, while others will not claim a clearance unless the perpetrator is arrested and charged for the instant offense. Clearance statistics are also affected by the amount of effort devoted to classifying reported crimes as "unfounded" when the police find no evidence that a crime was actually committed. This practice both reduces reported crime rates and increases reported clearance rates.

With administrative discretion playing such a large role in determining a department's clearance rates, any attempt to compare effectiveness among departments using clearance rates is evidently meaningless. Even comparisons over time within a single department are unreliable unless steps are taken to assure that no change occurs in administrative practices concerning clearances and classification of crimes. Arrest rates, too, are unreliable measures of effectiveness, since arrests can be made without resulting in any clearance.[11] The frequency of such events can be judged from the fact that, in half of all departments, the number of arrests for Part I crimes exceeds the number of clearances.[12]

Quite apart from their unreliability is the fact that arrest and clearance rates reflect activities of patrol officers and members of the public more than they reflect activities of investigators. Isaacs,[13] Conklin,[14] and our own study showed that approximately 30 percent of all clearances are the result of pickup arrests by patrol officers responding to the scene of the crime.[15] In roughly another 50 percent of cleared crimes (less for homicide and auto theft), the perpetrator is known when the crime report is first taken, and the main jobs for the investigator are to locate the perpetrator, take him or her into custody, and assemble the facts needed to present charges in court (see Table 1). This means that around 20 percent of cleared crimes could possibly be attributed to investigative work, but our own study showed that most of these were also solved by patrol, officers, or by members of the public who spontaneously provided further information, or by routine investigative practices that could also have been followed by clerical personnel.[16]

In fact, we estimate that no more than 2.7 percent of all Part I crime clearances can be attributed to special techniques used by investigators. (These are called "special action cases" in Table 2.) The remaining 97.3 percent of cleared crimes will be cleared no matter what the investigators do, so long as the obvious routine follow-up steps are taken. Of course, included in the 2.7 percent are the most interesting and publicly visible crimes reported to the department, especially homicides and commercial burglaries. But the thrust of our analysis is that all the time spent by investigators on difficult cases where the perpetrator is unknown results in only 2.7 percent of the clearances.

This finding has now been established for enough departments to leave little doubt of its general correctness, with some variation, for all departments. By establishing a restricted interpretation of what constitutes "routine processing," a department might find that investigative skill or "special action" contributes to as many as 10 percent of all its clearances. Even so, the basic conclusion

Table 1 Cleared Cases Having Initial Identification of Perpetrator (As a Percentage of All Cleared Cases)

Crime Type	Arrest at Scene	KANSAS CITY			Total Initial from Five Other Departments[c]
		Complete ID by Victim or Witness	Uniquely Linking Evidence[a]	Total Initial ID[b]	
Forgery/fraud	30.6	20.0	39.7	90.3	90.9
Auto theft	38.5	12.7	<7.8	>51.2[a]	47.4
Theft	48.4	8.6	17.2	74.2	70.0
Commercial burglary	24.4	16.9	16.9	58.2	80.0
Residential burglary	26.7	42.7	<6.2	>81.7[a]	80.0
Robbery	28.4	20.9	10.6	59.9	53.4
Felony morals	25.8	27.8	27.8	81.4	72.8
Aggravated assault	28.6	63.4	7.9	>91.1[a]	100.0
Homicide	28.3	34.8	10.9	74.0	42.9

NOTE: Numbers may not add to total because of rounding errors.

[a]If no cases of uniquely linking evidence were found in the sample, or if there were no cases other than those with initial identification, 95 percent confidence points are shown.

[b]I.e., the sum of the three preceding counties.

[c]Berkeley, Long Beach, and Los Angeles, California; Miami, Florida; and Washington, D.C.

remains the same. Only in cases of homicide, robbery, and commercial theft did we find that the quality of investigative effort could affect the clearance rate to any substantial extent. Conversely, the contribution of victims, witnesses, and patrol officers is most important to the identification and apprehension of criminal offenders.

Variations with Departmental Characteristics

Once the nature of investigators' contributions to arrest and clearance rates is understood, it must be anticipated that variations in these rates among departments will be explained primarily by characteristics that have nothing to do with the organization and deployment of investigators. This is in fact what we found from our survey data.[17] The three most important determinants of a department's arrest and clearance rates are the department's size, the region of the country it is located in, and its crime workload.

Large departments (measured by number of employees, budget, or population of the jurisdiction) claim more clearances per arrest in all crime categories than do smaller departments. However, the arrest rates of large and small departments do not differ.

Departments in the South Central states claim higher clearance rates than those in other regions, which follow in the order of North Central, South Atlantic, Northeast, and West. However, arrest rates vary in almost exactly the reverse order. Evidently, these differences reflect administrative practices or patterns of crime commission rather than differences in effectiveness.

Table 2 Special Action Cases (Percentage of All Cleared Cases)

| | KANSAS CITY | | FIVE OTHER DEPARTMENTS[a] | |
Crime Type	Sample Estimate	Maximum Estimate at 95% Confidence	Sample Estimate	Maximum Estimate at 95% Confidence
Forgery/fraud	0	5.7	0	12.7
Auto theft	0	6.9	0	14.6
Theft	0	3.2	0	25.9
Commercial burglary	4.9	12.4	10	39.4
Residential burglary	0	3.5	0	13.9
Robbery	7.1	16.6	9.5	15.6
Felony morals	0	14.5	9.1	36.4
Aggravated assault	0	5.9	0	25.9
Homicide	10.2	37.3	0	34.8
All types[b]	1.3	2.7		

[a] Berkeley, Long Beach, and Los Angeles, California; Miami, Florida; and Washington, D.C.

[b] This figure is shown for Kansas City only and reflects the relative numbers of cleared cases of each type in that city. The maximum estimate for the total is lower than the estimate for any single crime type, because the sample size is larger.

In regard to crime workload, we found that departments having a large number of reported crimes per police officer have lower arrest rates than other departments. This relationship works in the following way: The annual number of arrests per police officer rises nearly (but not quite) in direct proportion to the number of reported crimes per police officer until a certain threshold is reached. Beyond this threshold, increasing workload is associated with very small increases in the number of arrests per police officer. The thresholds are at approximately 35 Part I crimes per police officer per year and 3.5 crimes against persons per police officer per year. These thresholds are fairly high, as only about 20 percent of departments have greater workload levels.[18]

These findings are consistent with the assumption that a city can increase its number of arrests or decrease the number of crimes (or both) by increasing the size of its police force, but the effect of added resources would be greatest for cities above the threshold.

In regard to clearance rates, the data showed that departments with high crime workloads tend to claim more clearances per arrest than cities with low crime workloads. As a result, clearance rates are less sensitive to workload than arrest rates are. Although clearance rates for every crime type were found to decrease with increasing workload, the decreases were not significant for some types of crimes.

These workload relationships apply to all police officers, not just investigators. Although investigators are known to make more arrests per year than patrol officers, and our data confirmed this, the effect is small: we could not find a significant variation in arrest or clearance rates according to the fraction of the force in investigative units. In other words, if the total number of officers in a department is kept fixed, switching some officers into or out of investigative units is not likely to have a substantial effect on arrest or clearance rates.

Aside from the effects of size, region of country, and workload on clearance and arrest rates, we did find a few smaller effects of possible interest. Departments that assign a major investigative role to patrolmen have lower clearance rates, but not lower arrest rates, than other departments. This appears to reflect the fact that patrolmen cannot carry files around with them and therefore do not clear old crimes with new arrests. Departments with specialized units (concentrating on a single crime, such as robbery) were found to have lower arrest rates, but not lower clearance rates, for the types of crimes in which they specialize, as compared with departments having generalist investigators. Departments in which investigators work in pairs had lower numbers of arrests per officer than those in which they work singly. Since we did not collect data permitting a comparison of the quality of arrests produced by solo and paired investigators, this finding must be interpreted with caution. Still, the practice of pairing investigators, which is common only in the Northeast, is brought into sufficient question to warrant further research.

Most other characteristics of investigators were found to be unrelated to arrest and clearance rates. These include the nature and extent of the investigators' training, their civil service rank or rate of pay, and the nature of their interactions with prosecutors. However, the lack of correlation probably indicates more about the inadequacies of arrest and clearance rates as measures of effectiveness than about the inherent value of training and other characteristics.

How the Investigator's Time Is Spent

From an analysis of the Kansas City (Missouri) computer-readable case assignment file, and from observations during site visits, we determined that, although a large proportion of reported crimes are assigned to an investigator, many of these receive no more attention than the reading of the initial crime incident report. That is, many cases are suspended at once. The data show that homicide, rape, and suicide invariably result in investigative activity, and that at least 60 percent of all other serious types of cases receive significant attention (at least half an hour of a detective's time). Overall, however, less than half of all reported crimes receive any serious consideration by an investigator, and the great majority of cases that are actively investigated receive less than one day's attention. Table 3 shows, for several crime types, the percentage of cases that detectives worked on during the study period (1 May 1973 to 30 April 1974).

The net result is that the average detective does not actually work on a large number of cases each month, even though he may have a backlog of hundreds or thousands of cases that were assigned to him at some time in the past and are still theoretically his responsibility. Table 4 shows the number of worked-on cases per detective per month in the various units of the Kansas City Police Department.[19] Except in the case of the Missing Persons Unit, the number of worked-on cases per detective is generally under one per day. If we imagine that each case is assigned to a particular investigator as his responsibility, the

Table 3 Percentage of Reported Cases That Detectives Worked On

Type of Incident	Percentage
Homicide	100.0
Rape	100.0
Suicide	100.0
Forgery/counterfeit	90.4
Kidnapping	73.3
Arson	70.4
Auto theft	65.5
Aggravated assault	64.4
Robbery	62.6
Fraud/embezzlement	59.6
Felony sex crimes	59.0
Common assault	41.8
Nonresidential burglary	36.3
Dead body	35.7
Residential burglary	30.0
Larceny	18.4
Vandalism	6.8
Lost property	0.9
All above types together	32.4

SOURCE: Kansas City Case Assignment File; cases reported from May through November 1973.

Table 4 Average Number of Worked-On Cases per Detective per Month

Unit	No. of Cases
Crimes against persons	9.2
Homicide	11.2
Robbery	7.7
Sex Crimes	6.2
Crimes against property	16.9
Auto theft	19.5
Nonresidential burglary	9.4
Residential burglary/larceny	22.9
General assignment	18.6
Incendiary	7.8
Forgery/fraud/bunco	10.4
Shoplifting/pickpocket	20.9
Youth and women's	26.0
Missing persons	88.4

SOURCE: Kansas City Assignment File.

table shows the average number of cases that an investigator would be responsible for and work on in a month.

Our data revealed that most of an investigator's casework time is consumed in reviewing reports, documenting files, and attempting to locate and interview victims. For cases that are solved (that is, where a suspect is identified), an investigator spends more time in postclearance processing than in identifying the perpetrator.

For Kansas City, we found the following breakdown of investigators' time. About 45 percent is spent on activities not attributable to individual cases— doing administrative assignments, making speeches, traveling, reading tele-types, making general surveillances (of junkyards, pawnshops, gathering spots for juveniles, and the like), and occupying slack time (for example, in a unit that is on duty at night to respond to robberies and homicides). The remaining 55 percent of the time is spent on casework. Of this, 40 percent (or 22 percent of the total) is spent investigating crimes that are never solved; just over 12 percent (7 percent of the total) is spent investigating crimes that are eventually solved; and nearly 48 percent (26 percent of the total) is spent on cleared cases after they have been solved.[20] These figures, of course, apply only to Kansas City. But after reviewing them (and more detailed tabulations) with investigators from other cities, and after comparing them with our observational notes, we concluded that they are approximately correct for other cities, with variations primarily in the areas of slack time (if investigators are not on duty at night) and time spent in conference with prosecutors.

Thus, investigators spend about 93 percent of their time on activities that do not lead directly to solving previously reported crimes. How are they to be judged on the quality of these activities? The time they spend on cases after they have been cleared serves the important purpose of preparing cases for court: this activity will be discussed below. The time they spend on noncasework activities serves a general support function for casework and therefore may be useful in ways that are difficult to quantify. The time they spend on crimes that are never solved can only be judged in terms of its public relations value and possible deterrent value, because most of these crimes can be easily recognized at the start. (They are primarily the ones where no positive identification of the perpetrator is available at the scene of the crime.) Police administrators must ask themselves whether the efforts devoted to investigating crimes that are initially unsolved are justified by either the small number of solutions they produce or the associated public relations benefits.

Collecting and Processing Physical Evidence

A police agency's ability to collect and process physical evidence at the scene of a crime is thought to be an important component of the criminal investigation process. In our study, however, we analyzed only one aspect of the collection and processing of physical evidence—their role in contributing to the *solution* of crimes, as distinguished from their value in proving guilt once the crime is solved.

Earlier studies have shown that evidence technicians are asked to process the crime scene in only a small number of felony offenses.[21] And, even when the

Table 5 Productivity of Crime Scene Processing for Fingerprints, Residential Burglary Sample[a]

Item	Long Beach	Berkeley	Richmond
Percentage of cases where technicians were requested	58.0	76.6	87.6
Cases where prints were recovered, as percentage of cases where a technician was requested	50.8	42.0	69.1
Cases where prints were recovered, as percentage of total cases	29.4	32.2	60.5
Cases where perpetrator was identified as a result of lifted prints, as percentage of total cases	1.5	1.1	1.2

[a]The sample comprises 200 randomly selected residential burglary cases (cleared and uncleared) from each of three departments.

crime scene is processed, a significant portion of the available evidence may not be retrieved.[22] Police administrators, aware of these deficiencies, have begun to experiment with a variety of organizational changes designed to increase the number of crime sites processed for physical evidence.

Our analysis of the collection and processing of physical evidence in six police departments that employ different procedures[23] confirmed that a department can achieve a relatively high rate of recovery of latent prints from crime scenes by investing sufficiently in evidence technicians and by routinely dispatching these technicians to the scene of felonies. The latent print recovery rate is also increased by processing the crime scene immediately after the incident has been reported, rather than at a later time. Some of our data supporting these conclusions are shown (for burglary cases) in the first three lines of Table 5.

The last line of Table 5, however, shows that the rate at which fingerprints are used to identify the perpetrator of a burglary is essentially unrelated to the print recovery rate. From 1 to 2 percent of the burglary cases in each of three departments were cleared by identification from a latent print, despite substantial differences in operating procedures. In Richmond, evidence technicians are dispatched to nearly 90 percent of the reported burglaries and recover prints from 70 percent of the scenes they process, but the fraction of burglaries solved by fingerprints is about the same as in Long Beach or Berkeley, where evidence technicians are dispatched to the scene less frequently and lift prints less often.

Why does lifting more prints not result in a higher rate of identification? The most plausible explanation seems to be that police departments are severely limited in their capability for searching fingerprint files. If a suspect is known, there is little difficulty in comparing his prints with latent prints that have been collected. Thus, latent prints may help to confirm a suspect's identification obtained in other ways. But in the absence of an effective means of performing "cold searches" for matching prints (where the suspect is unknown), the availability of a latent print cannot help solve the crime.

From a comparison of the fingerprint identification sections in Washington, Los Angeles, Miami, and Richmond, we determined that, for all these departments, from 4 to 9 percent of all retrieved prints are eventually matched with those of a known suspect. However, the number of "cold-search" matches produced per man-year differed substantially among departments, according to the size of their inked print files and the attention devoted to this activity. In some departments, technicians performing cold searches produced far more case solutions per man-year than investigators.

We infer that an improved fingerprint *identification* capability will be more productive of identifications than a more intensive print *collection* effort. Although some techniques and equipment currently available to police departments were found to enhance identification capability, the technology needed to match single latent prints to inked prints is not fully developed and appears to us to be of high priority for research.

Preparing the Case for Prosecution

Police investigation, whether or not it can be regarded as contributing significantly to the *identification* of perpetrators, is a necessary police function because it is the principal means by which all relevant evidence is gathered and presented to the court so that a criminal prosecution can be made. Thus, police investigators can be viewed as serving a support function for prosecutors.

Prosecutors frequently contend that a high rate of case dismissals, excessive plea bargaining, and overly lenient sentences are common consequences of inadequate police investigation. The police, in response, often claim that even when they conduct thorough investigations, case dispositions are not significantly affected. We undertook a study to illuminate the issues surrounding this controversy about responsibility for prosecutorial failure.

On the basis of discussions with prosecutors, detectives, and police supervisors, we developed a data form containing 39 questions that a prosecutor might want the police to address in conducting a robbery investigation. When we used this form to analyze the completeness of robbery investigations in two California prosecutors' offices, chosen to reflect contrasting prosecutorial practices in felony case screening but similar workload and case characteristics,[24] we found that the department confronted by a stringent prosecutorial filing policy ("Jurisdiction A") was significantly more thorough in reporting follow-on investigative work than the department whose cases were more permissively filed ("Jurisdiction B"). Yet, even the former department fell short of supplying the prosecutor with all the information he desired: each of 39 evidentiary questions that prosecutors consider necessary for effective case presentation was, on the average, covered in 45 percent of the cases in Jurisdiction A. Twenty-six percent were addressed by the department in Jurisdiction B. (Table 6 lists the 39 questions. The summary entries indicate the percentage of cases where a question could be answered from information in the documents provided by the police to the prosecutor.)

We then determined whether the degree of thorough documentation of the police investigation was related to the disposition of cases, specifically to the rate of dismissals, the heaviness of plea bargaining, and the type of sentence imposed. Our analysis showed differences between the two jurisdictions.

Table 6 Presence of Information in Police Reports (In Percentages)

Case Information Desirable for Prosecution	Jurisdiction A[a] Information from at Least One Source[b]	Jurisdiction B[a] Information from at Least One Source[b]
1. What INTERVIEWS were conducted?	100.0	100.0
Offense		
2. Is there a verbatim report of the instant OFFENSE?	90.4	95.2
3. Is there a verbatim report of the FORCE USED?	95.2	36.5
4. What was the PHYSICAL HARM to the victim?	47.6	18.5
5. Is there a detailed description of the PROPERTY taken?	90.4	27.2
6. What was the method of S(uspect)'s ESCAPE?	71.4	45.4
7. What type of VEHICLE was used by S?	38.0	45.4
8. What type of WEAPON was used by S?	85.7	63.6
9. If a gun was used, was it LOADED?	19.0	13.5
10. If a gun was used, when was it ACQUIRED?	28.4	.0
11. Where is the LOCATION of the weapon now?	9.5	18.1
	(57.5%)	(36.2%)
Suspect		
12. Was S UNDER THE INFLUENCE of alcohol or drugs?	42.8	22.7
13. What are the details of S's DEFENSE?	18.9	.0
14. What is S's ECONOMIC STATUS?	14.2	4.5
15. Was S advised of his CONSTITUTIONAL RIGHTS?	100.0	63.6
16. If multiple suspects, what is their RELATIONSHIP?	42.7	.0
17. Is there evidence of PRIOR OFFENSES by S?	66.6	9.0
18. Is there evidence of S's MOTIVES?	47.6	18.1
19. Is there evidence of past PSYCHIATRIC TREATMENT of S?	9.5	4.5
20. What is S's PAROLE OR PROBATION status?	37.8	18.1
21. Does S have an alcohol or drug ABUSE HISTORY?	23.8	9.0
22. Where is S EMPLOYED?	28.5	4.5
	(39.3%)	(14.0)
Victim/Witnesses		
23. What is the RELATIONSHIP between S and V(ictim)?	4.7	9.0
24. What is the CREDIBILITY of the W(itnesses)?	9.5	.0
25. Can the W make a CONTRIBUTION to the case prosecution?	23.8	
26. Were MUG SHOTS shown to V or W?	51.7	4.5
27. If shown, are the PROCEDURES and RESULTS adequately described?	30.0	.0
28. Was a LINE-UP conducted?	53.0	.0
29. If conducted, are the PROCEDURES and RESULTS adequately described?	40.0	.0
30. Was an effort made to LIFT FINGERPRINTS at the scene?	41.0	4.5
31. If made, were USABLE FINGERPRINTS OBTAINED?	59.0	9.0
32. Were PHOTOS TAKEN at the crime scene?	35.0	4.5
33. Is the EXACT LOCATION from where the photos and prints were taken given?	29.0	.0
34. Did V VERIFY his statements in the crime report?	24.0	.0
35. Did V have IMPROPER MOTIVES in reporting the offense?	4.7	.0
	(31.1%)	(3.4%)

(continued)

Table 6 (*continued*)

Case Information Desirable for Prosecution	Jurisdiction A [a] Information from at Least One Source [b]	Jurisdiction B [a] Information from at Least One Source [b]
Arrest		
36. What was the legal BASIS FOR SEARCH AND SEIZURE?	23.8	36.3
37. How was the LOCATION OF EVIDENCE learned?	33.3	32.0
38. How was the LOCATION OF S learned?	66.6 ⎱ 52.3%	68.1 ⎱ 52.2%
39. How was the ARREST OF S made?	85.7	72.7
Overall	45.0%	26.4%

NOTE: The percentages within the matrix refer only to the presence of information the police chose to record; they may not represent a complete picture of the information gathered by the police in the course of the investigation. It is possible that certain police officers record only "positive" information and assume that an omission of information automatically implies that the information is either not applicable or inappropriate in a specific case.

[a] Twenty-one robbery cases in each sample.

[b] Percentage of cases that presented this information from at least one source.

Table 7 A Comparison Between A and B of Dispositions by Pleas of Guilty

Disposition	Percentage in Jurisdiction A	Percentage in Jurisdiction B
Plea of guilty to original charges	61.1	31.8
Plea of guilty to original charges but with special allegations stricken or not considered	27.7	22.7
Plea of guilty to 2d degree robbery reduced from 1st degree robbery	5.5	18.1
Plea of guilty to other lesser offense	5.5	4.5
Cases dismissed	—	22.7

NOTE: Because of rounding, columns do not add to 100 percent.

For example, none of the sampled cases was dismissed in Jurisdiction A; furthermore, 60 percent of the defendants pled guilty to the charges as filed. By comparison, in Jurisdiction B about one-quarter of the sampled cases were dismissed after filing, and only one-third of the defendants pled guilty to the charges as filed.

A comparison of the two offices' heaviness of plea bargaining is shown in Table 7. Although plea bargaining appears to be lighter in Jurisdiction A, this may simply reflect that the gravity of criminal conduct was less in the A than the B cases; that is, special allegations were considerably more frequent to begin with in B. One cannot conclude that only the quality of documentation of the police investigation accounted for the difference.

A similar conclusion applies to the type of sentence imposed: while there were differences in sentencing, the variations in other case characteristics indicate that these differences might not necessarily be related to thoroughness of documentation. This analysis leads us to suggest that the failure of police to document a case investigation thoroughly *may* contribute to a higher case dismissal rate and a weakening of the prosecutor's plea bargaining position.

Relations Between Victims and Police

Many investigators, as well as top-ranking police officials, have defended the investigative function, not because it contributes significantly to the identification of perpetrators, but because it is one of the principal contacts the police maintain with the victims of serious crimes. But, despite these verbal espousals of the public service function as an important part of the investigative role, our observations in departments across the country indicate that most police merely respond initially to the crime scene and file a cursory report; rarely do they subsequently contact the victims about the progress of the case. This is understandable, given the rising number of reported crimes and relatively constant police budgets.

While it seems reasonable to suggest that local police departments might win more public confidence by notifying the victim when the perpetrator has been identified, such a policy of routine feedback could be self-defeating. For example, if the police were to inform a victim that the perpetrator of his crime had been apprehended and was not being charged with his offense but being prosecuted on another, the victim, rather than feeling more confident in the police or the criminal justice system, might in fact become disillusioned. And a resentful victim could become highly vocal about his dissatisfactions and cause other citizens to be negative about police performance.

How much information to give the victim and when to give it were the questions behind a telephone survey we made of robbery and burglary victims. This study must be regarded as exploratory; the survey was conducted simply as an initial attempt to explore victims' feelings about receiving information feedback and about which types of information are most important.

The inquiry summarized by Table 8 was accompanied by two pairs of questions, with the first question of each pair addressing the victim's desire to have feedback on a specific matter and the second eliciting his probable reaction if the feedback occurred. Table 9 displays the responses on whether or not the victim wanted to be told of a police decision to suspend or drop investigative effort on his case if such a decision were made: these responses suggest a consistent preference for knowledge about this police decision, but with an observable tendency to the contrary in cleared robbery cases (which involve a relatively small segment of the underlying population). Table 10 exhibits the victims' responses to the question of what their reactions would be if they were told that no further investigation was intended on their cases. We note that approximately one-third of our sample would react negatively to unfavorable feedback (and the proportion would be higher if the data were weighted to reflect the relative numbers of each crime type).

To the extent that our survey results may reach beyond the confines of our small sample, they broadly support the belief that there is a strong market for information feedback to victims from the police. But they also tend to confirm

Table 8 Kind of Information Wanted by Victims

Survey Questions: As a Victim, Did You Want the Police to Inform You?	Yes	No	Indifferent	IF YOUR ANSWER WAS "YES," HOW IMPORTANT WAS IT TO YOU TO BE INFORMED?	
				Very	Somewhat
If your case was solved?	32 (89%)	1 (3%)	3 (8%)	26	6
If a suspect was arrested?	30 (83%)	5 (14%)	1 (3%)	22	8
If a defendant was tried?	27 (75%)	4 (11%)	5 (14%)	15	12
If a defendant was sentenced?	27 (75%)	4 (11%)	5 (14%)	16	11
What sentence was imposed?	27 (75%)	4 (11%)	5 (14%)	16	11
If the defendant was released from custody?	18 (50%)	11 (31%)	7 (19%)	11	7

Table 9 Respondent's Desire to Be Told of Police Decision to Suspend Investigation of His Case

Victim's Response	Burglary	Robbery	Total
Yes	16	10	26 (72%)
No	3	4	7 (19%)
Indifferent or no answer	1	2	3 (8%)
Total	20	16	36 (100%)

Table 10 Victim's Predicted Reaction to Information That Police Will Suspend Investigation of His Case

Victim's Prediction of His Own Reaction	Burglary	Robbery	Total	
Appreciative of being told and agreeable to police decision	3	1	4	(12%)
Understanding and resigned	11	7	18	(53%)
Disturbed and resistant	4	1	5	(15%)
Angry and resentful	2	5	7	(21%)
			34[a]	(100%)

[a]Two victims were omitted: the response of one was not applicable, and the other declined to answer.

the view that some victims, if given unfavorable information, will develop undesirable attitudes toward the police. Finally, our results suggest that other repercussions from information feedback, of which the police are sometimes apprehensive, are of slight significance. Few victims, no matter how distressed by information coming from the police, indicated that they would act inimically to police interests.

Proactive Investigation Methods

In a departure from the typically reactive mode (so called, because the investigator does not focus on the case until after a crime has occurred) of most investigators assigned to Part I crimes, some police departments have shifted a small number of their investigators to more proactive investigation tactics. Proactive units usually deal with a particular type of offender, such as known burglars, robbery teams, or active fences. A number of such units have been supported on an experimental basis with funds from the Law Enforcement Assistance Administration.[25]

The proactive team members often work quite closely with other investigators, but, unlike regular investigators, they are not assigned a caseload of reported crimes. Instead, they are expected to generate other sources of information to identify serious offenders. These other sources may include informants they have cultivated, their own surveillance activities, or undercover fencing operations operated by the police themselves.

The primary objective in establishing these units is to reduce the incidence of the target crime. The reduction is supposed to result from the containment achieved by successfully arresting and prosecuting offenders and from the deterrent effect on others of the publicity given the proactive programs. Therefore, the arrest rates of these units are typically used as a measure of their primary effect; and changes in the rate of incidence of the target crime are also cited. The chief problem in using these two measures is the difficulty of isolating the unique effects of the proactive unit from other activities of the police department and from external factors affecting crime or arrest rates.

In the course of our study, we looked at several such units by either examining evaluation reports or making direct observations. In general, they all seemed to produce a much higher number of arrests for the officers assigned than did other types of patrol or investigative activities. Consistent effects on targeted crime rates could not be identified.

In order to determine which activities of these units actually resulted in arrests, we examined in considerable detail a sample of cases from two units, the Miami Stop Robbery unit and the Long Beach (California) Suppression of Burglary unit.

From the sample of robbery cases in Miami, we determined that, although the Stop officers averaged 4 arrests per man-month, half of which were for robbery, in 10 out of 11 of these arrests the Stop officer was simply executing a warrant obtained by some other unit or accompanying another officer to make the arrest. In Long Beach, the Suppression of Burglary officers averaged 2.4 arrests per man-month, half of which were for burglary or for receiving stolen property. An analysis of 27 of the arrests disclosed that just half (13) resulted from the unit's own work; the remaining arrests were by referral or were the result of routine investigation that could have been handled by any other unit.

Our general conclusion was that proactive techniques can be productive in making arrests, particularly for burglary and fencing. To be effective, however, the units must be staffed with highly motivated and innovative personnel. And the officers' efforts must be carefully monitored to preclude their diversion to making arrests for other units and to ensure that their tactics do not become so aggressive as to infringe on individual liberties.

POLICY IMPLICATIONS

We have identified several distinguishable functions performed by investigators: preparing cases for prosecution after the suspects are in custody; apprehending known suspects; performing certain routine tasks that may lead to identifying unknown suspects; engaging in intensive investigations when there are no suspects or when it is not clear that a crime has been committed; and conducting proactive investigations. In addition, investigators engage in various administrative tasks and paperwork related to these functions.

We have enough information about the effectiveness of each function to begin asking whether the function should be performed at all and, if so, who should do it. The notion that all these functions must be performed by a single individual, or by officers having similar ranks or capabilities, does not stand up to scrutiny; in fact, many police departments have begun to assign distinguishable functions to separate units. Our own suggestions, to be presented below, support this development and extend it in certain ways. If a function now assigned to investigators can be performed as well or better, but at lower cost, by patrol officers, clerical personnel, or information systems, it should be removed from the investigators; if it serves the objectives of the prosecutor, then it should be responsive to the needs of the prosecutor; and, if especially competent investigators are required, the function should be assigned to a unit composed of such officers.

In this section we describe the implications of our findings for changes in the organization of the investigative function, the processing of physical evidence, and the role of the public.[26]

Preparing Cases for Prosecution

Postarrest investigative activity—not only important for prosecution but also one of the major activities now performed by investigators—can perhaps be done in a less costly or more effective manner.

Our observations indicate that the current coordination, or lack thereof, between the police and prosecutorial agencies does not support a healthy working relationship. It allows for a situation in which each can blame the other for outcomes in court that it views as unfavorable.

Most prosecutors do not have investigators on their staff. If they do, these investigators are usually occupied with "white-collar" offenses rather than street crimes. Generally, then, the prosecutor relies on police investigators to provide the evidence needed to prosecute and convict arrestees. But inherent in this situation is a conflict between prosecutor and police. An arrest is justified by *probable cause*—that is, by an articulable, reasonable belief that a crime was committed and that the arrestee was the offender. Often, the police are satisfied to document the justification for the arrest rather than expend further investigative effort to strengthen the evidence in the case. The prosecutor, on the other hand, may be reluctant to file the charges preferred by the police, or to file at all, he believes the evidence would not suffice for a conviction, that is, as *proof beyond a reasonable doubt*. Many cases appear to be affected by the conflicting incentives of police and prosecutor, as reflected in failures to file and in lenient filing, early dismissals, or imbalanced bargaining.

One way of ameliorating this problem is to make explicit the types of information that the prosecutor and police agree are appropriate to collect and document, given the nature of the crime. The form we designed for robbery cases (summarized in Table 6) gives an example of how such information can be made explicit. Each jurisdiction should develop appropriate forms for major categories of crimes. Such written documents would assist the police in becoming more knowledgeable about the type and amount of information that a prosecutor requires to establish guilt for each type of offense and in allocating their investigative efforts to provide this information.[27]

We observed that the prosecutor's strictness with respect to filing decisions can affect the thoroughness of case preparation. In turn, the thoroughness of documentation may affect the percentage of cases subsequently dismissed and the degree of plea bargaining. We suggest, therefore, that prosecutors be mindful of the level of investigative documentation in their jurisdictions, especially in offices where the officer presenting the case may not have participated in the investigation.

One rationale advanced in some police departments for minimizing the factual content of formal investigative reports is that these reports are subject to discovery by defense counsel and thereby facilitate the impeachment of prosecution witnesses, including policemen. Such departments believe that the results of detailed investigations are better communicated orally to the prosecutor's office. The results of our research, while not conclusive, tend to refute this argument. In the jurisdiction ("A") where detailed documentation is prepared, no such negative consequences were noted; but in the jurisdiction ("B") having less information in the documentation, oral communication failed in some instances to reach all the prosecutors involved in the case.

Above and beyond merely improving coordination between police and prosecutors, it is worthy of experimentation to assign the prosecutor responsibility for certain investigative efforts. We feel that a promising approach would be to place nearly all postarrest investigations under the authority of the prosecutor, either by assigning police officers to his office or by making investigators an integral part of his staff, depending on the local situation. A test of this arrangement would show whether it is an effective way of assuring that the evidentiary needs for a successful prosecution are met.

Apprehending Known Suspects

We have noted that, in a substantial fraction of the cases ultimately cleared, the perpetrator is known from information available at the scene of the crime. If he or she is already in custody, the case becomes a matter for postarrest processing, as discussed above. If the perpetrator is not in custody, it is important for the responding officer(s), whether from investigative or patrol units, to obtain and make a record of the evidence identifying the suspect. This requires that the responding officers be permitted adequate time to conduct an initial investigation, including the interviewing of possible witnesses, and that the crime-reporting form be designed in such a way that the presence of information identifying a suspect is unmistakably recorded.

Apprehending a known suspect may or may not be difficult. Assigning all such apprehension to investigators does not appear to be cost-effective, especially if the investigators are headquartered at some distance from the suspect's location and a patrol officer is nearby. We believe that certain patrol officers, whom we shall call generalist-investigators, could be trained to handle this function in such a way that the arrests are legally proper and a minimum number of innocent persons are brought in for questioning. Only when apprehension proves difficult should investigative units become involved.

Routine Investigative Actions

For crimes without initial identification of a suspect, we found that many of those eventually cleared are solved by routine investigative actions—for example, listing a stolen automobile in the "hot car" file, asking the victim to view a previously assembled collection of mug shots for the crime in question, checking pawnshop slips, awaiting phone calls from the public, and tracing ownership of a weapon.

One implication of this finding is that any steps a police department can take to convert investigative tasks into routine actions will increase the number of crimes solved. Technological improvements, especially in information systems, produced many of the clearances we identified as "routine." In the absence of good information systems, such clearances might never have occurred or might have been difficult to achieve. The ability of patrol officers to check rapidly whether a vehicle is stolen or, more important, whether the owner is wanted for questioning produced numerous case solutions in our samples. Well-organized and maintained mug-shot, *modus operandi,* or pawn-slip files also led to clearances.

A second implication is that it may not be necessary for *investigators,* who are usually paid more than patrol officers or clerks, to perform the functions that lead to routine clearances. We believe that an experiment should be conducted to determine the cost and effectiveness of having lower-paid personnel perform these tasks.

Once clerical processing is complete, some action by a police officer may still be needed; for example, the suspect may still have to be apprehended. Such action should be assigned to generalist investigators.

Investigating Crimes Without Suspects

Two basic objectives are served by taking more than routine investigative action when the suspect is unknown. One objective is to solve the crime; the other is to demonstrate that the police care about the crime and the victim. The latter objective can be carried out by generalist-investigators who are responsible to a local commander concerned with all aspects of police-community relations. This type of investigative duty does not require specialized skills or centralized coordination. The officers performing it could readily shift between patrol and investigative duties. In departments with team policing, such investigations could be a task rotated among team members.

If the objective is actually to solve the crime, police departments must realize that the results will rarely be commensurate with the effort involved. An explicit decision must be made that the nature of the crime itself or public concern about the crime warrants a full follow-up investigation. A significant reduction in investigative efforts would be appropriate for all but the most serious offenses. If, in a less serious offense, a thorough preliminary investigation fails to establish a suspect's identity, then the victim should be notified that active investigation is being suspended until new leads appear (as a result, for example, of an arrest in another matter).

Serious crimes (homicide, rape, assault with great bodily injury, robbery, or first-degree burglary) warrant special investigative efforts. These efforts can best be provided by a Major Offenses Unit, manned by investigators who are well trained and experienced in examining crime scenes, interpreting physical evidence, and interrogating hostile suspects and fearful witnesses, and who are aided by modern information systems. One reason for establishing such a unit is to identify the investigative positions that require special skills and training and that demand knowledge of citywide crime patterns and developments. Our observations suggest, by way of contrast, that current staffing patterns rarely allow most investigators to see these highly serious cases. Therefore, when such cases arise, the investigators are frequently ill equipped to cope with them and unduly distracted by the burden of paper work on their routine cases.

A Major Offenses Unit would concentrate its efforts on a few *unsolved* serious felonies. The team would consist of a relatively small number of experienced investigators closely supervised by a team commander. From our observations, it appears that the most serious impediment to high-quality investigative work is the traditional method of case assignment and supervision. In nearly every department, a case is normally assigned to an individual investigator as his sole responsibility, whether he is a generalist, specialist, or engaged in team policing. Supervisors do not normally review the decisions he makes on how to pursue the investigation, and his decisions are largely unrecorded in the case file. Consequently, the relative priority an investigator gives to the tasks on a given case assigned to him depends largely on the number and nature of his other case assignments and on his personal predilections and biases. Caseload conflicts and personal predilections frequently lead an investigator to postpone unduly or perform improperly the critical tasks of a particular case assignment.

Assigning cases to investigative teams rather than to individuals could eliminate this problem. For effective operations, the team should include approximately six men and be led by a senior investigator knowledgeable about the local crime situation, criminal law, and police management. The leader's primary responsibility would be to keep informed of progress on the cases assigned to his team and to make the broad tactical decisions on the team's expenditure of effort. Each day the subordinate investigators would perform individually assigned tasks. A clerk delegated to the team would prepare progress reports to document the daily accomplishment on open cases and to assist the leader in making the allocation for the following day. These reports would also help the leader identify which of his men were most effective at which tasks. Such an approach should assure that significant steps in an investigation are objectively directed by an experienced senior investigator.

Proactive Investigations

Our research into proactive units—let us call them "strike forces"—leads us to conclude that they can be relatively productive. In instances where such units were successful, they were manned by motivated and innovative personnel. The gain in employing them becomes illusory when mere quantity of arrests is emphasized, for then their efforts tend to be diverted into making arrests that are not the result of unique capabilities. We feel that departments should employ strike forces selectively and judiciously. The operation of strike forces necessitates careful procedural and legal planning to protect the officers involved and to ensure that the defendants they identify can be successfully prosecuted. These units also require close monitoring by senior officers to ensure that they do not become overly aggressive and infringe on individual privacy.

In all likelihood, the relative advantage of strike force operations in a particular department will not persist over a long period of time. The department must accustom itself to creating and then terminating strike forces, as circumstances dictate.

Processing Physical Evidence

Most police departments collect far more evidence (primarily fingerprints) than they can productively process. Our work shows that cold searches of inked fingerprint files could be far more effective than routine follow-up investigations in increasing the apprehension rate.

Fingerprint processing capabilities should be strengthened as follows. First, the reference print files should be organized by geographic area, with a fingerprint specialist assigned to each area; no area should have more than 5,000 sets of inked prints. Second, to assure a large number of "request searches," which imply a cooperative effort between investigator and fingerprint specialist, some communication links should be devised to help motivate and facilitate the reciprocal exchange of information between these two parties. Third, the fingerprint specialists should be highly trained, highly motivated, and not overloaded with other tasks that might detract from their primary function.

Several existing systems for storing and retrieving inked prints with specified characteristics (of the latent print or the offender) appear useful and were widely praised by departments that have them. However, further research might contribute a major technological improvement in the capability of police departments to match latent prints with inked prints.

Role of the Public

Our research persuaded us that actions by members of the public can strongly influence the outcome of cases. Sometimes private citizens hold the perpetrator at the scene of the crime. Sometimes they recognize the suspect or stolen property at a later time and call the investigator. Sometimes the victim or his relatives conduct a full-scale investigation on their own and eventually present the investigator with a solution. Collectively, these types of citizen involvement account for a sizable fraction of cleared cases.

Police departments should initiate programs designed to enhance the victim's desire to cooperate fully with the police. Such programs might both increase apprehension rates and improve the quality of prosecutions. Specifically, when major crimes are solved, police departments should announce the particular contribution of members of the public (respecting, of course, any person's desire for anonymity). A realistic picture of how crimes are solved will help eliminate the public's distorted image of detectives and will impress on them the importance of cooperating with police.

Reallocation of Investigative Resources

Ultimately, our suggestions imply a substantial shift of police resources from investigative to other units. However, such reallocations cannot be justified on the basis of current knowledge alone; they must await testing and evaluation of each of our recommendations. If we prove correct, most initial investigations would be assigned to patrol units under the direction of local commanders. To improve the quality of initial investigations, the patrol force would have to be augmented with a large number of generalist-investigators. These officers would also perform certain follow-up work, such as apprehending known suspects and improving communications with victims and witnesses of crimes. The resources needed to field generalist-investigators would be obtained by reducing the number of investigators.

Additional major reallocations of resources away from "traditional" reactive investigative units are implied by our suggestions to have clerical personnel and generalist-investigators perform routine processing of cases, to increase the use of information systems, to enhance capabilities for processing physical evidence, to increase the number of proactive investigative units, and to assign investigative personnel to the prosecutor for postarrest preparation of cases. If all these changes were made, the only remaining investigative units concerned with Part I crimes would be the Major Offenses Units. The number of investigators assigned to such units would ordinarily be well under half the current number of investigators in most departments.

In no way does our study suggest that total police resources be reduced. On the contrary, our analysis of FBI data suggests that such a reduction might lower arrest and clearance rates. Reallocating resources might lead to somewhat increased arrest and clearance rates, but our suggestions are intended primarily for the more successful prosecution of arrestees and for improved public relations.

We know that most of the changes we advocate are practical, because we observed them in operation in one or more departments. For example, a number of departments have recently introduced "case screening," whereby each crime report is examined to determine whether or not a follow-up investigation should be conducted. Our findings indicate that the decision rule for case screening can be quite simple. If a suspect is known, the case should be pursued; if no suspect is known after a thorough preliminary investigation, the case should be assigned for routine clerical processing unless it is serious enough to be assigned to the appropriate Major Offenses Unit. The definition of "serious" must be determined individually by each department, since it is essentially a political decision.

Another current innovation is "team policing," in which investigators are assigned to work with patrol officers who cover a specified geographical area. While there are many organizational variations of team policing,[28] most forms would permit the introduction of generalist-investigators having the functions we describe, and some already include such personnel.

We know of no jurisdiction in which the prosecutor currently administers postarrest investigations, although investigators have been assigned to several prosecutors' offices (for example, in Boston, New Orleans, and San Diego) to facilitate interactions with the police. Only a careful experiment will determine the feasibility and effectiveness of making the prosecutor responsible for postarrest investigations.

The National Institute of Law Enforcement and Criminal Justice has funded the introduction of revised investigative procedures in five jurisdictions. The experimental changes, which are based partly on the findings of our study, will be carefully evaluated to determine whether, to what extent, and under what circumstances they actually lead to improved effectiveness.

ENDNOTES

1. This article summarizes the work of all the Rand researchers engaged in the study. In addition to the authors, they are Robert Castro, Konrad Kellen, Eugene Poggio, Linda Prusoff, and Sorrel Wildhorn. The study was performed under Grant 73-NI-99-0037-G from the National Institute of Law Enforcement and Criminal Justice, Law Enforcement Assistance Administration, Department of Justice. The points of view or opinions stated here do not necessarily represent the official position or policies of the Department of Justice.

The latest version of the complete study is Peter W. Greenwood et al., *The Criminal Investigation Process* (Lexington, Mass.: D. C. Heath, 1977).

2. Part I crimes are criminal homicide, forcible rape, robbery, aggravated assault, burglary, larceny, and auto theft. Except in the case of homicide, the FBI definitions of these crimes include attempts.

3. The advisory board consisted of Cornelius (Neil) J. Behan (New York City Police Department); James Fisk (member of

the Los Angeles Police Commission); Thomas Hastings (Rochester, New York, Police Department); Jerry Wilson (former Chief of the Washington, D.C., Police Department); and Eugene Zoglio (professor, Prince George's Community College).

4. Consultants were Sydney Cooper, Carmine Motto, Albert Seedman, Seymour Silver, and Raymond Sinetar.

5. The complete results of the Rand survey are reported in Jan M. Chaiken, *The Criminal Investigation Process: Volume 11. Survey of Municipal and County Police Departments,* R-1777-DOI (Santa Monica, Calif.: The Rand Corporation, October 1975).

6. See, for example, National Criminal Justice Information and Statistics Service, "Expenditure and Employment Data for the Criminal Justice system" (Washington, D.C.: U.S. Government Printing Office, updated annually).

7. A crime is *cleared* when a perpetrator is apprehended or is identified as unapprehendable. The latter possibility is intended to apply in "exceptional" circumstances, such as when the perpetrator is dead.

8. Peter W. Greenwood, *An Analysis of the Apprehension Activities of the New York City Police Department,* R-529-NYC (New York: New York City-Rand Institute, September 1970). For the reader unfamiliar with this field, let us explain that more than one clearance can be claimed for a single arrest if the person arrested for a specific crime is then charged with, or admits to, crimes he committed elsewhere.

9. Bernard Greenberg et al., *Enhancement of the Investigative Function, Volume I: Analysis and Conclusions; Volume III: Investigative Procedures — Selected Task Evaluation; Volume IV: Burglary Investigative Checklist and Handbook* (Menlo Park, Calif.: Stanford Research Institute, 1972). (Volume II is not available.)

10. Chaiken, *Criminal Investigation Process: Volume 11,* pp. 36, 37.

11. In some jurisdictions, persons may be arrested "for investigation" without a crime being charged. In all jurisdictions, persons are occasionally arrested by error and are subsequently released by a prosecutor or magistrate without any clearance being claimed by the police.

12. Instances in which several perpetrators are arrested for a single crime may also explain an arrest/clearance ratio of over 1.

13. Herbert H. Isaacs, "A Study of Communications, Crimes, and Arrests in a Metropolitan Police Department," Appendix B of Institute of Defense Analyses, *Task Force Report: Science and Technology,* A Report to the President's Commission on Law Enforcement and Administration of Justice (Washington, D.C.: U.S. Government Printing Office, 1967).

14. John Conklin, *Robbery and the Criminal Justice System* (Philadelphia, Pa.: J. B. Lippincott Co., 1972).

15. After initial publication of the Rand study, this finding was further confirmed by a Police Foundation study, "Managing Investigations: the Rochester System," by Peter B. Bloch and James Bell (Washington, D.C., 1976). While that study was intended primarily to compare team policing with nonteam policing, the report presents data that make it possible to calculate the ratio of on-scene arrests to all clearances by arrest for three crimes. The data show that, in Rochester, 31.7 percent of burglary clearances by arrest, 31.1 percent of robbery clearances by arrest, and 28.7 percent of larceny clearances by arrest were the result of on-scene arrests.

16. See Peter W. Greenwood, Jan M. Chaiken, Joan Petersilia, Linda Prusoff, Bob Castro, Konrad Kellen, Eugene Poggio, and Sorrel Wildhorn, *The Criminal Investigation Process: Volume III. Observations and Analysis* R-1778-DOI (Santa Monica, Calif.: The Rand Corporation, October 1975), chap. 6.

17. See Chaiken, *Criminal Investigation Process: Volume II,* pp. 38–47.

18. The 1972 data revealed a linear relationship between arrests per officer and crime workload, up to the threshold, but the intercept of the straight line fit was at a positive value of arrests per officer. After 1972, crime rates in the United States generally increased. Since we did not perform any longitudinal analyses, we do not know whether the thresholds also increased or remained at the same levels.

19. "Worked-on" means that at least half an hour was spent on the case. The types

of cases assigned to each unit are described in Greenwood et al., *Criminal Investigation Process: Volume III,* pp. 53–55. For example, the homicide unit handles not only homicides but also suicides and un-attended deaths from natural causes.

20. Activities after the case is cleared can include processing the arrestees, vouchering property, meeting with prosecutors, appearing in court, contacting victims, and completing paper work.

21. See Brian Parker and Joseph Peterson, "Physical Evidence Utilization in the Administration of Criminal Justice" (Berkeley, Calif.: School of Criminology, University of California, 1972).

22. President's Commission on Crime in the District of Columbia, *Report of the President's Commission on Crime in the District of Columbia* (Washington, D.C.: U.S. Government Printing Office, 1966).

23. The six departments are those in Berkeley, Long Beach, Los Angeles, and Richmond, California; in Miami, Florida; and in Washington, D.C. For further details, see Greenwood et al., *Criminal Investigation Process: Volume III,* chap. 7.

24. Peter W. Greenwood et al., *Prosecution of Adult Felony Defendants in Los Angeles County: A Policy Perspective,* R-1127-DOJ (Santa Monica, Calif.: The Rand Corporation, March 1973) led us to expect significant differences in police investigative effort and prosecutorial posture between the two selected jurisdictions.

25. For a description of five antirobbery units of this type, see Richard H. Ward et al., *Police Robbery Control Manual.* (Washington, D.C.: National Institute of Law Enforcement and Criminal Justice, 1975).

26. For an expanded discussion of the policy implications, see Peter W. Greenwood and Joan Petersilia, *The Criminal Investigation Process: Volume I. Summary and Policy Implications,* R-177-DOJ (Santa Monica, Calif.: The Rand Corporation, October 1975).

27. Alternatives that might accomplish some similar aims include having the prosecutor provide the investigators with periodic evaluations of their case preparation efforts; training new investigators in case preparation; or having on-call attorneys assist in the preparation of serious cases.

28. See, for example, Peter B. Bloch and David Specht, *Neighborhood Team Policing* (Washington, D.C.: National Institute of Law Enforcement and Criminal Justice, December 1973).

The Relationship Between Evidence, Detective Effort, and the Disposition of Burglary and Robbery Investigations

STEVEN G. BRANDL
JAMES FRANK

T he police detective is commonly cast by the media and detective fiction as a highly skilled and intelligent investigator who, through the use of complex and extraordinary means, is capable of solving virtually any crime (Klockars, 1985; see also Garofalo, 1981). The public, in turn, has largely accepted this portrayal as an accurate reflection of reality (Wilson, 1975). Further, the police organization reflects and perpetuates this institutionalized belief by dividing the investigative task among detectives, who specialize in investigating crimes, and patrol officers, who perform the countless other tasks associated with police work.

With the appearance of empirical inquiries into the operations of the criminal investigation process, the capabilities of detectives in investigating crimes have been directly questioned. However, not only have these studies been relatively few in number, but they have also produced contradictory findings. For example, Greenwood, Chaiken, and Petersilia (1977) explain that "detective work is not characterized by hard work leading to case solutions . . ." rather, "the cases that get cleared are primarily the easy ones to solve" (p. 112). Thus, "any justification for the work of [detectives] must lie in areas other than crime solution" (p. 141). On the other hand, Eck (1983) argues that "the work of . . . detectives is extremely important with respect to the subsequent making of follow-up arrests" (p. 243). As a result of the divergent findings, definitive conclusions concerning the contributions of detectives in solving crimes cannot be drawn.

The analyses reported in this study are intended to cast additional light on the debate concerning the extent to which detective effort contributes to the identification and apprehension of criminals. Specifically, we test hypotheses that link burglary and robbery follow-up investigation arrests to the amount of

From *American Journal of Police* 13: 149–168. 1994.

time spent on follow-up investigations and the strength of the evidence associ-ated with the cases. The study addresses some shortcomings evident in the prior research and provides some empirical evidence where speculation has gone be-fore. In so doing, the study represents an extension of previous research.

PREVIOUS RESEARCH

In the first study to examine the contribution of detectives in solving crimes, Isaacs (1967) analyzed data on 1,905 crimes reported to two of 15 Los Angeles Police Department field divisions in January 1966. Isaacs found that of the 1,905 crimes, 336 (18%) resulted in an actual arrest while 146 (8%) resulted in "other clearances" (e.g., victim refused to prosecute, unfounded). Of the 336 cases that resulted in an arrest, only 27 (8%) were as a result of an arrest by a detective. Based on the limited statistical analyses performed on the data, the author concluded that "[o]ne of the most significant characteristics of a case, affecting its chances of being cleared, is whether the suspect was named in the crime report by the victim" (p. 96). For example, of the 1,905 crimes, 1,556 (82%) involved suspects who were not named in the initial crime report. Of these 1,556 cases, 1,375 (88%) were not cleared. Conversely, of the 1,905 crimes, 349 (18%) involved suspects who were named in the crime report. Of these cases, only 48 (14%) were not cleared.

Greenwood (1970), in an analysis of burglary, robbery, and grand larceny crimes that were reported to several precincts of the New York City Police Department during the first six months of 1967, also found that when a sus-pect could be named by the victim, the chances of an arrest were significantly greater compared to when only a description was provided, or other evidence was available. For example, the analyses showed that approximately 9 percent of reported robberies resulted in an on-scene arrest while the remaining 91 per-cent were initially unsolved. Of the unsolved cases, the victim could name a suspect in about 2 percent and could describe the suspect in 67 percent. For those cases with a named suspect, 46 percent resulted in an arrest, while only 2 percent of the cases with a description resulted in an arrest. Once again, cir-cumstances—namely, the victim providing the suspect's name—were por-trayed as determining the outcome of the case.

The study conducted by Greenwood, Chaiken, and Petersilia of the RAND Corporation in 1977 supported, and elaborated on, the conclusions of Isaacs (1967) and Greenwood (1970). Their results were derived from analyses of primarily two sets of data. First, based on an analysis of the computer-readable case assignment file maintained by the Kansas City (MO) Police Department, the researchers provided insight into how detectives spend their working time. In comparing the amount of time spent on uncleared cases with the amount of time spent on cleared cases, they found that the "time spent on uncleared cases [was] significantly higher than time spent prior to clearance on cleared cases with no initial patrol arrest" (p. 115).[1] On the basis of this comparison, they conclude that there are basically two types of investigations: "Some investigations are lengthy but do not result in a clearance. Others lead to a clearance after a small amount of work but entail substantial efforts by the investigator once the crime is cleared" (p. 116). Thus, "the cases that get cleared are primarily the easy ones to solve" (p. 112).

Second, a post hoc analysis of cleared crimes (homicide, aggravated assault, felony morals, robbery, burglary, theft, auto theft, and forgery/fraud) from five police departments (Berkeley, Long Beach, Los Angeles, Miami, and Washington, D.C.)[2] provided a means by which to describe the method in which cleared cases were solved. Greenwood et al. (1977) found that about 22 percent (38 of 172) of the cleared crimes resulted from an arrest by a patrol officer at the scene of the crime. In another 44 percent (76 of 172), the perpetrator was "known" when the crime report was first taken and, as described by the researchers, "the main job for the investigator in these cases [was] to locate and apprehend the perpetrator, and to assemble evidence adequate to charge him" (p. 135). The remaining 34 percent (58 of 172) of all cleared crimes were cleared primarily as a result of "simple routine actions" of detectives (e.g., showing mug-shot books, acting on precise and detailed informant tips). According to Greenwood et al. (1977), only about three percent of these cleared crimes could be attributed to "special actions" of detectives (e.g., preparation of investigative bulletins, matching latent prints to inked prints in a file organized by M.O.).

Like Isaacs (1967) and Greenwood (1970), Greenwood et al. (1977) explain that the overwhelming majority of solved crimes are solved because of arrests by patrol officers or because the identity of the perpetrator is known when the crime report reached the detective. "If information that uniquely identifies the perpetrator is not presented at the time the crime is reported, the perpetrator, by and large, will not be subsequently identified" (Greenwood, Chaiken, and Petersilia, 1976:65). Thus, "it is not true in general that the greater the investigative effort devoted to a crime the more likely it will be cleared" (p. 64).

Eck (1983) provides contrast with Isaacs (1967), Greenwood (1970), and Greenwood et al. (1977) by emphasizing, or at least not minimizing, the importance of detective effort in solving crimes. Using data collected from three police departments (DeKalb Co., GA, St. Petersburg, FL, and Wichita, KS), he examined activities performed by detectives and patrol officers to produce crime and/or suspect information, and the relationship between this information and a suspect being arrested. The study focused on burglaries and robberies. Eck found that certain types of information produced during the preliminary investigation (i.e., information pertaining to the suspect) were predictive of whether or not an arrest was made during the follow-up investigation as were some of the activities performed by detectives during the follow-up investigation (e.g., record checks, informant interviews). As such, Eck provides evidence to suggest that circumstances of criminal incidents *as well as* efforts of detectives contribute to the making of arrests during follow-up investigations.

On the basis of his analyses, Eck (1983) proposed what he referred to as the "triage hypothesis" (see also Eck, 1979). According to this hypothesis, cases can be grouped into three categories depending on the strength of the evidence (i.e., favorable circumstances) associated with the case. The hypothesis predicts that, first, cases with weak evidence will rarely conclude with an arrest, regardless of the investigative effort or time allocated to them. Second, cases with moderate evidence, where there are sufficient leads to suggest that the cases could be solved, will often result in an arrest but only if effort is allocated to them. Third, cases with strong evidence, where the suspect has been positively identified, will usually result in an arrest, even with only minimal investigative effort. Accordingly, based on this hypothesis, circumstances determine the outcome of the cases in the first and third group and thus, for these cases, the probability of an arrest does not increase with more time spent. However, effort determines the outcome of the cases in the second group and as a result, for these cases, the probability of an arrest does increase with more time spent on the investigation. Therefore, like Greenwood et al. (1977), Eck implies that, in general, the likelihood of an arrest may not increase with more effort devoted to the case. However, Eck (1983) suggests that this relationship—that more time spent on an investigation increases the probability of an arrest—does hold true for cases with moderate suspect information. And, as hypothesized by Eck (1979), it is cases in this second category that have the most time devoted to them.

There are several issues that need to be considered when judging the overall validity of the conclusions offered by the previous research. First, Isaacs (1967) and some of the analyses performed by Greenwood et al. (1977:97–119) used whether cases were "cleared" as the primary outcome variable.[3] A clearance, which is subject to administrative definition, can be obtained in ways other than by making an arrest (e.g., when the victim refuses to cooperate in the investigation);[4] therefore, a "cleared crime" should not be considered synonymous with a "solved crime." Whether or not at least one arrest was made for the particular crime under investigation appears to be a more accurate indicator of investigative success because it focuses more directly on the work product of detectives rather than on associated administrative practices or policies (cf. Greenwood, 1970; Eck, 1983; also see Bloch & Bell, 1976).[5] In addition, other analyses performed by Greenwood et al. (1977:121–32) focus only on cleared crimes, thus making it impossible to identify the actual impact of detective effort on case disposition.

Second, although Greenwood (1970) and Eck (1983) use "arrest" as the outcome variable, it is not clear whether they recognize that detectives are sometimes constrained in their abilities to make an arrest even when a suspect has been positively identified (see Eck, 1983:202–4). For example, a victim may not desire that the police conduct an investigation of the criminal incident. In another instance, it may be determined (either by the police *or* the victim) that a reported crime did not actually occur. It would be inappropriate to expect the police to pursue charges and make arrests in these types of cases and thus, it would be misleading to consider these types of cases as "no arrest" cases in the statistical analyses. It would seem more appropriate to consider such cases "constrained cases" and treat them independent of the "arrest" versus "no arrest" classification.

Third, while much of the previous research suggests that the evidence—namely, suspect information—available at the conclusion of the initial investigation determines the ultimate disposition of the case (Isaacs, 1967; Greenwood, 1970; Greenwood et al., 1977), the complexity of the construct has often escaped its operationalization. Saying that a suspect is "described," (Eck, 1983), "named" (Isaacs, 1967; Greenwood, 1970), or "known" (Greenwood et al., 1977) without specifying *how,* may invite erroneous conclusions. For example, a suspect could be "named" as a result of a victim guess or because an eyewitness saw the individual committing the crime. There is clearly variation in the strength of the information in these two situations but it is not captured with the simple "named" versus "not named" classification. Thus, to adequately determine the strength of suspect information, it is necessary to specify the basis of the information.

Finally, measures of detective effort have often been suspect in terms of their validity. Greenwood et al. (1977) used "hours spent" but activities that took less than one-half hour were not included in the estimate.[6] In addition, the activity categories on which to record time spent prior to an arrest were rather limited ("interrogation," "interview," "report writing," and "crime scene investigation"). Eck (1983) used, as the primary indicator of investigative effort, whether certain activities were performed in the investigation, but this measure does not account for the variation in the amount of time spent on specific activities (e.g., an interview that lasts two hours versus one that takes ten minutes). Most troubling, however, is that some analyses do not include any measure of detective effort but inferences about the contributions of detectives in solving crimes are made nonetheless (Isaacs, 1967; Greenwood, 1970; Greenwood et al., 1977: 121–132).

In this study, we attempt to address these issues. We focus on cases that were closed with either an "arrest" or "no arrest" and we explicitly realize that, independent of detective effort and strength of evidence considerations, detectives are sometimes constrained in their ability to make arrests even when a suspect has been identified. We use a measure of suspect information that enables us to test Eck's (1983) triage hypothesis. Finally, we include in the analyses an appropriate measure of detective effort. In making these methodological and conceptual refinements, the study may extend our understanding of the relationship between evidence, detective effort, and case dispositions.

METHOD

Study Site

The data for this study were obtained from a medium-sized midwestern municipal police department. At the time of the study, the department employed 245 sworn officers and 102 civilians. Thirty of the 245 officers were assigned to the investigations division. In 1989 the department served a community of approximately 130,000 people; 33 percent of whom were non-white.

Sample

The process of selecting cases for this study consisted of several steps. Initially, a list of all the burglaries and robberies that occurred between July 1, 1989 and June 30, 1990 was obtained from the department's computer system. This list identified 339 robberies and 1,674 burglaries. All of these cases, which were in chronological order within the records bureau, were then reviewed and several categories of cases were eliminated.

First, all of the cases that were not assigned to detectives were excluded (12 robberies, 1,219 burglaries).[7] Second, all of the reports which stated that an arrest was made prior to case assignment (i.e., during the initial investigation) were excluded (32 robberies, 73 burglaries). Third, cases that were assigned to detectives only after information became available that would allow the cases to be immediately "closed" (defined below) were excluded (e.g., a person confessed to committing a crime while being questioned about another crime) (no robberies, 32 burglaries). Fourth, cases that were missing from the files were excluded from the population (two robberies, 33 burglaries). As a result of the case selection procedure, 292 robbery cases and 317 burglary cases were included in the sample (N = 609). For each of the 609 cases, the initial and follow-up investigation reports were reviewed and a case data coding form was completed.

Measures

The independent variables in this study were (1) strength of suspect information at the conclusion of the initial investigation and (2) amount of detective time spent on the follow-up investigation. Data on "suspect information" were obtained from the initial investigation report. The variable incorporated what was known about the culprit (description, identification, name) *and* how this information was produced (on the basis of a victim or witness guess, an eyewitness to the crime, or some other witness account). A description refers to information about the physical characteristics of the culprit while an identification means that the witness could recognize the culprit if seen again. It is expected that this measurement scheme captures more of the construct's complexity than a simple tally of how many suspect-related solvability factors were present at the conclusion of the initial investigation (e.g., suspect named? suspect described? etc.) or stating that the suspect is "described," "known," or "named" without specifying how (e.g., a guess? an eyewitness account? as in Isaacs, 1967; Greenwood, 1970; Greenwood et al., 1977; and Eck, 1983). Although one might question the use of "suspect information" as the sole measure of "evidence," previous research has consistently shown that suspect information is the most powerful, if not the only, evidence consideration vis-à-vis the solvability of burglaries and robberies (Greenwood et al., 1977; see also Bloch and Bell, 1976).

To be congruent with, and test, the "triage" hypothesis identified earlier, the suspect information variable had three values: (1) *weak* suspect information (no significant suspect information available, a suspect was described and could be identified on the basis of a [victim] guess only, a suspect could be described by an eyewitness to the crime, a suspect could be named by a guess); (2) *moderate* suspect information (a culprit could be described and identified by an eyewitness to the crime, the culprit could be named by being seen in the area at about the time the crime occurred, the culprit could be named on the basis of a guess and supported by other witness information, the culprit could be named by an individual who saw the culprit with the stolen property, or heard the culprit confess to committing the crime, or the culprit could be named in some other way [i.e., through patrol activities]); and (3) *strong* suspect information (the culprit could be named by an eyewitness to the crime).

The operational definition of "suspect information" was developed on the basis of observations and discussions with the burglary and robbery detectives in the department.[8] The information classified as "moderate suspect information" consistently constituted "good leads" for detectives to follow; the information was of better quality and provided more direction in terms of activities to perform than the suspect information defined as "weak." However, "moderate suspect information" did not allow the detectives to conclude with any degree of certainty that the suspect could/would be arrested—as was the case if "strong suspect information" was present.

Data on the amount of time spent on follow-up investigations were obtained from "turn-back sheets" on which detectives recorded the amount of time spent on, and the activities performed in,[9] the investigation from the point when the initial investigation report was received until the case was closed (e.g., an arrest warrant was issued, all leads were exhausted, the crime was unfounded, victim did not wish to pursue the complaint, etc.). This measure did not include any time spent on the investigation subsequent to an arrest or any other case closure. The completion of the turn-back sheets was a standard procedure of the department.[10]

The dependent variable, case closure status, was also determined from the turn-back sheets. Detectives could assign one of several statuses to a case in order to terminate (i.e., "close") an investigation: (1) "No Further Investigation" (NFI; all leads were exhausted and the investigation could go no further); (2) "Prosecutor Refused to Issue" (PRF; a suspect was identified but the prosecutor's office would not issue an arrest warrant); (3) "Unfounded" (UNF; a reported crime was determined not to have been committed); (4) "Victim Canceled Investigation" (VCI; the victim no longer wished to pursue the complaint, did not cooperate in the investigation, or did not wish to prosecute the offense); (5) "Closed, Other Prosecution" (COP; the accused was not charged with the present crime but was charged with a different crime); or (6) "Warrant Pending Arrest" (WPA; an offender was identified and a warrant was issued by the prosecutor's office, or a juvenile offender was referred to probate court).

For most of the analyses, case closure status was dummy coded as "arrest made" versus "no arrest made." The "arrest" category consisted of (a) cases in which an arrest warrant was issued (WPA) and (b) cases that were investigated by detectives and the identity of the suspect was positively known but for some (unspecified) reason, the suspect was not charged with the crime (COP). The "no arrest" category consisted of cases in which (a) all leads were exhausted (NFI) and (b) the prosecutor declined to issue an arrest warrant (PRF). For reasons identified earlier, cases in which (a) the victim canceled the investigation (VCI) and (b) the crime was determined not to have occurred (UNF) were considered "constrained cases" and excluded from most of the analyses.

FINDINGS

Table 1 provides descriptive data on the uncollapsed values of suspect information and case status for burglary and robbery cases and also shows the mean amount of time spent on each category of cases. Of particular importance in Table 1 are the data concerning the characteristics of the "constrained cases"— cases that are excluded from the subsequent analyses. It is seen that relatively few burglary and robbery cases were closed with the "UNF" (Unfounded) status; only 14 of 317 (4.4%) burglaries and 11 of 279 (3.9%) robberies were closed in this manner. Given the relative rarity of this case closure status, it does not appear, at least on its face, that there was a widespread unjustified practice of unfounding (at least burglary and robbery) crimes in this department. As a result, there is little reason to believe that bias is introduced when these cases are excluded from the subsequent analysis. Overall, 64 of the 317 (20.2%) burglaries and 97 of the 279 (34.8%) robberies were excluded as a result of being closed with either the "UNF" or "VCI" status.

Tables 2 and 3 provide data on the collapsed categories of suspect information and case status for burglaries and robberies, respectively. The mean amount of time spent on each category of cases is also presented. Not surprisingly, Table 2 shows that the likelihood of a burglary investigation concluding with an arrest increases with stronger suspect information. Of the 133 cases with weak suspect information, 13 (10.8%) concluded with an arrest. This percentage increases to 33.7 percent with moderate suspect information, and to 62.1 percent with strong suspect information. The correlation between suspect information and case status is moderately strong ($r = .43$; $p < .001$).[11]

Also apparent from Table 2 is that, overall, more time was spent on burglary cases that concluded with an arrest than on cases that did not conclude with an arrest (3.23 versus 6.72 hours; $t = -3.65$; $p < .000$; t-tests not tabled). Overall, there is a slight relationship between time spent on burglary follow-up investigations and case status ($r = .31$; $p < .001$). In addition, most time was spent on cases with moderate suspect information (5.52 hours).

Table 3 shows that, as with burglaries, the likelihood of a robbery investigation concluding with an arrest increases with stronger suspect information. Of the 55 cases with weak suspect information, only 1 (1.8%) concluded with an arrest. Of the 121 cases with moderate suspect information, 43 (35.5%) concluded with an arrest. Of the 14 cases with strong suspect information, 9 (64.3%) concluded with an arrest. There is a moderately strong relationship between suspect information and case status ($r = .41$; $p < .001$).[12]

**Table 1 Suspect Information, Time Spent, and Case Statuses:
Descriptive Statistics for Burglary and Robbery
Follow-up Investigations**

| | | | CASE STATUS | | | | | | |
| | | | Arrest Made | | No Arrest Made | | Constrained Case | | |
Susp. Info	Mean Time on Case (in hours)	S.D.	WPA	COP	NFI	PRF	UNF	VCI	Totals
No Sig Info	3.8 (3.1)	5.6 (2.2)	1 (0)	0 (1)	34 (19)	1 (1)	2 (3)	5 (4)	43 (28)
Des/Id-guess	2.7 (−)	.9 (−)	0 (0)	0 (0)	2 (0)	0 (0)	0 (0)	0 (0)	2 (0)
Des-eyewit	3.1 (3.2)	2.7 (6.0)	0 (0)	0 (0)	9 (34)	0 (0)	0 (1)	0 (5)	9 (40)
Named-guess	2.8 (−)	2.8 (−)	12 (0)	0 (0)	69 (0)	5 (0)	5 (0)	10 (0)	101 (0)
Des/Id-eyewit	5.3 (5.2)	2.8 (6.2)	3 (30)	1 (11)	12 (76)	1 (3)	0 (5)	1 (56)	18 (181)
Named-saw in area	3.2 (−)	1.6 (−)	4 (0)	0 (0)	11 (0)	3 (0)	0 (0)	2 (0)	20 (0)
Named-guess w/other support	5.2 (6.1)	5.5 (−)	5 (0)	1 (0)	9 (1)	0 (0)	1 (0)	4 (0)	20 (1)
Named-saw w/prop or heard confess	6.1 (7.9)	11.1 (2.1)	5 (1)	0 (0)	11 (0)	1 (0)	3 (1)	1 (0)	21 (2)
Named-other	6.0 (6.7)	4.4 (3.4)	8 (3)	1 (0)	7 (0)	0 (0)	0 (0)	1 (2)	17 (5)
Named-eyewit	2.9 (2.8)	2.6 (1.5)	23 (9)	0 (0)	6 (2)	8 (3)	3 (2)	26 (19)	66 (35)
Totals			61 (41)	3 (12)	170 (130)	19 (7)	14 (11)	50 (86)	
Mean time spent on case (in hours)			6.8 (8.6)	6.2 (9.8)	3.2 (4.0)	3.4 (5.4)	2.1 (3.0)	1.9 (2.2)	
S.D.			7.6 (6.1)	3.1 (9.7)	3.3 (5.8)	3.2 (2.9)	2.2 (1.5)	1.7 (1.4)	

NOTES: (1) entries in crosstabulation are raw frequencies; (2) entries in parentheses are for robberies; (3) missing data are excluded from the analyses.

Table 3 also reveals that, overall, more time was spent on robbery cases that concluded with an arrest than on cases that did not (4.07 versus 9.12 hours; $t = -4.68$, $p < .000$). Overall, there is a slight relationship between time spent and case status ($r = 35$; $p < .001$). In addition, most time is spent on cases with moderate suspect information (6.66 hours).

To determine the effect of time spent on the likelihood of an arrest being made within each category of suspect information, and thus to directly test the triage hypothesis, logistic regression analyses were used. Separate analyses were

Table 2 Relationship Between Case Outcomes, Strength of Suspect Information, and Time Spent for Burglary Follow-up Investigations

		CASE STATUS		Mean Time
	N	**0 = No Arrest**	**1 = Arrest**	**Spent (hours)**
Strength of Suspect Information				
1 = Weak	133	120 (3.01)	13 (6.41)	3.35
2 = Moderate	83	55 (3.87)	28 (8.75)	5.52
3 = Strong	37	14 (2.56)	23 (4.44)	3.73
N =	253	189 (3.23)	64 (6.72)	

NOTES: (1) entries in parentheses are mean amount of time spent on each set of cases (in hours), other entries are raw frequencies; (2) missing data are excluded from the analyses.

Table 3 Relationship Between Case Outcomes, Strength of Suspect Information, and Time Spent for Robbery Follow-up Investigations

		CASE STATUS		Mean Time
	N	**0 = No Arrest**	**1 = Arrest**	**Spent (hours)**
Strength of Suspect Information				
1 = Weak	55	54 (3.32)	1 (6.50)	3.38
2 = Moderate	121	78 (4.63)	43 (10.35)	6.66
3 = Strong	14	5 (3.40)	9 (3.51)	3.47
N =	190	137 (4.07)	53 (9.12)	

NOTES: (1) entries in parentheses are mean amount of time spent on each set of cases (in hours), other entries are raw frequencies; (2) missing data are excluded from the analyses.

conducted on burglaries and robberies. In each model, a pair of interactive terms (or "slope dummy variables;" see Hanushek and Jackson, 1977) was included. Each model took the following form:

$$Y = a + b_1X_1 + b_2X_2 + b_3X_3 + b_4X_4 + b_5X_5 + e$$

where

a = a constant

X_1 = time spent

X_2 = time spent if suspect information is weak, 0 otherwise

X_3 = time spent if suspect information is strong, 0 otherwise

X_4 = 1 if suspect information is weak, 0 otherwise

X_5 = 1 if suspect information is strong, 0 otherwise

The results can be interpreted as follows: b_1 is the estimated effect of effort on case disposition (0 = no arrest; 1 = arrest) in cases with moderate suspect information; the sum of $b_1 + b_2$ is the estimated effect of effort in cases with weak suspect information; and the sum $b_1 + b_3$ is the estimated effect of effort in cases

Table 4 Logistic Regression of Time Spent as a Determinant of Arrests in Burglary and Robbery Follow-up Investigations

Regressors	Burglaries	Robberies
(X₁) Time Spent	.235**	.226**
	(.075)	(.061)
(X₂) Time Spent/Weak Cases	−.102	−.171
	(.093)	(.117)
(X₃) Time Spent/Strong Cases	.047	−.119
	(.189)	(.555)
(X₄) Suspect Info/Weak	−.857	−2.204
	(.615)	(1.261)
(X₅) Suspect Info/Strong	1.497*	2.247
	(.772)	(2.022)
Constant	−1.930**	−2.029**
	(.465)	(.425)
N	253	190
−2 log Likelihood	215.61	160.74

NOTES: (1) unstandardized coefficients reported with standard errors in parentheses; (2) * p < .05; ** p < .01, one-tailed test; (3) missing data are excluded from the analyses.

with strong suspect information. b_2 reflects the size of the difference in the effects of effort between moderate and weak suspect information cases and b_3 reflects the size of the difference in the effects of effort between moderate and strong suspect information cases. The effects of suspect information on case disposition are reflected in b_4 and b_5.

As seen in Table 4, the amount of time spent on the burglary follow–up investigation is a significant predictor of whether an arrest was made in the investigation for cases with moderate suspect information (b_1, p = .000). Separate logistic regression procedures (not tabled), using time spent on weak cases and strong cases as baseline measures show that the effect of effort in weak burglary cases is also significant ($b_1 + b_2$, p = .007) but the effect of effort in strong cases falls just short of a conventional level of significance ($b_1 + b_3$, p = .052). While the impact of effort on whether an arrest was made appears the strongest in burglary cases with moderate suspect information,[13] the results reported in Table 4 show that the size of the difference in the effects of effort between moderate and weak cases (b_2) and between moderate and strong cases (b_3) are not significant (p = .136 and p = .402; respectively).[14]

As for robberies, the amount of time spent on the follow–up investigation is, as with burglaries, a significant predictor of whether an arrest was made in the investigation for cases with moderate suspect information (b_1, p = .000). Separate logistic regression procedures (not tabled) demonstrate that the effect of effort on robbery cases with weak and strong suspect information is not significant ($b_1 + b_2$, p = .292; $b_1 + b_3$, p = .443, respectively). However, it is seen in Table 4 that the size of the difference in the effects of effort between moderate and weak cases (b_2) and between moderate and strong cases (b_3) are not significant (p = .071 and p = .415, respectively).[15]

CONCLUSION

Our findings cast some additional light on the relationship between detective effort, strength of the evidence associated with the case, and whether an arrest is made in the investigation. Specifically, the analyses show that in burglary and robbery cases with moderate suspect information, the probability of an arrest increased significantly with more time spent. In fact, the relationship between time spent and case outcome is the strongest in the cases with moderate suspect information. However, the magnitude of the effects across cases with varying strengths of suspect information is not significant; the effect of time spent on case outcome in moderate cases is not significantly different than the effect of time spent on case outcome in either weak or strong suspect information cases. Accordingly, while our findings offer only limited and qualified support for Eck's (1983) triage hypotheses, the results do contradict Greenwood et al. (1977) and others who have suggested that detective effort has no effect on whether crimes are solved. When considering the triage hypothesis in relation to the findings reported here however, one must be cognizant of the fact that in the study department, the (burglary) cases with the weakest suspect information are screened out. If such cases had been assigned to detectives, then one might expect to find greater support for the triage hypothesis—i.e., find the effects of effort in weak cases to be quite small and thus, differ significantly from the effects of effort in cases with moderate suspect information.

Consistent with the expectation of Eck (1979), the analyses show that more time is spent on cases with moderate suspect information than on cases with weak or strong suspect information. This is perhaps because of the detectives' reasonable expectation that with just a little more information these cases could conclude with an arrest. The analyses also show that, overall, significantly more time was spent on burglary and robbery cases that were solved than on cases that were not solved. This directly contradicts the conclusion of Greenwood et al. (1977) that "the cases that get cleared are primarily the easy ones to solve" (p. 112).

As a result of this study, some directions for future research have also been illuminated. First, it would be useful to ask about the extent to which the findings of this study are generalizable to the investigation of other types of crimes and to other organizational contexts. On the basis of the data analyzed here, it is seen that there are few differences between burglaries and robberies; however, there is little justification for this belief vis-à-vis other crime types. As a result, the question becomes: In what types of crime does detective effort have more or less impact on whether an arrest is made? It would also be useful to examine the relationships of interest across different organizational settings with varying organizational structures, workloads, and/or policies (especially case screening). In essence, the generalizability of the findings in these regards remain empirical issues.

Second, while this study focused on the impact of *time* spent on case status in burglary and robbery investigations, the study does not, because of data limitations, provide guidance as to what activities should consume investigative time. Accordingly, future efforts could be directed at identifying how detectives should most productively spend their case-related investigative time.

Finally, because the evidence associated with cases appears to limit (but not eliminate) the extent to which detectives can affect case outcomes, and because patrol officers are initially responsible for identifying and collecting evidence, it is important to examine the determinants of time spent on initial investigations and the corresponding role of evidence in this calculus. Studies focused on these issues could add another dimension to our understanding of the criminal investigation process.

ENDNOTES

1. The researchers considered a full range of crime types in these analyses including crimes against persons (e.g., homicide, rape, robbery, kidnapping), crimes against property (e.g., auto theft, theft from auto, burglary, larceny), other destructive acts (e.g., arson, vandalism) and acts of fraud (e.g., shoplifting, forgery). The same general finding was uncovered across most of the crime types including burglaries and robberies.

2. The reported findings were also confirmed with data from the Kansas City Police Department.

3. However, Greenwood et al. (1977) do not specify what constitutes a "clearance" in these analyses.

4. The difference between the number of clearances and the number of arrests can be substantial. For example, Eck (1983) found that in one agency, 58 percent of the burglaries that were cleared were as a result of an arrest. In another site, 100 percent of cleared cases resulted from an arrest. Greenwood (1970) found that of the burglary cases that were cleared, only 26 percent were by an actual arrest. Of the robberies that were cleared, 60 percent were as a result of an arrest.

5. See Sherman and Glick (1984) for a discussion of the validity and reliability of arrest statistics.

6. In assessing the validity of their data, Greenwood et al. (1977) explain that "some case-related activity presumably

takes place in blocks of less than a half-hour and therefore goes unreported" (p. 104).

7. For a case to be assigned to a detective for a follow-up investigation it had to survive two screening stages. First, the department operated a Differential Police Response (DPR) strategy of call management. As part of this strategy, certain types of complaints, which were identified by policy, were taken over the telephone by police telephone operators. Complaints handled in this manner were very rarely brought to the attention of the investigations division. Second, detective sergeants had the responsibility for screening cases that received an initial investigation and assigning only those deemed appropriate for follow-up investigations. Accordingly, of the 12 robberies not assigned, all 12 were screened out by the detective sergeants. Of the 1,219 burglaries not assigned, 697 received telephone reports and 540 were screened out by the detective sergeants.

8. For a period of 30 weeks, from September 1990 to March 1991, detectives were observed by the first author for 400 hours (approximately 50 eight-hour shifts). Time was split equally between the crimes against property squad (burglaries) and the crimes against persons squad (robberies). The primary focus of the observations was on examining how detectives made time allocation decisions (see Brandl, forthcoming). The observations informed judgments as to how detectives

considered and acted upon evidence, as well as other case information, and provided a means by which to judge the validity of the self-report measure of time spent (see note number 10).

9. Listed activities were similar to those identified by Eck (1983). They included interviewing victims, witnesses, informants, suspects, and others, conducting neighborhood canvasses, searching the crime scene, submitting evidence for analysis, searching departmental records or other files, conducting photo line-ups and physical line-ups, and showing mug-shot books. Although it could have been a useful analytic addition, time spent on each activity was not collected for this study.

10. The validity of the self-report measure of time spent may be subject to criticism (Manning, 1980; Waegel, 1981). However, on the basis of the observations, it is believed that little error in this measure was intentionally introduced by the detectives. While detectives were required to record the amount of time spent on the investigation, the information was not monitored or organizationally reported in any fashion. There was little feedback to the detectives or supervisors on the basis of these statistics. Detectives were not evaluated on this information. However, distortion was probably introduced through memory errors, which resulted when the activities performed and time spent were forgotten before completion of the case log, and calculation errors, which resulted from the difficulties of allocating time spent on certain activities to particular investigations (e.g., driving time, discussions with other personnel in the department, etc.).

11. When suspect information is kept in its raw form (i.e., 0 through 9), the correlation between suspect information and case status is .45, p < .001.

12. When suspect information is kept in its raw form (i.e., 0 through 9), the correlation between suspect information and case status remains at .41, p < .001.

13. One can rank the impact of variables based on their level of significance only when the variables are measured on the same scale, as is the case here (Johnson, Johnson, & Buse, 1987).

14. When "strength of suspect information" is coded so that "a name provided by a [victim] guess" is considered moderate rather than weak evidence and "a culprit named in some other way" is considered strong rather than moderate evidence, the results change minimally. In addition, when victim type (individual/business), dollar value of property loss (in dollars), and physical evidence present at the conclusion of the initial investigation (yes/no) are used as control variables in the analyses, essentially the same results are obtained.

15. Once again, when "strength of suspect information" is coded so that "suspect described by an eye-witness" is considered moderate instead of weak suspect information and "culprit could be named in some other way" is classified as strong instead of moderate suspect information, the results change minimally. In addition, substantially the same results are obtained when victim type, dollar value of property loss, physical evidence present, as well as weapon used in commission of offense (yes/no), and degree of victim injury (none, minor, serious) are used as controls in the analyses on robberies.

REFERENCES

Bloch, P. and J. Bell (1976). *Managing Investigations: The Rochester System.* Washington, DC: Police Foundation.

Brandl, S. (forthcoming). "The Impact of Case Characteristics on Detective Decision Making." *Justice Quarterly.*

Eck, J. (1983). *Solving Crimes: The Investigation of Burglary and Robbery.*

Washington, DC: Police Executive Research Forum.

——— (1979). *Managing Case Assignments: The Burglary Investigation Decision Model Replication.* Washington, DC: Police Executive Research Forum.

Garofalo, J. (1981). "Crime and the Mass Media: A Selective Review of Research." *Journal of Research in Crime and Delinquency,* 18:319–50.

Greenwood, P. (1970). *An Analysis of the Apprehension Activities of the New York City Police Department.* New York, NY: Rand.

Greenwood, P., J. Chaiken, and J. Petersilia (1976). "Response to: An Evaluation of the Rand Corporation's Analysis of the Criminal Investigation Process." *Police Chief,* 12:62–71.

———— (1977). *The Criminal Investigation Process.* Lexington, MA: Heath.

Hanushek, E. and J. Jackson (1977). *Statistical Methods for Social Scientists.* New York, NY: Academic Press.

Isaacs, H. (1967). "Police Operations: The Apprehension Process." In President's Commission on Law Enforcement and Administration of Justice, *Task Force Report: Science and Technology.*

Washington, DC: United States Government Printing Office.

Johnson, A., M. Johnson, and R. Buse (1987). *Econometrics: Basic and Applied.* New York, NY: Macmillan.

Klockars, C. (1985). *The Idea of Police.* Newbury Park, CA: Sage Publications.

Manning, P. (1980). *The Narc's Game: Organizational and Informational Limits on Drug Law Enforcement.* Cambridge, MA: MIT Press.

Sherman, L. and B. Glick (1984). *The Quality of Police Arrest Statistics.* Washington, D.C.: Police Foundation.

Waegel, W. (1981). "Case Routinization of Investigative Police Work." *Social Problems,* 28:263–75.

Wilson, J. (1975). *Thinking About Crime.* New York, NY: Vintage.

Team Policing

LAWRENCE W. SHERMAN
CATHERINE H. MILTON
THOMAS V. KELLY

FOREWORD

The police administrator faces a dilemma. He is aware that corruption and the abuse of authority are constant dangers on his force, that rioting and collective violence have occurred before in his city and may occur again, and that people are frightened and want visible evidence of a massive police presence that will reduce crime. He also knows that, however much the city council may complain of rising crime rates, it is also concerned

Source: Lawrence W. Sherman, Catherine H. Milton, and Thomas V. Kelly (1973). "Foreword," pp. ix–xii; Chapter 1, "Elements of Team Policing," pp. 3–7; Chapter 5, "Obstacles to Team Policing," pp. 91–96; Chapter 7, "Summary and Conclusions," pp. 107–108. In *Team Policing: Seven Case Studies.* Washington, DC: The Police Foundation. Reprinted by permission of The Police Foundation.

about rising tax rates and thus wants the police department run as economically as possible. For all these reasons, the police administrator is tempted to organize and operate his department along tight, quasi-military lines with strict supervision of patrol officers, a strong command structure that can deploy effectively large numbers of police in emergency situations, powerful and mobile tactical forces that can saturate areas experiencing high crime rates, and close controls over costs, scheduling, assignments, and discipline.

But he is also aware that his patrol officers exercise great discretion and thus can never be fully supervised, that much of their time is spent on noncriminal matters, that some parts of the community fear and distrust the police while other parts want closer contact with them, that massive displays of police power can sometimes exacerbate tense situations, and that quasi-military discipline can lower the morale and perhaps the effectiveness of many officers. For these reasons, he is tempted to organize his department along highly decentralized lines, with considerable discretionary authority to give patrol officers and their sergeants, great attention given to the resolution of community disputes and the provision of social services, and little use of tactical forces.

There are two reasons why the administrator regards this choice as posing a dilemma: First, he has very little evidence, other than his own hunches and the lore of his craft, which of these two models of policing is most likely to succeed, or even what "success" means. Second, being an experienced officer, he is aware that both theories of policing are correct in some measure, and thus gains from wholly adopting one will create costs from having forgone the other. For example, the military model may result in a prompt response to radio calls, but since answering all calls promptly means spending as little time as possible on any given call, an officer cannot learn much from or be of much help to a citizen who calls. On the other hand, the service model will enable the officer to devote time and expertise to helping a citizen who calls but at the cost of postponing answering other calls or referring them to officers who are not as familiar with the area.

Even if the administrator could be clear in his own mind as to what he wants, he faces two important constraints on his freedom of action, one internal to the department and the other external to it. His officers, in all likelihood, will be accustomed to one way of doing things and they will see any effort to change that as a threat, not only to their habits and expectations, but to their promotion prospects, work schedules, and authority. Community groups, on the other hand, will be divided as to what they want: some neighborhoods may welcome tough, vigorous policing as a way of keeping the streets safe and the "kids in their place," while others may prefer a police force that is closely integrated with the community and perhaps even subject to its control. Indeed, it is likely that any given community will want both things at once—be tough and concerned, visible and invisible, enforcement-oriented and service-oriented.

Team policing should be seen as an effort, one of many possible, to test these competing views and form a realistic and objective assessment of what kinds of police deployment produce what results under which circumstances. This is not to say that it is merely an experiment, designed to satisfy curiosity or gather data. Rather, it is a police strategy—or more accurately, a collection of somewhat similar police strategies—which some police administrators believe may be a partial solution to the dilemma they face. In theory it combines the advantages of a substantial police presence in a neighborhood, deployed to put the maximum number of officers on the street during times of greatest need and supervised so as to encourage the maximum use of information about the area and its citizens, with the advantages of a police style devoted to servicing complaints, helping citizens, and establishing good relations.

But so far it is only a theory. It is still too early to tell whether this strategy will real- ize the expectations of its creators. In presenting the case studies and analysis that follows, the Police Foundation is not suggesting that team policing, in any of its many variants, is the answer to the police dilemma, or even that we are now in a position to know what an answer is. We believe that it is a promising approach but one that is still somewhat vague in conception, weak in execution, and uncertain in results. In time, we hope that by care- fully designing and testing several different police strategies, various police departments will obtain information that can be widely disseminated as to circumstances under which one police strategy, or some combination of strategies, produces gains in crime control, citizen service, and community support. The Police Foundation is engaged in helping depart- ments try approaches they have formulated to see what works and what does not.

It is this approach—testing and evaluating—rather than the substantive content of any given strategy that is important. Not every city, or every part of any city, may be well served by a single police strategy. Yet in the past, our police strategies were picked, or rather they emerged out of historical forces, without much systematic reflection as to how well they might help control crime, or help citizens. Indeed, until recently we did not think in terms of a police "strategy" or "style" that could be deliberately chosen. We tended instead to accept either what existed as historically foreordained or what was pro- posed by "leading authorities" as unquestionably correct. At one time our cities were po- liced by watchmen who not only walked a beat, but who managed it and the people on it with a minimum of supervision and relatively few arrests. Some cities still display the watchman style. In reaction to this, advocates of centralized control, close supervision, and maximum enforcement arose, whose textbooks and personal example created a new era of policing that was called "professionalism." Now some of the doctrines of that school are being questioned by those who believe that professionalism separated the police from the community and over-emphasized writing tickets and making arrests.

It is not the purpose of this publication to offer any new dogma to replace the dogmas of yesterday. It is rather to show how some cities went about the task of finding new so- lutions to the police dilemma and to offer some preliminary findings about what will hap- pen as a result. In future publications, the Foundation will offer more systematic evidence on additional projects that are now under way.

JAMES Q. WILSON
SHATTUCK PROFESSOR OF GOVERNMENT
HARVARD UNIVERSITY
VICE CHAIRMAN, POLICE FOUNDATION

ELEMENTS OF TEAM POLICING

Police administrators in the 1960's confronted a dilemma in organizing their departments: the community wanted both more sensitive police and better crime control. Police administrators who attempted to professionalize their departments through more centralized control and motorized patrol were criticized by community leaders and riot commissions for having police who were insensitive to and isolated from the communities they were supposed to serve. Yet with rising crime rates, few police administrators could seriously consider a return to the inefficiencies of the traditional beat-cop. Team policing was one answer to this conflict of police goals and needs.

By the early 1970's team policing had become a popular idea among many police administrators. And yet, even now, no one really knows what it is, what it costs, or whether it is an improvement. This study cannot answer those questions; it can only describe what it looks like in a few cities.

Team policing is a term that has meant something different in every city in which it has been tried. But all of the team policing programs studied for this book—except Richmond—attempted to implement three basic operational elements which differ from conventional patrol concepts. These three elements are: geographic stability of patrol, maximum interaction among team members, and maximum communication among team members and the community.

1. *Geographic stability of patrol: i.e., permanent assignment of teams of police to small neighborhoods.* The geographic stability of patrol is the most basic element. The only city which did not assign its teams permanently to a neighborhood was Richmond, California. There, teams were assigned as units on staggered shifts. Each team remained on duty for eight hours, and a new team came on duty every four hours. We included Richmond in this study, however, because that city is small enough to function as a neighborhood and because the patrol officers function as team members in much the same way as those geographically-based teams, despite the assignment by time.

2. *Maximum interaction among team members, including close internal communication among all officers assigned to an area during a 24-hour period, seven days a week.* The element of encouraging interaction among team members was evident in all the team policing cities, but with considerable variation. Implicit in the concept of maximum interaction is exchange of information. One of the simplest means of accomplishing this exchange is through the scheduling of team conferences at regular intervals. Analogies may be found in the case conferences conducted by social workers or doctors, in which each professional describes several difficult cases of the previous week and opens them to discussion with his colleagues, soliciting criticism and advice. The police teams which followed a similar route with their conferences found that, in many instances, the cases were continuing problems covering more than one shift and required cooperation among several police officers. Those teams which did not have formal conferences had to rely on informal ways of communicating—a practice which was more successful when the team was stationed and thereby isolated in a separate building than when sharing a stationhouse with the regular patrol units. The other critical factor in communication was the team leader. When he encouraged sharing of information and was still able to instill a sense of teamsmanship, the members communicated more frequently and informally.

3. *Maximum communication among team members and the community.* The third element, maximum communication among team members and members of the community, seemed to be aided by regular meetings between teams and the

community. These meetings were a means of emphasizing the cooperative aspects of the peacekeeping function, facilitating the flow of information, and assisting in the identification of community problems. Such conferences have been a vehicle for eliciting community involvement in the police function. Another technique, participation of community members in police work, has been accomplished through auxiliary patrols, supply of information leading to arrests, and community voice in police policy-making. Such participation was designed to bring the police and community together in a spirit of cooperation. Finally, maximum communication among teams and the community has also been enhanced by an efficient system of referral of non–police problems (e.g., emotional problems, garbage collection, drug addiction) to appropriate service agencies. Teams that have developed their own neighborhood lists of social service units and names of social workers have made appropriate referrals far more quickly than through centralized traditional channels.

All of the cities in this study (except Richmond) attempted to achieve all three basic operational elements. The departments which were most successful in implementing these elements also had in common certain organizational supports: unity of supervision, lower-level flexibility in policy-making, unified delivery of services, and combined investigative and patrol functions.

1. *Unity of supervision.* Different supervisors controlling an area during the course of a day can create inconsistent police policies and approaches to community problems. It may be difficult, for example, for a group of young boys to understand why one police officer allows them to play baseball in the street between 8:00 a.m. and 4:00 p.m. while another forbids ball-playing from 4:00 p.m. to midnight. In order to maintain coherent and consistent police performance, then, it is preferable that one supervisor be responsible for a given area at all times and that his orders be obeyed. Unity of supervision is also useful for the effective performance of the officers as a team. If a team member has more than one supervisor giving him conflicting orders, he may determine that team policy-making is a myth and that the whole team concept is a hoax.

2. *Lower-level flexibility in policy-making.* Interaction among team members is most productive when the team has the flexibility to carry out its own operational decisions. Indeed, the very rationale for the sharing of information among team members is that they will use their increased knowledge to decide upon better strategies for the delivery of police services to their neighborhood. For example, decisions about mode of dress and duty schedules have been traditionally reserved for higher-ups, but several departments pushed those decisions down to the team level where information about neighborhood needs was most accurate.

The police administrators who advocated increased authority at lower levels of the hierarchy considered it a means of increasing responsibility and accountability of patrol officers. Former New York City Police Commissioner Patrick Murphy, for example, tried to loosen the strict rules governing behavior at all ranks in order to discourage "buck-passing" up the ranks. Supervisors at the precinct level were held accountable for the performance of patrol

Summary of Elements (The following summarizes the elements of team policing in each city.)							
Operational Elements	Dayton	Detroit	New York	Syracuse	Holyoke	Los Angeles (Venice)	Richmond
Stable geographic assignment	+	+	−	+	+	+	•
Intra-team interaction	−	+	−	−	+	+	+
Formal team conferences	−	+	−	−	+	+	+
Police-community communication	+	+	−	−	+	+	•
Formal community conferences	+	•	•	−	+	+	•
Community participation in police work	+	+	+	•	+	+	•
Systematic referrals to social agencies	+	−	−	•	•	•	+
Organizational Supports							
Unity of Supervision	+	+	−	+	+	+	+
Lower-level flexibility	−	−	−	+	+	+	+
Unified delivery of services	+	−	−	+	+	+	•
Combined patrol and investigative functions	+	+	•	+	+	+	+

Key:
+ the element was planned and realized
− the element was planned but not realized
• the element was not planned

officers in their precincts, team leaders for their team members, team officers for themselves.

3. *Unified delivery of services.* Some departments extended the concept of team decision-making to complete control over the delivery of all police services in the team neighborhood. This included the team's power to decide when specialized police units were needed or when they would be disruptive. This concept was also designed to make the best use of local community knowledge developed by the officers who patrol an area every day. It does not deny the value of the local police generalist to decide when they are needed.

4. *Combined investigative and patrol functions.* In the absence of information supplied by the community, apprehension of a criminal is difficult. As a part of a larger unified delivery of services, team programs should seek to combine patrol and investigative functions, for the intuitive judgments required for effective investigations are enhanced by familiarity with the life of the community. As Egon Bittner has observed:

To give circumstantial factors their correct weight in decision making it is necessary that they be intelligently appraised. That is, patrolmen must be able to draw on background information to be able to discern what particular constellations of facts and factors mean. In the case of the carefully deliberate policeman—by which is meant a man who organizes his activities with a view towards long-range peacekeeping and crime control objectives in the area of his patrol, knowing that what he does from case to case can create more or less calculable advantages or liabilities for himself in the future—the background information consists of an enormously detailed factual knowledge.[1]

When one considers that crimes of violence are usually committed by people known to the victim, it becomes clear that a knowledge of the human relationships in a community is of immeasurable value in solving crimes. It is instructive, though, that Bittner had to note the "case of the carefully deliberate policeman" as an exception to the rule. The cultivation of area knowledge has not been something for which the patrol officer has been rewarded in the United States. By contrast, an essential element in the English Unit Beat scheme is the "collator," the central receiver of daily area reports; each officer is evaluated partly according to how much quality information he feeds the collator.

The seven case studies that follow will describe the team policing programs in each city and the contexts in which they developed. Each will also discuss the three basic operational elements and four organizational supports of team policing in each city.

OBSTACLES TO TEAM POLICING

In addition to the inevitable influence of individual leaders, police department organization contributed three major obstacles to team policing: middle management, trial by peers, and dispatchers.

Middle Management

Team policing, as a method of decentralization, was designed to give more decision-making power to lower levels of the police organization. By fiat from the top, it gave powers to the bottom (patrol officers and sergeants) that had traditionally been reserved for the middle (lieutenants, captains, etc.). Thus team policing was a form of decentralization which gave less power to mid-management than it had under centralization. As a result, middle management often impeded their administrators' goals for team policing.

One way in which middle management limited the success of team policing was by failing, as precinct or division commanders, to deal with conflicts and problems arising out of team policing programs under their command. Conflicts frequently developed between team leaders and officers of the next higher rank—a problem apparently endemic to the team policing concept. It surfaced in England almost immediately, where despite the role definitions of inspectors as strategists and sergeants as tacticians, one Home Office study found that both ranks were confused and dissatisfied about their new roles. Detroit and New York had similar conflicts between lieutenants and sergeants that the precinct commanders simply ignored.

Another, more direct way in which middle management sometimes thwarted the goals of team policing was by simple bad-mouthing: sending out the word through informal channels of communication that this crazy team idea was a hoax. Precinct commanders were also able to undercut the operational freedom of the team leader. By limiting or discouraging the team leader's initiative on day-to-day issues, middle management could effectively defeat the program's goal of innovative team response to local conditions.

A third form of resistance by middle management was a frank expression to top management of disagreement about team policing issues. A Detroit precinct commander complained to the police commissioner that by implication the Beat Commander system criticized the precinct commander's performance, implying that his position was insufficient to insure adequate police service. In his frustration he exclaimed, "The people who wrote the guidelines for this thing didn't read the rules and regulations." The view that the rules and regulations are sacred and unchangeable subverts not only team policing, but any change at all.

Middle-management opposition is not unavoidable, however. If middle management is brought into the planning process for decentralization, it is entirely possible that its cooperation and support for the new system will be won. Although the commander of the first precinct in a city to try the team concept was usually involved in its planning (Detroit, New York, Los Angeles), most of the middle managers who would be affected by the program were not asked for their views, nor were they told about the program before its public announcement. But a participative and consensual form of planning with all middle management can cultivate their support for plans which might otherwise be resisted.

Most team programs have been perceived as giving more power to the bottom at the expense of the middle, a perception which has been the basis for middle management's opposition. It is possible, however, for the power of each level to be expanded simultaneously with benefits for the entire organization. A goal of team policing is to expand the effectiveness of the police in the community: talking to more people, establishing more positive and informal relationships, apprehending more criminals, and providing more and better service. This expanded role requires a new structure: the followers (patrol officers and sergeants) must do more leading of themselves, and the leaders (middle management) must lead in new and different ways. Mid-managers must analyze the new influx of information, plan for better manpower utilization in light of that information, and obtain more resources to support the expanded role of their officers—for example, arranging liaison with social service agencies, traffic and sanitation departments, and other city agencies. If their function is viewed more as support than as control, middle management can gain power under team policing rather than lose it.

Trial by Peers

Middle management was not the only obstacle to team policing. In most of the cities studied, the larger patrol force—those not involved in the team project—objected to team policing. The opposition was strongest when the project split a precinct or division. The first pilot teams formed new elites. The patrol officers had learned to accept the old elite forces (e.g., detectives), but they were not eager to accept new ones. The fact that the usefulness of the teams was necessarily unproven left them vulnerable to attack. Also, to outside patrol officers, the community aspects of team policing smacked of appeasement of hostile minorities.

There was also jealousy, in many instances stemming from the fact that the patrol officers first heard about the program through the news media—after the personnel had already been chosen. Not all patrol officers would have volunteered, but many would have liked to have had the chance to decide not to. When one is shut out of a newly-formed club, the natural response is to attack the club—and certain aspects of team programs were "clubby" and, superficially at least, elitist. The first Crime Control Teams in Syracuse wore white shirts while the rest of the patrol force wore blue, which prompted sarcastic remarks such as "the good guys wear white shirts." In New York, the Neighborhood Police Team in the 17th Precinct (midtown) was exempted from consulate guard duty, a detested detail. The apparent over-allocation of manpower to NPT areas (even though justified by workload figures) produced the charge from other precinct patrol officers that they had all the hard work. Detroit's Beat Command invited resentment by flaunting their accomplishment of reducing the average time required to complete radio runs from 40 minutes to 27. The freedom of team police officers in some cities produced irritation. In Syracuse, for example, the CCT was freed from roll calls. In New York, the orders establishing the Neighborhood Police Teams suspended portions of the Rules and Procedures manual—one that had been frequently violated in the field, anyway—to legitimize such things as chatting with neighborhood people and driving sick cases to the hospital. The overtime pay available to the Holyoke team was greatly resented by other patrol officers of the poorly paid department.

Given all of these irritations, one might expect the outside patrol officers' field cooperation to be affected. With the exception of Holyoke (where the team had virtually seceded from the rest of the department), this did not happen. The team members were always backed up by non–team cars. None of the physical acts that too often characterize racial or religious animosity in police departments (vandalizing lockers, insulting graffiti, and even fights) occurred between team officers and the regular patrols. Instead, the opposition was evidenced by strong vocal criticism and political maneuvers to keep the team idea from spreading.

Dispatchers

Another non-team group, the radio dispatchers, greatly hampered team policing, often without intent. The dispatcher is under constant pressure, and he is not particularly concerned with neighborhood or team boundaries. He must be converted to the primary assumption that the new neighborhood team should stay in its neighborhood. Teams frequently could not; New York teams often spent half their time outside their neighborhoods. When the team members found the neighborhood was a myth, many concluded that the team project was a hoax.

Sociologist Albert Reiss has made an observation on the Chicago Police Department's dispatching system, which should be applicable to other large cities:

> In Chicago in 1966, we observe that fewer than one-third of all criminal incidents were handled by beat cars in their own beat. . . . Many police administrators regard a patrolman's intelligence on a community to be of most importance in non-criminal matters, where an officer must exercise the greatest degree of discretion. However, despite this, officers in Chicago handled an even smaller proportion of all non-criminal incidents, arising from dispatches to their own beat, than criminal incidents. . . . Beat cars handled only one-third of all incidents, and one-fifth of all criminal incidents arising on their own beats.
>
> Based on these Chicago data, it appears conclusive that beat cars, whether dispatched or on routine preventive patrol, are more likely to handle incidents outside their own area than within it. . . . This problem may actually be due to the fact that beat cars are dispatched to handle incidents outside their beat. Once a car is dispatched to handle a call outside its beat, the probability of its handling outside calls increases, since, while that car is in service, any call to its beat must be assigned to a car from a neighboring beat. Calls to that beat in turn must be handled by a neighboring area. The problem of such chain effects is a familiar one in systems analysis.[2]

Today's radio systems give little latitude for the kind of screening which once occurred when calls came in at the precinct switchboard and the sergeant held the less important calls or threw out the ones from known neighborhood cranks. Computerized dispatch systems such as New York's SPRINT treat almost all calls as serious, and the widespread use of the "911" police telephone number has increased the volume enormously.

The Los Angeles Basic Car Plan attempted to cope with the dispatching problem. The "A" Basic Cars worked with "X" support cars on the heavy duty, 8:00 a.m. to 4:00 p.m. and 4:00 p.m. to midnight watches. The Basic Cars were to remain in their beats, while the X cars crossed boundaries. In practice, the distinction between A and X was often without substance. Dispatchers frequently assigned either, without regard for beats.

In Detroit, the Beat Command cars were out of their neighborhoods as much as a third of the time. Only after great pressure was placed on the dispatchers from the top did the percentage drop to 10–15%. The Detroit dispatchers were bitter about the pressure. They said the Beat Command car was often the closest car to the call, but they were forbidden to send it. In the end, the Detroit dispatchers gave the Beat Command cars no outside calls of any nature. They treated the two-sector area as an entirely separate precinct and sent cars from miles away to an emergency scene immediately adjoining the Beat Command boundaries even when the BC car was available. Obviously, city-wide application of this principle would be disastrous, turning the city into hundreds of non-cooperating police departments.

But the dispatchers are not the villains. Consider a huge roomful of clacking printers and blaring loudspeakers on a hot summer night with calls backlogged for two hours. Each dispatcher has 30 to 70 sector cars to dispatch. If an available car happens to be labelled team, he will assign that car to the necessary job regardless. Indeed, the pressure grows so intense that in one city on an especially busy evening, a captain tried to prod a dispatcher into faster clearing of calls; the dispatcher, in response, stood up, vomited, threw his shield to the floor, gave his captain an obscene gesture, announced that he was reporting sick, and walked away.

There were reasons why team cars were often the most frequently available. The size of a team may be determined by computation of precinct manpower to area workload. The logic of the method, however, had only one weakness: it was never used for the other sectors of the precinct. The result of making workload calculations for one area but not the others could result (and did) in the assignment of more officers to the team area and a decrease in the number in other areas. It was difficult to persuade others that team policing would make better use of available manpower when the apparent result was to double the manpower assigned to the team area while reducing it everywhere else. The second reason that the team cars in Detroit and New York were frequently available was that the number of team men on duty was (sometimes) related to time workload while the number of non-team men on duty was not. Teams which assigned the most officers during peak hours were unrushed while the rest of the precinct was backlogged with calls. Non-team officers concluded erroneously that the teams were not doing their share of the work.

The dispatching difficulty is not insurmountable, and it is not universal. There is relatively little boundary difficulty in Holyoke or Venice (LA). In the dispatching issue, small cities or self-contained units like Venice have a clear advantage—the pressure is less and the boundaries are easier to maintain.

SUMMARY AND CONCLUSIONS

On the basis of the team programs discussed in this report, it would be tempting to conclude that team policing had certain consequences for crime, community relations, and police morale and productivity. The data are far too scant, however, to make such conclusions final. More important is the question many readers will have: should we try team policing in our police department? Most important is the question: how can we decide whether team policing makes sense?

Team policing was conceived as a means to an end—a decentralized professional patrol style. In none of the cities studied has that end yet been achieved. The many problems and obstacles experienced by team policing projects merely demonstrate the depth of the change they attempt, which cannot realistically succeed overnight. In all the team policing cities, there were three major reasons that team policing either failed or reached only partial success. These were:

1. Mid-management of the departments, seeing team policing as a threat to their power, subverted and, in some cases, actively sabotaged the plans.

2. The dispatching technology did not permit the patrols to remain in their neighborhoods, despite the stated intentions of adjusting that technology to the pilot projects.

3. The patrols never received a sufficiently clear definition of how their behavior and role should differ from that of a regular patrol; at the same time, they were considered an elite group by their peers who often resented not having been chosen for the project.

Even if team policing can be implemented as conceived, it is still unclear what effects it may have. To the extent that team policing makes police more responsive to community demands, it might put the police in a crossfire of conflicting goals. On one hand, a decentralized professional model of policing is conceived by many police administrators as a means of making the police "nice guys": polite, observant of citizen's constitutional rights, sensitive to the management of conflict, and honest. On the other hand, the community may make strong demands for the police to be "tough guys" in order to clean up crime, in ways that, if not illegal, are in contradiction to the model conceived by police administrators. For example, data from the evaluation of the New York City program shows that some teams increased the use of aggressive tactics, specifically illegal stop-and-frisks.[3] Early data from the Cincinnati evaluation tentatively suggests the same trend.[4]

There is at present a great concern among police forces and in American cities at large to consider change, to make police officers more responsive to the community. This concern has surfaced in many projects in addition to those labelled "team policing."[5] Whether a specific community should adopt team policing, however, depends first on that community's goals, and second on that community's judgment of team policing's effectiveness within its own situation. Most of all, it depends on both the commitment and the available resources to manage a complex process of institutional and community change.

ENDNOTES

1. Egon Bittner, *The Functions of the Police in Modern Society* (National Institute of Mental Health, November 1970), p. 90.

2. Albert Reiss, *The Police and the Public* (New Haven: Yale University Press, 1971), pp. 98–99.

3. Peter B. Bloch and David I. Specht, *Evaluation Report on Operation Neighborhood* (Washington, D.C.: The Urban Institute, 1972).

4. Joseph H. Lewis, Director of Evaluation, Police Foundation, personal communication, August 3, 1973.

5. Efforts to reestablish foot patrol (the pinpoint patrol program in Kansas City) or bicycle patrol (in Baltimore, New York City, and Isla Vista, California) reflect the need on the part of both community and police for more personal contact between the two groups. The Urban Group in the New Orleans Police Department, the Beat Committees in Dallas, and the Pilot District Project in Washington all attempt to improve community relations.

Structural Change in Large Municipal Police Organizations During the Community Policing Era

EDWARD R. MAGUIRE

The organizational structures of large municipal police departments in the United States have changed substantially during the twentieth century. Many of these changes can be attributed to new technologies, increasing demands from communities to broaden the scope of their services, and efforts to prevent corruption. Precinct-based police organizations employing only sworn police officers have been transformed into highly centralized, specialized, formal organizations with tall hierarchies and large administrative units. Community policing reformers have attempted to reverse this progression toward more "bu-

An earlier version of this paper was presented at the annual meetings of the American Society of Criminology, held in Boston in November 1995. I would like to thank Steve Cox, Bill King, Joe Kuhns, Bob Langworthy, Dick Ritti, Jeff Snipes, Craig Uchida, and the anonymous reviewers for their assistance with this study and/or their helpful comments on earlier drafts.

Source: Maguire, Edward R. (1997) Structural Change in Large Municipal Police Organizations During the Community Policing Era. *Justice Quarterly* 14: 547–576. Reprinted with permission of the Academy of Criminal Justice Sciences.

reaucratic" organizational forms. They argue that police should thin out their adminis-
trative components to cut red tape and to focus more resources on the goals of the organi-
zation than on the organization itself; deformalize, eliminating unnecessary rules and
policies; despecialize, to encourage departmentwide problem solving; "delayerize," to en-
hance communications and decision making by flattening the organizational hierarchy;
and civilianize, to use departmental resources more efficiently. By altering many of their
key administrative arrangements, critics argue, police departments can develop more flex-
ible, more responsive service delivery. Using a quasi-experimental design combining data
from a variety of sources, this paper examines whether the community policing movement
has succeeded in altering the organizational structures of large municipal police depart-
ments over the six-year period from 1987 to 1993. The sample agencies experienced
only minimal changes in organizational structure during the study period, and there were
no significant differences in levels of change between agencies that claim to practice com-
munity policing and those which do not.

Despite some continuity with past forms and functions, police organization in the twentieth century has evolved in response to changes in technology, social organization, and political governance at all levels of society. . . . Bureaucratization of the police has produced numerous changes
within departments and has been strongly influenced by changing conditions from outside of departments. Community-based and problem-
oriented policing are reshaping the way in which some police organizations conduct their business. (Reiss 1992:51)

The organizational structures of large municipal police departments in the
United States have changed substantially throughout the twentieth century.
Many of these changes can be attributed to the emergence of new technologies such as the patrol car, mobile two-way radios, and advances in dispatching
technology; all of which served to centralize police territorially (Manning
1992; Reiss 1992). Rising crime rates during much of the century, coupled with
a change in focus on different types of crimes (e.g., drug violations, juvenile
crimes, bias crimes, drunk driving, environmental crimes, family violence),
led departments to modify their structures in a variety of ways, including the
development of formal written policies and/or specialized units for dealing
with these issues (Reiss 1992). Corruption problems, often concentrated more
heavily in specific precincts, led to the development of administrative mechanisms for preventing future corruption (Fogelson 1977). Responses varied by
department, but generally took the form of rigid control structures such as formal written policies, centralized operations, and larger administrative staffs.
Throughout the twentieth century, precinct-based police organizations employing only sworn police officers have been transformed into highly centralized, specialized, and formal organizations with tall hierarchies and large administrative units (Fogelson 1977; Reiss 1992).

Over the past few years, however, community policing reformers have attempted to reverse this progression toward more complex police organizations

by suggesting that police departments must modify their organizational structures to accommodate the new demands imposed by community policing. Bureaucratic departments, they argue, hinder efficient, effective, responsive service delivery. Police departments are now told that if they truly want to implement community policing, then they must begin by modifying their organizational structures. Specifically, they must decentralize, both territorially and administratively (Kelling and Moore 1988; Mastrofski and Ritti 1995; Moore and Stephens 1992; Skolnick and Bayley 1988); they must deformalize, eliminating unnecessary rules and policies (Goldstein 1990); they must despecialize, developing a front line of "uniformed generalists" (Mastrofski and Ritti 1995); they must "de-layerize" by shortening their rank structures (Mastrofski 1994; Moore and Stephens 1992); and they must civilianize by replacing sworn officers with civilians in a variety of clerical, technical, and professional duties (Crank 1989; Lutz and Morgan 1974; Skolnick and Bayley 1988). Community policing reformers argue that police departments can serve their communities in a more flexible, more responsive manner by altering many of their key administrative arrangements.

In this paper I examine whether the community policing movement has succeeded in altering some elements of formal organizational structures in large municipal police departments over the six-year period from 1987 to 1993. We might expect to find such changes for two reasons. First, as highlighted above, reformers have *explicitly* outlined the types of structural changes that police organizations should make. Second, as organization theorists have known for many years, changes in the operational technology of an organization should *implicitly* produce certain structural modifications as the organization drifts toward an appropriate "fit" between technology and structure (Woodward 1965). According to reformers, community policing represents a fundamental shift in the social technology[1] of policing, from one centered on people-*processing* to one centered on people-*changing* (Mastrofski and Ritti 1995). To make this shift, which is at the very heart of community policing, police officers require a flexible organizational environment that enables them to design creative solutions to distinctive social problems. If police organizations truly are moving toward community policing, we should find evidence of structural change for either of two reasons: because it is an explicit element of the reform prescription, or because it is an implicit result of the change in the way police do business.

The analysis of structural change and community policing was made possible by forming a unique database consisting of data from five sources: three waves of the Law Enforcement Management and Administrative Statistics series (1987, 1990, and 1993) produced by the Bureau of Justice Statistics (Reaves 1992); a national survey of community policing conducted by the Police Foundation in 1993 (Wycoff 1994); and another national survey of community policing conducted jointly by the National Center for Community Policing at Michigan State University and the FBI Behavioral Sciences Unit (Trojanowicz 1994). Together these data sources provide abundant information for examining the relationship between community policing and structural change in large municipal police organizations.

THE STRUCTURE OF POLICE ORGANIZATIONS

Organizational structure is the formal apparatus through which organizations accomplish two core activities: the division of labor and the coordination of work (Scott 1992). Mintzberg's definition of structure eloquently reflects these two dimensions:

> Every organized human activity—from the making of pots to the placing of a man on the moon—gives rise to two fundamental and opposing requirements: the division of labor into various tasks to be performed, and the coordination of these tasks to accomplish the activity. The structure of an organization can be defined simply as the sum total of the ways in which it divides its labor into distinct tasks and then achieves coordination among them. (1979:2)

Though all large municipal police organizations in this country perform similar functions, their structures vary widely, as in many other types of organizations. Scott (1992:1) comments, "[W]hile organizations may possess common generic characteristics, they exhibit staggering variety—in size, in structure, and in operating processes."

Organizational structures vary along numerous dimensions. Over the past three decades, organizational theorists and empirical researchers have identified dozens of individual structural variables. Some of these have been discussed widely in the literature; others have appeared only briefly. Some have achieved a broad consensus among organizational scholars as core elements of structure; others have been dismissed or ignored. Some overlap conceptually with others; some are considered conceptually distinct. But nearly all relate to the way an organization divides, controls, coordinates, and organizes its workers and its work. The core elements of organizational structure are differentiation, formalization, centralization, and administration (Blau and Schoenherr 1971; Child 1973; Hage and Aiken 1967; Hall, Haas, and Johnson 1967; Hsu, Marsh, and Mannari 1983; Kriesburg 1976; Mintzberg 1979; Rushing 1976; Scott 1992).

Elements of Organizational Structure

Differentiation, according to Langworthy (1986), takes four forms: vertical, functional, occupational, and spatial. Vertical differentiation focuses on the hierarchical nature of an organization's command structure, including its segmentation, concentration, and height. Organizations with elaborate chains of command are more vertically differentiated than those with "flatter" command structures. Segmentation is the number of command levels in an organization, concentration is the percentage of personnel located at various levels, and height is the social distance between the lowest- and the highest-ranking employees. Functional differentiation is the degree to which tasks are broken down into functionally distinct units. An organization with a sales force, a separate production staff for each product, a planning staff, and an engineering group is more functionally differentiated than an organization containing only one department. Occupational differentiation is the degree to which an organization uses specially trained workers.[2] Occupational and functional differentiation are sometimes, but not always, related. Functional differentiation measures the division of tasks; occupational differentiation measures the division of staff (Langworthy 1986). Spatial differentiation is the extent to which an organization is spread geographically (Bayley 1992; Langworthy 1986). A police agency with a headquarters and several precinct stations is more spatially differentiated than a department that operates out of a single police facility.

In addition to the four primary elements of differentiation, three other elements of organizational structure are centralization, formalization, and administration. Centralization is the extent to which the decision-making capacity in an organization is concentrated in a single individual or a small, select group. Formalization is the extent to which actors in an organization are governed by specific rules and policies. Administrative density or "administrative overhead" refers to the size of the administrative component in an organization (Crank 1990; Langworthy 1986; Monkkonen 1981; Scott 1992). In the organizational literature, these three structural elements are often known collectively as "control" or "coordination" mechanisms.

Other measures of structure have emerged as well: some are similar to those explained here but are named differently, and others are labeled mistakenly as elements of structure. The dimensions of organizational structure listed here are not exhaustive, but represent those appearing most frequently in the literature. These elements are not merely theoretical categories; they represent real choices faced by those seeking to design or redesign an organization. Taken together, like separate components of a personality, they define an organization's structure.

The Evolution of Police Organizational Structures

Organizational structures do not stand still: They have been targeted by reformers for decades, and they have evolved in response to a number of social, political, and technological themes prominent in American history. During the earliest stages of American policing, police departments were geographically based. Precinct Captains were the main source of power in the organization; each one running essentially a small-scale department. Officers walked beats, rang neighborhood callboxes, and were responsible for particular patches of "turf." Policemen were "amateurs"; often their authority was based on the man rather than the institution (Miller 1977). Partisan control of the police, and thus corruption, were prominent in the early days of policing (Fogelson 1977;

Miller 1977; Woods 1993). Police agencies were characterized by relatively simple organizational structures.

In the twentieth century, a variety of social and technological changes led to a gradual increase in the complexity of police organizations (Kelling and Moore 1988). The emergence of the patrol car and the mobile two-way radio led to the initial displacement of the old geographically based model. Police cars enabled officers to cover greater areas of territory, and emerging dispatch technologies enabled supervisors to exercise control over officers far away. According to Reiss (1992:52), "the span of technological control widened the span of administrative control," thereby laying the groundwork for police organizations to centralize both geographically and administratively. Problems with police corruption furthered the trend toward centralization as departments sought to buffer themselves from the threat of future corruption.

The emergence of new technologies (e.g., ballistics, automated fingerprinting, computerized crime analysis) led police departments to form specialized units for handling these functions and/or to hire new personnel with specialized skills. Newly emerging (or newly discovered) social problems fostered increasing functional differentiation as police agencies formed new squads to handle issues such as family violence, bias/hate crimes, and environmental crimes.

Increases in specialization and centralization led departments to expand their administrative components and implement an increasing number of formal rules, policies, procedures, and standards in order to manage the increasing organizational complexity. The result of this historical evolution in police organizational structures is the bureaucratic structural form that characterizes most police organizations today and has been attacked by critics and reformers for many years (Angell 1971; Bayley 1994; Cordner 1987; Skolnick and Bayley 1986).

Critics argue that the bureaucratization of large police organizations has insulated them from the communities they are supposed to serve (Kelling and Moore 1988). Past reform efforts have not succeeded in remedying these structural defects. Following the influential report of the President's Commission (1967), most police departments developed or expanded specialized community service units that focused mainly on community outreach activities. In team policing, which emerged in the early to mid-1970s, specialized squads of officers were decoupled from the "regular" patrol force to engage in a variety of problem-solving and community engagement activities (Walker 1993).

Neither community service units nor team policing squads were very successful in bringing police closer to the public. Both approaches separated the work of community outreach, community engagement, and problem solving into specialized units, thereby shifting the responsibility for performing these functions away from the entire department (or the whole patrol force). Thus community engagement and problem solving became isolated activities, practiced by only selected personnel in the organization. By isolating community activities into peripheral specialized units, police departments buffered their patrol operations from the demands of reformers, adopting a classical institutional response to external demands for reform: They implemented symbolic efforts at reform that were only loosely coupled with the day-to-day operations of the organization (Crank and Langworthy 1992; Manning 1971).[3] These early reform efforts had little impact on the structures of police organizations.

The failure of police reform efforts in the 1960s and 1970s, to bring police closer to communities set the stage for the emergence of community policing (Walker 1993). Community policing, as defined in the vast reform and research literatures, involves many of the same strategies as earlier reform efforts, such as community out-reach, problem solving, and community engagement. One major difference is that community policing is envisioned, in its ideal form, as a departmentwide activity *with distinct implications for the way police organizations are structured.*

COMMUNITY POLICING

Community policing is embraced by many as the "new orthodoxy" in American policing (Eck and Rosenbaum 1994). Over the last decade, the community policing movement has gained a great deal of support from scholars, reformers, politicians, and the public (Rosenbaum 1994). Police executives are pressured by citizens and local government officials to implement community policing strategies (Friedman 1994; Zhao 1996). It has been endorsed by a variety of national and international professional police organizations (Community Policing Consortium 1994). The last three U.S. presidents—Bill Clinton, George Bush, and Ronald Reagan—have supported it. And with the implementation of the 1994 Crime Act, particularly the $8.8 billion "Cops on the Beat" program, community policing has received a legislative seal of approval from the federal government (U.S. Congress 1994). Police agencies who want to receive federal aid to hire new police officers under the Crime Act *must* implement it. The message is simple and clear: Police departments who don't accept community policing aren't doing the right things.

Given the tremendous pressure on American police agencies over the past decade, to implement community policing, one might expect that many have succumbed to the pressures for reform. Indeed, in the sample of 236 large metropolitan American police agencies used in this study, 44 percent report that they have adopted community policing, 47 percent say they are currently in the planning or implementation process, and only 9 percent report that they have no plans to adopt community policing. Because of recent federal initiatives to promote community policing, it is likely that many of these "holdouts" will move toward community policing in the near future.

Although most large American police departments say that they already have implemented or are planning to implement community policing, it is uncertain to what extent they have actually made substantive changes. Community policing has become the new rhetoric of policing in the 1990s, and many people do not understand what the term means (Greene and Mastrofski 1988; Hunter and Barker 1993; Manning 1988). For some it means problem solving and order maintenance; cleaning up tattered neighborhoods, revitalizing depressed areas, and fixing "broken windows" (Wilson and Kelling 1982). For others it means community relations: instituting foot and bicycle patrols, becoming familiar with residents and business owners, and many other activities that are designed to bring police officers closer to the communities they serve. To the leaders of the movement, much of what is new in policing, from the mundane to the ambitious, is mislabeled as community policing (Goldstein 1994; Skolnick and Bayley 1988). To many critics, including some police officers, community policing is nothing more than image management or a public relations gimmick. As Bayley (1988:225–26) warms, "[I]t is a trendy phrase spread thinly over customary reality. Unless the state of affairs changes, . . . it will be remembered as another attempt to put old wine into new bottles."

Most scholars and police executives who support the community policing movement view it as a new philosophy of policing rather than a simple programmatic innovation. Two seminal articles in the movement, written by Goldstein (1979) and by Wilson and Kelling (1982), set forth the framework for a new vision of the police role (Walker 1993). To these authors, community policing means more than implementing ministrations and foot patrols, or setting up neighborhood watches. Community policing, in its ideal sense, means changing the traditional definition of policing from one of crime control to one of community problem solving and empowerment. In addition to redefining the police mission, a practical shift to a community policing strategy means changing the "principal operating methods, and the key administrative arrangements of police departments" (Moore 1992:103). To effectively implement this strategy, reformers argue, police departments must redesign their organizations from the ground up.

WHY COMMUNITY POLICING
MIGHT PRODUCE STRUCTURAL CHANGES

For two compelling reasons, we should expect to find evidence of structural change in police agencies that have implemented community policing. First, community policing reformers have *explicitly* included prescriptions for structural change in their overall reform agendas. Second, community policing represents a significant change in the core operational technology of the police. As organizational theorists have known for many years, changes in technology, whether social or material, often lead *implicitly* to changes in structure.

EXPLICIT STRUCTURAL CHANGE

Nearly every reference in the community policing literature mentions the need for police organizations to implement some form of structural innovation as part of their overall effort at implementation. The organizational structures of community policing departments are supposed to differ markedly from those of "traditional" departments. Manning (1989), for example, distinguishes between "community policing" and "bureaucratic" police departments, implying that the two are polar opposites. Similarly, in his discussion of the "Cedar City" Police Department's difficulty in adopting community policing, Scheingold observes that "it was one thing to direct the department along responsive lines and quite another to give up bureaucratic control to the extent required by community policing" (1991:113). Greene, Bergman, and McLaughlin believe that organizational structure is integral to the very survival of the movement:

> For community policing to become a central feature of American law enforcement, the institutional framework and organizational apparatus of police organizations must be altered. . . . The success or failure of community policing then is in large measure affected by the organizational structures and processes that characterize modern-day policing. (1994:93)

Because traditional organizational structures are blamed for many of the ills plaguing American police departments (Angell 1971; Goldstein 1977:114–15), the community policing literature overall argues forcefully that structural change is necessary for the survival of community policing.

If contemporary reformers are correct, then departments that implement the programmatic components of community policing without the structural changes required by an overall shift in philosophy will lack the appropriate infrastructure to support community policing activities, and will maintain or eventually revert to more traditional forms of policing. Major changes in an organization's structure are not accomplished by renaming divisions or by shuffling boxes on an organizational chart. They involve significant changes in the administrative apparatus of the department. Community policing reformers have exhorted police organizations to decentralize their operations and management, to reduce their reliance on specialized units, to flatten their chains of command, to reduce needless formal policies and procedures, to replace sworn officers with civilians where possible, and to reduce the size of their administrative components. These structural changes are supposed to produce leaner, more responsive police organizations (Mastrofski 1994; Mastrofski and Ritti 1995).

Yet there are significant obstacles to implementing such changes. Organizational inertia constrains reformers' ability to implement significant structural changes *in any type of organization* (Hannan and Freeman 1984), and police organizations are notoriously difficult to change (Guyot 1979; Sparrow, Moore, and Kennedy 1990; Tafoya 1990). Therefore departments probably vary widely in the quantity and quality of structural changes motivated by their plans for, or adoption of, a community policing strategy.

Reformers are uncertain whether structural change is a *component* of community policing (e.g., Skolnick and Bayley 1986, 1988), a necessary *precursor* to community policing (e.g., Greene et al. 1994), or simply a *helpful feature* that might enhance community policing (Goldstein 1979). The literature, although clear about highlighting the need for structural change, is unclear about where it fits temporally into the implementation process (Wycoff 1994). Yet despite this uncertainty, nearly all reformers agree that structural change should be included as at least one element in a department's efforts to implement community policing.

Implicit Structural Change

Community policing is a new way of doing police work. For many years, policing has been described as a people-processing enterprise characterized by a variety of impersonal techniques for "slotting" clients into categories and providing canned responses to unique social problems[4] (Lipsky 1980; Prottas 1978; Waegel 1981). Reformers argue that police should not be so obsessed with routine *people-processing* activities (e.g., making arrests, filling out reports, issuing citations), but should focus instead on *people-changing* activities (Mastrofski and Ritti 1995). These might include building up neighborhoods, designing custom solutions to local problems, forging partnerships with other community agencies, and various other nonroutine police activities.

Community policing, in its ideal sense, represents a dramatic change in the way police organizations operate—a fundamental change in their operational "technology." Organizational theorists generally define technology as "a system of techniques" for accomplishing work or transforming raw materials into outputs (Perrow 1967; Scott 1992; Thompson and Bates 1957:325). Whereas manufacturing organizations tend to rely on material technologies such as computers and mechanical devices, service organizations such as the police depend more on "social" technologies (Glisson 1978; Manning 1992; Mills and Moberg 1982; Reiss 1992). People are the raw material of police organizations, and the type of social technology that the police select dictates how they process their raw materials. Because community policing entails a fundamental shift in the way the police transform raw materials into outputs—from people-processing to people-changing—it is a new technology of policing (Mastrofski and Ritti 1995).

Changes in operational technology frequently produce changes in organizational structure. Technology lies at the heart of functionalist theories of organizations, which assume that *what organizations do* determines how they are structured. Since the influential work of Woodward (1965), organizational scholars have regularly employed measures of technology in models explaining organizational structure. Many researchers have confirmed that technological differences produce structural differences (Dewar and Hage 1978; Hage and Aiken 1969; Van de Ven and Delbecq 1974; Woodward 1965), though others have found that the relationship is weaker than expected (Hickson, Pugh, and Pheysey 1969; Hsu et al. 1983; Pugh et al. 1969). The lack of consensus on the effect of technology on structure may be attributable to the variety of measurement schemes used and to the diversity of organizations studied. Different types of organizations use widely different technologies, and capturing this variation is extremely difficult.

Still debated is whether there exists a "technological imperative" that implicitly dictates how organizations are structured.[5] If such a technological imperative exists in police organizations, we should find evidence of structural change in those agencies which practice community policing.

RESEARCH QUESTIONS

The formal structures of large organizations vary along a number of dimensions. Nearly all of the dimensions that I discussed above are relevant in some way to community policing reform. Unfortunately, however, not all of these variables are available in existing data sources on American police agencies. Specifically, the data used in this analysis contain no measures of centralization or spatial differentiation. Thus the number of structural elements included here represents only a subset of those which interest community policing reformers. In this study I examine patterns of change in five structural variables: functional differentiation, vertical differentiation, occupational differentiation, formalization, and administrative density.

Functional Differentiation

Functional differentiation, as described earlier, is the degree to which an organization's tasks are broken down into functionally distinct units (Langwsorthy 1986). Police organizations have become more and more functionally differentiated during the twentieth century (Reiss 1992).[6] Under community policing, however, police organizations are encouraged to develop a front line of "uniformed generalists" well versed in dealing with a variety of social problems. This arrangement avoids placing all responsibility for particular problems on a single unit because, as Moore (1992:135) suggests, "[O]nce a special squad is formed, everyone else in the department is seemingly relieved of responsibility."

Although police departments have become more functionally differentiated in recent decades, it might be expected that departments practicing community policing would experience a reversal of this trend. The first research question examines whether functional differentiation in police organizations decreased from 1987 to 1993, and whether there are discernible differences between agencies which claim to practice community policing and those which do not.

Vertical Differentiation

Height, one component of vertical differentiation, is the distance from the bottom to the top of the organization, or the amount of social space between the lowest- and the highest-ranking employees (Black 1976; Langworthy 1986). Smaller organizations generally tend to be flatter and larger organizations tend to be taller, but not all the variation in height can be explained by organization size.[7] Langworthy (1986:40) measured the height of police departments with a standardized pay differential that he constructed by "subtracting the lowest paid officer's salary from the highest paid officer's salary and dividing that difference by the lowest salary." The larger the difference, the greater the height of the organization. Police rank hierarchies have been described (and criticized) for decades as rigid, paramilitary control structures that stifle innovation and slow decision making (Angell 1971; Bayley 1994; Guyot 1979; Heisel and Murphy 1974; Moore 1992).

To overcome this state of affairs, community policing reformers suggest that police organizations must become flatter, either by developing more informal managerial methods that would give subordinates more flexible access to superordinates, or by formally reducing the number of command levels (Mastrofski 1994). In the second research question I address whether reformers have been successful in "flattening" police organizations, and whether there are differences between community-policing and noncommunity-policing agencies.[8]

Occupational Differentiation

Langworthy (1986) operationalized occupational differentiation as the proportion of employees who are not sworn police officers, or the degree of "civilianization" (Crank 1989; Lutz and Morgan 1974).[9] Proponents herald civilianization as a cost-effective means of redeploying more expensive sworn officers from duties that could be performed as well by nonsworn personnel. Many police agencies, however, have resisted civilianization because officers perceive civilians as a threat to future police hiring, as an affront to the militaristic image of policing, and as a technique used by police executives to gain more extensive control over departments (Crank 1989).

Civilianization was one of the recommendations for police reform made by the President's Commission in 1967, and in recent decades, police departments have employed increasing numbers of civilian personnel (Guyot 1979). Unlike the other elements of structural reform discussed here, civilianization is an ongoing trend that community policing reformers encourage rather than seeking to reverse. The third research question is whether civilianization has continued to increase in this sample of police agencies, and whether there are discernible differences between community-policing and noncommunity-policing agencies.

Formalization

Formalization is the degree to which an organization is governed by formal (written) rules, policies, procedures, and standards (Hall et al. 1967). Formalized organizations are characterized by mountains of rules, piles of forms, and rigid standards of conduct. Accounts of overformalistic police agencies are common. As an extreme example, Reiss (1992) cites the Kansas City (MO) Police Department, which has 356 separate forms for reporting police matters.

Community policing advocates often argue that formalization stifles creativity and encourages generic, stock responses to the complex social problems that the police face each day (Mastrofski 1994). Although police have become more formalized during the twentieth century (Reiss 1992), it might be expected that this trend would be reversed under community policing. Thus the fourth research question is whether formalization in police organizations decreased from 1987 to 1993, and whether there are discernible differences between agencies which claim to practice community policing and those which do not.

Administrative Density

Administrative density is the size of the administrative component (Langworthy 1985). In the general literature on organizational structure, studies often use this variable as an overall indicator of bureaucratization (Scott 1992).[10] The logic of this rationale is simple: The more people employed in administrative duties, the fewer people doing the actual core work of the organization. Police organizations have become increasingly bureaucratic since the late nineteenth century (Monkkonen 1981; Reiss 1992). Under community policing, however, police organizations are supposed to become less bureaucratic (Mastrofski 1994). Thus the fifth research question is whether administrative overhead has decreased in those agencies which claim to practice community policing.

DATA AND METHODS

I obtained data for this study by merging five separate databases. The first three of these databases are the three separate waves of the Law Enforcement Management and Administrative Statistics (LEMAS) series (1987, 1990, and 1993) produced by the Bureau of Justice Statistics (Reaves and Smith 1995). The LEMAS series provides a wide range of information on the organizational features of American police agencies, and is used here to measure the various elements of structure.

The fourth database used here is a national survey of community policing conducted by the Police Foundation in 1993 (Wycoff 1994). This survey was distributed to the same large police agencies as the LEMAS surveys, and thus offers an opportunity to link the separate data sources.

The fifth database is another national survey of community policing, conducted jointly by the National Center for Community Policing at Michigan State University and the FBI Behavioral Sciences Unit (Trojanowicz 1994). This survey contains only two variables of interest, one of which is not available in any other data source: how long agencies have been practicing community policing. Because the implementation of community policing is regarded in this study as a quasi-experimental "treatment" occurring between 1987 and 1993, I use this variable to verify the assumption that nearly all agencies began practicing community policing during or near this period.[11] The data are being released only to selected scholars by the National Center for Community Policing (e.g., Yeh 1994), but the Center was kind enough to supply me with information on two variables.

Together these data sources provide abundant information for examining the relationship between community policing and structural changes in large municipal police organizations.

The Sample

The sample of police agencies used in this study was not selected randomly. I seek to generalize only to large municipal police agencies employing 100 or more full-time (actual, not authorized) sworn officers. Because there are only about 435 such agencies[12] in the United States, according to the 1992 Directory Survey of Law Enforcement Agencies (Reaves 1993), it would have been advantageous to select the entire population for this analysis. Unfortunately, however, this was not possible because of survey and item nonresponse in one or more of the four primary data sets: To be selected for inclusion in this study, a department had to respond to all four of the surveys constituting the merged data set, and also must have completed every applicable survey item. Only 236 of the 435 eligible departments (54 percent) met these criteria. Thus, due to survey and item non-response, the data set used for this analysis is based on a nonrandom sample of large municipal police agencies.

To test for possible nonresponse bias, I compared sample data for the most recent panel (1993) with data from the 1993 LEMAS survey (Reaves and Smith 1995). Of the 435 departments constituting the population of interest, 413 (95 percent) responded to the 1993 LEMAS survey. I compared the 236 sample respondents with the 177 nonrespondents on all of the variables included in the analysis, and detected some nonresponse bias. Independent-samples *t*-tests revealed significant differences for four of the seven variables in the model: The sample used here contains agencies that, on average, are larger, taller, more functionally differentiated, and perform a greater scope of tasks than nonrespondents.[13] In subsequent multivariate analyses I attempt to control statistically for nonresponse bias.

Variables

Functional differentiation is an additive index consisting of responses to nine separate questions on whether the department has a full-time specialized unit to deal with each of a variety of issues. Each component item is scored 0 for no special unit and 1 for a full-time special unit.[14] Higher scores indicate greater functional differentiation. Height is measured as the difference between the chief's salary and the entry-level salary, divided by the entry-level salary (Langworthy 1986). Civilianization is the percentage of full-time actual employees who are not sworn officers. Formalization is an additive index consisting of responses to 10 separate binary questions about whether the department has a formal written policy on a number of subjects. A score of 7, for example, indicates that the department has written policies governing seven of the 10 specific subject areas. Administrative density is the percentage of full-time actual employees who serve an administrative function.

In addition to the five structural variables, two covariates are included in the multivariate analysis as controls. Size of the organization is measured as the number of full-time sworn and nonsworn personnel employed by the agency (Langworthy 1986). Most studies have found consistent positive relationships between organization size and structural complexity (Blau 1970; Blau and Schoenherr 1971; Child 1973; Hsu et al. 1983; Pugh et al. 1969; Terrien and

Table 1 Mean Values within Community Policing and Time Categories

Variables	Year	Not Implemented	Implementing	Implemented
Covariates				
Size	1987	306	811	872
	1990	326	852	876
	1993	329	879	907
Task scope	1987	9.27	9.09	9.14
	1990	8.86	8.70	8.56
	1993	9.23	8.82	8.60
Structural Variables				
Functional	1987	3.82	4.39	4.07
Differentiation	1990	3.77	4.67	4.60
	1993	3.77	4.95	5.07
Formalization	1987	8.00	8.31	8.13
	1990	8.09	8.26	8.08
	1993	8.14	8.11	8.19
Administrative density	1987	.070	.069	.071
	1990	.065	.063	.060
	1993	.047	.062	.062
Height	1987	1.45	1.59	1.57
	1990	1.34	1.36	1.25
	1993	1.30	1.41	1.40
Civilianization	1987	.195	.220	.217
	1990	.198	.222	.229
	1993	.214	.222	.226
Number of Cases	(N = 236)	22 (9%)	110 (47%)	104 (44%)

Mills 1955), though some have found a weaker effect than expected (Beyer and Trice 1979; Hall et al. 1967). A number of others argue that size is a less important predictor of structure than are organizational tasks or technologies (Aldrich 1972; Thompson 1967; Woodward 1965).

Task scope is an additive index consisting of responses to 17 binary questions on the primary functions performed by the department, such as "Does your agency have primary responsibility for enforcement of traffic laws?" (Reaves and Smith 1995). A score of 8 on the task scope index indicates that the department is responsible for performing eight of the 17 tasks listed. Agencies that perform more tasks probably exhibit greater structural complexity: Previous research found a modest causal link between task scope and structure (Dewar and Hage 1978; Van de Ven and Delbecq 1974). Although neither size nor task scope is of substantive importance to this study, I include them here as controls because changes in either variable may produce changes in structure.[15]

I grouped the sample according to level of community policing implementation, as reported to the Police Foundation in 1993. Three separate groups

Table 2 Mean Changes over Time: Full Sample

Variables	1987–1990	1990–1993	1987–1993
Covariates			
Size (# of employees)	22	24*	46***
Task scope	−.53***	.11	−.41***
Structural Variables			
Functional differentiation	.35*	.38**	.72***
Formalization	−.03	−.03	−.04
Administrative density	.00	.00	.00
Height	−.25***	.06	−.19***
Civilianization	.009**	−.003	.006

$*p < .05; **p < .01; ***p < .001$; (paired t-tests, two-tailed)

were formed: have not implemented community policing, planning to implement community policing, and have implemented community policing. I measured each structural variable at three time points (1987, 1990, and 1993) based on separate waves of the LEMAS series. Research has shown that six years is an ideal period in which to examine structural adaptation to changes in causal variables such as size or technology (Dewar and Hage 1978). Descriptive statistics for all variables are shown in Table 1.

Methods

First I used paired t-tests to test for changes in structure for the whole sample over each of the three data–collection points of the LEMAS series (1987, 1990, and 1993). The results are shown in Table 2. Next I conducted repeated-measures multivariate analyses of variance with covariates (MANCOVA) to examine differences in structure across levels of community policing implementation (groups), over time, and across the group-time interaction. To control for the sample selection bias discussed earlier, I calculated a "hazard rate" variable that represents the likelihood of exclusion from the sample.[16] Three covariates—size, scope of tasks performed by the agency, and the hazard rate—were included to control for the possibility that these variables, rather than group differences alone, may be responsible for the variance in structural change. The model provides an F-statistic to test the hypothesis that group, time, or group-time differences differ significantly from zero. The results of the model are shown in Table 3.

RESULTS

Table 2 shows, for the full sample, the mean changes in each variable from 1987 to 1990, from 1990 to 1993, and across the entire period, 1987 to 1993. I compute significance levels for each difference, using paired t-tests without any

Table 3 Results of MANCOVA Repeated-Measures Analyses with Group, Time, and Interaction Effects (Controlling for Size and Task Scope)

Scales	Community Policing	Time	Interaction
	F	F	F
Functional Differentiation	.67	3.74*	1.19
Formalization	.17	.09	.67
Administrative Density	.42	1.10	.40
Height	.46	14.38***	1.04
Civilianization	2.60	2.02	1.26
Model	.50	4.38***	1.00

$p < .05$; ***$p < .001$

controls. The two covariates—size and scope of tasks performed—are listed first. Police departments grew at an average rate of 3 percent over each period, for an average overall increase of 6 percent in the number of employees. The scope of tasks performed by the police decreased significantly from 1987 to 1990: Departments dropped an average of .5 tasks (out of a total of 17). Task scope did not change significantly from 1990 to 1993, but the initial change remained significant across the entire period.

Functional differentiation increased significantly across both periods: Departments added an average of .7 full-time special units between 1987 and 1993. Thus, despite the expectations of community policing reformers, departments appear to be increasing rather than decreasing their reliance on specialized units. Formalization did not change significantly across any of the periods, contrary to the expectations of community policing reformers, who suggest that departments should become less formalized. Similarly, although community policing reformers suggest that departments must focus more of their resources on the *ends* of the organization (accomplishing their core street-level tasks) than on the *means* (such as enforcing rules and policies) (Goldstein 1979), administrative density did not seem to change significantly over any of the periods.

Height decreased significantly from 1987 to 1990 but not from 1990 to 1993. The initial change remained significant across the entire period, from 1987 to 1993. The reduction in the height of police organizations is one indication that reformers may have succeeded in convincing police agencies to flatten their rank structures (Mastrofski 1994).[17] Civilianization increased significantly from 1987 to 1990, continuing the upward trend of the past several decades. This trend showed an insignificant reversal, however, from 1990 to 1993. The two changes canceled each other out, producing a statistically insignificant change in civilianization across the entire period, from 1987 to 1993.

The results of the MANCOVA analysis are displayed in Table 3. When the hazard rate and the differences in size and task scope are controlled, the F-statistics for the grouping variable show no significant differences in structural change between police departments who are not implementing, who are planning to implement, and who have implemented community policing. This result holds for each structural variable individually and for the model as a whole.[18] The F-statistics for the time variable show that police organizations indeed have modified their structures over the period from 1987 to 1993: Functional differentiation increased significantly, and height decreased significantly. Civilianization increased, but the change is not statistically significant ($p = .07$). Formalization and administrative density show no significant changes over time. The F-statistics for the group-time interaction reveal no significant differences over time and between groups from 1987 to 1993. Thus the MANCOVA analysis shows that the grouping (community policing) variable was unrelated to differences in either levels of structure (cross-sectional) or structural change (longitudinal) in police organizations.

DISCUSSION

For nearly a decade, reformers have tried to diffuse the community policing movement throughout the United States. One substantial element of this reform involves structural change in police organizations. Although this study focuses only on a subset of relevant structural variables, the results suggest that community policing reformers have not succeeded in convincing large metropolitan police agencies to modify their existing organizational structures.

Only two of the five structural variables examined in this study changed significantly from 1987 to 1993, and one of these changes was in the wrong direction. First, police departments showed a significant decrease in organizational height. Community policing reformers have called repeatedly for police departments to flatten their rank structures or "de-layerize" so as to speed decision making and enhance upward and downward communications (Mastrofski 1994). Although reformers might find this trend encouraging, further research should explore vertical differentiation using more complete data sources. Second, continuing a trend of several decades (Reiss 1992), functional differentiation in police departments increased significantly from 1987 to 1993. Community policing reformers apparently have been unable to convince large metropolitan police organizations to despecialize.

Unfortunately, the research design used here permits inferences only about whether large municipal police agencies have made structural changes over a six-year period; it does not allow for inferences about the *causes* of structural change. I now suggest four possible explanations for the results obtained in this study: the time frame of the analysis, the attitudes of police executives, the environments of municipal police agencies, and the degree of organizational commitment to community policing.

First, it is possible that six years is not enough time to expect core structural changes in police organizations. In theory, however, community policing represents the most fundamental shift in the way police do business since the invention of the automobile and the two-way radio. The six-year period between 1987 and 1993 saw the emergence of the single largest reform effort in the history of the police, when *community policing* became a household phrase. If ever we would expect to find structural changes in police organizations, it would be the period examined here.

Second, there is some evidence that police executives may disagree with the prescriptions for structural change that appear in the reform literature. In the Police Foundation study of community policing implementation, only 61 percent of the executives of large (100+ sworn) municipal police agencies agreed that "community policing requires major changes of organizational policies, goals, or mission statements," and only 34 percent believed that community policing "requires extensive reorganization of police agencies" (Wycoff 1994: 32). If police executives don't support the need for structural change, it is likely that community policing advocates will remain unsuccessful in their efforts to implement such change in American police agencies.

Third, the reforms promoted by community policing advocates often conflict with other demands placed on police organizations by their environments.[19] Under community policing, for example, police agencies are urged to become less formalized. Yet to become accredited, they must institute a number of formal written policies and therefore become more formalized (Brown 1995; Cordner and Williams 1996; Mastrofski 1986). Similarly, under community policing, police organizations are urged to despecialize. Yet, as Mastrofski and Ritti (1995) report, special units have a great deal of symbolic meaning for police departments: They represent a substantial effort by the department to "do something" about a particular problem (e.g., drunk driving) without actually disturbing the organization's day-to-day operations. Despecialization would be a symbolic gesture indicating that the problems formerly handled by special units are no longer important to the department. As institutional theorists have argued for many years, structural changes are most likely to occur under two conditions: when they have "symbolic" value for the legitimacy of the organization, and when they do not disrupt the day-to-day operations of the organization's "technical core," where most of the work is done (such as a factory's assembly line or a police department's patrol squad) (Crank and Langworthy 1992; Mastrofski 1994; Mastrofski and Ritti 1995; Meyer and Rowan 1977).[20]

Fourth, large municipal police agencies may not be implementing community policing in wholesale fashion. If police organizations are jumping onto the community policing bandwagon only for its symbolic appeal without implementing its actual substance, the adoption of this strategy might not represent a significant change in social technology; therefore we would not expect to find evidence of implicit structural change. I now discuss this possibility in greater detail as I examine the "community policing" label.

The "Community Policing" Label

What defines whether departments claim that they *have not implemented, are now implementing,* or *have already implemented* community policing? In discussing the Police Foundation survey of community policing practices, Wycoff highlights this common concern:

One of the things this survey cannot tell us is "Who is really implementing community policing?" . . . Some questioners want to know which
agencies are implementing practices and arrangements that, a priori, have
been defined as being the operational representation of the philosophy.
Others want to know whether the agency is doing these in an isolated and
experimental way or whether it already has moved the entire organization
in a new direction. Others want to know whether agencies know what
they are talking about when they say they are implementing community
policing: "Are they really doing community policing or do they just think
they are?" And some want to know whether agencies are being honest:
do they really *believe* they are implementing community policing . . . or
are they just *saying* they are in order to increase their popularity in the
community or, perhaps, to gain federal funding? (1994:133–34)

Wycoff points to a number of compelling reasons why police departments'
claims may not reflect their actual involvement in community policing. It is far
beyond the scope of this study to examine the validity of the "community
policing" label, but simple reliability checks reveal some interesting patterns.
Two studies have asked large municipal police agencies whether they have
implemented community policing: the Michigan State University (MSU) survey administered in the summer of 1992 (Trojanowicz 1994), and the Police
Foundation survey administered in May 1993.

After recoding the survey questions in both studies so that the response
categories were equivalent, I found the correlations between responses to be
only .43. Some of this discrepancy probably exists because the Police Foundation study was distributed approximately 10 months after the MSU study. Of
the 236 departments I sampled from the Police Foundation data, 196 responded
to the community policing question in the MSU study. Of these 196, 135 (69
percent) responded consistently by giving the same answers in both studies.
Eleven departments (6 percent) responded to the MSU study in the summer of
1992 that they were not doing community policing, but then told the Police
Foundation study in May 1993 that they were doing community policing.

Given the speed with which the community policing movement is sweep-
ing the nation, this change is not unreasonable: New departments adopt community policing strategies every day. Even so, 50 departments (26 percent)
responded to the MSU study in 1992 that they were currently practicing community policing, and then reported to the Police Foundation in May 1993 that
they were not. Although it is reasonable to expect some attrition in the number of departments practicing community policing over the 10-month period
between studies, the magnitude of the difference in this case suggests that the
responses may be somewhat unstable.[21] The "community policing" label, as
Skogan (1994) suggests, merits further inquiry.

If police departments' claims regarding their community policing status are
not reliable (and presumably not valid), then the construct of community
policing used here may mask the true relationship between community policing and police organizational structure. Regardless of this limitation, however,

this study has revealed two important findings about community policing and structure in large police organizations. First, by linking separate data sources, the study (serendipitously) has uncovered evidence that police agencies' claims about their involvement in community policing are temporally unstable. This finding may appear banal to those who might have guessed as much, but it is the first piece of empirical evidence (from study with a large N) to support what most scholars probably suspected already. Second, this study has established that there are no structural differences between those agencies which *claim* to practice community policing and those which do not. Again, whether there is a relationship between structure and actual community policing status cannot be established until a reliable and valid measurement model of community policing is developed and tested on a large sample of police agencies.[22]

CONCLUSION

In this study I found no significant differences in structural change between departments which claim that they have not implemented, are planning to implement, or have implemented community policing. When I collapsed these groups, only two significant findings emerged: Departments have decreased in height and have increased in functional differentiation from 1987 to 1993. Community policing advocates may find the decrease in height encouraging because they have suggested this structural reform for nearly a decade. On the other hand, advocates may be discouraged by the increase in functional differentiation because they have pressed police departments to despecialize as part of their overall reform prescriptions.

The other structural variables (formalization, civilianization, and administrative density) did not change significantly between 1987 and 1993. Overall it appears that in this sample of large metropolitan police agencies, community policing advocates have tended to be unsuccessful in implementing their structural reform agendas.

Although the research design of this study did not allow inferences about *why* structures change (or fail to change), I presented four possible explanations for the findings. All of these explanations should be considered as hypotheses that can be tested in future research. Longitudinal research will be needed to identify the causal mechanisms responsible for structural change and (more important for police organizations) for structural intransigence.

ENDNOTES

1. For a review of the difference between social and material technologies, see Mills and Moberg (1982).

2. Langworthy (1986) operationalizes this variable as the percentage of civilians employed by the agency. Although civil-

ians in police organizations perform a variety of functions that are not necessarily specialized (e.g., Lutz and Morgan 1974), they represent a separate occupational category from sworn police officers.

3. In addition, officers engaging in community-based work were often marginalized by other officers for not doing "real" police work. In fact, there is some evidence that community officers were selected for such duties because they were deemed unfit for "regular" police work (Skolnick and Bayley 1986). As Moore recalls, "[T]he community relations units became known as 'grin and wave' squads and 'rubber gun' squads" (1992:135).

4. The tendency to slot clients into categories is not restricted to the police; it is also common in other criminal justice agencies (McCoy 1993; Sudnow 1965) and in many other types of human service bureaucracies (Lipsky 1980).

5. Mohr (1971:452) explores an alternative possibility, that "technology may not actually force structure, but rather that organizations will be effective only insofar as their structures are *consonant* with, or follow the dictates of, their technologies." The consonance hypothesis has received qualitative support over the years from researchers noting how the "fit" between technology and structure is integral to organizational effectiveness (Burns and Stalker 1961; Mastrofski and Ritti 1995; Woodward 1965). If the consonance hypothesis holds, we may find evidence of structural changes only in those police organizations which are "effective." As with all human-service agencies, however, judging effectiveness in police organizations requires normative judgments about agency goals; therefore measuring effectiveness is difficult (Langworthy 1986; Ostrom 1973).

6. The police are famous for dealing with new problems by forming specialized units (Bayley 1994; Mastrofski 1994; Moore 1992). Sparrow, Moore, and Kennedy (1990) quote an appropriate London Metropolitan Police saying: "When in doubt, form a squad and rush about."

7. In Langworthy's (1986) study, size explained between 2 and 26 percent of the variance in height, depending on the sample used. Crank and Wells (1991) found that size has a nonlinear effect on height: The effects of size on height are greater in smaller departments.

8. Unfortunately, the data sets used in this study do not contain information on segmentation and concentration, the remaining two components of vertical differentiation.

9. Although we are interested in the theoretical concept of occupational differentiation, this variable has been operationalized in prior research as the level of civilianization. Because *civilianization* is a more straightforward term for describing the proportion of police employees who are not sworn officers, I use it throughout the remainder of this paper.

10. This study uses a measure of "horizontal" administrative density, which refers to the amount of resources devoted to administrative support. Some theorists contrast this usage with "vertical" administrative density, which refers to the size of the supervisory component.

11. The MSU data contains information on year of community policing (CP) implementation for 115 of the 236 agencies in this sample (recall that only 104 agencies in the Police Foundation data claimed to practice community policing). Only 68 (59 percent) of the agencies that reported to MSU the year they had implemented community policing later reported to the Police Foundation that they practiced CP. Thus 41 percent of the agencies reporting year of CP implementation to MSU *later reported to the Police Foundation that they didn't practice CP*. This issue is covered in greater detail in the "discussion" section.

12. Municipal police agencies are those which serve local governments; this definition excludes all special, county, state, and federal law enforcement agencies. There are 12,444 municipal police agencies in the United States serving 165,113,274 persons and employing 349,647 sworn full-time police officers. Although the 435 largest of these agencies account for only about 3 percent of the total, they serve 48 percent of the total population covered by all municipal police agencies, and employ 57 percent of the police officers.

13. The main source of the nonresponse bias was easy to locate. Whereas the 1990 and 1993 LEMAS surveys collected data from all law enforcement agencies with more than *100* sworn officers, and sampled

smaller agencies, the 1987 LEMAS survey collected data from all agencies with more than *150* sworn officers and sampled smaller agencies. Thus the sample used in this study contains all respondents with more than 150 sworn officers, and only a subset of agencies with 100 to 150 sworn officers. In the 100 to 150–officer category, only those agencies which were selected randomly for the 1987 LEMAS sample are included here.

14. Although functional differentiation (FD) has been measured in a number of ways, in this study I follow the method suggested by Reimann (1973:464), who operationalizes functional specialization as "the number of discrete, identifiable functions performed by at least one, full-time specialist." I obtained similar results from subsequent analyses that treated FD as an additive index composed of indicators in which 0 = no unit, 1 = part-time unit, and 2 = full-time unit. The part–time category, however, is a probable source of uncertainty in the FD construct because respondents may be unsure what exactly constitutes a part-time special unit. Walker and Katz (1995) discovered a substantial degree of measurement error in one of the LEMAS questions regarding specialized units: Among the departments that indicated in their LEMAS responses that they had a specialized unit for enforcing bias crime statutes, 37.5 percent reported that they never had such a unit when contacted subsequently by researchers. Similar problems presumably would affect questions about other types of special units, which are combined to form the composite FD index in this study.

15. Although size and task/technology are the primary explanations for structure in the organizational literature, there is some evidence that other factors may influence structure as well. Dozens of variables have been hypothesized to affect or constrain structure in a wide range of organizational types, but the two primary factors found in the policing literature are environment (Crank and Wells 1991; Langworthy 1986) and age of the organization (King 1994). Research has shown that relative to size and technology, neither factor exerts a very strong effect on organizational structure.

Because this study is not concerned with explicitly modeling structure, the exclusion of these controls should have little effect on the findings.

16. Sample selection bias resulting from nonrandom sampling procedures "is proportional to the probability of exclusion" (Berk 1983:392). In most studies the probability of exclusion is unknown; the data used in this study, however, offer the possibility of calculating the estimated probability of exclusion for each case. Using data from the 1993 LEMAS survey, which contains information on 413 of the 435 agencies in the population of interest (95 percent), I estimated a logistic regression equation predicting sample exclusion with the seven variables employed here. From this equation I calculated the predicted probability of exclusion from the sample and then introduced it as a covariate in the MANCOVA model.

17. The standardized pay differential between the highest- and the lowest-ranking employee has been used in the past to measure height (Langworthy 1986) but is a more abstract element of vertical differentiation than segmentation, or the number of command levels (Crank and Wells 1991; Langworthy 1986). Unfortunately, measures of segmentation are not available in the LEMAS series or in any other national data set on American police agencies.

18. If police agencies implemented community policing and made structural changes before 1987, these changes would not be reflected in this set of analyses and might explain some of the null findings. To examine this possibility, I dropped the 25 agencies that claimed to have implemented community policing before 1987, and reran the analyses. I found no significant differences between the two sets of models.

19. Williams and Wagoner (1992), for example, predict that police organizations will maintain their paramilitary bureaucratic structures because they must respond to competing demands from disparate elements of their environments.

20. Elements of the institutional approach were also implicit in earlier discussions of the police by Reiss and Bordua (1967) and Manning (1977).

21. It is unknown whether the instability is due to sloppy survey responses, to a general misunderstanding about the intent of the questions, or to respondents' effort to present the organization in a favorable light.

22. Some scholars have begun to establish various schemes for measuring levels and types of community policing activities, but nobody claims to have developed a "true" measurement model of community policing. Such an undertaking, although difficult, would be a tremendous contribution to the empirical study of community policing.

REFERENCES

Aldrich, H.E. 1972. "Technology and Organizational Structure: A Reexamination of the Findings of the Aston Group." *Administrative Science Quarterly* 17:26–43.

Angell, J. 1971. "Toward an Alternative to the Classic Police Organizational Arrangements: A Democratic Model." *Criminology* 9:185–206.

Bayley, D.H. 1988. "Community Policing: A Report from the Devil's Advocate." Pp. 225–237 in *Community Policing: Rhetoric or Reality?*, edited by J.R. Greene and S.D. Mastrofski. New York: Praeger.

———. 1992. "Comparative Organization of the Police in English-Speaking Countries." Pp. 509–546 in *Modern Policing*, edited by M. Tonry and N. Morris. Chicago: University of Chicago Press.

———. 1994. *Police for the Future*. New York: Oxford University Press.

Berk, R.A. 1983. "An Introduction to Sample Selection Bias in Sociological Data." *American Sociological Review* 48:386–98.

Beyer, J.M. and Trice, H.M. (12979). "A Reexamination of the Relations Between Size and Various Components of Organizational Complexity." *Administrative Science Quarterly.* 24:48–64.

Black, D. 1976. *The Behavior of Law.* New York: Academic Press.

Blau, P.M. 1970. "A Formal Theory of Differentiation in Organizations." *American Sociological Review* 35:201–18.

Blau, P.M. and R.A. Schoenherr. 1971. *The Structure of Organizations.* New York: Basic Books.

Brown, J.M. 1995. "Accreditation Breeds Professionalism." *Sheriff* 5/6:12.

Burns, T. and G.M. Stalker. 1961. *The Management of Innovation.* London: Tavistock.

Child, J. 1971. "Predicting and Understanding Organization Structure." *Administrative Science Quarterly* 18:168–85.

Community Policing Consortium. 1994. "Understanding Community Policing: A Framework for Action." Bureau of Justice Assistance Monograph, U.S. Department of Justice, Washington, DC.

Cordner, G. 1987. "Open and Closed Models of Police Organizations: Traditions, Dilemmas and Practical Considerations." *Journal of Police Science and Administration* 6:22–34.

Cordner, G. and G. Williams. 1996. "Community Policing and Accreditation: A Content Analysis of CALEA Standards." Pp. 243–62 in *Quantifying Quality in Policing*, edited by L.T. Hoover. Washington, DC: Police Executive Research Forum.

Crank, J.P. 1989. "Civilianization in Small and Medium Police Departments in Illinois, 1973–1986." *Journal of Criminal Justice* 17:167–77.

———. 1990. "The Influence of Environmental and Organizational Factors on Police Style in Urban and Rural Environments." *Journal of Research in Crime and Delinquency* 27:166–89.

Crank, J.P. and R. Langworthy. 1992. "An Institutional Perspective of Policing." *Journal of Criminal Law and Criminology* 83:338–63.

Crank, J.P. and L.E. Wells. 1991. "The Effects of Size and Urbanism on Structure among Illinois Police Departments." *Justice Quarterly* 8: 170–85.

Dewar, R. and J. Hage. 1978. "Size, Technology, Complexity, and Structural Differentiation: Toward a Theoretical Synthesis." *Administrative Science Quarterly* 23:111–36.

Eck, J.E. and D.P. Rosenbaum. 1994. "The New Police Order: Effectiveness, Equity, and Efficiency in Community Policing." Pp. 3–26. In *The Challenge of Community Policing,* edited by D.P. Rosenbaum. Thousand Oaks, CA: Sage.

Fogelson, R.M. 1977. *Big-City Police.* Cambridge, MA: Harvard University Press.

Friedman, W. 1994. "The Community Role in Community Policing." Pp. 263–269 in *The Challenge of Community Policing,* edited by D.P. Rosenbaum. Thousand Oaks, CA: Sage.

Glisson, C.A. 1978. "Dependence of Technological Routinization on Structural Variables in Human Service Organizations." *Administrative Science Quarterly* 23:383–95.

Goldstein, H. 1977. *Policing a Free Society.* Cambridge, MA: Ballinger.

———. 1979. "Improving Policing: A Problem-Oriented Approach." *Crime and Delinquency* 25:236–58.

———. 1990. *Problem-Oriented Policing.* New York: McGraw-Hill.

———. 1994. "Foreword." Pp. viii–x in *The Challenge of Community Policing,* edited by D.P. Rosenbaum. Thousand Oaks, CA: Sage.

Greene, J.R., W. Bergman, and E. McLaughlin. 1994. "Implementing Community Policing: Cultural and Structural Change in Police Organizations." Pp. 92–109 in *The Challenge of Community Policing,* edited by D.P.

Rosenbaum. Thousand Oaks, CA: Sage.

Greene, J.R. and S.D. Mastrofski. 1988. *Community Policing: Rhetoric or Reality?* New York: Praeger.

Guyot, D. 1979. "Bending Granite: Attempts to Change the Rank Structure of American Police Departments." *Journal of Police Science and Administration* 7:253–84.

Hage, J. and M. Aiken. 1967. "Relationship of Centralization to Other Structural Properties." *Administrative Science Quarterly* 12:72–92.

———. 1969. "Routine Technology, Social Structure, and Organization Goals." *Administrative Science Quarterly* 14:366–77.

Hall, R.H., J.E. Haas, and N.J. Johnson. 1967. "Organizational Size, Complexity, and Formalization." *American Sociological Review* 32:903–12.

Hannan, M.T. and J. Freeman. 1984. "Structural Inertia and Organizational Change." *American Sociological Review* 49:149–64.

Heisel, W.D. and P.V. Murphy. 1974. "Organization for Police Personnel Management." Pp. 1–16 in *Police Personnel Administration,* edited by O.G. Stahl and R.A. Staufenberger. Washington, DC: Police Foundation.

Hickson, D.J., D.S. Pugh, and D.C. Pheysey. 1969. "Operations Technology and Organization Structure: An Empirical Reappraisal." *Administrative Science Quarterly* 14:378–97.

Hsu, C., R.M. Marsh, and H. Mannari. 1983. "An Examination of the Determinants of Organizational Structure." *American Journal of Sociology* 88:975–96.

Hunter, R.D. and T. Barker. 1993. "BS and Buzzwords: The New Police Operational Style." *American Journal of Police* 12(3): 157–168.

Kelling, G. and M. Moore. 1988. *The Evolving Strategy of Policing.* Washington, DC: National Institute of Justice.

King, W.R. 1994. "Do Older Police Departments Have More Wrinkles?

The Age-Structure Relationship." Presented at the annual meeting of the American Society of Criminology, Miami.

Kriesburg, L. 1976. "Centralization and Differentiation in International Non-governmental Organizations." *Sociology and Social Research* 61:1–23.

Langworthy, R.H. 1985. "Administrative Overhead in Municipal Police Departments." *American Journal of Police* 4:20–37.

———. 1986. *The Structure of Police Organizations*. New York: Praeger.

Lipsky, M. 1980. *Street-Level Bureaucracy: Dilemmas of the Individual in Public Services*. New York: Russell Sage Foundation.

Lutz, C. and J. Morgan. 1974. "Jobs and Rank." Pp. 17–44 in *Police Personnel Administration,* edited by O.G. Stahl and R.A. Staufenberger. Washington, DC: Police Foundation.

Manning, P.K. 1971. "The Police: Mandate, Strategies, and Appearances." In *Crime and Justice in American Society,* edited by J.D. Douglas. New York: Bobbs-Merrill.

———. 1977. *Police Work: The Social Organization of Policing*. Cambridge, MA: MIT Press.

———. 1988. "Community Policing as a Drama of Control." Pp. ___ in *Community Policing: Rhetoric or Reality,* edited by J.R. Greene and S.D. Mastrofski. New York: Praeger.

———. 1989. "Community Policing." Pp. 395–405 in *Critical Issues in Policing: Contemporary Readings,* edited by R.G. Dunham and G.P. Alpert. Prospect Heights, IL: Waveland.

———. 1992. "Information Technologies and the Police." Pp. 349–398 in *Modern Policing,* edited by M. Tonry and N. Morris. Chicago: University of Chicago Press.

Mastrofski, S.D. 1986. "Police Agency Accreditation: The Prospects of Reform." *American Journal of Police* 5:45–81.

———. 1994. "Community Policing and Police Organization Structure." Presented at the Workshop on Evaluating

Police Service Delivery, Centre for Comparative Criminology, University of Montreal.

Mastrofski, S.D. and R.R. Ritti. 1995. "Making Sense of Community Policing: A Theory Based Analysis." Presented at the annual meeting of the American Society of Criminology, Boston.

McCoy, C. 1993. *Politics and Plea Bargaining*. Philadelphia: University of Pennsylvania Press.

Meyer, J. and B. Rowan. 1977. "Institutionalized Organizations: Formal Structure as Myth and Ceremony." *American Journal of Sociology* 83:340–63.

Miller, W.R. 1977. *Cops and bobbies*. Chicago: University of Chicago Press.

Mills, P.K. and D.J. Moberg. 1982. "Perspectives on the Technology of Service Organizations." *Academy of Management Review* 7:467–78.

Mintzberg, H. 1979. *The Structure of Organizations*. Englewood Cliffs, NJ: Prentice-Hall.

Mohr, L.B. 1971. "Organizational Technology and Organizational Structure." *Administrative Science Quarterly* 16:444–59.

Monkkonen, E.H. 1981. *Police in Urban America*. New York: Cambridge University Press.

Moore, M.H. 1992. "Problem Solving and Community Policing." Pp. 99–158 in *Modern Policing,* edited by M. Tonry and N. Morris. Chicago: University of Chicago Press.

Moore, M.H. and D. Stephens. 1992. "Organization and Management." Pp. 22–58 in *Local Government Police Management,* edited by W.A. Geller. Washington, DC: International City Managers Association.

Ostrom, E. 1973. "On the Meaning and Measurement of Output and Efficiency in the Provision of Urban Police Services." *Journal of Criminal Justice* 1:93–112.

Perrow, C. 1967. "A Framework for the Comparative Analysis of Organizations." *American Sociological Review* 32:194–208.

President's Commission on Law Enforcement and Administration of Justice. 1967. *Task Force Report: The Police.* Washington, DC: U.S. Government Printing Office.

Prottas, J.M. 1978. "The Power of the Street-Level Bureaucrat in Public Service Bureaucracies." *Urban Affairs Quarterly* 13:285–312.

Pugh, D.S., D.J. Hickson, C.R. Hinings, and C. Turner. 1969. "The Context of Organization Structures." *Administrative Science Quarterly* 14:91–114.

Reaves, B. 1992. *Law Enforcement Management and Administrative Statistics, 1990: Data for Individual State and Local Agencies with 100 or More Officers.* Washington, DC: Bureau of Justice Statistics.

———. 1993. *Census of State and Local Law Enforcement Agencies, 1992.* Washington, DC: Bureau of Justice Statistics.

Reaves, B. and P. Smith. 1995. *Law Enforcement Management and Administrative Statistics, 1993: Data for Individual State and Local Agencies with 100 or More Officers.* Washington, DC: Bureau of Justice Statistics.

Reimann, B.C. 1973. "On the Dimensions of Bureaucratic Structure: An Empirical Reappraisal." *Administrative Science Quarterly* 18:462–76.

Reiss, A.J., Jr. 1992. "Police Organization in the Twentieth Century." Pp. 51–98 in *Modern Policing,* edited by M. Tonry and N. Morris. Chicago: University of Chicago Press.

Reiss, A.J., Jr. and D.J. Bordua. 1967. "Environment and Organization: A Perspective on the Police." Pp. 25–55 in *The Police: Six Sociological Essays,* edited by D.J. Bordua. New York: Wiley.

Rosenbaum, D. 1994. *The Challenge of Community Policing: Testing the Promises.* Thousand Oaks, CA: Sage.

Rushing, W.A. 1976. "Profit and Nonprofit Orientations and the Differentiations-Coordination Hypothesis for Organizations: A Study of Small General Hospitals." *American Sociological Review* 41:676–91.

Scheingold, S.A. 1991. *The Politics of Street Crime.* Philadelphia: Temple University Press.

Scott, W.R. 1992. *Organizations: Rational, Natural, and Open Systems.* 3rd ed. Englewood Cliffs, NJ: Prentice-Hall.

Skogan, W. 1994. "The Impact of Community Policing on Neighborhood Residents: A Cross-Site Analysis." Pp. 167–181 in *The Challenge of Community Policing,* edited by D.P. Rosenbaum. Thousand Oaks, CA: Sage.

Skolnick, J.H. and D.H. Bayley. 1986. *The New Blue Line: Police Innovation in Six American Cities.* New York: Free Press.

———. 1988. "Theme and Variation in Community Policing." Pp. 1–37 in *Crime and Justice: A Review of Research,* vol. 10, edited by M. Tonry and N. Morris. Chicago: University of Chicago Press.

Sparrow, M., M. Moore, and D. Kennedy. 1990. *Beyond 911: A New Era for Policing.* New York: Basic Books.

Sudnow, D. 1965. "Normal Crimes: Sociological Features of the Penal Code in a Public Defender's Office." *Social Problems* 12:255–76.

Tafoya, W.L. 1990. "Understanding Resistance to Change: Implications for the Future of Police." *American Journal of Police* 9:183–88.

Terrien, F.W. and D.L. Mills. 1955. "The Effect of Changing Size upon the Internal Structure of Organizations." *American Sociological Review* 29:11–13.

Thompson, J.D. 1967. *Organizations in Action.* New York: McGraw-Hill.

Thompson, J.D. and F.L. Bates. 1957. "Technology, Organization, and Administration." *Administrative Science Quarterly* 2:325–43.

Trojanowicz, R. 1994. *Community Policing: A Survey of Police Departments in the United States.* Washington, DC: U.S. Department of Justice.

United States Congress. 1994. *Congressional Record: Proceedings and Debates of the 103rd Congress, Second Session,* 140 (120): H8772-H8878. Washington, DC: U.S. Government Printing Office.

Van de Ven, A.H. and A. Delbecq. 1974. "A Task Contingent Model of Work-Unit Structure." *Administrative Science Quarterly* 19:183–97.

Waegel, W. 1981. "Case Routinization in Investigative Police Work." *Social Problems* 28:263–75.

Walker, S. 1993. "Does Anyone Remember Team Policing? Lessons of the Team Policing Experience for Community Policing." *American Journal of Police* 12:33–55.

Walker, S. and C. Katz. 1995. "Less Than Meets the Eye: Police Department Bias-Crime Units." *American Journal of Police* 14:29–48.

Williams, F.P., III, and C.P. Wagoner. 1992. "Making the Police Proactive: An Impossible Task for Improbable Reasons." *Police Forum* 2(2): 1–5.

Wilson, J.Q. and G. Kelling. 1982. "Broken Windows: The Police and Neighborhood Safety." *Atlantic Monthly,* March, pp. 29–38.

Woods, G. 1993. *The Police in Los Angeles.* New York: Garland.

Woodward, J. 1965. *Industrial Organization, Theory and Practice.* London: Oxford University Press.

Wycoff, M.A. 1994. "Community Policing Strategies." Unpublished report, Police Foundation, Washington, DC.

Yeh, S. 1994. "Diffusion of Innovation: An Explanatory Study on Community Policing." Presented at the annual meeting of the American Society of Criminology, Miami.

Zhao, J. 1996. *Why Police Organizations Change: A Study of Community-Oriented Policing.* Washington, DC: Police Executive Research Forum.

Improving Policing: A Problem-Oriented Approach

HERMAN GOLDSTEIN

The police have been particularly susceptible to the "means over ends" syndrome, placing more emphasis in their improvement efforts on organization and operating methods than on the substantive outcome of their work. This condition has been fed by the professional movement within the police field, with its concentration on the staffing, management, and organization of police agencies. More and more persons are questioning the widely held assumption that improvements in the internal management of police departments will enable the police to deal more effectively with the problems they are called upon to handle. If the police are to realize a greater return on the investment made in

The author is indebted to the University of Wisconsin Extension Department of Law for making the time available to produce this article as part of a larger effort to reexamine the university's role in research and training for the police.

improving their operations, and if they are to mature as a profession, they must concern themselves more directly with the end product of their efforts.

Meeting this need requires that the police develop a more systematic process for examining and addressing the problems that the public expects them to handle. It requires identifying these problems in more precise terms, researching each problem, documenting the nature of the current police response, assessing its adequacy and the adequacy of existing authority and resources, engaging in a broad exploration of alternatives to present responses, weighing the merits of these alternatives, and choosing from among them.

Improvements in staffing, organization, and management remain important, but they should be achieved—and may, in fact, be more achievable—within the context of a more direct concern with the outcome of policing.

> Complaints from passengers wishing to use the Bagnall to Greenfields bus service that "the drivers were speeding past queues of up to 30 people with a smile and a wave of a hand" have been met by a statement pointing out that "it is impossible for the drivers to keep their timetable if they have to stop for passengers."[1]

All bureaucracies risk becoming so preoccupied with running their organizations and getting so involved in their methods of operating that they lose sight of the primary purposes for which they were created. The police seem unusually susceptible to this phenomenon.

One of the most popular new developments in policing is the use of officers as decoys to apprehend offenders in high-crime areas. A speaker at a recent conference for police administrators, when asked to summarize new developments in the field, reported on a sixteen-week experiment in his agency with the use of decoys, aimed at reducing street robberies.

One major value of the project, the speaker claimed, was its contribution to the police department's public image. Apparently, the public was intrigued by the clever, seductive character of the project, especially by the widely publicized demonstrations of the makeup artists' ability to disguise burly officers. The speaker also claimed that the project greatly increased the morale of the personnel working in the unit. The officers found the assignment exciting and challenging, a welcome change from the tedious routine that characterizes so much of regular police work, and they developed a high esprit de corps.

The effect on robberies, however, was much less clear. The methodology used and the problems in measuring crime apparently prevented the project staff from reaching any firm conclusions. But it was reported that, of the 216 persons arrested by the unit for robbery during the experiment, more than half would not have committed a robbery, in the judgment of the unit members, if they had not been tempted by the situation presented by the police decoys. Thus, while the total impact of the project remains unclear, it can be said with certainty that the experiment actually increased the number of robberies by over 100 in the sixteen weeks of the experiment.

The account of this particular decoy project (others have claimed greater success) is an especially poignant reminder of just how serious an imbalance there is within the police field between the interest in organizational and procedural matters and the concern for the substance of policing. The assumption, of course, is that the two are related, that improvements in internal management will eventually increase the capacity of the police to meet the objectives for which police agencies are created. But the relationship is not that clear and direct and is increasingly being questioned.

Perhaps the best example of such questioning relates to response time. Tremendous resources were invested during the past decade in personnel, vehicles, communications equipment, and new procedures in order to increase the speed with which the police respond to calls for assistance. Much less attention was given in this same period to what the officer does in handling the variety of problems he confronts on arriving, albeit fast, where he is summoned. Now, ironically, even the value of a quick response is being questioned.[2]

This article summarizes the nature of the "means over ends" syndrome in policing and explores ways of focusing greater attention on the results of policing—on the effect that police efforts have on the problems that the police are expected to handle.

THE "MEANS OVER ENDS" SYNDROME

Until the late 1960s, efforts to improve policing in this country concentrated almost exclusively on internal management: streamlining the organization, upgrading personnel, modernizing equipment, and establishing more business-like operating procedures. All of the major commentators on the police since the beginning of the century—Leonhard F. Fuld (1909), Raymond B. Fosdick (1915), August Vollmer (1936), Bruce Smith (1940), and O.W. Wilson (1950) —stressed the need to improve the organization and management of police agencies. Indeed, the emphasis on internal management was so strong that professional policing was defined primarily as the application of modern management concepts to the running of a police department.

The sharp increase in the demands made on the police in the late 1960s (increased crime, civil rights demonstrations, and political protest) led to several national assessments of the state of policing.[3] The published findings contained some criticism of the professional model of police organization, primarily because of its impersonal character and failure to respond to legitimate pressures from within the community.[4] Many recommendations were made for introducing a greater concern for the human factors in policing, but the vast majority of the recommendations that emerged from the reassessments demonstrated a continuing belief that the way to improve the police was to improve the organization. Higher recruitment standards, college education for police personnel, reassignment and reallocation of personnel, additional training, and greater mobility were proposed. Thus the management-dominated concept of police reform spread and gained greater stature.

The emphasis on secondary goals—on improving the organization—continues to this day, reflected in the prevailing interests of police administrators, in the factors considered in the selection of police chiefs and the promotion of subordinates, in the subject matter of police periodicals and texts, in the content of recently developed educational programs for the police, and even in the focus of major research projects.

At one time this emphasis was appropriate. When Vollmer, Smith, and Wilson formulated their prescriptions for improved policing, the state of the vast majority of police agencies was chaotic: Personnel were disorganized, poorly equipped, poorly trained, inefficient, lacking accountability, and often corrupt. The first priority was putting the police house in order. Otherwise, the endless crises that are produced by an organization out of control would be totally consuming. Without a minimum level of order and accountability, an agency cannot be redirected—however committed its administrators may be to addressing more substantive matters.

What is troubling is that administrators of those agencies that have succeeded in developing a high level of operating efficiency have not gone on to concern themselves with the end results of their efforts—with the actual impact that their streamlined organizations have on the problems the police are called upon to handle.

The police seem to have reached a plateau at which the highest objective to which they aspire is administrative competence. And, with some scattered exceptions, they seem reluctant to move beyond this plateau—toward creating a more systematic concern for the end product of their efforts. But strong pressures generated by several new developments may now force them to do so.

1. *The Financial Crisis*

   The growing cost of police services and the financial plight of most city governments, especially those under threat of Proposition 13 movements, are making municipal officials increasingly reluctant to appropriate still more money for police service without greater assurance that their investment will have an impact on the problems that the police are expected to handle. Those cities that are already reducing their budgets are being forced to make some of the hard choices that must be made in weighing the impact of such cuts on the nature of the service rendered to the public.

2. *Research Findings*

   Recently completed research questions the value of two major aspects of police operations—preventive patrol and investigations conducted by detectives.[5] Some police administrators have challenged the findings[6]; others are awaiting the results of replication.[7] But those who concur with the results have begun to search for alternatives, aware of the need to measure the effectiveness of a new response before making a substantial investment in it.

3. *Growth of a Consumer Orientation*

   Policing has not yet felt the full impact of consumer advocacy. As citizens press for improvement in police service, improvement will increasingly be measured in terms of results. Those concerned about battered wives, for example, could not care less whether the police who respond to such calls operate with one or two officers in a car, whether the officers are short or tall, or whether they have a college education. Their attention is on what the police do for the battered wife.

4. *Questioning the Effectiveness of the Best-Managed Agencies*

   A number of police departments have carried out most, if not all, of the numerous recommendations for strengthening a police organization and enjoy a national reputation for their efficiency, their high standards of personnel selection and training, and their application of modern technology to their operations. Nevertheless, their communities apparently continue to have the same problems as do others with less advanced police agencies.[8]

5. *Increased Resistance to Organizational Change*

   Intended improvements that are primarily in the form of organizational change, such as team policing, almost invariably run into resistance from rank-and-file personnel. Stronger and more militant unions have engaged some police administrators in bitter and prolonged fights over such changes.[9] Because the costs in terms of disruption and discontent are so great, police administrators initiating change will be under increasing pressure to demonstrate in advance that the results of their efforts will make the struggle worthwhile.

Against this background, the exceptions to the dominant concern with the police organization and its personnel take on greater significance. Although scattered and quite modest, a number of projects and training programs carried out in recent years have focused on a single problem that the public expects the police to handle, such as child abuse, sexual assault, arson, or the drunk driver.[10] These projects and programs, by their very nature, subordinate the customary priorities of police reform, such as staffing, management, and equipment, to a concern about a specific problem and the police response to it.

Some of the earliest support for this type of effort was reflected in the crime-specific projects funded by the Law Enforcement Assistance Administration.[11] Communities—not just the police—were encouraged to direct their attention to a specific type of crime and to make those changes in existing operations that were deemed necessary to reduce its incidence. The widespread move to fashion a more effective police response to domestic disturbances is probably the best example of a major reform that has, as its principal objective, improvement in the quality of service delivered, and that calls for changes in organization, staffing, and training only as these are necessary to achieve the primary goal.

Are these scattered efforts a harbinger of things to come? Are they a natural development in the steadily evolving search for ways to improve police operations? Or are they, like the programs dealing with sexual assault and child abuse, simply the result of the sudden availability of funds because of intensified citizen concern about a specific problem? Whatever their origin, those projects that do subordinate administrative considerations to the task of improving police effectiveness in dealing with a specific problem have a refreshing quality to them.

WHAT IS THE END PRODUCT
OF POLICING?

To urge a more direct focus on the primary objectives of a police agency requires spelling out these objectives more clearly. But this is no easy task, given the conglomeration of unrelated, ill-defined, and often inseparable jobs that the police are expected to handle.

The task is complicated further because so many people believe that the job of the police is, first and foremost, to enforce the law: to regulate conduct by applying the criminal law of the jurisdiction. One commentator on the police recently claimed: "We do not say to the police: 'Here is the problem. Deal with it.' We say: 'Here is a detailed code. Enforce it.'"[12] In reality, the police job is perhaps most accurately described as dealing with problems.[13] Moreover, enforcing the criminal code is itself only a means to an end—one of several that the police employ in getting their job done.[14] The emphasis on law enforcement, therefore, is nothing more than a continuing preoccupation with means.

Considerable effort has been invested in recent years in attempting to define the police function: inventorying the wide range of police responsibilities, categorizing various aspects of policing, and identifying some of the characteristics common to all police tasks.[15] This work will be of great value in refocusing attention on the end product of policing, but the fact that it is still going on is not cause to delay giving greater attention to substantive matters. It is sufficient, for our purposes here, simply to acknowledge that the police job requires that they deal with a wide range of behavioral and social problems that arise in a community—that the end product of policing consists of dealing with these *problems*.

By problems, I mean the incredibly broad range of troublesome situations that prompt citizens to turn to the police, such as street robberies, residential burglaries, battered wives, vandalism, speeding cars, runaway children, accidents, acts of terrorism, even fear. These and other similar problems are the essence of police work. They are the reason for having a police agency.

Problems of this nature are to be distinguished from those that frequently occupy police administrators, such as lack of manpower, inadequate supervision, inadequate training, or strained relations with police unions. They differ from those most often identified by operating personnel, such as lack of adequate equipment, frustrations in the prosecution of criminal cases, or inequities in working conditions. And they differ, too, from the problems that have occupied those advocating police reform, such as the multiplicity of police agencies, the lack of lateral entry, and the absence of effective controls over police conduct.

Many of the problems coming to the attention of the police become their responsibility because no other means has been found to solve them. They are the residual problems of society. It follows that expecting the police to solve or eliminate them is expecting too much. It is more realistic to aim at reducing their volume, preventing repetition, alleviating suffering, and minimizing the other adverse effects they produce.

DEVELOPING THE OVERALL PROCESS

To address the substantive problems of the police requires developing a commitment to a more systematic process for inquiring into these problems. Initially, this calls for identifying in precise terms the problems that citizens look to the police to handle. Once identified, each problem must be explored in great detail. What do we know about the problem? Has it been researched? If so, with what results? What more should we know? Is it a proper concern of government? What authority and resources are available for dealing with it? What is the current police response? In the broadest-ranging search for solutions, what would constitute the most intelligent response? What factors should be considered in choosing from among alternatives? If a new response is adopted, how does one go about evaluating its effectiveness? And finally, what changes, if any, does implementation of a more effective response require in the police organization?

This type of inquiry is not foreign to the police. Many departments conduct rigorous studies of administrative and operational problems. A police agency may undertake a detailed study of the relative merits of adopting one of several different types of uniforms. And it may regularly develop military-like plans for handling special events that require the assignment of large numbers of personnel.[16] However, systematic analysis and planning have rarely been applied to the specific behavioral and social problems that constitute the agency's routine business. The situation is somewhat like that of a private industry that studies the speed of its assembly line, the productivity of its employees, and the nature of its public relations program, but does not examine the quality of its product.

Perhaps the closest police agencies have come to developing a system for addressing substantive problems has been their work in crime analysis. Police routinely analyze information on reported crimes to identify patterns of criminal conduct, with the goal of enabling operating personnel to apprehend specific offenders or develop strategies to prevent similar offenses from occurring. Some police departments have, through the use of computers, developed sophisticated programs to analyze reported crimes.[17] Unfortunately, these analyses are almost always put to very limited use—to apprehend a professional car thief or to deter a well-known cat burglar—rather than serving as a basis for rethinking the overall police response to the problem of car theft or cat burglaries. Nevertheless, the practice of planning operational responses based on an analysis of hard data, now a familiar concept to the police, is a helpful point of reference in advocating development of more broadly based research and planning.

The most significant effort to use a problem orientation for improving police responses was embodied in the crime-specific concept initiated in California in 1971[18] and later promoted with LEAA funds throughout the country. The concept was made an integral part of the anticrime program launched in eight cities in January 1972, aimed at bringing about reductions in five crime categories: murder, rape, assault, robbery, and burglary.[19] This would have provided an excellent opportunity to develop and test the concept, were it not for the commitment that this politically motivated program carried to achieving fast and dramatic results: a 5 percent reduction in each category in two years and a 20 percent reduction in five years. These rather naive, unrealistic goals and the emphasis on quantifying the results placed a heavy shadow over the program from the outset. With the eventual abandonment of the projects, the crime-specific concept seems to have lost ground as well. However, the national evaluation of the program makes it clear that progress was made, despite the various pressures, in planning a community's approach to the five general crime categories. The "crime-oriented planning, implementation and evaluation" process employed in all eight cities had many of the elements one would want to include in a problem-oriented approach to improving police service.[20]

DEFINING PROBLEMS
WITH GREATER SPECIFICITY

The importance of defining problems more precisely becomes apparent when one reflects on the long-standing practice of using overly broad categories to describe police business. Attacking police problems under a categorical heading—"crime" or "disorder," "delinquency," or even "violence"—is bound to be futile. While police business is often further subdivided by means of the labels tied to the criminal code, such as robbery, burglary, and theft, these are not adequate, for several reasons.

First, they frequently mask diverse forms of behavior. Thus, for example, incidents classified under "arson" might include fires set by teenagers as a form of vandalism, fires set by persons suffering severe psychological problems, fires set for the purpose of destroying evidence of a crime, fires set by persons (or their hired agents) to collect insurance, and fires set by organized criminal interests to intimidate. Each type of incident poses a radically different problem for the police.

Second, if police depend heavily on categories of criminal offenses to define problems of concern to them, others may be misled to believe that, if a given form of behavior is not criminal, it is of no concern to the police. This is perhaps best reflected in the proposals for decriminalizing prostitution, gambling, narcotic use, vagrancy, and public intoxication. The argument, made over and over again, is that removing the criminal label will reduce the magnitude and complexity of the police function, freeing personnel to work on more serious matters and ridding the police of some of the negative side effects, such as corruption, that these problems produce. But decriminalization does not relieve the police of responsibility. The public expects drunks to be picked up if only because they find their presence on the street annoying or because they feel that the government has an obligation to care for persons who cannot care for themselves. The public expects prostitutes who solicit openly on the streets to be stopped, because such conduct is offensive to innocent passersby, blocks pedestrian or motor traffic, and contributes to the deterioration of a neighborhood. The problem is a problem for the police whether or not it is defined as a criminal offense.

Finally, use of offense categories as descriptive of police problems implies that the police role is restricted to arresting and prosecuting offenders. In fact, the police job is much broader, extending, in the case of burglary, to encouraging citizens to lock their premises more securely, to eliminating some of the conditions that might attract potential burglars, to counseling burglary victims on ways they can avoid similar attacks in the future, and to recovering and returning burglarized property.

Until recently, the police role in regard to the crime of rape was perceived primarily as responding quickly when a report of a rape was received, determining whether a rape had really occurred (given current legal definitions), and then attempting to identify and apprehend the perpetrator. Today, the police role has been radically redefined to include teaching women how to avoid attack, organizing transit programs to provide safe movement in areas where there is a high risk of attack, dealing with the full range of sexual assault not previously covered by the narrowly drawn rape statutes, and—perhaps most important—providing needed care and support to the rape victim to minimize the physical and mental damage resulting from such an attack. Police are now concerned with sexual assault not simply because they have a direct role in the arrest and prosecution of violators, but also because sexual assault is a community problem which the police and others can affect in a variety of ways.

It seems desirable, at least initially in the development of a problem-solving approach to improved policing, to press for as detailed a breakdown of problems as possible. In addition to distinguishing different forms of behavior and the apparent motivation, as in the case of incidents commonly grouped under the heading of "arson," it is helpful to be much more precise regarding locale and time of day, the type of people involved, and the type of people victimized. Different combinations of these variables may present different problems, posing different policy questions and calling for radically different solutions.[21]

For example, most police agencies already separate the problem of purse snatching in which force is used from the various other forms of conduct commonly grouped under robbery. But an agency is likely to find it much more helpful to go further—to pinpoint, for example, the problem of teenagers snatching the purses of elderly women waiting for buses in the downtown section of the city during the hours of early darkness. Likewise, a police agency might find it helpful to isolate the robberies of grocery stores that are open all night and are typically staffed by a lone attendant; or the theft of vehicles by a highly organized group engaged in the business of transporting them for sale in another jurisdiction; or the problem posed by teenagers who gather around hamburger stands each evening to the annoyance of neighbors, customers, and management. Eventually, similar problems calling for similar responses may be grouped together, but one cannot be certain that they are similar until they have been analyzed.

In the analysis of a given problem, one may find, for example, that the concern of the citizenry is primarily fear of attack, but the fear is not warranted, given the pattern of actual offenses. Where this situation becomes apparent, the police have two quite different problems: to deal more effectively with the actual incidents where they occur, and to respond to the groundless fears. Each calls for a different response.

The importance of subdividing problems was dramatically illustrated by the recent experience of the New York City Police Department in its effort to deal more constructively with domestic disturbances. An experimental program, in which police were trained to use mediation techniques, was undertaken with obvious public support. But, in applying the mediation techniques, the department apparently failed to distinguish sufficiently those cases in which wives were repeatedly subject to physical abuse. The aggravated nature of the latter cases resulted in a suit against the department in which the plaintiffs argued that the police are mandated to enforce the law when *any* violation comes to their attention. In the settlement, the department agreed that its personnel would not attempt to reconcile the parties or to mediate when a felony was committed.[22] However, the net effect of the suit is likely to be more far reaching. The vulnerability of the department to criticism for not having dealt more aggressively with the aggravated cases has dampened support—in New York and elsewhere—for the use of alternatives to arrest in less serious cases, even though alternatives still appear to represent the more intelligent response.

One of the major values in subdividing police business is that it gives visibility to some problems which have traditionally been given short shrift, but which warrant more careful attention. The seemingly minor problem of noise, for example, is typically buried in the mass of police business lumped together under such headings as "complaints," "miscellaneous," "noncriminal incidents," or "disturbances." Both police officers and unaffected citizens would most likely be inclined to rank it at the bottom in any list of problems. Yet the number of complaints about noise is high in many communities—in fact, noise is probably among the most common problems brought by the public to the police.[23] While some of those complaining may be petty or unreasonable, many are seriously aggrieved and justified in their appeal for relief: Sleep is lost, schedules are disrupted, mental and emotional problems are aggravated. Apartments may become uninhabitable. The elderly woman living alone, whose life has been made miserable by inconsiderate neighbors, is not easily convinced that the daily intrusion into her life of their noise is any less serious than other forms of intrusion. For this person, and for many like her, improved policing would mean a more effective response to the problem of the noise created by her neighbors.

RESEARCHING THE PROBLEM

Without a tradition for viewing in sufficiently discrete terms the various problems making up the police job, gathering even the most basic information about a specific problem—such as complaints about noise—can be extremely difficult.

First, the magnitude of the problem and the various forms in which it surfaces must be established. One is inclined to turn initially to police reports for such information. But overgeneralization in categorizing incidents, the impossibility of separating some problems, variations in the reporting practices of the community, and inadequacies in report writing seriously limit their value for purposes of obtaining a full picture of the problem. However, if used cautiously, some of the information in police files may be helpful. Police agencies routinely collect and store large amounts of data, even though they may not use them to evaluate the effectiveness of their responses. Moreover, if needed information is not available, often it can be collected expeditiously in a well-managed department, owing to the high degree of centralized control of field operations.

How does one discover the nature of the current police response? Administrators and their immediate subordinates are not a good source. Quite naturally, they have a desire to provide an answer that reflects well on the agency, is consistent with legal requirements, and meets the formal expectations of both the public and other agencies that might have a responsibility relating to the problem. But even if these concerns did not color their answers, top administrators are often so far removed from street operations, in both distance and time, that they would have great difficulty describing current responses accurately.

Inquiry, then, must focus on the operating level. But mere questioning of line officers is not likely to be any more productive. We know from the various efforts to document police activity in the field that there is often tremendous variation in the way in which different officers respond to the same type of incident.[24] Yet the high value placed on uniformity and on adhering to formal requirements and the pressures from peers inhibit officers from candidly discussing the manner in which they respond to the multitude of problems they handle—especially if the inquiry comes from outside the agency. But one cannot afford to give up at this point, for the individualized practices of police officers and the vast amount of knowledge they acquire about the situations they handle, taken together, are an extremely rich resource that is too often overlooked by those concerned about improving the quality of police services. Serious research into the problems police handle requires observing police officers over a period of time. This means accompanying them as they perform their regular assignments and cultivating the kind of relationship that enables them to talk candidly about the way in which they handle specific aspects of their job.

The differences in the way in which police respond, even in dealing with relatively simple matters, may be significant. When a runaway child is reported; one officer may limit himself to obtaining the basic facts. Another officer, sensing as much of a responsibility for dealing with the parents' fears as for finding the child and looking out for the child's interests, may endeavor to relieve the parents' anxiety by providing information about the runaway problem and about what they might expect. From the standpoint of the consumers—in this case, the parents—the response of the second officer is vastly superior to that of the first.

In handling more complicated matters, the need to improvise has prompted some officers to develop what appear to be unusually effective ways of dealing with specific problems. Many officers develop a unique understanding of problems that frequently come to their attention, learning to make important distinctions among different forms of the same problem and becoming familiar with the many complicating factors that are often present. And they develop a feel for what, under the circumstances, constitute the most effective responses. After careful evaluation, these types of responses might profitably be adopted as standard for an entire police agency. If the knowledge of officers at the operating level were more readily available, it might be useful to those responsible for drafting crime-related legislation. Many of the difficulties in implementing recent changes in statutes relating to sexual assault, public drunkenness, drunk driving, and child abuse could have been avoided had police expertise been tapped.

By way of example, if a police agency were to decide to explore the problem of noise, the following questions might be asked. What is the magnitude of the problem as reflected by the number of complaints received? What is the source of the complaints: industry, traffic, groups of people gathered outdoors, or neighbors? How do noise complaints from residents break down between private dwellings and apartment houses? How often are the police summoned to the same location? How often are other forms of misconduct, such as fights, attributable to conflicts over noise? What is the responsibility of a landlord or an apartment house manager regarding noise complaints? What do the police now do in responding to such complaints? How much of the police procedure has been thought through and formalized? What is the authority of the police in such situations? Is it directly applicable or must they lean on somewhat nebulous authority, such as threatening to arrest for disorderly conduct or for failure to obey a lawful order, if the parties fail to quiet down? What works in police practice and what does not work? Are specific officers recognized as more capable of handling such complaints? If so, what makes them more effective? Do factors outside the control of a police agency influence the frequency with which complaints are received? Are noise complaints from apartment dwellers related to the manner in which the buildings are constructed? And what influence, if any, does the relative effectiveness of the police in handling noise complaints have on the complaining citizen's willingness to cooperate with the police in dealing with other problems, including criminal conduct, traditionally defined as much more serious?

Considerable knowledge about some of the problems with which the police struggle has been generated outside police agencies by criminologists, sociologists, psychologists, and psychiatrists. But as has been pointed out frequently, relatively few of these findings have influenced the formal policies and operating decisions of practitioners.[25] Admittedly, the quality of many such studies is poor. Often the practitioner finds it difficult to draw out from the research its significance for his operations. But most important, the police have not needed to employ these studies because they have not been expected to address specific problems in a systematic manner. If the police were pressured to examine in great detail the problems they are expected to handle, a review of the literature would become routine. If convinced that research findings had practical value, police administrators would develop into more sophisticated users of such research; their responsible criticism could, in turn, contribute to upgrading the quality and usefulness of future research efforts.

EXPLORING ALTERNATIVES

After the information assembled about a specific problem is analyzed, a fresh, uninhibited search should be made for alternative responses that might be an improvement over what is currently being done. The nature of such a search will differ from past efforts in that, presumably, the problem itself will be better defined and understood, the commitment to past approaches (such as focusing primarily on the identification and prosecution of offenders) will be shelved temporarily, and the search will be much broader, extending well beyond the present or future potential of just the police.

But caution is in order. Those intent on improving the operations of the criminal justice system (by divesting it of some of its current burdens) and those who are principally occupied with improving the operating efficiency of police agencies frequently recommend that the problem simply be shifted to some other agency of government or to the private sector. Such recommendations often glibly imply that a health department or a social work agency, for example, is better equipped to handle the problem. Experience over the past decade, however, shows that this is rarely the case.[26] Merely shifting responsibility for the problem, without some assurance that more adequate provisions have been made for dealing with it, achieves nothing.

Police in many jurisdictions, in a commendable effort to employ alternatives to the criminal justice system, have arranged to make referrals to various social, health, and legal agencies. By tying into the services provided by the whole range of other helping agencies in the community, the police in these cities have taken a giant step toward improving the quality of their response. But there is a great danger that referral will come to be an end in itself, that the police and others advocating the use of such a system will not concern themselves adequately with the consequences of referral. If referral does not lead to reducing the citizens' problem, nothing will have been gained by this change. It may even cause harm: Expectations that are raised and not fulfilled may lead to further frustration; the original problem may, as a consequence, be compounded; and the resulting bitterness about government services may feed the tensions that develop in urban areas.

The search for alternatives obviously need not start from scratch. There is much to build on. Crime prevention efforts of some police agencies and experiments with developing alternatives to the criminal justice system and with diverting cases from the system should be reassessed for their impact on specific problems; those that appear to have the greatest potential should be developed and promoted.[27] Several alternatives should be explored for each problem.

1. *Physical and Technical Changes*

   Can the problem be reduced or eliminated through physical or technical changes? Some refer to this as part of a program of "reducing opportunities" or "target hardening." Extensive effort has already gone into reducing, through urban design, factors that contribute to behavior requiring police attention.[28] Improved locks on homes and cars, the requirement of exact fares on buses,[29] and the provision for mailing social security checks directly to the recipients' banks exemplify recent efforts to control crime through this alternative.

   What additional physical or technical changes might be made that would have an effect on the problem? Should such changes be mandatory, or can they be voluntary? What incentives might be offered to encourage their implementation?

2. *Changes in the Provision of Government Services*

   Can the problem be alleviated by changes in other government services? Some of the most petty but annoying problems the police must handle originate in the policies, operating practices, and inadequacies of other public agencies: the scattering of garbage because of delays in collection, poor housing conditions because of lax code enforcement, the interference with traffic by children playing because they have not been provided with adequate playground facilities, the uncapping of hydrants on hot summer nights because available pools are closed. Most police agencies long ago developed procedures for relaying reports on such conditions to the appropriate government service. But relatively few police agencies see their role as pressing for changes in policies and operations that would eliminate the recurrence of the same problems. Yet the police are the only people who see and who must become responsible for the collective negative consequences of current policies.

3. *Conveying Reliable Information*

   What many people want, when they turn to the police with their problems, is simply reliable information.[30] The tenant who is locked out by his landlord for failure to pay the rent wants to know his rights to his property. The car owner whose license plates are lost or stolen wants to know what reporting obligations he has, how he goes about replacing the plates, and whether he can drive his car in the meantime. The person who suspects his neighbors of abusing their child wants to know whether he is warranted in reporting the matter to the police. And the person who receives a series of obscene telephone calls wants to know what can be done about them. Even if citizens do not ask specific questions, the best response the police can make to many requests for help is to provide accurate, concise information.

4. *Developing New Skills among Police Officers*

The greatest potential for improvement in the handling of some problems is in providing police officers with new forms of specialized training. This is illustrated by several recent developments. For example, the major component in the family-crisis intervention projects launched all over the country is instruction of police officers in the peculiar skills required to de-escalate highly emotional family quarrels. First aid training for police is being expanded, consistent with the current trend toward greater use of paramedics. One unpleasant task faced by the police, seldom noted by outsiders, is notifying families of the death of a family member. Often, this problem is handled poorly. In 1976, a film was made specifically to demonstrate how police should carry out this responsibility.[31] Against this background of recent developments, one should ask whether specialized training can bring about needed improvement in the handling of each specific problem.

5. *New Forms of Authority*

Do the police need a specific, limited form of authority which they do not now have? If the most intelligent response to a problem, such as a person causing a disturbance in a bar, is to order the person to leave, should the police be authorized to issue such an order, or should they be compelled to arrest the individual in order to stop the disturbance? The same question can be asked about the estranged husband who has returned to his wife's apartment or about the group of teenagers annoying passersby at a street corner. Police are called upon to resolve these common problems, but their authority is questionable unless the behavior constitutes a criminal offense. And even then, it may not be desirable to prosecute the offender. Another type of problem is presented by the intoxicated person who is not sufficiently incapacitated to warrant being taken into protective custody, but who apparently intends to drive his car. Should a police officer have the authority to prevent the person from driving by temporarily confiscating the car keys or, as a last resort, by taking him into protective custody? Or must the officer wait for the individual to get behind the wheel and actually attempt to drive and then make an arrest? Limited specific authority may enable the police to deal more directly and intelligently with a number of comparable situations.

6. *Developing New Community Resources*

Analysis of a problem may lead to the conclusion that assistance is needed from another government agency. But often the problem is not clearly within the province of an existing agency, or the agency may be unaware of the problem or, if aware, without the resources to do anything about it. In such cases, since the problem is likely to be of little concern to the community as a whole, it will probably remain the responsibility of the police, unless they themselves take the initiative, as a sort of community ombudsman, in getting others to address it.

A substantial percentage of all police business involves dealing with persons suffering from mental illness. In the most acute cases, where the individual may cause immediate harm to himself or others, the police are usually authorized to initiate an emergency commitment. Many other cases that do not warrant hospitalization nevertheless require some form of attention: The number of these situations has increased dramatically as the mental health system has begun treating more and more of its patients in the community. If the conduct of these persons, who are being taught to cope with the world around them, creates problems for others or exceeds community tolerance, should they be referred back to a mental health agency? Or, because they are being encouraged to adjust to the reality of the community, should they be arrested if their behavior constitutes a criminal offense? How are the police to distinguish between those who have never received any assistance, and who should therefore be referred to a mental health agency, and those who are in community treatment? Should a community agency establish services for these persons comparable to the crisis-intervention services now offered by specially organized units operating in some communities?

Such crisis-intervention units are among a number of new resources that have been established in the past few years for dealing with several long-neglected problems: detoxification centers for those incapacitated by alcohol, shelters and counseling for runaways, shelters for battered wives, and support services for the victims of sexual assault. Programs are now being designed to provide a better response to citizen disputes and grievances, another long-neglected problem. Variously labeled, these programs set up quasi-judicial forums that are intended to be inexpensive, easily accessible, and geared to the specific needs of their neighborhoods. LEAA has recently funded three such experimental programs, which they call Neighborhood Justice Centers.[32] These centers will receive many of their cases from the police.

Thus, the pattern of creating new services that bear a relationship with police operations is now well established, and one would expect that problem-oriented policing will lead to more services in greater variety.

7. *Increased Regulation*

Can the problem be handled through a tightening of regulatory codes? Where easy access to private premises is a factor, should city building codes be amended to require improved lock systems? To reduce the noise problem, should more soundproofing be required in construction? The incidence of shoplifting is determined, in part, by the number of sales-people employed, the manner in which merchandise is displayed, and the use made of various anti-shoplifting devices. Should the police be expected to combat shoplifting without regard to the merchandising practices by a given merchant, or should merchants be required by a "merchandising code" to meet some minimum standards before they can turn to the police for assistance?

8. *Increased Use of City Ordinances*

Does the problem call for some community sanction less drastic than a criminal sanction? Many small communities process through their local courts, as ordinance violations, as many cases of minor misconduct as possible. Of course, this requires that the community have written ordinances, usually patterned after the state statutes, that define such misconduct. Several factors make this form of processing desirable for certain offenses: It is less formal than criminal action; physical detention is not necessary; cases may be disposed of without a court appearance; the judge may select from a wide range of alternative penalties; and the offender is spared the burden of a criminal record. Some jurisdictions now use a system of civil forfeitures in proceeding against persons found to be in possession of marijuana, though the legal status of the procedure is unclear in those states whose statutes define possession as criminal and call for a more severe fine or for imprisonment.

9. *Use of Zoning*

Much policing involves resolving disputes between those who have competing interests in the use made of a given sidewalk, street, park, or neighborhood. Bigger and more basic conflicts in land use were resolved long ago by zoning, a concept that is now firmly established. Recently, zoning has been used by a number of cities to limit the pornography stores and adult movie houses in a given area. And at least one city has experimented with the opposite approach, creating an adult entertainment zone with the hope of curtailing the spread of such establishments and simplifying the management of attendant problems. Much more experimentation is needed before any judgment can be made as to the value of zoning in such situations.

IMPLEMENTING THE PROCESS

A fully developed process for systematically addressing the problems that make up police business would call for more than the three steps just explored— defining the problem, researching it, and exploring alternatives. I have focused on these three because describing them may be the most effective way of communicating the nature of a problem-oriented approach to improving police service. A number of intervening steps are required to fill out the processes: methods for evaluating the effectiveness of current responses, procedures for choosing from among available alternatives, means of involving the community in the decision making, procedures for obtaining the approval of the municipal officials to whom the police are formally accountable, methods for obtaining any additional funding that may be necessary, adjustments in the organization and staffing of the agency that may be required to implement an agreed-upon change, and methods for evaluating the effectiveness of the change.

How does a police agency make the shift to problem-oriented policing? Ideally, the initiative will come from police administrators. What is needed is not a single decision implementing a specific program or a single memorandum announcing a unique way of running the organization. The concept represents a new way of looking at the process of improving police functioning. It is a way of thinking about the police and their function that, carried out over an extended period, would be reflected in all that the administrator does: in the relationship with personnel, in the priorities he sets in his own work schedule, in what he focuses on in addressing community groups, in the choice of training curriculums, and in the questions raised with local and state legislators. Once introduced, this orientation would affect subordinates, gradually filter through the rest of the organization, and reach other administrators and agencies as well.

An administrator's success will depend heavily, in particular, on the use made of planning staff, for systematic analysis of substantive problems requires developing a capacity within the organization to collect and analyze data and to conduct evaluations of the effectiveness of police operations. Police planners (now employed in significant numbers) will have to move beyond their traditional concern with operating procedures into what might best be characterized as "product research."

The police administrator who focuses on the substance of policing should be able to count on support from others in key positions in the police field. Colleges with programs especially designed for police personnel may exert considerable leadership through their choice of offerings and through the subject matter of individual courses. In an occupation in which so much deference is paid to the value of a college education, if college instructors reinforce the impression that purely administrative matters are the most important issues in policing, police personnel understandably will not develop their interests beyond this concern.

Likewise, the LEAA, its state and local offspring, and other grant-making organizations have a unique opportunity to draw the attention of operating personnel to the importance of addressing substantive problems. The manner in which these organizations invest their funds sends a strong message to the police about what is thought to be worthwhile.

EFFECT ON THE ORGANIZATION

In the context of this reordering of police priorities, efforts to improve the staffing, management, and procedures of police agencies must continue.

Those who have been strongly committed to improving policing through better administration and organization may be disturbed by any move to subordinate their interests to a broader concern with the end product of policing. However, a problem-oriented approach to police improvement may actually contribute in several important ways to achieving their objectives.

The approach calls for the police to take greater initiative in attempting to deal with problems rather than resign themselves to living with them. It calls for tapping police expertise. It calls for the police to be more aggressive partners with other public agencies. These changes, which would place the police in a much more positive light in the community, would also contribute significantly to improving the working environment within a police agency—an environment that suffers much from the tendency of the police to assume responsibility for problems which are insolvable or ignored by others. And an improved working environment increases, in turn, the potential for recruiting and keeping qualified personnel and for bringing about needed organizational change.

Focusing on problems, because it is a practical and concrete approach, is attractive to both citizens and the police. By contrast, some of the most frequent proposals for improving police operations, because they do not produce immediate and specifically identifiable results, have no such attraction. A problem-oriented approach, with its greater appeal, has the potential for becoming a vehicle through which long-sought organizational change might be more effectively and more rapidly achieved.

Administrative rule making, for example, has gained considerable support from policy makers and some police administrators as a way of structuring police discretion, with the expectation that applying the concept would improve the quality of the decisions made by the police in the field. Yet many police administrators regard administrative rule making as an idea without practical significance. By contrast, police administrators are usually enthusiastic if invited to explore the problem of car theft or vandalism. And within such exploration, there is the opportunity to demonstrate the value of structuring police discretion in responding to reports of vandalism and car theft. Approached from this practical point of view, the concept of administrative rule making is more likely to be implemented.

Long-advocated changes in the structure and operations of police agencies have been achieved because of a concentrated concern with a given problem: The focus on the domestic disturbance, originally in New York and now elsewhere, introduced the generalist-specialist concept that has enabled many police agencies to make more effective use of their personnel; the problem in controlling narcotics and the high mobility of drug sellers motivated police agencies in many metropolitan areas to pool their resources in special investigative units, thereby achieving in a limited way one of the objectives of those who have urged consolidation of police agencies; and the recent interest in the crime of rape has resulted in widespread backing for the establishment of victim-support programs. Probably the support for any of these changes could not have been generated without the problem-oriented context in which they have been advocated.

An important factor contributing to these successes is that a problem-oriented approach to improvement is less likely to be seen as a direct challenge to the police establishment and the prevailing police value system. As a consequence, rank-and-file personnel do not resist and subvert the resulting changes. Traditional programs to improve the police—labeled as efforts to "change," "upgrade," or "reform" the police or to "achieve minimum standards"—require that police officers openly acknowledge their own deficiencies. Rank-and-file officers are much more likely to support an innovation that is cast in the form of a new response to an old problem—a problem with which they have struggled for many years and which they would like to see handled more effectively. It may be that addressing the quality of the police product will turn out to be the most effective way of achieving the objectives that have for so long been the goal of police reform.

ENDNOTES

1. Newspaper report from the Midlands of England, cited in Patrick Ryan, "Get Rid of the People, and the System Runs Fine," *Smithsonian,* September 1977, p. 140.

2. The recent study in Kansas City found that the effect of response time on the capacity of the police to deal with crime was negligible, primarily because delays by citizens in reporting crimes make the minutes saved by the police insignificant. See Kansas City, Missouri, Police Department, *Response Time Analysis,* Executive Summary (Kansas City, 1977).

3. See President's Commission on Law Enforcement and Administration of Justice, *The Challenge of Crime in a Free Society* (Washington, D.C.: Govt. Printing Office, 1967); National Advisory Commission on Civil Disorders, *Report of the National Advisory Commission on Civil Disorders* (Washington, D.C.: Govt. Printing Office, 1968); National Commission on the Causes and Prevention of Violence, *To Establish Justice, to Insure Domestic Tranquility,* Final Report (Washington, D.C.: Govt. Printing Office, 1969); President's Commission on Campus Unrest, *Report of the President's Commission on Campus Unrest* (Washington, D.C.: Govt. Printing Office, 1970); and National Advisory Commission on Criminal Justice Standards and Goals, *Police* (Washington, D.C.: Govt. Printing Office, 1973).

4. See, for example, National Advisory Commission on Civil Disorders, *Report,* p. 158.

5. George L. Kelling et al., *The Kansas City Preventive Patrol Experiment: A Summary Report* (Washington, D.C.: Police Foundation, 1974); and Peter W. Greenwood et al., *The Criminal Investigation Pro-*

cess, 3 vols. (Santa Monica, Calif.: Rand Corporation, 1976).

6. For questioning by a police administrator of the findings of the Kansas City Preventive Patrol Project, see Edward M. Davis and Lyle Knowles, "A Critique of the Report: An Evaluation of the Kansas City Preventive Patrol Experiment," *Police Chief,* June 1975, pp. 22–27. For a review of the Rand study on detectives, see Daryl F. Gates and Lyle Knowles, "An Evaluation of the Rand Corporation's Analysis of the Criminal Investigation Process," *Police Chief,* July 1976, p. 20. Each of the two papers is followed by a response from the authors of the original studies. In addition, for the position of the International Association of Chiefs of Police on the results of the Kansas City project, see "IACP Position Paper on the Kansas City Preventive Patrol Experiment," *Police Chief,* September 1975. p. 16.

7. The National Institute of Law Enforcement and Criminal Justice is sponsoring a replication of the Kansas City Preventive Patrol Experiment and is supporting further explorations of the criminal investigation process. See National Institute of Law Enforcement and Criminal Justice, *Program Plan, Fiscal Year 1978* (Washington, D.C.: Govt. Printing Office, 1977), p. 12.

8. Admittedly, precise appraisals and comparisons are difficult. For a recent example of an examination by the press of one department that has enjoyed a reputation for good management, see "The LAPD: How Good Is It?" *Los Angeles Times,* Dec. 18, 1977.

9. Examples of cities in which police unions recently have fought vigorously to oppose innovations introduced by police

administrators are Boston, Massachusetts, and Troy, New York.

10. These programs are reflected in the training opportunities routinely listed in such publications as *Police Chief, Criminal Law Reporter, Law Enforcement News,* and *Crime Control Digest,* and by the abstracting service of the National Criminal Justice Reference Center.

11. See, for example, National Institute of Law Enforcement and Criminal Justice, Law Enforcement Assistance Administration, "Planning Guidelines and Program to Reduce Crime," mimeographed (Washington, D.C., 1972), pp. vi–xiii. For a discussion of the concept, see Paul K. Wormeli and Steve E. Kolodney, "The Crime-Specific Model: A New Criminal Justice Perspective," *Journal of Research in Crime and Delinquency,* January 1972, pp. 54–65.

12. Ronald J. Allen, "The Police and Substantive Rulemaking: Reconciling Principle and Expediency," *University of Pennsylvania Law Review,* November 1976, p. 97.

13. Egon Bittner comes close to this point of view when he describes police functioning as applying immediate solutions to an endless array of problems. See Egon Bittner, "Florence Nightingale in Pursuit of Willie Sutton," in *The Potential for Reform of Criminal Justice,* Herbert Jacob, ed. (Beverly Hills, Calif.: Sage, 1974), p. 30. James Q. Wilson does also when he describes policing as handling situations. See James Q. Wilson, *Varieties of Police Behavior: The Management of Law and Order in Eight Communities* (Cambridge, Mass.: Harvard University Press, 1968), p. 31.

14. I develop this point in an earlier work. See Herman Goldstein, *Policing a Free Society* (Cambridge, Mass.: Ballinger, 1977), pp. 30, 34–35.

15. In the 1977 book I presented a brief summary of these studies. Ibid., pp. 26–28.

16. For an up-to-date description of the concept of planning and research as it has evolved in police agencies, see O. W. Wilson and Roy C. McLaren, *Police Administration,* 4th ed. (New York: McGraw-Hill, 1977), pp. 157–81.

17. For examples, see National Institute of Law Enforcement and Criminal Justice, *Police Crime Analysis Unit Handbook* (Washington, D.C.: Govt. Printing Office, 1973), pp. 90–92, 113–21.

18. For a brief description, see Joanne W. Rockwell, "Crime Specific . . . An Answer?" *Police Chief,* September 1972, p. 38.

19. The program is described in Eleanor Chelimsky, *High Impact Anti-Crime Program,* Final Report, vol. 2 (Washington, D.C.: Govt. Printing Office, 1976), pp. 19–38.

20. Ibid., pp. 145–50, 418–21.

21. For an excellent example of what is needed, see the typology of vandalism developed by the British sociologist, Stanley Cohen, quoted in Albert M. Williams, Jr., "Vandalism," *Management Information Service Report* (Washington, D.C.: International City Management Association, May 1976), pp. 1–2. Another excellent example of an effort to break down a problem of concern to the police—in this case, heroin—is found in Mark Harrison Moore, *Buy and Bust: The Effective Regulation of an Illicit Market in Heroin* (Lexington, Mass.: Lexington Books, 1977), p. 83.

22. See Bruno v. Codd, 90 Misc. 2d 1047, 396 N.Y.S.2d 974 (1977), finding a cause of action against the New York City Police Department for failing to protect battered wives. On June 26, 1978, the city agreed to a settlement with the plaintiffs in which it committed the police to arrest in all cases in which "there is reasonable cause to believe that a husband has committed a felony against his wife and/or has violated an Order of Protection or Temporary Order of Protection." See Consent Decree, Bruno against McGuire, New York State Supreme Court, index #21946/76. (Recognizing the consent decree, the New York Appellate Court, First Department, in July of 1978 [#3020] dismissed an appeal in the case as moot in so far as it involved the police department. From a reading of the court's reversal as to the other parts of the case, however, it appears that it would also have reversed the decision of the lower court in sustaining the action

against the police department if there had not been a consent decree.)

23. It was reported that, on a recent three-day holiday weekend in Madison, Wisconsin, police handled slightly more than 1,000 calls, of which 118 were for loud parties and other types of noise disturbances. See "Over 1,000 Calls Made to Police on Weekend," *Wisconsin State Journal* (Madison, Wisc.: June 1, 1978).

24. See, for example, the detailed accounts of police functioning in Minneapolis, in Joseph M. Livermore, "Policing," *Minnesota Law Review,* March 1971, pp. 649–729. Among the works describing the police officers' varying styles in responding to similar situations are Wilson, *Varieties of Police Behavior;* Albert J. Reiss, Jr., *The Police and the Public* (New Haven, Conn.: Yale University Press, 1971); Jerome H. Skolnick, *Justice without Trial: Law Enforcement in Democratic Society* (New York: John Wiley, 1966); and Egon Bittner, *The Functions of the Police in Modern Society: A Review of Background Factors, Current Practices, and Possible Role Models* (Washington, D.C.: Govt. Printing Office, 1970).

25. See, for example, the comments of Marvin Wolfgang in a Congressionally sponsored discussion of federal support for criminal justice research, reported in the U.S., House, Committee on the Judiciary, Subcommittee on Crime, *New Directions for Federal Involvement in Crime Control* (Washington, D.C.: Govt. Printing Office, 1977). Wolfgang claims that research in criminology and criminal justice has had little impact on the administration of justice or on major decision makers.

26. For further discussion of this point, see American Bar Association, *The Urban Police Function,* Approved Draft (Chicago: American Bar Association, 1973), pp. 41–42.

27. Many of these programs are summarized in David E. Aaronson et al., *The New Justice; Alternatives to Conventional Criminal Adjudication* (Washington, D.C.: Govt. Printing Office, (1977); and David E. Aaronson et al., *Alternatives to Conventional Criminal Adjudication: Guidebook for Planners and Practitioners,* Caroline S. Cooper, ed. (Washington, D.C.: Govt. Printing Office, 1977).

28. The leading work on the subject is Oscar Newman, *Defensible Space: Crime Prevention through Urban Design* (New York: Macmillan, 1972). See also Westinghouse National Issues Center, *Crime Prevention through Environmental Design— A Special Report* (Washington, D.C.: National League of Cities, 1977).

29. For a summary of a survey designed to assess the effect of this change, see Russell Grindle and Thomas Aceituno, "Innovations in Robbery Control," in *The Prevention and Control of Robbery,* vol. 1, Floyd Feeney and Adrianne Weir, eds. (Davis, Calif.: University of California, 1973), pp. 315–20.

30. In one of the most recent of a growing number of studies of how police spend their time, it was reported that, of the 18,012 calls made to the police serving a community of 24,000 people in a four-month period, 59.98 percent were requests for information. Police responded to 65 percent of the calls they received by providing information by telephone. See J. Robert Lilly, "What Are the Police Now Doing?" *Journal of Police Science and Administration,* January 1978, p. 56.

31. *Death Notification* (New York: Harper & Row, 1976).

32. The concept is described in Daniel McGillis and Joan Mullen, *Neighborhood Justice Centers: An Analysis of Potential Models* (Washington, D.C.: Govt. Printing Office, 1977): See also R. F. Conner and R. Suretta, *The Citizen Dispute Settlement Program: Resolving Disputes outside the Courts— Orlando, Courts— Orlando, Florida* (Washington, D.C.: American Bar Association, 1977).

Broken Windows

The Police and Neighborhood Safety

JAMES Q. WILSON
GEORGE L. KELLING

In the mid-1970s, the state of New Jersey announced a "Safe and Clean Neighborhoods Program," designed to improve the quality of community life in twenty-eight cities. As part of that program, the state provided money to help cities take police officers out of their patrol cars and assign them to walking beats. The governor and other state officials were enthusiastic about using foot patrol as a way of cutting crime, but many police chiefs were skeptical. Foot patrol, in their eyes, had been pretty much discredited. It reduced the mobility of the police, who thus had difficulty responding to citizen calls for service, and it weakened headquarters control over patrol officers.

Many police officers also disliked foot patrol, but for different reasons: it was hard work, it kept them outside on cold, rainy nights, and it reduced their chances for making a "good pinch." In some departments, assigning officers to foot patrol had been used as a form of punishment. And academic experts on policing doubted that foot patrol would have any impact on crime rates; it was, in the opinion of most, little more than a sop to public opinion. But since the state was paying for it, the local authorities were willing to go along.

Five years after the program started, the Police Foundation, in Washington, D.C., published an evaluation of the foot-patrol project. Based on its analysis of a carefully controlled experiment carried out chiefly in Newark, the foundation concluded, to the surprise of hardly anyone, that foot patrol had not reduced crime rates. But residents of the foot-patrolled neighborhoods seemed to feel more secure than persons in other areas, tended to believe that time had been reduced, and seemed to take fewer steps to protect themselves from crime (staying at home with the doors locked, for example). Moreover, citizens in the foot-patrol areas had a more favorable opinion of the police than did those living elsewhere. And officers walking beats had higher morale, greater job satisfaction, and a more favorable attitude toward citizens in their neighborhoods than did officers assigned to patrol cars.

James Q. Wilson is Shattuck Professor of Government at Harvard and author of *Thinking About Crime.* George L. Kelling, formerly director of the evaluation field staff of the Police Foundation, is currently a research fellow at the John F. Kennedy School of Government at Harvard.

These findings may be taken as evidence that the skeptics were right—foot patrol has no effect on crime; it merely fools the citizens into thinking that they are safer. But in our view, and in the view of the authors of the Police Foundation study (of whom Kelling was one), the citizens of Newark were not fooled at all. They knew what the foot-patrol officers were doing, they knew it was different from what motorized officers do, and they knew that having officers walk beats did in fact make their neighborhoods safer.

But how can a neighborhood be "safer" when the crime rate has not gone down—in fact, may have gone up? Finding the answer requires first that we understand what most often frightens people in public places. Many citizens, of course, are primarily frightened by crime, especially crime involving a sudden, violent attack by a stranger. This risk is very real, in Newark as in many large cities. But we tend to overlook or forget another source of fear—the fear of being bothered by disorderly people. Not violent people, nor, necessarily, criminals, but disreputable or obstreperous or unpredictable people: panhandlers, drunks, addicts, rowdy teenagers, prostitutes, loiterers, the mentally disturbed.

What foot-patrol officers did was to elevate, to the extent they could, the level of public order in these neighborhoods. Though the neighborhoods were predominantly black and the foot patrolmen were mostly white, this "order-maintenance" function of the police was performed to the general satisfaction of both parties.

One of us (Kelling) spent many hours walking with Newark foot-patrol officers to see how they defined "order" and what they did to maintain it. One beat was typical: a busy but dilapidated area in the heart of Newark, with many abandoned buildings, marginal shops (several of which prominently displayed knives and straight-edged razors in their windows), one large department store, and, most important, a train station and several major bus stops. Though the area was run-down, its streets were filled with people, because it was a major transportation center. The good order of this area was important not only to those who lived and worked there but also to many others, who had to move through it on their way home, to supermarkets, or to factories.

The people on the street were primarily black; the officer who walked the street was white. The people were made up of "regulars" and "strangers." Regulars included both "decent folk" and some drunks and derelicts who were always there but who "knew their place." Strangers were, well, strangers, and viewed suspiciously, sometimes apprehensively. The officer—call him Kelly— knew who the regulars were, and they knew him. As he saw his job, he was to keep an eye on strangers, and make certain that the disreputable regulars observed some informal but widely understood rules. Drunks and addicts could sit on the stoops, but could not lie down. People could drink on side streets, but not at the main intersection. Bottles had to be in paper bags. Talking to, bothering, or begging from people waiting at the bus stop was strictly forbidden. If a dispute erupted between a businessman and a customer, the businessman was assumed to be right, especially if the customer was a stranger. If a stranger loitered, Kelly would ask him if he had any means of support and what his business was; if he gave unsatisfactory answers, he was sent on his way. Persons who broke the informal rules, especially those who bothered people waiting at bus stops, were arrested for vagrancy. Noisy teenagers were told to keep quiet.

These rules were defined and enforced in collaboration with the "regulars" on the street. Another neighborhood might have different rules, but these, everybody understood, were the rules for *this* neighborhood. If someone violated them, the regulars not only turned to Kelly for help but also ridiculed the violator. Sometimes what Kelly did could be described as "enforcing the law," but just as often it involved taking informal or extralegal steps to help protect what the neighborhood had decided was the appropriate level of public order. Some of the things he did probably would not withstand a legal challenge.

A determined skeptic might acknowledge that a skilled foot-patrol officer can maintain order but still insist that this sort of "order" has little to do with the real sources of community fear—that is, with violent crime. To a degree, that is true. But two things must be borne in mind. First, outside observers should not assume that they know how much of the anxiety now endemic in many big-city neighborhoods stems from a fear of "real" crime and how much from a sense that the street is disorderly, a source of distasteful, worrisome encounters. The people of Newark, to judge from their behavior and their remarks to interviewers, apparently assign a high value to public order, and feel relieved and reassured when the police help them maintain that order.

Second, at the community level, disorder and crime are usually inextricably linked, in a kind of developmental sequence. Social psychologists and police officers tend to agree that if a window in a building is broken *and is left unrepaired,* all the rest of the windows will soon be broken. This is as true in nice neighborhoods as in run-down ones. Window-breaking does not necessarily occur on a large scale because some areas are inhabited by determined window-breakers whereas others are populated by window-lovers; rather, one unrepaired broken window is a signal that no one cares, and so breaking more windows costs nothing. (It has always been fun.)

Philip Zimbardo, a Stanford psychologist, reported in 1969 on some experiments testing the broken-window theory. He arranged to have an automobile without license plates parked with its hood up on a street in the Bronx and a comparable automobile on a street in Palo Alto, California. The car in the Bronx was attacked by "vandals" within ten minutes of its "abandonment." The first to arrive were a family—father, mother, and young son—who removed the radiator and battery. Within twenty-four hours, virtually everything of value had been removed. Then random destruction began—windows were smashed, parts torn off, upholstery ripped. Children began to use the car as a playground. Most of the adult "vandals" were well-dressed, apparently clean-cut whites. The car in Palo Alto sat untouched for more than a week. Then Zimbardo smashed part of it with a sledgehammer. Soon, passersby were joining in. Within a few hours, the car had been turned upside down and utterly destroyed. Again, the "vandals" appeared to be primarily respectable whites.

Untended property becomes fair game for people out for fun or plunder, and even for people who ordinarily would not dream of doing such things and who probably consider themselves law-abiding. Because of the nature of community life in the Bronx—its anonymity, the frequency with which cars are abandoned and things are stolen or broken, the past experience of "no one caring"—vandalism begins much more quickly than it does in staid Palo Alto, where people have come to believe that private possessions are cared for, and that mischievous behavior is costly. But vandalism can occur anywhere once communal barriers—the sense of mutual regard and the obligations of civility—are lowered by actions that seem to signal that "no one cares."

We suggest that "untended" behavior also leads to the breakdown of community controls. A stable neighborhood of families who care for their homes, mind each other's children, and confidently frown on unwanted intruders can change, in a few years or even a few months, to an inhospitable and frightening jungle. A piece of property is abandoned, weeds grow up, a window is smashed. Adults stop scolding rowdy children; the children, emboldened, become more rowdy. Families move out, unattached adults move in. Teenagers gather in front of the corner store. The merchant asks them to move; they refuse. Fights occur. Litter accumulates. People start drinking in front of the grocery; in time, an inebriate slumps to the sidewalk and is allowed to sleep it off. Pedestrians are approached by panhandlers.

At this point it is not inevitable that serious crime will flourish or violent attacks on strangers will occur. But many residents will think that crime, especially violent crime, is on the rise, and they will modify their behavior accordingly. They will use the streets less often, and when on the streets will stay apart from their fellows, moving with averted eyes, silent lips, and hurried steps. "Don't get involved." For some residents, this growing atomization will matter little, because the neighborhood is not their "home" but "the place where they live." Their interests are elsewhere; they are cosmopolitans. But it will matter greatly to other people, whose lives derive meaning and satisfaction from local attachments rather than worldly involvement; for them, the neighborhood will cease to exist except for a few reliable friends whom they arrange to meet.

Such an area is vulnerable to criminal invasion. Though it is not inevitable, it is more likely that here, rather than in places where people are confident they can regulate public behavior by informal controls, drugs will change hands, prostitutes will solicit, and cars will be stripped. That the drunks will be robbed by boys who do it as a lark, and the prostitutes' customers will be robbed by men who do it purposefully and perhaps violently. That muggings will occur.

Among those who often find it difficult to move away from this are the elderly. Surveys of citizens suggest that the elderly are much less likely to be the victims of crime than younger persons, and some have inferred from this that the well-known fear of crime voiced by the elderly is an exaggeration: perhaps we ought not to design special programs to protect older persons; perhaps we should even try to talk them out of their mistaken fears. This argument misses the point. The prospect of a confrontation with an obstreperous teenager or a drunken panhandler can be as fear-inducing for defenseless persons as the prospect of meeting an actual robber; indeed, to a defenseless person, the two kinds of confrontation are often indistinguishable. Moreover, the lower rate at which the elderly are victimized is a measure of the steps they have already taken—chiefly, staying behind locked doors—to minimize the risks they face. Young men are more frequently attacked than older women, not because they are easier or more lucrative targets but because they are on the streets more.

Nor is the connection between disorderliness and fear made only by the elderly. Susan Estrich, of the Harvard Law School, has recently gathered together a number of surveys on the sources of public fear. One, done in Portland, Oregon, indicated that three fourths of the adults interviewed cross to the other side of a street when they see a gang of teenagers; another survey, in Baltimore, discovered that nearly half would cross the street to avoid even a single strange youth. When an interviewer asked people in a housing project where the most dangerous spot was, they mentioned a place where young persons gathered to drink and play music, despite the fact that not a single crime had occurred there. In Boston public housing projects, the greatest fear was expressed by persons living in the buildings where disorderliness and incivility, not crime, were the greatest. Knowing this helps one understand the significance of such otherwise harmless displays as subway graffiti. As Nathan Glazer has written, the proliferation of graffiti, even when not obscene, confronts the subway rider with the "inescapable knowledge that the environment he must endure for an hour or more a day is uncontrolled and uncontrollable, and that anyone can invade it to do whatever damage and mischief the mind suggests."

In response to fear, people avoid one another, weakening controls. Sometimes they call the police. Patrol cars arrive, an occasional arrest occurs, but crime continues and disorder is not abated. Citizens complain to the police chief, but he explains that his department is low on personnel and that the courts do not punish petty or first-time offenders. To the residents, the police who arrive in squad cars are either ineffective or uncaring; to the police, the residents are animals who deserve each other. The citizens may soon stop calling the police, because "they can't do anything."

The process we call urban decay has occurred for centuries in every city. But what is happening today is different in at least two important respects. First, in the period before, say, World War II, city dwellers—because of money costs, transportation difficulties, familial and church connections—could rarely move away from neighborhood problems. When movement did occur, it tended to be along public-transit routes. Now mobility has become exceptionally easy for all but the poorest or those who are blocked by racial prejudice. Earlier crime waves had a kind of built-in self-correcting mechanism: the determination of a neighborhood or community to reassert control over its turf. Areas in Chicago, New York, and Boston would experience crime and gang wars, and then normalcy would return, as the families for whom no alternative residences were possible reclaimed their authority over the streets.

Second, the police in this earlier period assisted in that reassertion of authority by acting, sometimes violently, on behalf of the community. Young toughs were roughed up, people were arrested "on suspicion" or for vagrancy, and prostitutes and petty thieves were routed. "Rights" were something enjoyed by decent folk, and perhaps also by the serious professional criminal, who avoided violence and could afford a lawyer.

This pattern of policing was not an aberration or the result of occasional excess. From the earliest days of the nation, the police function was seen primarily as that of a night watchman: to maintain order against the chief threats to order—fire, wild animals, and disreputable behavior. Solving crimes was viewed not as a police responsibility but as a private one. In the March, 1969, *Atlantic,* one of us (Wilson) wrote a brief account of how the police role had slowly changed from maintaining order to fighting crimes. The change began with the creation of private detectives (often ex-criminals), who worked on a contingency-fee basis for individuals who had suffered losses. In time, the detectives were absorbed into municipal police agencies and paid a regular salary; simultaneously, the responsibility for prosecuting thieves was shifted from the aggrieved private citizen to the professional prosecutor. This process was not complete in most places until the twentieth century.

In the 1960s, when urban riots were a major problem, social scientists began to explore carefully the order-maintenance function of the police, and to suggest ways of improving it—not to make streets safer (its original function) but to reduce the incidence of mass violence. Order-maintenance became, to a degree, coterminous with "community relations." But, as the crime wave that began in the early 1960s continued without abatement throughout the decade and into the 1970s, attention shifted to the role of the police as crime-fighters. Studies of police behavior ceased, by and large, to be accounts of the order-maintenance function and became, instead, efforts to propose and test ways whereby the police could solve more crimes, make more arrests, and gather better evidence. If these things could be done, social scientists assumed, citizens would be less fearful.

A great deal was accomplished during this transition, as both police chiefs and outside experts emphasized the crime-fighting function in their plans, in the allocation of resources, and in deployment of personnel. The police may well have become better crime-fighters as a result. And doubtless they remained aware of their responsibility for order. But the link between order-maintenance and crime-prevention, so obvious to earlier generations, was forgotten.

That link is similar to the process whereby one broken window becomes many. The citizen who fears the ill-smelling drunk, the rowdy teenager, or the importuning beggar is not merely expressing his distaste for unseemly behavior; he is also giving voice to a bit of folk wisdom that happens to be a correct generalization—namely, that serious street crime flourishes in areas in which disorderly behavior goes unchecked. The unchecked panhandler is, in effect, the first broken window. Muggers and robbers, whether opportunistic or professional, believe they reduce their chances of being caught or even identified if they operate on streets where potential victims are already intimidated by prevailing conditions. If the neighborhood cannot keep a bothersome panhandler from annoying passersby, the thief may reason, it is even less likely to call the police to identify a potential mugger or to interfere if the mugging actually takes place.

Some police administrators concede that this process occurs, but argue that motorized-patrol officers can deal with it as effectively as foot-patrol officers. We are not so sure. In theory, an officer in a squad car can observe as much as an officer on foot; in theory, the former can talk to as many people as the latter. But the reality of police–citizen encounters is powerfully altered by the automobile. An officer on foot cannot separate himself from the street people; if he is approached, only his uniform and his personality can help him manage whatever is about to happen. And he can never be certain what that will be— a request for directions, a plea for help, an angry denunciation, a teasing remark, a confused babble, a threatening gesture.

In a car, an officer is more likely to deal with street people by rolling down the window and looking at them. The door and the window exclude the approaching citizen; they are a barrier. Some officers take advantage of this barrier, perhaps unconsciously, by acting differently if in the car than they would on foot. We have seen this countless times. The police car pulls up to a corner where teenagers are gathered. The window is rolled down. The officer stares at the youths. They stare back. The officer says to one, "C'mere." He saunters over, conveying to his friends by his elaborately casual style the idea that he is not intimidated by authority. "What's your name?" "Chuck." "Chuck who?" "Chuck Jones." "What'ya doing, Chuck?" "Nothin'." "Got a P.O. [parole officer]?" "Nah." "Sure?" "Yeah." "Stay out of trouble, Chuckie." Meanwhile, the other boys laugh and exchange comments among themselves, probably at the officer's expense. The officer stares harder. He cannot be certain what is being said, nor can he join in and, by displaying his own skill at street banter, prove that he cannot be "put down." In the process, the officer has learned almost nothing, and the boys have decided the officer is an alien force who can safely be disregarded, even mocked.

Our experience is that most citizens like to talk to a police officer. Such exchanges give them a sense of importance, provide them with the basis for gossip, and allow them to explain to the authorities what is worrying them (whereby they gain a modest but significant sense of having "done something" about the problem). You approach a person on foot more easily, and talk to him more readily, than you do a person in a car. Moreover, you can more easily retain some anonymity if you draw an officer aside for a private chat. Suppose you want to pass on a tip about who is stealing handbags, or who offered to sell you a stolen TV. In the inner city, the culprit, in all likelihood, lives nearby. To walk up to a marked patrol car and lean in the window is to convey a visible signal that you are a "fink."

The essence of the police role in maintaining order is to reinforce the informal control mechanisms of the community itself. The police cannot, without committing extraordinary resources, provide a substitute for that informal control. On the other hand, to reinforce those natural forces the police must accommodate them. And therein lies the problem.

Should police activity on the street be shaped, in important ways, by the standards of the neighborhood rather than by the rules of the state? Over the past two decades, the shift of police from order-maintenance to law-enforcement has brought them increasingly under the influence of legal restrictions, provoked by media complaints and enforced by court decisions and departmental orders. As a consequence, the order-maintenance functions of the police are now governed by rules developed to control police relations with suspected criminals. This is, we think, an entirely new development. For centuries, the role of the police as watchmen was judged primarily not in terms of its compliance with appropriate procedures but rather in terms of its attaining a desired objective. The objective was order, an inherently ambiguous term but a condition that people in a given community recognized when they saw it. The means were the same as those the community itself would employ, if its members were sufficiently determined, courageous, and authoritative. Detecting and apprehending criminals, by contrast, was a means to an end, not an end in itself; a judicial determination of guilt or innocence was the hoped-for result of the law-enforcement mode. From the first, the police were expected to follow rules defining that process, though states differed in how stringent the rules should be. The criminal-apprehension process was always understood to involve individual rights, the violation of which was unacceptable because it meant that the violating officer would be acting as a judge and jury—and that was not his job. Guilt or innocence was to be determined by universal standards under special procedures.

Ordinarily, no judge or jury ever sees the persons caught up in a dispute over the appropriate level of neighborhood order. That is true not only because most cases are handled informally on the street but also because no universal standards are available to settle arguments over disorder, and thus a judge may not be any wiser or more effective than a police officer. Until quite recently in many states, and even today in some places, the police make arrests on such charges as "suspicious person" or "vagrancy" or "public drunkenness"—charges with scarcely any legal meaning. These charges exist not because society wants judges to punish vagrants or drunks but because it wants an officer to have the legal tools to remove undesirable persons from a neighborhood when informal efforts to preserve order in the streets have failed.

Once we begin to think of all aspects of police work as involving the application of universal rules under special procedures, we inevitably ask what constitutes an "undesirable person" and why we should "criminalize" vagrancy or drunkenness. A strong and commendable desire to see that people are treated fairly makes us worry about allowing the police to rout persons who are undesirable by some vague or parochial standard. A growing and not-so-commendable utilitarianism leads us to doubt that any behavior that does not "hurt" another person should be made illegal. And thus many of us who watch over the police are reluctant to allow them to perform, in the only way they can, a function that every neighborhood desperately wants them to perform.

This wish to "decriminalize" disreputable behavior that "harms no one"—and thus remove the ultimate sanction the police can employ to maintain neighborhood order—is, we think, a mistake. Arresting a single drunk or a single vagrant who has harmed no identifiable person seems unjust, and in a sense it is. But failing to do anything about a score of drunks or a hundred vagrants may destroy an entire community. A particular rule that seems to make sense in the individual case makes no sense when it is made a universal rule and applied to all cases. It makes no sense because it fails to take into account the connection between one broken window left untended and a thousand broken windows. Of course, agencies other than the police could attend to the problems posed by drunks or the mentally ill, but in most communities—especially where the "deinstitutionalization" movement has been strong—they do not.

The concern about equity is more serious. We might agree that certain behavior makes one person more undesirable than another, but how do we ensure that age or skin color or national origin or harmless mannerisms will not also become the basis for distinguishing the undesirable from the desirable? How do we ensure, in short, that the police do not become the agents of neighborhood bigotry?

We can offer no wholly satisfactory answer to this important question. We are not confident that there *is* a satisfactory answer, except to hope that by their selection, training, and supervision, the police will be inculcated with a clear sense of the outer limit of their discretionary authority. That limit, roughly, is this—the police exist to help regulate behavior, not to maintain the racial or ethnic purity of a neighborhood.

Consider the case of the Robert Taylor Homes in Chicago, one of the largest public-housing projects in the country. It is home for nearly 20,000 people, all black, and extends over ninety-two acres along South State Street. It was named after a distinguished black who had been, during the 1940s, chairman of the Chicago Housing Authority. Not long after it opened, in 1962, relations between project residents and the police deteriorated badly. The citizens felt that the police were insensitive or brutal; the police, in turn, complained of unprovoked attacks on them. Some Chicago officers tell of times when they were afraid to enter the Homes. Crime rates soared.

Today, the atmosphere has changed. Police-citizen relations have improved—apparently, both sides learned something from the earlier experience. Recently, a boy stole a purse and ran off. Several young persons who saw the theft voluntarily passed along to the police information on the identity and residence of the thief, and they did this publicly, with friends and neighbors looking on. But problems persist, chief among them the presence of youth gangs that terrorize residents and recruit members in the project. The people expect the police to "do something" about this, and the police are determined to do just that.

But do what? Though the police can obviously make arrests whenever a gang member breaks the law, a gang can form, recruit, and congregate without breaking the law. And only a tiny fraction of gang-related crimes can be solved by an arrest; thus, if an arrest is the only recourse for the police, the residents' fears will go unassuaged. The police will soon feel helpless, and the residents will again believe that the police "do nothing." What the police in fact do is to chase known gang members out of the project. In the words of one officer, "We kick ass." Project residents both know and approve of this. The tacit police-citizen alliance in the project is reinforced by the police view that the cops and the gangs are the two rival sources of power in the area, and that the gangs are not going to win.

None of this is easily reconciled with any conception of due process or fair treatment. Since both residents and gang members are black, race is not a factor.

But it could be. Suppose a white project confronted a black gang, or vice versa. We would be apprehensive about the police taking sides. But the substantive problem remains the same: how can the police strengthen the informal social-control mechanisms of natural communities in order to minimize fear in public places? Law enforcement, per se, is no answer. A gang can weaken or destroy a community by standing about in a menacing fashion and speaking rudely to passersby without breaking the law.

We have difficulty thinking about such matters, not simply because the ethical and legal issues are so complex but because we have become accustomed to thinking of the law in essentially individualistic terms. The law defines *my* rights, punishes *his* behavior, and is applied by *that* officer because of *this* harm. We assume, in thinking this way, that what is good for the individual will be good for the community, and what doesn't matter when it happens to one person won't matter if it happens to many. Ordinarily, those are plausible assumptions. But in cases where behavior that is tolerable to one person is intolerable to many others, the reactions of the others—fear, withdrawal, flight—may ultimately make matters worse for everyone, including the individual who first professed his indifference.

It may be their greater sensitivity to communal as opposed to individual needs that helps explain why the residents of small communities are more satisfied with their police than are the residents of similar neighborhoods in big cities. Elinor Ostrom and her co-workers at Indiana University compared the perception of police services in two poor, all-black Illinois towns—Phoenix and East Chicago Heights—with those of three comparable all-black neighborhoods in Chicago. The level of criminal victimization and the quality of police-community relations appeared to be about the same in the towns and the Chicago neighborhoods. But the citizens living in their own villages were much more likely than those living in the Chicago neighborhoods to say that they do not stay at home for fear of crime, to agree that the local police have "the right to take any action necessary" to deal with problems, and to agree that the police "look out for the needs of the average citizen." It is possible that the residents and the police of the small towns saw themselves as engaged in a collaborative effort to maintain a certain standard of communal life, whereas those of the big city felt themselves to be simply requesting and supplying particular services on an individual basis.

If this is true, how should a wise police chief deploy his meager forces? The first answer is that nobody knows for certain, and the most prudent course of action would be to try further variations on the Newark experiment, to see more precisely what works in what kinds of neighborhoods. The second answer is also a hedge—many aspects of order-maintenance in neighborhoods can probably best be handled in ways that involve the police minimally, if at all. A busy, bustling shopping center and a quiet, well-tended suburb may need almost no visible police presence. In both cases, the ratio of respectable to disreputable people is ordinarily so high as to make informal social control effective.

Even in areas that are in jeopardy from disorderly elements, citizen action without substantial police involvement may be sufficient. Meetings between teenagers who like to hang out on a particular corner and adults who want to use that corner might well lead to an amicable agreement on a set of rules about how many people can be allowed to congregate, where, and when.

Where no understanding is possible—or if possible, not observed—citizen patrols may be a sufficient response. There are two traditions of communal involvement in maintaining order. One, that of the "community watchmen," is as old as the first settlement of the New World. Until well into the nineteenth century, volunteer watchmen, not policemen, patrolled their communities to keep order. They did so, by and large, without taking the law into their own hands—without, that is, punishing persons or using force. Their presence deterred disorder or alerted the community to disorder that could not be deterred. There are hundreds of such efforts today in communities all across the nation. Perhaps the best known is that of the Guardian Angels, a group of unarmed young persons in distinctive berets and T-shirts, who first came to public attention when they began patrolling the New York City subways but who claim now to have chapters in more than thirty American cities. Unfortunately, we have little information about the effect of these groups on crime. It is possible, however, that whatever their effect on crime, citizens find their presence reassuring, and that they thus contribute to maintaining a sense of order and civility.

The second tradition is that of the "vigilante." Rarely a feature of the settled communities of the East, it was primarily to be found in those frontier towns that grew up in advance of the reach of government. More than 350 vigilante groups are known to have existed; their distinctive feature was that their members did take the law into their own hands, by acting as judge, jury, and often executioner as well as policeman. Today, the vigilante movement is conspicuous by its rarity, despite the great fear expressed by citizens that the older cities are becoming "urban frontiers." But some community-watchmen groups have skirted the line, and others may cross it in the future. An ambiguous case, reported in *The Wall Street Journal,* involved a citizens' patrol in the Silver Lake area of Belleville, New Jersey. A leader told the reporter, "We look for outsiders." If a few teenagers from outside the neighborhood enter it, "we ask them their business," he said. "If they say they're going down the street to see Mrs. Jones, fine, we let them pass. But then we follow them down the block to make sure they're really going to see Mrs. Jones."

Though citizens can do a great deal, the police are plainly the key to order-maintenance. For one thing, many communities, such as the Robert Taylor Homes, cannot do the job by themselves. For another, no citizen in a neighborhood, even an organized one, is likely to feel the sense of responsibility that wearing a badge confers. Psychologists have done many studies on why people fail to go to the aid of persons being attacked or seeking help, and they have learned that the cause is not "apathy" or "selfishness" but the absence of some plausible grounds for feeling that one must personally accept responsibility. Ironically, avoiding responsibility is easier when a lot of people are standing about. On streets and in public places, where order is so important, many people are likely to be "around," a fact that reduces the chance of any one person acting as the agent of the community. The police officer's uniform singles him out as a person who must accept responsibility if asked. In addition, officers, more easily than their fellow citizens, can be expected to distinguish between what is necessary to protect the safety of the street and what merely protects its ethnic purity.

But the police forces of America are losing, not gaining, members. Some cities have suffered substantial cuts in the number of officers available for duty. These cuts are not likely to be reversed in the near future. Therefore, each department must assign its existing officers with great care. Some neighborhoods are so demoralized and crimeridden as to make foot patrol useless; the best the police can do with limited resources is respond to the enormous number of calls for service. Other neighborhoods are so stable and serene as to make foot patrol unnecessary. The key is to identify neighborhoods at the tipping point—where the public order is deteriorating but not unreclaimable, where the streets are used frequently but by apprehensive people, where a window is likely to be broken at any time, and must quickly be fixed if all are not to be shattered.

Most police departments do not have ways of systematically identifying such areas and assigning officers to them. Officers are assigned on the basis of crime rates (meaning that marginally threatened areas are often stripped so that police can investigate crimes in areas where the situation is hopeless) or on the basis of calls for service (despite the fact that most citizens do not call the police when they are merely frightened or annoyed). To allocate patrol wisely, the department must look at the neighborhoods and decide, from first-hand evidence, where an additional officer will make the greatest difference in promoting a sense of safety.

One way to stretch limited police resources is being tried in some public-housing projects. Tenant organizations hire off-duty police officers for patrol work in their buildings. The costs are not high (at least not per resident), the officer likes the additional income, and the residents feel safer. Such arrangements are probably more successful than hiring private watchmen, and the Newark experiment helps us understand why. A private security guard may deter crime or misconduct by his presence, and he may go to the aid of persons needing help, but he may well not intervene—that is, control or drive away—someone challenging community standards. Being a sworn officer—a "real cop"—seems to give one the confidence, the sense of duty, and the aura of authority necessary to perform this difficult task.

Patrol officers might be encouraged to go to and from duty stations on public transportation and, while on the bus or subway car, enforce rules about smoking, drinking, disorderly conduct, and the like. The enforcement need involve nothing more than ejecting the offender (the offense, after all, is not one with which a booking officer or a judge wishes to be bothered). Perhaps the random but relentless maintenance of standards on buses would lead to conditions on buses that approximate the level of civility we now take for granted on airplanes.

But the most important requirement is to think that to maintain order in precarious situations is a vital job. The police know this is one of their functions, and they also believe, correctly, that it cannot be done to the exclusion of criminal investigation and responding to calls. We may have encouraged them to suppose, however, on the basis of our oft-repeated concerns about serious, violent crime, that they will be judged exclusively on their capacity as crime-fighters. To the extent that this is the case, police administrators will continue to concentrate police personnel in the highest-crime areas (though not necessarily in the areas most vulnerable to criminal invasion), emphasize their training in the law and criminal apprehension (and not their training in managing street life), and join too quickly in campaigns to decriminalize "harmless" behavior (though public drunkenness, street prostitution, and pornographic displays can destroy a community more quickly than any team of professional burglars).

Above all, we must return to our long-abandoned view that the police ought to protect communities as well as individuals. Our crime statistics and victimization surveys measure individual losses, but they do not measure communal losses. Just as physicians now recognize the importance of fostering health rather than simply treating illness, so the police—and the rest of us— ought to recognize the importance of maintaining intact, communities without broken windows.

Militarizing Mayberry and Beyond: Making Sense of American Paramilitary Policing

PETER B. KRASKA

LOUIS J. CUBELLIS

National-level data, derived from a survey of all police agencies serving 25,000 to 50,000 people, document a previously unrecognized phenomenon: the growth in the number, an expansion of the activities, and the movement toward the normalization of small-locality police paramilitary units (PPUs). Beside examining the implications of these findings for small-locality policing, we situate this phenomenon within broader

We would like to thank the four anonymous reviewers for their insightful suggestions, especially reviewer number 2 who provided the information for footnote 12. Please send any correspondence to Peter B. Kraska, Department of Police Studies, Eastern Kentucky University, Richmond KY 40475.

Source: Kraska, Peter B. and Louis J. Cubellis (1997) Militarizing Mayberry and Beyond: Making Sense of American Paramilitary Policing. *Justice Quarterly* 14: 607–629. Reprinted with the permission of Academy of Criminal Justices.

paramilitary changes in the police. To begin the process of making theoretical sense of PPUs, we refute the commonsense notion that their rise is a response to changes in crime. We then contextualize the phenomenon by discussing the lingering influence of the military model, the recent popularity of paramilitary subculture, changing police tactics in the war on drugs, police reform efforts, and the quest to modernize the criminal justice apparatus. Noting similar developments in corrections, we conclude that this phenomenon should not be seen merely as a peculiar manifestation of get-tough policies. Instead it corresponds closely to attempts by the state, in times of high modernity, to further refine its administration of violence.

Crime and justice studies have a fundamental interest in society's formal reaction to the breaking of laws (Sutherland, Cressey, and Luckenbill 1992). Consequently criminologists have examined and debated the changing nature of the criminal justice enterprise. Some penological scholars argue, for instance, that correctional ideology and practice are aligning themselves more closely with the features of a postmodern or high-modern society (Christie 1994; Feeley and Simon 1992; Garland 1990, 1995). Policing scholars, on the other hand, focus predominantly on the "quiet revolution" occurring within the modern police institution, namely community and problem-oriented policing reforms (Kelling 1988).

Despite the democratic rhetoric connected with this "revolution," the discourse associated with military activity and war remains a core feature of crime-control ideology (e.g., the war on drugs, crime fighters). Indeed the military model, the armed forces, and a fear of martial control have all been influential in the development of police (Bailey 1995; Bittner 1970; Enloe 1980; Fogelson 1977; Manning 1977). Early police scholarship examined in depth the military model's theoretical and practical importance for civilian law enforcement (Bittner 1970; Fogelson 1977; Manning 1977). Contemporary discussions, however, rarely include the military model as a central influence on the police institution.

An important exception is Skolnick and Fyfe's (1993) recent discussion, similar to Bittner's in 1970, of the continued harmful influence of the military paradigm in contemporary policing. They argue that despite the recent rhetorical turn toward democratic reforms, the military model still lingers as a central feature of police culture and operation. One important manifestation of this paradigm which Skolnick and Fyfe overlooked is the adoption of the military special operations model,[1] embodied in what the international literature calls police paramilitary units (PPUs) (Brewer et al. 1988; Enloe 1980; Jefferson 1990; Reiner 1992). These units are known most commonly in the United States as SWAT or special response teams.

At first glance, the police paramilitary unit imagery exhibited at Waco and Ruby Ridge hardly appear to support the notion that a component of policing is moving toward a military approach. These events were sensational and alarming, but could be regarded as unique events that portended little about trends in law enforcement overall. Kraska and Kappeler (1997), however, in a national study of PPUs in medium-sized to large police departments, found that these units have not only grown in numbers but have become increasingly proactive.

The research presented here stems from a separate national survey of small-locality police agencies. Descriptive and longitudinal data on small-locality PPUs are presented, followed by the implications of these findings. In an effort to begin making theoretical sense of these data, we then situate the small-locality findings with the larger PPU phenomenon. We present additional analyses and discuss how the rise and normalization of PPUs correspond closely to macro-level changes in formal social control.

THE MILITARY MODEL AND PARAMILITARY UNITS

In this study we shed light on two neglected areas of scholarship in criminology. First, Weisheit (1993:217) charges crime and justice studies with urban ethnocentrism when reviewing the scant literature on rural crime and justice issues. Although the literature includes some case studies of small police departments (Decker 1979; Gibbons 1972; Marenin and Copus 1991), few systematic examinations of these agencies exist (Weisheit, Falcone, and Wells 1996). The existing literature characterizes small-locality police as oriented toward crime prevention and social service.

Second, until recently no scholarly research on PPUs existed except in the international literature (Jefferson 1990; Reiner 1992).[2] Few police scholars have acknowledged that the military and the police have an inherent political connection: both possess a monopoly on and the prerogative to exercise the state-legitimized use of force (Bittner 1970; Enloe 1980; Kraska 1994; Turk 1982). Even internationally, police rarely organize and administer force along any other lines than the military-bureaucratic model, although the degree of militarization varies widely (Brewer et al. 1988; Chevigny 1995; Enloe 1980).

Police academics, however, have criticized the military model as playing a central role in numerous problems that plague policing (Angell 1971; Bittner 1970; Fogelson 1977; Fry and Berkes 1983; Klockars 1985; Skolnick and Fyfe 1993). The military-bureaucratic model, epitomized in the professional model of policing, acts as a barrier to police-community ties by fostering a "we/they" attitude. Military ideology and organization are also antithetical to more democratic approaches, both internal and external to a police agency. Finally, the military model encourages overemphasis on the crime-fighting function of police work and promotes a warlike approach to crime and drug problems.

In the "era" of community- and problem-oriented policing, it may seem inappropriate to examine trends toward rather than away from the military paradigm, particularly in smaller police jurisdictions. Yet today, the military model's influence on the police may be no less significant (Chevigny 1995; Kraska 1994; Skolnick and Fyfe 1993).

Cop-on-the-Beat Police versus Police Paramilitary Units

It is important to distinguish traditional police from policing with PPUs. In the images constructed by the media, PPUs are highly trained and disciplined teams of police officers housed in the largest agencies, which respond to the rare hostage, sniper, barricaded person, or terrorist. Police paramilitary units can be distinguished from what Enloe (1980) calls "cop-on-the beat policing" most simply by their appearance, their heavy weaponry, and their operations.

For a more exact identification, we must clarify the term *paramilitary unit*. We must distinguish between indications that are *necessary* in applying the PPU label and those which would only *contribute* to labeling these units and their activities as paramilitaristic.

First among the necessary factors, the unit must train and function as a military special operations team with a strict military command structure and discipline (or the pretense thereof). Examples include the U.S Navy Seals teams and foreign police paramilitary squads such as the British Special Patrol Groups. This status as a unique team within a larger organization perpetuates the belief that these units and their members are "elite," a sentiment supported by their administrators (Kraska and Paulsen 1997).[3]

Second, the unit must have at the forefront of their function to threaten or use force collectively, and not always as an option of last resort (e.g., in conducting a no-knock drug raid).[4] Operationally, PPUs are deployed to deal with situations that require a team of police officers specifically trained to be use-of-force specialists. Historically they have operated as *reactive* units, handling only strictly defined, high-risk situations already in progress.

Finally, the unit must operate under legitimate state authority, and its activities must be sanctioned by the state and coordinated by a government agency. This criterion would exclude common thuggery, militia organizations, and guerrilla groups.

Contributing indicators include the hardware they employ and their garb. These teams generally outfit themselves with black or urban camouflage BDUs (battle dress uniforms), lace-up combat boots, full-body armor, Kevlar helmets, and ninja-style hoods. PPUs' weapons and hardware include submachine guns, tactical shotguns, sniper rifles, percussion grenades, CS and OC gas (tear and pepper gas), surveillance equipment, and fortified personnel carriers.

It would seem improbable, given the crime prevention and service orientation attributed to small-locality police agencies, that they would want, need, or be willing to fund these expensive units.[5] Ethnographic research, however, uncovered a flourishing PPU movement in small-town police departments in the north central United States (Kraska 1996); this work overcame our doubts about using resources and time to conduct a national survey of these agencies.

METHODOLOGY

We designed and administered a 40-item (100-variable) survey to collect data on the formation, prevalence, and activities of PPUs in small localities. We developed a sampling frame of all U.S. police agencies (excluding federal agencies), serving jurisdictions between 25,000 and 50,000 citizens.[6] This list yielded a population of 770 law enforcement agencies. In March 1996 we made an initial mailing of the survey to this population of police agencies; the mailing included a letter of introduction and a copy of the survey instrument. Because police agencies are secretive and suspicious (Manning 1978; Skolnick 1966; Westley 1956), and because of the difficulty in researching sensitive topics in policing, the letter was written on a recognized sponsor's letterhead. It was signed by both the principal researcher (the first author) and the director of the professional organization that was sponsoring the research. It also noted the researchers' university affiliation. The language used in the survey encouraged respondents to recognize the study as administratively oriented. It is likely that this orientation, coupled with the authors' familiarity with PPU rhetoric and the promise of confidentiality and anonymity, aided our response rate.

Within five weeks, the first mailing yielded 433 completed surveys, a 56 percent response rate. After approximately six weeks, we mailed a second wave of surveys to the remaining 337 nonrespondents. In the second mailing we emphasized the high level of participation by other police agencies and urged cooperation from departments without a PPU. After six additional weeks, this follow-up mailing yielded an additional 119 surveys for a total response rate of 72 percent ($n = 552$).

Of the 552 returned surveys, we excluded 79 departments that employed more than 100 sworn officers, and thus obtained a more accurate representation of policing in small localities ($N = 473$).[7] The resulting sample of departments contained an average of 62 officers and a median of 60.

Of the 473 agencies, we selected 40 to provide identification and telephone information for semistructured follow-up phone interviews. We sought information on missing data and inquired into some of the more sensitive PPU activities, such as proactive patrol work. Interviews lasted five minutes to one hour; most lasted about 30 minutes.

ANALYSIS AND RESULTS

Demographic and Descriptive Characteristics

Over 65 percent ($n = 311$) of the departments responded that they had a SWAT team. Of the remaining agencies (those without a PPU), 28 percent ($n = 46$) responded that they planned to develop a team within the next few years. The highest proportion of these agencies (24 percent) used the traditional acronym SWAT. Other departments employed an array of labels for the reorganized or more recently formed PPUs, including SRT (special response team, 21 percent) and ERU (emergency response unit, 15 percent).

Most of the units we surveyed were equipped with the latest "tactical gear." Over 80 percent of the departments had MP5 submachine guns, tactical semi-automatic shotguns, night vision equipment, sniper rifles, flash-bang grenades, tactical shields, battle-dress uniforms, and specialized "dynamic entry tools." Over 50 percent had electronic surveillance equipment, tactical helmets, tactical communication headsets, and a mobile command center (i.e., a SWAT van). Seven percent had armored personnel carriers.

Most of the officers responding to the survey were police supervisors. Thirty-eight percent ($n = 119$) could be categorized as high-level administrators (chief, sheriff, deputy chief, major, or captain); 50 percent were either sergeants or lieutenants ($n = 154$); the remainder were patrol officers or deputy sheriffs.

Because the departments were relatively small, it was important to understand how PPUs fit into these agencies' organizational structures. Seven percent ($n = 22$) of the PPUs were maintained full-time; 93 percent, were classified as a part-time arrangement ($n = 288$). Almost 74 percent ($n = 230$) of the PPUs served only one department, while 18 percent ($n = 58$) were multi-jurisdictional. Follow-up phone interviews revealed that many extremely small departments offset the high costs of forming and operating a paramilitary unit by participating in regional units. Some of these multijurisdictional operations involved 50 to 60 smaller agencies.[8]

There were 17.7 paramilitary officers for every 100 sworn persons. We realize that this finding is due mainly to departmental size. As we discuss later, the proximity of paramilitary police officers to regular patrol officers (in fact, most officers in small-town PPUs function as both) is important in assessing the potential cultural and operational effects of these units on the larger organization.

PPU Activities over Time

Analysis of the longitudinal data revealed important trends in the periods during which PPUs were formed (see Figure 1). Only 20 percent ($n = 63$) of today's PPUs existed at the beginning of 1980. By the end of 1984, the number had risen to 121, a 92 percent increase. This increase foreshadowed the developments in the second half of the 1980s. The number of PPUs formed between 1985 and 1990 increased sharply: 130 new units came into existence during this period, bringing the total to 251 and representing an increase of 107 percent. Between 1985 and 1995, the number of paramilitary units in agencies serving small jurisdictions increased by 157 percent. This growth is likely to continue. If we consider that 46 of the departments surveyed responded that they would establish a unit within the next few years, three-fourths of departments employing 100 or fewer officers and serving 25,000 to 50,000 persons will have a PPU by the turn of the century.

The formation of numerous but relatively inactive units, however, would lessen the significance of these data. Therefore we collected baseline data on the number of call-outs performed by each department beginning in 1980; we re-

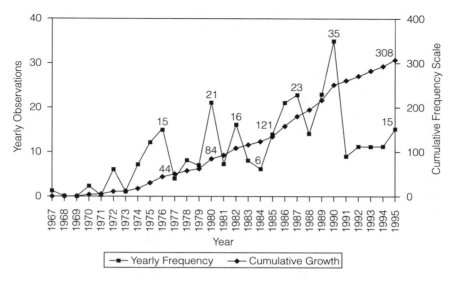

FIGURE 1. Cumulative Growth of PPUs, Showing Number of New PPUs Formed Each Year

quested longitudinal data from 1980 to the end of 1995. "Call-outs" included any activity requiring deployment of the unit, such as barricaded persons, hostages, terrorists, civil disturbances, and the serving of high-risk search and arrest warrants. These data do not include activities related to proactive patrol work by PPUs.

The number of call-outs from 1980 to 1984 remained relatively stable at an average of 3.6 to 3.8 per year (see Table 1). Beginning in 1985, the mean number increased steadily from 4.5 in 1985 to slightly over 12 by the end of 1995. The median rose from 4 in 1985 to 9 in 1995. Between 1980 and 1995 the mean number of call-outs increased by 238 percent.

The total number of call-outs, because of the increase in the number of PPUs in the last 10 years, illustrates more clearly the aggregate rise in police paramilitary activities (see Table 1). In 1980 the total was 220. By 1985 the number had more than doubled to 481, by 1988 it had quadrupled to 960, and by the end of 1995 it had reached 3,715, a total increase of 1,589 percent.

For 1995, traditional reactive functions associated with SWAT units accounted for a surprisingly small proportion of call-outs. Hostage situations ($n = 193$; 5 percent), civil disturbances ($n = 52$; 1 percent), and terrorist incidents ($n = 5$; .1 percent) were quite rare. Barricaded persons accounted for a higher proportion ($n = 874$; 24 percent). By far the most common use of these units was for executing search and arrest warrants: 66 percent ($n = 466$) of the units' call-outs belonged to this category.[9]

Figure 2 displays the number of departments each year that began using their paramilitary units to execute warrants. The total number of departments using

Table 1 Selected Characteristics of Call-Out Data

Year	Mean	Median	Number of Call-Outs	Percentage Increase[a]
1980	3.7	3.0	220	N/A
1981	3.7	3.0	244	10.9
1982	3.6	3.0	274	24.6
1983	3.7	3.0	322	46.4
1984	3.8	3.0	350	59.1
1985	4.5	4.0	481	118.6
1986	5.5	4.0	685	211.4
1987	6.7	4.5	960	336.4
1988	7.1	4.0	1,151	423.2
1989	8.9	5.0	1,633	642.3
1990	10.3	5.0	2,311	950.5
1991	11.1	6.0	2,610	1,086.4
1992	12.1	7.0	3.052	1,287.3
1993	12.0	8.0	3,255	1,379.6
1994	12.2	8.0	3,452	1,469.1
1995	12.5	9.0	3,715	1,588.6

[a]Within the percentage increase column, 1980 is the base year for all calculations.

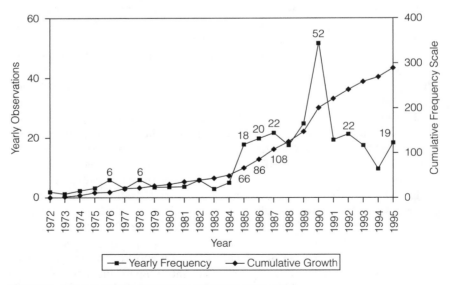

FIGURE 2. Years in Which PPUs Began Warrant/Drug Raids

Table 2 Proportion of PPUs Conducting Warrant Work for Selected Years

	Number of Units in Existence	Number of Units Used for Warrants	Percentage Engaged in Warrant Work
1984	121	48	39.67
1985	135	66	48.89
1990	251	203	80.88
1995	311	292	93.89

PPUs for this purpose has increased steadily over the last 20 years, and increased exponentially (342 percent) between 1985 and 1995. Even though the overall number of units has increased, the percentage of units engaged in warrant work has grown significantly as well. For instance, as shown in Table 2, only 40 percent of PPUs were used in this capacity in 1980. This number had risen to 49 percent by 1985, to 81 percent by the end of 1990, and to 94 percent by the end of 1995. These data indicate a dramatic shift in PPUs' activity.

Serving warrants should not be interpreted as a "reactive" deployment of the unit when a felony arrest warrant is served on a high-risk suspect after a thorough investigation. Phone interviews revealed that warrant work consisted almost exclusively of proactive, no-knock "raids" for the purpose of investigating a residence and collecting evidence such as drugs, guns, and money. About 10 percent of the small-locality departments served 20 to 120 investigatory search warrants a year.

Possibly an even more controversial use of PPUs was their deployment as a patrol force. Seventeen percent of the departments with a paramilitary unit ($n = 55$) used the unit as a proactive patrol force in "high-crime" areas within their jurisdiction. Although a few PPUs performed this function before 1989 ($n = 6$), most of the increase has occurred since then ($n = 49$, a 717 percent increase; see Figure 3). Phone interviewees described a variety of approaches used to deploy these units as patrol teams. Some PPUs patrolled in BDUs and carried MP5 submachine guns. These units responded only to the most serious call for service; they spent most of their time conducting "terry-stops."[10] Other departments used similar tactics but dressed less like a military unit (in jeans and jackets identifying their unit) and carried only 9mm service revolvers and semiautomatic shotguns.

Finally, the PPUs' training deserves mention. Training holds a central place in the police paramilitary subculture (Kraska 1996; Kraska and Paulsen forthcoming). As with military special operations teams such as the Navy Seals and the Army Rangers, these units' elite status is based in part on their reputation for receiving extensive training in "tactical or special operations."

In medium-sized to large police organizations, each officer in a paramilitary unit receives an average of 225 hours of formal training per year (Kraska and Kappeler 1997). Most PPU commanders agreed that if a department is moderately active in conducting call-outs (two per month), a tactical officer needs at least 220 hours of training a year. If the unit conducts relatively few call-outs

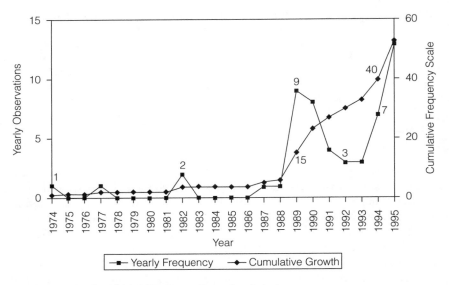

FIGURE 3. Years in Which PPUs Began Proactive Patrol

(three a year), it should provide at least an additional 50 hours of formal training per year. The PPUs housed in the small-locality departments studied here conducted a yearly average of only 106 hours of formal training per officer. Almost 53 percent of these departments conducted 100 or fewer hours of training per year; 20 percent provided their tactical officers with 50 or fewer hours.

Police paramilitary teams often draw their expertise and training from actual military special operations teams such as the Navy Seals and the Army Rangers (Kraska and Kappeler 1997). Surprisingly, even in these smaller jurisdictions, 32 percent ($n = 101$) of the respondents answered "yes" when asked whether they trained with active-duty military experts in special operations. Thirty-one percent ($n = 96$) responded that they were influenced by "police officers with special operations experience in the military." The two most popular sources of PPU training and/or expertise were the FBI and for-profit, tactical training schools. Forty-one percent ($n = 129$) of the PPUs worked with the FBI; 63 percent ($n = 196$) used private tactical schools.

IMPLICATIONS FOR SMALL LOCALITIES: THE DANGERS OF MILITARIZING MAYBERRY

The data demonstrate a significant growth in the number of PPUs and a precipitous rise in PPU activity in small jurisdictions. Because small-locality PPUs engage in proactive patrolling and serve investigatory search warrants, these findings also document the normalization of the PPU approach into small-town police work. Most likely we captured these trends in the midst of their development.[11]

Previous research assessing macro-level shifts in police practices focused mainly on "big-city policy" (Fogelson 1977). Our research adds a new dimension to the underresearched area of small-locality policing by raising questions about the assumption that these agencies are exclusively service-oriented. Paramilitary units in small towns are even more significant than in big cities because urban police officials and politicians can justify, at least partially, a paramilitary approach to crime and drugs in the media-constructed image of a hostile, crime-ridden, urban environment. How do we reconcile this same type of paramilitary policing imagery and activity in "Mayberry"?

It would be tempting to marginalize this paramilitary phenomenon as an interesting appendage of the multidimensional nature of modern police. Not only do the findings on the normalization of small-locality PPUs into routine police work neutralize this argument, it is also critical to recall that there are almost 18 police paramilitary officers for every 100 regular patrol officers in these small localities. Most of these PPU officers serve in the organization as regular patrol officers during their normal duties. In addition, police administrators view these officers as the "elite" or the "cops' cops" (see footnote 3). These factors add credence to the possibility that the paramilitary team model today represents a significant cultural and operational influence on small-locality police organizations as a whole (and possibly will do so more strongly in the future).

The small number of training hours in these PPUs raises another important issue: the degree to which these teams approximate the ideal of highly trained, proficient squads of use-of-force specialists. In keeping with the decentralized nature of American policing, departments form these squads in an ad hoc fashion, with no regulatory body or set of standards. Expertise in "tactical operations" often is gained from reading books, watching videotapes, and possibly visiting a 3- to 5-day for-profit, paramilitary training camp.

In view of these conditions, strict military discipline, a rigid command structure, and tight administrative oversight may not be the norm in Mayberry. PPU members in this study claimed autonomy from direct administrative supervision. As one team commander stated, "We're left alone. The brass knows that we know what we're doing more than they do. One of the reasons we're so effective is we have the freedom to handle situations and problems as we see best." Bock (1995) documents how the autonomy enjoyed by these PPUs, even at the federal level, carries high potential for abuse, particularly in serving no-knock search warrants.

Another development that must be tracked closely are departments' tendency to expand paramilitary units' range of applications, especially if we consider their high cost (see footnote 5) and the extreme concern about officers' safety in the police subculture (Skolnick 1966; Van Maanen 1978). PPUs are not only creeping into proactive functions; their existence in small localities also might be contributing to a broader definition of reactive situations requiring a paramilitary response. One small-locality SWAT commander gave the following justification for an inordinately large number of PPU deployments for barricaded suspects in relation to a departmental policy that requires patrol officers to ask "barricades" only once to surrender:

> If the subject refuses once, the SWAT unit is called in, and we almost always either gas 'em or toss in a flash-bang grenade. We're not gonna hang around for hours and beg, and we're sure not going to get killed because we're indecisive.[12]

BEYOND MAYBERRY: EXPLAINING PARAMILITARY UNIT POLICING

Theoretical and Causal Analysis

To understand the PPU phenomenon more clearly, we must situate small-locality PPUs within broader changes in the police institution and in formal social control in general. We attempt here to make theoretical sense of the rise and normalization of paramilitary policing.

Trends in small-locality policing lag, by roughly three years, nearly identical shifts in larger departments (see Kraska and Kappeler 1997). Small-locality paramilitary policing thus follows an even more significant movement in medium-sized to large police agencies. If we combine the data from larger departments with those cited in this study, we see that the paramilitary unit approach is becoming an integral part of contemporary policing in all departments serving localities with 25,000 or more people. In 1995 over 77 percent of police departments had paramilitary units, an increase of almost 48 percent since 1985. The returned surveys alone documented 29,962 paramilitary deployments in 1995, a 939 percent increase over the 2,884 call-outs of 1980. Over 20 percent of all departments with PPUs use the units for proactive patrol work, a 257 percent increase since the beginning of 1989.

Our assertion that these data represent a shift in the police institution should not be interpreted as the announcement of a mutually exclusive shift—that is, the only shift. The police institution has probably shifted as well toward the rhetoric and activities associated with community policing. National-level longitudinal data documenting the degree to which the police institution has structurally transformed and engaged in activities associated with community policing over time, however, have yet to surface (see Maguire forthcoming).[13] As we argue below, it is likely that the two approaches are increasing simultaneously.

As with any macro-social shift, an explanation for the rise of PPUs will likely involve a multitude of intersecting and overlapping factors forming a complex theoretical mix of social, political, economic, and cultural influences. Because of the shortage of relevant longitudinal, national-level data, valid theory testing and model building will be difficult.

Nonetheless we attempted to determine what factors accounted for variance in the dependent variables, paramilitary unit formation and paramilitary unit call–outs ($n = 846$). We collected 73 national–level independent variables that measured economic trends and trends in crime rates, drug use, fear of crime, and criminal justice activity. Using varimax factor analysis and multiple regression, as well as "differencing" to control for the influence of time (Lafree and Drass 1996), we found that no single variable or construct accounted for a significant amount of variance in our depedent variables.[14]

The inability to account for variance by using these independent variables may be important in itself. We were especially interested in additional testing of the commonsense notion that the rise of PPUs represents a rational reaction by police to changes in crime. Therefore we tested, agency by agency, whether PPU activity corresponds to the occurrence of violent crime. We compared call–out rates from 1980 to 1995, for each jurisdiction, to a UCR violent-crime composite for each of those jurisdictions. We derived the UCR composite by summing the homicide, rape, and robbery rates for each of the responding locations for each year from 1980 through 1995. We excluded aggravated assault rates on the basis of recommendations in the literature (Gove, Hughes and Geerken 1985; Lafree and Drass 1996).

Because the data revealed time-based dependence, we differenced the call–out and crime measures at the first level to make them stationary (i.e., to remove the effects of time). A canonical analysis, using the 15 call–out variables and the 15 crime variables for each jurisdiction, revealed that the canonical correlation value of .59 differed significantly from zero at the .000 level. The Stewart-Love index of redundancy, which is directly analogous to the R^2 statistic in multiple regression and is interpreted similarly (Hair et al. 1995), allowed us to determine that only 6.63 percent of the variance in the call–out data was explained by the violent crime composites. Thus we could reasonably exclude changes in violent crime as an important factor explaining the activities of PPUs.

Beyond the Numbers: A Theoretical Exposition

To make sense of this phenomenon beyond the commonsense notion that it reflects a rational response to crime, we must first recognize that the specter of the military model still haunts the real world of contemporary policing, despite the recent rhetoric of democratic reforms. In learning that a component of the police institution is reorganizing itself and conducting operations that could be characterized as militaristic, we find strong support for the thesis that the military model is still a powerful force guiding the ideology and activities of American police. This should not be surprising considering the war/military paradigm remains an authoritative framework for crime-control thinking and action by politicians, bureaucrats, the media, and much of the public (Sherry 1995).

To understand the revival of militarism in policing, we must point out the close identification between the police paramilitary subculture associated with PPUs and the recent growth of a larger paramilitary culture in the United States during the Reagan-Bush era, and especially since the end of the cold war (Gibson 1994; Hamm 1993; Kraska 1996). Gibson (1994) believes that a ubiquitous culture of paramilitarism has arisen in the last 15 years. Indications include the popularity of paramilitary themes in films, movies, politics, and the news media during the 1980s; the rise of PPUs at the federal and local levels; the popularity of military special operations teams such as the Navy Seals, the Army Rangers, and the Delta Force; the rise of informal militia/paramilitary groups; and the paramilitarism found in some urban gangs (Gibson 1994).

Within this larger culture, the police paramilitary subculture contains a status hierarchy with military special operations squads such as the Navy Seals at the top, followed by FBI, and BATF police paramilitary teams, large metropolitan paramilitary units, and, finally, PPUs in smaller jurisdictions (Kraska 1996). In the past decade an enormous police paramilitary community has developed, which includes a 10,000-member professional organization, numerous periodicals, and even its own artwork.

A complex of for-profit training, weapons, and equipment suppliers heavily promotes the culture at police shows, in police magazine advertisements, and in police paramilitary training programs sponsored by gun manufacturers such as Heckler and Koch and Smith and Wesson. As evidenced by data in this study, the U.S. armed forces also participate, particularly since the end of the cold war (Kraska 1996). The allure of police paramilitary subculture stems from the enjoyment, excitement, high status, and male camaraderie that accompany the heavy weaponry, new technologies, dangerous assignments, and heightened anticipation of using force in most PPU work (Kraska 1996; Kraska and Paulsen 1997).

Ideologically the government's latest war on drugs, with its rhetoric and actions associated with doing battle (drug war boot camps, drugs as a threat to national security, and the use of the U.S. armed forces), dovetails nicely with Gibson's thesis on the growth of paramilitary culture. The drug war—beginning in the early 1980s, peaking in the late 1980s, and continuing through the 1990s—has profoundly affected all aspects of the criminal justice system (Irwin and Austin 1997; Miller 1996). It is no coincidence that the police cracked down on drugs in economically deprived areas concurrently with the great increase in investigatory, no-knock drug raids, conducted mostly by PPUs. Indeed, most of the increases in paramilitary deployments began in 1988, at the apex of drug war activity and hysteria. Nearly all police officials ($n = 126$) in small and large agencies explained in phone interviews that their agency either formed its PPU or dramatically increased the activities of its PPU to conduct raids on private residences in search of drugs, guns, and "drug money."

The escalation of the drug war and the increase in PPUs coincide as well with reformers' calls for the police to alter their operational focus. Reformers advocate a change from *reacting* to individual calls for service with one or two officers to adopting a *proactive* model, which establishes "teams" of officers that work collectively to "maintain order" or solve "community problems" (Goldstein 1990; Kelling 1988; Trojanowicz and Bucqueroux 1990). As we found in this research, and according to data from larger departments (Kraska and Kappeler 1997), police paramilitary teams are used as proactive patrol forces to "suppress" highly politicized problems such as guns, drugs, gangs, and community disorder in economically deprived areas. In fact, 63 percent of police agencies serving 25,000 people or more agreed or strongly agreed that PPUs "play an important role in community policing strategies." One PPU commander clarified the rationale behind this belief:

> We conduct a lot of saturation patrol. We do "terry stops" and "aggressive" field interviews. These tactics are successful as long as the pressure stays on relentlessly. The key to our success is that we're an elite crime-fighting team that's not bogged down in the regular bureaucracy. We focus on *"quality of life"* issues like illegal parking, loud music, bums, neighbor troubles. We have the freedom to stay in a hot area and clean it up—particularly gangs. Our tactical enforcement team works nicely with our department's emphasis on community policing (emphasis added).

At first glance one might assume that a trend toward militarization must be in opposition to the community policing "revolution." In the real world of policing, however, some police officials are interpreting the reformers' call to adopt a proactive stance, and to "actively create a climate of order" (Bayley 1996), as requiring a more aggressive, indeed militaristic approach to enforcing law and order among the "dangerous classes." At least in their minds, PPUs do not supplant a CP or POP approach; they operate in harmony. This reasoning is exemplified most clearly in the recent crackdown on crime and drugs by New York city politicians and police officials.[15]

The rise and the normalization of PPUs, then, correspond to changes in popular culture, drug control operations, and police reform efforts. It should be apparent that a complex combination of factors plays a role in this phenomenon. To explain the final and perhaps most compelling way in which the rise of PPUs corresponds to larger shifts in formal social control, we must revisit the essence of paramilitary unit functioning: PPUs are deployed to deal with situations that police agencies perceive as requiring a team of officers with a strong focus on the threatened or actual use of violence. Street-level policing has always been individually based, discretionary, and unregulated (Bittner 1970; Skolnick 1966). Does this shift in policing, away from individual, situational uses of violence and toward the collective use of violence by "well-managed" teams of officers, coincide with larger trends in formal social control?

A comparable development in scope, form, and function is occurring in corrections. It cross-validates the notion that paramilitary units may indicate *modernizing* changes in the handling of violence by social control agents in the larger criminal justice apparatus (Christie 1994; Feeley and Simon 1992; Garland 1990). Correctional administrators have adopted the paramilitary unit model in attempting to *rationalize* (in the Weberian sense) correctional officers' use of violence through the establishment of "special operations" or "emergency response" teams. As has occurred in policing, "many departments of corrections created their own emergency response teams modeling them after Police SWAT Teams and military commando units such as the Army Green Beret Special Forces and the Navy Seal Teams" (Bryan 1995:2). These units, originally designed to react to only the most serious inmate disturbances, have expanded their range of functions in the last few years to include cell searches, lesser inmate disturbances, "extractions" of inmates from cells, and the forced administration of medicines (Beard 1994; Bryan 1995).

Why is this paramilitary model so appealing to both corrections and policing? As noted above, part of the answer lies generally in the seductive powers of paramilitary unit subculture as promoted by for-profit industry. The techno-warrior garb, heavy weaponry, sophisticated technology, hypermasculinity, and "real-work" functions are nothing less than intoxicating for paramilitary unit participants and those who aspire to work in such units (Kraska 1996; Kraska and Paulsen 1997).

An additional source of allure is the hope that bureaucracies, by creating "violence specialists," can finally control, manage, and make more efficient the state-administered force which is their prerogative. This faith in professionalizing violence by adopting the military model has a long history in both corrections and policing. Thus, to much of the practicing criminal justice community, the recent implementation of the military special operations model represents not a regression in the administration of justice but a step toward further modernizing and refining state violence.

In sum, militarizing state force does not only signal a falling back on a culture of militarism and crude state power in the war on crime and drugs. It also corresponds closely to developments documented by Christie (1994), Cohen (1985), Ericson (1994), Feeley and Simon (1992, 1994), Garland (1990, 1995), Manning (1992, 1993), and of course Foucault (1977). All of these scholars have theorized on what they view as an unpromising, fundamental shift in formal social control: an acceleration of criminal law agencies' uncritical implementation of practices consistent with the tenets of "high-modernity"—accentuated standardization, routinization, technical efficiency, scientificazation, risk minimization, technologicalization, actuarial thinking, the "what works" fetish, moral indifference, and a focus on aggregate populations—in a quest to more efficiently manage those who threaten state order. The rise and the normalization of PPUs represents, therefore, an adaptation to conditions of high-modernity in the crime war.

POLICY SCIENCE AND
GENERAL SCHWARTZKOPF

We cannot assume, however, that this quest for rationality will lead to rational outcomes. Ritzer (1993:121) draws from Weber in asserting that "rational systems inevitably spawn a series of irrationalities that serve to limit, ultimately compromise, and perhaps even undermine, their rationality." The central policy issue related to PPUs is the degree to which this phenomenon constrains police violence, as intended, or escalates it. Except for individual departments, no systematic data have been compiled on the extent to which these units use force. The first author interviewed officials from large and small police departments who claimed that their units had never discharged weapons during a deployment; others stated that they often discharged their weapons on call-outs; some admitted shooting innocent people; and some described casualities to officers caused by "friendly fire."

The paramilitary community is adamant about PPUs' life-saving potential. Few could argue against using well-trained specialists to respond to serious terrorist or hostage situations. Even within these narrow reactive functions, however, we need only recall Waco and Ruby Ridge to appreciate what the adaptation of the paramilitary model implies for civilian law enforcement. Valid systemwide data on PPUs' use of force is needed but will be difficult to obtain.

To determine the rationality of this approach, however, we must consider issues broader than whether these units "save lives" and how often weapons are discharged. Researchers also must track and assess PPUs' "mission creep" into mainstream policing functions. As evidenced by the broad definition of "barricades" in some small-locality agencies, the normalization of the PPU approach carries high potential for expanding the use-of-force options available to the police and the circumstances in which they are utilized in a type of police violence net widening. "Less-lethal technologies," for instance, are becoming extremely popular among PPUs (Kraska 1996).

These data also demonstrate the expansion of police power in conducting contraband raids. PPUs provide the police institution with a new tool for conducting a crude form of investigation into drug and gun law violations inside private residences. This new approach to drug and gun law enforcement is not necessarily a reaction to a dangerous existing condition (such as a hostage situation). Rather, it is a police-initiated *proactive* approach, which itself manufactures dangerous situations.

Policy research as it applies to police militarization, however, can provide only limited guidance. The debate on paramilitary policing in the British literature illustrates clearly that normative concerns play a central role in assessing its desirability (Jefferson 1990; Reiner 1992). This issue involves heartfelt beliefs, values, and morals. To many people, even among academics, the military model represents constraint, discipline, honor, control, competence, and even a type of patriotism. To others it stands for tyranny, state violence, human rights abuses, war, and an ideology which stresses that problems are best handled by technologized state force. Some will see the rise and normalization of PPUs as a necessary and rational approach to today's crime, gang, and drug problems; others will view it as bureaucracy building and as evidence of a government in crisis moving toward a police state.

Crime and justice academicians nevertheless must be careful not to succumb to what Ericson calls "General Schwartzkopf criminology": an uncritical policy science approach that emphasizes "how military-type bureaucracy, discipline, technology, deployment and coercion fight criminal sources of insecurity" (Ericson and Carriere 1994:100). The ideological trappings of the General Schwartzkopf approach lie in its close association with military professionalism, scientific rationality, advanced technology, and expedient, value-neutral problem solving through the use or threat of force. Scholars must remain skeptical about applying these tenets of high-modern militarism to the criminal justice apparatus, and must watch closely for the irrationalities it is likely to spawn.

ENDNOTES

1. For a more thorough discussion of the war/military paradigm and its connection to paramilitary policing, see Kraska (1996).

2. *The Iron Fist and the Velvet Glove* (Crime and Social Justice Associates 1983) was the first work to identify and critique the SWAT phenomenon. Chambliss (1994) conducted field research on the Washington, DC rapid deployment unit (RDU) and discussed its "repressive" tendencies. Stevens and MacKenna (1988) conducted survey research on PPUs in 1986, which yielded only a 40 percent response rate. Their research focused on administrative issues.

3. Ninety-six percent ($n = 45$) of the police chiefs responding to this survey agreed or strongly agreed with the statement "Being part of a tactical unit is a prestigious position in the department."

4. One department of 75 officers sent us professionally made trading cards depicting its 15-man unit. One of the cards was a photograph of the SRT posed around an armored personnel carrier. Members were dressed in full tactical gear; nylon-mesh masks covered their faces. The back of the card read, "When citizens need help they call the police. When the police need help they call SRT." The SRT's self-image as the cops' cops illuminates members' self-perception as specialists in the use of force.

5. In phone interviews with two departments that had just established PPUs, the informants estimated that start-up and first-year costs of a 15-member unit would be $200,000 to $250,000. This figure includes all "tactical gear" and first-year training costs.

6. The demographic literature makes the break between smaller and larger cities at 50,000 (McGregor-Matlock and Woodhouse 1987; Shannon and Ross 1977). In labeling this study "small-locality," as opposed to "small-town," we included 37 county agencies that serve 25,000 to 50,000 people and employ 100 or fewer officers.

7. Although the N is reduced by truncating the population subset at the 100-officer level, analysis of the larger data set revealed no appreciable differences in our findings.

8. Some police administrators in small towns and rural counties are developing multijurisdictional PPUs by using existing arrangements designed to assist small communities in natural disasters. A paper agency is formed when departments participating in the disaster relief arrangement also donate one to three officers and associated funds to be a part of a fully operational 40- to 60-member PPU. Several interviewees claimed that their multijurisdictional PPUs gradually developed an independence from political and community oversight; this left them free to collaborate with state police agencies, with little political or community scrutiny.

9. Three percent ($n = 125$) of call-outs were categorized as "other."

10. Interviews revealed that when paramilitary units conducted proactive patrols, they were not required to answer routine calls for service. These units instead were deployed into "high-crime" neighborhoods to conduct street interrogations of "suspicious" pedestrians, occupants of automobiles, and even persons in "drug houses." Three departments said that it was not unusual for their units to conduct "warrantless dynamic entries" into private residences if they saw suspected drug dealers entering a residence to elude police interrogation.

11. Evidence for this assertion includes the large number of police departments planning to establish a PPU in the future, the recent steep growth in PPUs doing warrant and patrol work, and the fact that

much of these data comes from newly formed units.

12. One of the anonymous reviewers of this paper claimed that similar changes are taking place in hostage/barricade situations:

> Instead of following the tried and true 25-year-old practice of negotiating for a bloodless resolution no matter how long it takes, some departments seem to have adopted the practice of turning scenes over to SWAT after a relatively short time. . . . SWAT then attempts to implement a "tactical resolution" which usually ends in one or more dead bodies. Indeed, members of one SWAT team even told me that their department has given up on negotiating for a bloodless resolution no matter how long it takes. Instead, they have adopted the "LA procedure" which consists of negotiating with hostage takers or barricaded persons for the purpose of putting them in position for a "tactical resolution": an "instantly catastrophic" shot by a sniper to the cerebral cortex.

13. On the basis of data from 1987–1993, Maguire (forthcoming) finds no significant differences in the extent of structural change between agencies that identify themselves as community policing departments and agencies that do not.

14. Currently we are collecting data relevant to social threat theory for each of the 846 jurisdictions for 1995. The objective is to determine which (if any) social threat variables account for the variance in paramilitary deployments across jurisdictions.

15. NYPD officials, with support from the Harvard School of Government, are quite vocal in claiming that their unique brand of proactive, aggressive policing has reduced crime dramatically. In April 1996, NYPD launched a "3,000"-officer offensive to "crush drug trafficking and the drug business," employing the same tactics as discussed in this research (Kraus 1996:1). NYPD is also aggressively marketing its "success strategy" to other police agencies via national conferences.

REFERENCES

Angell, J.E. 1971. "Toward an Alternative to the Classic Police Organizational Arrangements: A Democratic Model." *Criminology* 9:195–206.

Bailey, W.G. 1995. *The Encyclopedia of Police Science,* 2nd ed. New York: Garland.

Bayley, D.H. 1994. *Police for the Future.* New York: Oxford University Press.

Beard, J.A. 1994. "Using Special Management Units to Control Inmate Violence." *Corrections Today* (August): 88–91.

Bittner, E. 1970. *The Functions of Police in Modern Society.* Chevy Chase: National Clearinghouse for Mental Health.

Bock, A.W. 1995. *Ambush at Ruby Ridge: How Governmental Agents Set Randy Weaver Up and Took His Family Down.* Irvine, CA: Dickens.

Brewer, J.D., A. Guelke, I. Hume, E. Moxon-Browne, and R. Wolford. 1988. *The Police, Public Order and the State.* New York: St. Martin's.

Bryan, D. 1995. "Emergency Response Teams: A Prison's First Line of Defense." *Corrections Compendium* 20(7): 1–13.

Chambliss, W.J. 1994. "Policing the Ghetto Underclass: The Politics of Law and Law Enforcement." *Social Problems* 41:177–94.

Chevigny, P. 1995. *Edge of the Knife: Police Violence in the Americas.* New York: Free Press.

Christie, N. 1994. *Crime Control as Industry: Toward GULAGS, Western Style.* New York: Routledge.

Cohen, S. 1985. *Visions of Social Control: Crime, Punishment and Classification.* Cambridge: Polity.

Crime and Social Justice Associates. 1983. *The Iron Fist and the Velvet Glove: An Analysis of the U.S. Police.* 3d ed. San Francisco: Garret.

Decker, S. 1979. "The Rural County Sheriff: An Issue in Social Control." *Criminal Justice Review* 4:97–111.

Enloe, C. 1980. "Police, Military, and Ethnicity: Foundations of State Power." New Brunswick, NJ: Transaction.

Ericson, R. 1994. "The Division of Expert Knowledge in Policing and Security." *British Journal of Sociology* 45:149–70.

Ericson, R. and K. Carriere. 1994. "The Fragmentation of Criminology." Pp. 89–109 in *The Futures of Criminology* edited by D. Nelken. Beverly Hills: Sage.

Feeley, M. and J. Simon. 1992. "The New Penology." *Criminology* 39:449–74.

———. 1994. "Actuarial Justice: The Emerging New Criminal Law." Pp. 173–201 in *The Futures of Criminology,* edited by D. Nelken. Beverly Hills: Sage.

Fogelson, R.M. 1977. *Big-City Police.* Cambridge, MA: Harvard University Press.

Foucault, M. 1977. *Discipline and Punish: The Birth of the Prison.* New York: Vintage.

Fry, L.W. and L.J. Berkes. 1983. "The Paramilitary Police Model: An Organizational Misfit." *Human Organization* 42:225–34.

Garland, D. 1990. *Punishment and Modern Society: A Study in Social Theory.* Chicago: University of Chicago Press.

———. 1995. "Penal Modernism and Postmodernism." Pp. 181–210 in *Punishment and Social Control: Essays in Honor of Sheldon L. Messinger,* edited by T.G. Blomber and S. Cohen. New York: Aldine.

Gibons, D.C. 1972. "Crime in the Hinterland." *Criminology* 10:177–91.

Gibson, J.W. 1994. *Warrior Dreams: Manhood in Post-Vietnam America.* New York: Hill and Wang.

Goldstein, H. 1990. *Problem-Oriented Policing.* New York: McGraw-Hill.

Gove, W.R., M. Hughes, and M. Geerken. 1985. "Are Uniform Crime Reports a Valid Indicator of the Index Crimes? An Affirmative Answer with Minor Qualifications." *Criminology* 23:111–20.

Hair, J.F., Jr., R.e. Anderson, R.L. Tatham, and W.C. Black. 1995. *Multivariate Data Analysis with Readings.* 4th ed. Upper Saddle River, NJ: Prentice-Hall.

Hamm, M.S. 1993. *American Skinheads: The Criminology and Control of Hate Crime.* Westport, CT: Praeger.

Irwin, J. and J. Austin. 1997. *It's About Time: America's Imprisonment Binge.* Belmont, CA: Wadsworth.

Jefferson, T. 1990. *The Case against Paramilitary Policing.* Bristol, PA: Open University Press.

Kelling, G.L. 1988. *Police and Communities: The Quiet Revolution.* Washington, DC: National Institute of Justice.

Klockars, C.B. 1985. *The Idea of Police.* Beverly Hills: Sage.

Kraska, P.B. 1994. "The Police and the Military in the Post-Cold War Era: Streamlining the State's Use of Force Entities in the Drug War." *Police Forum* 4:1–8.

———. 1996. "Enjoying Militarism: Political/Personal Dilemmas in Studying U.S. Police Paramilitary Units." *Justice Quarterly* 13:405–29.

Kraska, P.B. and V.E. Kappeler. 1997. "Militarizing American Police: The Rise and Normalization of Paramilitary Units." *Social Problems* 44:1–18.

Kraska, P.B. and D.J. Paulsen. 1997. "Grounded Research into U.S. Paramilitary Policing: Forging the Iron Fist inside the Velvet Glove." *Policing and Society* 7:253–70.

Kraus, C. 1996. "NYC Police to Start Big Drug Offensive Using New Approach." Posted on World Wide Web, April 4. *New York Times* Company.

LaFree, G. and K.A. Drass. 1996. "The Effects of Changes in Intraracial Income Inequality and Educational Attainment on Changes in Arrest Rates for African Americans and Whites, 1957 to 1990." *American Sociological Review* 61:614–34.

Maguire, E.R. Forthcoming. "Structural Changes in Large Municipal Police Organizations during the Community Policing Era." *Justice Quarterly.*

Manning, P.K. 1977. *Police Work: The Social Organization of Policing.* Cambridge, MA: MIT Press.

———. 1978. "The Police: Mandate, Strategies and Appearances." Pp. 53–70 in *Policing: A View from the Street,* edited by P.K. Manning and J. Van Maanen. Chicago: Goodyear.

———. 1992. "Economic Rhetoric and Policing Reform." *Criminal Justice Research Bulletin* 7:1–8.

———. 1993. "The Preventive Conceit: The Black Box in Market Context." *American Behavioral Scientist* 36: 639–50.

Marenin, O. and G. Copus. 1991. "Policing Rural Alaska: The Village Public Safety Officer (VPSO) Program." *American Journal of Police* 10:1–26.

McGregor-Matlock, L. and L. Woodhouse. 1987. "The State of the Small City: A Survey of the Nation's Cities and Towns under 50,000." Washington, DC: National League of Cities.

Miller, J.G. 1996. *Search and Destroy: African-American Males in the Criminal Justice System.* New York: Cambridge University Press.

Reiner, R. 1992. *The Politics of the Police.* Toronto: University of Toronto Press.

Ritzer, G. 1993. *The McDonaldization of Society: An Investigation into the Changing Character of Contemporary Social Life.* Thousand Oaks, CA: Pine Forge.

Shannon, J. and J. Ross. 1977. "Cities: Their Increasing Dependence on State and Federal Aid." Pp. 211–29 in

Small Cities in Transition: The Dynamics of Growth and Decline, edited by J. Herrington. Cambridge, MA: Ballinger.

Sherry, M.S. 1995. *In the Shadow of War: The United States since the 1930s.* New Haven: Yale University Press.

Skolnick, J.H. 1966. *Justice without Trial: Law Enforcement in a Democratic Society.* New York: Wiley.

Skolnick, J.H. and J.J. Fyfe. 1993. *Above the Law: Police and the Excessive Use of Force.* New York: Free Press.

Stevens, J.W. and D.W. MacKenna. 1988. "Police Capabilities for Responding to Violent Criminal Activity and Terrorism." *Police Studies* 11:116–23.

Sutherland, E.H., D.R. Cressey. and D.F. Luckenbill. 1992. *Principles of Criminology.* Dix Hills, NY: General Hall Inc.

Trojanowicz, R. and B. Bucqueroux. 1990. *Community Policing: A Contemporary Perspective.* Cincinnati: Anderson.

Turk, A. 1982. *Political Criminality: The Defiance and Defense of Authority.* Beverly Hills: Sage.

Van Maanen, J. 1978. "Kinsmen in Repose: Occupational Perspectives of Patrol-men." Pp. 28–39 in *Police and Policing: A View from the Street,* edited by P.K. Manning and J. Van Maanen. Chicago: Goodyear.

Weisheit, R.A. 1993. "Studying Drugs in Rural Areas: Notes from the Field." *Journal of Research in Crime and Delinquency* 30:213–32.

Weisheit, R.A., D.N. Falcone, and L.E. Wells. 1996. *Crime and Policing in Rural and Small-Town America.* Prospect Heights, IL: Waveland.

Westley, W.A. 1956. "Secrecy and the Police." *Social Forces* 34:254–57.

QUESTIONS FOR
DISCUSSION AND REVIEW

1. Describe how the Kansas City Preventive Patrol Study was conducted. What were the major findings of the study?

2. The Kansas City Preventive Patrol Study (KCPPE) and the study by Sherman and Rogan (1995) both examined the effects of police patrol on crime. How did the Sherman and Rogan study differ from the KCPPE in how it was conducted? Which study do you think provided for a more valid test of the impact of police on crime? Why?

3. Considering the Kansas City Preventive Patrol Experiment and the study by Sherman and Rogan (1995), can the police impact crime through patrol activities? Under what circumstances? Explain.

4. According to Chaiken et al. (1977), how do detectives spend most of their time? How are most cases solved?

5. Given the findings of the study by Chaiken et al. (1977), what are the implications for the criminal investigation function in police departments?

6. According to Brandl and Frank (1994), what are the major problems with the study conducted by Chaiken et al. (1977)?

7. How do the findings of Brandl and Frank (1994) differ from the findings offered by Chaiken et al. (1977)?

8. According to Sherman et al. (1973), what was team policing? How did team policing differ from community policing, which came later? How are community policing and team policing similar?

9. Based on the discussion provided by Maguire (1997), has the community policing movement succeeded in altering the organizational structure of police departments in the United States? Why or why not?

10. According to Goldstein (1979), what is the "means over ends" syndrome and how does it relate to policing?

11. According to Goldstein (1979), what is the end product of policing and what are the four different results that can be measures of success?

12. What is the significance of "broken windows," according to Wilson and Kelling (1982)?

13. Explain the relationship between disorder, fear of crime, and actual crime as discussed by Wilson and Kelling (1982).

14. What are the major findings of the study conducted by Kraska and Cubellis (1997)?

15. "The military model still lingers as a central feature of police culture and operation" (Kraska and Cubellis, 1997:608). Explain the significance of this statement in light of the findings presented by Kraska and Cubellis (1977). How can this statement be reconciled with notions of community policing?

16. If the trend described by Kraska and Cubellis (1997) continues, what will the future of policing look like? What evidence is there to believe that this trend will continue?

Name Index

Aaronson, D.E. 374
Adamson, C. 70, 73, 89
Adorno, T.W. 131, 168
Agnew, S. 63
Aiken, M. 329, 335, 350
Aldrick, H.E. 340, 349
Allen, R. J. 373
Alpert, G.P. 130, 133, 168
Anderson, D. 133, 169
Anderson, E. 55, 66
Anderson, K.R. 24
Anderson, R.E. 406
Angell, J.E. 331, 334, 337, 389, 405
Arnold, W.J. 349
Austin, T. 59, 60 66, 400, 406

B

Balch, R.W. 131, 169
Balkan, S. 82, 85, 89
Banton, M. 213, 214
Barker, T. 332, 350
Barlow, D.E. 2, 3, 68, 71, 89, 110, 111
Barlow, M.H. 2, 3, 68, 71, 81, 89, 110, 111
Barr, R. 268, 274
Bastian, D. 59, 67
Bates, F.L. 335, 352
Bayley, D.H. 25, 84, 85, 89, 138, 140, 164, 169, 328, 330, 331, 333, 334, 337, 347, 349, 352, 401, 405

Bayley, P.H. 198, 214
Beard, J.A. 402, 405
Becker, H.S. 212, 213, 214
Bell, J. 298, 303, 305, 313
Bennett, L. 90
Bergman, W. 334, 350
Berk, R.A. 272, 274, 349
Berk, S.F. 129, 130, 169
Berkes, J.M. 340, 349
Berkley, G.E. 213, 214, 218, 230
Berlin, I. 45
Binder, A. 138, 169, 272, 274
Bittner, E. 3, 92, 111, 129, 169, 194, 210, 214, 319, 320, 326, 373, 388, 389, 401, 405
Black, D. 113, 114, 129, 130, 139, 141, 168, 169, 184, 194, 196, 197, 198, 214, 231, 336, 349
Black, W.C. 406
Blau, P.M. 329, 339, 349
Bloch, P.B. 133, 169, 298, 299, 303, 305, 313, 326
Blomberg, A. 406
Blumberg, M. 130, 133, 169, 171
Bock, A.W. 397, 405
Bogess, S. 58, 67
Bohannan 195
Boland, B. 134, 143, 172
Bordua, D.J. 193, 197, 348, 352

Subject Index